Praise for *The (*

"Every quilter needs this book—I can't ima... it. It is everything wrapped in one perfect package."

—ALEX ANDERSON, COHOST OF *THE QUILT SHOW*

"I am so impressed. . . . This is a comprehensive, indispensable book for quilters."

—JEAN WELLS, FOUNDER OF THE SISTERS OUTDOOR QUILT SHOW IN SISTERS, OREGON

"This book brings quilt history up-to-date. . . . The pages are loaded with information, from useful tips to valuable resources. This is a must-have book for every quilter's library, for quilt collectors, and for anyone who loves quilts!"

—BONNIE BROWNING, EXECUTIVE SHOW DIRECTOR
FOR THE AMERICAN QUILTER'S SOCIETY, PADUCAH, KENTUCKY

"*The Quilter's Catalog* is an essential companion for quilters and quilt-lovers."

—SANDRA DALLAS, AUTHOR OF *TALLGRASS* AND OTHER NOVELS

"This is the book quilters have been waiting for. Whether you are a novice or an advanced quilter, this all-encompassing, broad-ranging sourcebook is simply the best!"

—DR. CAROLYN L. MAZLOOMI, INDEPENDENT CURATOR AND WRITER

"It's all here. For those new to quilting, buy and devour this book. For those who already love and live quilting, the author has written our family history."

—JODIE DAVIS, QNNTV.COM

"This is huge. . . . I assure you that *The Quilter's Catalog* will be my bedside and sewing room reading for years to come!"

—MARK LIPINSKI, *QUILTER'S HOME MAGAZINE*

"Wow! This is the best resource for everything you would ever want to know about quilting. The perfect quilt resource book . . . There is something for everyone, from quilt history to great projects."

—YVONNE PORCELLA, QI

BY MEG COX

WORKMAN PUBLISHING
NEW YORK

For my late mother

Jo Cox

who taught me.

 Published simultaneously in Canada by Thomas Allen & Son Limited.

Library of Congress Cataloging-in-Publication Data
Cox, Meg.
The quilter's catalog: a comprehensive resource guide / by Meg Cox.
p. cm.
ISBN-13: 978-0-7611-3881-5 (alk.)
1. Quilting. 2. Quilts. I. Title.
TT835.C6933 2007
746.46'041—dc22 2007036314

This book references websites that may be of interest to the reader. Every effort has been made to ensure that the information about these websites is correct and up-to-date as of press time.

Cover design by Janet Parker
Book design by Janet Parker *with* Katherine Tomkinson and Beverly McClain

Workman Publishing Company, Inc.
225 Varick Street
New York, NY 10014-4381
www.workman.com

Printed in the U.S.A.
First printing January 2008

10 9 8 7 6 5 4 3 2 1

Acknowledgments

FIRST, THANKS TO PETER WORKMAN FOR SAYING "No" to this book—twice. After each "No," I spent a year doing research. By the time Peter said "Yes," the proposal was one hundred pages long. All the extra time I put into researching this book, plus the months of additional work my editor squeezed out of me after I thought it was done, have made it the fat, full thing you are holding, a book of which I'm very proud. I've wanted to be a Workman author ever since I profiled the company for *The Wall Street Journal* in 1990: The experience has exceeded my high expectations.

At Workman, I was incredibly lucky to have Suzanne Rafer as my editor. Suzanne took a somewhat disjointed collection of writings and shaped them into a cogent resource guide. She got me to switch out of my "*Wall Street Journal* impassive observer voice." If the book seems personal, even occasionally humorous, thank Suzanne. About a third of the sidebars were her idea, as was the chapter for beginners. She made this book so much deeper than it might have been.

My copy editor, Barbara Mateer, should be anointed for sainthood. This book had so many moving parts, but she never balked. Her patience over details like how to sew a binding was endless. We all wanted to make this book as beginner-friendly as possible: Thanks to Barbara, I think we succeeded. There are so many publishing wizards at Workman, but I must single out Helen Rosner, Janet Parker, the book's designer, Elara Tanguy, Kate Tomkinson, Brian Belfiglio, Brianna Yamashita, Amy Corley, and Peter Bohan.

Until now, I hadn't tried to write quilting directions and didn't realize how difficult it is to do well. A big thank-you to freelance quilting expert Eleanor Levie, who helped with technical editing on the twelve projects and wrote the first draft of the directions for my five.

Today's quilt world is a vast territory, and it took many guides to explore it. Chief among them is the indispensable Liza Prior Lucy, a wonderful quilter and generous teacher who knows everyone and who became a valued friend. Liza did everything from recommending teachers and tools to reading every chapter. She even helped me pick out fabric for one of the project quilts and consoled me over lunches at our favorite hangout when I suffered from book burnout. I think of her as more than a mentor: Liza is the godmother of this book. Bless you.

My knowledge of quilt history owes much to the nonprofit Alliance for American Quilts, an extensive and reliable database on both historic quilts and contemporary quilters. Alliance cofounder Shelly Zegart, a quilt collector and appraiser, was one of my first interview subjects. Her vital role in the twentieth-century quilt renaissance made her an invaluable resource, and she was unfailingly generous with both her time and knowledge.

Shelly persuaded me to join the alliance board, and foremost among the board colleagues who aided me was Karen Musgrave, an art quilter and teacher who is the prime force behind the alliance's impressive oral history project, Quilter's S.O.S.–Save Our Stories. Karen read the first draft of this book with a critical eye and made numerous helpful suggestions. She's got great taste and spent many hours helping make this book better. That she also chose to interview me for the QSOS project was an unexpected and gratifying bonus.

I also want to thank other alliance board members who shared their expertise both casually and in formal interviews, especially quilt historians Marsha MacDowell and Merikay Waldvogel and pioneering art quilter Yvonne Porcella. To the rest of the board and staff, especially executive director Amy Milne, thanks for all your support and friendship!

The best place to get a crash course in quilting trends is at the nation's premier quilt shows. Thanks to all the people who helped me during my visits to Paducah, Kentucky, and Houston. Special thanks to Bonnie Browning, the imperturbable leader of the American Quilter's Society Show in Paducah. Bonnie made so many introductions and answered so many questions in 2002, exerting herself way beyond the call of duty—all for a writer who hadn't yet secured a contract for a book on quilting.

No quilt is ever perfect—and the same is true for books. After seventeen years at *The Wall Street Journal*, I know the importance of fact-checking and of going to top experts for help and that's what I did here. Whenever possible, I also had top experts review whole sections and chapters to catch my mistakes, and they found some. I have no doubt that some crept in anyway, and I take full responsibility for those.

But I must express my unending gratitude to the many experts who helped check my facts, as follows: Thanks to Donna Wilder, former head of FreeSpirit fabrics, and Irwin Bear, president of P&B Textiles, for reading the chapter on fabric. Teacher and quilt shop owner Harriet Hargrave also read big chunks of the text on fabric. Patricia Slaven, who tests sewing machines for Consumer's Union, helpfully reviewed most of the section on sewing machine technology, as did Sharon Darling, author of *Picking a Sewing Machine You'll Love*. Thanks to longarm gurus Janet-Lee Santeusanio and Linda Taylor for reading the sections on midarm and longarm quilting machines. Thank-you to longarm pioneer Marcia Stevens for reading the sidebar on finding a finisher. Thanks to fabric-dyeing wizard Carol Soderlund for checking the section on fabric dyeing. Thanks to quilter Scott Murkin for reading the sidebar on male quilters and to curator Carolyn Mazloomi for reading the section on African American quilters. For looking over the sections on computers and quilting, thanks to art quilter and Web designer Gloria Hansen and Rob Holland, who rules over PlanetPatchwork.com.

I'm extremely grateful to the twenty top teachers who agreed to be profiled. These are all amazingly accomplished quiltmakers, and it was an honor getting to know them. I demanded a lot of time from each of them, especially the seven who contributed projects to the book.

Since I began my research in 2001, I have interviewed hundreds of individual quilters in person and by phone, on top of the hundreds who filled out my questionnaire on their quilt histories. I'm grateful to every one of you for taking the time to share your passion. Those who filled out my questionnaire taught me so much about why this ancient craft is booming in the twenty-first century. A number of you are quoted by name in chapter one, but I'm grateful to all of you for your insights.

Two vital resources in researching this book were e-mail lists, the Quiltart list and the QHL or quilt history list. Reading the postings every day helps keep me abreast of developments in the quilt world. More important, these lists work like an instant focus group at times. On multiple occasions, I asked QA members especially to share their favorite teachers, books, tools, and techniques, and their feedback was detailed and precise. This virtual community extends well off the screen, and the connection prompted me to invite art quilter and teacher Robbi Joy Eklow to have dinner with me before the Houston show in 2004. Robbi shared the artfully loopy traditions of the annual "tiara parade" and much more.

My development as a quilter owes a great deal to the deliciously laid-back guild I joined, the Hopewell Valley Quilters. Long after my husband and son banned "the Q word" at home, my guild friends eagerly followed stories of my quilt world adventures and would pat me on the back every month, even when I was too busy writing to make quilts for show-and-tell. Ever since I met guild president Nancy Breland on the plane coming back from Paducah in 2002, she's been especially helpful. A prize-winning quilter who has taken many classes, Nancy had a role in picking the list of quilt teachers to watch for. And Sandy Merritt, a longarm quilter who belongs to the guild, has been a lifesaver when I'm on a deadline: She beautifully quilted most of my projects in the book.

Every author seeks an agent who has business savvy and great publishing connections. I found those qualities and much more in Chris Tomasino, who nurtured me and this book through all the discouraging times.

I can never express adequately my love and gratitude to my husband, Dick Leone, and my son, Max, for keeping me centered and happy. They may be sick of quilts, but they don't seem to tire of me. Endless gratitude goes to my sister, Tracy Hagen Smith, who has been a soul mate and cheerleader all my life (except for a few of those rocky teenage years). A highlight for me was when I dragged Tracy off for a visit to the Quilt National show in 2005 and she turned to me at the end and said, "teach me."

Every quilt is a labor of love, often created for a specific person. This book is a tribute to my mother, who taught me to quilt but didn't get the chance to see that it changed my life.

Contents

CHAPTER FOUR

Fabulous Fabric and Where to Find It

CHAPTER FIVE

Great Teachers: So Many Ways to Learn

Classic Revival: Alex's Album, *detail of a group quilt made under Elly Sienkiewicz's direction.*

Opposite page: A detail of Anna Williams' quilt XLV.

CHAPTER SIX

For the Beginner

CHAPTER SEVEN

Putting It Together

Twelve Projects from Notable Quilters

Sue Benner's Wild and Crazy Fused Heart Ornament

CHAPTER EIGHT

Shoot It, Show It, Ship It, and More!

The Nebraska State Quilt Guild displays its work at the 2003 Nebraska State Fair.

INTRODUCTION

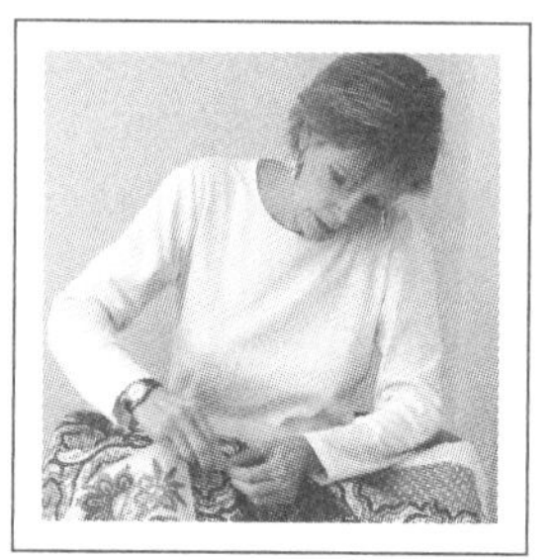

My Quilt History

I LEARNED HOW TO QUILT DURING A NORTH CAROLINA snowstorm. The year was 1989, and I was visiting my parents for Christmas, traveling from New York City where I worked as a reporter for *The Wall Street Journal*. I had asked my mother earlier to teach me quilting, and when I arrived at their house, she handed me a beautiful basket she had prepared. Inside were all the squares needed for a simple crib quilt she had designed, alternating squares of white fabric with primary colors. There was a paper pattern of the finished quilt to guide me, but making it even simpler, she had stacked the squares of fabric in order so that each little pile was one complete row, and the rows were numbered. Also in the basket was a pair of small, supersharp Gingher sewing scissors, as well as thread, needles, and everything else I might need to complete the quilt top.

I suppose I might have taken to quilting even without the snowstorm, but it multiplied the length of my lesson and made the learning seem fated. Soon after I arrived, a freak southern blizzard closed the airport and all the roads. There I was for several days, snowbound at my parents' house in front of a roaring fire, with all the ingredients for a quilt. The snow piled up outside, and the neat bundle of rows piled up in my lap. I barely stopped piecing except to eat and sleep, and by the time I flew back to New York, my first quilt top was finished. I was hooked.

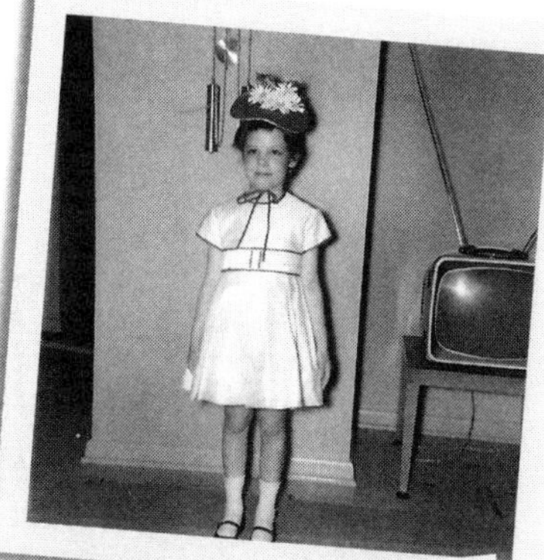

For me, quilting started as a way to rekindle a childhood connection with my mother, who had taught me to sew (although it was my Barbie doll who sparked the desire to learn). My mother, with a master's degree in art, had worked at everything from cartography to puppetry, but once she had kids, the bulk of her toil was managing the four of us and my father. She did this as artfully as possible on a small budget. Except for the underwear she ordered from the Sears catalog, she sewed virtually everything we wore: play clothes and school clothes, pajamas and robes, Halloween costumes, even pastel coats for Easter with matching flower-covered hats (for the three girls). Not to mention an endless succession of stuffed animals and rag dolls. There should have been smoke coming out of the Singer sewing machine she kept in her bedroom.

Easter 1959 (top). The Easter parade: dresses, hats, and coats all handmade by my mother (bottom).

By the age of eight, I was begging my mother for fabric scraps, and she taught me how to sew simple suits and dresses for my classic brunette Barbie. By the time I was ten, I had inherited my mother's Singer when she got a new model, and she taught me how to use it. The sewing machine was moved into the basement, where I began sewing clothes for myself: This being the sixties, they tended to be minidresses.

When I left suburban Cleveland for college, I left behind both the machine and any interest in sewing clothes—for good. I was too busy getting through college, then I was off building a career in journalism, starting at a small newspaper in Ohio.

The idea of my making a quilt might never have occurred to me, except that sometime in the early eighties in North Carolina, when my father retired, my mother decided to try making a quilt. Her sister Dorothy, the domestic goddess of the family, claims she was the one who got Mother started.

From the first, my mother loved what turned out to be the perfect outlet for both her needle skills and her artist's sense of composition and color. Her first quilt, a traditional eight-point star done simply with just three fabrics (off-white, maroon, and a delicate flower print that used both colors) won a blue ribbon in the local quilt guild show. Although she sewed all her clothes by machine, she was a fierce devotee of handwork in her quilts: All were pieced and quilted by her arthritic hands, yet her tiny stitches were awesomely even.

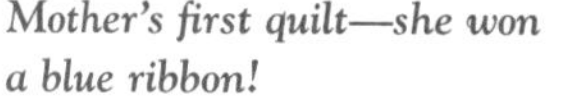

Mother's first quilt—she won a blue ribbon!

Mother became active in her quilt guild, taking classes, buying books, trying new techniques. She made bold appliqué samplers; designed abstract, pastel wall hangings; completed a flawless white-on-white bed quilt; and sewed brightly colored quilted vests for virtually every member of the family.

I believe she was diagnosed with emphysema about the time she started quilting, and it may be that one of Mother's motivations was to leave a legacy behind, something that would outlast the Raggedy Anns and smocked dresses we outgrew in childhood. Then again, I think most of what kept her quilting was pure pleasure. In her final years, quilting and calligraphy were the only activities she continued pursuing daily.

Passing the quilt bug on to me was definitely not part of a conscious plan. I was a divorced, compulsive career woman living in a tiny walk-up apartment in New York's East Village, and I'm confident she didn't imagine that the thing missing from my life was quilting. I can't really say why I asked to learn, but her obvious pleasure in it was one factor. Her first quilt, the prizewinner, had been made for me and covered my bed at the time. Mother said later she suspected that I asked to learn quilting just to make her happy but was delighted when she discovered that wasn't true—or not the whole truth.

I continued my quilt progress slowly, with no one to consult but her. She gave me tips and answered my questions by phone and in regular letters accompanied with tiny, detailed drawings. When it came time to complete that first quilt, Mother sent me batting and backing, and on my next visit south, she showed me how to quilt by hand and "bury the knot."

My mother hard at work on her calligraphy.

When the crib quilt was finished, I folded it up and set it aside and immediately searched for a new project. I wasn't expecting to be a mother at that point but couldn't imagine giving away my first quilt. My mother found some fabric that reproduced a quaint patchwork pattern with primitive animals in squares and mailed it off to me. A dear friend had just had a baby, so I tried a simple whole-cloth quilt. Mother sent me instructions in a letter explaining how to tie the layers together with embroidery floss, as an alternative to the slow process of hand quilting. The tied quilt was done in a flash, and my friend was thrilled with this "heirloom."

The incomparable Quilts! Quilts!! Quilts!!! *by Diana McClun and Laura Nownes.*

Then Mother gave me *Quilts! Quilts!! Quilts!!! The Complete Guide to Quiltmaking*, by Diana McClun and Laura Nownes, an invaluable book that has turned many a beginner into a lifelong quilter, and I immediately started making the colorful sampler featured there. Here was a way to experiment with more than a dozen appealing traditional blocks: Drunkard's Path, Log Cabin, Bear Paw, Pine Tree, Wild Geese, Nine Patch, and more. Still, I never set foot in

. . . it may be that one of Mother's motivations was to leave a legacy behind, something that would outlast the Raggedy Anns and smocked dresses we outgrew in childhood.

a fabric shop: To simplify things, my mother kept mailing me fabric from her stash.

Wanting to share the results of my months of hand sewing, done in evenings and on weekends when I didn't have a reporting assignment eating up time, I took all the finished blocks of the sampler down to North Carolina. How well I remember trying out all the different combinations of blocks on the carpet in my parents' living room, using the floor like a design wall. (Veteran quilters often have a designated wall in the sewing room that is covered with neutral-colored flannel. Fabric patches stick to it so the quilter can audition different color combinations. But I had no design wall—and no sewing room.) Like most beginning quilters, I took the layout of blocks in the book's pattern as only a suggestion and felt perfectly confident rearranging them to suit myself. (I still think the Drunkard's Path block looks better in the center than the Madison House.)

After that, quilting receded in my life for a while, as I got distracted with other things. Perhaps the impulse would have died out, except that I remarried in my late thirties and was pregnant at forty. The crib quilt that was my first project came out of the closet and became my son's "tiny special blanket," a description he took from a favorite children's book.

Alas, my mother never got to witness Max's devotion to the quilt she designed. She died suddenly the very week she was supposed to meet my infant son. Her memorial service was a tribute to a life of creativity, as family members filed into the church wearing all those handmade quilted vests. There were so many patchwork vests, it looked like the family uniform, and we seemed like the opposite of a mourning procession.

Losing my mother made quilting much more important to me. Quilting has been a way to make the connection between us feel profoundly alive. It's not just that I inherited her vast fabric stash and her collection of quilting books, one of the other things I inherited is my mother's bone structure, and sometimes when I look down in my lap and see my hands quilting, I get a physical jolt of déjà vu—they look exactly like hers.

The final legacy from my mother's estate was the quilt she was working on when she died, a complicated appliqué bed quilt that she had designed for my sister's daughter, Jenny. All in pinks, purples, and pale greens, the quilt featured reverse appliqué hearts and vines in each of four horizontal panels. Mother had finished the appliqué in the panels, but the four strips were not attached to each other and only a small portion of the quilting was done.

The quilt seemed beyond my skill level, and grief delayed me further. But I had promised Jenny at the memorial service that I would finish Grandma's quilt and so I did, though it took me more than five years. After all the quilting was done, I got stumped trying to figure out what borders would match and how to finish it, but the ladies at my local quilt shop (where I was a regular by now) knew just the thing: a thin border of striped fabric that echoed all the solid colors, with a wider border of deep purple at the edges.

My mother's last quilt: She designed and appliquéd it, and I completed it after her death.

Even though the quilt arrived in the mail on a day when she was engaged in an episode of full-out teenage angst, I learned that Jenny took one look at the finished quilt and wept. The quilt was stunningly beautiful, but I believe that, after waiting all those years, she was overcome with the palpable essence of two generations of love and perseverance.

Since then, building on what my mother taught me has brought me tremendous satisfaction. I would never say I'm "doing it for her," because I would never spend this much time doing something that didn't bring me joy. But I know the very fact that it does bring me joy would have been a source of endless delight for her.

While writing extensively on family traditions during my son's childhood, including completing and publishing two books, my quilting was done in spurts. I'd throw together a crib quilt when a friend got pregnant or adopted a baby, and I picked up a pattern here and there from a quilt shop to make myself a wall quilt.

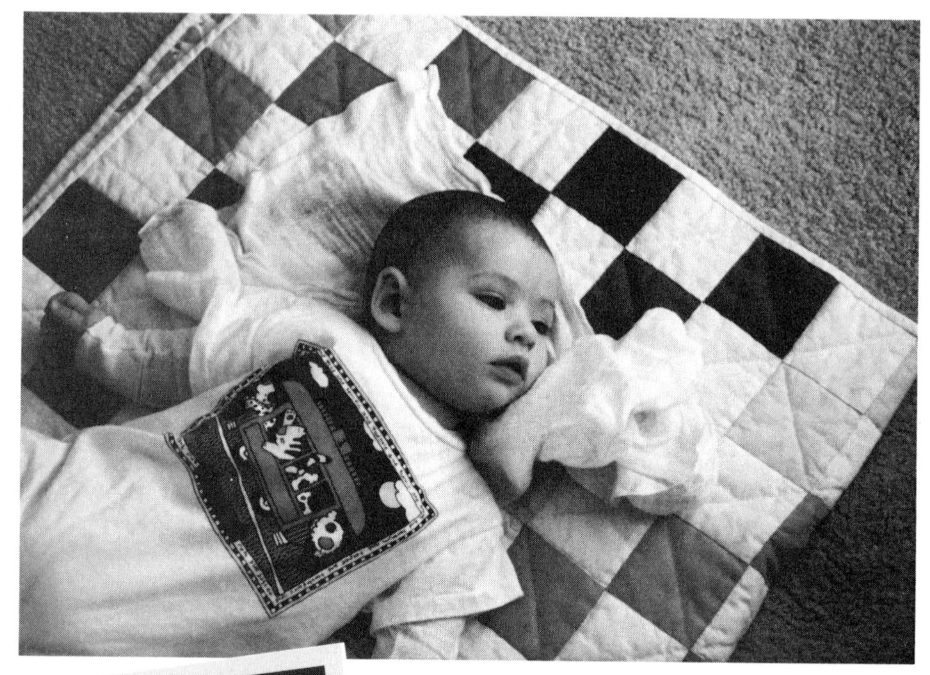

Me back in North Carolina, learning to hand quilt my first project. My son Max on my first quilt (top).

Although I have a high-tech sewing machine, a gift from my husband, and I've taken some machine-quilting classes, I continue to both piece and quilt by hand. That's not because I'm a snob about machine-done quilts or because I slavishly follow my mother's preferences, but simply because that's what works best in my life now.

As a writer, I spend my days sitting in front of a machine (my computer). As a wife and mother, I don't want to spend my evenings in front of a different machine. After dinner, I prefer to work in my lap, in the family room, where I can simultaneously supervise my son's homework, engage in conversation, or watch television. Also, hand piecing and quilting are as mobile as I need to be. I can quilt at school meetings, the pediatrician's office, and on long family car trips.

Like thousands of quilters everywhere, I've learned that a mere half hour of hand quilting each day can lead to an astounding number of finished quilts. Some day, I vow to myself, I'll take quilt cruises, enter my quilts in shows, and go on quilt retreats. For now, in this hectic period of my very domestic life, simply to be producing beautiful quilts is joy enough.

Why This Book?

SOME YEARS AGO, WHILE SEARCHING FOR IDEAS for a new book, I began to realize that I was holding an incredibly rich subject material in my own two hands. I saw that there were hundreds of how-to and project books, but there didn't seem to be any books that guided readers through the increasingly complex quilt world. The number of resources for quilters was multiplying exponentially. By the start of the twenty-first century, the number of quilt shops in the United States exceeded 2,500. A list of quilt-related websites could fill a fat volume all by itself. How could quilters ever determine the best tools for their own purposes out of so many choices?

I also became obsessed by this basic question: Why were more and more women in a high-tech, "liberated" era taking up this very old-fashioned pursuit? It seemed so counterintuitive. My journalist's nose smelled a trend story, and I followed it straight to the annual American Quilter's Society 2002 show in Paducah, Kentucky. While there, I peeked in on classes, interviewed prize-winning quilt teachers, and buttonholed quilters everywhere I went, even in parking lots and ladies' rooms. "Why do you do this?" I asked repeatedly, followed by "Why do you love it so much?"

I also became obsessed by this basic question: Why were more and more women taking up this very old-fashioned pursuit?

The photo quilt I made for my son's fifth grade class.

By this time, I had begun taking my questions to quilters across the country via a printed list of a dozen questions about quilters' histories. I posted notices about the questionnaire on quilters' message boards all over the Internet. I mailed questionnaires to quilt shops. The Keepsake Quilting catalog carried a listing describing my survey.

Responses flooded in, and quilters poured their hearts out. After receiving hundreds of completed questionnaires, I began to get a clearer picture of this modern quilt boom, what motivates quilters and what they want from their quilt life. And I decided I could help meet their needs. I've spent six years combing the vast quilt world and digging up riches, tracking down great sources of quilt supplies, quilt education, and quilt inspiration.

The purpose of this book is to help every reader, no matter what her (or his) skill level, grow and deepen as a quilter. Because what I found from the hundreds of quilters who have shared their dreams with me is an enormous thirst for more. A desire to make quilts that are even more expressive, accomplished, and original than the ones they've already made. Quilters vary enormously in their histories, techniques, and goals, I learned, but as a whole, they are a driven breed.

Anyone who has quilted for even a short time recognizes this pull. The feeling that quilting is rooted in a rich tradition going back hundreds of years provides a wonderfully grounded feeling. But most quilters are pointed forcefully ahead, almost giddy with a sense of excitement about the next quilt and the next technique. They seem to feel part of a great adventure, both personally and collectively: The possibilities for today's quilters to create and experiment are tantalizing and limitless.

My fervent hope is that this book helps lead you toward that exciting future faster—to being the best quilter you can possibly be.

A traditional Amish quilt from the late nineteenth century (top). Make Me Gotta Holler, *by Penny Mateer, from the early twenty-first century (bottom).*

Six Quilt Myths Debunked

MYTH ONE: LIKE JAZZ, QUILTING IS AN AMERICAN INVENTION.

A QUILT IS A FABRIC SANDWICH, WITH A WARM stuffing material nestled between two layers of cloth and sewed tightly together. Sometimes the top layer is made of many pieces of fabric sewn together, a so-called patchwork, but what makes it a quilt is the three layers, not the patchwork. This technique has been traced back thousands of years to ancient Egypt, where it was used especially in the making of warm clothing. Medieval knights wore such padded garments under their armor, as did their horses.

The oldest quilted bedcover to survive dates back to fourteenth-century Sicily. Starting in the 1600s, quilted bedcovers made in India were a popular import item for the British market. By the time America was colonized, there was a well-established quilting tradition throughout Europe, especially in England and Holland. Most of these quilts were made from large pieces of a single fabric; what were whole-cloth quilts. Later, colorful patchwork quilts made from scrap fabric became a symbol of American thrift and resourcefulness. Today, America's quilters stand out for their artistry and technical innovation. But quilting itself was a borrowed craft.

A fourteenth-century Italian quilted blanket illustrating the story of Tristan and Isolde.

MYTH TWO: QUILTING WAS BIG IN COLONIAL AMERICA.

THE FIRST WOMEN TO COME TO AMERICA SURELY brought needle skills with them, but there is scant evidence that they brought quilts. Household inventories from the seventeenth century rarely mention quilts. The relatively few intact quilts dating back to the first third of the eighteenth century tend to be whole cloth (not patchwork) made of wool or imported silk.

Early on, American women had practical reasons for not quilting: After working in the fields, cooking the food, caring for children, and spinning, weaving, and sewing to keep their families clothed, there was little time to quilt. Some garments were quilted, but blankets were generally made of wool and often imported from England. Those colonists who did own quilts prized them, but most of these treasures were imported. Quilting and quilting bees started becoming popular sometime after 1750, but historians agree that the peak of early American quiltmaking came later, from 1830 to 1870. That coincides with the production of good quality, affordable cotton from America's own mills and the cult of domesticity that praised fine needlework as the height of womanly accomplishment.

A silk and ribbon quilt from the 1740s.

An American mill worker in 1916, winding cotton thread onto a cone.

MYTH THREE: QUILTING IS ONLY FOR THE FRUGAL.

Fabric scraps and worn-out clothing have been used by Americans to make quilts since colonial times; during the Depression such quilts were commonplace. But art and luxury are as much a part of quilt history as craft and necessity. When making an album quilt, for example, no two quilt blocks are the same. Baltimore album quilts up the ante, featuring elaborate appliquéd blocks of flowers, animals, and people. In the 1840s, these were all the rage, elaborately stitched by ladies with lots of leisure time. Crazy quilts, a rampant fad in the 1870s, were made almost entirely by well-off women who competed to use the most lavish imported silk, velvet, and lace, set off with extravagant embroidery. These were not bedcovers made to keep families warm but elegant throws for the parlor sofa.

A typical crazy quilt from the 1890s, made with fine fabrics, such as velvet, and lavishly embroidered.

Lately the line between art and necessity has become blurred. The Gee's Bend quilters, African American women living in a remote area of Alabama, make striking quilts from such humble material as their husbands' worn overalls. Lauded for their strong, simple designs, these quilts are now being exhibited in top art museums, including the Whitney in New York City and Boston's Museum of Fine Arts.

Today quilters probably quilt more for joy than out of necessity. The hunt for bargain fabrics can be a sport. The majority of quilters own both sewing machines—whether it's an old clunker or state-of-the-art—and computers. And it's likely that when quilters decide to reuse fabric or clothing it's for nostalgic reasons, such as making T-shirt quilts for a family memento.

MYTH FOUR: QUILTS WERE USED TO GUIDE RUNAWAY SLAVES TO THE UNDERGROUND RAILROAD.

WHEN A BOOK CALLED *HIDDEN IN PLAIN VIEW: A Secret Story of Quilts and the Underground Railroad*, written by Jacqueline L. Tobin and Raymond G. Dobard, was published in 1999, with the claim that slaves used a series of specific quilt blocks to find safe havens on the Underground Railroad, it made a big splash. Quilt kits were designed to correspond to the book's stories, and the book was adapted for elementary school curriculums all across the country. But it was based solely on the family stories of one (now deceased) quilt vendor from Charleston, South Carolina, Ozella McDaniel Williams, and historians have not been able to corroborate its claims. One of the criticisms directed at the book is that some of the blocks cited as guiding slaves didn't exist until much later.

In addition, government-sponsored interviews with hundreds of former slaves in the 1930s didn't turn up a single personal remembrance of a quilt the blocks of which were used in this fashion. Although there is a rich tradition of African American quilts and there are antique quilts that commemorate the Underground Railroad, the use of coded quilts to guide slaves appears unlikely. Some quilt historians have made a near crusade of trying to nip this myth in the bud, but already it seems as deeply rooted as George Washington's cherry tree.

MYTH FIVE: OLD QUILTS ARE ALWAYS WORTH A LOT OF MONEY.

This quilt is valuable because it covers Calvin Coolidge's childhood bed.

IN 1991, AN ANTIQUE QUILT SOLD FOR $264,000 AT a Sotheby's auction, but the circumstances were unusual. It was a Civil War–era quilt—these are rare; it was beautiful; and it was in excellent condition, all vital factors influencing the quilt's worth. Furthermore, two determined quilt dealers engaged in a fierce bidding war, pushing the price to historic levels. Well-preserved Civil War quilts are almost always sought after. On the other hand, many rare, old quilts are falling apart, drained of color or otherwise not pleasing to look at, and thus fail to fetch a high price.

Quilt lovers who frequent garage sales and flea markets constantly find stunning old quilts and quilt tops in good shape that they pick up for a song. Some of these go on to sell for hundreds of dollars, but it takes a practiced eye to tell a faded modern copy from a rare antique quilt. Even a gorgeous old quilt in excellent condition may not fetch a great deal, if it is made with a very common pattern. Unless, perhaps, the quilt was made or owned by someone famous. The quilt on President Calvin Coolidge's boyhood bed isn't exceptional except for the fact that it was made by Coolidge. If this quilt were ever to come on the market (which is unlikely), it would probably fetch a bundle.

MYTH SIX: SERIOUS QUILTS ARE MADE ONLY BY HAND, NOT BY MACHINE.

As long as there have been sewing machines, quilters have made use of them. The sewing machine came on the market in the 1850s and was a must-have appliance within twenty years. Quilt historians say that quilters immediately started using sewing machines to piece together their patchwork tops, which led them to try new complex geometric patterns. By one estimate, 75 percent of the quilts made between 1860 and 1940 had at least some machine stitching in them, even those produced by the Amish in some parts of the country. Nonetheless, most quilters continued to mix machine and hand work, doing the actual quilting of the three layers together by hand, partly because their machines couldn't handle something as big or thick as a quilt.

An early sewing machine.

When the most recent quilt renaissance started in the 1970s, many quilters did everything by hand and said that anyone who quilted by machine was a "cheater." But by the late 1980s, machine quilting was widely recognized as a valid design choice, not just the last resort of a lazy quilter looking for shortcuts. Quilts that were sewn entirely by machine were winning some of the top quilt prizes, showcasing dazzling new quilting techniques that took hours of patient practice.

Much of the information here comes from three excellent books on quilt history: *Quilts: Their Story, and How to Make Them*, by Marie D. Webster, *Old Patchwork Quilts and the Women Who Made Them*, by Ruth E. Finley, and *The American Quilt: A History of Cloth and Comfort 1750–1950*, by Roderick Kiracofe and Mary Elizabeth Johnson.

On Choosing the Word *Quilter*

It says volumes about the increased sophistication and complexity of the quilt world that people have warned me against using the word *quilter*. The differences between the people who create quilts today sometimes seem greater than the similarities. There is a vast distance on the continuum from those who stick with historical patterns and methods to art quilters who challenge every notion of what a quilt looks like, and between the casual hobbyist quilters and those who earn their living making quilts.

Even among traditionalists there is now a division of labor: More and more, there are people who only make quilt tops and others who are professional quilt finishers. Some denizens of the quilt world believe that only those people who sew the three layers together, whether by hand or machine, should be called quilters.

Katrina Blues, *by Susan Shie*.

"I don't get offended when someone calls me a quilter," says art quilter Susan Shie, whose distinctive quilts are reminiscent of the best folk art. "But I know that when you tell someone you're a quilter, your goose is cooked. They get a flash image of a little old lady sewing a traditional quilt. I am an artist who happens to use the quilt form to create, so I call myself an art quilter."

Other art quilters have different preferences. Some prefer to be called textile artists or fiber artists. Quilting teacher Karen Musgrave says she would rather be called a quiltmaker. Instead of becoming tangled up in labels for the people and quilts described here, I have chosen to use the word *quilter* in general, clarifying with additional descriptive words when they seemed necessary. I have tried to write a book that will be useful to anybody who makes quilts, collects quilts, or loves quilts.

CHAPTER ONE

Who Quilts Today and Why

A WOMAN USING THE SCREEN NAME "STARBUCKS" posted this item on an Internet message board for quilters in 2001: "Okay, I just did the math. I'm forty-three years old. I make about fifteen quilts a year. If I live another thirty years, that's four hundred and fifty more quilts. And the scary part is that I've already got enough fabric to make them!!!!"

Starbucks went on to say she had recently taken an oath to stop "sport shopping for fabric," and she wondered whether other quilters were curbing their own fabric lust. Typical of the posts that followed was this: "My oath lasted until I went into Rite Aid to buy some Depends for my mother. I came out with twelve yards of patterned flannel. . . ."

The Quilting in America study made by CKMedia looked most closely at what it calls "dedicated quilters," the 5 percent of the group who spend more than $600 a year on their hobby. These well-educated, well-off women buy more than one hundred yards of fabric a year and start an average of fourteen projects annually. Most are computer-savvy, own multiple sewing machines, and have a special room just for quilting.

These women are citizens of the twenty-first-century quilt world, a place that would amaze quilters from earlier eras in American history, and a place that nonquilters don't even know exists.

This modern quilt world is a place where quilters use cutting-edge technology to practice an ancient craft on a whole new scale, sometimes making as many quilts in a year as a nineteenth-century quilter produced in an entire lifetime. These quiltmakers use computer-powered sewing machines, download quilt software onto their PalmPilots, and buy fabric online from all over the world. They probably belong to a local quilt guild, but if they have a technique question before its next meeting, they'll post a query in one of dozens of online quilting forums, where the virtual quilting bee never ends.

The growing legions of passionate American quilters have almost single-handedly saved the makers of fabric and sewing machines in this country from extinction, creating a vast, sophisticated web of vendors, suppliers, and teachers that, in turn, produce products and designs that inspire quilters to make even more quilts.

Quilting nearly died out in America after World War II but is now thriving like never before, as a renaissance that began in the late sixties continues to build. There are an estimated 27.7 million quilters in this country, up from 15.5 million in 1993, when magazine publisher CKMedia (then Primedia Inc.) first commissioned a survey to count them. If all the quilters in the country lived in one state, its population would

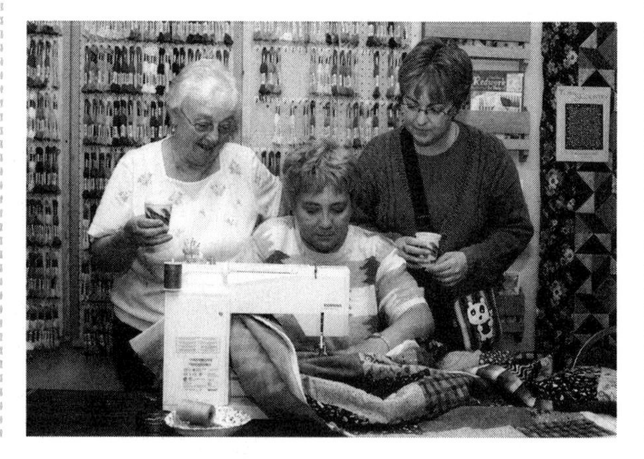

Linda Laegergren, center, of New London, Minnesota, flanked by Dorothy Rudland and Christine Paynter, of Bristol, England, at the Flying Goose Quilt Shoppe.

rival that of Texas, and those would be some very warm and happy cowgirls (according to CKMedia, 99 percent of quilters are women).

Although there are particular "hotbeds" of quilting activity in the Midwest, in New England, and on the West Coast, quilters thrive in every state of the union, and they travel far and wide to take classes and buy quilt supplies. The International Quilt Festival, the biggest annual quilt show in the United States, is run by Quilts, Inc. and attracts more than fifty thousand people to Houston. Most years, it's the biggest convention in town. The other major annual national quilt show, the AQS Quilt Show & Contest, in Paducah, Kentucky, run by the American Quilter's Society, is second only to the Kentucky Derby in the tourist dollars it brings into that state, filling up hotels fifty miles away. Regional and local quilt shows flourish and their numbers grow yearly.

A booth at the 2006 Machine Quilters Exposition in Manchester, New Hampshire (top), and a demonstration of the Aranya method of fabric dyeing at the 2006 Festival of Quilts in Birmingham, England (bottom).

Lime Light, by Phillippa Naylor, won Best of Show at the 2003 AQS Quilt Show in Paducah, Kentucky.

These days, the stakes for prizewinners are high. Top quiltmakers don't just compete for pin money or the blue ribbon at the county fair. The total prize money every year at the Paducah show alone exceeds $100,000 when you combine all of the categories.

Contrary to the myth of quilting as a boon for the poor and frugal, America's quilters love to shop, supporting more than 2,500 quilt stores and spending an estimated $3.3 billion each year on their hobby. Instead of recycling old clothes, they're scooping up top-of-the-line cotton fabric, along with $100 custom-fitted thimbles and $1,000 sewing machines.

The myth that most quilters are rural and poor has likely been fueled in recent years by such events as the wildly popular quilt show that toured the country's art museums featuring stunning quilts from Gee's Bend, Alabama. Before they became the subject of books and television documentaries, these African American women spent decades living quiet lives in hardscrabble conditions. After working in the fields by day, they would come home to make quilts to keep their families warm. Although they still live in a remote hamlet, the women of Gee's Bend today sell their quilts for hundreds of dollars, sometimes thousands. Though not rich, they have become famous. Many of them have toured the country giving interviews and signing autographs, as erudite museum directors gush over them. When at home, most of them still quilt.

Meanwhile, fellow quilters across the country are as apt to be teachers and investment bankers as farmwives, and to live in suburbs and cities as often as in farm towns. And though some still sew by hand, the quilt craze is essentially fueled by a technology boom. Quilting retains many of its traditional charms for women, as both a uniquely satisfying craft and an excuse for pleasant social interaction, but the craft has traveled far from its early roots to become big, brassy, and very modern.

In today's quilt world, sewing machine companies chase celebrity quiltmakers like Nike courts basketball stars, featuring them in ad campaigns and new product press conferences (although they pay them

The Gee's Bend quilters, here at the Museum of Fine Arts in Boston, sometimes sing spirituals at their appearances and have even recorded an album. Below, some of the quilters at home in Gee's Bend, Alabama.

Art quilter Nancy Crow at work on one of her masterpieces.

much less). Top quilt teachers endorse specific brands of thread and hawk their own fabric lines, magazines, books, and instructional DVDs.

Quilting has become a fashion business, with between forty thousand and sixty thousand new fabric patterns introduced every year, largely for this market. Quilt publishing has exploded too, both in books and magazines: Amazon.com alone lists more than three thousand quilt titles.

Knitting is booming as well, prompted by some of the same primal needs women have to create, socialize, and give meaningful gifts to their loved ones. Today's knitting world has also become flashier and trend driven. But one of the striking differences between the two disciplines is that quilting is taken seriously not only as a pastime but also as an art form.

The movement of artists into quilting in the sixties and seventies was a central factor in shaping the quilt boom, and the ripple effects are very wide. It was a time of ferment, when crafts of all sorts were being reevaluated and elevated in the art world and the lines between art and craft were purposely blurred. Robert Rauschenberg produced an artwork in 1955 called *Bed* in which he painted over parts of a traditional quilt. By the time acclaimed quiltmaker Michael James went to art school in the late sixties, he says that painting seemed dead to him, but the medium of textiles was on the verge of exploding, and he became a quiltmaker instead of a painter.

In those years, traditional quilts were being seen anew by curators and critics immersed in abstract art, and they were dazzled by the colors and composition. This led to a groundbreaking 1971 exhibition at the Whitney museum called Abstract Design in American Quilts. The sixty-two bed-size quilts were mostly traditional patterns and were made between 1840 and 1930, but major critics raved that they were masterpieces that ranked with the best contemporary art. And it wasn't just New Yorkers who saw and praised these quilts: For nearly four years, the show crisscrossed the United States and Europe.

This critical attention literally pulled quilts off of beds. First, the chorus of accolades increased the number of quilt collectors and the perceived value of quilts. Just as important, the hoopla liberated quiltmakers, inspiring them to stop thinking of their works as utilitarian household artifacts.

Today, most who consider themselves art quilters virtually never make a quilt that will be used as a bed covering. Art quilts can be any size and shape imaginable and are made of everything from metal scraps to matchsticks—materials that no one would fancy sleeping under. But even an ordinary quilter quietly pursuing the traditional hobby makes a choice each time as to whether to make a wall hanging, a bed quilt, a tote bag, an iPod case, or something else.

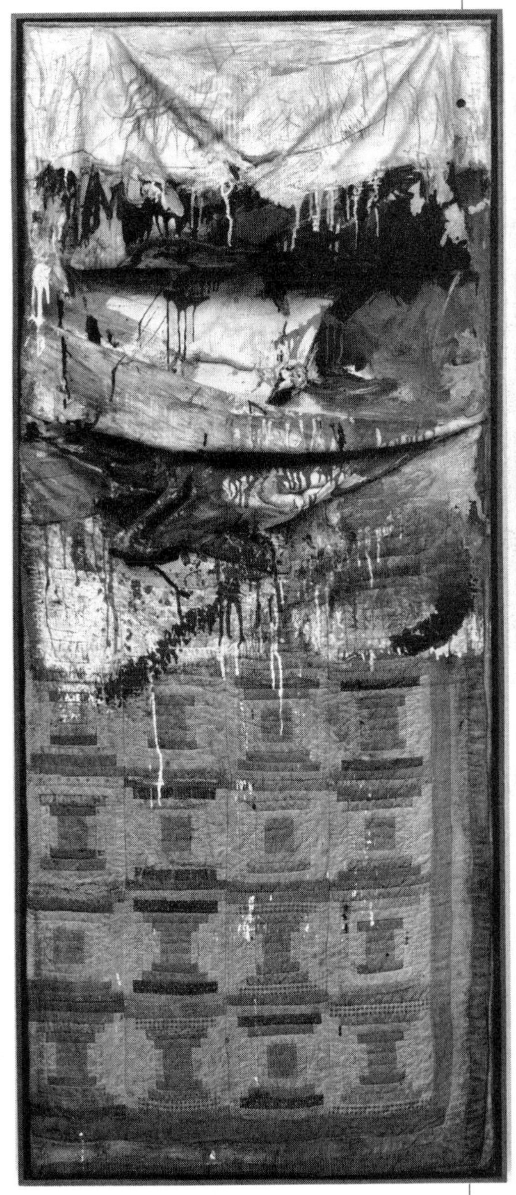

Robert Rauschenberg's 1955 artwork Bed.

The complex quilt world of the early twenty-first century encompasses crafters of every level of sophistication. There are millions of casual hobbyists content to work at a leisurely pace, trying out traditional block patterns that are hundreds of years old. They might advance to a difficult Mariner's Compass or take up Baltimore album quilts, in which each block is a different appliqué pattern. Their goal might be to make a quilt for every single member of their extended family.

At the other end are quilters pushing the envelope in every conceivable way, dyeing their own fabrics, inventing their own patterns, and creating abstract quilts or pictorial quilts. They're making quilts as a form of expression rather than a gift for their parents' fiftieth wedding anniversary (which doesn't mean they won't take a break to do that, too). They may spend months of each year on the road, teaching all over the world, and they have made quilts a profession rather than a hobby.

But all the different parts of the quilt world get a glimpse of the others at major quilt shows, in magazines and catalogs, and online, and they inevitably influence one another. Even hobbyist quilters who just want to make crib quilts for their pregnant friends are aware that some quilts sell for thousands of dollars and hang on museum walls. Knitters usually don't wonder if the products of their labor will some day wind up in a sweater museum. For quilters, the knowledge that their work stands on a continuum leading toward art creates an extra sense of satisfaction—and aspiration.

And yet, all this hovers out of sight, a subculture of zealous crafters and artists who remain invisible to the nonquilting nation and the big-city media not located in places where quilting shows are a staple on local PBS. Bonnie Browning, executive show director of the quilt show in Paducah, says with a sigh, "I wish I had a quarter for every person I've met who said, 'Oh, quilts. My grandma made those.' "

The quilting nation may not remain invisible much longer, considering the rapid growth in both the number of quilters and the money they spend. Rob O'Brian, a direct-marketing executive who knew nothing about quilting until he was hired to run retailer Keepsake Quilting in 2005, was flabbergasted at the size and complexity of the world he walked into. "Quilting today is where NASCAR was ten years ago," he says. Perhaps before long, *Time* magazine will be writing about savvy politicians who are setting out to court the "quilt vote."

One of Carol Bruce's Needlesongs *patterns (top), and Roberta Horton's book* The Fabric Makes the Quilt.

Why Quilt Now?

IT ISN'T LIKE "EVERYBODY" QUILTS, WHICH WAS essentially true in America in the nineteenth century, when virtually every girl was taught to sew and most quilted. In many parts of the country, a young woman coming of age was expected to enter her marriage with a dowry of quilts she had made herself. (Indeed, many a quilting bee was scheduled to finish up a batch of quilt tops in time for an impending wedding.) But these days, making quilts is purely a matter of choice.

But why do quilters quilt? What's the bug that gives them this itch? For quiltaholics, what's the nature of the high that fuels their addiction? In sorting through the responses to the quilt questionnaire that I circulated for this book, some answers to the question of why quilting is booming emerged. And to why those who start to quilt often abandon every other craft they once pursued.

Home economics hasn't been obligatory since the 1960s, and women in their twenties and thirties haven't learned the basics of sewing like their mothers did in high school. This creates a potential problem for nurturing the next generation of quilters (although the sewing fad that followed TV's *Project Runway* might help). But in the baby boom generation, the bedrock of today's quilting population, it's hard to find a woman who didn't sew at least an apron in high school. In the 1950s and early 1960s, the home-sewing market flourished, and every department store had a vast stock of fabric and a wide selection of patterns. (In New York, Macy's fabric department took up an entire floor, one full city block long and one block wide.) Sewing one's own clothes was not only frugal, but a girl could make the trendy garments her mother wouldn't possibly consider buying.

For quilters, the knowledge that their work stands on a continuum leading toward art creates an extra sense of satisfaction—and aspiration.

A lot of those sewing skills went dormant as women entered the workforce in droves in the sixties and seventies. The vast majority of these striving women stopped sewing their own clothes, which tipped over a long line of dominoes. Sewing machine sales plummeted. Department stores closed their fabric departments. Fabric companies went bankrupt.

To be sure, there were grandmothers and mothers who had been quilting for decades who didn't put down their needles, but their numbers diminished and they had trouble finding the fabrics and other supplies they needed. It didn't take many attempts for them to discover that stretchy polyester made lousy quilts.

Macy's fabric department in its heyday.

The smattering of women who never stopped quilting continued their work alone and unsung. Nobody really knew about these die-hard throwbacks until Bonnie Leman started a mail-order business selling quilt patterns in the 1960s. Leman, a Denver, Colorado, mother of seven, inherited a whole cache of mimeographed quilt patterns from her mother and decided to try to supplement the family income with a home-based business selling to quilters. She also sold thin plastic templates in the shape of popular quilt block patterns: Quilters could put these templates on fabric and draw and cut around them to make their patchwork pieces.

Bonnie Leman holds the first-ever Quilter's Newsletter Magazine.

Sales grew nicely, so in 1969, Leman created a modest little newsletter to pad out her catalog of patterns. She called it *Quilter's Newsletter Magazine* and printed a first edition of five thousand copies. The newsletters sold out immediately, much to her surprise, so she printed more issues in bigger and bigger numbers. By 1985, she had a paid circulation of 150,000.

Women basting a quilt in the 1940s.

As Leman was beginning her newsletter, major changes in the culture of the country were quietly sowing the seeds of a quilting revival that would bring in new, younger blood, as hippies and conservationists tried out crafts and self-sufficiency. It may seem like everybody was making lopsided macramé plant holders, but some people were also attempting to sew quilts. Others were buying old quilts at flea markets and yard sales, engaged in a frugal and aesthetically pleasing form of recycling.

Shelly Zegart, a prominent quilt appraiser, collector, and cofounder of the nonprofit group The Alliance for American Quilts, says, "I believe what really started the revival were these artsy people who didn't want regular jobs. They discovered they could make a living buying up old quilts, then selling them out of their beat-up minivans."

The Alliance for American Quilts

The Alliance for American Quilts is a key organization behind the nationwide drive to preserve quilt history. In 1981, Shelly Zegart, quilt collector and appraiser, founded the first state quilt documentation project in Kentucky. A few years later, she met Karey Bresenhan and Nancy O'Bryant, cousins who founded Quilts, Inc., which runs the International Quilt Festival, and the nonprofit Texas Quilt Search, a documentation project in that state. As the years went by, more and more states began concerted efforts to document quilts, with thirty state projects initiated just between 1985 and 1988.

The Center for the Quilt Online.

In the early 1990s, these strong women decided to join together to actively preserve quilts and quilt history on a national basis, fueled by both technology and controversy. The Kentucky Quilt Project had held a notable conference on using new computer technology to store and share quilt images and historical data, and Zegart, Bresenhan, and O'Bryant felt this technology should be widely available. At the same time, the Smithsonian Institution provoked a controversy when it licensed overseas reproduction of some of the prime quilts in its collection. American quilters were up in arms, saying these Asian imports would cheapen the image of America's treasures. After receiving thousands of angry letters and hearing congressional testimony by Bresenhan, among others, the Smithsonian canceled the reproduction license. But the controversy convinced Zegart, Bresenhan, and others that American quilts and quilters needed a voice and a way to preserve their history, and they cofounded the alliance, a 501(c)3 nonprofit, in 1993.

Since then, The Alliance for American Quilts has grown exponentially and the fruits of its many projects can be found at the Center for the Quilt Online **(www.centerforthequilt.org).** The website showcases several ongoing oral history projects, including Quilters' S.O.S.—Save Our Stories, fascinating interviews with more than six hundred quilters, from the famous to the dabbler, who all share personal stories. Browsers here can also find the Quilt Index, an online listing soon to exceed fifty thousand photographs and records from many museum collections and state documentation projects.

Now based in Asheville, North Carolina, The Alliance for American Quilts continues to expand its mission to preserve and share the story of quilts and provides free downloads of instructions on how to document local quilts.

Zegart remembers meeting one of these laid-back quilt sellers near her home in Louisville, Kentucky, in 1976, and though she knew absolutely nothing about quilts, she fell in love with these beautiful objects. She had no interest in sewing, but Zegart started passionately collecting quilts and researching their history. From then on, much of her energy was devoted to quilts and their history, as she helped start a statewide project in Kentucky in the early 1980s to document old quilts and the stories of their makers. This effort has since spread across the country, spawning documentation efforts in many states.

It was a short trip from appreciating old quilts to trying to make new ones. But appreciation came first, powered by the patriotic fever leading up to America's bicentennial in 1976. Suddenly, quilt shows were popping up at museums all across the country, and the products of America's patchwork history were uncovered as the treasures they are. All the top antiques stores in Manhattan sold exquisite examples of Baltimore album and other elaborate quilts, and the quilted look even influenced the fashion scene. In 1969, dress designer Adolfo, credited with popularizing harem pants "and the bolero jacket, introduced the patchwork look." The heiress Gloria Vanderbilt was photographed wearing a patchwork skirt.

Patricia Crews, director of the International Quilt Study Center.

Eager to capitalize on the quilt craze, all of the major women's magazines showcased antique quilts in beautiful living rooms and bedrooms, and started featuring new quilt patterns. But printing patterns wasn't enough: Modern women wanted to make quilts that looked like the historic ones, but they were loathe to use cumbersome tools like room-size frames. At the time, there were commercial wood frames available to hold the fabric in place for quilting—even Sears, Roebuck offered quilt frames in its catalog then. But the younger generation that rediscovered quilting demanded new techniques.

In her groundbreaking 1973 book, *The Perfect Patchwork Primer,* Beth Gutcheon was already suggesting to modern women that, if they didn't enjoy quilting, they hire somebody else to finish the tops they had pieced. As for frames, she wrote, "You can use a quilting frame if you like (and, more to the point, if you have room). Traditional quilters feel that a frame is essential, but I think that's part habit, part horseradish."

Gutcheon suggested that those who didn't want to use a frame could simply roll up part of their basted quilt, weigh it down with phone books at that end, then work on the other end, possibly letting it hang down from an ironing board. "You can sit cross-legged on the floor, with the work in your lap. . . ." she wrote.

Thus began a whole era in which a new generation of quilt teachers was born with the mission of making quilting easy. In *American Quiltmaking: 1970–2000,* a book documenting the quilt renaissance, author Eleanor Levie quotes one of the boom's founding mothers, Marti Michell. In 1977, Michell had come to *Woman's Day* magazine with her kit for making a Log Cabin quilt using a simple method that dispensed with the frame. Women could make the quilt by hand, in their laps, and Michell proved it was quick by making one over a weekend for an editor at the magazine.

Shortly thereafter, a promotion ran in *Woman's Day* for what the magazine called "the quickest quilt in the world." Michell told Levie that the promotion was a "blockbuster." She and her husband filled all the orders themselves and had eighteen-wheel semitrucks pulling up to their house to cart off fabric and patterns. Michell says she doesn't have an exact count on how many quilt kits sold, but it was "millions of dollars worth."

Even before the bicentennial, there were stirrings of a quilt revival as part of a blossoming crafts movement in California. One of the pioneering quilt teachers was Roberta Horton, who had been a teacher of home economics. In the late sixties, Horton and her husband were adopting a baby girl, and that's when she decided she should apply her sewing skills to making a quilt.

Two of the first books aimed at making quilting fun and accessible: Beth Gutcheon's The Perfect Patchwork Primer, *and Christine Barnes and Steve W. Marley's* Quilting, Patchwork & Appliqué.

"At the time, there was hardly any information available and only one pattern book I could find," says Horton. "In 1970, I went to my first quilting event and there were lots of quilts there and a speaker who had consulted on the first quilt book published by Sunset. I became a quiltmaker from that day on."

First Horton taught quilting in a classroom she rented from a grocery chain in Berkeley, advertising in the store's flyers for students. For a decade, she taught in adult education programs. "We worked in such isolation as quiltmakers in the early days," she marvels. "I think the quilt world has advanced so much since then that a beginning quilter today can pick up in two years what we learned in ten. They don't have to reinvent the wheel because there is such a rapid exchange of information now."

Many of the early quilt teachers translated what instructions there were into the simplest possible terms. When Eleanor Burns started teaching quilting in 1978, she had been a special education teacher and was dyslexic, so she methodically broke everything down into the shortest, easiest steps. The name of her class, Quilt in a Day, became her motto and the name of her company. Burns became the "Pied Piper of quilting," leading a long line behind her.

The Shelton Bicentennial Quilt, *a group quilt commemorating the history of the town of Shelton, Connecticut, through 1976.*

Burns' other trademark was her corny sense of humor, and that was also a tool of another early enabler, Mary Ellen Hopkins. At the quilt shop she opened in Santa Monica in 1978, called Crazy Ladies and Friends, Hopkins challenged the conventional wisdom of the day, which held that there were rigid rules about quilts. Those rules related not just to how quilts were made but even to how they should be used. Never sit on a quilt was one hard and fast rule, the reason being that "it will weaken the stitches." So Hopkins called her first book *The It's Okay if You Sit on My Quilt Book*, and told every class she taught, "There are no quilt police!"

Pioneering quilt teachers were pulling in new quilters in other parts of the country too, especially through the early quilt television shows. Georgia Bonesteel, whose contribution was to teach lap quilting—how to break quilts down into smaller, more manageable pieces—had her first show on North Carolina public television in 1979. In 1981, Penny McMorris started broadcasting a quilting show from Bowling Green, Ohio. The honchos at PBS were stunned when fifty stations all across the country signed up for the thirteen-episode series. McMorris followed up with a second thirteen-week series the next year.

It's surprising how quickly quilting pulls women in. Alex Anderson, host of the long-running television show *Simply Quilts*, recalls an e-mail she got from a woman who had just started quilting. "She sent me this very serious message about how obsessive she was becoming and she asked me, 'Is this healthy?' " recalls Anderson, with a laugh. What did Anderson write back? "Welcome to the club."

Squared Illusions IV, *by Gloria Hansen.*

All these great teachers got enormous help popularizing quilting with the introduction of a nifty new tool in the late 1970s: the rotary cutter. This simple, inexpensive gadget looks something like a pizza cutter, but in the quilt world, it sparked a revolution comparable to the effect of the food processor on home cooking. Instead of having to laboriously cut each single piece of fabric, rotary cutters whipped through many layers like a hot knife through butter. Pattern makers instantly created new construction techniques that used the rotary cutter, in turn allowing quilters to make quilts even faster and spawning a whole series of new books, such as Bethany Reynolds' Stack-n-Whack books, referring to her own trademarked shortcuts for rotary cutting and speed-sewing quilts.

A rotary cutter: the food processor of the quilt world.

Quilting Is Simple

THEIR METHODS AND PERSONALITIES MAY HAVE been different, but the secret all these early teachers passed along was the same: Basic quiltmaking is actually quite simple. And those who decided to give quilting a try soon learned that for themselves. It turns out that quilting is one of those impressive-sounding domestic projects like roasting a turkey that is actually loads easier than it looks, especially with the new quicker techniques. Virtually anybody who can sew a straight line can make a basic quilt by machine or by hand. And it's a very forgiving medium.

By simply cutting and sewing neatly, it's possible to produce something quite beautiful without a guidebook or guru. A small crib quilt for a new baby is a project that can be completed swiftly and easily but will be met with gasps of admiration and appreciation from the recipient. It's a gift that becomes a treasured possession for generations, long after the cute onesies are outgrown.

Pat Slaven, who studied textiles in India and has tested sewing machines for Consumers Union, says she both quilts and knits, but that she finds quilting less time-consuming. "Because I do everything but bindings by machine and use time-saving tricks for cutting, I can finish a quilt pretty fast," says Slaven. "But a sweater is a big commitment: It usually takes me several months, partly because I dye my own wool."

Emily Ronning, a River Falls, Wisconsin, resident, started quilting right after graduate school and says she doesn't know many people her age who quilt. She thinks one reason for this is the misperception that quilting is difficult. "So many people say to me, 'Oh, I could *never* do that!'" says Ronning. "But the reality is anyone can do it. Certainly, some patterns or types of quilting require more time and skill than others. But ultimately, anyone can do it and be good at it. It's just taking that first step that's scary."

Unlike some crafts, like macramé, that boomed then busted, quilting isn't quickly outgrown. There's always something more to learn. In fact, quilting can also be incredibly complicated, full of hard-to-sew curves and intricate embellishments. There's endless room to grow, for those so inclined.

Even without being a gifted artist, a quilter can keep going deeper into the craft and produce more and more sophisticated work. More time and effort leads to greater satisfaction, which leads to quilters eagerly taking on new challenges. Even fairly new quilters often alter a purchased pattern and are soon emboldened to design their own quilts. Then they go on to local and national quilt shows, take classes, join quilt groups, and seek out craft museums. They might start selling their own patterns and usually progress from making quilts that cover their beds to art quilts for their walls.

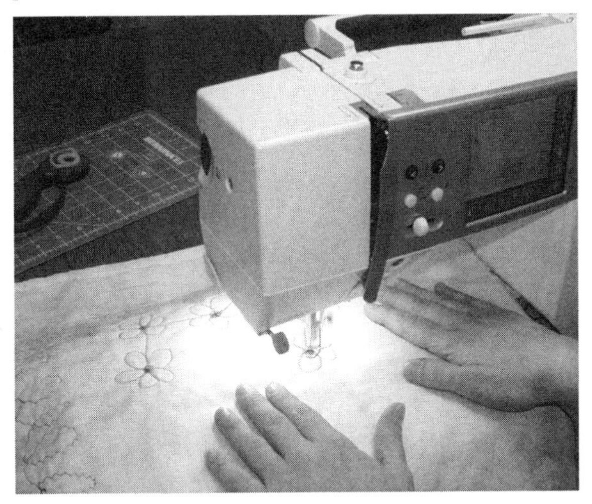

An at-home quilting setup: a sewing machine, rotary cutter, and quilter's ruler.

"The quilt boom took off because there is something for Ms. Overachiever and stuff for Ms. Klutz," says Mary Ellen Hopkins, the comical early quilting instructor who joked about the "quilt police."

Quilting Is Addictive

BETWEEN THE "SIMPLIFIERS" AND THOSE PUSHING quilts to new levels, quilting has become a hobby that is both easy to start and hard to stop. Many of the quilters who filled in the research questionnaire for this book reported that they were hooked after a single class or the completion of their first project.

Psychiatrist Jeri Riggs of Dobbs Ferry, New York, is a typical example—she made her first quilt for her first baby: Someone in her mother's circle of friends quilted and got her interested. By the time Riggs dropped her medical practice in 1992, she was ready to make quilting her life's work, and she has. She belongs to a group of art quilters called Fiber Revolution, exhibits her quilts in galleries, and maintains a website showcasing her work.

Jeri Riggs (above) and her quilt Thinking Inside the Box.

Janet Steadman who lives in Clinton, Washington, laughs at the thought that she took up quilting because she bought a round bed in the early 1980s and couldn't find a bedspread that fit. Since then, she has made more than 135 quilts, studied with legendary art quilters, and won top prizes at prestigious quilt shows.

It took just one episode of Alex Anderson's television show about quilting, *Simply Quilts*, to convince Geraldine Congdon of Santa Rosa, California, that this was for her. "I saw an episode with quilt teacher Katie Pasquini Masopust, and I thought, 'Wow! This is what I want to do,' " she recalls. Once she retired in 1999, Masopust started quilting constantly, completing more than fifty quilts in the first four years and moving from store-bought fabrics to dyeing her own.

And, Cathy Rogers in Schaumburg, Illinois, says she took her first quilting class in 1986, after she and a friend noticed pretty quilts in the window of a nearby shop called A Touch of Amish. She loved quilting immediately and dreams of retiring from her job as a school nurse to quilt full-time. All right, maybe not *everyone* catches the bug—Rogers' friend still hasn't finished a quilt.

Form and Spirit, *by Jeri Riggs.*

Quilting Is Portable and Family-Friendly

ANOTHER SELLING POINT FOR quilting is that women have always been multitaskers, and quilting fits beautifully into a busy woman's life. As the late Hilary Fletcher, formerly head of the biennial art quilt show called Quilt National, put it: "You can always put your needle down when the baby cries. You can't stop so easily in the middle of an oil painting."

Indeed, Denmark, Wisconsin, resident Julie Duschack stopped working as a stained glass artist when her son was born because "glass chips, soldering irons, and acid are not a good mix with a newborn." Her mother convinced her to try quilting as a creative outlet instead, and she's been a quilt artist ever since.

Award-winning quilter Sandra Leichner of Albany, Oregon, says she never would have switched from being a painter to being a quiltmaker except for her three small children. "I did watercolor, which dries quickly and you can't stop in the middle," Leichner explained in an interview with The Alliance for American Quilts.

Although one doesn't see as many quilters as knitters on subways and buses, quilting can be rendered

YOU CAN TAKE IT WITH YOU

Teri Reath D'Ignazio, a travel agent in Oxford, Pennsylvania, gets a lot of quilting done when she takes her teenage daughter to cheerleading events. Suzanne Sanger of Naples, Florida, says, "I quilt on cars, planes, trains, and boats, leaving a trail of snipped threads wherever I go." Charlotte Bull, a grandmother who lives in the Ozark Mountains of Missouri, insists she has quilted absolutely everywhere, "Even once in a canoe," she boasts. "I had a deadline!"

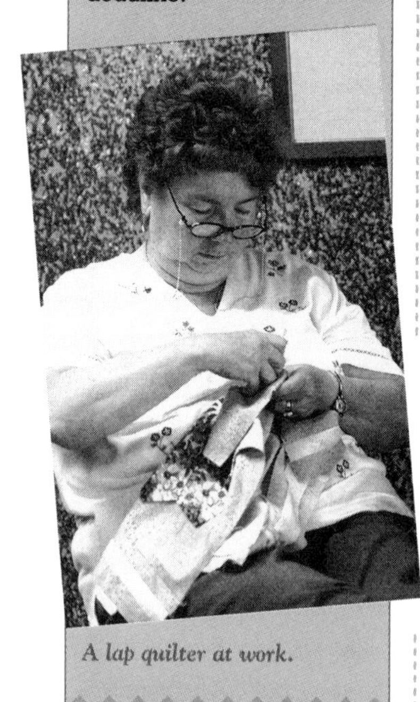

A lap quilter at work.

just as portable. There are times when a nearly finished bed-size quilt will take up a lot of room, but single patchwork blocks are very easy to take along to the pediatrician's office or a child's soccer practice. It's a perfect hobby for anyone who works all day and wants to unwind in front of a television set at night: Keep the handwork in a basket by a comfy chair.

Being made from bits and pieces as it is, quilting serves as an apt and very satisfying metaphor for many. Patchwork manages to take scraps of fabric, like the fragmented pieces of time, and turn them into a beautiful whole. This makes quilters feel that all of the scattered pieces of their lives can add up to something worthwhile and appealing as well.

Quilting Marks Milestones

QUILTING HAS PROVED ADAPTABLE TO THE TIMES on many levels. It has always been the case that big occasions inspired women to make a particular quilt, and that still holds true. It's just that the occasions that inspire quiltmaking are sometimes very different. Making a quilt for a new baby is still quite popular. But, whereas an early nineteenth-century quilter might have made a quilt to honor a new preacher at her church, today's quilters mark the myriad milestones of their own generation.

Shannon Smith of Billings, Montana, made a quilt to celebrate her divorce. "I spent my married years making quilts that would fit the decor of my house, in colors my husband didn't think were too feminine," she says. "The day I went to court for divorce, I left the courthouse and went straight to the quilt shop and spent two hours picking out bright, happy fabrics. It's my favorite quilt."

Suzanne Mouton Riggio, who lives in Wauwatosa, Wisconsin, made a quilt she calls *Celebration of Sight* to mark her successful cataract surgery. "Five panels chronicle my journey," she explains, starting out with blurry images of the city where she lives and gradually becoming crystal clear. She took the actual eye patches she had to wear during her treatment, embellished

them, and attached them to the surface of the quilt.

In Brooklyn, quiltmaker Wendy Menard made a quilted prayer shawl, or tallis, for her daughter's bat mitzvah, using as part of the fabric "a piece from the tallis my father wore at his bar mitzvah."

Some historians have documented a tradition in the early nineteenth century of making so-called freedom quilts for young men when they turned twenty-one years old, an age when some men became free from the bounds of professional apprenticeships. Today, celebrating a different milestone of freedom and separation, quilters save their children's favorite childhood T-shirts, then present them with a T-shirt quilt when they leave for college.

Further encouraging the urge to preserve memories in quilts is the latest technology that makes it easy for anyone with a home computer and printer to transfer favorite photographs onto fabric. Anything from a photo of a bride and groom kissing to a cute baby on a blanket can quickly be printed on fabric and made into quilts, which are more portable and cuddly than the photos that inspired them. Such occasions as graduations, major birthdays, retirements, and fiftieth wedding

Celebration of Sight, *by Suzanne Riggio, pictured above.*

Historical Markers

It's not just personal milestones that prompt people to make quilts; historical milestones are also a significant spark. The country's bicentennial celebration in 1976 is considered one of the key elements in fueling the modern quilt revival. Untold thousands of women, often in groups, decided that making a quilt was the perfect tribute to America's big birthday. Block patterns from the nineteenth century were revived, and red, white, and blue fabric flew off the shelves. Many of the women who made these Bicentennial quilts were surprised that they couldn't wait to make another quilt.

For contemporary quilters, the next big milestone was the millennium, and the craze in the late 1990s was making Y2K quilts with 2,000 or 2,001 pieces of fabric.

New Yorkers from all five boroughs, putting the finishing touches on a community bicentennial quilt in 1976.

To make it even more challenging, many millennium quilts were made with no two pieces cut from the same fabric. This is a very old quilt tradition called a charm quilt, but it was much harder to make one in the nineteenth century when fabric selection was relatively paltry. Today's quilters had the Internet to help them, and they found quilters in cyberspace from all over the globe eager to swap fabrics for millennium quilts.

Cathy Neri, who lives in Sombers, New York, used 2,001 pieces and called her quilt *Y2Quilt? Because I Stash.* (A stash is what quilters call the pile of fabrics they've bought even though they didn't fit into any current project.)

Worcester, Massachusetts, resident Yvonne Dawkins, who collected much of the fabric for her millennium quilt's two thousand three-inch squares by swapping with quilters via cyberspace, brags that she got fabric from quilters in all fifty states and quite a few foreign countries.

anniversaries especially lend themselves to photo quilts featuring multiple images.

Whether they use photographs or not, the making of personalized milestone quilts has even become a profession for some. Jennifer Olson-Hyatt of Wisconsin had little sewing experience when she decided to make a quilt after her mother's death from breast cancer in 1994. Making that quilt made her realize how powerful quilts were as preservers of memories and, drawing on her background as an MBA graduate, she got the idea for a business making special quilts for different milestones in people's lives. In 2002, Olson-Hyatt started Legacy Quilts, which got a big boost when Olson-Hyatt was chosen out of twelve thousand entrants in a Build Your Own Business contest run by Oxygen Media. (For more information about Legacy Quilts, Olson-Hyatt's website is www.elegacyquilts.com.)

An American quilt from 1850 with patriotic imagery.

Quilting Can Be a Sisterhood

SAY THE WORD *QUILTING* AND IT WILL LIKELY invoke an image of a nineteenth-century quilting bee, of normally isolated women happily gathered around an enormous quilt frame. Quilting get-togethers occur frequently today, but they aren't called bees and rarely involve a group of women working together on the same quilt. Indeed, at many guild gatherings there is no actual quilting going on, although guilds may meet a few times a year to work as a group on charity projects. But many guilds have mini groups within the larger guild that meet weekly or monthly to work in the same room, with everyone stitching individual projects, by hand or by machine. And many women organize small groups of six to ten friends who get together weekly to quilt and chat.

Unlike in the quilting bees of an earlier era, quilters today aren't pulled together out of economic necessity and the dictates of a cumbersome process best accomplished by many hands. Nonetheless, the easy,

Quilters (and a young onlooker) gathered around a quilt frame in the 1930s.

comforting exchange of gossip, advice, and encouragement is as treasured by quilters now as it has been throughout the history of the craft.

With more women working outside the home, many find a greater need now to schedule regular get-togethers with friends. As with book groups and knitting circles, quiltmakers enjoy the virtuous feeling that they aren't merely loafing but accomplishing something practical or edifying at quilt gatherings.

The joy of fellowship is cited as one of the major attractions of the craft. Shannon Banks, who lives in San Marino, California, said she started quilting with a group of faculty wives in Rochester, New York, in 1988. The women started getting together to make a baby quilt for a mutual friend. "Our group was so much fun, that we kept meeting twice a month even when the quilt was done," recounts Banks. "The camaraderie was the real reason we gathered. It was an outlet for us to share feelings, vent frustrations, and just enjoy each other's company."

The long-running television show *Simply Quilts* host Alex Anderson thinks this sisterly fellowship is deeply rooted in quilting and an important factor in its revived popularity. "I think the quilt boom is so much more than the quilting itself. There is a community," she says. "I've gotten to the point where I don't even know what the best part of quilting is. Is it the fabric? The craft? The community? Or is it winning best of show, which only happened to me once in my life?"

Fellowship isn't the only benefit. Lindi Wood, a librarian in Seattle, Washington, says she wouldn't have progressed nearly so fast in her quilting if it wasn't for a group of about one hundred she belongs to called the Contemporary QuiltArt Association. Wood says this group meets monthly, usually to hear a featured speaker before the part of the meeting in which members share their current projects. During the showcase segment, members can ask other quilters to critique their work, but only those who are comfortable with criticism do. In addition to all the support the members give one another, Wood says CQA is great because it actively seeks to get its members' work exhibited, and not just in shows featuring the group's quilts.

Quilters say that belonging to quilt groups and guilds makes them feel part of something bigger and gives them a sense of membership in a sorority that goes way back in history. The warmth and sympathy that pulls quiltmakers together—no matter how different their personalities—is captured especially well in the series of popular quilting novels written by Jennifer Chiaverini. These books center around a fictional master quilter who runs "quilt camps" at her family's estate in rural Pennsylvania, helped by her friends the Elm Creek Quilters. The Chiaverini books are set in the present, and make quilt groups and classes sound so inviting that they've inspired many readers to try quilting even when they don't know anybody else who does it.

A gathering of quilters in 2007.

Peter Mancuso, who with his brother, now runs quilt shows around the country, says it was partly the joyful attitude of quilters in groups that got the Mancuso brothers to branch out from their antiques shows. "I had gone to Chicago to see about doing an antiques show there and I came downstairs in my hotel, and there must have been three million women in the lobby and I asked, 'What is going on here?' " Mancuso recalls. "Someone told me there was a quilt show downtown, and I couldn't believe it. I never saw that many women at an antiques show! I have to add that before doing this, I came from nine years on the New York State commission on family violence. I saw women who struggled and were victims of abuse, and I stumbled into this world where women were just having a wonderful time. It is so upbeat."

Quilters say that belonging to quilt groups and guilds makes them feel part of something bigger and gives them a sense of membership in a sorority that goes way back in history.

Quilting Is for Men, Too

MALE QUILTERS ARE A TINY MINORITY, AN estimated 1 percent of the whole. But their contributions are greater than their numbers would suggest, and they've been part of the quilt world for much of its history. For example, during the late nineteenth century when quiltmaking was widespread in America, many boys were versed in the craft. President Calvin Coolidge pieced a quilt in the popular Tumbling Blocks pattern in 1882, when he was ten years old. This quilt can still be viewed in the bedroom of his Vermont boyhood home.

President Dwight D. Eisenhower, who was born in 1890, is said, along with his brothers, to have helped his mother make quilts. One of those quilts can be seen in the Eisenhower Birthplace museum in Denison, Texas. The book *Quilts in America,* by Patsy and Myron Orlofsky includes a photograph of the Eisenhower quilt, and a caption says that the fabric was left over from men's shirts and women's dresses.

The Shelburne Museum in Vermont has an excellent collection of historical quilts, including one made by a Union soldier during the Civil War. That soldier's quilt represents a major trend in the history of male quilters: A significant portion of early quilts made by men were sewn by guys temporarily confined—in hospitals, jails, or the military—and in need of activity. This is true in England too, which has a well-documented history of military quilts, especially those from the Crimean War, often pieced from scraps of red and black uniforms.

However, none of the male quilters whose work was included in the exhibit The Twentieth Century's Best American Quilts produced his masterwork as the result of being confined. Of the hundred quilts chosen for this show, seven were produced by five men.

The oldest quilt in the top one hundred was made in 1900 by a German immigrant tailor as a wedding gift for his daughter. Carl Kleinicke made an elaborate bed quilt of his own design using scraps of elegant dress fabrics from his shop. Another quilt was made in the 1930s by Albert Small, who was determined to break the record for the most individual pieces in a quilt. His rather gaudy mosaic quilt is composed of 123,200 hand-pieced hexagons. At the time of his accomplishment, the press made much of the contrast between this gentle domestic hobby and Small's daytime occupation: He earned his living blowing up rock in quarries.

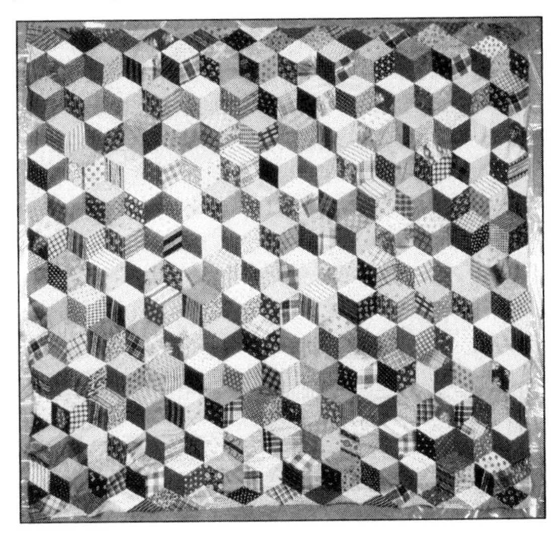

Calvin Coolidge's block quilt.

The other three men whose quilts were picked for the top hundred are quilting today, and the fact that they list quiltmaking as their profession speaks volumes about how times have changed. The most prominent is Michael James, one of a handful of pioneering quiltmakers who got the critical establishment to consider quilts as an art form. With a bachelor's and a master's degree in art, James planned to be a painter but decided while in college in the sixties that painting's time was over. The bold solid colors of his quilts are reminiscent of the abstract paintings of Frank Stella and the op art works of the sixties, but they also play off such traditional quilt patterns as Drunkard's Path and the formal style of Amish quilts. Quilts by Michael James are in the collections of some of the nation's top museums, including the Renwick Gallery at the Smithsonian, and two of his quilts were voted into the top one hundred of the twentieth century.

Bee All

A quilting bee is a gathering of friends and neighbors for the chief purpose of finishing a quilt or quilts. Historically, bees focused on quilting, sewing the three layers of quilts together, which usually required the use of large, bulky frames. Quilt tops were saved for bees, so that many hands could make short work of finishing the quilts and maximize use of frames. Some houses were too small to hold a frame and all the helpers; in those cases, bees were reserved for warm weather seasons, when the work could be done outdoors. It's reported that the women reputed to possess the finest needle skills attracted the most invitations to quilting bees. Those known for large stitches or sloppy work might get invited less often or be relegated to kitchen duty.

Quilters at a bee, 1948.

A bee hostess preparing refreshments in her kitchen.

Historian Ruth Finley describes quilting bees, which were also known as quiltings or quilting parties, in her classic book *Old Patchwork Quilts and the Women Who Made Them,* published in 1929. "So, starting from the grimness of economic need, the quilt became a social factor," she writes. "Soon no function was more important than the quilting-bee in town or country. For many years, it was the most popular form of feminine hospitality."

Finley writes that up to twelve women could fit around a quilt frame, but that the usual number attending a bee was seven or eight, to avoid overcrowding. These frames took up so much room in the small houses of the time that sometimes they were suspended from rings in the parlor or kitchen ceiling when not in use. Most of the frames were simple, utilitarian structures made of four lengths of wood fastened at the corners by bolts or pegs. The boxy frames were typically supported on the backs of chairs, so the three layers to be quilted would be held in place for the participants at about chest level.

Finley says a woman often waited until she had several quilt tops pieced by hand before sending invitations to a quilting bee, so she could get more than one quilt finished at a time. This usually required her quilting friends to work for several days—and spend several nights—and there was often a festive chicken or turkey dinner and a dance in the evening. Some quilting bees lasted for as long as ten days.

These quiltings did not just happen on the frontier, either. In their book *Quilts in America,* authors Patsy and Myron Orlofsky estimate that some housewives in nineteenth-century New England would "participate in as many as twenty-five or thirty quilting bees in a single winter."

Cutting off extra batting.

Another contemporary art quilter, Jonathan Shannon, also boasts two quilts in the top hundred. Shannon was the first man to win Best of Show in the big annual show of the American Quilters Society in Paducah, Kentucky, in 1993. His winning quilt was called *Air Show* and features a colorful appliqué collage of early airplanes, which could be said to be very masculine imagery.

Shannon is equally famous for being rejected two years later by the AQS for his quilt *Amigos Muertos*, a vivid portrayal of dancing skeletons meant to commemorate a generation of artists who died of AIDS. Shannon was told it was too "upsetting," but the outcry that followed his rejection made the quilt famous and generated a worthwhile discussion about the legitimacy of provocative, politically pointed quilts. *Amigos Muertos* quilt *was* chosen for the top one hundred.

Men are increasingly visible among the ranks of popular quilt teachers, and some aren't shy about exploiting the novelty of their gender. Flamboyant teacher Ricky Tims, who was born in Texas and formerly made his living as a musician, called one of his early classes Quilting Caveman Style. San Francisco–based quiltmaker Joe Cunningham offers a lecture titled Quilter in a Strange Land, promising "a rare glimpse into the mind of a male quilter."

A gentleman helps out at an outdoor, multiquilt bee.

Some men claim to experience a form of discrimination from quilt shop clerks who assume they are ignorant or shopping for their wives—that's a feeling any woman who has ever entered a hardware store knows. There have been rare cases of male quilters being rejected by guilds that prefer sticking with an all-women membership policy.

But most male quilters agree with prize winning quilter Scott Murkin, a physician in Asheboro, North Carolina, that the benefits of being a minority in this case outweigh the disadvantages. "Men have a distinct advantage in the quilt/fiber world because we stick out," he says. "It's much easier for me to have my name remembered with a lot less effort because it's not Linda, Sharon, etc. I'm sure I get some teaching, lecturing, and judging jobs because of the novelty. Hopefully, the repeat gigs are for other reasons."

To ask the obvious question, do men approach quilting differently than women? Some men say yes.

"For the first ten years, I used to say I just wanted to be one of the girls," says Joe Cunningham, who started quilting in 1979. "But really, I wanted to be king of the quilt world. I did what I think men always do when they enter a woman's arena: They turn it into a business, or they're aggressive about getting blue ribbons. Men just seem more competitive." A full-time quiltmaker, Cunningham sells his quilts and earns money doing workshops and lectures.

Noshi, *by Scott Murkin.*

Quilter Kevin Key in Chicago, who like many male quilters finds himself the only guy in the local guild, says, "Maybe it's because I quilt with a group of elderly Mennonite ladies, but in general I find they are afraid of breaking the 'rules' of quilting and I could care less. I'm much more of a risk taker."

Although nobody seems to expect a huge increase in the percentage of men who quilt, their visibility is undeniably growing as their numbers do. In recent years, a number of museum exhibits have highlighted the quilts of men, including Man Made, an invitational juried show organized in 2003 by the Museum of the American Quilter's Society in Paducah, Kentucky.

This exhibit of twenty-three quilts by men has since traveled to venues around the country, with a written comment from each quiltmaker about his story. If gender weren't declared, observers would have a hard time guessing what links this group of diverse quilts together. "Modern quiltmaking knows no gender," reads a brochure for the show, but the exhibit's very existence seems to suggest otherwise, at least for now.

Joe Cunningham (top) in front of his quilt Snake in the Garden. *Below, a detail of Cunningham's* Straw Into Gold.

Quilter Scott Murkin (above) and his quilt Giving Tree.

Quilters of Color

African Americans have been part of the sisterhood of quilters going back to the days of slavery. As historian Barbara Brackman writes in her book *Facts & Fabrications: Unraveling the History of Quilts & Slavery*, many slaves came to the United States with needle skills, from countries with a rich tradition of patchwork. Once here, they stitched quilts for both slave owners and their own families.

A late-nineteenth-century quilt illustrating Bible scenes, by African American quilter Harriet Powers.

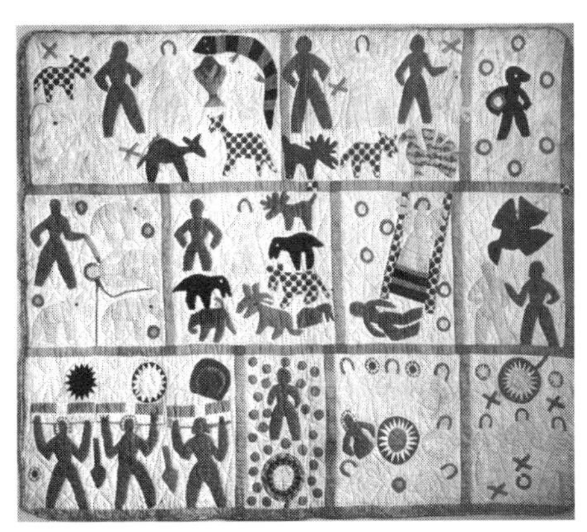

In her 2003 book *Black Threads: An African-American Quilting Sourcebook*, black quilter Kyra Hicks begins her quilt timeline in the first half of the nineteenth century and singles out Harriet Powers, calling her the "mother" of African American quilting. Born into slavery in 1837, Powers exhibited a magnificent pictorial appliqué quilt featuring Bible stories at a Georgia fair in 1886. Later, during a time of desperate need, Powers sold her beloved Bible quilt to a white woman for five dollars. That quilt is now owned by the Smithsonian. A second Bible quilt made by Powers is in the permanent collection of the Boston Museum of Fine Arts.

Artist Kim McKinney uses Civil War–era quilt patterns as inspiration for her contemporary African Slave Quilt series.

There is no reliable headcount available of today's African American quilters. Hicks puts the number at around one million, but others think that's too high. Clearly, there are more black quilters than male quilters in this country (although some are both, like prominent narrative quiltmaker Michael A. Cummings). But one thing is clear: African American quilters have made a profound contribution to the art and craft of quilts that is greater than their numbers.

Scholars who have compared traditional textiles from Africa to quilts made by several generations of African American quilters note that both often employ bold colors, asymmetrical designs, and improvisation. The improvisation has sometimes been the result of the poverty of quilters who couldn't afford to purchase fabric, patterns, or tools. They used what they could find or recycle, such as old clothes. Their methods were often unorthodox, sometimes leading to arrestingly original designs.

Such was the case with the quilters of Gee's Bend, Alabama, whose bold quilts have been hanging on the walls of art museums in recent years. These quilts became such icons of national creativity that in 2006 they were featured on postage stamps, a rare honor.

Anna Williams, another accomplished African American quilter given to improvising, has influenced some of the top art quilters in the country. While living in Baton Rouge, Louisiana, and working as a domestic, Williams started making quilts in her late fifties. A professor whose house she cleaned gave her some fabric and Williams began adapting patterns she had learned from her grandmother, combining long, thin strips of fabric in bright colors with triangles and other geometric shapes. Williams did all her cutting freehand with scissors, giving her quilts a slightly off-kilter, free-form look.

These dazzling quilts attracted the attention of renowned quilt artist Nancy Crow in the late 1980s, and Crow has publicly credited them with helping to

drastically change her style and way of working. Crow says Williams gave her the inspiration to work more freely, without rulers and templates, and she saw to it that Anna Williams' quilts were exhibited and widely seen, spreading the influence of these fine works. In her old age Williams is said to be no longer making quilts, but her works will outlast her.

Anna Williams (top) sewing in her home and her quilt XLV (bottom).

Not all prominent black quiltmakers began as outsider artists or work in this style. Many come from a fine arts background. Faith Ringgold, to name one, started as a painter and sculptor before beginning to create quilts in the 1980s. On her website, the artist says she was inspired to make her painted quilts because "I thought it would be a good way to get people to read my stories and maybe that way I could get one of them published as a book."

Faith Ringgold (below) and her quilt Tar Beach 2.

Ringgold's quilt *Tar Beach,* which appeared in a Caldecott medal-winning picture book by the same name published in 1991, is now in the collection of the Guggenheim museum. She went on to make dozens more story quilts and to publish a number of children's books illustrated with quilts, including in 2001, *Cassie's Word Quilt.*

The rich diversity of styles within the African American quilt community is the chief message that historian and curator Carolyn Mazloomi emphasizes in her books, lectures, and exhibits. "We're not just about improvisational quilts: African American quilts are as varied as the people who make them," says Mazloomi, who was working as an aerospace engineer for Lockheed when she started to make quilts.

In her exquisitely illustrated book *Spirits of the Cloth: Contemporary African American Quilts*, Mazloomi includes both traditional patterns and abstract art quilts. There are protest quilts, quilts using African fabrics, a Kwanzaa quilt, and a quilt that celebrates the childhood sport of jumping rope, among many others.

After she began quilting, she rarely met or heard about other black quilters, says Mazloomi, so she put an ad in a popular quilt magazine asking African American quiltmakers to contact her. Thus was born the Women of Color Quilters Network, which she founded in the 1980s to bring together black quilters who felt isolated around the country.

But what started as a hobbyist group has been transformed in recent years into an organization designed to promote and assist professional art quilters. Only those whose quilts have been in at least three museum or gallery exhibitions can join the Women of Color Quilters Network, which offers members workshops on marketing and access to major curators. "I want men and women to be able to show and sell their quilts," says Mazloomi.

For African American quilters with a more casual bent, there are numerous guilds around the country, including the Brown Sugar Stitchers of Lawrenceville, Georgia, and the Uhuru Quilters Guild of Clinton, Maryland. One of the oldest guilds for black quilters is the Daughters of Dorcas and Sons, a prominent Washington, D.C.–based group with well over two hundred members.

Dr. Carolyn Mazloomi, founder of the Women of Color Quilters Network.

RESOURCES

For African American Quilting

The books and websites here are far from being the only resources on African American quilts and quiltmaking, but these stand out for their quality. At the very minimum, give yourself a treat and check out some of the stunning quilts shown on the websites.

Books

FACTS & FABRICATIONS: UNRAVELING THE HISTORY OF QUILTS & SLAVERY,
by Barbara Brackman,

***C&T Publishing;* $27.95**

Historian Barbara Brackman has combed through the historic record to write a book that dispels myths about slave-made quilts. It's a fascinating account made livelier by period photos, first-person accounts, and nine projects. Not just for historians!

SPIRITS OF THE CLOTH: CONTEMPORARY AFRICAN AMERICAN QUILTS,
***by Carolyn Mazloomi, Clarkson Potter;* $40**

A remarkable book, with a preface by Faith Ringgold, Carolyn Mazloomi's *Spirits of the Cloth* includes stunning photos of 150 quilts, plus biographical information about their makers. Each featured quilt is accompanied by an explanation of what inspired it.

STITCHED FROM THE SOUL: SLAVE QUILTS FROM THE ANTEBELLUM SOUTH,
***by Gladys-Marie Fry, University of North Carolina Press;* $27.50**

A folklore professor, Gladys-Marie Fry's great-great-grandmother was a slave and a gifted seamstress. With more than one hundred photos of quilts, Fry's book traces the influence of African culture in American quilts.

Websites and Blogs

AFRICAN AMERICAN ART QUILTERS

To see the diverse work of African American art quilters, explore this great website. You can visit a virtual gallery of work by black art quilters and follow links to the websites of such noted quiltmakers as Michael A. Cummings and Keisha Roberts.

www.AfricanAmericanArtQuilt.com

CENTER FOR THE QUILT ONLINE

Learn more about the personal stories of traditional African American quilters through the website of The Alliance for American Quilts, where an online oral history project called Quilters' S.O.S.—Save Our Stories includes interviews with Viola Canady, the army seamstress who founded the Daughters of Dorcas guild in Washington, D.C., in 1980. There are two interviews with Canady here, as well as interviews with other Dorcas members.

www.centerforthequilt.org

QuiltEthnic.com

A great resource on the ethnic quilting worldwide. If you click on the words *African American*, there's a link to dozens of quiltmakers and groups, including guilds around the country for quilters of color (look under Networking at the end of each section).

www.quiltethnic.com

Eli Leon

View a collection of improvisational African American quilts at the website of Eli Leon, a noted curator and author on the topic.

www.elileon.com

Faith Ringgold

You'll find biographical information and photos of quilts by Faith Ringgold on her website, which is unusually rich in content, including a chronological listing of all the images she has created since 1963. Click on any one to enlarge it, the better to examine such trademark techniques as meshing paint on canvas with intricate quilted fabric borders.

Hybrid quilt paintings like *Tar Beach* and *Dancing on the George Washington Bridge* are characteristic of Ringgold's work, which often features colorful crowd scenes with a folk art exuberance. She updates a very traditional art form to comment on issues of race and gender. The site even includes a story written by Ringgold, "How the People Became Color Blind," that can be printed and shared.

www.faithringgold.com

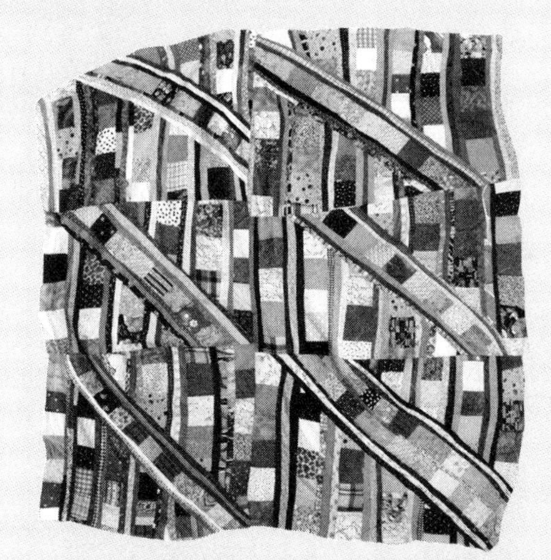

An Anna Williams quilt.

Anna Williams

View the striking improvisational quilts of Anna Williams at a site run by quilt authority Susan Druding. There is an exuberance and color confidence to these quilts that makes them unique.

www.straw.com/equilters/annawilliams/index.html

Black Threads

The tagline for this blog is "Explorations in African American Quilting, Quilt History, Fabrics and Other Fanciful Topics." Blogger Kyra Hicks, a resident of Alexandria, Virginia, is an author and quilter who has turned her blog into *the* national bulletin board for African American quilts and quilt events. This is a fun, newsy blog with gorgeous photos.

blackthreads.blogspot.com

Kyra Hicks.

Quilting Is Artistic

ONE OF THE BIGGEST DIFFERENCES BETWEEN today's quilters and their foremothers is that women in the age of "compulsory" quilting rarely thought of themselves as artists. Many contemporary quiltmakers believe that if they aren't making art yet, they have the potential to do so—if only they can take more classes and devote more of their time to quilting. And they've got the role models to prove it.

A number of the women (and a few men) whose quilts hang in museums, art galleries, and corporate headquarters have résumés that don't look all that different from that of the average quilter. Although some have fine art backgrounds, many do not, and most began working in vastly different fields.

Star art quilter Caryl Bryer Fallert was an airline stewardess before earning her living as a quilter and teacher. Adrienne Yorinks, whose quilts have been commissioned by national organizations and have been used to illustrate books, formerly ran a dog-grooming business in New York. She got fascinated with fabric while making designer kerchiefs for her doggy clients. Award-winning art quilter Yvonne Porcella worked as an operating-room nurse for nineteen years and, like many quilters, is entirely self-taught.

That isn't to say that there aren't plenty of quilters like Gayle Reece of Tyler, Texas, who just want to have fun. "I'm not a master quilter and I don't want to be," states Reece. "My quilts get used on couches and picnics and each one has a bed to live on and a person to sleep under it."

But partly because quilts are respected as an art form now, more quilters than ever aspire to make art. Unlike earlier eras where the creativity of quilting was mostly limited to embellishments within the confines of standard patterns, all the rules are gone, and quilters have license to be wildly creative. Add to that the fact that new technologies allow them to try more techniques and different materials and make more quilts per year, and you get a fluid, frisky quilt world in which quilters are often astounded by their own creative development.

RESOURCES

Whether you make art quilts or just love to look at them, here are some of the best guides to the art side of the quilting path.

Internet Resources

The Quiltart group is the network for people interested in quilts as art. To become a member, go to the group's website **www.quiltart.com.** *There is a suggested fee of $15 a year, which is used to help maintain the list. Anyone can join; you don't need to prove you're an artist (or they would have turned me down for sure).*

Many top quilt artists have inspiring websites. You can view the work of some of the artists mentioned in Quilting Is Artistic at the following sites:

PAULINE BURBIDGE
www.paulineburbidge-quilts.com

NANCY CROW
www.nancycrow.com

CARYL BRYER FALLERT
www.bryerpatch.com

MICHAEL JAMES
www.unl.edu/mjames_quilts

JOAN LINTAULT
www.mjlintault.com

THERESE MAY
www.theresemay.com

FAITH RINGGOLD
www.faithringgold.com

"I never thought I was artistic until I tried quilting," says Ginny Gowden, who's a resident of Dunmore, Pennsylvania.

"This helped me get over the F I got in third-grade art," says Milwaukeean Susan Burczyk. "At first I just quilted to escape and unwind, but it's been so rewarding to hear people say things like 'You have such a good sense of color.'"

"I think we all have a primal need to make something pretty, and what is more joyous than playing with color?" asks Liza Prior Lucy, a professional quilter and coauthor with Kaffe Fassett of numerous pattern books. "I can't draw a tree but I can make a quilt and it turns out pleasing. I rarely find women who don't love quilting at first try."

Among the evidence that more quilters are taking the artistic road is the steep rise in quilts entered in shows and contests. Quilt National, the biennial premier art quilt show in the United States, began in 1979 with 390 entries. The 1,288 entries in 2005 came from forty-seven states and twenty-one countries, but only eighty were chosen for the juried show. There is no doubt that making a living as an art quilter is still difficult; however, clearly, more quiltmakers than ever are trying to make that leap.

"I'm going to continue making quilts because I'm driven," pioneering art quilter Nancy Crow is quoted as saying in the book *The Art Quilt*, by Penny McMorris and Michael Kile. "I fully believe that the quilt's time has come; only the fact that it's made from fabric has held it back until now."

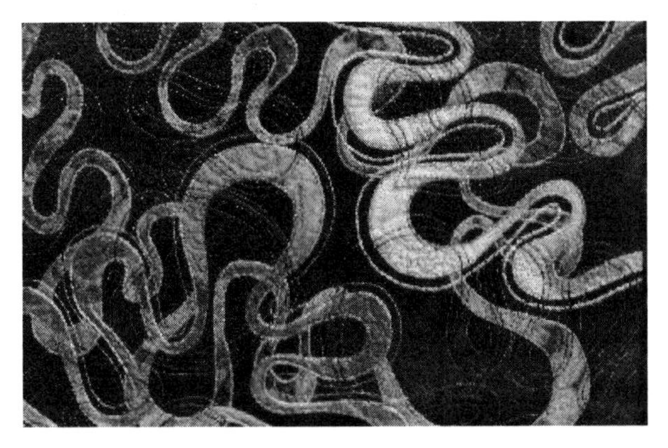

Foliage, *by Libby Lehman.*

Other Resources

QUILTING ARTS MAGAZINE

This bimonthly magazine is a visual feast with plenty of how-to features. *Quilting Arts Magazine* is a must for would-be art quilters and anyone interested in the ongoing evolution of quilts.

P.O. Box 685
Stow,
Massachusetts 01775
(866) 698-6989;
(978) 897-7750
www.quiltingarts.com

STUDIO ART QUILT ASSOCIATES

An association for art quilters, the members of Studio Art Quilt Associates include quiltmakers, collectors, curators, and teachers. Membership benefits include a quarterly journal, exhibits, lectures, and referrals.

P.O. Box 572
Storrs,
Connecticut 06268-0572
(860) 487-0572
www.saqa.com

What Is an Art Quilt?

The quilt world is roughly divided into two camps: those who want to create art and those who just want to have fun. It's not quite that simple, but the distinction is part of what makes quiltmaking so exciting in the twenty-first century. Those who create quilts are motivated by many things and have vastly different goals. Some want to make beautiful coverlets and wall hangings for their own pleasure and for loved ones, while others aspire to have their work hang in art museums and galleries. The variations in intention make for dramatic differences in the results.

Art quilters strive for originality in both design and materials. They're trying to constantly push the envelope and experiment, while still clinging to some aspect of the traditional quilt, whether it's the number of layers of fabric or the use of recognizable patterns as a jumping-off point.

Art quilter Nancy Crow at work in her studio.

Art quilts bend the rules. For example, those entered into the biennial show called Quilt National in Athens, Ohio, don't have to be made of three layers, but they "must be predominantly fabric or fabric-like material," according to the rules. That leaves plenty of room for unusual embellishments. Since the first Quilt National show in 1979, entries have been decorated with such items as bottle caps, matchsticks, dental floss, candy wrappers, paper clips, and burned birthday candles.

The shapes of art quilts aren't set in stone either. Some have jagged edges, some aren't rectangular. Themes and titles of art quilts may include disturbing images or address such topics as pollution, politics, sexual abuse, AIDS, or death.

In his groundbreaking (and gorgeous) book *The Art Quilt*, published in 1997, curator and historian Robert Shaw wrote, "The art quilt is a new artistic medium that has developed over the past quarter century and is now the focus of hundreds of artists worldwide. . . . Often made by academically trained artists, art quilts are meant to be seen and judged solely as works of visual art."

Why did quilts start traveling down this artsy road?

Certainly a pivotal event was the 1971 Whitney Museum of American Art show entitled Abstract Design in American Quilts, in which traditional bed quilts made between 1840 and 1930 were hung on the museum's white walls. The show was organized by quilt collectors Jonathan Holstein and Gail van der Hoof, who argued that these quilts were authentic masterpieces that should be recognized within the art world. Quilts had been displayed for years, but never in such a major museum or with such acclaim. Both influential critics and the public embraced the show and agreed with the premise.

New York Times critic Hilton Kramer was among those gushing. He wrote, "For a century or more preceding the self-conscious invention of pictorial abstraction in European painting, the anonymous quilt-makers of the American provinces created a remarkable succession of visual masterpieces that anticipated many of the forms that were later prized for their originality and courage."

Although the quilts in the Whitney show were all made before 1930, this declaration had a profound effect on artists working in the 1970s: Quilts were now "officially" labeled as art, and as such, the medium of fabric became legitimized.

During the 1960s and 1970s, the art world was in turmoil anyway. Art was affected by rock and roll, by the women's movement, and by the back to the earth movement. Crafts in general were being elevated in the art world, including ceramics, glass, and jewelry. Old-school media like paint seemed boring. Art was being made out of found objects and junkyard leavings. It was all about installations, and happenings, and conceptual art.

Markings #1: The Known and Unknown, *by Nancy Crow.*

Although the top art quilters come from many different educational and work backgrounds (Caryl Bryer Fallert was a

The Way Home, *by Joe Cunningham.*

in Ohio, helped create the educational institutions, juried shows, and professional associations art quilters needed. Crow was one of the major forces behind Quilt National, the internationally renowned biannual art quilt show, which is still held in the former dairy barn she helped renovate. In 1990, Crow was also instrumental in starting the Quilt Surface Design Symposium, a revered training ground for art quilters that offers several weeks of classes every summer in Columbus, Ohio (for more about the Quilt Surface Design Symposium, see page 386).

Today, art quilters have their own associations, publications, websites, and suppliers. There are multiple magazines for art quilters, ranging from glossy magazines like *Quilting Arts* to almost handmade "zines" that go to a few hundred subscribers and may have plastic baggies of fabric and beads stapled to the pages. There are also a growing number of blogs, in which quilt artists share their creative process, one project at a time.

Indeed, the Internet is an important factor in the growth and development of the art quilt movement because it pulls together people who are geographically far-flung, allowing them to share ideas and feel part of a bigger group.

One such vital Internet resource is the Quiltart group, a sort of virtual guild for art quilters. Quiltart was founded in 1995 by Washington, D.C. quilter Judy Smith, who works full-time for *The Washington Post.* Smith started an Internet mailing list in which members send e-mails that are shared with every other member (most members choose the "digest" option

stewardess), a good number of the pioneers in the field attended art school in the sixties and seventies, including Michael James, Therese May, and Joan Lintault, in the United States, and Pauline Burbidge, in England. Experimentation was encouraged and people sampled lots of media, but fabric especially seemed new and full of possibilities.

Many, like James, started by making very traditional quilts, but they quickly veered off in a more original direction, using sewing and quilting techniques in new ways. Some well-known artists such as Miriam Shapiro and Faith Ringgold mixed paint and fabric in their works. Ringgold, for one, sometimes framed her paintings with pieced fabric squares.

Many of these pioneering art quilters had to find their own way without a lot of institutional support. But since then, art quilters have carved out a vibrant community within the larger quilt world. Some major early figures like Nancy Crow, and get bundles of eight or ten e-mail messages at a time). This creates a sort of public bulletin board on which Quiltart members can share techniques, debate what's art, and ask for advice.

"There are a lot of questions about how to put together a portfolio or a résumé, or other steps toward becoming more professional," says Smith, "but often people just like to share what they're working on at the moment."

Over the years, the Quiltart list has morphed into something more than a virtual guild, becoming a public force in the art quilt movement. By the time the list celebrated its ten-year anniversary in 2005, it had well over two thousand members and was creating actual, live quilt shows. Every so often, list members issue challenges online, such as a challenge to make self-portraits, or one to make a quilt about the eighth deadly sin. Originally these quilts were only displayed on the Quiltart website **(www.quiltart.com)**, but the group has also had shows in such venues as the Houston International Quilt Festival.

As the art quilt movement has grown and developed, there have been bumps on the road. Some art quilters complain that they still are treated like second-class citizens in the general art world and have trouble finding galleries, collectors, and publications that receive them with open arms.

But there is no question that art quilts are here to stay and deserve credit for being one of the chief engines driving the modern quilt renaissance. Curator Robert Shaw wrote in his 1997 book, *The Art Quilt*, that the incredible outpouring of quilts in the twenty-five years prior to his book "rivals that of a hundred years earlier, the so-called Great Age of Quiltmaking." This new golden age of quilts is possible because art and originality are stressed above mere workmanship.

So what exactly is an art quilt? When does a quilt become art? Shaw says: "As in any other form of art, the overarching criteria used in making this judgment should be originality of concept, power of expression, interest and balance of color, line, pattern, texture, and other formal elements, and most important, the cohesion and integrity of the overall work." Which, Shaw stresses, includes the artist's recognition that the object she or he has made is still a quilt.

Constructions #82: Breaking Control, by Nancy Crow.

Shaw closed his masterful introduction to *The Art Quilt* with this statement: "The art quilt represents the future of quilting, its best chance to remain active and vibrant into the next [twenty-first] century."

Quilting Can Be a Career

FOR INCREASING NUMBERS OF WOMEN (AND MEN), twenty-first century quilting isn't a hobby, but a business. There has been a wonderful grassroots entrepreneurial impulse propelling the quilt boom all along. Over the past several decades, quiltmakers and quilt lovers have perceived various needs in the quilt market and enthusiastically raced to fill them, resulting in topsy-turvy growth and a patchwork of many small businesses.

When computer graphics became commonplace there wasn't any software made specifically for quilters. No problem—Penny McMorris, the host of one of the nation's first quilt television shows in the early eighties, enlisted the help of her computer programmer husband, Dean Neumann. McMorris got too busy to make quilts herself, but her quiltmaking knowledge was crucial in helping to build the company she and Neumann named Electric Quilt. More than twenty years later, Electric Quilt is still the leading provider of quilting software. By 2006, the company was introducing a sixth version (for information on the different types of quilt software, see pages 168–75).

Scissors are forbidden on airlines now? No problem—within a couple months after post-9/11 security changes were initiated there were at least three devices on sale at quilt shops that allowed quilters to cut thread on a plane trip without being mistaken for a terrorist.

Some of the inventions and businesses have been very humble kitchen-table operations that never outgrew the kitchen. But others just mushroomed.

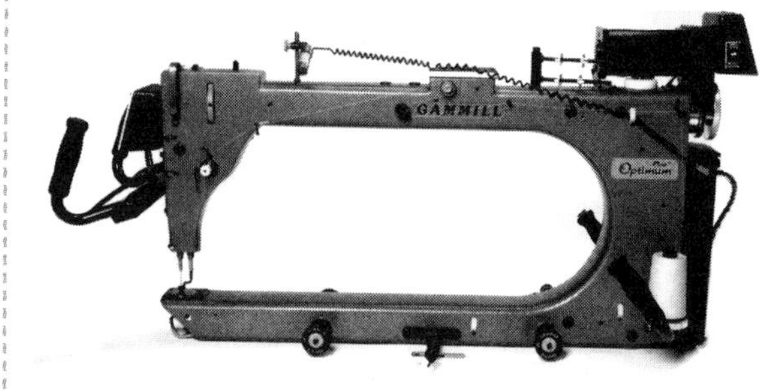

A Gammill longarm sewing machine.

THE QUILT FESTIVAL AND QUILT MARKET

The stunning growth of Houston's annual consumer quilt show, International Quilt Festival, and quilt trade show, International Quilt Market, have helped prove beyond any doubt that today's quilt market is big, vital, and sophisticated. The first Quilt Festival was staged by Karey Bresenhan in Houston in 1974, and it quickly became a major convention there, drawing more and more quilters from all over the world. Attendance now tops fifty thousand every fall.

Bresenhan and her company Quilts, Inc. followed up the success of the Houston Festival by starting another annual consumer quilt show in 2003, this time held in Chicago. Called International Quilt Festival/Chicago, it draws more than twenty thousand quilters every spring.

In between starting the big shows in Houston and Chicago, Bresenhan recognized that the boom was traveling overseas, so Quilts, Inc. began a European version of the festival in 1988 called

Take the experience of Karey Bresenhan, a fifth-generation Texas quilter, who opened a Houston quilt shop called Great Expectations with her mother in 1974. The shop did well, and after that first year Bresenhan and her mother gave a thank-you party for their customers that included a quilt show. Two years later, they invited the public to a local quilt show they called Quilt Fair. Quilt Fair, now known as the International Quilt Festival, became an annual event, and attracts quilters from farther and farther away. But Bresenhan didn't stop there either.

Because she continued to own a quilt shop, Bresenhan was acutely aware in the mid-1970s how hard it was for quilters to find the fabric and supplies they craved. This was the era when all the department stores had shuttered their fabric departments. What fabric was available was of poor quality, with limited choices of colors and designs.

So while continuing to host the Quilt Fair each year, in 1979 Bresenhan was moved to start another venture she called Quilt Market at which vendors from all over the country could sell their wares directly to the growing legions of quilt shop owners. That first year, the wholesale Quilt Market attracted forty-eight vendors. By 2000, the number of vendors had grown to 450, and by 2006, it was close to 600.

An emphatic, dark-haired woman who dresses in bright colors, Bresenhan likes to joke she would never have started the Quilt Market if she hadn't been exasperated by "the impossibility of finding yellow fabric" (which she pronounces "yellah" in her Texas twang). The search for the source of one color of fabric led to the establishment of something groundbreaking and enormous, thanks to Bresenhan's indefatigable energy and drive. Her brilliant move soon made Houston the epicenter of the burgeoning quilt business, establishing the annual market as *the* place to debut new fabrics and quilt products of every kind. (For more about the International Quilt Market and related shows, see sidebar.)

Eventually, all the quilting moms running businesses out of their living rooms began to be joined by larger companies, as the quilt boom grew and became more sophisticated. Commercial outfits of all

Patchwork & Quilt Expo. This consumer show was held in even-numbered years in various countries, but was dropped after 2006 because the European quilting community began mounting their own shows.

Bresenhan has also been receptive to the needs of quilt business owners. Her fall trade show, International Quilt Market, is always scheduled in Houston right before the consumer show. But she believed that many of the buyers attending the quilt market, mostly quilt shop owners, would prefer not having to travel so far to meet suppliers and keep up with trends. So in 1981, Quilts, Inc. started also offering a spring quilt market. Unlike the fall version, which always takes place in Houston, the spring trade show travels from year to year.

For more on the Quilt Festival and Quilt Market, go to **www.quilts.com,** the website of Karey Bresenhan's company. For insider tips on getting the most from the International Quilt Festival and other major quilt shows, see page 543.

sorts began to realize the quilt market had depth and reach and that many quilters didn't pinch pennies when it came to their passion. Those fabric companies that revamped their businesses to appeal to quilters were soon joined by competitors. Sewing machine companies began buying up notions companies and fabric companies, and so on.

Through it all, countless small enterprises have continued to bloom, remaining mom-and-pop—or mom-only—businesses. Thus, among those six hundred vendors at the 2004 Quilt Market were not just international corporations but also individuals like Carol Bruce, who started a tiny quilt pattern business in 2001 from her home in Las Vegas. Bruce sold her patterns on the side, while working full-time in the wardrobe department for the Siegfried and Roy wild animal show. When a tiger attack ended the show and put all the employees out of work, Bruce switched full-time to expanding her pattern business, Needlesongs (www.Needlesongs.com). By paying for a booth at the Quilt Market, Bruce could present her patterns to hundreds of quilt shop owners in one place.

One of the most popular at-home quilting businesses today is to become a professional quilt finisher. Many quilters love to make quilt tops, eagerly experimenting with every fabric, pattern, and technique that comes along. But they get bored with the next part, the sewing together of the three layers that is the actual quilting. Doing this by hand can take months, and doing it by machine requires patience and finesse. As a result, the average quilter usually has a growing pile of single-layer quilt tops, often known as UFOs (for unfinished objects), about which she feels pangs of guilt, but to which she keeps adding nonetheless.

Along came a major technological development, the introduction in the 1990s of large commercial quilting machines into the home market. These so-called longarm machines cost thousands of dollars and take up most of a small room. But, the longarms make it possible to complete a bed-size quilt in as little as an hour or two.

Despite their size and expense, longarms soon became the fastest-growing segment of the sewing

A Needlesongs pattern designed by Carol Bruce (top), and one of Karen McTavish's many books.

machine business. By the beginning of the twenty-first century, there were thousands of quiltmakers across the country who had bought these behemoths, and most bought them for business reasons, advertising their finishing services through quilt stores and publications.

Karen McTavish of Duluth, Minnesota, is a nationally known and lauded professional quilt finisher, and her story is instructive partly because of her unusual route into the business. While many get into the custom-quilting business because they love to quilt, McTavish wasn't even a quilter when she began.

According to an interview published in *The Professional Quilter* magazine, McTavish was a single mom doing accounting work in California when her mother back in Minnesota declared she had found the perfect new career for her. She told her daughter that all she had to do was buy one of these giant sewing machines, and she could work at home, finish eight quilts a day, and support her daughter. Although McTavish had never even *seen* a longarm machine, let alone made a quilt herself, she was ready for a change, so in 1996 she moved back to Minnesota and took her mother's advice .

Within a year, McTavish was supporting herself entirely by custom quilting. But she has since gone well beyond that, writing books, winning awards, and becoming a very popular teacher, practically a poster child for the business potential of quilting. Her work includes the quilting on half a dozen of the quilts featured in the bestselling project book *Quilts from "The Quiltmaker's Gift,"* by Joanne Larsen Line and Nancy Loving Tubesing. McTavish is a staunch advocate of professional quilters being compensated fairly and teaches others not just how to finish quilts, but also how to make a business of it.

Three of Karen McTavish's intricately quilted designs.

THE QUILTERS HALL OF FAME

Like Cleveland's Rock and Roll Hall of Fame, The Quilters Hall of Fame was inducting honorees long before it had a physical space in which to immortalize them. Historian Hazel Carter launched The Quilters Hall of Fame in 1979 and named six people who had made outstanding contributions to the world of quilting, but the organization's headquarters didn't open until 2004. Multiple individuals were named each year until 1991, when the tradition of selecting one person a year was established, bringing the total receiving the award to thirty-seven by 2007.

The Hall of Fame is now located in the restored Marion, Indiana, home of Marie Webster, a quilt designer and early historian of the craft. Her pivotal book, *Quilts: Their Story and How to Make Them*, was first published in 1915 (the 1990 edition from Practical Patchwork, $20.00, is still widely available).

Carter's purpose in starting the organization was to celebrate and preserve both the history

Karen McTavish manning her longarm sewing machine.

Quilting Lasts

OVER AND OVER, QUILTERS SAY THEY FEEL THAT making a quilt is the one way they have, besides raising children, of leaving something of themselves for posterity.

"We make the bed this morning, but we'll still have to do it again tomorrow," says Georgia-based quilter Merryl Gillingham. "As a teacher, I teach something today but even if the students understood it, I'll still have to teach the same thing to a new group of students next year. Everything has to be done again—except quilting. When I put a stitch in a quilt, it's done, I never have to make that stitch again. It's the sense of permanence that draws me to quilting."

This is a topic about which many quilters speak fervently. Their belief that they will pass both their creativity and their love down to future generations sustains them.

Quilt artist JoAnn Peraino of Ann Arbor, Michigan, says she was traumatized by the news that she couldn't have children and felt there was a hole in her life. But she says she discovered that making quilts was another profound way of giving her life meaning. "I make art—both paintings and quilts—to express myself, to leave a tangible record of my existence."

Why do today's quilters believe so firmly in their immortality through quilts? All the lauding, cataloging, and collecting of old quilts has given them proof that quilts can outlast their makers. They see that beautiful, old quilts are hung on museum walls and sold at Sotheby's even when the maker is listed as anonymous. They don't intend their own quilts to be anonymous, and in the interest of creating future heirlooms, most quiltmakers are reasonably good at documenting each completed quilt. Labels are carefully sewn on the backs, giving the makers' names and the date of completion, and most quilters take a photograph of every single quilt they give away. Some go farther, keeping elaborate quilt journals.

Quilters also have the evidence of their own eyes. Beloved quilts get saved and treasured. Quilts with a cotton surface that is worn and torn are pulled out of the closet for snuggling in on the sofa on a cold night. Even those who don't expect to be inducted into The Quilters Hall of Fame sleep better at night knowing that when they're gone, the quilts they made will still keep children and grandchildren warm at night. (There's more about The Quilters Hall of Fame at left.)

Quilting Is Therapy

MANY RECENT BOOKS AND ARTICLES ABOUT knitting stress the meditative aspects of the craft, asserting that the repetitive motions and the sound of clicking needles are soothing. The pleasure is multiplied knowing that the meditation results in not just an improved state of mind but a useful tangible object, as well. Time isn't wasted. One can meditate but also create a warm sweater or scarf.

Quilters are equally quick to ascribe similar therapeutic benefits to their craft. Sometimes this is done jokingly. One popular slogan on merchandise for quilters, including luggage tags, reads: "Quilting in Houston *is* my therapy: I'm preshrunk!"

But for many quilters the assertion that quilting is therapy is a serious one; they say the proof is in their own lives. Amy Lafferty, a teacher living in California, says, "Quilting is a meditation for me. The needle going

and art of quiltmaking, and the inductees have included historians, such as Barbara Brackman and Cuesta Benberry; renowned quilt teachers, such as Georgia Bonesteel and Yvonne Porcella; and quilt collectors, such as Jonathan Holstein and Gail van der Hoof, who organized the famous 1971 Whitney museum show on quilts as art.

Every July, The Quilters Hall of Fame hosts what it calls Celebration in the Marie Webster House to honor that year's inductee. These events include lectures, quilt exhibits, how-to workshops, and such history-related topics as learning how to date antique fabrics. Except for the months of January and February, when it is closed, the Marie Webster House operates as a museum, with changing quilt-related exhibits and a museum shop.

The Hall of Fame's website includes the biographies of all of its inductees.

The Quilters Hall of Fame
926 South Washington St.
Marion, Indiana 46952
(765) 664-9333
www.quiltershalloffame.net

in and out, up and down, calms me and enables me to hear others better. Quilting slows me down to my 'proper pace.'"

"Quilting can be both stimulating and soothing," observes Diane Doro of Des Moines, Iowa, a mother of two and a part-time proofreader. "Choosing fabrics is energizing for me, but sewing mile after mile of quarter-inch seams on my machine as I string piece hundreds of small shapes is almost a meditative experience. I put soft music on my CD player and experience a sense of 'flow.'"

A quilt made using fabric designed by Jane Sassamon.

Dr. Susan Delaney Mech, a Plano, Texas, psychiatrist who quilts, goes even further in making health claims for the craft. In her book *Rx for Quilters: Stitcher-Friendly Advice for Every Body*, Dr. Delaney, who goes by her maiden name now, provides tips to help quilters avoid sore fingers, tired eyes, and carpal tunnel syndrome. But she also says that quilting is "good for you," claiming that quilting lowers blood pressure and the heart rate and leaves people less likely to succumb to colds and flu.

The Distance Between Us, *by Penny Mateer.*

"The health benefits for sewing in general and quilting in particular are incredible—and there are studies to prove it," says Dr. Delaney. "For example, a few years back, a company in the sewing business commissioned a psychologist in New York City to test for actual physical changes in a group of women doing a simple sewing exercise. They were piecing together two patches of fabric by hand, a typical action for a quilter. The psychologist found that their heart rate and blood pressure readings went down while they were sewing, and that the activity produced a relaxation response in the body."

Some quilters themselves report explicitly therapeutic results, and a few starkly claim that quilting saved their lives. Tina Wilson, a mother of four, works as a drugstore clerk and has been sewing since the age of three. She declares, "I keep quilting because it keeps me sane and alive. I couldn't stop breathing either. Quilting is something that is all mine, I only do it because I love it and I can completely control it. There are few things in my life that fit that description."

In short, life is messy, but quilting is neat. The "high" a quilter experiences when sewing a binding onto a completed quilt, thus burying all those pesky loose ends, comes from the feeling of control and the ever-elusive psychological Holy Grail, closure.

A poster for the 1933 World's Fair, held in Chicago.

Quilting Keeps Changing

WE'RE ADDICTED TO NOVELTY. ARTS, HOBBIES, and pastimes of all sorts become stagnant and die out if they don't change over time. Would your kids keep playing their video gaming devices week after week if there were no new games? Restaurants that don't vary their menus from time to time don't stay popular when new trends in food emerge.

Indeed, plain old monotony is one of the primary reasons quilting nearly went extinct during the forties and fifties. Earlier in the twentieth century, quilting had both waxed and waned. The craft was in a lull as the 1900s began but got a big push during the Depression, both from the necessity of housewives having to make do and because of efforts by the Works Progress Administration (WPA) to document and laud the country's best craftspeople, including quiltmakers.

The Century of Progress exhibition in Chicago from 1933 to 1934 included a generous display of quilts. Sears, Roebuck and Company, based there, announced a national quilt contest that drew twenty-five thousand entries, and the winning quilt was given to First Lady Eleanor Roosevelt. There was also a major quilt contest in 1939 as part of the New York World's Fair.

But by the end of World War II, quilting seemed on the verge of becoming a lost art. Many women considered themselves too modern for this old-fashioned craft, while others associated it with hard times and frugality—and now they could afford store-bought bedcovers.

RESOURCES

Here are some excellent websites and a book to help you explore the massive cross-pollination between American quilters and quilters abroad.

Websites

QuiltEthnic

The QuiltEthnic site allows you to look at quilts from around the world without getting out of your chair by clicking on such categories as Native American, Haitian, or African. Selecting Japanese quilts, for example, will link you to photos of gorgeous art quilts by prizewinning quilter Keiko Goke or a site on the history of kimonos.

www.quiltethnic.com

Pauline Burbidge: A Master Art Quilter Working in Scotland

Perhaps the most famous quilter in Great Britain, Pauline Burbidge, creates collagelike quilts that have been collected by such august institutions as the Victoria and Albert Museum in London. You can view her work on her website. Burbidge usually schedules an annual open house at her art studio, located about an hour's drive from Edinburgh; you'll find details about this and other exhibits on the website. And, she is now marketing a series of what

Quilt blocks of denim chenille.

Some historians and writers, including Penny McMorris, believe that the precut quilt kits that were widely available starting around 1910 also had a hand in downgrading the craft by removing all the creative aspects. Like the early cake mixes, the kits left women feeling like they had nothing to add. McMorris makes a comparison to paint-by-number kits, in which hobbyists go through the motions of making a picture but don't create any shapes or choose any colors. Making it worse, the fabrics available in quilt kits were generally somber, with few choices available.

But the quilting renaissance that began in the late sixties is no monochromatic Johnny-one-note affair. Instead of reheating the same old dish, it has become a lavish all-you-can-eat buffet, in which every technique, every pattern, every quilting tradition ever practiced is available to sample.

Like music buffs who can go from listening to baroque chamber music to hip-hop in an instant, quiltmakers can also cruise through and select from a diverse number of possibilities. They can find out more about nineteenth-century block patterns than most women living at the time knew and choose among them. Then, they can take a class with the most cutting-edge art quilter around, unleashing their creative juices through quilt software to make a wall hanging of their own unique design. Speed and shortcuts can coexist with painstaking quilt artistry.

Quilters who want to control every aspect of a quilt—from design, to cutting, to piecing and quilting—have unlimited options. Those who want to do most of the piecing and quilting but prefer to follow the patterns of others can choose from thousands of available quilt patterns sold in individual packets in quilt shops or in books that feature multiple patterns and directions. Scores of free patterns can be downloaded online. Those quilters willing to pay for packaged convenience can buy complete quilt kits with precut fabric and just do the sewing part.

Fabric and other materials also change and develop constantly: First bright batiks were all the rage, then fabrics imported from Africa, then Japanese kimono silks. Pictorial quilts have gotten big, and there are teachers who specialize in how to make only flower quilts—or tree quilts—or quilts that feature portraits of people. Classes can range everywhere from Crazy Quilting for the Precision Impaired to Creating Realistic Rock and Wood Imagery.

Often when a little-known quilter wins the top prize at one of the major national shows, she or he

Manhattan Threads, *by Jeri Riggs.*

she calls "practical" quilts meant to be thrown on a bed, not hung on a wall.

www.paulineburbidge-quilts.com

CELIA EDDY'S QUILTSTORY

An online British quilt "magazine" run by author and quilter Celia Eddy, QuiltStory provides her invaluable comments on European quilt history along with dozens of links to British quilt groups, notices of major European quilt shows, and more.

www.quilt.co.uk

Book

QUILTED PLANET: A SOURCEBOOK OF QUILTS FROM AROUND THE WORLD,
by Celia Eddy,
Clarkson Potter; $40.00

Celia Eddy has written a gorgeous coffee table book loaded with photographs of quilts both old and new, from all over the world. She discusses such different quilting traditions as *kanthas*, Indian quilts made from layers of old saris, and Swedish wedding cushions.

CANADA'S QUILT OF BELONGING

Canadian quilters have their own versions of the resources that American quilters rely on: inspiring shows, welcoming guilds, and creative shops. What the Canadians have that Americans don't is the *Quilt of Belonging*. This vividly colored quilt is composed of 263 blocks, linked hexagons, representing every ethnic group and nation that has people living in Canada. When all eight panels are attached, the *Quilt of Belonging* stretches 120 feet long and 10½ feet high, with blocks for 192 immigrant nationalities (basically, every nation on the planet is represented) and 71 aboriginal groups, such as the Inuit. The imagery and materials represent the various cultures, so the quilt's blocks were created not just from fabric but also from feathers, fur, bark, beads, sealskin, and other materials, embellished with lavish needlework of many styles.

The brainchild of visual artist Esther Bryan, this massive handmade

becomes the next hot teacher, the flavor of the month in the quilt world, popping up to endorse products, design a new fabric line, write books, and deliver lectures and trunk shows at guilds across the country.

The new blood, the new ideas just keep coming. In the late nineties, dyeing one's own fabric became the trendy thing. One minute even quilts displayed at major museums were full of busy, colorful fabric patterns available at the corner quilt shop; the next moment it seemed that just about every art quilt hung in a show came with a display label reading "fabric dyed by the artist." Thus, a whole new rush and bustle began as rank-and-file quilters across the country signed up for fabric-dyeing lessons, and how-to books and websites sprang up immediately.

Technological change also adds new wrinkles constantly. The latest sewing machines are either powered by internal computers or sold with cables to link them to PCs. Things that used to be difficult, like scanning photographic images onto fabric, are now simple and available to the average quilter, who can buy multiple brands of paper-backed cotton that feed right into the average computer printer. Suddenly, everyone is making memory quilts for milestone birthdays and anniversaries, presenting their loved ones with quilts covered in dozens, even hundreds, of images from throughout their lives.

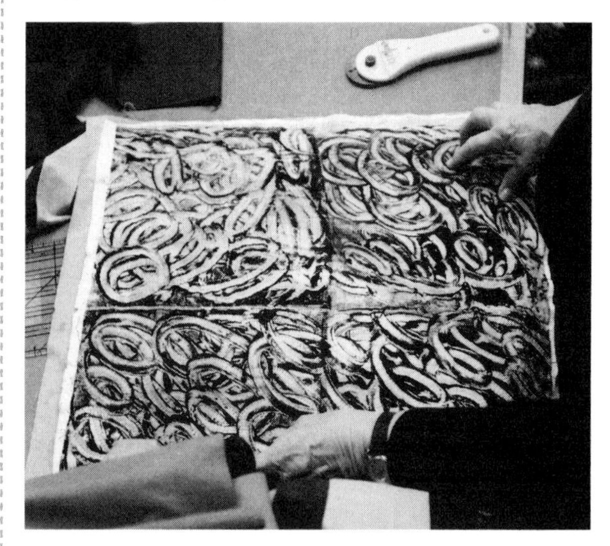

Hand-painting blocks of fabric.

Software for designing quilts has also continued to boom since the introduction of Electric Quilt in 1981. Now users of EQ software have access to a database of virtually every quilt block ever documented. They can play with hundreds of different fabrics on screen, plugging them into the existing quilt blocks or designing blocks of their own. They can scan the actual fabric pattern they plan to use into the on-screen schematic. And then the software will help them create templates for cutting out fabric, it will figure the yardage—do everything but sew.

This constant swirl of revival and invention keeps quilters giddy with anticipation. Quilters say over and over that if they were to live forever, they wouldn't be able to execute all the ideas for quilts stored in their brains, nor use all the tempting fabric squirreled away in their stashes.

The All-ness of Quilting

THE QUILTING RENAISSANCE SHOWS NO SIGN OF abating. Quilters asked to name their favorite almost always pick their current project, but they can't wait to get to the next one, and the one ten quilts on, when they will finally get to use a fabric or technique they've been saving for years.

Quilting not only survives but flourishes today because its pleasures are both multiple and profound. The merging of the beautiful and the practical, and the sense that quilts confer meaning and celebrate relationships, continues to attract new practitioners to the craft.

There are so many possibilities and ambitions to contemplate, plan for, and fantasize about, but meanwhile, the satisfactions of working on a quilt every day at one's current level of competence are sumptuous. For passionate quilters, to call this a hobby is a gross understatement. For them, it's a way of life.

"When I first started quilting, it was just for something to do. Now it's something I am," says Donna Merritt of Hancock, Michigan, a full-time professional quilter who alternates between her own designs and commissioned works.

metaphor for global community took hundreds of volunteers more than six years to complete. It was officially launched in 2005 at the Canadian Museum of Civilization in Gatineau, Quebec, and later began a four-plus year tour of Canada. The *Quilt of Belonging* traveled to the United States in 2007, and will come to rest at a permanent home in Canada.

If you want to learn more about this remarkable quilt, go to the website **www.quiltofbelonging.ca.** The well-designed site includes a photo gallery of the quilt on display as well as a feature that allows you to look at each block individually. There is a bookstore on the site that sells a beautiful comprehensive paperback book about the project, *Quilt of Belonging: The Invitation Project,* by Esther Bryan and friends (Boston Mills Press; $29.95). *Quilt of Belonging: Stitching Together the Stories of a Nation,* is a smaller version for children. Both books are available in the United States, including on Amazon.com.

The Quilt Boom Overseas

America didn't invent quilting but *is* largely responsible for the current quilt boom worldwide. There are long and rich quilting traditions in Europe, Asia, and elsewhere, but by the middle of the twentieth century, quilting had nearly died out in many countries even more so than it had in the United States. Although American colonists brought quilts from Europe, the current quilt renaissance started in the New World and traveled back to the Old. In the past decade or so, the American quilt bug has turned out to be more contagious than bird flu.

There are several explanations. For one thing, quilts are pretty portable: The pivotal American museum show in the 1970s that presented quilts as serious art traveled widely, as did the 1995 movie *How to Make an American Quilt,* starring Winona Ryder. The Internet also has played a major role. Thanks to the explosion in quilt websites, quilters all over the globe can easily buy American quilt books and supplies, download patterns, and ask for advice. They don't need to have a great little quilt shop down the road when they can get everything they need by computer.

A growing number of quilters are crossing oceans to take classes here, especially at the big annual shows in Houston and Paducah, Kentucky. And the major quilt contests in this country include more and more quilts entered by overseas quilters, some of whom are earning top prizes.

"Of course, the briefest glance at today's patchwork and quilting scene will confirm that the amazing revival inaugurated in America, which swept to Europe, Japan, South Africa, and Australia, is also booming in the U.K." writes British quilter and historian Celia Eddy in her online "magazine" QuiltStory (**www.quilt.co.uk**). "The exhibition The Pieced Quilt: An American Design Tradition, which was brought to England in 1975 by Jonathan Holstein and Gail van der Hoof, is largely responsible for the British resurgence in patchwork and quilting, but it in turn has led to an increased interest in our home-grown traditions."

In an interview, Eddy said she doesn't know of any attempts to count the number of British quilters, but she says there are more than seven thousand members in The Quilters' Guild of the British Isles, "which is quite large for a membership based on a specific interest."

After observing the enormous popularity of America's major quilt shows and the willingness of British quilters to travel to Texas and Kentucky and other overseas locations, British entrepreneurs have originated large quilt shows at home that have taken off. One of the largest is The Festival of Quilts, an annual show in Birmingham, England, which started in 2003. More than 24,000 visitors came to the 2006 show from dozens of countries, including Iceland, Russia, and South Africa, and more than 1,500 quilts were entered into competition.

Similar crowds were drawn to the Patchwork & Quilt Expo, held biennually from 1998 to 2006 in various European cities. The Patchwork & Quilt Expo was

about twenty-five years ago."

Even more stunning is the growth of quilting's popularity in Japan. The Tokyo International Great Festival lasts more than a week and pulls in about 300,000 visitors, making it bigger than any single quilt show staged in the United States. The Japanese quilt boom is taken seriously by many Japanese media leaders, including NHK, the Japanese equivalent of the BBC or PBS, which sponsors many cultural events. Seeing the growing popularity of quilting, NHK began sponsoring quilt shows, as well as offering quilting courses on television and at community culture centers.

Jacqueline M. Atkins, a textile historian who is the Kate Fowler Merle-Smith Curator of Textiles at the Allentown Art Museum in Pennsylvania, wrote a master's thesis for Columbia University on Japanese quilting and spent about a year in that country studying the quilt boom. "Based on my estimates, there were about one and a half million Japanese quilters in the 1990s," says Atkins. "I've gone back since to judge major quilt shows, and I'm sure it's higher now."

Early on, Japanese quilters were more likely to slavishly follow American patchwork designs and were drawn to classic floral appliqué designs and block patterns such as the Log Cabin. But in more recent years, Japanese quilters have adapted the craft to their own aesthetic and materials, working with Japanese silks like those used in kimonos and using such Japanese hand-stitching techniques as *sashiko,* which translates as "little stabs" and employs large stitches sewn with a thick white thread. Similarly, in England, as the boom has grown and matured,

actually run by Texan Karey Bresenhan, an entrepreneurial American, who founded and runs the extremely successful International Quilt Festivals in Houston and Chicago every year. Rather than keeping it in one location, Bresenhan varied the venues for the European version of her spectacular quilt show, setting up in Austria, the Netherlands, Germany, France, Denmark, and Spain.

"When we started the Patchwork & Quilt Expo, there were no large shows in Europe whatsoever, just little ones," says Bresenhan. "Now, there are a number of significant shows. And what's wonderful is that some of these countries are rediscovering their own quilt heritage: In France, they had forgotten they *had* a quilting tradition until they rediscovered it

Britain's Festival of Quilts: bamboo pole wrap dying (top), and Michael James lecturing (bottom).

quilters have become interested in such older, home-grown traditions as making whole-cloth quilts, in which the top is made from a single fabric and the quilting provides the design and embellishment.

Even when foreign quilters copy American designs, their approach to quilting is often quite different, especially in the way quilting is taught. In the United States, quilting is learned in a very ad hoc way, with quilters piecing together their knowledge from each other, books, shops, and the occasional class. The British and Japanese have very formal training systems available. Although not every quilter learns this way, many follow this structured, systematic approach, which results in technical proficiency and a certificate to prove it.

At the Festival of Quilts in Birmingham, England.

In Britain, part-time quilting courses are widely available, organized by a national training agency that offers accreditation in the craft. These courses are generally available at a number of colleges (with weekend versions being the most popular), but there are also correspondence courses and Internet versions. The best known courses have been offered since the early 1990s by something called The City & Guilds of London Institute, a very old educational organization that offers courses in many other subjects as well. The requirements of City & Guilds' two-year course in patchwork and quilting are quite rigorous. Students have to master a whole portfolio of techniques, including both hand and machine quilting.

In Japan, the requirements for student quilters are even more demanding, according to the textile historian Atkins. "In Japan, it is very hierarchical, with a sensei, or teacher, at the top of it," says Atkins. "The Japanese teach quilting the way they teach many traditional arts, like Noh, martial arts, or the tea ceremony. It is very disciplined and the teacher is the master. The teacher assigns the students projects such as a specific block pattern or floral design for a quilt, and she might even choose the fabric, not just the pattern."

The level of technical proficiency among Japanese quilters as a group is outstanding, says Atkins, but until recently they were not on par with Americans in terms of the originality of their designs. Now there are Japanese quilters who are executing exquisite designs, and with their amazing technical expertise, these quilters are winning major prizes and appearing in American museums.

The quilt world grows smaller all the time, as quilters from all over the world learn from each other. Among others, highly respected Japanese art quilter Keiko Goke is starting to teach occasionally and have her work exhibited in the United States. At the same time, quilt tourism is growing fast, and there is a steady stream of quilters going abroad to be inspired by other quilting traditions. American quilters have more opportunities than ever to study abroad, with quilt tours and cruises that travel to England, France, Italy, Japan, Tahiti, Australia, Guatemala, New Zealand, South Africa, and elsewhere.

Suzanne Sanger of Naples, Florida, has been quilting since the 1970s but says her enthusiasm is still growing. "At first, what appealed to me most about quilting was the connection to the past, especially my Aunt Blanche," says Sanger. "In the beginning, I clung to the traditional patterns and didn't think art quilters were really quilting." But then Sanger saw a display of art quilts at the biennial Quilt National show in the midnineties, and what she saw exploded all her notions of the craft.

"Wow! Here were quilts made from funny fabrics—even wood!—metallic threads, machine work everywhere! What freedom. What creativity. Suddenly, I couldn't wait to get home and try these new ideas. Now I feel as though I can do anything I imagine, and I spend hours on the computer playing with ideas."

She is not alone in finding that her quilt dreams keep expanding as the years go by. "In 1981, my dream was to own a quilt shop," says Charlotte Bull, who quilts in Missouri's Ozarks. "In 1991, my dream was to write a quilt book. In 2001, my fantasy was to be either a quilt museum curator or a certified quilt appraiser. But I'll settle for ten more years of quilting, wherever it takes me."

Like music buffs who can go from listening to baroque chamber music to hip-hop in an instant, quiltmakers can also cruise through and select from a diverse number of possibilities.

What's Great About Quilt Guilds

During the many years Alex Anderson hosted the popular television program *Simply Quilts*, viewers would constantly approach her and gush about how much they loved the show. Anderson always thanked them and then asked, "Do you belong to a guild?" If the answer was no, she would retort, "You've got to join. No matter what level you're at as a quilter, they'll embrace you."

Anderson explains that she feels like a teacher first and a TV personality second, and she believes that guilds are the ultimate educational tool for quilters. A wide variety of techniques have been demonstrated on *Simply Quilts* and other quilt shows still on the air, but these are no substitute for a firsthand personal connection between quilters.

GOTTA GET A GUILD

It's not always easy to find a guild to join, especially for a beginning quilter or a newcomer to town. Karen Musgrave, an accomplished art quilter, who moves often because of her husband's work, says joining a new guild has helped her find like-minded friends in new communities. "I've been a member of guilds in five states and two foreign countries," says Musgrave. While living in Aruba, she couldn't find a guild to join and started her own, called Quilting by the Sea.

When Musgrave moves to a new city, her technique is to find a quilt shop in the phone book's business listings (guilds are rarely listed there), sign up for a quilt class, and "pump the other women for information about the local guild."

There are several good websites that list guilds around the country. One is **www.QuiltIndex.com;** go to the home page, click on Community, and then click on Quilt Guilds. A second website that has extensive listings is: **www.quiltguilds.com.**

An enormous amount of the socializing people associate with quilting happens at guild meetings; guilds are also like permanent but portable, flexible, instructional academies. For quilters who didn't grow up playing under Grandma's quilt frame, there is always an older or more experienced quilter who knows how to finish a bias binding or what's the best batting for machine quilting—and when the local quilt shop is going to have a sale. Most guilds also host regular workshops and lectures.

Virtually every guild includes some form of show-and-tell as part of its regular meetings, so that quilters can also pick up know-how and find inspiration by regularly examining the work of fellow guild members. Many quilters find that just being in a room full of people who share their passion keeps them energized and focused and reignites their flame of enthusiasm when it threatens to burn out. Some guild members report that just knowing they'll have nothing to share at the next show-and-tell gooses them along to complete their projects. The result of all these interactions is that quilters who belong to guilds tend to move faster along the learning curve than they would otherwise.

"I joined a guild and got involved with an online group when I moved to North Carolina and both the quantity and quality of my quilts took off," says Diane Gregg, a Greenville, North Carolina, math teacher.

Over and over, quiltmakers cite their sisterhood with other quilters as one of the main sources of joy in their craft. And although some quilters may also break off into more intimate groups, the guilds are where the action begins, and most of these quilters maintain their guild memberships as well.

There is no way to count exactly how many guilds there are in the United States. Considering how vigorously quilting grew from the nineties into the twenty-first century, the overall numbers have clearly risen sharply. What makes the number of quilters in guilds untrackable is that there is no single organization to which they all belong, and guilds tend to be staffed entirely by volunteers, with officers that change every year or so. Even guilds with $50,000 or $100,000 in the bank generally meet at the local school, library, or church and don't have official headquarters.

At one extreme are low-key guilds that don't charge dues or elect officers but provide members a regular place and time to gather with other quilters. (My wonderful guild, the Hopewell Valley Quilters, fits this description.) These are mostly local guilds covering a community or county. Usually, at least coffee and a snack are served at meetings, and quilters share their latest quilting projects.

The other end of the continuum is occupied by large guilds with hundreds of members and many committees. There are ten guilds in the San Francisco area alone, and some of those guilds boast more than six hundred members. Many states have statewide guilds that run statewide annual shows, but it's hard to get that many people gathered together often. Maine's nonprofit Pine Tree Quilters Guild counts more than two thousand members in its ranks, but they are scattered across seventy-five chapters. Most activities take place at the local guild level.

The larger guilds generally charge dues (not exorbitant ones, maybe $30 a year), elect officers, and offer a structured program of workshops and lectures, generally one a month. The speakers can be local quilters but often are prizewinners and top teachers from out of town, who are paid for their appearances.

A multi-generational quilting group.

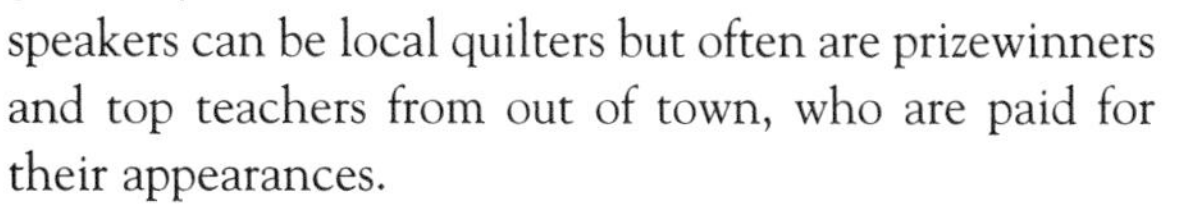

Big local guilds frequently have a major show of members' quilts every other year, and these shows are used to raise money through admission fees and quilt raffles. Many guilds organize regular charity projects, publish a newsletter, and maintain a website to keep members informed. Some also keep a lending library of quilt books.

THE SEWATHON!

The Los Alamos Piecemakers Quilt Guild in New Mexico conducts an annual charity event it calls a Sewathon! At the evening event, guild members sew crib-size quilts to give away to needy babies, often shipping them to a national charity, such as Project Linus (see page 87).

For this event, the guild is broken down into teams that consist of cutters, sewers, and pressers (who iron the seams). The teams produce the quilts in assembly-line fashion, says Rosemary Sallee, of the Museum of International Folk Art in Santa Fe, New Mexico.

Sallee, who belongs to the Piecemakers, wrote about her guild as part of a master's thesis in American studies. She describes how teams compete to see which can finish a quilt top the fastest. Prizes are also awarded in such categories as quietest team, most organized, and most disorganized. The pattern that will be used is kept a strict secret beforehand to make the contest fair and more exciting. Later, guild members finish the quilts.

Guilds have their own, sometimes idiosyncratic traditions, such as pet projects and special awards. The Austin Area Quilt Guild in Texas invented an award, The Order of the Fat Quarter, to recognize any of the 575 members who have "given service to our guild above and beyond the call of duty." Most months at least one person is given this award, which includes a fat quarter of fabric in a golden hue and a special lapel pin decorated with a gold star.

The majority of guilds are flexible and welcome quilters who have a wide range of techniques and approaches. There are some guilds with requirements that free spirits may find chafing, such as strict design parameters for elaborately quilted member name tags and that sort of thing. Art quilters sometimes grumble that their more traditional fellow guild members malign or misunderstand their work, but that seems to be more the exception than the rule. And there is always the option of forming a small, private group of totally like-minded quilters. Guilds might not be every quilter's cup of tea, but most feel at home there.

How to Start a Small Quilting Group—and Why

OVERALL, GUILDS ARE GREAT, BUT LIKE ALMOST everything else in life, with the good comes the not so good. The bigger guilds tend to be large and diverse; they can also be bureaucratic and demanding. There are meetings to attend, officers to elect, dues to pay, raffle quilts to make, and shows and workshops to organize. Because guilds have to meet the needs of a large group of people, they can't possibly tailor their programs and schedules to satisfy just a few individuals.

This is where small quilting groups come into the picture. These groups, often formed by people who also belong to large guilds, are able to hold more intimate gatherings of like-minded individuals. Guilds are generally open to whoever shows up at meetings, but these small groups are invitation-only affairs. Some meet weekly and some monthly, and many convene at members' homes instead of the school gyms, libraries, and churches where guilds typically gather.

Most small groups meet to quilt and try new techniques, but members also chat while they sew. The smaller gatherings make intimate conversation possible. Such groups have more in common with the quilting bees of old, partly because they are personal and home based.

The experiences of Judy Keim, who belongs to the Ohio Valley Quilters' Guild as well as to a smaller group called the Serial Quilters, are fairly typical. Keim says the guild has about 130 members, while the local group has fewer than 20. Ironically, many of the women actually met online in a chat room, only to discover they lived in the same area. One of the women decided to host a get-together at her house, and Keim's horrified son said, "Mom, you met these people on the Internet. How do you know they're not serial killers?" It turned out none of them were, says Keim, and the women couldn't resist naming themselves the Serial Quilters.

"We get together every Friday morning and spend the better part of the day quilting and talking," says Keim. "Usually between six and ten people show up each week. Part of the group meets Tuesday evenings instead because they can't come days. At first, we only met to work on quilts for charity, but now we also show up with our own personal projects. It's been a great opportunity to learn new things."

Accomplished quiltmaker and teacher Liza Prior Lucy, who makes quilts for designer and coauthor Kaffe Fassett, has been in a weekly quilt group for more than a decade in New Hope, Pennsylvania. The group was started by a few women who met at a quilt shop class, she says, and still only has about ten members.

"I love that there are no rules, no formal structure. That would make me crazy," says Lucy. "It's a social thing. We all work on our own stuff and we talk a lot, about sick husbands, tough pregnancies, whatever is going on. We quilt, we talk, we eat dessert, and that's all. And we get a lot of affirmation from each other."

Interviews with thriving quilt groups across the country yielded the following practical advice for those interested in starting a small group.

Most small groups meet to quilt and try new techniques, but members also chat while they sew. The smaller gatherings make intimate conversation possible.

FIND KINDRED SPIRITS

Start with a few friends from work or approach quilters you meet at a quilt shop class or guild meeting. Mix friends with strangers and young with old to make it lively. What's important isn't necessarily that you're all at the same level of competence but that you agree on the basic purpose and structure of the group. If some members want unstructured time for sewing and chatting, while others want to rigorously pursue challenging new techniques, it may not be a workable group.

Some weekly groups organize around the mission of making progress on their "UFOs," aka unfinished objects. Many quilters have piles of partly completed quilt tops gathering dust in their sewing rooms, and working methodically through them with friends finally makes a dent. Also worth discussing is whether food will be served. Most quilt groups have coffee and dessert at a minimum, but many share lunch or dinner.

. . . it isn't surprising that there is a long tradition of quilting for charity.

PICK A CLEVER NAME

Thinking up a name that is descriptive and humorous is a good way to further the sense of camaraderie: A group that meets during lunch hours at the CIA in Washington, D.C. calls itself the Undercover Quilters. Several groups around the country playfully call themselves Women Who Run with Scissors, after the bestselling book *Women Who Run with the Wolves*. Ann Rhode belongs to an easygoing group of about ten quilters in California that meets twice a month, once for breakfast and once in the evening. One of its few rules is: Don't clean your house before meetings. The group is called the No Problem Quilters.

KEEP IT SMALL

Most groups number between six and twelve members, which makes it possible to fit comfortably into members' living rooms. Kathy Harte, an accomplished quilter in Anchorage, Alaska, says her group of advanced art quilters sticks to just six because each session is devoted to experimenting with a new technique, such as fabric painting, and the quilters need space to work.

STRETCH YOURSELVES

Use the group's supportive atmosphere to try things and take artistic risks. Judy Mathieson in Santa Rosa, California, is part of a group that started when one young quilter put out a call for other art quilters to join her. There was no screening process and the group was closed when membership reached a dozen. Mathieson loves the group; she says the founder really pushes them artistically. She has organized several challenges in which each member writes one word or design concept on a piece of paper. Four pieces are arbitrarily picked out of a hat, and over the next few months everyone makes a quilt inspired by those words. One time, the quilters had to incorporate these four things or concepts: something yellow, a fabric depicting life forms, light and shadow, and "ethnic." Fittingly, this group calls itself Extreme Quilters. Many quilt groups also plan a once-a-year retreat of at least a weekend, giving them a chance to deepen their ties and learn new techniques.

Quilt Charities

QUILTMAKERS ARE EXCEPTIONALLY GENEROUS, often giving away many more of their quilts to loved ones than they keep for themselves. So it isn't surprising that there is a long tradition of quilting for charity. During the Civil War, quilts were made and donated to both Union and Confederate soldiers. During both World Wars, boatloads of quilts were made for refugees and orphans in Europe. Many of these quilting efforts were organized. For example, during the Civil War, women in the North did a lot of volunteer work through the United States Sanitary Commission, a precursor of the Red Cross. This included making quilts for the Union soldiers, says quilt historian Merikay Waldvogel: Some quilts were made specifically for the soldiers and others were raffled off to raise money to help the men.

Recipients of quilts from More Than Warmth.

WHO NEEDS QUILTS WHERE YOU LIVE?

You don't have to ship a quilt far away to make a difference. If you want to make a quilt for charity, consider your own community. Remember to ask first and sew later.

◆ Ask the local fire department or police if it could use a few sturdy, colorful quilts to warm and comfort kids who get picked up during a fire, domestic dispute, or other emergency.

◆ See if a hospital in your community has children who could use a soft quilt to hold while undergoing difficult procedures.

◆ Make a quilt for the next big fundraiser at the school your children attend. It could be auctioned off or sold in a raffle.

◆ Call a local soup kitchen or women's shelter. A formerly homeless woman once told me that the quilt she was given at a shelter helped turn her life around knowing someone thought she was worthy of something so special.

A small part of the AIDS quilt.

What's interesting is that in the twenty-first century, making a quilt still seems to be among the first impulses of a compassionate person wanting to help the sick and the grief stricken. The AIDS quilt was started in the 1980s as a memorial to those who died of the disease and as a statement of political protest in the Reagan era. Each panel is six feet by three feet, the size of a coffin. Technically speaking, some may say The AIDS Memorial Quilt isn't a quilt, in that most panels are not three layers stitched together. But it is the most famous example of patchwork in modern times, and there is no denying that it has provided enormous cathartic comfort for countless families who lost loved ones to AIDS. (To learn more about the AIDS quilt, go to www.aidsquilt.org.) Its fame has also likely contributed to the flourishing number and variety of contemporary quilt charities. These days, every high-profile tragedy sparks an immediate frenzy of quilting. Quilts were made for all the families of Oklahoma City bombing victims and for thousands of families who lost loved ones on 9/11. And there are multiple organized efforts to make quilts for soldiers who fought in Afghanistan and Iraq.

Quilt guilds today generally list the making of charity quilts as one of their central missions, and many have a particular charity that they've worked with for years. In addition, quilters and quilting groups often contribute a quilt they have made to a nonprofit organization holding a fund-raiser. These donated quilts are

Spotlight on Quilts for Kids

Interior decorator Linda Arye noticed huge plastic bags full of fabric swatches discarded after a trade show she attended in Philadelphia in 2000. Inside the bags were discontinued designer fabrics, mostly cottons and chintzes for home decor priced as high as $400 a yard. The bags were earmarked for drop-off at a local landfill.

"It just seemed so horribly wasteful that I asked if I could have them instead," says Arye, who lived in nearby Yardley, Pennsylvania. "They said nobody had ever wanted the remnants before, so fine. But then I had to decide what to do with fifteen hundred pounds of fabric in my house!" The swatches were fairly large, many measuring twelve inches square, but that wasn't enough to cover a chair or make a shirt.

Inspiration struck as Arye remembered a time when her daughter, then four, had to be hospitalized with a serious virus and the hospital wouldn't let the girl keep her beloved teddy bear by her side. "Too germy," Arye was told by the nurses. Arye somehow flashed on the idea of using the fabric patches she rescued to make quilts—quilts that could be washed over and over and, unlike the bear, be clean enough to comfort a child in the hospital.

Arye got the idea of having quilts made for kids with cancer, AIDS, and other life-threatening illnesses. Although Arye later learned to quilt, at that time she didn't sew at all, but that didn't stop her. First she persuaded her Aunt Barbara to take a quilting class and to make some quilts from the discarded swatches. And then, being a practiced networker, Arye set about recruiting what would become thousands of volunteers.

Quilts for Kids now has fifty chapters in the United States and abroad, groups that are given donated designer fabric swatches from which to make quilts. Arye works full-time for the nonprofit, signing up additional design centers around the country to donate fabric instead of tossing it out, distributing quilts, and raising money to mail the completed quilts to hospitals. Quilts for Kids has sent more than forty thousand quilts to sick children and saved nearly a million pounds of fabric from the nation's landfills.

To handle the huge shipments of fabric and quilts, Arye has had to build an addition onto her house. As the quilts go out, stories come back. For the children who heal, the quilts they clutched in the hospital become treasured keepsakes.

It might seem that decorator fabrics would be too heavy for quilts, but Arye says that the heaviest ones are used for projects like tote bags designed to hang on wheelchairs. Lighter fabrics are perfect for quilts; chintz, for example, will lose its stiffness and sheen after just one washing.

There are patterns on the Quilts for Kids website, **www.quiltsfor kids.org,** but volunteer quilters are welcome to use their own. The directions include the size required: A kid in the hospital can't drag a full-size bed quilt through the corridors. Along with fabric, volunteers get a Quilts for Kids label, with its trademark of a quilt being hugged by two arms, which they can sew to the back. All quilts must be pieced and quilted by machine so they'll stand up to lots of machine washing.

Visitors to the John F. Kennedy Presidential Library and Museum in Boston, Massachusetts, view a quilt made in memory of the victims of 9/11.

used to sell raffle tickets or they're auctioned off to the highest bidder, with all the monies going to the charity. Quilt groups often hold quilt raffles, but many of the charities are not quilt related: They may be raising money for a school or medical research, for example. It's a simple fact that attractive quilts fetch eager bidders when many other standard auction items don't. The book *Hearts and Hands: Women, Quilts, and American Society*, by Pat Ferrero and others, explains how deep such philanthropic roots run in quilt history, displaying a photo of a quilt made in 1836 specifically for a crafts fair to benefit the antislavery movement.

The philanthropic urges of quiltmakers show no signs of abating now that new technology allows quilters to dramatically increase their quilt output. As catastrophes arise, quiltmakers will rally to aid their victims, but there are also a number of notable ongoing charities that have become well established in the past decade and are always looking for donated quilts.

You'll find a list here of quilt charities geared toward both guilds and individuals. It is far from comprehensive, but these are all well-run organizations with reliable track records. The recipients of the quilts differ, as do the requirements of the charities, so please check in with them before donating. In addition, local guilds and shops and quilt magazines are all good resources for information about where donated quilts would be welcome.

RESOURCES

Quilting Charities

PROJECT LINUS

One of the best-known quilt charities, this national organization is named for the *Peanuts* character who keeps a tight hold on his security blanket. Blankets must be homemade and washable but don't have to be quilts. All are given to seriously ill or traumatized children. More than a million and a half blankets have been donated since 1995. There are more than 385 chapters of Project Linus nationwide, and all volunteers (or blanketeers as they are called) must work through their local chapter. Chapter coordinators must agree to abide by the group's requirements, which are spelled out in detail in a handbook. To find the nearest chapter, contact the Bloomington, Illinois, headquarters.

P.O. Box 5621
Bloomington,
Illinois 61702
(309) 664-7814
www.projectlinus.org

QUILTS FOR KIDS

This charity delivers quilts to children with life-threatening illnesses, often while they are in the hospital. Quilts for Kids is unusual among quilt charities in that most of the fabrics are provided to the quilters who make the quilts. This twist is related to the nonprofit's origins and founder Linda Arye's desire to recycle designer fabric swatches (for the full story, see Spotlight on Quilts for Kids on page 85). Volunteers, who don't need to be members of a Quilts for Kids chapter, can get patterns from the charity or use their own.

11 Effingham Road
Yardley,
Pennsylvania 19067
(215) 295-5484
www.quiltsforkids.org

ALZHEIMER'S ART QUILT INITIATIVE

Many guilds and individuals donate quilts or give financial support to this organization launched by Ami Simms, whose mother suffers from Alzheimer's disease. The Alzheimer's Art Quilt Initiative organized a juried show of fifty-two quilts interpreting the disease. Called Alzheimer's Forgetting Piece by Piece, the quilts will tour the United States through 2009, and can also be seen in the book of the same name. On its website, the organization holds regular auctions of donated quilts; quilters at every level are welcome to contribute their work. All funds go to the Alzheimer's Association.

www.alzquilts.org or call **(800) 278-4824.**

WRAP THEM IN LOVE

Emphasizing needy children, especially those living in dire poverty in the United States and abroad, Wrap Them in Love was started by a woman who adopted children from Korea in 1980 and 1983 and wished she could provide quilts for all those left in the orphanage. Quilts are shipped all over the world, but the founder has a special relationship with the Rose bud Indian reservation in South Dakota. Because most quilt charities concentrate their efforts on domestic recipients, this is a good choice for quiltmakers who want to help needy children in other parts of the world.

2522-A Old Highway 99S
Mt. Vernon,
Washington 98273
(360) 424-9293
www.wraptheminlove.org

PRAYERS & SQUARES, THE PRAYER QUILT MINISTRY

This charity makes quilts for both children and adults who are struggling with a crisis, medical or otherwise.

All the quilts are tied (some are quilted, too), because prayer plays a key role here: With every knot, a prayer is said for the quilt's recipient. Since Prayers & Squares was founded in 1992, more than 550 chapters have sprung up in the United States and abroad, many based at churches of various denominations. Many of the quilts are blessed by ministers during regular Sunday services, and then the quilts are put on a table so members of the congregation can add their prayers. For more information on the "Three Commandments of Prayers & Squares" and how to locate a nearby chapter, go to the website **www.prayerquilt.org**. There is also a book about the group, *Fabric of Faith: A Guide to the Prayer Quilt Ministry*, by Kimberly Winston.

Children helped by More Than Warmth.

More Than Warmth

Helping elementary school children in the United States make simple quilts to be sent to needy children all over the world, More Than Warmth was launched by Tennessee teacher Judith Biondo Meeker after 9/11, when she organized one hundred fourth-graders to make quilts for Afghanistan. Before long, the project took over her life, and she now runs it full-time. More than seven hundred quilts have been sent to thirty-plus countries, thanks to more than five thousand students. Meeker has contacts who deliver the quilts in person, and recipients include young boys in India who were formerly slaves in rug factories and refugees fleeing genocide in Africa. Teachers can choose a country on the nonprofit's website and download related lesson plans for math, art, and social studies to use in their classes, as well as instructions for making the quilts.
More Than Warmth needs funds to support its work, as well as people to donate fabric, quilters to finish the pieced tops, and volunteers to lead local school projects. The website is **www.morethanwarmth.org** or send a fax to **(615) 799-7729.**

CHAPTER TWO

Sewing Now: Tools, Technology, Techniques

QUILTERS LOVE THE LENGTHY HISTORY OF THEIR craft and cherish the many aspects of it that remain unchanged. But one of the major attractions of quilting now is the gee-whiz gadgets and cutting-edge technology that now simultaneously reduce the drudgery and multiply the design opportunities.

If you choose to piece and quilt by hand, you'll have access to tools and materials your grandmother never dreamed of. You can design original quilts on your computer and order fabric online—anything from reproductions of Civil War fabrics to thirties prints, if you want—and use a handcrafted, ergonomically designed thimble and hoop to sew by hand. If you work by machine, your choices of tools will be nearly overwhelming.

Quilting's evolution is analogous to what has happened to home cooking in recent decades. Both these staid and comfy pastimes have become trendy and competitive. It's not enough to serve up a pleasing plate or stitch a snug blanket; you've got any number of ways to do these with flair, using more cool gizmos than James Bond does when he's dispatching a sadistic villain.

Just as tools like the food processor have revolutionized cooking, quilting has been altered radically by things like the rotary cutter and computerized sewing machines. Quilters collect and compare new gadgets constantly and are always looking for the best system for cutting a perfect circle or guiding a bulky quilt through a home sewing machine.

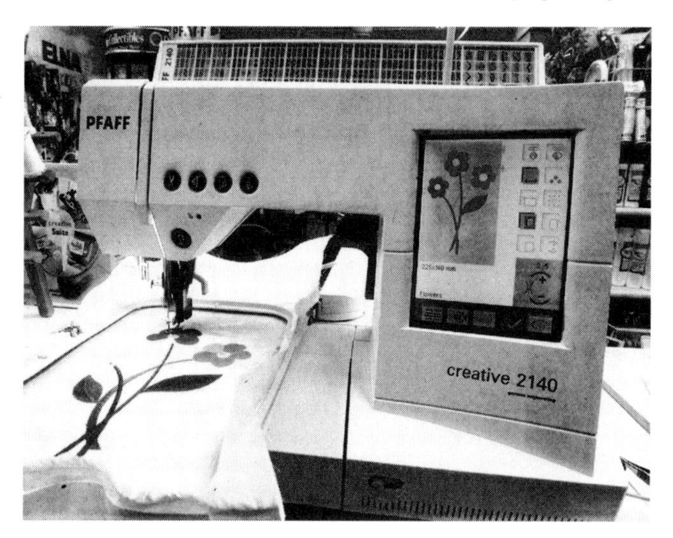

A Pfaff sewing machine with embroidery software.

Of course, the final results do matter; most of us think that we are more sophisticated cooks than our mothers. Quilters, too, are creating staggering works of craft and art using all these new tools.

This chapter explores the evolution of quilting techniques from hand work to the use of increasingly sophisticated—and large—sewing machines. In the chapter that follows you'll find descriptions of other hot techniques like fabric dyeing, printing photos on fabric, and using quilting software. No book can stay abreast of technology in real time. Every year the sewing machine companies retire old models and release new ones, adding competitive features. Trends change quickly and quilters seem willing to pay up for new technology. Still, the general discussion, descriptions of specific sewing machines, and detailed resources you'll find here will guide you to a thorough understanding of the major trends in sewing machine technology and help you sort out which machines will be most valuable for meeting your quilting goals.

QUILTING BY HAND

In this magical, high-tech quilt world, where computerized sewing machines do just about everything but serve latte, why would people continue to piece and quilt by hand? The reasons are multiple and compelling. As with knitting, where it's just yarn, two needles, and you, making quilts by hand feels satisfying. In a high-tech world where it seems like you can't do anything without an electronic device, creating something practical with the simplest of tools and your own two hands can make you feel self-sufficient, accomplished, frugal, and at peace. When you're done, you have something that will keep you warm or decorate your wall—and impress your friends. How cool is that?

As a quilter who personally prefers piecing and quilting by hand, I find I develop a comforting rhythm when I work. Quilting on my lap, I'm much more aware of the tactile pleasures of the fabric and thread. Almost every evening when I'm at home with my family, I settle into my favorite armchair and work on a quilt. During the day, just thinking about my small basket of tools and a pile of fabric squares on the table nearby makes me look forward to the end of the day.

All the new techniques and possibilities have made many quilters impatient, and they rush through one project to get to the next. To me, taking my time is part of the pleasure. Quilting is my hobby, not my work; I'm doing this to have fun, not fill a quota. Yet, the quilts get done. Like hand-quilting guru Jinny Beyer, I find that working by hand each day, I produce a lot more finished quilts than I would have expected.

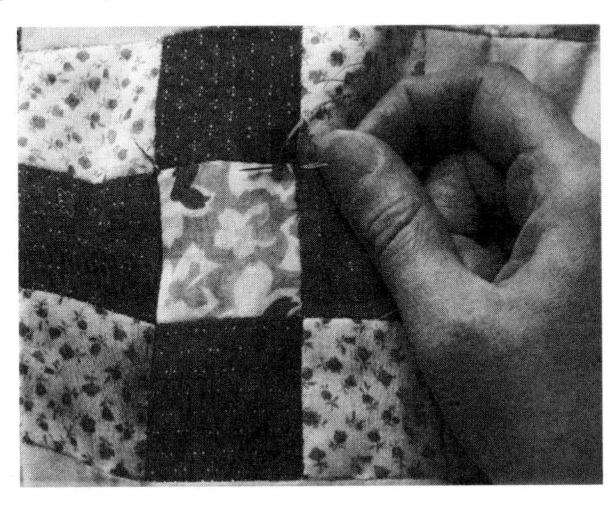

Hand quilting a basic Nine Patch block.

This isn't to say that I piece and quilt every single project by hand. If I've got a deadline on a quilt because it's for a baby that's due any minute or because I promised to make it for a charity to raffle, then I will get out my sewing machine to piece it. And I've gotten in the habit of sending a good number of my hand-pieced quilts out to be finished by a longarm machine quilter in my guild, Sandy Merritt (she quilted three of the five projects that I designed for this book). Knowing the quality of her work, I trust my precious quilts to her.

There are many quilters who constantly shift back and forth between handwork and machine work. They may save their masterpiece or heirloom projects for hand quilting but finish their "utility," experimental, and quickie quilts by machine. Some prizewinning quilters say they use both hand and machine quilting on the same project because they're trying for different effects. They may choose to piece a quilt top by machine, then use hand appliqué and embroidery to embellish it. Sometimes you want a more homemade or folk art look for a quilt, and having precisely even stitches doesn't produce the effect you're after.

It's not surprising that the explosive development in new tools has affected handwork, too. There are dozens of different types of thimbles now, for example, made of everything from leather to plastic to sterling silver. There are more types of thread and needles, hoops and frames, and devices for lighting your work. And there are hand-quilting experts, with books, classes, and DVDs, demonstrating new, improved techniques for a very old craft.

It may be hard to predict the next high-tech toy to captivate the quilt market, but one thing is clear: Quilters are going to continue working with their hands for a very long time to come.

One of Dierdra McElroy's thimbles.

Battle of the Thimble Gurus

As if proof were needed that hand quilting is still a popular method in the twenty-first century, there are actually competing thimble experts who both sell expensive handcrafted thimbles and teach their own methods of hand quilting.

The more established "thimble guru" is Dierdra "Didi" McElroy, who has a master's degree in biomedical science from Texas A&M. McElroy's mother became a quilter while McElroy was in college, and noticing that her mother could hand quilt for eight hours a day without pain, McElroy decided to write her master's thesis on the orthopedics of a hand quilter.

McElroy went on to invent and patent a thimble she swears is the "Cadillac of thimbles," the most comfortable, orthopedically correct, and best made on the market. Her thimbles come in four different metals, including sterling silver and gold plate, and sixteen sizes and are priced from $45 to $100.

McElroy is based in California, but her rival Liuxin Newman lives in Australia. Newman, who calls herself "Thimble lady," has made a splash with her books and DVDs and has taught classes at quilt shows in the United States and appeared on television's *Simply Quilts*.

A quilter and a metalsmith, Newman has developed her own style of thimble: It's cylindrical, with one flat side, and comes in inexpensive plastic models and ones made from precious metals.

A collection of McElroy's "Cadillac" thimbles (top). The classic Thimblelady thimble (right).

Dierdra "Didi" McElroy

On McElroy's website, **www.thatperfectstitch.com**, you can order a thimble; buy a book, pattern, or quilt kit; check her teaching itinerary; or book one of her guided tours to Tahiti (McElroy lived there as a child). Her book, *That Perfect Stitch*, contains one hunded photographs and eighty line drawings and there's a video in which she demonstrates her technique. Information is also available at (800) 993-4445.

Liuxin Newman, "Thimblelady"

Although Newman is based in Australia, you can use her website, **www.thimblelady.com**, to watch a video about her thimble technique, check out her teaching schedule, or order her thimbles and other notions. Newman has written two books, each with a companion DVD: *Perfect Hand Quilting Without Pain*, and *Perfect Hand Appliqué with Thimblelady*.

Frames, Hoops—or Neither

THERE USED TO BE NO QUESTION—EVERYBODY hand quilted on a frame. But now there are many choices. From seeing grainy old photos and movies, we can all visualize old-style quilting bees, in which all the quilters sat around a full-size quilt stretched on a frame. In those days, quilters spent months sewing on their laps to hand piece quilt tops. Once they had several tops that needed to be attached to batting and backings, the quilters would schedule a quilting bee and assemble their big wooden quilting frame. The frame filled the whole room, and setting it up was part of the extended ritual of completing a quilt.

When the quilt revival began in the late 1960s and early 1970s, one of the factors that fueled the boom was the relaxing of all of the old rules. Many of the early teachers viewed their purpose as making quilting easier, more fun, and more satisfying, so they took apart the whole process and reinvented it to suit modern lives.

Lap quilting using a hoop.

Among the teachers was Georgia Bonesteel, who has had a quilting show on television for more than thirty years and invented what she called lap quilting. "It began for me when I signed up to teach a class at the local community college and realized that they all couldn't finish their quilts on the single frame we had," says Bonesteel. She broke down the process and taught the women to quilt their projects in sections, on their laps, and then sew those sections together at the end.

"Other people started doing something similar, and a few books called it apartment quilting or quilt-as-you-go," says Bonesteel. It offered a new freedom and portability for quilters, which they quickly embraced.

Over the years, quilting has evolved to offer a wide range of options to crafters and artists. They can quilt by hand on their laps without any hoops or frames, which is the way I was taught and have always done it. I find it easy and the results are excellent, as long as I'm extremely careful in basting the three layers together first. I always use the living room floor for that purpose, taping the backing right to the wood floor, then positioning the batting and the top over it. I use great big basting stitches, starting in the center and working out to the edges.

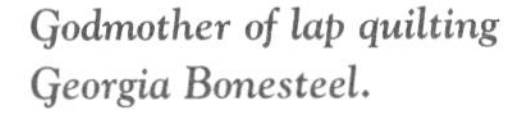

Godmother of lap quilting Georgia Bonesteel.

However, that's just one method. Many hand quilters prefer to quilt on their laps using a hoop, usually made of wood or plastic. These come in many sizes, and some are on stands. This option is also good for apartment dwellers or those who crave portability.

For hand quilters who want to work across the entire surface of a quilt there are more choices of frames than ever before. Some are big, requiring loads of space, and once erected are meant to stay that way. But many are made of light-weight materials, such as plastic piping, and can easily be assembled and disassembled. One advantage of using a frame is that the quilt usually doesn't have to be basted before the three layers are sewn together, which saves time.

Finally, the option of quilting a hand-pieced quilt by machine is also becoming more popular, and there are loads of techniques for doing this and special frames that can be added to extend the surface area of a standard sewing machine (see Expanding Your Quilting Area on pages 132–33 for more about these).

How to choose? Try different methods, ask other quilters what works for them, and see what frames and techniques your local quilt shop recommends.

"There should never be any guilt if you are not quilting in a hoop or frame," says Bonesteel. "I still do lap quilting myself, but I often use a hoop because I don't always make my quilts in sections any more. I think that all our hands are not the same and all our laps are not the same. But the advice I always give is that if you are going to do lap quilting, it's imperative that you baste the three layers together first, on a flat surface, and make sure they are stable."

A quilting hoop made by Hinterberg Design, set on a stand.

RESOURCES

For Piecing and Quilting by Hand

Frankly, I don't know how long it would have taken me to learn hand quilting without having my mother teach me. Seeing her do it, then immediately practicing it myself, I was quilting by hand in well under an hour (if not expertly, then at least comfortably).

Although learning to piece by hand is relatively simple—you just thread a needle and sew a simple running stitch, pulling the needle through the fabric—doing the actual quilting by hand is a bit more complicated, and there are a number of methods to choose from. There are plenty of books and websites that are worthwhile, but there's no substitute for hands-on learning (pun intended) from a quilter. So check out the resources listed here, but also take a class at your local quilt shop and ask for advice from more experienced quilters in your guild.

Websites

It's difficult to find complete, sustained directions on the Internet for making quilts by hand, but here are some helpful resources.

HANDQUILTER

Handquilter is the site of Candy Goff, a Montana-based quilter who loves to piece and quilt entirely by hand and has won major awards, including a first-place prize at the prestigious International Quilt Festival in Houston, Texas. Her well-designed site is packed with tips and practical information in the section marked Handquilting 101 and features inspiring photos of Goff's quilts.

www.handquilter.com

JINNY BEYER

Probably the most famous advocate of piecing and quilting by hand, Jinny Beyer gives classes and runs a shop. You'll find her first-rate book about handwork listed on the facing page, but there is also some excellent how-to information on her website. In her discussion of hand piecing and even stitches, for example, Beyer explains how she holds the fabric in both hands and pulls her hands away from each other slightly to create tension. To read her description, once you have gone to her website, click on Quilt Tips, set your cursor on Back to Basics, and then click on Hand Piecing.

www.jinnybeyer.com

THREADS

The Taunton Press publishes a popular magazine called *threads*, that covers all types of sewing, not just quilting. Its Web page **www.taunton.com/threads/pages/t00024.asp** has a long address, but it's worth the trouble to type it all in. This reprints an article by quilt teacher Mary Stori called "Perfect Your Hand-Quilting Stitch," and it includes not just invaluable advice but also very clear, close-up photographs of how to make her version of a "rocking stitch," a favorite for hand quilting. If you've never had a demonstration of how a quilter uses a thimble to help push a tiny needle through three layers, this will be a help.

Books

Some of these books cover just piecing or just quilting, while some cover both, so pick whatever serves your needs and level of expertise.

HAND QUILTING WITH ALEX ANDERSON: SIX PROJECTS FOR HAND QUILTERS,
by Alex Anderson, C&T Publishers; $12.95

Alex Anderson, the longtime host of the popular television show *Simply Quilts*, has written a good primer (you'll find a profile of Anderson on page 307). Her forty-page book includes instructions for five wall hangings and a pillow. The author swears that none of them took her longer than ten hours to complete.

Quilting with a hoop.

QUILTMAKING BY HAND: SIMPLE STITCHES, EXQUISITE QUILTS,
by Jinny Beyer, Breckling Press; $29.95

This is the bible for both piecing and quilting by hand. Just like Jinny Beyer's stunning, prizewinning quilts, the book is beautifully constructed. It's full of tips and tricks, illustrations, and recommended tools. If you buy just one book on handwork, it should be this.

The CD-ROM *Hand Piecing with Jinny Beyer*, from Breckling Press ($19.95) makes an excellent companion to her book. For anybody who can't take quilting lessons in person, the next best thing is following these detailed, how-to instructions from Beyer. You can watch over her shoulder while she demonstrates, then click on step-by-step photos that supplement what she just showed. Even basics like how to thread a needle are covered.

QUILT SAVVY: HAND QUILTING,
by Virginia Hedrick, American Quilter's Society; $21.95

Part of a series of practical how-tos from the American Quilter's Society published in skinny spiral-bound books, Hedrick's volume contains lots of good basic information from a teacher and longtime quilter. The many close-up photos of hands are invaluable.

QUILTERS AND THE SEWING MACHINE

In 1989 there was a near scandal at the annual American Quilter's Society show in Paducah, Kentucky. For the first time ever, the AQS bestowed its top prize on a quilt that had been quilted using a sewing machine. Listening to the outraged hand quilters complain, you would have thought that winner Caryl Bryer Fallert had cheated when making *Corona #2: Solar Eclipse*. The stunning contemporary quilt, which later appeared in the exhibit The Twentieth Century's 100 Best American Quilts in Houston in 1999, shows spiraling swirls of reds, yellows, and oranges flowing from a blue/black ball.

There were quilters who labored endlessly to make tiny, even stitches who didn't think it fair to have to compete with a machine.

There were quilters who labored endlessly to make tiny, even stitches who didn't think it fair to have to compete with a machine. What they didn't realize is that to execute the intricate, swirling stitches that Fallert made using a machine requires at least as much practice, skill, and artistry as those possessed by these hand quilters. A more sophisticated awareness of the technique would come later, but at this moment, machine quilting was dismissed by many. For these people, Fallert's AQS victory seemed like the end of the world.

For sure, it was the end of an era.

"Some people were really angry," Fallert recalled more than a decade later. "But I wasn't trying to make fake hand quilting. My goal was to produce the best machine quilt I possibly could."

In truth, Fallert's victory was just the peak of a long climb for machine quilting. Machine-finished quilts had been creeping into the mix for years, and one had garnered the top prize at the International Quilt Festival in Houston six months before Fallert's win. But the AQS show in Paducah has long been considered the more conservative venue, the bastion of traditional quilting. For an original design that was machine quilted to win Best of Show at Paducah was big news.

The shock soon faded, and before long, Fallert found herself the object of gratitude rather than scorn. Everywhere she traveled, fellow quilters rushed up to thank her. "So many people said to me: 'Thank you so much! I can finish my quilts now. I have a full-time job, and your victory has given me permission to quilt by machine.' "

Before this, it was okay to quilt by machine if you were in a hurry. But there was a slightly guilty feeling that it wasn't quite kosher, that it didn't qualify as one's best work and surely couldn't compete with the finest work of master hand quilters.

The prizewinning Corona #2: Solar Eclipse, *by Caryl Bryer Fallert—a victory for all machine quilters.*

Once machine-made quilts started winning major prizes, it didn't take long before the floodgates opened. Machine quilting became more than acceptable, and many of the top art quilters started experimenting, finding fresh methods to produce creative results that could *only* be done by machine. They were followed en masse by hobby quilters, although these soon learned that Fallert wasn't exaggerating when she said that anybody could make their sewing machine do what hers did, "if they practice for two hundred to three hundred hours."

Before long, sewing machine companies took up the cause and made more and more adjustments to their equipment so that artistic machine quilting would be easier—thereby making it even more common.

Bonnie Browning, who runs the AQS show in Paducah, recalls that in 1989 she spent the entire convention justifying Fallert's award to every quilter she met. But in the years that followed, more machine-finished quilts were entered in the AQS contest until by 2002 the majority of entries were quilted by machine, another major milestone in the technology of quilting.

When in 2005 the AQS decided to initiate a separate category for quilts produced entirely by hand, in both the piecing and the quilting, conventional

Linda Roy (far right) accepting the 2004 Best of Show award in Paducah for her quilt Spice of Life.

wisdom held that there would never be enough entries to make for a real competition. But, as is often the case, conventional wisdom was wrong: There were plenty.

By then, a small army of teachers and quilters who preferred handwork for all sorts of reasons had come forward with classes, books, patterns, and breathtaking quilts and made the convincing case that hand quilting was alive and well, and as valid and creative as ever.

As it turns out, the Best of Show winners at AQS in both 2004 and 2005 were made entirely by hand. As the quilt renaissance continues to spread and deepen in nuance, the pendulum keeps swinging from handmade to machine-made quilts, producing some amount of tension as it swings. The fact that it doesn't stop permanently in one spot is testimony to the continuing fluidity and vitality of the quilt boom.

But the march of technology remains relentless, giving today's quilters a range of choices for their craft that is incredibly liberating, though at times a bit overwhelming. Let's take a look at some of the technological revolutions that have boosted the growth of machine quilting in recent years.

The Sewing Machine Revolution

TO BE SURE, QUILTERS HAVE BEEN USING SEWING machines for a very long time. Invented in the 1850s, the sewing machine became a must-have home appliance within twenty years. This was a boom time for quilting in America, so it shouldn't come as too much of a surprise that many quilters used their machines in some part of the sewing process.

But quilters mostly concentrated their efforts on using sewing machines to piece together the tops of their quilts. Some used the machine for quilting also, to sew the so-called fabric sandwich of two layers of fabric with a layer of batting in between, but this was the exception to the rule.

Bonnie Browning says there are antique quilts that clearly display machine stitching around appliquéd shapes. "These ladies wanted everybody to notice they had a machine and that they knew how to use it!" These were not lazy quilters trying to get away with a shortcut. Still, for many years most of the actual quilting was done by hand, and a major reason for this was that home sewing machines simply weren't equipped to handle a big, bulky quilt.

Interestingly, all machine ties to quilting seem to have been forgotten back in the early 1970s when the first stirrings of the current quilt boom began. Quilting was part of a major crafts movement that stressed handwork above all as a badge of authenticity and purity. And although most of the early revivalists knew perfectly well how to sew clothes on a machine, many were adamant about both piecing and quilting by hand.

An 1851 Singer sewing machine, one of the earliest models.

This 1981 book said machine quilting was just fine . . . for potholders.

In 1985, Harriet Hargrave's book helped launch the machine quilting revolution.

This practice held for some years, but by examining both pattern and how-to books of the late seventies and early eighties you can almost feel the growing impatience with this slow way of working. A 1981 book called *Quilting, Patchwork & Appliqué,* by Christine Barnes and the editors of Sunset Books, gives equal emphasis to hand piecing and machine piecing in its instructions. When it comes to appliqué, only hand methods are mentioned. And when it comes to quilting, most of the instructions are for handwork.

Nonetheless, the authors comment in an almost plaintive tone that machine quilting has its place. "Though purists scoff at anything but hand quilting, there are times when quilting with a sewing machine is appropriate," Barnes writes. The book goes on to state that machine quilting is justified if the quilter is in a rush or when the project is quite small, like a potholder. But it is clear in the writing that Barnes is justifying an exception to the general rule and not advocating that machine quilting should become the norm.

It took a number of home quilters and quilt teachers many years to make the "radical" switch. To do the actual quilting by machine, to make those machine-made stitches visible for all the world to see, seemed like quilting's final frontier.

Many date the switch to the 1985 publication of Harriet Hargrave's seminal how-to book, *Heirloom Machine Quilting,* which Caryl Bryer Fallert herself cited as an influence when she won the big AQS award. As Hargrave wrote in the introduction to a later edition of the book, "I feel that we spend too much energy debating whether machine or hand is best. There are enough quilts in all our heads that need to come out, that as long as the workmanship is of high quality, it should not matter what technique is used."

In retrospect, the switch to machine quilting seems inevitable, and it's part of the growing commercialism of the quilting boom. Embracing quilts finished by machine was obviously in the interests of virtually every player in the burgeoning business of quilting. Fabric shops were eager to foster this trend, adding machine-quilting classes nationwide.

If quilters used machines for more of the sewing process, they could make more quilts in less time, which would lead them to buy more of everything: more fabric, more thread, more patterns, more books, more sewing tools, and even more sewing machines.

To do the actual quilting by machine, to make those machine-made stitches visible for all the world to see, seemed like quilting's final frontier.

Sewing Machines—Then and Now

THE SINGER COMPANY'S FIRST SEWING machines were heavy industrial models, and they sold for $125 each. The earliest machines weren't really envisioned for the home market, and most households could not have afforded one anyway. Eventually sales took off, in part due to founder Isaac Merritt Singer's theatrical ways of marketing and

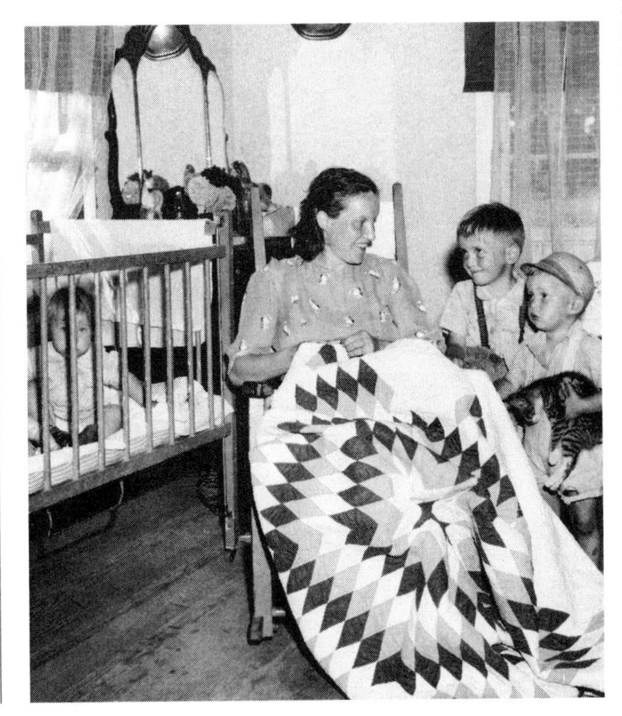

Quilts bring the whole family together.

ALL NATIONS
USE
SINGER SEWING
MACHINES.
ITALY.
SPAIN (VALENCIA)
TUNIS
SPAIN.
JAPAN.
BURMAH
SERVIA
INDIA
SWEDEN.
SPAIN
SPAIN.
PORTUGAL (VIANNA)

selling the machines (often employing pretty young women to demonstrate the devices) and then due to his pressing relentlessly into international markets. Singer is widely credited with creating the first American multinational corporation.

As mass production evolved, sewing machines got progressively better, less expensive, and lighter in weight, and sales soared in the home market. By 1870, the price had dropped almost by half, from $125 to $64, and the practice of paying over time made the sewing machines affordable to many more families.

But while sewing machines were embraced by grateful women everywhere, the last thought in I. M. Singer's mind was to lighten their workloads. "What a devilish machine!" he is quoted as saying early in his work on the project. "You want to do away with the one thing that keeps women quiet, their sewing!"

Fast-forward one hundred years, and the sewing machine is about as common as such household appliances as the toaster, washing machine, and lawn mower. By 1950, roughly forty million American consumers owned a sewing machine, and overall the sewing industry in the United States pulled in revenues of more than $1 billion a year.

But sadly, bumpy times were coming for the sewing business in general and Singer in particular. As lower-priced machines from overseas flooded the market, Singer lost its near global monopoly. In the United States, women were beginning to find other ways to spend their time. Sewing machines imported from Japan were cheaper, and Singer's market share dropped from 66 percent to 33 percent by the end of the 1950s.

Millions of women raised in the fifties had been taught by their mothers to sew clothing, and many more learned sewing basics in obligatory home economics classes in high school. But when equal rights for women became the next generation's theme song, even those women who liked to sew packed up their sewing machines in attics and basements and forgot them. Not only was making one's own clothing no longer hip, by then it wasn't even economical. Cheap, imported clothing flooded into every mall and megastore and kept up with the latest fashion trends. Jeans and T-shirts were the uniforms of youth.

While sewing machines were embraced by grateful women everywhere, the last thought in I. M. Singer's mind was to lighten their workloads.

A nineteenth-century Singer sewing machine advertisement (facing page).

FOR HISTORY BUFFS

The early history of the sewing machine is extremely rich—fraught with false starts, warring inventors, and larger-than-life personalities. As author Ruth Brandon explains in her book *A Capitalist Romance: Singer and the Sewing Machine*, Isaac Merritt Singer didn't invent the sewing machine. By the time he got involved, at least four versions had already been invented throughout the world, including a model patented by Elias Howe.

Like the other early attempts, Howe's patented device didn't work very well, and he had so much trouble drumming up interest in his invention that, during a particularly bleak period living in England, he pawned the patent for $100 so he could raise the money to return home to America.

Singer, a flamboyant womanizer who fathered more than twenty-five children by five different women, would much rather have made his career as an actor, and if he had succeeded, would likely be unknown today. But he was also a gifted mechanic,

Singer rushed to diversify with other products, especially in the aerospace and defense industries. The sewing machine division became a tiny part of the company, and it was spun off to shareholders as the Singer Sewing Machine Co. in the mid-1980s.

Singer's business had been gravely wounded by imported sewing machines, not just from Japan but also those made by such European manufacturers as Husqvarna Viking and Pfaff. However, the entire sewing machine industry was in serious trouble during the decades when women fled the unpaid monotony of

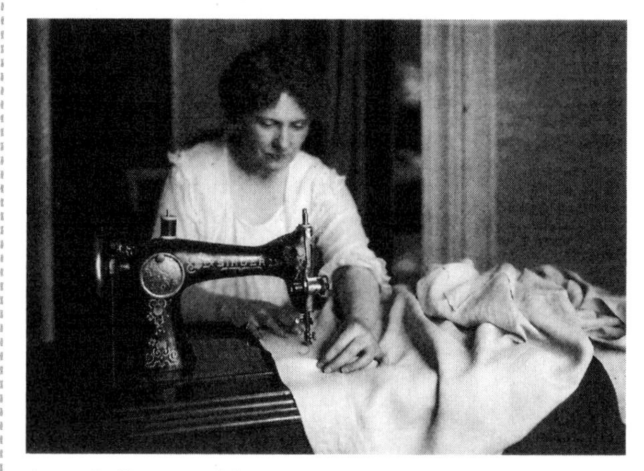

An early Singer model.

a housewife's life for careers of their own. At the time, dire reports by marketing researchers predicted that the market for high-priced American-made sewing machines would soon dry up entirely.

Nancy Jewell, the head of public relations for Husqvarna Viking in the United States, has been in the sewing machine business for more than twenty years, including a long stint at Singer. She has had a front-row seat for what became the sewing machine revolution and has observed the vital role quilting has played in the historic turnaround. "In the 1960s and 1970s, women ripped off their bras and said, 'I'll never do a domestic task again,' " says Jewell. While there were still some grandmothers plugging away making comfortable pants and some thrifty younger women whipping up curtains, the sewing machine market was becalmed. "When I came into this industry in 1984, it was just flat. There was no growth, nothing stimulating interest," Jewell recalls.

It took a combination of technological advances and the renaissance in quilting to revive the market. "Around 1985, Singer introduced a machine called a serger," Jewell says. "It's a domesticated version of an industrial machine and it sews twice as fast as a regular one. It was sort of the sewing equivalent of the microwave. Suddenly you started seeing things like a twenty-minute dress," and that pulled some of the home sewers back to their old hobby.

The other big innovation of the 1980s and 1990s was the electronic sewing machine. Putting microprocessors into sewing machines was a major breakthrough. As a *New York Times* reporter described it in an August 2004 article, "In essence, sewing machines are now computers with needles and thread." The *Times* reporter, Marc Weingarten, noted that the computerized machines allowed the inclusion of advanced embroidery packages that let sewers pick from hundreds of stitches and color palettes at the touch of a button. He compared the ability to embroider using a standard sewing machine as "analogous to having DVD drives on computers," and noted that even though high-end machines come with hundreds of preloaded stitches, enthusiasts insist on downloading more from the Internet, like teenagers surfing for tunes to plug into their mp3 players.

But what the *Times* didn't pay much attention to was how quilters were interacting with these high-tech machines or how quilters were being wooed by sewing machine makers. The biggest surge in the market for sewing machines came in the nineties, when quilting exploded. So many famous and not-so-famous teachers had come along by then and taught legions of quilters easy ways to use their sewing machines to make quilts faster and faster.

There was Eleanor Burns stitching away on her Elna on the PBS show *Quilt in a Day*, demonstrating ultraquickie shortcut methods of piecing a bed-size quilt. Burns, and others, were doing things like assembly-line "speed piecing," sewing a whole line of triangles or squares in a row without stopping and cutting the threads in between.

Sewing machine makers began adding more features that quilters craved. Consider that people using a sewing machine to make a garment are used to having to stop

and years of poverty, spent wandering the East Coast with a small acting troupe, forced Singer to support his family with his mechanical abilities.

After first trying to make a profit on a machine he invented for carving the type used for typesetting, Singer was asked to improve the frustratingly inept early sewing machine models. His breakthrough improvements included the invention of the presser foot. According to biographer Brandon, "There are ten essential features to a practical working sewing machine," and only two of them came from Singer.

Contentious and swaggering, Singer refused for years to acknowledge that he had borrowed some of the key elements of his device. But Howe, seeing the market for his invention take off, was able to raise the $100 to get his patent back, and he got all the sewing machine companies but Singer to pay him royalties. Singer didn't pay him until after there was a rancorous battle fought out in both the press and the courts. In the end, both men grew rich.

and start. For example, in order to carefully fit a curved sleeve inside a shoulder seam, the seamstress needed to use her hands to coax the fabric pieces together and expected to have to manually lift the presser foot, a metal attachment that holds the fabric firmly to the machine. But quilters, especially when zipping through miles of straight lines, had become speed demons who wanted to keep both hands on the fabric.

Once quilters started to use their home sewing machines to quilt as well as to piece tops, it became even more important to be able to keep their hands on the quilt. So sewing machine companies started adding hands-free features like knee lifters, also called knee lift levers. A knee lifter allows a quilter to raise the presser foot using a knee, instead of a hand, and was considered a major breakthrough. Bernina's so-called Free Hand System (FHS) was patented in Switzerland in 1983.

As Eleanor Levie describes the innovation in her excellent book *American Quiltmaking: 1970–2000*, "The knee lever lifted the presser foot for stops and restarts, leaving hands free to guide the work as the piecer sped through a chain of paired patches like a NASCAR racer on a mission."

Also, sewers who make clothes generally need their sewing machines to sew only straight or gently curved lines, forward and backward. But machine quilters want to be able to use the needle more like a pencil, drawing swirls and feathers and flowers and whatever else they feel like, and this requires different attachments that will allow free movement of the fabric underneath the needle.

By the late 1980s and early 1990s, when machine quilting became not only acceptable but chic, the sewing machine had been elevated to a new status in the quilt world. It became an object of fashion and obsession. Quilters could debate the advantages and disadvantages of different makes and models for hours. It has now become common for passionate quilters to own a whole stable of sewing machines, some for home, some for travel, with some they prefer for piecing, some for quilting, and some for embroidery.

Eleanor Burns, host of Quilt in a Day*.*

"I find it amazing how many of my customers have many sewing machines," says Sue Fox, a Janome dealer in Jacksonville, Illinois. "We gave a prize at our Christmas party last year to the lady with the most sewing machines at home. She has nineteen!"

The book of quilting surveys *Quilting in America* put out by CKMedia (formerly Primedia) tracks the trends in quilt styles and the way quilters use their machines. In 1994, 42 percent of quilters surveyed said they hand quilted exclusively. By 2003, almost a decade later, only 20 percent did all their quilting by hand. The numbers for machine quilting are almost a mirror image: In 1994, only 13 percent of passionate quilters said they did all their quilting on a sewing machine. By 2003, 31 percent, or nearly a third, did all their quilting by machine. Those numbers translate into huge sales for sewing machine companies, and they have gone after the machine quilting market with a vengeance.

Mastering the Machine

"RIGHT NOW, QUILTING IS DRIVING THE industry," says Jennifer Gigas, the director of education and training for Bernina of America. And Bernina has been especially canny in catering to quilters. Bernina makes a fine, well-crafted sewing machine and actively attempts to attract quilters through its advertising, promotions, and special resources, all of which has given it a cachet, almost a mystique, in the quilt world especially when it comes to machine quilting.

"Some quilters think if you can't get a Bernina, don't get anything," says Sharon Darling, who runs the Quilter's Review website and wrote a book called *The Quilter's Review Guide to Picking a Sewing Machine You'll Love*. "I think celebrity endorsements matter a lot, and they see Alex Anderson in the Bernina ads and hear Caryl Bryer Fallert talk about her Bernina in workshops. People always ask someone who's teaching a quilt class, 'What sewing machine do you use?'"

One reason for Bernina's popularity is its high-tech improvements, including something called the Bernina

QUILTS VS. CLOTHES

Quilters would seem to be an obvious target for sewing machine companies. But in truth, even in the eighties, many sewing machine manufacturers still thought of quilters as handworkers, not as their customers; it took the sewing machine companies a while to catch up. And quilters have different needs and desires than dressmakers.

Sewing hobbyists who make clothes, for example, sew just about all their garments with a 5/8-inch seam, whereas for quilts, the seam allowance is only a skimpy 1/4-inch, a vast difference. It wasn't until the late eighties and early nineties that sewing machine manufacturers caught on to such nuances and started offering feet for their sewing machines that were marked for 1/4-inch seams.

stitch regulator (BSR), which makes it easier to do free-motion machine quilting. Keeping stitches even is something every sewing machine is designed to do under normal conditions, but engineering did not anticipate free-motion quilting. Free-motion quilting is tricky to master because to do it the quilt must be released from some of the devices that would normally grip the fabric firmly on the sewing machine. In free-motion quilting, instead of letting the machine guide the flow of fabric, the quilter pushes the fabric under the needle in whatever direction is desired. This can be liberating and produce creative designs, but it typically takes many hours of practice to learn how to do it smoothly. In the meantime, the quilter will do a lot of jerky starting and stopping and pulling, which causes the length of stitches to vary all over the place.

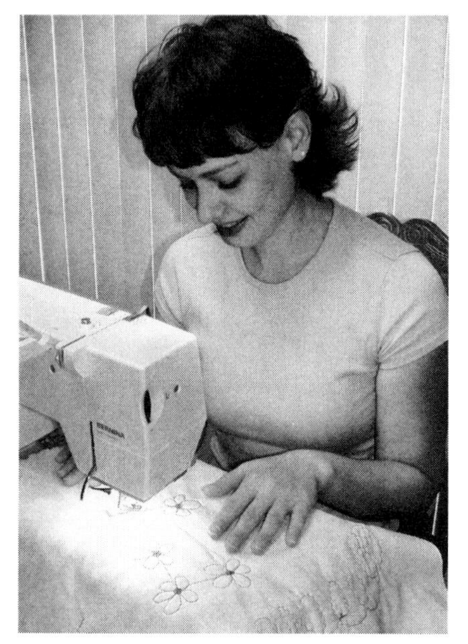

Quilting by machine: easy, approachable, and increasingly popular.

The stitch regulator changed all that. "It's like the difference between a slide rule and a calculator," says Pat Slaven, who tests sewing machines for *Consumer Reports*. Or even simpler—a calculator allows you to do complex math problems without knowing all the detailed mathematical stuff. In a similar way, the stitch regulator allows you to skip a major part of the learning curve in free-motion quilting.

When the stitch regulator was introduced in 2004, it created a big buzz at every quilt show and guild meeting. While some quilters pooh-poohed the device, others welcomed it with open arms and great relief. Bernina's Gigas says that even though the company anticipated a positive reaction to the innovation, it was actually overwhelmed with initial orders for this new machine. Although other sewing machine companies are following with their own versions of the stitch regulator, Bernina was well ahead of the curve.

The enthusiasm for the stitch regulator illustrates a fact of life that was becoming clear to quilters: Machine quilting, which once seemed like cheating, isn't all that easy. Quilts can be finished much more quickly by machine than by hand, but to make them look good requires hours of patient practice and a certain amount of sheer muscle. Some quilters found they didn't have the patience to learn or couldn't get over the fear of failure. The specter of sticking their gorgeous quilts under a powerful, fast-moving needle and potentially ruining them forever proved unshakable for some.

Those like Harriet Hargrave, who teaches machine quilting (and helped start the machine revolution), get frustrated at the difficulty of pushing quilters over this barrier. "I hear the same thing over and over again. My students say they hate machine quilting, they can't do it, it's just too hard," says Hargrave. "They *can* do it. They just want instant gratification. I tell them to buck up. We're wrestling a big quilt through a piece of steel! And you simply must spend ten to twenty minutes a day for six months practicing the techniques I teach" to gain proficiency.

Hargrave's point is an important one: Machine quilting can be mastered, but not quickly. And it turns out, although there are legions of quilters who love to use their home sewing machines to piece quilt tops, many of them *don't* have the patience to practice machine quilting daily. The ratio of effort to results can be just too big a barrier. But, sewing machines are still a powerful tool.

By adding the stitch regulator, a special presser foot with a small plastic attachment at the back, Bernina made it much easier for beginning machine quilters to make nice, neat stitches quickly and easily.

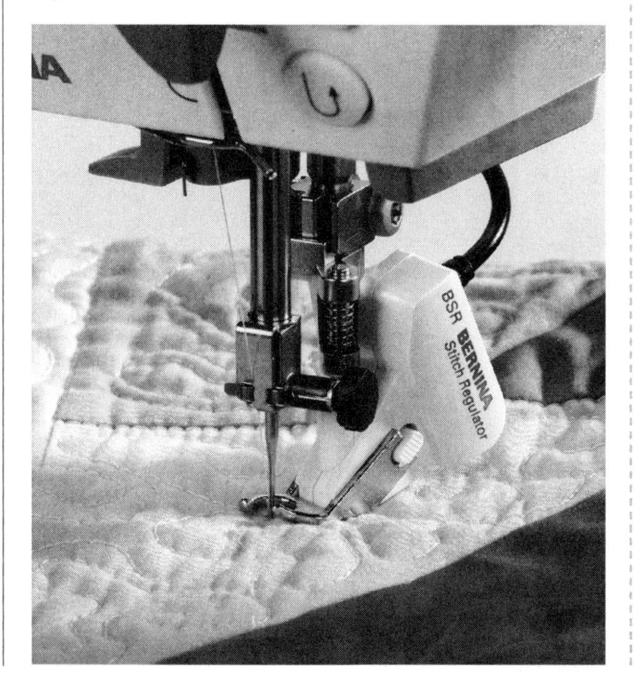

Machine quilters welcomed innovations like the stitch regulator.

The Cult of the Featherweight

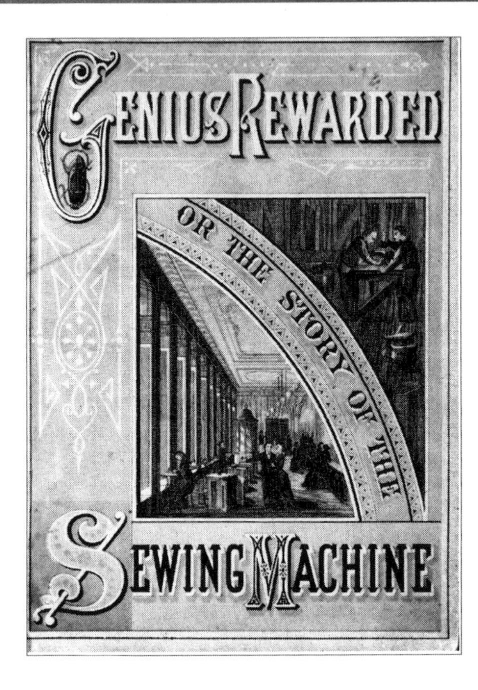

Despite the high-tech sophistication of today's sewing machines, one of the most popular machines among quilters is old, plain, slow, and can't even manage a zigzag stitch. Not only that, this sewing machine has been out of production for decades.

The Singer Sewing Machine Company manufactured well over a million of its model 221 units, dubbed the Featherweight because the machine was designed to be portable and weighed only eleven pounds. Singer Featherweights were manufactured between 1933 and 1964, and the popular affordable sewing machines helped Singer establish its reputation as a global brand name.

Three early ads for Singer sewing machines.

Why would quilters used to computer-equipped machines rave ecstatically about a toy-size model that only stitches forward and backward?

Beverly Macbeth, a quilter from Grafton, Ohio, who owns five Featherweights explains, "These machines execute a perfect stitch, the motor is incredibly quiet, and the machine is so easy to carry with me when I meet with other quilters. The Featherweight is so reliable I never worry that it will go on the fritz in the middle of a project. And it's so darned cute!"

Another appealing aspect of the Featherweight mentioned by many mechanically challenged users is its sheer simplicity. "It's so easy to maintain, clean, and oil that I can take care of it myself, which is very empowering," says one.

Cult isn't too strong a word for the growing band of quilters with an intense emotional attachment to their Featherweights. Indeed, there is a private e-mail group numbering hundreds of paid members called the Featherweight Fanatics. Many Featherweight owners have multiple models and name their favorites as though they were pets. Floridian Julia Squires Vernon calls her Featherweight "Hummer, because she hums as she sews."

Sarah Ann Smith in Maine named her Featherweight, too, and like many others, used the serial number to research when and where her machine was made. "My FW was born in Elizabeth, New Jersey, on September 23, 1935," says Smith. Indeed, a number of Featherweight lovers obsessively search for a Featherweight that has the same "birthday" they have.

One caveat about these light weight machines is that they are great for piecing a quilt top but less than ideal for machine quilting. Indeed, the motor may burn up with such hard use. Nonetheless, there are Featherweight owners who swear they quilt without problems on their machines.

Although rare Featherweights, including those produced in colors other than black, have sold for upward of $1,000, it's still possible to find these nifty little machines at flea markets and yard sales and on eBay for $50 or less. Dealers generally charge more, but are more likely to have cleaned the machines and replaced any missing parts.

In recent years, many sewing machine companies have attempted to create new sewing machines that can compete with the Featherweight in their portability and ease of use. Some of these models sell quite well, but none has attracted the fervent following of this old-timer.

Resources for Featherweight Fans

The book to buy is *Featherweight 221: The Perfect Portable and Its Stitches Across History,* by quilt teacher and designer Nancy Johnson-Srebro (C&T Publishing; $24). Along with the history and lore of the Featherweight, the book reproduces most of the original manual for the machine, which is great for quilters whose secondhand Featherweight came without these important directions.

The Featherweight Fanatics can be found at **www.featherweightfanatics.com**, and although it costs $15 to become a member and gain access to message boards and other features, there is quite a bit of information available to anybody who goes to the site. Here you'll find Singer's toll-free number for learning when and where your Featherweight was made, along with links to other related websites. One of the reasons fans of the machine pay to join this list is to find sources of Featherweight replacement parts, including feet and needles.

It's good news that all the major sewing machine makers woo quilters.

Home Sewing Machines

WITHIN THE SEWING MACHINE BUSINESS, standard home sewing machines are broken down into three sewing categories.

MECHANICAL MACHINES

Mechanical sewing machines are basic, starter machines that are good for beginner quilters or those who want a simple back-up machine to take to class. They can be great for piecing quilts but are generally not recommended for quilting. Except for some of the really bare-bones machines like the Singer Featherweight (see pages 112–13), many mechanical machines are often capable of sewing more than a simple straight stitch, but nothing is automatic. Adjustments for tension and so forth must generally be done manually.

PRICE RANGE: LESS THAN $500

ELECTRONIC MACHINES

Most quilters buy electronic machines. They have bigger motors and more features, including many fancy stitches, special feet that make quilting simpler, and plenty of microprocessor push-button controls. There are often features like knee presser lifts that let a quilter keep hands on the fabric instead of fiddling with knobs and levers. Prices vary as enormously as the number of features do. See the section on sewing machine companies (pages 121–31) to get an idea of what different manufacturers offer.

PRICE RANGE: $500 TO $4,000

COMPUTERIZED EMBROIDERY MACHINES

It isn't that these machines are the Cadillacs of the sewing machine business, per se, because not every quilter wants to do sophisticated machine embroidery. But these machines do include cutting-edge computer technology and allow quilters to take any image they can download or design and embroider it on fabric. The software powering fancy touch screens can display thousands of colors, and some machines include a vast updatable database of available thread types and colors.

Say you want to embroider a butterfly and you find a particular shade of deep purple for its wing: You can tell the machine what brand of thread you prefer, choose the type of thread you want to use, and the sewing machine will tell you the color and manufacturer's identifying number for the thread to buy. (Some newer embroidery machines cost less than $1,000, but they must be plugged into a home computer to work.)

PRICE RANGE: $4,000 TO $8,000

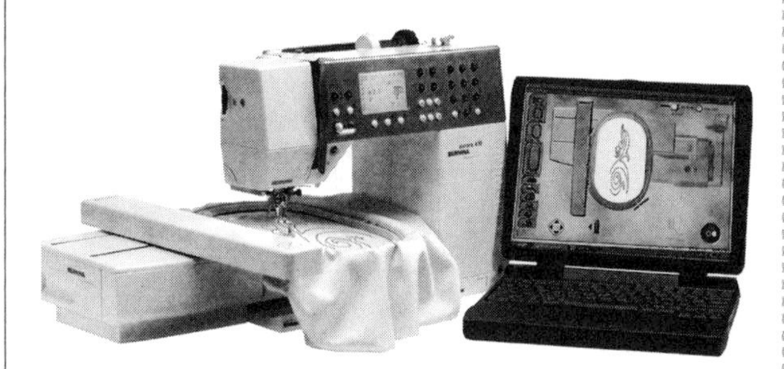

How to Buy a Sewing Machine

BUYING A SEWING MACHINE TODAY IS AS confusing as buying a new television and can be just as expensive. The features that are available and the prices are all over the lot. Do you want to spend $200 or $20,000? Are fifteen built-in stitches enough, or do you require six hundred? Do you want a sewing machine with a computer inside or one that plugs into your home PC?

It's good news that all the major sewing machine makers woo quilters, but that's also part of what makes choosing so difficult. The special features of the different machines vary, many differences are not quantifiable, and new models are introduced constantly.

What's a quilter to do?

"As far as I'm concerned, there is no perfect machine," says Sharon Darling, author of the book *The Quilter's Review Guide to Picking a Sewing Machine You'll Love*. "Even when sewing machines in a given category have the same basic features, they don't work the same way. You have to find out what works best for you."

WHAT IS A STITCH REGULATOR?

One of the biggest challenges for machine quilters is keeping stitches the same length: They tend to stretch out or contract based on the variations of the speed at which the machine is being operated. There is no question that when quilting by hand it's easier to produce the tiny, uniform stitches we all crave.

Technology has come to the aid of quilters with the relatively recent invention of the stitch regulator, which helps control the length of stitches. These attachments are now available not just on some models of home sewing machines (Bernina was the pioneer) but also on longarm machines as well.

As any teacher of machine quilting will tell you, stitch regulators help ease but don't completely eliminate the learning curve for quilters. Expect these devices to become both more advanced and more prevalent in the coming years.

But, don't expect stitch regulators to eliminate the need for practising machine quilting.

EMBROIDERY MACHINES' HIDDEN COSTS

If you're shopping for one of those high-end embroidery machines that are all the rage, don't forget to calculate the hidden cost of adding extra designs. Although many of the fancy sewing machines come preprogrammed with hundreds of designs, many quilters find that they want even more.

Russell Moline, the owner of The Moses House Quilt Shop in Keene, New Hampshire, sells a range of sewing machine brands including Baby Lock, Pfaff, and Elna. "I try to educate my consumers to consider when they buy an embroidery machine, they need to think about how they'll obtain additional designs," says Moline. "Although there are some designs you can download free on the Internet, most cost something. Many embroidery design websites charge ten or fifteen dollars to download a single design. One alternative is to buy programmed plug-in cards that contain a dozen or more designs, but those generally cost one hundred to one hundred

Darling has lots of good advice for quilters who are shopping for sewing machines, both in her book and on her website, www.QuiltersReview.com. Darling reviews new models and features on the website, along with quilt books and other products.

In general, Darling says, "I warn people about buying a low-end sewing machine if they are going to use it for quilting. Those machines are made for the casual home sewer who is going to make a pillowcase or dress. Quilters run their machines long and hard and through several layers of fabric, so my advice is to buy the best machine you can possibly afford."

Darling suggests reviewing your own needs and some basic options *before* you start shopping for a machine. Otherwise, she says, "You may get snowed by the razzle-dazzle" of a good salesperson.

QUESTIONS TO ASK YOURSELF

Start by methodically assessing your needs and wants. How will you use your machine? Just for quilting, or for household sewing, too? Would you prefer a lightweight model so you can haul it to quilting classes? What features are essential? If you don't plan on doing a lot of embroidery, one of the high-end machines with customized, computerized embroidery features isn't worth its high price. If you're older, your eyes will surely appreciate a model with a self-threading needle.

If you've been quilting awhile or belong to a guild, do an informal survey: What brands do your friends use, and how satisfied are they? Ask around at the local quilt shop: What models do they use in the shop and at home? Go to online message boards dedicated to quilters and post questions. And if you take quilting classes where machines are provided, you'll have a chance to try different brands and models.

There are subtle and not so subtle differences among all the brands. Only Pfaff has something called an "even-feed system," which Darling likes because it helps machine quilters move all three layers of the quilt smoothly under the needle. Bernina was the first company to have a model with a built-in stitch regulator, a breakthrough lauded by novice machine quilters because it assures them of making precisely even stitches, rather than unpredictably big or small ones.

FINDING A SEWING MACHINE DEALER

You may see what look like great deals on the Internet, but if you don't know sewing machines well, you won't know if they're for real. And what happens when the machine breaks down? Although you can save hundreds of dollars when you order a machine from a bargain Internet site or purchase one from a budget store like Target or Kmart, they won't have someone on staff to answer questions or a place for you to drop off your machine for repairs. If you buy from a local sewing machine dealer you'll have someone who can lead you through the ins and outs of your specific model before you buy. And should you have questions once you get the machine home, the dealer will be available to answer them.

To find a dealer, check under Sewing Machines in the printed Yellow Pages or whichever Internet Yellow Pages you like. Often, you'll find a locally owned "sew and vac" store that sells and repairs both sewing machines and vacuum cleaners. It will likely carry a range of brands and models, so you can try out lots of sewing machines at one time.

All of the major sewing machine companies have websites, and generally you can search their lists of dealers to find one nearby. Some dealers will carry several manufacturers' brands, others only one kind.

A good share of fabric shops also double as sewing machine dealers, and if your quilt shop is one of these, this is generally a good place to start looking. At the very least, you'll be doing business with a sewing machine dealer who understands what quilters need. Some dealers offer classes for quilters; you can learn about the machine and improve your quilting at the same time. One more reason for buying from a dealer: If you grow as a quilter and want to trade up to a fancier sewing machine later, you can trade in your starter machine and get a better deal.

TAKE A TEST-DRIVE

When it comes to buying a new sewing machine, taking a test-drive is critical. The two best places to do this are at quilt shows and by going to sewing machine dealers. Dealers show off their latest models at quilt shows and try to dazzle passersby with glitzy features and special deals. Try to avoid buying on the spot: Many "show

and fifty dollars per card. You can also buy software to create your own custom designs."

When shopping for an embroidery machine, check to see how many designs are included and what it will cost you to purchase more. If you're a savvy bargainer, you might be able to talk your dealer into providing a free card or some software.

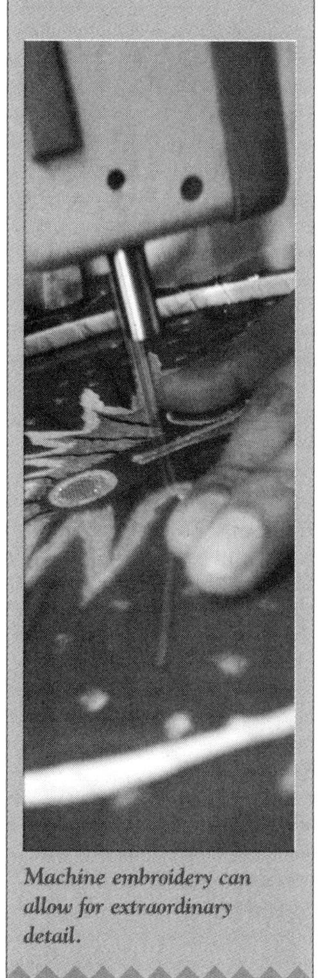

Machine embroidery can allow for extraordinary detail.

specials" will extend up to a month after the show.

Take at least a couple of sewing machines in your price range for a spin before you buy. You'll be surprised how many good entry-level machines are available for between $200 and $500 and each with different features and a different look and feel. Don't make your decision based solely on a friend's rave; even if your friend loves a particular machine, try several other brands before committing.

The importance of a good dealer cannot be overstressed. Sewing machine dealers today offer a range of services, especially for top-of-the-line machines. Dealers not only repair and clean machines but usually provide a roster of classes and ongoing hand-holding. Some dealers sell a wide range of makes while others carry just one or two brands, so again, it's good to have some idea of which brands you want to try before you go.

BUY A STURDY MACHINE—AND DON'T FORGET ATTACHMENTS

There are some basic machines that will work just fine for sewing fabric together—piecing a quilt top, for example (some frugal consumers favor an entry-level Kenmore). But if you plan to try machine quilting, then you need a more powerful model with an engine that won't blow out when you plow through two layers of fabric and the batting. Also check whether the model comes with a table extension: Machine quilters often want a bigger work surface around their machine than what comes built-in on a regular home sewing machine.

And, it's a lot easier to produce perfect quarter-inch seams if you have a special foot for that purpose. There are also special "open feet" that quilters like to use when machine quilting—these allow you to see the stitching directly under the needle. The very fact that such feet are packaged with a particular model is an indication that this machine has been made with quilters in mind.

SHOP PREPARED

In order to test-drive sewing machines, you'll need to bring fabric with you. Darling's most detailed advice relates to how to test a sewing machine before you make your selection. Here's a list of supplies she suggests bringing to the dealership.

PERFECT PITCH

Quilting magazines are just stuffed with ads from the top sewing machine makers touting their latest advances—features to make a machine quilter weak in the knees. Features that have hiked up the prices of sewing machines, many starting at $1,000 and going way up from there.

The ads stress creativity and technology. Husqvarna Viking says "Let Your Creativity Sparkle: Swedish Innovation is the Joy of Sewing." Janome asks "What will you create?" and boasts of its customer service. ("We have the best customer service in the business. Although it may be years before you find out.")

In 2007 Bernina celebrated its seventy-fifth anniversary by touting its stitch regulator, which makes free-motion quilting easier—"This is *your* year to play with free-motion. Come experience the Bernina Stitch Regulator. One of the most creative innovations in our 75-year history."

And, to launch its top-of-the-line machine, Brother bragged "Introducing Duetta. Do it All. Do it Better."

- A spool of the thread you use most often.
- Spools of any specialty threads you use, such as metallic thread, which some sewing machines don't handle well.
- Two dozen accurately cut two-inch squares of cotton quilting fabric. Darling sews two squares together, then measures to make sure the quarter-inch seam allowance is accurate and consistent. She suggests running this test for each of the feet that come with the machine.
- A small quilter's ruler with one-quarter inch clearly marked.
- A resealable plastic bag, labeled with the name and model number of the machine to be tested. To hold the fabric swatches you sew.
- Several fabric hearts, each ironed onto a six-inch fabric square by using fusible web. The hearts can be used to test appliqué and embroidery stitches; the heart shape is perfect for this because it has straight edges, curves, an "innie" point and an "outie" point.
- Two twelve inch–square quilt sandwiches made from cotton muslin and batting that have been basted together using whatever method you normally use. You can use these to run a test of machine quilting on the model in question.

Using these supplies, don't be afraid to really take your time and get to know the machine you are testing. Darling even suggests unthreading and rethreading the machine and using up all the thread on the bobbin to see what happens when it runs out and how hard it is to rewind.

If the dealer balks at your extensive testing, or can't answer most of the questions you ask, says Darling, take your business elsewhere.

Be sure to ask if the dealership has a promotion coming up soon: You might be able to snag your machine for the sale price.

HOW TO BARGAIN

Sharon Darling tells readers they shouldn't be shy about trying to bargain when buying a new sewing machine. It is sometimes tricky to figure out the manufacturer's suggested retail price for a particular model, but dealers often have leeway in what they charge. I've confirmed that with the dealers I've spoken to while researching this book. Be sure to ask if the dealership has a promotion coming up soon: You might be able to snag your machine for the sale price. And always ask if the dealer might enhance the package with extra classes or a free tune-up. A quilter who posted an online review at Epinions.com of a lightweight Janome Jem machine in 2004 boasted that the list price was $300, but because a new model was about to be introduced, she got her new Jem for $195, and the dealer threw in a quilting kit as a free bonus.

BRINGING HOME THE BABY

Like any new baby, this one needs some space—and the bottom of the closet is definitely not it. I've known passionate quilters who have worked for years with their sewing machine on the family's dining room table, but this is far from ideal. Having to unplug and put away your sewing machine every time you quilt is the worst: It's hard to get into the rhythm and flow of the process. And there is so much supporting paraphernalia with quilting that also has to be moved. Before unpacking your new machine, try and negotiate for a permanent spot, perhaps in a corner of your bedroom or a guest room. Maybe my father was unusually understanding, but throughout my entire childhood, my mother's sewing machine was as much a part of their bedroom as the bed.

Eleanor Burns in her home studio.

BASIC SEWING MACHINE CARE

Even if your sewing machine is running well, plan to take it back to the shop about once a year for a tune-up. We don't expect our cars to perform well without regular maintenance and the same is true with sewing machines.

In between, regularly clean out the lint that gets caught in the bobbin and feed dog areas. This lint can mess with the machine's tension or cause it to skip stitches. Your machine may come with a little lint brush, or you can use a cotton swab.

When you clean your sewing machine, you may need to oil the bobbin area, using the type of oil recommended by the machine's manufacturer. However, some new machines don't require oil. Follow the directions that come with your machine!

Sewing Machine Manufacturers

The major sewing machine manufacturers that follow have actively pitched and adapted their products for the quilt market. It's not practical to list each brand's models, features, and prices because it would take pages and things change too frequently. But the capsule descriptions will give you an idea of the different makes and their price points and will guide you to additional information and resources. The websites listed generally provide an index of dealers and lots of information about available models. Some also allow downloads of patterns, projects, or software or offer free e-mail newsletters.

Just because some sewing machine companies court quilters doesn't mean that there aren't other terrific machines available for making quilts. Before bringing a machine home, know your needs and price range and take the time for a thorough test-drive. After you've bought the machine, make time to read the manual and learn your way around its various features. Then, surf the Internet for a users' group devoted to that sewing machine; this will give you quick access to other quilters who know its quirks and capabilities.

BERNINA

Making excellent, innovative sewing machines, Bernina has arguably tried the hardest to attract quilters. The company actively sponsors quilt shows and has hired Alex Anderson, longtime host of the television show *Simply Quilts*, as its spokesperson and the star of its print ads. It offers classes and other goodies, including free quilt patterns and a quilting message board on the Bernina website.

Many nationally known quilt teachers swear by the company's top-tier machines. Among the famous machine quilters who praise their Berninas publicly are Caryl Bryer Fallert, Diane Gaudynski, Harriet Hargrave, Ricky Tims, and Michael James (whose wife was a longtime Bernina dealer, but he insists he'd use one anyway).

Bernina of America
3702 Prairie Lake Court
Aurora, Illinois 60504
(630) 978-2500

Bernina boasts a user-friendly website, which includes free software downloads, online classes, and a directory of dealers. Go to **www.berninausa.com.**

Bernina has been a high-tech leader in electronic machines, introducing a sewing machine powered by Microsoft's Windows software in 2002. The company has invited star machine quilters like Libby Lehman to its factory in Switzerland to offer advice. "I had some input into the design of the stitch regulator" (a device that regulates stitch length and makes machine quilting easier for beginners), says Lehman. "But I agreed not to discuss what I saw there. I was surprised by how much was still done by hand in the factory." When Bernina introduced its stitch regulator in 2004, it was the talk of the quilt world. (For a description of the stitch regulator, see page 115.)

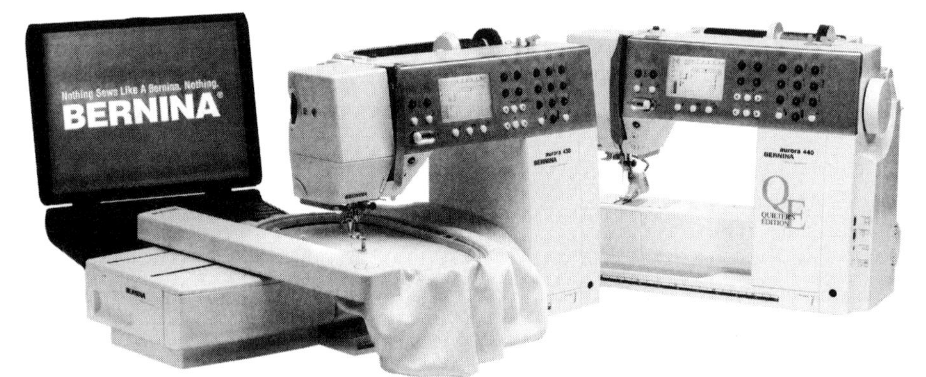

The Bernina aurora 430 (left) and aurora 440; both models let quilters take advantage of Bernina's groundbreaking stitch regulator.

As a result of all these factors, "Bernina is huge with quilters," says Sharon Darling, author of *The Quilter's Review Guide to Picking a Sewing Machine You'll Love.* "Some people think if you can't get a Bernina, don't get anything. They are great, but there's no one perfect machine for everyone."

Bernina is generally viewed as a maker of deluxe, high-priced machines, but the company also produces simpler, less costly machines for the school and beginner markets. A new line of entry-level electronic machines called activa came out in 2004, with one of the three models, the 230 PE (for patchwork edition), pitched directly to quilters.

"I liken the Berninas to the finest tools for a woodworker," explains Bernina dealer Debbie Byrne, who is located in New Britain, Pennsylvania. "This company is known for having the widest range and highest quality of feet [metal attachments that hold the fabric securely under the needle and often resemble feet]. To give an example, they have four different kinds of what are called pintuck feet in various sizes. [Pintuck feet make tucks in fabric.] Most sewing machines come with one of these.

Among those four feet is one that quilters like to use for adding fine piping to their bindings. You could certainly use a regular foot to do this, but the specialized foot makes it easier. That's what Bernina is known for."

An entry-level Bernina, such as an activa, can be purchased for around $700, while the top-of-the-line artista, a fancy embroidery and sewing machine, goes for ten times that price, around $7,000. Especially popular is the Bernina 440 QE (for quilter's edition) with the Bernina stitch regulator, which sells for about $3,000 without an embroidery unit.

A Bernina walking foot.

HUSQVARNA VIKING

Founded in 1689 to make firearms for the king of Sweden, Husqvarna (pronounced husk-varna) Viking has been making sewing machines since 1872 and selling them in the United States since the 1940s. Like Bernina, it has gone the extra mile to add features that quilters crave, especially those who can afford top-of-the-line sewing machines. For example, Husqvarna Viking observed that quilters wanted the widest possible space between the needle and the arm of the machine, so there was room to push a bed-size quilt through, and the company dramatically increased the work space on its machines.

The high-tech Husqvarna Viking Designer I, which offers such features as six hundred built-in stitches, a color touch screen, free updates of embroidery stitches, and software accessible via the Internet, was widely heralded when it premiered in the late 1990s. The online consumer site ConsumerSearch.com said of this machine at the time that "expert reviewers and sewing enthusiasts alike are ceaseless in their praise for this computerized machine" but noted that with an estimated price of $5,000, it was out of range for many.

In 2005, Husqvarna Viking introduced the Designer SE (for simply excellent), with even more bells and whistles for quilters and a bigger price tag. The company prides itself on not copying other manufacturers but coming up with its own design innovations. These include a unique patented lighting system called E Light, which allows quilters to adjust the intensity and color tone (from warm to cool and from reds to whites on the color spectrum) and virtually eliminate shadows on their quilt in progress. There is also a sensor system that gauges the thickness of the fabric pushed under the needle: Quilters don't have to lift their

Husqvarna Viking USA
VSM Sewing Inc.
31000 Viking Parkway
Westlake, Ohio 44145
(800) 358-0001

For lots more information, go to the Husqvarna Viking website, **www.husqvarna viking.com/us/**.

hands from the quilt sandwich to raise the presser foot or make other adjustments because the computerized machine automatically adjusts to the fabric's thickness.

"This is a big part of why Viking machines are attractive to my quilting customers," says Richard Jung, co-owner with his wife, Sue, of the Singing Dog Quilt Works in Placerville, California, a fabric shop as well as a Husqvarna Viking dealer. "The company puts a lot of thought into reducing the steps you have to take to adjust your sewing machine, so you can spend as much of your time as possible quilting. When we demonstrate the Sensor System, we do it by sewing a star shape on top of a background fabric, like you would appliqué a quilt top. With a regular machine, every time you come to a corner you'd have to put your needle down into the fabric, lift the presser foot, pivot the fabric, put the presser foot back down, whereas with the Husqvarna Viking, you just keep your hand on the fabric and the machine takes care of the rest."

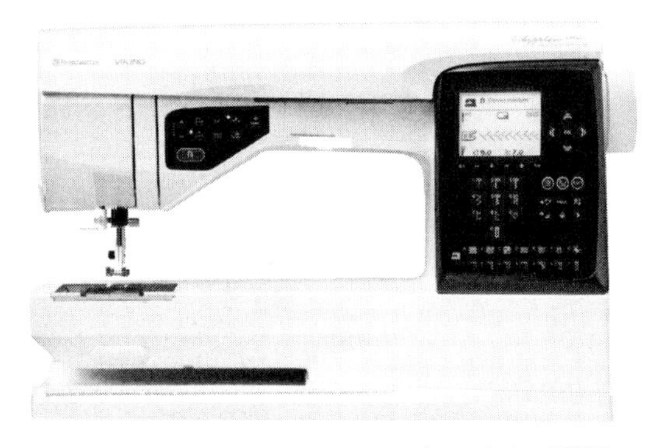

The Husqvarna Sapphire 870

Although expensive, these well-engineered machines are in line with prices for other high-end machines. Some of the Designer series sewing machines sell for less than $3,000, but the Husqvarna Viking machines that come with computerized embroidery capabilities are much more expensive. The suggested retail price for the Designer SE limited edition, introduced in 2007, is $7,999, but this machine includes cutting-edge 3-D interactive embroidery features. Among other things, the machine's computer can recommend the type of needle, thread, and stabilizer to use. The price includes a huge package of extras, such as project DVDs and a $500 voucher to buy embroidery designs.

For those who aren't shopping for a high-end embroidery machine, Husqvarna Viking introduced the Sapphire 870 Quilt in late 2007, an outstanding quilt-focused sewing machine that retails for $2,299. This machine has a repertoire of 163 stitches, some designed especially for machine quilting, and what the company claims is the largest work space available on a regular sewing machine, ten inches between the needle and the post that holds the controls. Other electronic features include self-adjusting thread tension and programmable alphabet fonts.

JANOME

Janome is the leading Japanese manufacturer of sewing machines, and its machines are said to be perhaps the quietest and smoothest on the market. Many quilters swear by their Janome. *Janome* (pronounced ja-NO-me) is Japanese for "eye of the snake" and was so named in the twenties when the company's founder began to use the round metal bobbins that are so familiar to home sewers: He thought they looked like a snake's eye.

"People who have a Janome love the way it works and the way it feels, and if they have one, they buy another," says author Sharon Darling. Also, she adds, Janome has a reputation for "trying to give buyers a lot for their money. The machines may cost as much as a comparable machine of another brand, but the Janome will probably include more features and feet." (Different feet are used for different kinds of sewing.)

On its website, Janome boasts that it's been on the cutting edge of sewing technology for years, having introduced one of the first computerized sewing machines, the Memory 7, back in 1979. Janome says it launched the revolution in electronic embroidery features in 1990, with the Memory Craft 8000.

"I think Janome is unusually receptive to what consumers want," says Dave LaValley, whose Bittersweet Fabric Shop near Concord, New Hampshire, has long been one of the biggest Janome dealers in New England. "I know this because this shop has sent prototypes of several innovations to the company in Japan for things like special feet for quilters, and they listened. They know we understand what customers want, and I think our sales show that. At this dealership, we sell four hundred to six hundred Janome sewing machines a year, but we get fewer than fifteen trade-ins a year. That's because people love these machines, and if they upgrade, they'll save their old one for a grandchild rather than turn it in."

Janome has made a number of machines specifically to attract quilters, including the Memory Craft 6600 Professional Sewing & Quilting Machine. This is a souped-up machine with great speed, an extrapowerful motor, and a large work space. It boasts lots of cool, practical features like a special motor that allows you to keep

Janome America, Inc.
10 Industrial Avenue
Mahwah,
New Jersey 07430
(201) 825-3200

For more information, go to Janome's website at **www.janome.com.**

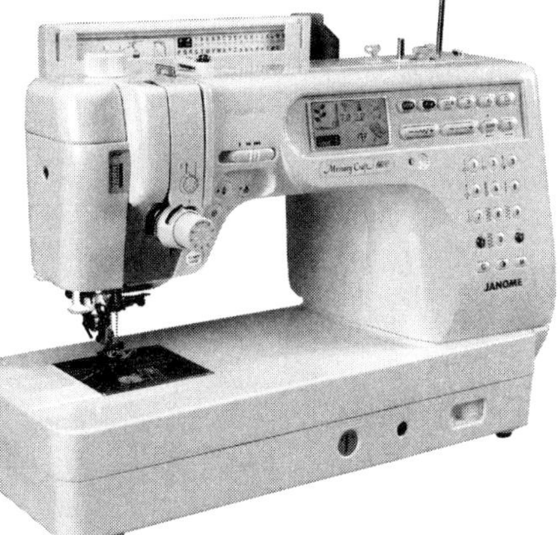

The Janome Memory Craft 6600, a machine designed specifically for quilters.

sewing even when the bobbin is being wound with thread. On quilt-related message boards, quilters who own the 6600 tend to gush, and those who don't, fantasize about it. These cost roughly $1,500.

Although it's not considered a budget sewing machine company, Janome has done more than most manufacturers to satisfy sewers and quilters looking for a modestly priced, lightweight portable they can take to classes. Their Jem series machines weigh only about twelve pounds and don't have a lot of customized features but sew perfectly well. Unlike many low-priced portables, the company brags, the Jems have metal rather than plastic gears. In addition to quilters looking for portables, the Janome Jems are popular with beginning sewers and college students, says Sue Fox, an all-Janome dealer in Jacksonville, Illinois.

Janome continues to upgrade the models in its Jem line. The Platinum Jems still weigh only twelve pounds, like the Gold Jems before them, but contain a choice of up to sixty different stitches. And while the earlier Jems didn't allow quilters to change the length of the stitches or the width of decorative ones, like zigzags or buttonhole stitches, the new ones do. Dealer prices of a new Platinum Jem will vary, but they usually cost $350 to $450.

PFAFF

Pfaff Sewing Machines
3100 Viking Parkway
Westlake, Ohio 44145
(800) 997-3233

Visit Pfaff's website at **www.PfaffUSA.com.**

Pfaff (pronounced faf) claims that its German precision engineering makes it "the premier sewing machine brand in the world," and among quilters its machines have a reputation for quality. Like Bernina and Husqvarna Viking, Pfaff is known for cutting-edge technology, and its machines come with a price tag to match. There are a number of signs that Pfaff has been actively courting quilters, starting with the naming of its machines, particularly the Pfaff GrandQuilter, an extremely fast machine. (The Grand-Quilter had a list price of $1,349 in 2007 but can sometimes be found for less.)

Now owned by the same investment company that owns Husqvarna Viking, Pfaff makes machines that have several exclusive features appealing to quilters. The primary one is what Pfaff calls Integrated Dual Feed, a built-in feature that feeds fabric through the machine from below and above simultaneously. Most sewing machines only feed fabric from below, using the grooved grippers called feed dogs. Dual feed pleases quilters because when they machine quilt, they're moving three layers through the machine and don't want the layers traveling at different speeds. Pfaff offers dual feed on many models, including its ClassicStyle Quilt 2027.

Pfaff has a number of terrific sewing machines that are more expensive than the GrandQuilter, including the Pfaff performance 2058, a top-of-the-line sewing machine with 240 decorative stitches that retails for about $3,000. For embroidery buffs, Pfaff has been busy designing new machines with extralarge touch screens for selecting embroidery designs. Among these is a deluxe sewing and embroidery machine called the Pfaff creative vision. Introduced in September 2007 for $8,499, the creative vision boasts a high-definition touch screen!

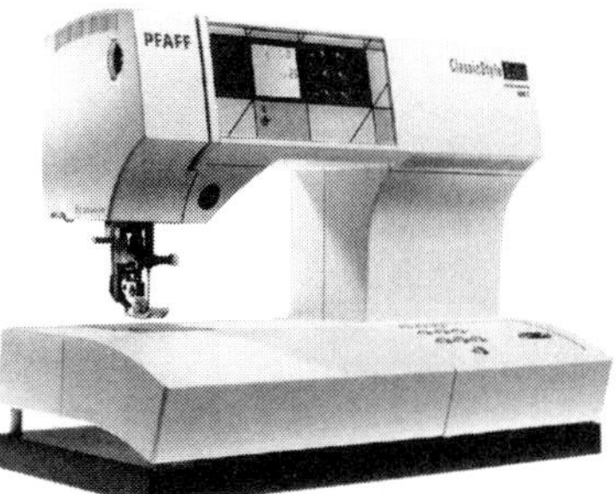

Pfaff's ClassicStyle Quilt 2027.

Whether you already own a Pfaff or are considering buying one, there's lots of information in the various user groups on the Internet. One site, www.pfafftalk.com, includes both chat rooms and message boards (it isn't affiliated with the company). Yahoo! has eight or ten user groups, some that are general in nature and others that focus on specific models. Go to http://dir.groups.yahoo.com/dir/HobbiesCrafts and search for Pfaff sewing machines. And, Pfaff is affiliated with the site www.nowsewing.net, which is loaded with tips and projects—and not just for quilting.

ELNA

A Swiss company, now owned by Janome, Elna has made sewing machines since the 1940s. Its profile in the quilt world isn't nearly as high as most of the companies listed here, but Elna makes fine machines and set out to attract quilters with its Quilter's Dream line. Still, although it advertises in many quilt magazines and frequently appears on the list of sponsors for quilt shows, Elna isn't one of the companies that offers lots of special products and events targeted at quilters.

While some of the higher-priced sewing machine models have flaunted their association with art quilters, Elna's print ads for the Quilter's Dream long featured down-to-earth teacher Eleanor Burns, host of the popular PBS television show *Quilt in a Day* (you'll find her profile on page 319). Burns switched her association to Baby Lock sewing machines in 2007, and when this book went to press, Elna hadn't yet named her replacement, although the company said it was in negotiations with a new spokesperson.

Elna USA
1822 Brummel Drive
Elk Grove Village,
Illinois 60007
(800) 848-3562 or
(847) 640-9565

For more information, go to the Elna website **www.elnausa.com.**

Elna executives insist that their commitment to quilters is growing, not shrinking, and that Elna's innovative machines prove it.

A lot of the sewing machine companies are trying to create a sort of hybrid machine that's bigger and faster than a conventional home machine but not the size of or as expensive as a longarm machine, which can only be used for quilting. Elna competes in that part of the market with its Elna PRO Quilting Queen, which can do a thousand stitches per minute and includes an extension table to broaden the sewing area. All that, and the machine is priced well under $2,000.

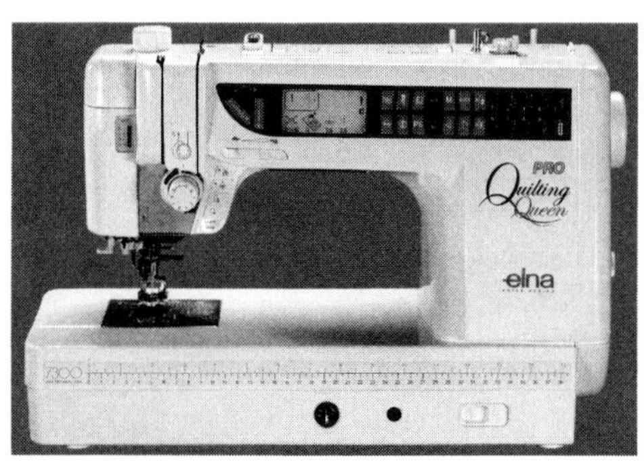

Elna's Pro Quilting Queen, loaded with useful features.

This machine was followed by the Elna 7300, introduced in September 2007, which is also very fast and has a raft of features for quilters that include a knee lifter, start-stop button, automatic thread cutter, lots of special feet that make machine quilting easy, and more than 230 built-in stitches. The suggested retail price is just a little more than $2,000.

Finally, Elna is pitching the Elna 2600 as an excellent machine for beginning quilters. This is a mechanical rather than computerized sewing machine and offers only nineteen stitches, but it's sturdy and affordable, priced at $399. Sometimes, Elna will throw in a free quarter-inch walking foot and a free-motion foot with this machine, important aids to machine quilting.

SINGER

Call it the "Comeback Kid." The Singer company had many prosperous years but also had some wild ups and downs that continued until the recent past and culminated in a Chapter 11 bankruptcy filing in 1999. Cut to the present and you find a company that has worked very hard to get its act together, and that includes actively courting the quilt market.

"Quilters don't automatically think of getting a Singer, but they've put out some very worthy machines at several price points," says author Sharon Darling. "They certainly have some competitive machines for quilters with regard to the number of features you get for the money."

Now that Singer is part of SVP Worldwide, which also owns Husqvarna Viking and Pfaff, the strategic thinking is that Singer shouldn't try to compete directly with those makers of high-end sewing machines. Rather, the current

Singer Sewing Company
1224 Heil Quaker Boulevard
P.O. Box 7017
LaVergne, Tennessee 37086
(800) 474-6437

Singer's official website is **www.SingerCo.com**. You'll find more about Singer's history on pages 103–107, and **www.singermemories.com** is a fascinating website with information about some of the company's colorful past.

owners have revamped Singer's line-up to emphasize sturdy, reliable machines that are attractive and affordable for beginners and the budget minded. The new line of Inspiration sewing machines for beginners were introduced at prices between $169 and $249, and some quilters have snapped them up as good lightweight carry-to-class machines.

But Singer hasn't ignored those quilters who also want to embroider. When fancy embroidery machines took off in 2004, Singer introduced its Futura, which sold for $700 to $800. Embroidery designs, instead of being stored within the sewing machine, were downloadable via a USB cable connecting the sewing machine to a PC. In 2007, Singer unveiled updated versions, including the Futura CE-250 and CE-350. These babies do tricks like transform clip art or personal photographs into embroidery designs. The Futura CE-250 and CE-350 sell for $1,099 and $1,399, respectively, a bargain for embroidery junkies.

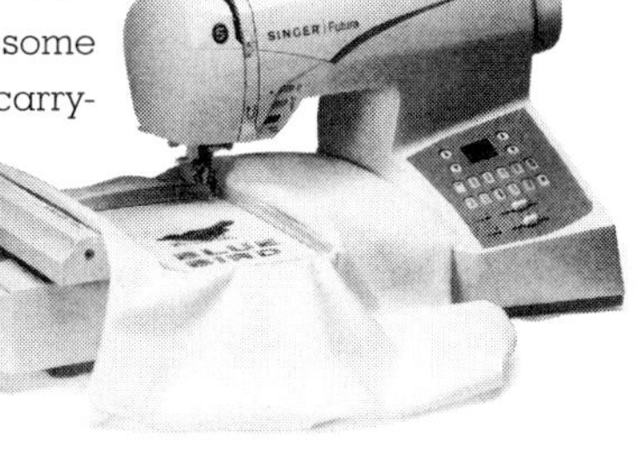

The Singer Futura: the first sewing machine powered by a personal computer.

BABY LOCK

The Baby Lock sewing machine brand was developed in Japan in the 1960s, and although it doesn't have quite as high a profile in the quilt world as some others, the company is known for well-made machines that are reasonably priced.

"For the love of sewing" is Baby Lock's corporate slogan, and its chief spokesperson in the United States is Nancy Zieman, whose PBS show *Sewing with Nancy* has been on the air for more than twenty years. Zieman isn't exclusively a quilt world celebrity in that her show covers many aspects of sewing. However, Baby Lock has targeted quilters in both its products and marketing and in 2007 signed up beloved quilt teacher Eleanor Burns (see her profile on page 319) to serve as spokesperson for the company's Quilter's Dream series. That series includes the Espire, the Quest, the Quilter's Choice, and the Quilter's Choice Professional, with new models to come.

Such Baby Lock models as the Quilter's Choice are endowed with lots of features quilters crave like an extrawide work surface and preprogrammed fancy stitches. The Baby Lock brand frequently advertises in quilting publications and often sponsors quilt shows and contests.

Baby Lock machines generally get very good word-of-mouth reviews from both users and dealers who carry

Baby Lock
1760 Gilsinn Lane
Fenton, Missouri 63026
(800) 422-2952

The website for Baby Lock is **www.babylock.com.**

multiple brands of sewing machines. On the website Epinions.com, Karen Nelson gave five stars to her Baby Lock Espire sewing machine, calling it "the best machine on earth." Nelson said this "quiet, idiot-proof" machine gives her five hundred built-in decorative stitches and four separate monogram alphabets and cost her less than $1,000.

Although the precise model Nelson describes eventually went out of production, Baby Lock reintroduced the Espire in 2006 with even more features for quilters. The new Espire has a knee lifter and lots of special feet that help make free-motion quilting easier. This model came out with a manufacturer's suggested retail price of $3,499.

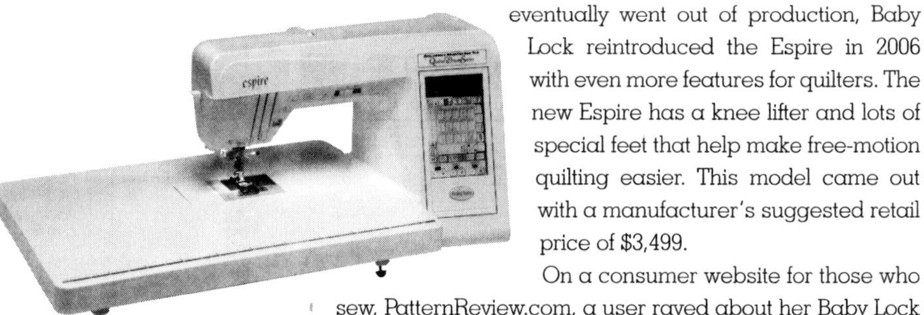

The Baby Lock Espire has an expanded workspace for larger quilting projects.

On a consumer website for those who sew, PatternReview.com, a user raved about her Baby Lock Quilter's Choice machine. She said it came with "many feet, a quilter's package, plus a table extension," and she praised it for great features and an easy-to-follow manual. She adds that she looked at other sewing machines for a lot more money but found they had nothing more to offer, and sometimes less. "This one was the right fit for me and for the money."

Ronald Spaulding, owner of Pottstown Sewing & Crafts in Pottstown, Pennsylvania, sells both Elna and Baby Lock sewing machines and is also impressed. "For intuitive ease of use, I haven't found anything better than a Baby Lock," he says. "I get great feedback on these machines. Plus, I think the manuals are especially easy to follow." Top-of-the-line Baby Locks with quilter-friendly attachments typically retail for between $1,000 and $3,000—sometimes less with special discounts.

BROTHER

Brother International
100 Somerset Corporate Boulevard
Bridgewater, NJ 08807
(908) 704-1700

Find out more about Brother's sewing machines at its website, **www.brother-usa.com.**

Another solid brand making machines in multiple price ranges is Brother, a $5 billion Japanese company that also makes fax and copy machines and industrial sewing machines. Today's Brother International has evolved from the Yasui Sewing Machine Company, founded by two brothers in Japan in 1908. The company later changed its name to Brother and began exporting sewing machines in 1947.

In the United States Brother hasn't hired a spokesperson from the quilt world; the company doesn't provide free quilt patterns on its website or follow some of the other practices of the sewing machine companies that aggressively court quilters. Brother does frequently cosponsor quilt contests and it regularly mans a booth at the major quilt shows. But, mostly Brother lets its sewing machines speak for themselves.

Both basic and computerized models of Brother machines have been selected as "best buys" in recent years by the magazine *Consumer Reports,* which lauds them for their "ease of sewing." While Brother still sells a basic sewing machine for less than $100, a lot of its effort lately has been directed toward competing for the well-heeled quilters who want every possible bell and whistle. Proof of Brother's commitment to the upscale market can be found in such recent models as the Innov-is QC-1000 (the latest in the company's Quilt Club series), introduced in the fall of 2006. This is an especially fast machine, capable of sewing a thousand straight stitches a minute, with a good supply of decorative stitches (121), and an extralarge extension table. It comes with its own rolling travel bag and a collection of quilting supplies and is marketed at a suggested retail price of $2,499.

That quilter-friendly machine was followed just a year later, in 2007, with the Duetta 4500D, a deluxe quilting, sewing, and embroidery machine with a suggested price of $7,999. The Duetta includes a raft of special features, such as automatic push-button needle threading and a pivoting function that makes it easy to change directions. The Duetta also has what the company calls an Automatic Height Adjuster that adjusts the tension after the machine senses the thickness of the layers of fabric being sewn (this also comes with the QC-1000). The Duetta boasts a larger than usual embroidery field (twelve by seven inches). There are two USB ports so you can connect the Duetta to your computer and to a special mouse (included) that helps you do things like drag and drop embroidery designs on the Duetta's LCD screen. All that on top of a huge library of built-in embroidery designs that includes 134 designs featuring Disney characters—which explains the tiny mouse ears logo on the machine.

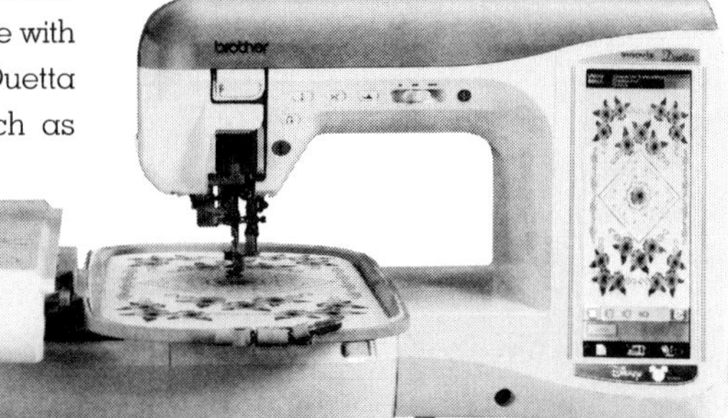

Brother's Duetta 4500, designed for quilters and emroiderers.

Expanding Your Quilting Area

Most people who use their home sewing machines to quilt on a regular basis face the frustrating problem of space: It's hard to create work area directly under the needle that's big enough to quilt easily. This is partly a function of the length of the sewing machine arm, but it's also a result of the size of the work area surrounding the needle.

Ultimately, you can make only modest adjustments to the work space within the confines of a regular sewing machine. Even if you buy one of those souped-up machines that boasts extrabig throat spaces (the area under the needle), you will still have to deal with the bulky, rolled-up edges of your quilt as you work. It's because of this that many prolific quilters either buy a longarm machine or hire professional quilt finishers to tackle their largest bed quilts.

However, there are multiple other ways to maximize the quilting area of a home sewing machine. Here are four solutions.

1. Buy a simple extension table. These can be acrylic boards with stubby, adjustable legs that will work with many models of sewing machines. Although they are called tables, they are more the size of a kitchen cutting board. Check to make sure the brand of extension table you buy is compatible with your sewing machine: The edges should be flush with your machine's base. Lots of quilters swear by these simple extenders, which come in different sizes up to roughly twenty-four by twenty-four inches. There are three popular brands.

Sew Steady Portable Table
The Website is **www.sewsteady.com** or call (800) 837-3261.

SewAdjusTables
The Website is **www.sewingmates.com** or call (503) 829-4013.

3 in 1 P.E.T.
The 3 in 1 P.E.T. (portable extension table) also includes a narrow drawer under the table to hold pins and needles and other tools.
Go to **www.3in1pet.com** or call (888) 346-1738.

ESTIMATED COST: $35 TO $110.

---

2. Check out extension tables available specifically for your brand and model of sewing machine. Go to your sewing machine dealer or the local "sew and vac" store and see what they're selling for your type of machine. This kind of extension table may give you a slightly snugger fit.

ESTIMATED COST: $30 TO $100.

---

3. Buy a combination table and cabinet from a sewing machine furniture company. Most companies sell tables with a well set into them, so when you place your machine in it, the sewing surface will be level with the surrounding table. This is a good way to expand your work area fairly dramatically.

Generally the major makers sell a full line of cabinets and tables. You can put together an elaborate matched set for your quilt studio, including additional cabinets, shelves, and storage units, or just buy a single simple table. The fancier cabinets have electronic lifters to make it easy to raise the sewing machine from a recessed place under the tabletop up to a sewing position, flush with the work surface. The price will depend on the materials used, the size of the table, and its design.

Arrow Companies LLC

Based in Elkhorn, Wisconsin, Arrow Companies LLC products include sewing cabinets that come in a variety of price ranges and sizes. Go to **www.arrowcompanies.com** (click on sewing cabinets) or call (800) 533-7374.

Arrow Companies' 300 series cabinet.

Horn of America

Widely considered the Cadillac of sewing machine furniture makers, Horn of America's sturdy tables and cabinets come in many styles, some with names like Quilter's Dream. The website is **www.hornofamerica.com** or call (800) 882-8845.

Koala Cabinets

This Australian company doesn't have a website, but you can find out about Koala Cabinets' cabinets by going to **www.koalacabinets.com**, the website for an American distributor, Waddington Sewing Center, or calling the toll-free number (877) 554-4739.

Roberts Manufacturing

An American firm, Roberts Manufacturing makes a variety of sewing tables and cabinets, some of which come with electronic lifts. The website is **www.robertsmfg.com** or call (800) 658-8795.

ESTIMATED COST: $100 TO $1,000.

---

4. Buy a large quilting frame on which to mount a home sewing machine, allowing it to function much like a longarm or midarm quilting machine. When your sewing machine is positioned on one of these large frames, it will have handles. You can work from either side of the machine and can quilt the width of a bed quilt.

Like longarm and midarm machines, these frames are quite wide and require a lot of space in your sewing room. And, if you are going to use your sewing machine for both piecing and quilting, you'll need additional furniture because you'll be shifting your machine back and forth between the frame, when you want to quilt, and a table, when you piece or do other types of sewing. These frames aren't as sturdy as the big industrial longarms and midarms, and of course, they don't make your machine as powerful or fast as the sewing mechanisms on those quilting-only machines.

There are many companies that make this type of quilting frame, but two of the best known are:

The Grace Company

The website is **www.graceframe.com** or call (800) 264-0644.

Hinterberg Design

The website is **www.hinterberg.com** or call (800) 443-5800.

ESTIMATED COST: $500 TO $1,000 OR MORE.

THE ANATOMY OF A LONGARM BEAST

These big, industrial-strength machines can be daunting at first glance. As with any other profession requiring complex gear, it takes a bit of time to learn the lingo and find your way around a longarm machine.

In her book *The Ultimate Guide to Longarm Machine Quilting* (C&T Publishing; $29.95), longarm guru Linda Taylor provides a helpful tip on how to tell the back from the front of a longarm. Taylor says to think of a longarm as a type of animal, with the cord being the tail: Where you see the cord dangling down is always the back. Longarm machines can be operated from either the front or the back and come with sets of handles located both at the front and at the back of the arm. The handles on the front are set higher, generally at chest level. Think of the higher handles as horns and you will always be clear which end is the front of your animal—er, longarm machine.

On page 150 you'll find a photo of a longarm in action.

The Longarms

WHAT IS A LONGARM? THESE ENORMOUS machines, which cost as much money and take up as much space as the family car, are engineered for high-speed quilting. The car comparison refers only to size and cost and is *not* meant to imply that the relationship between a regular sewing machine and a longarm is like that of a standard car and an SUV. Longarms are not simply supersize versions of home sewing machines; they are specialized machines designed for quilting—when you aren't making a quilt, you wouldn't use your longarm to make a dress.

Massive industrial longarm sewing machines have been workhorses in factories and small home decor firms for years, but in the early 1990s they began to make the leap into quilters' sewing rooms, living rooms, garages, and basements. The arm is the part of a sewing machine that extends out to support the needle and the foot (the foot being what anchors fabric as it is sewn). On a longarm machine, the arm is a minimum of eighteen inches in length and can be as long as thirty inches—compare this to a standard home sewing machine, where the arm is less than a foot long. That extra work space enables a longarm sewing machine to cover a huge swath of fabric at a fast clip. And even though they're as big as compact cars and cost thousands of dollars, longarms have become the fastest-growing part of the sewing machine business.

Longarms save time for quilters because they eliminate the basting step and take advantage of automation and scale. The machine's operator can quilt the entire width of a king-size bed quilt in one swath, guiding the needle by holding two sturdy handles that look like joysticks.

On a regular sewing machine, the metal (or sometimes plastic) arm that arches over the needle runs crosswise to the person doing the sewing. On a longarm, the arm isn't in profile like that, but head-on. Imagine you are sitting at your Bernina or your Singer, then stand up and walk to your left. Face the machine, with the needle end closest to you: That approximates

Longarm Linda

Linda Taylor built a 4,200-square-foot studio equipped with nine longarm machines on her ten-acre Texas property. There she and her staff hold one- and two-day longarm quilting classes almost every week. Sure, there are students from the Dallas area, but others come from as far away as Canada and New Zealand. The studio also houses the Gammill quilting machine business Taylor runs with her husband.

In 2006, the couple opened Linda's Longarm Lodge, a residential summer "camp" for longarm quilters near Jackson Hole, Wyoming. Students can sign up for a full week of classes at the lodge, or they can just stay for a day or two and learn the basics.

Taylor bought her first Gammill longarm to assist with a home decor business she ran, never thinking that she would become a top authority in longarm quilting. But Taylor has worked hard to change the perception that quilting done by longarm machines is inferior. People used to assume, she says, that longarms could only do boring repeat patterns that look like "the quilting on a mattress cover," so she set out to make award-winning quilts with a longarm. She uses her longarm not just to sew lines of stitches but also for thread painting, making elaborate freestyle decorative patches of colored thread.

Taylor has succeeded in her goal: Working in tandem with quiltmaker Cheri Meineke-Johnson, she has won first place for two-person quilts multiple times at the Houston quilt festival. "Cheri does gorgeous appliqué on the tops but leaves big open spaces, which give me lots of room to do my thread painting," says Taylor. "We do about two show quilts a year, which we enter in contests and then sell."

On Linda Taylor's website you can buy a Gammill longarm machine, book a class with Taylor or her staff, order videos of her TV series *Linda's Longarm Quilting*, or buy one of her instructional videos.

Linda Taylor (left), with guest Cathy Franks, on the set of Linda's Longarm Quilting.

For information about classes at Linda's Longarm Lodge, Taylor's Wyoming summer retreat, or at her Texas facility, go to the website, **www.lequilters.com** or call (800) 893-2748.

the quilter's relationship to a longarm machine in action, although the arm on a longarm extends much farther and is larger in scale in every way.

The biggest difference: When you quilt on a regular sewing machine, you push the fabric sandwich under the needle. When you use a longarm quilting machine, working standing up, you maneuver the needle (and the whole inner workings of the machine) across the fabric, which is held firmly in place on rollers. The sewing mechanism for a longarm is mounted on a large frame and is usually operated by handles on either side of the "head," the part to which the needle is attached. The sewing head shuttles back and forth across the quilt on small wheels, traveling along a set of parallel tracks that allow the head to "float" across the top of the quilt, stitching as it goes.

Quilts can be finished on a longarm by sewing either from left to right or from right to left across the width of the quilt. You can operate the head from either its front or back. Before quilting can begin, the quilt top, batting, and backing must be layered together and wound tightly around two sturdy rollers that run the length of the machine and are about three inches in diameter. After a swath of quilt that is about fifteen inches deep has been quilted, the longarm quilter has to stop the machine and roll up the quilted section to expose another section of unfinished quilt. It's a lot like writing on a scroll: You complete a section then roll it up, out of your way, until you get to a blank area in which to write a couple more paragraphs.

Two longarms by Nolting: Series 24 and Series 30.

Longarms sit on tables that are generally three to four feet wide and ten to fourteen feet long; these are also sold by the manufacturers. Naturally, the machines are not only big but heavy, and it can be a bit of a workout for longarmers who push the head from side to side manually. Setting up the machine and mounting the quilt on rollers can be time-consuming and frustrating, but doing it properly is essential to avoid creating lumps and puckers or producing a lopsided quilt.

SO HOW DOES A LONGARM QUILT?

There is more than one way to quilt on a longarm. One common method involves using a pantograph, which is an overall repeated quilting pattern printed on paper that is ten to fourteen feet long (matching the longarm table's length). Imagine you're standing by the head and handles of your longarm at the back of the machine (the back is where the cord sticks out). The pair of handles on that side is lower than the pair in front, about waist high—the height of a longarm can be adjusted according to the operator's height—and the quilt is stretched out roughly six inches below that. The table supporting the longarm machinery is lower still, about hip high, and at the back of the machine that table juts out beyond the handles. This creates a surface at least a foot wide that runs the full width of the supporting table, and that's where you spread out a pantograph. Longarms come with a narrow sheet of heavy, clear plastic used to hold the pantograph in place, so the sides don't roll up.

So, how do you transfer the paper design to stitches in the quilt? On older longarm models you trace the pattern and direct the needle using a metal stylus or pointer shaped like a pencil that is built into the machine. Most models now use a built-in laser light. Grasping the handles at the back of the machine, the longarmer follows the continuous line of the design with the laser light (only the light "touches" the paper), and the exact design is simultaneously sewn into the quilt.

Like tracing, this sounds simple but isn't foolproof: The quilter has to follow an often complex line with a steady hand while constantly checking that the thread tension is correct, that the stitches are uniform in length (if there isn't an automatic stitch regulator on the machine), that the machine hasn't run out of thread, and so forth. Longarm operators may repeat that same pantograph design, row after row, until the quilt is finished, or they may choose a different pattern for the center of the quilt and repeat the original design in the other borders.

Using pantographs is the quickest way to quilt with a longarm and costs the least. But experienced longarm quilters can also do free-form quilting, creating their own custom design for each quilt, making stars or

DESIGNED BY YOU

Who decides what quilting patterns to use when a quilt is finished on a longarm? You do. Professional quilt finishers offer many patterns or will make custom suggestions. But when you pay someone else to finish your quilt, you get to determine what it looks like, including the overall design, thread colors, and details.

Longarmers can do many of the same things any quilter might do on a machine, including "stitching in the ditch" along seam lines or "echo quilting" that traces around patterns or shapes on a quilt top. They can also execute simple repeat patterns of random wavy lines or draw free-form flowers or other shapes. Professional finishers will also have a library of pantograph patterns they have designed or patterns they have paid to use commercially.

Jodi Beamish, one of the most prolific creators of longarm quilting patterns, has examples of good pantograph designs on her website, **www.willowleafstudio.com.**

The Ultimate Longarm Website

Whether you're seriously considering buying a longarm quilting machine or merely curious about them, you won't do better than to check out the House of Hanson website, **www.houseofhanson.com**. The odd name sounds corporate and doesn't mention longarms or quilting—it isn't immediately obvious that this is one of those extravagantly informative websites that is a pure labor of love.

Jackie and Jeff Hanson registered the domain name in 1997, about the time that crafts-oriented Jackie decided to buy a longarm quilting machine and couldn't find any resources to help her. The couple lived in California, and both worked part-time certifying pilots for the FAA. With a degree in physics and a ham radio license, Jeff got pulled into the longarm world as a gadget guy who also loved tinkering with a website.

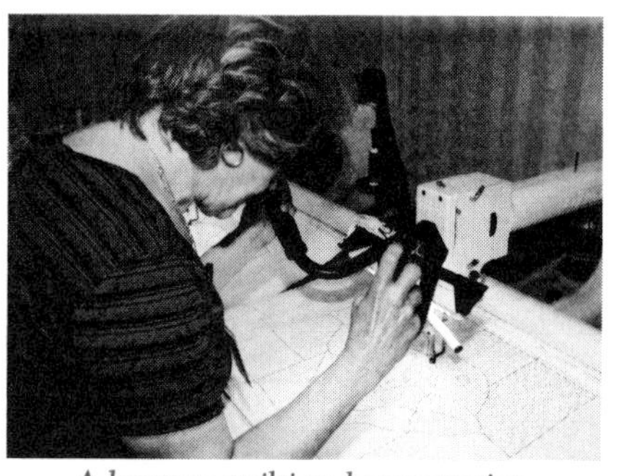

A longarm quilting demonstration.

Early on the couple bought a Statler Stitcher attachment so they could computerize their longarm quilting business and either one could operate the machine. Houseofhanson.com soon became the unofficial bulletin board for people starting up a home business for longarm quilting. Jeff posted all sorts of free articles about how to use the machines and how to build a business; he even posted digital photos of the first longarm quilt shows.

Thoroughness was one of the site's trademarks, and the articles that remain are written by some of the industry's savviest pioneers, like Marcia Stevens, who bought her first longarm in 1986. Stevens was the founder of the first longarm show, Machine Quilters Showcase, and the first magazine on longarm quilting, *Unlimited Possibilities* (both show and magazine still thrive under new owners; see Resources for Longarm Quilters on page 148).

An especially notable item on the Hanson site is the excellent article by professional quilter, author, and teacher Carol Thelen titled "Which Machine to Buy?" You'll find it in the Resources for Machine Quilters section (look for the link to this section in the list of Longarm Information Pages on the site's home page).

Sadly, Jackie Hanson died of bone cancer in January 2006. Jeff decided to sell the couple's longarm equipment and leave the business but vowed to maintain the website in Jackie's memory. This he has done, and the site receives frequent updates.

By going to House of Hanson you will find just about every resource and link you might need, including professional organizations, trouble-shooting tips, lists of classes on longarm quilting, e-mail groups to join, and much more.

waves or vines or whatever shapes they wish. (When doing free-form quilting, longarm users stand at the front of the machine, using the chest-high handles; they don't need the table that sticks out at the back to hold a pattern.)

Longarm professionals can also vary their design by using special decorative threads and embroidery stitches. This kind of quilting requires more craftsmanship, takes longer, and costs more if you are hiring someone else to do it.

There are also computerized systems that can be hooked up to longarm machines and programmed so that the quilting is automated. The operator picks the pattern and gets the machine started but then literally steps back from the longarm, and the design is rapidly reproduced. The Statler Stitcher and CompuQuilter, to name two major makers of computerized add-ons, can automatically reproduce purchased designs like pantographs or can be programmed to execute an original design that has been scanned into the computer's database. But adding a computerized add-on to a longarm creates a hybrid machine with a combined price tag of $26,000 to $32,000, so these are going to be used only by longarm quilters with high-volume businesses.

As time goes on, more and more features are being added to longarm machines, and more companies are entering the business. The market leader for the machines is still Gammill Quilting Systems of West Plains, Missouri, which has been in the business since 1980. Gammill has done a lot to lift the profile of longarm quilting by advertising in quilt publications and doing demos at county fairs and quilt shows nationwide.

Gammill also funds prizes and, since 2002, has been awarding one for the best longarm quilting at the American Quilter's Society show in Paducah, Kentucky, says Stacy Gammill, son of the company's founder and current marketing director. In 2004, Gammill put up the funding to sponsor the first television show devoted exclusively to longarm quilting. (Previously, Gammill had helped fund general quilting shows, but those only aired an occasional segment on longarms.) Called *Linda's Longarm Quilting*, the show is hosted by Linda Taylor, who with her husband runs a Gammill dealership in Melissa, Texas, outside of Dallas.

RESOURCES

Major Makers of Computerized Attachments for Longarms

STATLER STITCHER
8801 East
Columbus Court
Columbia,
Missouri 65201
(866) 830-3738
www.statlerstitcher.com

COMPUQUILTER
6412 West
Southgate Road
Rogers, Arkansas 72758
(479) 273-9926
www.compuquilter.com

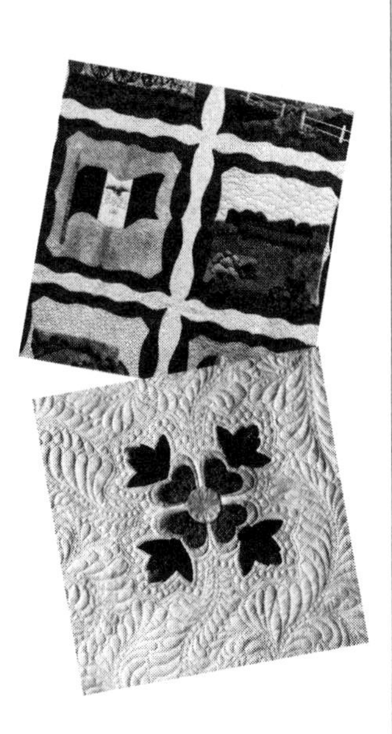

Two examples of professional longarm quilter Dawn Cavanaugh's intricate work.

> *Marcia Stevens says, "I'm stunned when I hear a woman has bought one of these $10,000 longarm machines just for her own use, but the response I get is usually something like, 'Well, my husband just bought a boat!'"*

In its first two seasons, *Linda's Longarm Quilting* aired on more than ninety PBS stations across the country, from Florida to California.

Taylor is fast becoming the Eleanor Burns of the longarm crowd, an enterprising "simplifier" who is a popular teacher with a multimedia reach. Taylor's book *The Ultimate Guide to Longarm Machine Quilting* has become a must-have primer, and she has self-published additional guides.

LONGARM QUILTING AS A PROFESSION

Starting in the early 1990s, word spread that buying a longarm machine and custom-finishing quilts could be a great home-based business for quilters. A big part of Taylor's television audience and many of her prospective students are women who aspire to become professional longarm quilters. This trend moved fast, quickly blanketing the country, so to speak. By time the twentieth-first century arrived, virtually every area where quilters live was supporting a number of custom quilters who worked full-time finishing the quilts of others. Nobody knows how many professional longarm quilters have set up shop, but the growth has been nothing short of phenomenal, says Ann Collet, head of the Home Machine Quilting Association.

Collet says she helped start a group for longarm quilters near Salt Lake City, who would meet monthly to share ideas, tips, and encouragement. Within four years, the group went from twenty quilters meeting in the city to four groups meeting all over the state—a total membership of nearly four hundred longarm quilters.

"The amazing thing is as fast as our ranks are growing, there are enough people out there making the quilts to keep us all busy! Everybody I know who does this with any skill has a waiting list virtually all the time," says Collet. "It's like a snowball rolling downhill: Quiltmakers see how easy it is to get their quilts finished, so they keep making more and more."

Nonetheless, getting started professionally can take some time, and that was especially true when the trend was new. When Dawn Cavanaugh of Ankeny, Iowa, bought her longarm in 1994 from APQS (American Professional Quilting Systems), Cavanaugh had only been quilting for about three years and found learning to operate the behemoth machine had its challenges. "The longarm has an X and a Y axis and you have to learn to get both hands working together," she explains. "Running a longarm is a lot like trying to draw on an Etch A Sketch. You can do great boxes on it, but it takes a lot of practice to make curves." (Newer models have stitch regulators, which have made longarms easier to manipulate.)

At the time Cavanaugh got her machine, longarms weren't prevalent and machine quilting was still scorned by many. In order to overcome this prejudice and the perception that longarm quilting was of poor quality, Cavanaugh recalls, "I suckered six of my quilting buddies into letting me practice on their quilts, and then I told them to all come to the next guild meeting and bring those quilts for show-and-tell. That was it! I have gotten all my business from word of mouth since that night."

Once she had experienced using her longarm, Cavanaugh named her business Rockin' Bobbin Quilting, Inc. and decided to emphasize custom freehand finishing for clients. "Some gals just stipple on their longarms, but I like to create a special design related to the client's top and make the quilt sing." (Stippling is an easy way to fill empty space on a quilt, making continuous wavy lines that circle around each other but never cross.) Cavanaugh has won the blue ribbon for best machine quilting at the Iowa State Fair three years in a row and has finished more than three thousand quilts for other people. She quilts full-time, and boasts a three-month waiting list for her services.

Not every longarm quilter is as diligent and artistic as Dawn Cavanaugh, and not everyone who tries to set up a finishing business succeeds. But she is part of a growing subculture within the quilt world. Longarm users have banded together to form their own support groups and shows; they create their own websites and publish their own magazines. Events such as the Machine Quilters Showcase, the annual conference and show run by the International Machine Quilters Association, continue to grow in size and sophistication.

Manufacturers of longarm machines refuse to divulge their sales numbers, but Marcia Stevens has a pretty good idea of how many longarmers are active because she was among the first to organize these quilters.

DON'T DO IT YOURSELF

A rising percentage of quilters have decided that even if they *can* machine finish their quilts, they'd simply rather not. And since quilting has become a hobby where frugality isn't an issue and quilters already spend top dollar for fabric, books, patterns, computer software, and other tools, many have decided why not spend a little extra to pay for someone else to handle what they consider the drudgery?

According to author Eleanor Levie, an estimated 10 percent of quilters were sending out their tops to be quilted in 1995. By the end of the twentieth century, she says that number was up to 40 percent, and experts estimate that well over half of all quilters have someone else finish their quilts now. What makes that possible is the proliferation of the longarm sewing machines, massive industrial machines that are large enough and powerful enough to quilt a full-size bed quilt in an hour or two if a simple, repeated pattern is used.

Top Longarm Manufacturers

There are three established companies that together dominate the market. The "Big Three" have each been in business for more than twenty years and have marked the additional business milestone of passing from their founders to new owners.

Longarm machines require a serious investment, ranging from around $5,000 for a small or secondhand machine up to about $20,000 for a new, high-end machine. Those that are computerized are even costlier and can be more than $30,000. Expect the purchase price to include a table, lots of accessories, and good customer service, but not necessarily installation. Be sure to find out whether you'll have to assemble the machine yourself!

GAMMILL QUILTING SYSTEMS

Gammill has a reputation for making strong, sturdy machines, sort of the SUVs of the longarm world, and for having a good network of dealers. The company has promoted itself and the reputation of longarm quilting by such activities as, since 2002, funding an annual longarm machine award at the American Quilter's Society show in Paducah, Kentucky. Gammill also sponsors a number of television quilting shows, particularly a PBS show devoted to longarm quilting that is hosted by the popular teacher Linda Taylor, who is herself a Gammill dealer in Texas.

A Gammill Classic Plus.

Gammill Quilting Systems
1452 West Gibson Street
West Plains, Missouri 65775
(800) 659-8224

The Gammill website, **www.gammill.net**, details features of the various models and lists authorized dealers and upcoming quilt shows where its machines will be on view. You can also download service manuals there.

AMERICAN PROFESSIONAL QUILTING SYSTEMS (APQS)

APQS has a sort of Avis/Hertz relationship with Gammill and has worked very hard in recent years to match its competitor in such areas as customer service. Its eagerness to reach out to customers can be seen in a website that is informative, interactive, and at times, even playful, reflecting the personalities of the men who currently own the company.

In addition to the obligatory lists of products and dealers, the APQS site is especially strong in tips on starting a professional quilting business and offers a free business starter kit, as well as a video on the topic and an extensive online forum. On the forum, you can ask current APQS owners such questions as how they price their services or make design decisions. There are also photographs of quilts made on APQS machines by teachers and quilt artists affiliated with the company. Among those are the quilt teachers and TV hosts Marianne Fons and Liz Porter; the two have made a series of humorous ads for APQS. (There's a link to www.fonsandporter.com, Fons and Porter's quirky website, which even reprints some of their recipes.)

American Professional Quilting Systems
8033 University Avenue,
Suite F
Des Moines, Iowa 50325
(800) 426-7233

You'll find APQS's website at **www.apqs.com.**

NOLTING MANUFACTURING

Nolting is a distant third to the other two major longarm manufacturers. Its website isn't flashy, and the company doesn't have a huge dealer network. But Nolting has weathered a very competitive market for many years, and its longarms definitely have their champions. Nolting has a reputation for giving quilters a lot for their money, and there are some people who just prefer the way the machines work.

Nolting Manufacturing
1265 Hawkeye Drive
Hiawatha, Iowa 52233
(319) 378-0999

For more about Nolting's longarms, go to **www.nolting.com.**

Nolting's Longarms have a faithful following.

FINDING ROOM FOR A LONGARM

The "footprint" for most popular longarm quilting machines is almost exactly the same as that for my Honda CRV. At more than thirteen feet long and about four feet wide, my baby SUV fits easily inside my half of the garage. But I'd have trouble using a longarm machine in there unless I booted my husband's car out, too, because you need room to move around a longarm, especially while loading a quilt.

The space requirements for a longarm are dictated by the extralong table and rollers that are essential to the machine. You can buy a standard longarm with a customized table that is ten or eleven feet long—and at quilt shows manufacturers demonstrate longarms that are only eight feet long. But if you want to be able to finish king- and queen-size bed quilts, which most professional longarmers do, you'll need a twelve- or fourteen-foot-long table.

Although it's possible to push one end of a longarm machine up against a wall, you will still need at least three feet at the other end,

Stevens was one of the pioneer teachers of longarm quilting, and anybody who has taken one of her classes or read the magazine she founded, *Unlimited Possibilities*, knows that her Nolting brand longarm machine is such an early model that she gave it the nickname "T. Rex."

"I've had my machine since 1986, so it really is a dinosaur in this world, but it still works great," jokes Stevens, who also has newer machines in her studio. She was one of the first to test using a laser to guide the stylus, now a feature that is routine, and has exerted enormous influence on this quilting subculture.

In 1995, Stevens organized the first show for longarm quilters, hosting it in Duluth, Minnesota, near her home. The show included classes, a vendor mall, and an exhibit of quilts done on longarm machines. About 250 quilters attended that first year. By the third show, there were one thousand. Seven years later, Stevens sold the show to the International Machine Quilters Association, now based in Kansas. Her magazine, *Unlimited Possibilities*, continues under a new publisher.

"As far as the future, I still don't think we've reached saturation levels of longarms in this country, and the growth abroad is now catching up to ours," says Stevens. "I think the trends will move toward more computerized machines and toward quilt artists playing more with these and raising the bar creatively. I also think the prices of machines will fall, and we'll see even more home sewers buying them."

It's fair to say that some tensions continue to exist among the different camps, and there are those who think longarm quilting takes machine quilters even farther away from the purity of their roots. Some worry that cheating goes on and quilters aren't always admitting when their quilts are finished by experts. The quilt world generally operates on the honor system, and since so many quilts are finished by machine now, who's to tell who did which part of the work, or whether the machine was operated by a computer or a person?

But most agree that longarm quilters have staked out a place in the quilt world that isn't based solely on speed and that the best of them are capable of original design and stunning craftsmanship. Now the annual quilt festival in Houston has a regular award category for quilts made by two people. With the increasing practice of quiltmakers sending their tops out to be finished by professional quilters, it seemed only right.

"At the end of the twentieth century, people were ruining quilts with these things [longarms] in my view," says Alex Anderson, who hosted the popular television show *Simply Quilts*. "People bought these machines for business reasons and couldn't take the time to create the Mona Lisa of quilts. But now, it's becoming an artistic tool. The level of craftsmanship that is going on now with longarm quilters is just staggering."

For their part, professional machine quilters assert that they aren't out to undermine anything or cheat anybody. The quilt world is getting bigger and more complicated, and there is room for everyone, they say.

"Hand quilting will never be replaced by machine quilting," insists Lois Knight, a longarm owner since 1997, who runs her custom quilting business Waltzing Needle Quilts from her home in Broomfield, Colorado. "Each kind of quilting has its own distinctive look. But if done properly, machine quilting can be more durable. So if you don't quilt yourself but inherit some quilt tops, they can be turned into family heirloom quilts. If you do quilt, sending your tops to a longarmer allows you to concentrate more on piecing quilts and spending more time at the fabric store, rather than wrestling that huge fabric bulk through a home sewing machine."

so you can maneuver around the machine.

Longarms are generally about four feet wide, but because they can be operated from the front and the back, you'll need about a three-foot clearance in front and in back for working space.

Altogether the amount of space you need to comfortably operate a standard longarm is approximately twenty by ten feet, says Janet-Lee Santeusanio, founder of the Machine Quilters Exposition.

As for working out of your garage, there are plenty of professional longarm users who do, but many prefer to take over a guest room or home office.

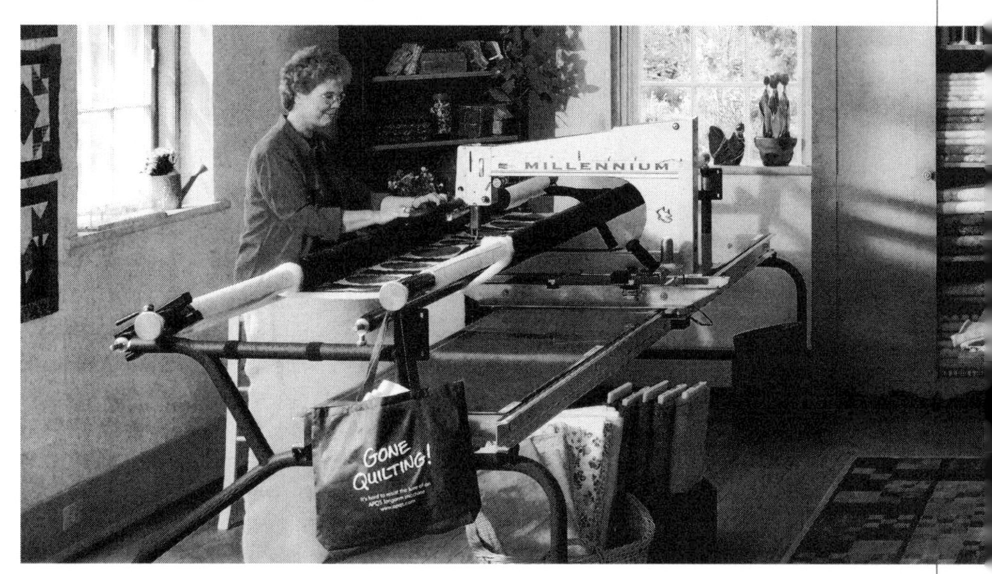

The Millennium Quilting Machine from American Professional Quilting Systems.

Do the Math on Longarms

There are some quilters who use their longarm machines to earn a living and others who consider them more of a hobby, using the machines mostly to finish their own quilts and taking an occasional commission from friends and fellow guild members. It's important for you to figure out how you plan to use the longarm before you purchase one, because it affects what sort of machine you should buy and how much you spend.

"If someone expects to use a longarm quilting machine as a business, then they should do some research and create a business plan first," says Janet-Lee Santeusanio, a New Hampshire quilter who runs a commercial quilting business, teaches longarm quilting, and started a show for longarmers, the Machine Quilters Exposition. "Threads and batting are especially expensive and people need to take that into account. If they set themselves up as a business, they'll be able to buy thread, batting, and other supplies at wholesale prices."

Would-be pro quilters also have to figure out what prices to charge for their quilting work. Quilts finished using a pattern called a pantograph can sometimes be completed in a few hours, but custom quilting patterns can take much longer and the rates for these are much higher.

Santeusanio has been openly critical of a longarm machine manufacturer that said on its website that a $17,000 machine could be paid for in a year by someone who only completed a couple of quilts a week. "That's just not realistic," she says.

Pieces quilted by longarmer Sandy Merritt.

"It's possible that if you work virtually full-time quilting you could pay off that machine in a year, but not everybody can or wants to work that hard. People have to know how long they can tolerate standing up every day."

Sandy Merritt, of Ewing, New Jersey, knew from the start that she didn't want to make quilt-finishing a full-time job but did want to use her longarm to help pay for itself, leaving plenty of time for her to quilt her own projects. She started by doing the math.

"I figured out that if I made two full-size bed quilts a month or four small projects (wall hangings or crib quilts), that it should take me about five years to pay off the line of credit I needed to buy the machine," says Merritt. "After three years, I think I'm pretty much on schedule, though it may take as long as six years." Merritt has been able to make her plan work without paying for a single ad, working almost exclusively for people she knows.

TIPS ON BUYING A LONGARM QUILTING MACHINE

Before buying a longarm machine, you really need to spend at least a few hours trying out the various features. It's fine to use a quilt show to get a sense of the competing makers and their newest models. But, shows are often crowded, and dealers don't have room to display their full lines.

Longarm companies frequently give their deepest discounts during quilt shows, so you may be smart to buy one then—but only if you've already spent lots of time test-driving the various machines and are confident that you've found the right make and model for your needs. Coming to that conclusion isn't as difficult as it may sound. Many dealers offer free tryouts and daylong classes in their dealerships. If you buy a machine after taking such a class, the class fee should be deducted from the price. Check with the dealership beforehand.

Here are several things to look for in a longarm test-drive.

- How difficult is it to load a quilt into the machine?
- Is it easy to adjust the frame for your height and reach?
- Longarm machines all have wheels that run on tracks; does the "ride" of the wheels feel bumpy or smooth?
- Do you feel in firm control of the machine?

Also, ask the longarm users in your community about their level of satisfaction with the brands they use, and search out online postings from current owners. Buying one of these machines is like buying a car, the experts say—not just because they cost so much but because, although the machines all do the same basic job, their operational "feel" and style vary considerably.

On pages 142–143 you'll find descriptions of the three major longarm manufacturers.

Details of intricate masterpieces from Dawn Cavanaugh.

The 2006 Machine Quilters Exposition.

The population of quilters who own longarm quilting machines, which are generally used for finishing the quilts of paying customers, has exploded in recent years. So has the number of resources available to serve them. These include not just places to find technical advice but also fellowship; longarm quilting can be a lonely pursuit. Here are some of the most respected sources for information and support.

Trade Associations

International Machine Quilters Association (IMQA)

Founded in 1996 by pioneering longarm quilter Marcia Stevens, the IMQA runs the annual Machine Quilters Showcase, a major trade show featuring classes, vendors, and quilts on display. There are regional IMQA groups as well as the national association, so longarmers can meet more often with their peers. The modest membership fee includes a quarterly publication called *On Track*. For information on membership and the trade show, go to the IMQA website (for those seeking a professional quilt finisher, the website includes a state by state listing of IMQA members who run longarm quilt businesses).

International Machine Quilters Association
P.O. Box 6647
Monona, Wisconsin 53716
(608) 222-9505
www.imqa.org

Home Machine Quilting Association (HMQA)

A newer group, the HMQA has a slightly different focus, reflecting recent trends in quilting. The IMQA was founded exclusively as an organization for longarm quilters. The smaller HMQA sprang up a decade later with the goal of including not just longarm quilters but also users of the smaller machines called midarms (see page 151), as well as welcoming home quilters who use standard domestic sewing machines to finish quilts. Members gain access to a very active website that includes many forums, information on training, discounts on or free samples of products related to machine quilting, and a newsletter. The HMQA also runs the annual Home Machine Quilting Show.

Home Machine Quilting Association
869 East 725 South
Centerville, Utah 84014
(801) 298-3844
www.hmqa.org

Shows

All three of the shows listed here are excellent and feature many of the top teachers and vendors. Pick the one that's nearest you.

Home Machine Quilting Show

The Home Machine Quilting Association runs the annual Home Machine Quilting Show in Salt Lake City, Utah. Begun in 2004, the regional show already boasts more than 120 exhibitors, more than 100 classes, and in excess of $14,000 in cash and prizes given to quilters who win awards in the juried quilt competitions. Originally focused mostly on people who use their domestic sewing machines to quilt, the Home Machine Quilting Show has broadened its reach to users of midarm and longarm quilting machines. Go to **www.hmqa.org** for more about this show.

Machine Quilters Exposition (MQX)

A fast-growing national show that attracts thousands of longarm and other machine quilters, MQX rivals the IMQA's Machine Quilters Showcase in size and scope. This show has been held every April in New Hampshire since 2003. Featuring lots of vendors, classes, and two hundred machine-made quilts, MQX is run by two women who have commercial quilting businesses and also teach longarm quilting, Janet-Lee Santeusanio and Mary Schilke. Some describe MQX as a giant family reunion for quilters. Go to **www.mqxshow.com** for information.

Machine Quilters Showcase

An annual show since 1995, the Machine Quilters Showcase is run by the IMQA (International Machine Quilters Association). More than fifteen thousand attend this Kansas show, which was originally modeled on the International Quilt Festival in Houston. See the association's website, **www.imqa.org**, for details.

Magazine

While the longarm quilters' associations have their own periodicals, *Unlimited Possibilities* is the best general publication to date. It contains reviews, interviews, show listings, and technical advice. Founded by longarm pioneer Marcia Stevens, *Unlimited Possibilities* is now published by Vicki Anderson, a former editor and writer for sewing and craft publications. *Unlimited Possibilities* is published in full color and has increased its issues from four to six a year. Anderson has expanded coverage to include users of all types of stand-up quilting machines, not just longarms.

Unlimited Possibilities
Meander Publishing
P.O. Box 918
Fort Lupton,
Colorado 80621
(720) 988-0753
www.upquiltmag.com

Book

The library of books about longarm quilting is growing, including pattern books and ones giving advice on how to run a business, but this is the classic: *The Ultimate Guide to Longarm Machine Quilting: How to Use Any Longarm Machine; Techniques, Patterns and Pantographs; Starting a Business; Hiring a Longarm Machine Quilter*, by Linda Taylor (C&T Publishing; $29.95). Taylor, a well-known teacher and host of a longarm quilting show on PBS, has written a comprehensive guide. Published in 2003, it is still hard to beat for covering the bases. It's a wise first investment if you think you want to enter the longarm business and includes thirty-two pages of original patterns.

Internet Resources

You'll find a number of longarm user groups on the Web. These often function as communal message boards. More than two thousand people belong to the Yahoo! group for longarmers, which is free to anybody interested in the big machines but requires you to sign up for membership. Find it at **http://groups.yahoo.com/group/Machine_Quilting_Professional.**

Another popular online user group can be found at **www.LongarmChat.com**. There are some three thousand registered users here, and while many forums are free, some require a membership fee.

DVDs

I'VE GOT A LONGARM (AND I'M NOT AFRAID TO USE IT!),
by Mindy Caspersen, Angel Threads Quilting;
$30.00

This is an excellent DVD for beginning and wannabe longarm quilters, covering all the basics about loading a quilt, adjusting thread tension, and maintaining your longarm machine. Caspersen is a well-known teacher and dealer who sells longarms and midarms, as well as frames. The DVD is available through her website, **www.angelthreadsquilting.com**, and many other quilting suppliers.

MASTERING THE ART OF MCTAVISHING,
by Karen McTavish, On-Word Bound Books;
$24.95

McTavish (read more about her on page 65) has emerged as one of the celebrities in the artistic end of longarm quilting, and this accompanying DVD and paperback book show her trademark lavish designs. It isn't exactly a nuts-and-bolts primer for using a longarm machine (and some readers at Amazon.com say they have adapted her design ideas to quilts they made on their regular sewing machines), but for professional quilters looking for design inspiration, it's a great choice.

Although it's expensive, you could also purchase past seasons of Linda Taylor's PBS show, *Linda's Longarm Quilting*. You get a whole season of thirteen episodes (five and a half hours) on four disks for $99.95. See Taylor's website, **www.lequilters.com**.

A longarm demonstration at the 2006 MQX.

Midarms: Another Solution

WHILE LONGARM MACHINES HAVE BECOME far more prevalent, they have also created an appetite for speed among quilters who can't afford the behemoths or don't have room for them. Entrepreneurs have sprouted forth with all kinds of solutions to this problem, including a raft of special frames on which to mount regular sewing machines to make them function more like longarms.

Another approach came with the creation of a category of sewing machines that do only quilting, like longarms, but are lighter and cheaper. These are usually referred to as midarms and are growing in popularity. Utah-based entrepreneur Laurel Barrus helped create this subcategory of machines. A quilter with a business degree, Barrus felt that Gammill, American Professional Quilting Systems, Nolting, and others had the market covered for quilters who wanted to make custom finishing a business. She realized her fellow quilters were increasingly fed up with paying $50 or more to have their quilts finished but also didn't want to pay $10,000 for a machine to do it themselves. And she felt that there was an underserved market of women who wanted to finish their own quilts but found it miserable work on a regular sewing machine.

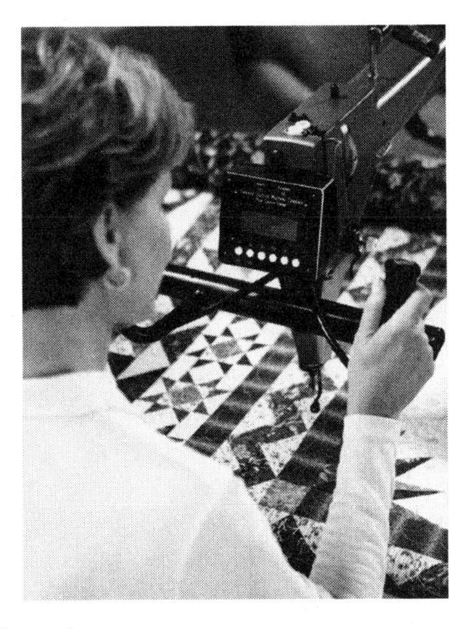

Manning the Gammill 140.

"In 2000, we brought out a frame, that allowed home quilters to put their existing sewing machine on a tray that was on wheels, so it could be used like a longarm," says Barrus. "We were selling lots of the frames but felt that our customers really wanted a bigger machine they could use for quilting but that wasn't one of those big industrial things. With a regular machine, you still feel cramped when you try to quilt, even with the greater freedom of a frame. It's like the difference between cooking in a camper kitchen versus a chef's kitchen. If you have all the space you need, creativity soars." Barrus saw the need for quilters to own a second machine, reserving their original one for sewing quilt tops. She began making machines in 2002.

"Quilters today often have as many sewing machines as they do pairs of scissors," says Barrus. "Why should my machine do piecing when they already have a machine that does that well? Our machine has a stitch regulator and is easy to use for the casual quilter who doesn't want a steep learning curve. It's lighter than a big industrial machine and costs about a third as much. Besides, those big longarms look industrial, like gray metal battleships. I created my Handi Quilter to look domestic, even feminine, with lavender accents on a white background. It's a girl machine!"

Initially, most of the men in the longarm machine world scoffed at the very notion of a woman making sewing machines and didn't give Barrus an easy time of it. But her claim that the Handi Quilter was "a machine made by quilters, for quilters" attracted many women to try it, and sales soon soared. Competing midarm manufacturers have emerged or raised their profiles with new models and increased marketing budgets. Plus, many makers of longarms now make downsized versions of their machines and pitch them to quilters who don't want to start a business but do want to finish their quilts more easily.

And so, the entrepreneurial wheel keeps turning. It's anybody's guess what new technology will come from the sewing machine market next. But it seems clear that the innovations will continue and that, no matter what follows, they will only increase the possibilities for passionate quilters.

The luxury of having a regular sewing machine always ready to piece, while a midarm is always set for quilting, is one that a substantial number of passionate quilters clearly want and can afford.

TIPS ON BUYING A MIDARM QUILTING MACHINE

Midarms may be a relatively new category of sewing machines, but their popularity is growing fast. Generally speaking, midarm machines have an "arm" that is much longer than that of a traditional domestic sewing machine. The arm area, which is also known as throat space, is important because it has a direct impact on the work space available for quilting. (The throat plate is that metal plate located over the bobbin compartment and under the needle. The throat space or throat area is the "real estate" around that metal plate over which you can manipulate the fabric sandwich as you quilt.)

Like longarms, midarms are generally used only for quilting and are most often operated while you are standing up. Midarms tend to weigh and cost much less than the industrial-size longarm machines, but the basic principles for operating them are like the longarm: You move the entire machine head with its needle across the quilt, as opposed to a traditional sewing machine where you move the quilt while the needle stays in one place. Also like longarms, midarms can be operated from either the front or the back, depending upon whether you trace a pattern (pantograph) or quilt freehand.

Midarms are targeted for home quilters who want to finish their own quilts and find it difficult to do so on their home sewing machine. While longarms are most often used by professional quilt finishers and cost in the range of $10,000 to $20,000, a midarm can generally be purchased for $4,000 to $7,000, so they are priced at anywhere from half to a third of the longarms.

These machines wouldn't be so popular if it weren't for the fact that today's well-heeled quilters are willing to own multiple sewing machines. Fans of midarm machines like the fact that they don't have to keep resetting their regular sewing machines when they want to do quilting—multiple steps are required to prepare a home sewing machine for quilting, including switching from the type of foot used for normal sewing to one that is more open in design and easier to see underneath. In a way, the action of quilting subverts the usual function of a sewing machine, because a quilter wants to stop the machine from controlling the way the fabric feeds under the needle and transfer that control to the quilter's hands. Taking back that control requires adjustments to the machinery, including lowering the "feed dogs," those metal teeth that grip and pull the fabric from below.

Usually, lowering the feed dogs involves adjusting a single lever or switch, but sometimes the adjustment is more complex, especially on a sewing machine that doesn't allow the quilter to drop the feed dogs. In that case, a special plate may have to be installed over the feed dogs so the quilt will move more smoothly. Obviously, this process is loads easier than, say, changing a tire on a car. But ours is a culture that loves gadgets and shortcuts and isn't afraid to pay plenty to get both. Midarms recognize the reality of how today's multitasking quilters

LONGARMS VS. MIDARMS

How they are the same

- Both longarm and midarm machines are used only for quilting.
- The quilter stands when operating both machines.
- Both can be operated from the front or the back.
- Both require a much longer table than a regular sewing machine—from ten to twelve feet.

How they differ

- Midarms have a slightly shorter arm—eleven to seventeen inches.
- Midarms usually weigh less than longarms.
- Midarms cost much less, about half to a third the price of longarms.

Who buys which

The rule is that you buy a midarm if you want to finish your own quilts and a longarm if you want to go into business. That said, there are always exceptions to the rule.

Some Popular Midarm Machines

Here are three of the bestselling brands of midarms. These three models are either sixteen or seventeen inches long, so they are just slightly shorter than the smallest longarms, but they cost considerably less—between $3,000 and $9,000. This is a fast-growing segment of the quilt market, so there may be some great newer brands on the market soon, but do your homework before buying one, being sure to test the machines thoroughly and get in touch with others who have had experience using them.

HANDI QUILTER

This is the manufacturer of the midarm originally designed by Laurel Barrus to be lighter and cheaper than a longarm. The number sixteen in the name of its HQ Sixteen Quilting Machine model refers to the length of the arm in inches.

The HQ's price is higher than some other midarms, partly because of the extra care taken to make it pleasing to the feminine eye, but it is a well-made machine with an excellent track record and is considered to be the dominant brand in this market. The HandiQuilter comes with a stitch regulator and frame and costs between $7,500 and $8,500, depending upon whether you buy a table for it.

Handi Quilter
76 South Orchard Drive
North Salt Lake, Utah 84054
(877) 697-8458

Handi Quilter's excellent website, **www.handiquilter.com**, provides lots of information, including tutorials, a dealer locator, and so forth.

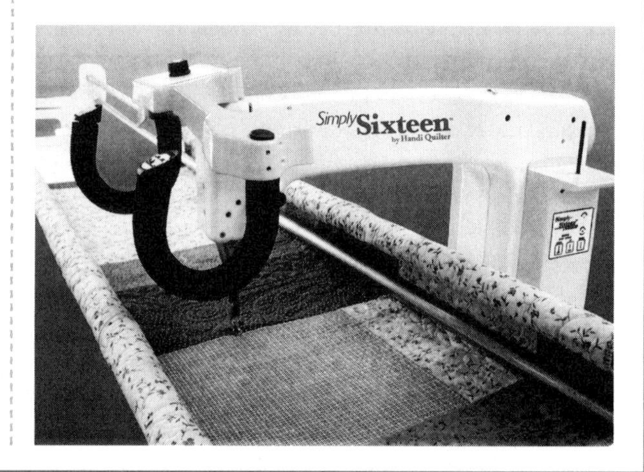

Handi Quilter.

VOYAGER 17

A newer brand of midarm, the Voyager 17 is made by the Hinterberg company, which is best known for making frames for midarm and regular sewing machines that facilitate machine quilting. Hollywood, Maryland, resident Mindy Caspersen, who sells the Voyager machines, says they are "stretched" machines, industrial sewing machines—that have been sliced open, added on to, and then welded together to create a much longer arm (seventeen inches, in this case). As a result, this machine looks more like a regular home sewing machine, and some midarm users like that familiarity. But because it is made from a heavy industrial sewing machine, the Voyager 17 weighs considerably more than some other midarms.

The basic Voyager machine costs about $2,000. You must buy a frame to go with it, such as Hinterberg's ten-foot frame, which costs $899 plus shipping. A stitch regulator, which is expected to become available soon, will cost extra.

Hinterberg Design
2805 East Progress Drive
West Bend, Wisconsin 53095
(800) 443-5800

For details about the Voyager 17, go to the website of the parent company, Hinterberg Design, **www.hinterberg.com.**

FUN QUILTER

Made by Nolting, a well-known manufacturer of longarms (see page 143), the Fun Quilter is positioned by the company as "the compact longarm for your tabletop quilting frame." In fact, at seventeen inches, the arm is only one inch shorter than the smallest longarm. This is a very lightweight machine, weighing thirty-five pounds, and Nolting really has tried to make it "fun." In profile it looks like a slightly simplified version of a longarm, with an actual smile under the logo, and this metal machine comes in colors like purple and light green. That said, this is basically a downsized longarm machine and has a powerful motor.

The Fun Quilter costs $4,400 without a stitch regulator and $5,900 with one. The cost of a frame is extra; the Fun Quilter can be mounted on the Hinterberg frame mentioned above ($899). Alternatively, you can buy the Fun Quilter with a twelve-foot Nolting commercial frame, which will cost a total of $6,400 without a stitch regulator or $7,900 with the regulator.

Nolting Manufacturing
1265 Hawkeye Drive
Hiawatha, Iowa 52233
(319) 378-0999

You'll find a lot of details, including photos, a list of dealers, and trouble-shooting tips for Nolting's Fun Quilter at the excellent website **www.funquilter.com.**

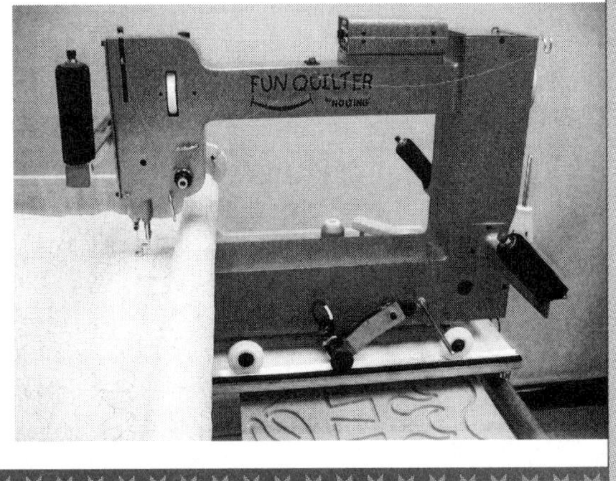

Nolting's Fun Quilter.

HOW MUCH QUILTING AREA?

As you graduate from a traditional home sewing machine to a midarm or longarm quilting machine, the throat space, which determines how large an area can be quilted at one time, increases. The actual work space available on midarm and longarm machines may be less than what the manufacturers claim because the take-up rollers can usurp some of the available work space.

The throat space measurements here cover the area from the needle to the back of the throat (up against the thick column that holds the machinery). Some sewing machine makers measure differently, partly to claim the maximum space for quilting. Says sewing machine dealer Mindy Caspersen, "I have seen nine-inch machines that advertised themselves as longarms! It is definitely a case of buyer beware."

Average Throat Space
Home sewing machine
7 to 9 inches
Midarm quilting machine
11 to 17 inches
Longarm quilting machine
18 to 30 inches

work: At any one time most have multiple quilts at different stages of completion. They may start quilting something and then need to start piecing a crib quilt for a baby due soon or need to finish the next block in the block of the month quilt at the quilt shop, meaning they would have to get their machine switched back for piecing, then reset it for quilting in a few days when they return to the original project.

Furthermore, the bigger the quilt, the harder it is to physically fit it through the small window between the needle and the fixed arm of a regular sewing machine; while one section of a quilt is being finished, the rest has to be draped or rolled out of the way and then wrestled with throughout the process.

The luxury of having a regular sewing machine always ready to piece, while a midarm is always set for quilting, is one that a substantial number of passionate quilters clearly want and can afford. Advice given elsewhere in this book about test-driving sewing machines also applies here. This is a big-ticket item, and the features and handling ability of the different brands of midarms vary a lot. Don't just take a five-minute test-drive at the next quilt show; be sure to find out if the company has a reputation for good customer service and training, and check to see if anybody you know uses the brand you are considering. Surf the Internet looking for other midarm quilting machine users, and haggle for the best price.

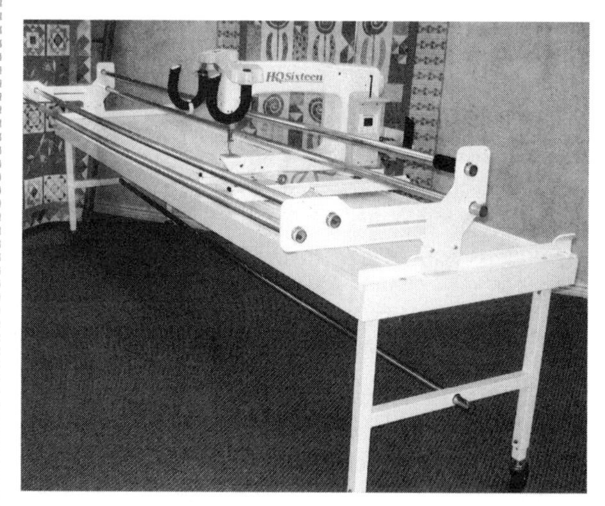

A midarm sewing machine with a king-size work surface.

CHAPTER THREE

More Revolutionary Tools

SEWING MACHINES HAVE BEEN A PIVOTAL PIECE OF the high-tech revolution fueling the quilt boom, but they aren't the only modern tools that have changed the face and pace of quilting. Other new tools have opened up whole fields of creativity. And with every innovation, a burst of entrepreneurial activity unleashes related devices that enhance the quilting experience. This section will explore some of these tools, including computer software.

What new devices will replace our current tools? How will they change the look of quilts in decades to come? It's impossible to predict, but gadget-happy quilters will keep searching quilt shops and shows for the next thing that allows them to work faster or better. And if they don't find it, they'll invent it.

Rotary Tools and Strip Piecing

Rotary cutters came on the market in the late 1970s and did for quilters what the food processor did for home cooks.

BEFORE QUILTERS SEW A QUILT THEY HAVE TO cut out the fabric, and that's an area in which speed has come to rule. It's hard to oversell the importance of the rotary cutter, a tool that looks a lot like a pizza cutter and makes it possible to slice swiftly through eight to twelve layers of fabric at once. A rotary cutter's blades are razor sharp and must be used with a companion tool, a thick, rubber "self-healing" mat, which protects whatever surface it rests on from nicks and cuts. Rotary cutters came on the market in the late 1970s and did for quilters what the food processor did for home cooks. The rotary cutter brought precision and speed to cutting fabric and launched a mania for gadgets in the quilt world.

The first cutter embraced by quilters was made by Olfa, a Japanese company that manufactures industrial cutters of all kinds and developed the rotary version for cutting kimono silk. American quilters went crazy when the device was imported, and before long, cutters were manufactured in multiple sizes with dozens of accessories. Soon there were competing brands. Manufacturers came out with larger blades that cut even more layers of fabric. Then, once quilters started coming down with carpal tunnel syndrome, cutters with ergonomic handles hit the market. Now, some cutters even come with built-in lights.

The popularity of the rotary cutter spawned the production of a vast quantity and variety of thick plastic rulers to be used for cutting triangles, hexagons, and every other possible fabric shape. Quilt teachers raced to start rotary cutting classes and create patterns and books featuring the new equipment.

Like everything else, there was a learning curve with the rotary cutters. Part of the lesson was cautionary: Tales spread from guild to guild and on the Internet about careless quilters who sliced off fingertips, or pets who walked across blades. "Always cut away from your body!" became one of the principle mantras of quilting.

Rotary cutters didn't just speed things up by enabling quilters to pile up layers of fabric. With this tool, a whole new way of cutting and designing quilts evolved. By using the rulers, quiltmakers improved their accuracy and raced through a novel method of strip piecing. Long strips of fabric were sewed together horizontally, then those pieced strips were cut lengthwise and rearranged, creating instant blocks. So the change in how quickly a quilt could be made wasn't just incremental but exponential.

"I had some reservations about the rotary cutters at first, largely because people were cutting on the crosswise grain, which is stretchy," says Judy Martin, who has written more than seventeen books and created more than nine hundred quilt patterns. But the cutters took off, and before long, once Martin became more familiar with them, she changed her mind about the gadget. "I realized I could just cut the other way—lengthwise." Martin took her time and did the math to figure out how to cut different shapes in many sizes using a ruler and rotary cutter. One of her most successful books is *Judy Martin's Ultimate Rotary Cutting Reference* (Collector Books; $7.95), which gives detailed cutting instructions for all the standard shapes used in quilt patterns, from simple squares and triangles to trapezoids, hexagons, and prisms. A lot of the book is simply charts: If quilters want to make, say, half-square triangles that measure three inches on the long side and two and an eighth inches on the short sides, this book will tell them which type of ruler to use, where to place it on the fabric, and how many triangles they can cut from a given length of fabric.

As Martin points out, the rotary cutter was also one of the factors that spurred machine piecing. Because precision is required to make a quilt block fit together, when quilters sew by hand, they generally need a line marked on the cloth that tells them where to stitch and they use a template to trace that line.

With a sewing machine, there is no need to draw on a stitching line because the machine has seam markings on the metal throat plate and often on the presser foot, too. Quilters just need to line up the fabric with the correct seam allowance to start and keep sewing a straight line. Using a rotary cutter and an acrylic ruler as a guide, a machine piecer can skip the templates and cut fabric much faster.

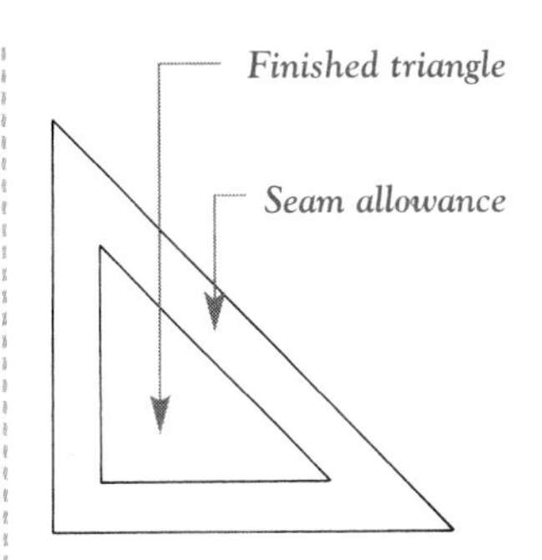

A half-square triangle—it's easy to cut one with a rotary cutter.

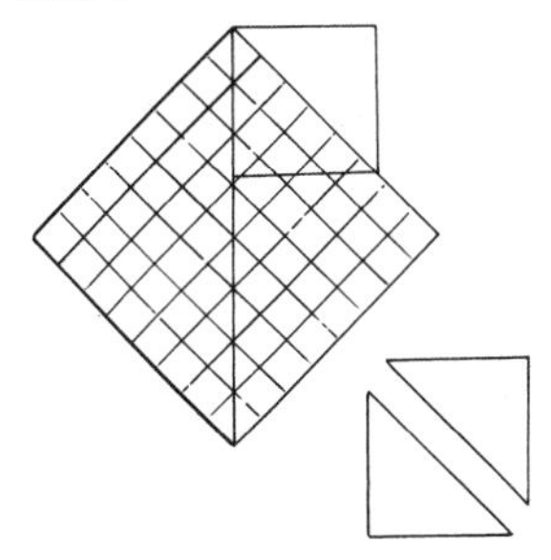
After cutting out squares of fabric, use the rotary cutter and an acrylic ruler to cut each square in half, corner to corner to form triangles.

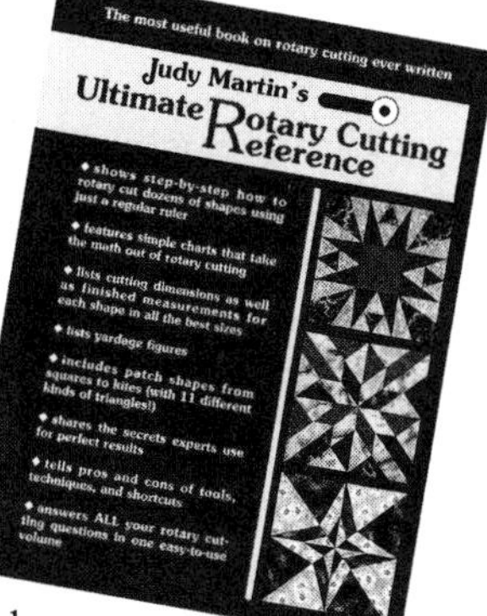

The standard-bearer: Judy Martin's book on rotary cutting.

Making the Cut: Tips on Rotary Cutting

Many quilters love rotary cutters. I've met some who insist they wouldn't still be quilting if it weren't for these handy tools. They cut through multiple layers of fabric like the proverbial hot knife through butter. When paired with the right sort of ruler, rotary cutters often eliminate the need for plastic and paper templates. Just by shifting and angling a ruler and slicing with a rotary cutter, quilters can swiftly produce triangles, hexagons, and any number of other shapes.

For example, to cut a whole bunch of three-inch squares, you could make a plastic template of that size and draw around it with a pencil on the wrong side of the fabric, then cut out each square individually. Instead, using a rotary cutter and a long, acrylic ruler, you can cut three-inch strips across the width of the fabric, then with the ruler to help guide you, go back across the strips making cuts every three inches to finish your squares. Much quicker!

However, that old reliable tool, a pair of scissors, also works well and there is no rule saying you *must* use a rotary cutter. At the least, I think it's important that beginners know there is a learning curve for most people with rotary cutters. And here's a time for true confessions: I haven't traveled very far along that curve myself. Although I own several rotary cutters and a cutting mat, I still feel like I'm all thumbs when I try to use them, and so I rarely do. I'm a pretty klutzy person, and some of my reluctance to use a rotary cutter is the fear that I will be one of those people who wind up in the ER with a dangling fingertip.

Part of it comes down to your personality as a quilter. I'm someone who finds pleasure in taking my time. It doesn't matter to me that it may take hours to position and reposition a plastic template on fabric and laboriously draw around it, then cut out the individual shapes one piece at a time. But a lot of quilters are speed freaks who want to know every shortcut to get to the finished product quicker and start on another quilt. If that describes you, you'll probably love rotary cutters. Rotary cutters can save a great deal of time; however, they are dangerous if used incorrectly. They are essentially circular razor blades attached to a handle, and they cut through skin as easily as fabric. Be sure to follow these safety tips.

- Always use one of those thick cutting mats to protect your table.
- Always cut against the side of a sturdy quilter's ruler: It will help you cut straight lines and keep the blade where it should be.
- Always roll the rotary cutter away from your body.
- Always use the built-in blade guard after every cut: If the cutting edge is left exposed on a table you might pick it up and cut yourself—or your children might. Also, pets have been known to walk across rotary cutters left open on tabletops, with disastrous consequences for their paws.
- Avoid cutting anything other than fabric, including pins and needles. The blade edges of a rotary cutter are easily

damaged by cutting over a pin, and if this happens, the fabric will have uncut gaps when you try to use the cutter again.

- If you are new to rotary cutting, start off by practicing with scrap fabrics. It takes a little time to get used to the feel of the cutter and to make straight, smooth cutting strokes.
- Don't worry about not knowing how to manipulate a rotary cutter and ruler so you get the fabric pieces you need for a project. Many quilt books, especially those that stress speed of production, come with explicit rotary-cutting instructions for the projects included.

Buy a 45-millimeter rotary cutter to start with, along with a cutting mat. The cutters are available with both bigger and smaller blades, but a 45-millimeter blade is the standard. An extralarge blade of 60 millimeters might feel better to someone with large hands, but for most people, a 45-millimeter cutter is comfortable to hold and is easier to control.

There are left-handed rotary cutters on the market and special ergonomic models. In addition to the standard blades, you can buy wavy blades that are used for cutting decorative edges. Art quilter Melody Johnson loves to use these to jazz up her collagelike quilts.

The number of brands of rotary cutters has proliferated. When the first issue of *Quilter's Home* magazine came out in June 2006, editor in chief Mark Lipinski had his "posse" that tests products try out eight different types of rotary blades made by seven different companies. In addition to Olfa, the major brands include Omnigrid, Dritz, Fiskars, and Clover. The *Quilter's Home* testers' favorites included the Olfa 45-millimeter deluxe rotary cutter. At $23.49, it was deemed a bit pricey (basic cutters cost about $15.00), but the magazine testers said its ergonomic handle made it easier to use than others and its automatic retractable blade made it safer.

On pages 418–419 you'll find step-by-step instructions for using a rotary cutter.

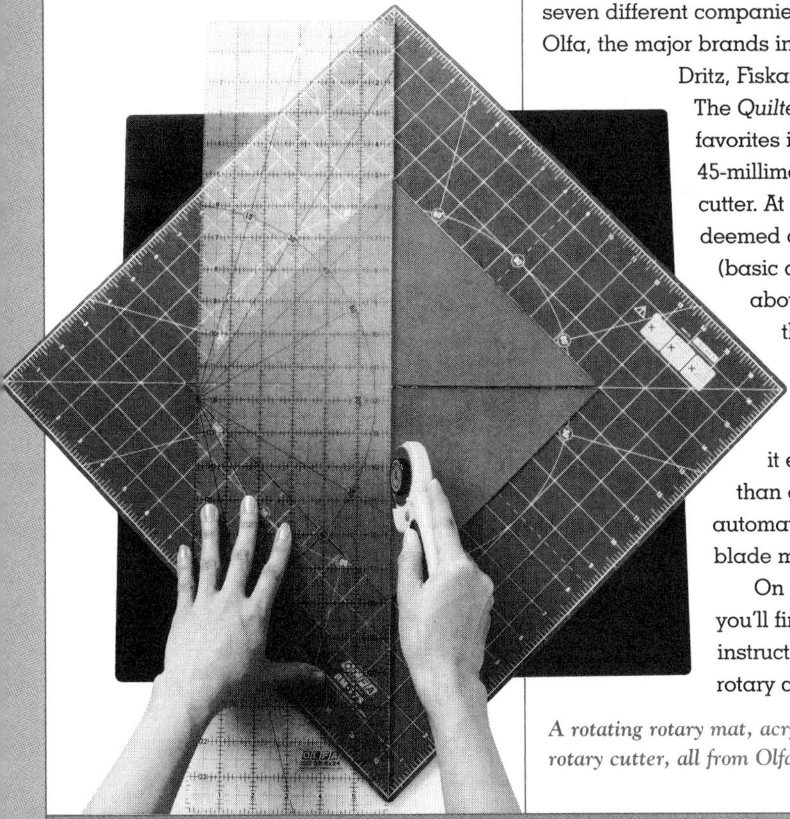

A rotating rotary mat, acrylic ruler, and rotary cutter, all from Olfa.

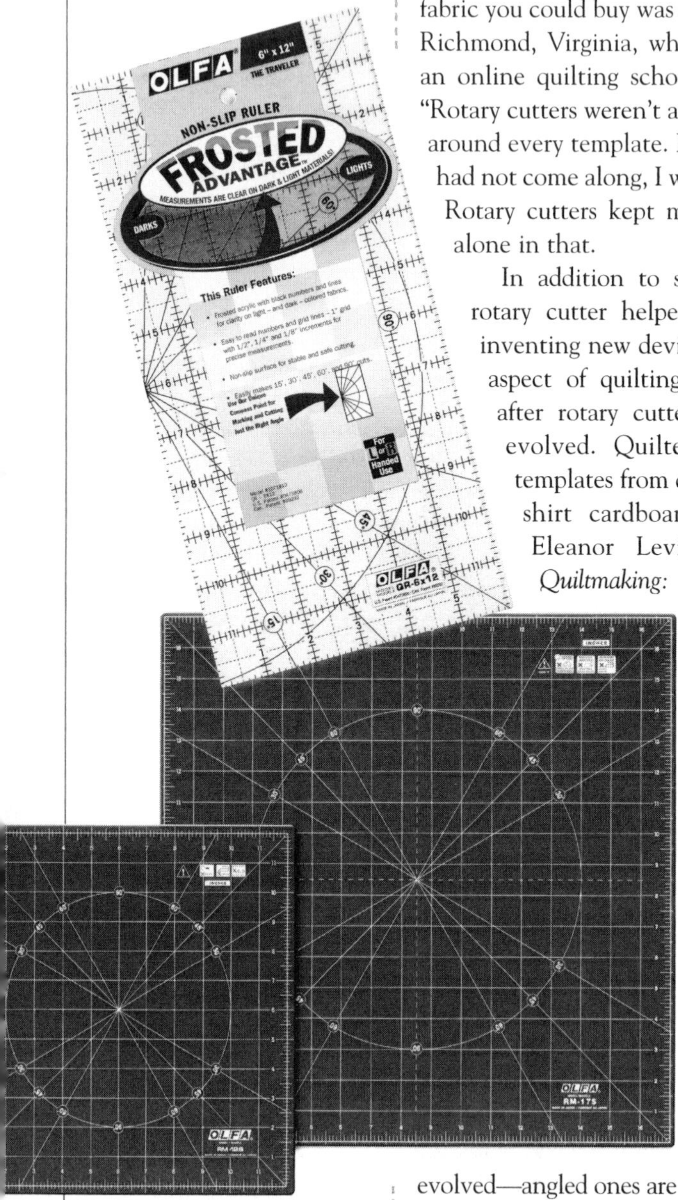

"When I began making quilts in 1979, people made them from two colors and a background, and the only fabric you could buy was calico," recalls Carol Miller of Richmond, Virginia, who now runs Quilt University, an online quilting school (www.quiltuniversity.com). "Rotary cutters weren't around yet and I hated drawing around every template. It was so slow! If rotary cutters had not come along, I would have definitely given up. Rotary cutters kept me in quilting!" Miller is not alone in that.

In addition to speeding up the process, the rotary cutter helped create a general frenzy of inventing new devices and materials to aid every aspect of quilting. Templates didn't disappear after rotary cutters came out, but they, too, evolved. Quilters had been cutting their templates from discarded household items like shirt cardboard and cereal boxes, notes Eleanor Levie in her book *American Quiltmaking: 1970–2000*. In the eighties, many quilters began experimenting, making templates with lots of other materials, especially sheets of clear plastic and less stiff alternatives such as freezer paper; these had crisper edges than cardboard templates, which became frayed with use. Judy Martin, for one, was happy to be rid of her cardboard templates.

Even the technology of the straight pin has changed; quilt shops now offer a variety of lengths and types. And safety pins have evolved—angled ones are particularly useful for machine quilters. The bend in the pins makes them easy to use to baste the layers of a quilt sandwich together. Basting with thread can be a nightmare for machine quilters because the basting threads get tangled up with the quilting threads, making them difficult to remove. These new pins were embraced immediately as a good alternative.

Essential rotary cutting accessories: a translucent acrylic ruler (top) and "self-healing" cutting mats (bottom).

Fusibles and Other Sticky Stuff

THE LIST OF NEW QUILT TOOLS AND PRODUCTS goes on and on, and for anyone coming fresh to the vast subculture of quilting, the complexity of materials can be a staggering surprise. Every revolutionary change, such as the switch to widespread machine quilting, unleashes a barrage of related tools. For example, some quilters found it frustrating work to guide the quilt layers through a sewing machine. Suddenly there were dozens of products to speed the process, from special gloves that grip the fabric better to sprays said to decrease friction from the machine's work surface.

And even old tools like thread, needles, and thimbles got more complicated. Thread comes in many more colors and types (you can read about them in Thread Basics on page 403), and even the humble thimble now comes in many more shapes, styles, and materials (see page 93 for some thimble innovations).

"I was away from sewing for about twenty-five years, and when I came back and started quilting, I was blown away by all the new gadgets, tools, and techniques," says Pat Slaven, who tests all sorts of appliances, including sewing machines, for *Consumer Reports*. "Now there are adhesives (spray-on, iron-on, tape-on, you name it), stabilizers, soluble stabilizers, tear-away stabilizers, water soluble thread, and on and on."

The **adhesives** mentioned by Slaven have been particularly important and are just one example of how new products led to an explosion of change and creativity. Adhesives can be found in several forms. Spray-on fabric adhesive comes in a can and is sometimes used to baste quilt layers together. There are also basting glues that come in a plastic bottle with a long tip, like crafter's glue. Some machine quilters love using the spray or glue for basting because it saves time and eliminates the headache of sewing around basting thread or safety pins.

Another variety of fabric adhesive that's especially popular for appliqué quilts is an iron-on bonding material often called **fusible web.** This comes in sheets

"If rotary cutters had not come along, I would have definitely given up. Rotary cutters kept me in quilting!"

of various thickness, usually with a paper backing. With fusible web, the adhesive is activated by ironing a sheet of web against a piece of fabric: The heat melts the adhesive and glues the fusible sheet to the quilt fabric. A quilter can cut a shape out of that fabric—say a flower—peel off the paper backing, and then iron the piece of fabric again to stick the back of the flower to the fabric of a quilt top.

This is an incredible help to someone who does appliqué, because there is no need for pins to hold the shape in place to stitch it down. Partly because of fusible web, what's called raw edge appliqué has become very popular. Quilters don't bother with the tedious work of turning under every edge of the flower, or whatever it may be, and then sewing it down; they simply sew around the cut edge of the fused shape, often using one of their sewing machine's decorative embroidery stitches. This serves the same purpose as turning the edge, which is to prevent the raw edge of the fabric from fraying.

"I was away from sewing for about twenty-five years, and when I came back and started quilting, I was blown away by all the new gadgets, tools, and techniques."

Fusibles fall under the big category of **interfacings,** which are used in clothing and all sorts of sewing projects. Interfacings are the invisible innards that give garments, cloth handbags, and handcrafted items the shape and crispness that fabric alone can't provide. Interfacing falls into two categories: the type that must be sewn in place and the fusible type. All of this has gotten more complex with the introduction of new products and technologies: The website for Pellon, one of the major producers of interfacing, lists dozens of types of interfacing products that it sells, including more than twenty for the crafts, home decor, and quilting market (to find out more, go to www.pellonideas.com).

The market for fusibles keeps growing as quilters find more ways to use them and new products are continually introduced. There are fusible battings, for example—battings that have adhesive applied to them. This eliminates the need to baste. And there is fusible fleece. All of these are used for convenience and speed in assembling quilts, quilted tote bags, quilted garments, and the like. Different products have different uses and qualities. Fusible fleece for example, is puffier and fatter than interfacing. You might use it for a tote bag you didn't want to be stiff. (The sides of the tote in the quilting project on page 448 are stiffened with fusible interfacing.) You can also buy fusible versions of the treated cotton sheets that are used to print photographs using a home computer (see page 205); crafters can stick these fabric photos onto a quilt or T-shirt or tote.

Art quilters in particular have made fusing hip. Melody Johnson, one of the teachers profiled in chapter five (see page 346), has embraced fusing with fabric adhesives as a way for quilters to work quickly and creatively. With several other prominent art quilters, including Laura Wasilowski and Frieda Anderson, Johnson invented the "Chicago School of Fusing" in the late 1990s, which espouses the use of fusible web in art quilts. Although the "school" is largely fictional, the quilters identified with it actually teach fusing techniques to guilds and at quilt shows around the country.

In general, fabric adhesives don't discolor fabric and don't gum up sewing machine needles. The spray-on fabric adhesives dissolve when the quilt is washed (and wash off your hands with soap and water), so for most quilts they're just a temporary measure to hold fabric together until it can be sewn. On the other hand, most makers of fusible web claim that it makes a permanent bond once it has been ironed to fabric. Over time, the adhesive can still be weakened by washing, so anybody using fusible web for a bed quilt or wall quilt that will be washed at some point should also anchor the appliqué pieces to the quilt top using decorative stitches.

One final cautionary note. After some curators reported that some wall quilts made with fusible webs had signs of yellowing and stiffness in the fabric, a study was conducted to see whether these products leave a residue that will harm quilts over time. The study has been controversial, and since the adhesives are relatively new, it will take more time to determine the effects. But there is no evidence that quilters are reducing their use of these helpful products. It seems clear fabric adhesives are here to stay, and there's no doubt these vital tools will continue to keep evolving and improving.

PRESSING CLOTHS

When you iron fusible web onto fabric for a project, you'll be partially melting the adhesive in the fusible web with the heat from your iron. You want to make sure that none of that gluey gunk messes up either your ironing board or your iron.

You can always use an old clean cloth, like a kitchen towel, to create a barrier where the fusible might touch your iron or the board. But there are also reusable sheets made of Teflon for this purpose: Any fusible residue that cakes on them can simply be scraped off. One brand is June Tailor, which makes a reusable Teflon pressing sheet that is eighteen inches square and costs about $10.

Cool Tools

Alongside the tools that have truly revolutionized modern quilting are many that are invaluable on a less universal scale. Here are some of the standouts in this category.

Reducing Glass

The opposite of a magnifying glass, a reducing glass provides a quick, easy way to check out the overall cohesiveness and impact of a quilt design. Prominent quilters like Liza Prior Lucy (you'll find her profiled with Kaffe Fassett on page 331) like to use reducing glasses while fiddling with a quilt in progress on a design wall. How many of us have sewing rooms spacious enough to stand back twenty feet from a quilt to evaluate the total composition? You should be able to pick up a reducing glass at a quilt shop or online for less than $10.

Sandboard

Essentially a piece of fine sandpaper attached to a hard, flat surface, a sandboard keeps pieces of fabric from slipping. It's primarily used to hold fabric securely while tracing patterns on it or sewing appliqué stitches.

Whether called sandboards or sandpaper boards, these come in various sizes, some square and some rectangular, and cost from $12 to $25. Appliqué masters Becky Goldsmith and Linda Jenkins, the Piece O' Cake Designs duo (profiled on page 339), say this may be their favorite tool ever.

Mini Iron on a Stick

The mini iron was introduced by Clover a few years back and was immediately embraced by quilters, especially those who do a lot of appliqué. This tool looks a bit like a curling iron, with a thick handle attached to a cord. At the tip is a small, triangular piece of flat metal that makes it easy to iron tiny pieces of fabric that would get lost under a regular-size iron. The standard retail price is about $25.

Gloves for Machine Quilting

More and more quiltmakers are attempting to quilt using their home sewing machines and are finding that, with the feed dogs lowered, it's tough to push the quilt sandwich around under the needle. The fabric is slippery, your fingertips get dry, and control is hard to maintain. One of the more ingenious solutions to this problem has been the invention of gloves for machine quilting.

Although some quilters use dishwashing gloves or gardening gloves, there are two popular types of wrist-length gloves made specifically for machine quilting: cotton gloves with tiny gripper pads that cover the palm and fingers, and Machingers nylon gloves with reinforced tips (these are thin enough to wear while removing pins). Most quilt shops carry both types, and you can usually buy a pair for less than $10.

A selection of Steam-A-Seam products, each tailored to a specific use.

LEARNING MORE ABOUT FUSIBLES

How do you know which brand and thickness of fusible web to buy? If you're using it for appliqué, you will likely want to try one of the popular lines of fusible web carried by many quilt shops, including such brands as Wonder-Under, Steam-A-Seam, and HeatnBond. But keep in mind that these adhesive products come in a very wide range of thicknesses. Many art quilters swear by the sheer fusible web called Misty-Fuse, created by quiltmaker Esterita Austin (for more about Austin, see page 310), which comes in both white and black. At the opposite end of the range is Timtex, a very thick fusible used to stiffen the sides of fabric bowls. If you're not sure which product is right for your project, ask your local quilt shop for advice, query other quilters in your guild, or pose your question on one of the quilting message boards online.

For those who want to learn to play with fusibles, a good book is *Fusing Fun! Fast, Fearless Art Quilts*, by Laura Wasilowski (C&T Publishing; $24.95). You can purchase the book through Wasilowski's website, www.artfabrik.com, where you can also find a schedule of her classes and buy some of the products you need for fusing. Other general quilting retail websites, such as www.equilter.com, carry a more complete line of fusible webs and spray fabric adhesives.

Laura Wasilowski's excellent guide to beginning to work with fusibles.

Quilting and Computers

These days, quilters use their PCs and Macs almost as much as their Berninas and Singers. It's not an overstatement to say that computers have revolutionized the craft and art of quilting. A careful examination of the place where computers and quilting intersect reveals how deeply the quilt revival is a product of our high-tech age. Quilting wouldn't be nearly as popular as it is today without computers.

"From early on, quilters just seemed to be more computer savvy. I can't explain why that is; perhaps quilters are more mathematical."

"Quilters have always been adopters of new technology," says Rob Holland, founder of the informational website PlanetPatchwork.com. "People think a bunch of ladies cutting fabric into bits and sewing it back together would be Luddites. But if you give quilters a better rotary cutter or a good software program to design quilts, they'll snap it up in a minute. They get comfortable fast with technology that helps them."

"I've been involved with computer forums since before the World Wide Web existed, and I think quilters were using the Internet way before knitters and weavers and other textile people," observes Susan Druding, a knitter and art quilter who was the host of the quilting forum on About.com until 2006. "From early on, quilters just seemed to be more computer savvy. I can't explain why that is; perhaps quilters are more mathematical or something."

Needless to say, there's a great intersection of quilting and computers in sewing machines themselves, where microprocessor chips have become an expected part of the package for high-end machines. Those technical innovations have had enormous impact on how quilters work, and you can read about them in Electronic Machines on page 114. The section here has loads more ground to cover examining the ways in which quilters use computers *outside* of their sewing machines.

QUILT SOFTWARE

Quilt design software works like a virtual design wall. Once you decide you want to make a quilt with a star block, you can search the computer database for the one that best suits your project. Then, you can experiment with an unlimited number of color combinations and border designs before spending a penny on fabric. When you pick what you want, the software will even tell you how much fabric to buy.

At home with Electric Quilt software.

The vast majority of quilters today cite their computers as an indispensable tool, but according to the 2003 Quilting in America survey conducted for CKMedia (formerly Primedia), only about 30 percent of avid quilters own quilt design software. Still, that percentage represents many thousands of quilters; the numbers of classes, books, and websites available show that quilt software is being broadly adopted as a tool. With good reason: The sophistication of the software has advanced exponentially. Every time a quilt wins a major prize and its maker mentions that it was designed using quilt software, more quilters get up the nerve to try this new technology.

There are only a handful of providers of specialty quilt-design software, but the market is intensely competitive, resulting in frequent updates, extra features, and improved service. The dominant player in the field has long been The Electric Quilt Company, which is based in Bowling Green, Ohio, and run by veteran quilter Penny McMorris and her mathematician husband, Dean Neumann. A few small firms have come and gone in recent years, but the two companies that still compete with EQ, as The Electric Quilt Company is frequently referred to, are Quilt-Pro Systems and PCQuilt.

McMorris was an established quilt world personality when she and her husband started the EQ software venture in 1991. By then, McMorris had already hosted several television series on quilts for PBS, which is where the earliest version of Electric Quilt was introduced.

"For a lot of people, quilt design software is a killer application. We heard that some people bought their computer in order to use our software, which in turn taught them how to use the computer."

"My husband loves quilts and art, and he thought it would be neat if quilters could have a way to try out different patterns and colors very quickly, rather than having to make drawings and color them by hand, or to audition fabrics and designs by cutting into them," McMorris explains. "He had met many of the wonderful quilters I interviewed on the show, and he thought that a computer program would let them invent new designs and free them creatively."

Neumann began tinkering with a software program for quilt design in 1989, and an early version was demonstrated on his wife's television show two years later. "We did a small segment, where the camera was on me, but he was actually working the computer keyboard because I had no clue how to use the program," McMorris recalls, laughing. "The camera would cut away, and Dean would put something else on the screen, then the camera would cut back to me saying 'Wasn't that easy?' It was a real Mickey Rooney/Judy Garland thing we were doing by the seat of our pants. But then, people started phoning the station to say they wanted to know how to buy the design program." Before long, McMorris and her husband had both quit their day jobs to expand the Electric Quilt business, improving their quilt software, while slowly building a customer base as word spread.

"For a lot of people, quilt design software is a killer application," says McMorris. "We heard that some people bought their computers in order to use our software, which in turn taught them how to use the computer."

Over the years, Electric Quilt's customers became noticeably more tech savvy. "When we first started the company, women were afraid to call with questions. They'd put their husbands on the phone," recalls McMorris. "That has dropped way off."

As new versions of EQ were released, the design functions got better and the database of possible quilt blocks, borders, and colors became more extensive. From a library of about five hundred different quilt blocks, EQ's database has soared to more than four thousand. Users can click on these block patterns and drag them into a diagram for a quilt top, then audition different colors and actual fabrics for the blocks. EQ6 allows users to plug in five thousand specific commercial

Quilt Software Tutorial

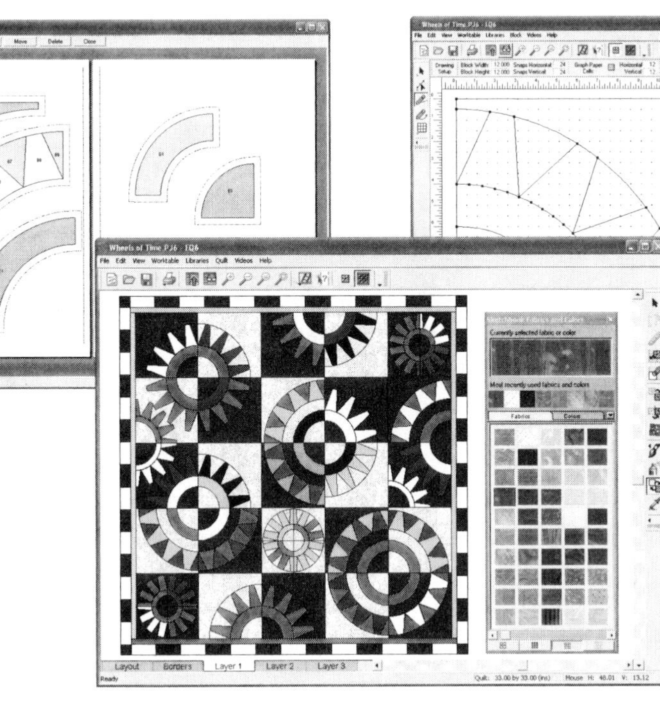

Eugénie Werdmuller von Elgg, who is from the Netherlands, used EQ to design her original quilt *Wheels of Time* for the birthday of a friend who loves cars, contemporary art, and the era of the Industrial Revolution.

Von Elgg designed her Gears quilt blocks on her computer. (She could also have used any of the four thousand blocks EQ6 has in its library of quilt blocks.)

Next, she colored the blocks of the quilt and chose a layout, deciding how many blocks she wanted and what size they should be. As Von Elgg adjusted the layout she could watch the quilt size change. Then she chose a simple border.

Von Elgg arranged the layout of the quilt blocks and colored in the border strips. She tried rotating some of the blocks, and it produced the effect of movement. When designing a quilt on the computer, it's easy to try out variations in the blocks and borders, changing the composition until you see what you like best.

When she was ready to sew the quilt, Von Elgg directed the computer program to number the quilt pieces for her. EQ also separated the pieces, so that she could print and cut out each template, then follow the numbered sewing sequence to piece the quilt top.

The EQ computer program will isolate the patches of a quilt block so you can make templates. It also shows you the overall pattern of the quilt you design.

"If I fall in love with a quilt in a magazine, I still want to change it, so I use a computer program to manipulate the design and audition the changes I think I want to try."

fabric patterns, and quilters have the additional option of scanning in fabric that isn't in the database.

"They have a lot of traditional layouts with straight blocks and sashing, but you can also mix blocks, alter blocks, even use tools that allow you to freehand draw a shape onto your hypothetical quilt top," explains Barb Vlack, a quilter who teaches classes on EQ software and has written several manuals for it. "You can print out paper or plastic templates that you need for cutting out blocks or foundation piecing, and the program will also compute how much fabric you need." (Some users complain that the fabric computation feature isn't always accurate, but if it errs, it tends to be on the side of recommending that a quilter buy more than is needed, not less.)

Vlack says she personally loves using software because she hates to copy existing designs. "I love to make quilts that nobody else has made. If I fall in love with a quilt in a magazine, I still want to change it, so I use a computer program to manipulate the design and audition the changes I think I want to try. For example, I had a commercial pattern for a quilt with twelve appliqué blocks, laid out in straight rows. I wanted something different, so I created a design for an eight-pointed star and set the appliqué blocks in the spaces between the arms of the star."

One of EQ's chief competitors is Quilt-Pro Systems, run by Miriam Neuringer, a Texas-based quilter with a graduate degree in art history. Neuringer is married to a computer programmer, Jim Salamon, who is also her partner in the business. She says her husband was cool to her proposal that they start a software company until she took him to the Dallas guild quilt show in 1991. When he saw there were already two other programs on the market, including the first version of EQ, "that perked him up," she says. By 1994, Quilt-Pro had the first version of its software on the market. After orders started pouring in, Jim quit his job and made Quilt-Pro his full-time work, says Neuringer.

Like EQ, Quilt-Pro has changed over the years, adding many new features and, eventually, a version for Macintosh users. Mostly what the company has learned through studying quilters, says Neuringer, is that "they don't want a long learning curve. We invited a bunch of

Dallas quilters in for a focus group to watch them use our software and decided it needed to be easier to use without sacrificing any flexibility." Neuringer says the reason Quilt-Pro doesn't sell all the companion books to users that Electric Quilt does is that "our software is so easy to use, you don't need all these companion books."

Computer quilt design teacher Vlack says it's worth the time it takes to master Electric Quilt. "I didn't have any computer savvy at all when I started working with the EQ program. Actually, I learned to use a computer just so I could use the first Electric Quilt software, and it took practice for me to be good at it," says Vlack. "You don't learn the program in ten minutes. But now it's a tool I can't live without. I would never go back to designing on paper again."

Indeed, Vlack says that with the improvements in software and her own greater knowledge, many times she finds it satisfying to complete her quilts only virtually. "I have designed thousands of quilts using EQ but have only made about one hundred of those," she confesses. "My creative urge is satisfied sometimes just by doing the design on my computer. Every once in a while, a design comes up that is such a winner, I absolutely *must* make it into a quilt, and then I do."

Two of EQ's most popular software packages.

Vlack concedes that many quilters haven't yet developed her comfort zone with computer design. And although she has worked hard to write such how-to volumes as *EQ4 Magic* and *EQ5 Quilt Design: Border, Layout, and Setting Secrets*, she says many quilters "don't want to follow a manual. They want to go to a class on software and be shown, step-by-step." Vlack has had students confide after one of her classes, "I bought the software but never took it out of the box. But now that I've taken some classes on how to use it, the world has changed. I get it now!"

In recent years, the makers of quilt software have worked hard to reach passionately creative quilters who aren't computer geeks by introducing software for beginners. Such products as Electric Quilt's Quilt Design Wizard and Quilt-Pro's 1-2-3 Quilt! offer

RESOURCES

Quilt Software at a Glance

How to choose which software to buy? Here's a list of the major makers of quilt design software. When possible, the best way to research these products is to go to the makers' websites and download demonstrations. Also, ask your friends and fellow guild members what they use and like. And, many quilt shops offer classes in using software, especially that from Electric Quilt.

A good website for information—and to buy software from—is ***www.softexpressions.com****. Run by quilter and computer expert Sharla Hicks, the site offers lots of background, including free tutorials, downloads, and extensive links. You can also subscribe to its free e-newsletter, "Computer Quilting BYTES."*

THE ELECTRIC QUILT COMPANY

Electric Quilt's very detailed website provides lots of specifics about what each of its programs can do, and there are demos to explore. You can buy EQ software directly from the company if you wish.

All EQ software is designed to run on PCs and the latest, EQ6, is compatible with Microsoft's Vista operating system. The company says that programs like Virtual PC will allow Mac users to use EQ software, but it may be slightly slower.

EQ6 software is sophisticated and complex, but the company also makes software for beginners. Quilt Design Wizard was created for those who are new to quilting, both as a sewer and in its virtual form, and includes such basic information as how to use a rotary cutter. Those who buy the quilt Design Wizard can download a free monthly quilt pattern from a sister website, **www.quiltdesignwizard.com**. The patterns come with complete instructions.

Prices range from $30 for Quilt Design Wizard, to $150 for the latest version of EQ software.

Go to **www.electricquilt.com** or call **(800) 356-4219**.

QUILT-PRO SYSTEMS

Quilt-Pro 5 comes in versions for both Macintosh and PCs, and Quilt-Pro's extensive website provides an unusual amount of hand-holding. There are forums where users having technical difficulties can have their questions answered, as well as video lessons to download.

You can buy the software directly from the company, if you wish. Prices range from $40 for the beginner software, 1-2-3 Quilt! (which can be used free for a thirty-day trial period) to as little as $80, a sale price, for Quilt-Pro 5.

Go to **ww7w.quiltpro.com** or call **(800) 884-1511**.

PCQUILT

In online reviews, PCQuilt for Windows has been called a "sophisticated" and "compact" program. It bills itself as the simplest quilt design software to learn and to use, and it is priced competitively. The software can be ordered directly from the company: To lower the price, PCQuilt changed to a system where, after paying, users download the software directly into their computers. The website provides demos and describes the software's features. An earlier version of the PCQuilt software has been adapted for Macintosh computer users.

Prices range from $35 for the "Baby Mac" program to $50 for PCQuilt for Windows Version 2.

Go to **www.pcquilt.com** or call **(866) 487-3359**.

hundreds of quilt blocks rather than thousands and are simpler to use. Not only that, they cost a fraction of the cost of the top-of-the-line quilt software.

Despite the considerable improvements in quilt-specific software, there are some art quilters who prefer to use software developed for graphic designers, such as CorelDRAW and Adobe Illustrator. Award-winning quilter Caryl Bryer Fallert has espoused CorelDRAW in particular and has taught many classes to quilters on how to use this software. Information on how and why she uses it can be found at her website, www.bryerpatch.com.

Quilt software has come a great distance but for all the amazing things that it does now, it will likely seem elemental compared to the new versions yet to come.

HOW COMPUTERS HAVE CHANGED QUILTING

As they use their computers to buy supplies, meet other quilters, look at masterpiece quilts, and learn new techniques, quilters have found themselves transformed by technology, and that transformation isn't finished. Quilters from around the world have reached out to each other in cyberspace, cross-pollinating their ideas and techniques. Asian and European quilters can buy books and fabrics from American suppliers. Quilters in this country can view quilt exhibits posted on Japanese websites—the visual language of quilts needs no translation.

The Internet has helped to simultaneously define and expand the boundaries of the quilt world. This is one of the many reasons predictions that the quilt boom will peak have proven erroneous time and time again. Computers help give quilting momentum; they accelerate the changes in techniques and tools by broadcasting them quickly to an ever-widening audience.

"When we went into business, only the really technically forward-looking quilters wanted to consider using a computer to design with," programmer Dean Neumann of The Electric Quilt Company told an interviewer for the Planet Patchwork website. "Recently, though, it seems to have been gaining considerable momentum. The Internet is a huge factor because quilters are naturally interested in sharing."

The Internet has helped to simultaneously define and expand the boundaries of the quilt world.

FOR ART QUILTERS ONLY

Corel Corporation is a Canadian company making software that is used by professional graphic designers. Although the software has no quilt features, some of the top art quilters swear by CorelDRAW. They don't want a vast database of traditional blocks, and this software helps them create abstract forms and manipulate photos in sophisticated ways. The software is available for PCs only.

Caryl Bryer Fallert (profiled on page 327) and Barbara Webster, an award-winning maker of complex photo quilts, are two art quilters well known for using CorelDRAW, and both teach classes in how to use it.

Webster uses CorelDRAW Graphics Suite X3, which retails for $379, although she admits that much of the program she's paying for isn't applicable to her work. Webster says of the software, "DRAW has some features I use every day, like PowerClip. This one feature is worth the price of the program. It lets you place a chosen part of your image into a shape, then you can resize

An excellent example of the ways in which computers have become inextricably woven into the lives of quilters and accelerated their development is that of Chris Pascuzzi, a mother of three who lives in Virginia Beach, Virginia. Pascuzzi has worked with fabric all her life, including a stint as education coordinator for a large fabric store. She earned a degree in fashion merchandising and design from the University of Delaware in 1985.

Flash forward to 1998, when Pascuzzi, then thirty-five, quit her full-time job after the birth of her second child. She was working part-time for the local Bernina sewing machine dealer and teaching the occasional class there, when she and her husband decided it was finally time to buy a home computer, she says, "and see what this Internet thing was."

"One of the very first things I did was to type the word *quilting* into the Yahoo! search engine," recalls Pascuzzi, and one of the sites it led her to was the Quiltart e-mail list. She joined the list immediately, and reading the daily postings led to multiple payoffs she never would have imagined.

"Quiltart became a lifeline between myself and the art quilting community and it continues to provide a wealth of information and inspiration," says Pascuzzi. "About three years ago, I read about QuiltUniversity.com on the list, contacted Carol Miller who runs it, and sent her some photos of my work. The next thing you know, I was on the faculty there, teaching a project class and also one called Tools of the Trade about different sewing machine tools and techniques like bobbin work and couching."

Pascuzzi also picked up a tip from the Quiltart list that a company was looking for designers to create block of the month projects (see page 264), to be carried by major fabric chain stores. That company subsequently accepted some of Pascuzzi's designs. It's not surprising that Pascuzzi uses her computer to create those designs, using Electric Quilt software. "I thought EQ5 would be fun, and it really has been," she says.

"A computer is required in so many aspects of my work now," says Pascuzzi. "I also use my computer to print photos and images on fabric. Not to mention that I have a computerized embroidery machine with digitizing software that I use to add machine embroidery to my quilts. My progress and success as a quilter is simply unthinkable without my computer."

QUILTERS AND THE INTERNET

A large number of quilters use their computers to connect them to the Internet and the rich virtual quilt world that resides there. According to the 2006 Quilting in America study conducted by CKMedia, 73 percent of avid quilters surveyed had visited a quilting website in the past month. The top reasons for doing this included seeking free quilt patterns, shopping for quilting supplies, searching for fabrics, and learning new techniques and tips.

The bottom line is that the Internet allows quilters to do the three things they love most in the world: They can buy quilt stuff, learn how to make their quilts better, and see gorgeous quilts made by others. When you stop and think about it, these are precisely the activities that draw hordes of avid quilters to major quilt shows all over the country. But with the Internet, the quilt show comes to them. It literally never ends, and quilters can watch and participate to their hearts' content, wearing comfy slippers and with a cup of tea at their elbow. "People who were working in isolation suddenly found out, 'Hey, other people do this too!'" says quilt teacher Liza Prior Lucy (see page 331 for more about her). "And then they began to share resources."

There are plenty of general sites for quiltaholics (including Quiltaholics.com) and online guilds that operate much like local ones. But the sites get much more specific than that. There are websites devoted entirely to Sunbonnet Sue. The appliqué crowd hangs out at the website for the nonprofit Appliqué Society (www.the appliquesociety.com), while members of the Crazy Quilt Society flock to crazyquilt.com. And, art quilters can find other art quilters.

Just about every quilting technique and brand of sewing machine has a discussion group and bulletin board. Those who are enthralled with old-fashioned Singer Featherweight machines can join a group called the Featherweight Fanatics, which has members numbering in the thousands. Those who love both cats and quilts gravitate to www.CatsWhoQuilt.com, a

or position it exactly where you want." She says she just doesn't find existing quilt-design software to be as comprehensive and design oriented, especially when it comes to photos, which she uses often.

To find out more about how quilters use Corel-DRAW, go to Fallert's website, **www.bryerpatch.com**, and click on FAQ followed by computers and Quilting. Fallert has a lesson there on how to use the PowerClip feature.

Also, go to Webster's website, **www.starforestquilts.com**, to see the amazing quilts she has produced using this software (you can also purchase it here). Webster has written a handbook for quilters on how to use CorelDRAW, which includes step-by-step tutorials and a CD with photographs that correspond to the lessons. Corel's website is **www.corel.com**.

Early Days: Internet Quilting Pioneers

Although Sue Traudt, a Connecticut-based computer professor and software designer, started quilting as a child in the 1960s, she didn't combine her interests in quilting and computers until the early 1990s. At that time, she remembers, America Online was actively recruiting interest groups to start forums for the then fledgling service. Nonetheless, repeated requests to start a quilting forum on AOL met with repeated rejections.

Color Fields I, *by Gloria Hansen.*

"At the time, I had gotten heavily back into quilting," recalls Traudt. "I met some other quilters online, but we just simply could not get AOL to let us have a forum. Eventually, more than twenty of us decided to actually make a quilt for America Online, to literally bribe them. We each made a square that expressed something about ourselves: Mine was images of fish because my name is pronounced trout. And you know, it worked! We heard back right away, and within six months of the quilt's arrival, there was a quilt forum at AOL. For years, that quilt was hanging in the corporate headquarters."

About a year later, in 1994, Traudt's husband, a database manager and software designer, decided he wanted to try to create a website and asked Sue to choose the topic. "I was both a knitter and a quilter, but I decided there was more to talk about with quilting and so that would make a more interesting website," says Traudt. "I had done some foundation piecing patterns and my husband just grabbed them and stuck them up on the site. In those days, you didn't really need to register a domain name, you just staked one out by using it, so we grabbed **www.quilt.com**. It was that simple, and that crazy."

In May of 1994, Traudt started adding all sorts of informational pages, while juggling her duties at work and at home—she's also the mother of four sons. She called the new enterprise the World Wide Quilting Page and ran it initially from an old Macintosh computer in her home.

"I decided one way to build traffic was to ask quilting teachers if they would like a free web page, so I attracted people like Ami Simms, Carol Doak, and Mary Stori," says Traudt (for more about Simms, Doak, and Stori, see pages 366, 379, and 390, respectively). "We got picked by this guy who ran a Cool Site of the Day website, and computer magazines started mentioning us. I just kept writing more and more pages of instructions and posting them on the site, things like instructions for rotary cutting and foundation piecing and how to choose a sewing machine. If someone wanted to know how to do something or needed a pattern, it was here, and free. I started doing guild listings and store listings and a bulletin board, where people could post questions and get answers."

Kudos from the quilt world rolled in and keep on coming. In their 1999 resource guide *Free Stuff for Quilters on the Internet,* authors Judy Heim and Gloria Hansen wrote, "Sue's was the first quilt page on the web, and it continues to be the best." Although Traudt makes some money through Google ads, the site is far heavier in content than commercials.

More and more quilters are discovering the site, and Traudt keeps adding material, although at a slower pace. "We have more than three thousand active pages, about one thousand of them picked up by Google, and we attract more than five thousand people a day to our site," she marvels. "It's a lot of work to keep the site up, but I have strong feelings about the way it should be done. My philosophy has always been to keep everything as simple as possible, so as many people as possible can use it, no matter what sort of computer they have. I just can't see myself selling it. It's like one of my children," says Traudt.

Computer geeks were skeptical about quilters. Before collaborating with Hansen, Judy Heim published a successful book in 1995 called *The Needlecrafter's Computer Companion: Hundreds of Easy Ways to Use Your Computer for Sewing, Quilting, Cross-Stitch, Knitting, & More!* But despite the book's popularity, Heim couldn't get computer magazines to write about it. She says the caustic response from New York–based editors was "Quilting? I suppose that happens in the Midwest."

This anecdote was recounted in the introduction to a 1997 book that Heim cowrote with Gloria Hansen called *The Quilter's Computer Companion.* As the coauthors put it, "If quilters are misunderstood, their use of computers is even more so. What possible use can an appliance that was born of the need to chart the distance between the earth and the moon have for people who spend their time sewing centuries-old pineapple designs onto fabric?"

The two go on to answer their question in the introduction of that book (now out of print): "The fact is there are some pretty amazing things that you as a quilter can do with a home computer, and you don't need the latest $4,000 Beyond-Pentium to do it. You can design quilt blocks, templates, appliqué patterns, and stencils. You can print photos on muslin, organize your fabric stash, and prowl the Internet for art to use in your quilt designs. You can exchange e-mails with other quilters around the globe. Heck, you can put your quilts on display in cyberspace for everyone to see."

These days, Heim and Hansen don't have to convince anybody that computers and quilting go together. *Free Stuff for Quilters on the Internet* went through multiple editions and sold many thousands of copies. Hansen's subsequent book, *Free Stuff for Traveling Quilters on the Internet* went through three editions. All the titles in the Free Stuff series are now out of print, Hansen says.

Hansen now designs websites for quilters all over the world and uses her own computer extensively to design quilts, print her own designs on fabric, and display her finished quilts at her website, **www.GloriaHansen.com.** "Foremost for me, the computer is a tool. It allows me to get done what I visualize in my mind in more efficient ways," she says. "I use the program Photoshop to design my quilts. I use pigmented ink in my home printer and dye my designs on fabric and it's gorgeous stuff. I just marvel at how much better all the tools are now."

whimsical website that includes everything from free quilt patterns featuring cats to safety tips for kitties in the sewing room.

In an era when quilters make up a small minority of the overall population, the virtual quilt world provides a comforting reminder that peers are plentiful. With the click of a mouse, quilters can pass through a portal to a parallel universe where everyone knows what a fat quarter is, and nobody wonders if a Bernina is an exotic cocktail served in trendy urban bars. All of this creates an amazing sense of community.

A selection of printed mud cloth fabrics from Culturedexpressions.com.

"When I started to quilt in the 1970s, the quilt renaissance was just beginning," recalls Judy Smith, who started Quiltart, an e-mail list for art quilters, in 1995. "In the seventies, you never knew about quilt shows taking place anywhere, except locally. You couldn't find out what sewing machine to buy or what the hot new fabric was. The Internet has opened up a whole new world of quilting and gotten people to try new things and grow and learn."

Sharing information has proved invaluable to quilters wherever they live and advanced their quilting in all sorts of ways, but Internet shopping has been another prime attraction. The growth in quilt-related e-commerce just keeps on booming. Whereas a good-size quilt shop might carry about two thousand bolts of fabric at any given time, on the Internet, quilters can multiply their choices exponentially by surfing through the stock of hundreds of out-of-town shops plus hundreds more e-tailers. They may expect to find an excellent selection of, say, imported African fabrics the next time they travel to a large quilt show, but meanwhile, if they want to purchase handwoven mud cloth from Mali, hand-embroidered Kuba cloth (made of woven raffia) from Central Africa, or batiks from Ghana, they can go online anytime and buy it (for more about buying fabric online, see pages 271–77).

A COMMUNITY OF QUILTERS ONLINE

While the computer has had many advantages for quilters, creating a sense of community is perhaps its most valuable asset. Judy Smith is another Internet pioneer who was poking around looking for other quilters online in the early 1990s and fondly remembers quilt groups on both the Prodigy and GEnie online services. Smith recalls that some of the quilters she bonded with online started an annual tradition of meeting each year at a quilt show in Lancaster, Pennsylvania.

Various of these online groups folded over time but Smith, who lives in Washington, D.C. and works for *The Washington Post*'s obituary department, kept looking for new online companions. She actually got kicked off one quilt list, she confesses, because she thought the rules were too strict and she complained. In response, Smith decided to start her own online group and in 1995 launched the Quiltart list. "It was hard in the beginning," she says. "It was free, but messages could take two weeks to show up. Eventually I found someone with the expertise to manage the list, and now messages flow quickly. I kept it free, because that was important to me, and the only two rules are: No talking about politics or religion."

"Quiltarters" consider their membership a badge of honor—a part of their identity that is not merely virtual.

Smith's vision for the list was eagerly embraced by many like-minded art quilters who wanted a place to meet in cyberspace where they could speak their minds. Over the years, the Quiltart membership has swelled to well in excess of two thousand members. More impressive than the size of Quiltart's membership, however, is the group's high profile within the quilt world.

The list has attracted many quilt celebrities, including award-winning art quilter Caryl Bryer Fallert (see page 327) and Karey Bresenhan, the powerful woman who runs the Houston International Quilt Festival (see page 62). Many of those who post regularly are not only smart and experienced but also feisty and funny, like award-winning quilter and teacher Robbi Joy Eklow. Eklow writes a popular column in *Quilting Arts Magazine* called "Goddess of the Last Minute," and her irreverent tone and generosity in sharing technical information are typical of what makes this list so lively. Computer guru and art quilter Gloria Hansen also posts frequently on the Quiltart list, so when members need advice on how to print fabric in their computers or what software to use for quilt design, they can get advice from a top expert.

Such luminaries attract many up-and-coming teachers, as well as novices and traditional quilters who are eager to expand their horizons. Some of the people who join mostly "lurk," too intimidated to post their own queries and comments, but they still glean invaluable advice and information.

Discussions on the Quiltart list are wide-ranging. Some are quite technical, about how to use specific fabrics, dyes, and embellishments. Members will ask advice before buying a new sewing machine and share their views of a current quilt book or show. From time to time, there are heated philosophical discussions of what makes an art quilt "art," but many of the postings concern such practical daily issues as how to create professional-looking photos, so masterpiece quilts have their best chance of getting accepted into upcoming shows.

"Quiltarters" consider their membership a badge of honor—a part of their identity that is not merely virtual. One way in which that sense of community has leaped off the screen has been the many quilt challenges proposed by list members that are open to everyone on Quiltart. Anyone can suggest a topic for a challenge, as long as she or he is willing to manage it personally; this includes setting design parameters and deadlines and collecting digital photos of all entries to display online. Entries to some of the previous challenges can be viewed by going to the Quiltart site. (For more information about quilt challenges, see page 256–57.)

Quilters who want to join the list simply go to Quiltart.com and sign up, indicating whether they want to receive members' e-mail messages at the time they are posted or in several batches, or digests, per day. Until they unsubscribe or unless they suspend message delivery while on vacation, every message sent to the list will be forwarded to all members. No one has to prove she or he is acknowledged as a quilt artist, and members are free to read the views expressed without posting their own.

When Judy Smith was looking for ways to celebrate the tenth anniversary of Quiltart in 2005, she asked

THE TIARA PARADE

Quiltart members have initiated an appropriately offbeat annual event that takes place during the International Quilt Festival in Houston each fall. The "Tiara Parade" consists of Quiltart members who make their way through the convention center on Saturday, many wearing homemade tiaras, the more outlandish the better, and blowing kazoos. They trek to the office of the show's president, Karey Bresenhan, where the tiaras are viewed and judged. Those who get the most votes receive rhinestone tiara pins bestowed with some ceremony. The noisy bunch then marches to a Chinese restaurant around the corner from the convention center.

Although initially an ad hoc event created by quilt teacher Robbi Joy Eklow, the Tiara Parade is a great metaphor for the Quiltart members to post messages about how the list had affected their quilting and their lives. She was astounded and gratified by the passionate responses she received.

"If not for Quiltart, I would not be making quilts," wrote Sherry Boram in one posted message. "I found the list via Google about the time my husband and I began our retirement travels. If I hadn't been inspired by Quiltart, I would be playing bridge, making counted cross-stitch doodads, or reading trashy novels. (No offense to those who like doing these things.) The knowledge and expertise graciously shared on this list give me more than I can express. I get camaraderie and creative inspiration, and I learn about techniques and tools. I've done more than a dozen Quiltart challenges. Wherever we travel in our RV, I have my sewing machine and my laptop, so I take my quilting community with me wherever I go."

Art quilter Michelle Verbeeck stays in one place, but she lives in the heart of Amish country in Pennsylvania and says Quiltart was her lifeline to a new way of quilting. "I started making traditional quilts, but I felt like I needed more," says Verbeeck. "I was searching around on the Internet and it was like making a wrong turn when you travel and finding paradise. I found the site of Maria Elkins, an art quilter, and wrote to her about how enthralled I was with her quilt *Wedding Dreams*. She told me about the Quiltart list online, and I checked it out and joined.

"At first I was overwhelmed by the information that was being thrown around on the QA list," says Verbeeck. "I just kept reading, researching, looking up products, reading books, and taking it all in. I discovered that these wonderfully talented people at Quiltart will help you through anything. The list provides not only community and the ability to connect with others who share in my joy of this art, but I get to watch their talent grow and share in their stories and techniques. I feel like we are pioneering this field of art quilting together. I find myself referring to this creative group of people in my daily life, as if I know them personally."

As time goes by, more of the Quiltart listers actually can and *do* meet in person. After posting messages to say what quilt show they will be attending, they link up with others from the Quiltart list who are going as well.

list because it is raucous, fun, and creative. Eklow confesses that it began as something of a joke, and she never expected it to become a tradition.

"People know I wear wild colors and once taught a class wearing a velvet dress and lime green gym shoes," says Eklow. "When a quilt of mine won an award at the Houston show, someone suggested I wear that outfit again, plus a tiara. I wore the tiara while walking around the show and happened to mention the fact in a message I posted on QA, which prompted someone to suggest that in future, everybody from the Quiltart list who comes to Houston should wear a tiara. We've been doing it since 2001, and it gets more elaborate every year. Dozens of people show up wearing these crazy creations. How wild is that?"

RESOURCES

Indispensable Websites for Quilters

There are thousands of websites for quilters. Most are commercial in nature, including those selling fabric and quilting tools and the ones that promote quilters and their work. Quilters who spend a lot of time on the Internet probably already have a list of bookmarked sites they love and may quibble with a few of the choices here. But for me this list represents the cream of the crop, well-established sites that have been repeatedly recommended by passionate quilters—along with some of my special favorites.

If this were a website itself, this would be the feature called Links, and you'd be able to just click on the addresses. But these websites are worth the effort it takes to type!

General-Interest Websites

Planet Patchwork

Established in 1995, this omnibus site lives up to its billing as "The Ultimate Address in Quilting." Rob Holland and his quilter wife, Lynn, have packed Planet Patchwork with basic information on tools and techniques, including an excellent section providing resources for beginning quilters. Planet Patchwork has much more than listings and links. Its interviews with top quilters, product reviews, and travel essays on quilt shops and shows are trustworthy and witty. The vast site offers just about everything, including free patterns and bulletin boards, and it sells quilting software. Many of the reviews and activity listings are part of a blog. To see these, click on News on the Planet Patchwork home page or go directly to **www.quiltchannel .com**.

www.PlanetPatchwork.com

WorldWide Quilting Page

Comprising more than three thousand pages, the WorldWide Quilting Page has been informing quilters all over since Sue Traudt got it started back in 1994. The extensive offerings include lists of quilt blocks, stores, museums, and shows. There are also bulletin boards and chat rooms, classified ads, and contests. The depth of its free how-to information on tools, techniques, and patterns is unmatched.

www.quilt.com

BlockCentral.com

Kim Noblin, a high school band director in Alabama, started this site in 1998, and it is rich in resources for quilters. Best known for an alphabetical listing of more than three thousand quilting blocks, BlockCentral.com also offers tons of free patterns and many other features, including a block swap and a place for users of Electric Quilt software to exchange their original designs. The forums are active and everything is free. Noblin operates the site as a labor of love, and the advertising is minimal.

www.BlockCentral.com

About.com Quilting

Part of the vast About.com empire, this impressive site is now hosted by longtime quilter Janet Wickell. Although not as extensive as it once was, the site is still impressive. Sign up for Wickell's free weekly newsletter and you will get multiple links to free projects and information. Each newsletter focuses on a theme like variations on Log Cabin blocks or how to make a T-shirt quilt. There are several active forums at the About.com quilting site covering a range of topics. Users of the forums also participate in a great many fabric and block swaps.

www.quilting.about.com

Study Online

Quiltmaking in America at the Library of Congress

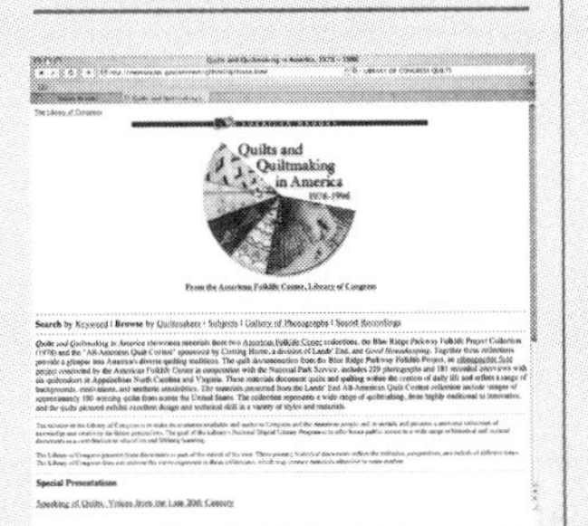

The site that documents two of the collections housed at the Library of Congress's American Folklife Center is an excellent resource for understanding the quilt revival. One collection contains more than 400 images and 181 segments of recorded interviews with quiltmakers around the Blue Ridge Parkway, an area near the Virginia and North Carolina border. These interviews were conducted between 1978 and 1981.

The center is also home to a collection of winning quilts from national contests cosponsored in the 1990s by the home decorating division of Lands' End and *Good Housekeeping* magazine. An essay by folklorist Laurel Horton explains how these quilts fit into the context of America's quilting history.

http://memory.loc.gov/ammem/qlthtml/qlthome.html

Quilt University

Take quilt classes at home, at any hour of the day or night. Quilt University offers dozens of courses taught by a faculty that includes well-known teachers. Here's a chance to study with a teacher based in Africa or England or to take a more advanced design class than those that are held at your local quilt shop. The classes provide a text, photos, and illustrations, which can be downloaded one lesson at a time. As you complete each exercise, you can ask the instructor and other students questions via an online message board. A typical class includes three or four lessons.

www.QuiltUniversity.com

Womenfolk

The Web is a great place to study the fascinating history of quilting, especially at the America's Quilting History part of the Womenfolk site, a labor of love created by retired teacher Judy Anne Johnson Breneman. It's addictive to browse through, including everything from myths about quilting to the stories behind famous patterns. You'll also find links to many other history-related sites.

www.womenfolk.com

FabricLink

Maintained by such companies as Monsanto and Amoco Fabrics and Fibers, FabricLink includes a wealth of information on textiles. Click on Fabric University to learn about the history of fabric as well as the proper care of cotton and simple tests to determine whether a fabric is pure cotton or blended with synthetics.

www.fabriclink.com

Personal Favorites

Hundreds of quilters maintain their own websites, and many of these are exemplary, useful resources. However, there are a small number of celebrated quilters whose websites transcend the medium, so to speak, offering more than just a virtual résumé with photos. This is a brief and idiosyncratic listing of some of my favorite quilter-focused sites. (Warning: Not for lovers of muted tones and pale pastels.)

Bryerpatch Studio

There are few quilt websites as lauded as this one, for obvious reasons. That's because award-winning art quilter Caryl Bryer Fallert goes way past pretty visuals on her site, offering a raft of tutorials on her techniques. This is a rich site where one can view Fallert's stunning quilts, but she is also unusually generous in sharing her expertise on such topics as machine quilting, fabric dyeing, and printing photographs on fabric using a home computer printer (click on FAQ). In addition, Fallert sells products she recommends related to those techniques and CD-ROMs of her most popular workshops.

www.BryerPatch.com

Nancy Crow

A famously demanding teacher, there is no denying Nancy Crow is one of the true pioneers of the art quilt movement. Crow's bold quilts are distinctive and her influence is extensive. Her website provides gorgeous photos of some of her signature works, as well as information on her classes and guided tours abroad.

www.NancyCrow.com

Jane A. Sassaman

Jane Sassaman is an art quilter most famous for her exquisite flower quilts. Now that she has raised her profile as a teacher and a fabric designer, Sassaman has turned her website into an unusually inspiring visual feast. You can view her award-winning quilts, read her biography, and check out her teaching schedule, but there are also free patterns using her new fabrics and photos of quilts that others have made and submitted using those fabrics. Sassaman provides a list of books and other resources that inspire her.

www.JaneSassaman.com

Kaffe Fassett Studio

Kaffe Fassett is an American-born designer living in London whose palette is electric and whose creative range is breathtaking, which explains why he was the first living textile artist to have his work exhibited at the Victoria and Albert Museum. Fassett began as a painter, then revolutionized knitting with his wild colors and patterns before learning to quilt. He also creates designs for mosaics, needlepoint, china, home furnishings, and more. This site provides a showcase of all things Fassett.

www.KaffeFassett.com

Kaffe Fassett.

Quilt Blogs

Quilters have long eagerly embraced any technology that lets them make quilts quicker, easier, or more beautiful. Now they're fast becoming converts to high-tech ways of showing off their creations. A blog, short for web log, is an online journal or newsletter, generally mixing both text and images, and is often highly personalized. Blogs are a perfect medium for quilters to share their work with family, friends, and total strangers because they're fairly simple to create and can be updated instantly. Although there are some blogs intended to disseminate news and trends in the quilt world, most blogs share the work, philosophy, tips, and musings of a single quilter, who often shows the creation of new quilt projects one step at a time.

Here I'm listing some of my favorites from the ranks of established blogs, choosing ones that are especially good examples of the medium. Be advised that many blogs start up and fade away quickly. There's no guarantee that all of these bloggers will still be active as you read this, but there will be plenty more worth checking out. One way to do this is to go to ***www.google.com*** *and type in the words* quilt blogs; *you're sure to find quite a few. I predict that a wealth of quilters will enter the blogosphere in the years to come, making it a more beautiful and inspiring place to visit for all of us.*

Liz Berg

Liz Berg is one of the pioneering quilt bloggers; her capsule description of what she blogs about is "the musings, trials, and tribulations of an art quilter on the long haul journey." Berg is especially generous about showing how she creates her stunning art quilts.

www.lizcreates.blogspot.com

Gina Halladay

A quilter and quilt designer, Gina Halladay also runs a longarm quilting business in California. Her entertaining blog is less like a personal journal than a trade journal. Halladay spotlights trends, products, and personalities in the quilt world. If you can't make it to the big quilt show in Houston, for example, check in at Halladay's QuiltersBuzz to see the hot new fabrics.

www.quiltersbuzz.com

Kyra Hicks

This is a broad, newsy blog rather than a personal one. Kyra Hicks is the author of an important book on African American quilting, *Black Threads: An African American Quilting Sourcebook*, and her own quilts have been widely exhibited. She has turned her blog, Black Threads, into a vital bulletin board on black quilters and quilt news where you can find information about upcoming exhibitions, books retreats, and other news—not to mention the occasional recipe.

www.blackthreads.blogspot.com

Sabrina Zarco

A Mexican American quilter living in Little Rock, Arkansas, Sabrina Zarco makes quilts that draw on her Chicana heritage. Although her quilts have appeared in a number of exhibits and publications, like many art quilters Zarco has to work a day job to make a living. She explained to me that "with limited resources, blogging is one way for me to get my images out."

www.sabrinazart.blogspot.com

E-MAIL LISTS FOR QUILTERS

Here are some of the best places to look for e-mail lists. The basic formula is that you sign up online and receive every e-mail message sent by anyone in that group.

◆ For a wide-ranging catalog of e-mail groups go to **www.quilt.com /MailingListPage.html.**

◆ Search under quilts at **http://groups.yahoo.com** for a group that matches your interests. Some Yahoo! groups are private, but most are open to all.

◆ For art quilters and would-be art quilters, try **www.quiltart.com.**

◆ For quilt history enthusiasts, there's **www.quilthistory.com**—click on Join QHL.

◆ Those in quilt-related businesses, including shop owners and quilters who sell patterns, will find **www.planetpatchwork. com/quiltbiz.htm** helpful. You need to send an e-mail to the list managers and describe your business, but membership is free.

A VAST PATCHWORK OF WEBSITES

If you type the word *quilts* into Google, it will instantly find upward of ten million listings. Many of the sites that turn up will be commercial in nature. In most cases, quilting is not a business with huge profit margins even for the most successful entrepreneurs in the quilt world, so television or radio advertising is out of the question. Print advertising in quilting publications is reserved mostly for major companies selling fabric or big-ticket items like sewing machines. But websites provide a way for small companies to reach more quilters. Just as important, the Internet is a visual medium, and quilt suppliers exploit this fully to make their case.

But, not only do a vast number of brick-and-mortar quilt shops operate companion websites that keep their customers informed about upcoming classes and sales, a growing number of guilds and individual quilters have their own websites, too. The explosion of quilt listings underscores the entrepreneurial impulse in the quilt world, and the Internet has been a major factor in making that boom possible. Quilt teachers post their résumés, brag about their awards, and list upcoming classes. Quilters hoping to raise their profiles enough to make a living selling their work can create a showcase for themselves, whether or not their quilts have been accepted into galleries. Those quilters who earn money finishing the quilts of others use cyberspace as a place to hang their virtual shingles.

Beyond all the commercialism exists a fascinating and ever-changing collection of quilting websites that run on pure enthusiasm and can only be described as labors of love. It is these sites, above all, that help keep the virtual quilt world humming, that keep quilters coming back to the net to be inspired and connected. These are websites like the one started by retired home economics teacher Judy Anne Johnson Breneman, which covers the history of quilting in America with distinction and some depth.

"I had started quilting in the nineties and was looking for historical information on the Internet, and I was just amazed how little there was at the time," recalls Breneman. "I began reading books, doing

How to Join an E-Mail Quilt List

While an online forum is like a public square, a place you travel to that is open to whomever comes along, an e-mail list delivers more narrowly focused content directly to you. Sometimes you must join as a member, and there may be a fee. Every message posted by a member of the list is sent to the e-mailboxes of all the other members. You don't have to surf a website to find out what people are thinking and saying.

The groups are usually centered around a type of quilting, such as art quilting, or a particular tool, such as longarm sewing machines or quilting software. There are user groups for most manufacturers of sewing machines, sometimes for specific models. There is also a very active e-mail group for quilt historians, both amateur and professional.

You can track down groups by using a search engine, such as **www.google.com**, and typing in your area of interest plus keywords like *online group* or *e-mail list*. Another good place to look is at **http//groups.yahoo.com**; Yahoo! has tons of registered groups. If you type *quilting* in the search box, you'll find hundreds of quilt-related groups covering every imaginable aspect of the craft. There are Yahoo! groups for beginning quilters and some that exist only to swap fabrics. You can click on the ones that interest you for details. If membership is required this usually just means filling out a form online.

Most groups are free, but some like the Quilt History group have a suggested donation to defray expenses. A handful charge an annual subscription fee, like the Featherweight Fanatics group, but the fee is modest. In rare cases, you have to provide some sort of credentials to join a list, as with the QuiltBiz group, reserved for people who are involved in quilting as a business in one way or another. Many quilt designers and independent shop owners swap advice on this list.

E-mail groups are generally friendly and welcoming to newcomers, but it may be smart to spend a few days soaking up the atmosphere and gathering information before firing off posts. Some terms and acronyms may be unfamiliar at first (for example, LQS stands for local quilt shop, as in "I always try to give most of my business to my LQS").

Those who host these sites and their longtime users will expect that some in the group aren't there because they already own the particular software or sewing machine under discussion, but because they're trying to decide whether it suits their needs. Members of these groups will patiently reply to basic queries from newbies, within limits.

Some groups are more serious than others about staying on topic: Members of the Quiltart list are careful to preface off-topic comments with the notation NQR for nonquilt related, and if the ratio of NQR posts gets too high, someone will inevitably chide the group.

A major strength of e-mail groups is that they tend to be focused and efficient. A negative for some of them is that the flow of e-mails can become overwhelming, but you can always choose to unsubscribe temporarily—or permanently.

FREE QUILT PATTERNS ON THE INTERNET

The Internet is one of the best sources of free patterns and quilting directions, but many of the web resources are inconsistent in quality or provide only a few designs. The major fabric companies will usually have some good free patterns, as will the websites for quilt magazines, so be sure to go there. And, the five websites below have been around for a good while and provide a rich range of diverse patterns and how-tos.

About.com's quilting page
www.quilting.about.com

FreeQuilt.com
www.freequilt.com

The Quilter's Cache
www.quilterscache.com

Scrapquilts.com
www.scrapquilts.com

World Wide Quilting Page
www.quilt.com

research, going to the few sites I could find, and then joining a group of historians in the American Quilt Study Group. Then I took the plunge and started www.womenfolk.com in 1998.

"I began by writing articles on things and posting them with lots of links to more scholarly and detailed articles," says Breneman. "Unlike academics, I try to write in an introductory way for someone who is casually interested. Then, if someone wants to go deeper, she can follow the links I've embedded in the site. What is great about a website as opposed to a book is that as my knowledge gets more sophisticated, I can easily update, adding information, things about Amish quilts, or whatever the topic may be."

Breneman recalls that some of the biggest hurdles were technological: She had to teach herself how to write code in order to set up the site. "I learned HTML on my own by looking at other people's code, and it was like learning another language. The visual appeal and graphic design aspect is also part of the attraction for me. On the technical end of things, making web pages is a lot like making a quilt—except it's easier to fix your mistakes. You can just delete instead of having to rip out stitches."

Selling ads to quilt businesses and Amazon.com covers her expenses and pays for her travel to quilt history seminars, but Breneman hasn't really made money from the site and says that's fine with her. "I get about a thousand visitors a day, and the site attracts a lot of students and teachers," she says. "Thanks to the Internet, I feel like the quilt history scene is blossoming, and I love being a part of it."

The high-tech world is thought of as "hard," while the quilt world is undeniably "soft," and the place where the two come together creates curious and practical partnerships. Computers use "cold" numbers to create exact codes that allow a single image or text to be transmitted identically to millions, while quilts are personal one-of-a-kind objects. The Internet allows millions of people to simultaneously appreciate a unique quilt without being in the same room. Turning blocks and stitches into pixels allows quilts to be shown off on a wider stage, with some surprising results.

Linda Taylor on the set of Linda's Longarm Quilting *television show.*

QUILT TV MOVES ONLINE

Quilters have been learning their craft by watching television practically since the quilt renaissance began, and such popular teachers as Eleanor Burns continue producing new seasons of television shows. But the latest trend has been the migration of quilt television to the Internet.

It began in April 2005, with the launch of Quilter's News Network, now called QNNtv. At this site, quilters can watch quilt programming twenty-four hours a day, seven days a week, in the form of what is sometimes called streaming video. Most of the shows are how-to programs currently airing on television, including some of the most established quilt TV shows. Among these are Eleanor Burns' *Quilt in a Day* show, Linda Taylor's program on longarm quilting, and the *Love of Quilting* show hosted by Marianne Fons and Liz Porter. This programming is interspersed with material produced by QNNtv, with titles like *Quilter's Coffee* and a regular block of the month segment.

Then celebrity quilter Ricky Tims, who has a history of innovation and ambition (you'll find his profile on page 369), announced a radical new concept that he would inaugurate in 2007: a forty-five-minute show produced directly for computer viewing but that would be taped in front of a live audience. *The Quilt Show* pairs Tims with cohost Alex Anderson, a celebrity of equal or greater stature (see page 307), whose long-running show *Simply Quilts* was cancelled by HGTV in 2006. Tims snapped her up as soon as her noncompete clause ran out.

Eleanor Burns hosts Quilt in a Day.

Ricky Tims, an online host of The Quilt Show.

Making the concept even more radical, Tims and Anderson announced that people would have to pay to see their show. People either pay an upfront fee to view a complete season of thirteen shows, or they can buy a DVD of the entire season later on. Either way, Tims and Anderson are asking quilters to pay for something they habitually received for free. There was definitely grumbling on various quilt message boards, but thousands of quilters paid for memberships long before the first show aired in April 2007.

Tims has plans ultimately to build an audience for *The Quilt Show* that will number in the millions; eventually the features on the website will be translated into Japanese, Spanish, and other languages. He believes that the growing fusion of video and computers is a perfect mix for quilters and he plans to invite his audience into the picture as well. "We would love to have members submit video content to the site," says Tims. "It would be like YouTube for quilters."

Both *The Quilt Show* and QNNtv employ some of the community-building aspects of the Internet. QNNtv watchers can download free patterns, sign up for quilt challenges, and read tips. *The Quilt Show* includes such online features as chat rooms, a blog, and a listing of quilt shops and classes, plus users can create a profile page that includes photos of some of their quilts.

Watch the Web Shows

Quilt Web Shows

QNNtv

You can watch quilt television programs 24-7 on QNNtv (formerly the Quilters News Network), including those featuring many of the nation's top quilting talents and teachers. Members can search through more than one thousand hours of quilting television shows and download patterns, but even browsers who pay nothing will find useful content.

www.qnntv.com

The Quilt Show

While there is a subscription fee to view entire episodes of *The Quilt Show*, some segments are broadcast online without charge. Plus there are many free features, such as blogs and forums.

www.thequiltshow.com

Quilt Podcasts

Podcasts are like radio programs that play on your computer or MP3 player. The content is free.

If you haven't got a high-speed Internet connection, you may have trouble downloading podcasts. Otherwise, it's pretty simple: Just download the file and play it on your computer's music player, such as iTunes or Winamp.

Here are four pioneers in podcasting for quilters, with very different approaches.

Alex Anderson, *host of Alex Anderson's Quilt Connection*

Alex Anderson is one of the most polished podcasters online. Her *Quilt Connection* podcasts include interviews with some of the top players in the quilt world. Anderson already has a wide following, but the podcasts are a special treat because they showcase her relaxed, wisecracking side, along with her deep knowledge of quilting. In most cases, the podcasts are supplemented by photographs posted on her website. For more about Alex Anderson, see page 307.

www.alexandersonquilts.com

Bonnie Lyn McCaffery, *Quilt Artist*

Bonnie Lyn McCaffery describes her series of podcasts as "life lessons of a traveling quilt artist." These tend to be brief and often philosophical. McCaffery has also begun offering free "VidCasts" on her website, which include demonstrations of the techniques that McCaffery uses in her own work.

www.bonniemccaffery.com

Annie Smith, *host of Quilting Stash*

A quilt designer and teacher who lives in California, Annie Smith produces her chatty but substantive *Quilting Stash* shows about once a week. Smith talks about her own inspiration, interviews top quilters, and takes her microphone to quilt shows, shops, and guild meetings.

www.simplearts.com

International Quilt Study Center at the University of Nebraska–Lincoln

The International Quilt Study Center has one of the premier collections of historical quilts and is an excellent resource. The center hosts many lectures by top historians and quilt experts, and a number of those talks can now be downloaded in podcast form. There is a notable lecture by folklorist Laurel Horton, "The Underground Railroad Quilt Controversy: Looking for the Truth."

www.quiltstudy.org/education/public_programs.html

Seeing Quilts Online

Nothing beats seeing quilts in person, being able to walk up close to see the texture and check nuances of embellishment and stitching. That's why big shows that attract masterpiece quilts are so popular. But the fact is, travel is wearing, and it's hard to find time and money to attend all the major quilt shows.

When it comes to seeing antique quilts, there are additional complications. Although there are a growing number of quilt museums, they are geographically scattered. And, many of the greatest historical quilts are in the collections of major museums with enormous holdings in other areas, so they are rarely on view. For example, thanks to recent acquisitions, the Art Institute of Chicago now boasts one of the premier quilt collections in the country, but its masterpieces are rarely seen by the public. The Baltimore Museum of Art owns an extensive collection of historic Baltimore album quilts, but again, those beauties aren't often displayed. The Metropolitan Museum of Art last put on a quilt show (featuring Amish quilts) in 2004, but chances to see the full collection of the Met's historic quilts are few.

Because of these limitations, having the opportunity to see many quilts online is extremely valuable, even if it's the second-choice viewing option. Luckily, technological improvements in computers, plus a heightened awareness of quilts' historical and artistic importance, have made it possible to see more great quilts online than ever before. And the near future will include a vast increase in quilts online.

The exterior of the Art Institute of Chicago.

The single best site for viewing lots of important quilts, both old and new, is the website for the nonprofit Alliance for American Quilts. This group's mission is to share the historical and personal stories of quilts and quilters and spread knowledge about this vital craft and art.

One of the alliance's founders was quilt appraiser and collector Shelly Zegart of Louisville, Kentucky, much of whose personal collection is now owned by the Art Institute of Chicago. Zegart was active in the first statewide project to document historic quilts, the Kentucky Quilt Project. It began in 1981, and over the course of two years there were a dozen "quilt days" during which Kentucky residents could bring quilts from their attics, closets, and beds and have them photographed and their histories recorded.

Similar projects were launched in Illinois, Tennessee, and Michigan, revealing a wealth of information about long-forgotten quilts. Many were worn, everyday bedcovers, while others were masterpieces that had been labored over diligently for years. They all came flying out of the cupboards.

From early on, the alliance vowed to work closely with universities, and one of the benefits of this was access to cutting-edge computer technology. Hundreds of historic quilts from the four state-documentation projects were scanned and their images and information were saved within the alliance's online Quilt Index, run in partnership with Michigan State University. Later, museum collections were added, along with more state-documentation projects, like that of North Carolina, bringing the total number of documented quilts into the thousands. Not just for scholars, any member of the public can browse through this still growing collection of old quilts simply by going to **www.quiltindex.org.**

The alliance also wanted to play a role in recording the unfolding history of the quilt renaissance in America and so began to conduct interviews with some of the top quilters and quilt teachers in the country. Their stories were collected, along with fascinating stories about ordinary grassroots quilters. Hundreds of these interviews have been posted in text form on the site along with photographs of signature quilts made by the interviewees (go to the Quilters' S.O.S.—Save Our Stories feature at the alliance website, **www.centerforthequilt.org**). In addition, the alliance and Michigan State historians began making and posting mini documentaries about the early pioneers of the quilt renaissance; you'll find these in the Quilt Treasures section of the alliance site.

The University of Nebraska–Lincoln's International Quilt Study Center (IQSC) has a vast and noteworthy collection of quilts. Founded in 1997, the center has been a key player in the increasingly scholarly attention paid to quilts, and the university hosts many seminars, graduate programs, and summer institutes. But only so many quilters can make a pilgrimage to Nebraska, and even for those who do, the vast bulk of the university's holdings will be in storage at any given time. Anyone interested in quilts can view the hundreds of them in the Nebraska collection by going to the website **www.quiltstudy.org** and browsing at will. All of the quilts in the collection have been photographed, and by clicking

An untitled crazy quilt, 1978, by Zenna Todd, from the collection of the Library of Congress.

for more information browsers can learn the history of each quilt along with such details as how it was made and how many stitches per inch the maker averaged in its construction.

An architectural model for the proposed home of the International Quilt Study Center.

The IQSC collection includes about two thousand quilts, both cutting-edge modern ones and antique quilts, from the collection of Ardis and Robert James. There is also a noteworthy collection of Amish quilts and of African American quilts. And in 2003, the university quilt center received one of the world's great quilt collections, that of Jonathan Holstein, which includes the sixty quilts exhibited in a groundbreaking 1971 show at New York's Whitney Museum of American Art. That show, called Abstract Design in American Quilts, was instrumental in getting scholars, artists, critics, and the general public to reconsider the artistic merit of this old-fashioned domestic craft.

In addition, of course, there are the thousands of websites maintained by contemporary quilters. As the photo-tech revolution puts a digital camera in nearly every household, more and more quilters are learning how to photograph their quilts and mount displays of them in cyberspace. Art quilters are especially likely to have their own websites and to use them to enhance their reputations and attract students and buyers of their quilts.

So, e-mail lists like the Quiltart group feature many messages posted by group members inviting the couple thousand people on the list to visit a new site or come see the latest work posted on an existing site.

Sometimes quilters want to scope out quilts on the Internet for ideas and inspiration, and sometimes they're looking for quilts to buy. For those who have that dual agenda, another good place to see quilts is eBay. At any given time, there are hundreds of quilts for sale at this popular website, running the gamut from Civil War–era quilts to contemporary ones. Even if you don't collect quilts, looking at those on eBay is like taking a glimpse into the nation's attics: These are the quilts people inherited from their grandmothers, as well as the ones antiques dealers are peddling. Looking at the bids can provide some clues as to what is considered valuable among quilt collectors.

Liza Prior Lucy, quilt teacher and coauthor of pattern books with Kaffe Fassett, says she is a frequent browser of the eBay quilt section, but she offers some caveats about the goods there. "Many of the quilts listed are *not* antique but brand-new, despite the claims, and many are junk. People need to read the descriptions very carefully. That said, I still think eBay is the best place on the web to see wonderful quilts for sale."

RESOURCES

Best Places to See Quilts Online

*When it comes to contemporary quilts, there are many wonderful options, including excellent websites maintained by contemporary quilters to showcase their own work. You'll find a listing of some of the best art quilters' sites on page 186. In addition, such major quilt shows as the International Quilt Festival in Houston (**www.quilts.com**) display the winning quilts from their contests online each year. And you can read interviews with more than six hundred contemporary quiltmakers and see some of their work at the Quilters' S.O.S.–Save Our Stories project of The Alliance for American Quilts (**www.centerforthequilt.org**).*

Sadly, many of the best museum quilt collections are not available online. If the public's interest in quilts and quilt history continues to grow, that may change in coming years. For now, the four best websites for looking at old and historic quilts are the ones listed here. As additional important older quilts are scanned and displayed online, these four sites will be good portals for finding out about the new postings.

The Quilt Index

A groundbreaking database, The Quilt Index allows you to search for images and information about thousands of old quilts. Documentation projects in four states provided the initial images, but many more collections, including those of museums, have been added recently. You can search by pattern, period, and the name of the quilter, among other choices. The Quilt Index is operated by a partnership of The Alliance for American Quilts (for more, see page 27), Michigan State University's MATRIX: Center for Humane Arts, Letters, and Social Sciences Online, and the Michigan State University Museum.

www.quiltindex.org

International Quilt Study Center

The International Quilt Study Center at the University of Nebraska–Lincoln was begun in 1997 and provides a wealth of information. The center has a collection of more than two thousand historic quilts, and its excellent site allows you to search through them by period, pattern, and so forth by clicking on Search Collections on the home page. I find the easiest way to do this is through the "advanced search" function, which lists hundreds of traditional quilt blocks.

www.quiltstudy.org

Womenfolk

Diligent quilt-history lover Judy Anne Johnson Breneman maintains the best list of online museum quilt exhibits in cyberspace. If you go to her website you'll find links to the sites of various quilt museums and historical societies where you can view their quilts. Among the links is a site showing some of the vast collection of quilts owned by the Smithsonian Institution's National Museum of American History.

www.womenfolk.com/quilt_history_websites/lmuseum.htm

eBay

In terms of quality, what goes on sale here is a totally mixed bag. eBay is the opposite of a curated exhibit and many quilts are not as old or rare as the sellers claim (some of the sellers are simply ignorant, while others mislead on purpose). Before buying anything, research both the item and the seller. There's no charge for browsing: This site is like a free quilt exhibit that changes daily. Once you are on the home page, click on Antiques, then choose Quilts from the Textiles, Linens list.

www.ebay.com

Cutting-Edge Techniques

A LOT OF INNOVATIVE TOOLS WERE BORN OF the movement to make quilts more quickly. But some revolutionary tools and techniques are not aimed at increasing speed. Instead, these hot new techniques expand the design vocabulary, giving quilters a whole range of new looks.

Barbara Webster's intricate photo-based November Goldenrod.

An exciting chunk of the tech boom that has changed quilting and kept it vital has to do with techniques for manipulating the fabric itself. These days, most quilters buy commercial fabric at quilt shops and shows and make it into quilts using someone else's designs or buy a complete kit with the fabric precut. But more and more quilters are becoming adventurous, creating their own patterns and looking for ways to take store-bought fabric and personalize it.

Gone are the days when quilts were judged mostly on neatness—how many stitches per inch and whether the seams all lie flat. Originality is now highly prized—literally. To win top awards, quilters have to be creative. And the increase in the speed of quilting also encourages creativity. Now quilters can make quilts so much faster that they can take the risk of making mistakes. If you can sew a quilt in a weekend instead of a year, you don't have to be nearly as conservative in your colors, techniques, or designs. You can be more playful and reach further out of your comfort zone; after all, if the quilt doesn't quite satisfy you, you can always sew another one.

Two of the techniques that have blossomed are printing photographic images onto fabrics for quilts and making quilts from fabric dyed by the quilter.

Adventurous art quilters led the way in both areas, creating stunning effects that caught the eye of casual quilters at shows and in magazines and books. Over time, the methods for both techniques have been simplified and the tools improved, making them accessible to still more quilters.

PHOTOS ON FABRIC

Transferring photographic images to fabric is something that has been doable for quite some time. One of the earliest processes was cyanotype—the making of blueprints. According to Barbara Hewitt's 1995 book *Blueprints on Fabric: Innovative Uses for Cyanotype* (now out of print), the process was invented by a British astronomer in 1842. And commercial machines that could make blueprints became available in the nineteenth century as well.

Textile artists have been fiddling with the process virtually ever since, and the method is still fairly simple. The chemicals ferric ammonium citrate and potassium ferricyanide are applied to fabric, then the fabric is allowed to dry. Objects are placed on the surface of the fabric, which is then exposed to sunlight. The object, whether a photographic negative, a dried flower, a toy, or whatever you want, blocks some of the light and leaves an image imprinted on the fabric. After the fabric is rinsed, the chemicals come off but the image remains.

Beautiful effects can be created in this way, but not everyone who sews at home wants to work with messy chemicals, wearing rubber gloves and a protective mask. So art-supply companies began selling fabric (and paper, too) pretreated with the necessary chemicals. Quilters can buy this fabric, mostly on the Internet, in squares and by the yard, and immediately experiment with all sorts of unusual visual effects.

Still, printing blueprinted images hasn't caught on with quilters the way that the direct transfer of photographs has, partly because the technological developments in digital photography and home computer printers have been so widely publicized and become so instantly popular. Printing one's own photos is becoming as common as downloading music, something that people simply take for granted. It was inevitable that

CYANOTYPE RESOURCES

Blue Prints on Fabric carries both pretreated fabric and, for do-it-yourselfers, the chemicals needed to sensitize fabric for the cyanotype process. At the website, **www.blueprintsonfabric.com**, you will find detailed instructions for making cyanotypes, along with a wide range of pretreated products, including cotton and silk fabric and even cotton T-shirts. You can also order these by phone at (800) 631-3369.

The business was founded by Barbara Hewitt, author of the book *Blueprints on Fabric: Innovative Uses for Cyanotype*, and when Hewitt retired, it was taken over by Linda Stemer, whose new book *Blueprints on Fabric: The Magic of Cyanotype* includes historical background, lots of instructions, and a gallery of quilts made using the technique.

Pros and Cons of Photo Printing

Photo quilts are one of the hottest trends in quilting today and are one of the techniques most appealing to beginners. But when you set off to the local quilt shop or surf the major quilt e-tailers, you may be shocked at all the choices that confront you. Here are the basic options (on pages 210–11 you'll find a list of the supplies you'll need for each of the methods). You may want to experiment with several varieties of the methods to see which gives you the most satisfying results.

Photo Transfers

Anything labeled photo-transfer sheets will be for a *paper,* not fabric, transfer. Once a photograph is printed on that paper, that image will have to be transferred onto fabric, generally by ironing. Some photo-transfer papers can be printed using a computer printer at home (either ink-jet or laser, depending on the paper), but others require a transfer process using the kind of big, sophisticated color laser copiers found only at commercial copy shops, like Kinko's and OfficeMax. Check the package carefully to see whether the transfer sheets can be printed at home or must be taken to a copy shop.

A floral photo quilt.

Photo transfer pros

- The price of transfer paper is generally less than the cost of the specially treated fabric that is used for directly printing photos at home.
- If the transfer is done by a copy shop, some people say the photo quality is better.

Photo transfer cons

◆ The photo transfer can leave the fabric somewhat stiff.

◆ It can be less convenient if you can't do all the steps at home.

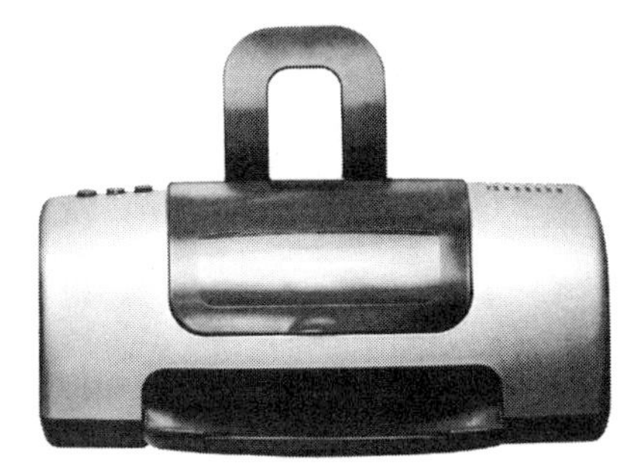

The basic tool of photo transfer: a home printer.

Printing Photos Directly on Fabric

Quilters love the option of printing right on fabric because they can do it themselves at home, using their own computer printers. Pretty much any brand of computer printer will work, but it *must* be a color ink-jet printer, not a laser printer. Any photo or image that can be scanned or downloaded into your computer can be printed on fabric using this technique. You may want to experiment with fabrics, but the experts recommend natural fibers like cotton or silk.

You can't just stick a sheet of fabric into your Epson or HP and press Print because fabric is too floppy. The fabric must be stuck to a sheet of paper to stiffen it. To secure the dyes and make the photo waterproof, you must use fabric that has been treated with a chemical solution.

But there is still a choice to make: Do you use pretreated fabric sheets with a peel-off paper backing? Or will you prepare your own fabric sheets?

Store-bought pretreated fabric sheet pros

◆ Instant gratification—when you're ready, you just open the pack and start printing the photos on fabric.

◆ The dyes may be somewhat brighter and last longer than if you treat the fabric yourself because the chemicals must be somewhat diluted for home use.

◆ The fabric photos will be soft and supple. Although the fabric photos will be a trifle harder to sew through than regular fabric, they won't have the residue of glazed dye left by the paper photo-transfer method. (The fabric will be equally soft whether you use pretreated sheets or treat your own.)

Store-bought pretreated fabric sheet cons

◆ Store-bought fabric sheets are considerably more expensive than fabric you prepare yourself. The cost will be comparable to or higher than the total cost of a paper photo transfer, where you have to pay for the transfer paper plus any copy shop fees.

◆ You will have limited choices in the color and type of fabric.

Do-it-yourself fabric treating pros

◆ It's less expensive.

◆ There's greater design flexibility in the fabric choices.

Do-it-yourself fabric treating cons

◆ The chemicals are messy: Using rubber gloves is urged.

◆ Doing the fabric treating yourself is time-consuming.

these printing technologies would captivate quilters, who get more and more tech savvy by the hour.

Pioneering art quilter Jean Ray Laury explained it this way in her 1999 book *The Photo Transfer Handbook: Snap It, Print It, Stitch It!* "Changing technology is catapulting quilting into the twenty-first century, and quilters now position their computers, scanners, and printers right next to their sewing machines. The possibilities for including photos, words, and drawings in our quilts seem unlimited and irresistible."

Art quilters such as Caryl Bryer Fallert were eager to use photographic images in their contemporary quilts and had suffered through many messy and less than perfect methods. Fallert writes in the introduction to her excellent handbook *Quilt Savvy: Fallert's Guide to Images on Fabric* that she had experimented with "photo silk screen, photocopying, and transfer sheets, as well as several formulas that were supposed to set color ink-jet printer ink. Unfortunately, none of these methods was entirely satisfactory, and many didn't work at all."

Some quilters went to copy shops to do what is called photo transfer, in which images are copied at the shop onto transfer paper. That paper can then be placed facedown on fabric and pressed with a hot iron; the heat transfers the image from the paper onto the fabric. But this method often produces shiny images and adds so much thickness to the fabric that quilting becomes difficult. The quality of the images varies widely depending on such factors as the heat of the iron.

Despite this bother, intrepid quilters experimented with photo-transfer imagery, and some still swear by it, including teacher and author Ami Simms. Simms, who loves to take photos of her favorite places and people and has written two books about photo-transfer quilt techniques, also sells transfer paper for this process on her website. She makes it clear that this paper is *not* to be used for printing in a home computer printer and must be taken to a copy shop for printing on a color copier. Then at home, the quilter can iron the image onto fabric.

"I'm not the only person who prefers photo-transfer images to those printed on a home computer printer," says Simms. "Which do you think is going to take a

MONEY-SAVING TIP

Even when bought in bulk, pretreated fabric for ink-jet printing usually costs more than a dollar a sheet, which adds up fast. All the pros advise that once you've scanned or downloaded the image you want to print on fabric, you practice printing it on paper first. On fabric the colors will be slightly different and the picture will be less crisp, but if you print the photo on paper first, you'll be sure you've got the basic look and composition you want without wasting any fabric.

better picture, your HP printer that you bought for $150 or a commercial color copier that costs $30,000? The colors from the commercial copier are much more vibrant, and I'll happily trade that for slightly stiffer fabric any day."

However, she adds, "I may not always have that choice to make. Copy machines are changing and the newer ones cannot run the paper used for photo transfers." Simms worries that eventually the photo-transfer paper she prefers will be impossible to find. But as long as it's available, she vows to use it for her own photo quilts and to keep selling it on her website, www.amisimms.com. Whether or not this particular technique will continue to be practiced, Simms' enthusiasm for it and the stunning memory quilts she has produced have helped build the appetite for photo quilts.

Fallert's primer on transferring photos to fabric.

At the dawn of the twenty-first century, several technological developments occurred to simplify the process of transfer to fabric and vastly increase the popularity of photo quilts. One major breakthrough was the 1999 release of a product called Bubble Jet Set that, as Fallert explains in her guidebook, "chemically bonded printer-ink molecules to fiber molecules," making it possible to print photographs that were permanent and washable by running properly prepared fabric through a home computer printer. Unlike photo-transfer prints, printing this way doesn't leave the fabric stiff.

Once pure cotton fabric has been soaked in a solution of Bubble Jet Set and has dried, the treated fabric is stuck onto sheets of freezer paper by using a home iron (the paper's only purpose is to stiffen the fabric enough to feed it through a printer successfully). Trimmed to the size of letter paper, the sheets of paper-backed fabric can then be run through an ink-jet printer, printing an image from a computer directly onto the fabric. After the paper backing is pulled off, the fabric is put in a rinse.

Bubble Jet Set, the breakthrough fabric treatment for photo transfers.

Like many art quilters, Fallert was ecstatic about this new process.

"This is what we have all been waiting for—a magic formula that allows us to print color images directly onto fabric, at home, on our own ink-jet printers," Fallert writes in her *Images on Fabric* handbook. Fallert quickly embraced the new technique, turning out stunning quilts like her *Stars of Africa* from 2001, a colorful quilt including images from photographs she took on a seven-week trip to South Africa. Fallert created brilliant kaleidoscopic stars that look like flower patterns cut from commercial fabric until one gets up close and picks out the repeated images of zebras, exotic birds and flowers, and so on.

Caryl Bryer Fallert's Stars of Africa, *which incorporates photographic elements.*

Other technically savvy and artistically motivated quilters shared Fallert's excitement about these new tools, but many casual quilters weren't sold. Preparing fabric with a chemical solution that required rubber gloves and special handling, followed by the bother of bonding the fabric to paper and carefully trimming off any little stray threads (so they didn't snag and muck up the printer), discouraged some potential users.

Technological improvements kept coming, and a few short years after the advent of Bubble Jet Set, came a new tool that made putting photos on fabric a breeze—pretreated fabric that was already attached to paper and could be directly fed into home printers. Although this new technology allows even beginning quilters a chance to print photos on fabric, some quiltmakers aren't as enthusiastic because of its limitations and cost. Art quilters like Fallert want total control and flexibility, including the ability to print words and images onto any color or type of fabric. Commercially treated fabric costs as much as $3.50 a sheet. Quilters who prepare their own fabric can do so at a fraction of the cost.

RESOURCES

Best Brands of Pretreated Fabric Sheets for Ink-jet Printers

Virtually every quilt shop carries packs of paper-backed fabric sheets that are ready to pop into your ink-jet printer. But many quilt shops stock just one or two brands. Here is a list of commonly available brands and the companies that make them. Sometimes you can buy directly from the manufacturer's website, but even if you can't, you'll find those websites to be useful resources.

While these are not the only makers of fabric sheets for photo printing, they are the major players, and retailers report a high level of satisfaction among people who use their products. When choosing a brand, don't rely just on price: Experts say that the various makes of ink-jet printers use different chemicals and that these react differently to the chemicals found in the pretreated fabric sheets. You'll need to see which brand works best with your printer.

A final word of caution: Follow the directions on the package very carefully. Once some treated fabrics have been printed with ink-jet photos, they cannot be washed in a washing machine. And all ink-jet photos will fade if the quilt is hung in a sun-filled room.

Printed Treasures

The first pretreated fabric for photos to reach the quilt market, Printed Treasures is made by Milliken & Company, a textile manufacturer. The Printed Treasures website includes project ideas and lets you find a nearby store that carries the product line. You can also buy the fabric sheets online.

www.printedtreasures.com

EQ Printables

The quilting design software pioneer, Electric Quilt, makes these fabric sheets. The company claims its EQ Printables are the best quality for the money, and EQ sells its fabric sheets in several sizes. Your quilt shop may carry them, but you can also order packs of six or fifty sheets of EQ Printables from the website or by calling (800) 356-4219.

www.electricquilt.com

Miracle Fabric Sheets

These fabric sheets are made by C. Jenkins, the company that invented Bubble Jet Set, the chemical solution that adheres the dyes in ink-jet printers to the molecules in fabric. (People who prepare their own fabric sheets for ink-jet printing use Bubble Jet Set.) While the competing products usually come in packs of three to six sheets, Miracle Fabric comes in packages of ten. You can buy Miracle Fabric Sheets from retailers or the website, which also sells Bubble Jet Set directly to consumers.

www.cjenkinscompany.com

Color Plus

Color Plus paper-backed fabric sheets come in multiple sizes and a variety of fabrics, including silk, cotton, poplin, and rayon crepe. This paper-backed fabric is also sold by the roll. The manufacturer is Color Textiles Inc., a Las Vegas–based company that has been a groundbreaker in the technology and sells to both retailers and consumers. You can order Color Plus sheets in packs of six, thirty, or one hundred, and there are sample packs. The sample pack cotton includes seven different types of fabric.

www.colortextiles.com

For quilters seeking pretreated fabrics of a more exotic nature, such as silk organza, poplin, linen, and art canvas, e-tailer Sharla Hicks, owner of the Soft Expressions website, recommends two suppliers with their own websites.

www.jacquardproducts.com
www.thevintageworkshop.com

The new technology was a major hit in the rest of the quilt world, trumpeted via ads in quilt magazines, demonstrations at quilt shows, and a raft of how-to classes at quilt shops nationwide, which quickly picked up this hot new product. A pioneer in this technology was Milliken & Company, a textile manufacturer in South Carolina that came out with a branded product called Printed Treasures.

These treasures were pricey, costing about $18 for only five letter-size sheets, but quilters were quick to seize on the fun new product. For its part, Milliken reached out to quilters in various ways, particularly through its website, www.printedtreasures.com, offering free quilt project ideas, a message board for quilters, and a free e-mail newsletter. "Printed Treasures is more than a quilting accessory. It's a community. And we'd love to hear how you use Printed Treasures, as would many other quilters," it says on the website.

Competing products started joining Printed Treasures on the market, including the paper-backed fabric sheets sold by The Electric Quilt Company, which markets quilt-design software. And the Electric Quilt people got smart and started offering their product, called EQ Printables, in a variety of sizes, including eleven by seventeen–inch fabric sheets and thirteen by nineteen–inch sheets.

Meanwhile, makers of printers were beginning to take notice of how quilters used their machines, and Hewlett-Packard got into the printable fabric game. HP started selling software for quilters in 2002, with the release of its Custom Quilt Label Kit. Most quilters like to attach labels to all their quilts, especially those they give away as gifts to loved ones. Previously, such labels, whether simple or elaborate, tended to be handwritten.

EQ's brand of printable fabric sheets (top), and one of the many excellent books on incorporating photos into quilting (bottom).

Hewlett-Packard figured out a way to bring quilt labels into the twenty-first century. As more and more people bought digital cameras, stored photos on their computers, and used them to send the pictures to friends and family, soon there was software to edit and

***Not all photo quilts are photo transfers: Marilyn Belford used a photo as the inspiration for her quilt* My Parents.**

manipulate the photographs, and home printers got better at printing out the photos.

The Hewlett-Packard product is essentially graphic-design software that has been tweaked for quilters, providing special templates in which they can type in the name of the recipient of the quilt, the date it was finished, and the quiltmaker's name. A clip-art database of about five hundred images can be pasted onto the quilt label without any copyright issues, and there is a series of borders and backgrounds designed for quilters. A grandmother making a baby quilt can feature the baby's photo on the label, or a photo of herself, if she wishes. Someone making a quilt for a girlfriend could use an image of the two of them together as part of the quilt label's design.

To help boost sales, Hewlett-Packard devotes space on its website to quilting and has hired quilters to help design projects to post there. Sue Anderson of Vancouver, Washington, who worked as a freelance technical writer for the company's ink-jet printer division, was one of these quilters. For several years Anderson wrote for the company's website as part of HP's effort to promote printing on fabric for crafters, and this inspired her to start her own company, Quilt Pics, in 2003. From her website, www.quiltpics.com, Anderson sells kits that include printable fabric sheets along with templates and patterns to make quilts with photographs.

TRANSFERRING PHOTOS TO FABRIC WITHOUT A COMPUTER

Just in case you aren't confused enough, here's one more option for printing photographs on fabric that doesn't require a computer or a scanner.

Sharla Hicks, who runs the Soft Expressions website, uses her home copier to print photos on the pretreated fabric sheets normally used in ink-jet printers. With this method, you put your photograph on the copier, load in a paper-backed fabric sheet, and simply press the button to copy. "A lot of these cheap color copiers are made by the same companies that make the printers, and they use exactly the same ink-jet cartridges," says Hicks.

Of course, when you use this method, you don't have the tools of scanner and computer software to manipulate images, tweak colors, and so forth, but Hicks says that, when she sets it for high-quality printing, she has had good results with a Canon color copier she bought on sale for less than $100.

FINDING PHOTOS YOU CAN LEGALLY USE

Go right ahead and use your own family photos to make picture quilts, but remember that you can't use any other photographs for which you don't hold the legal rights. Generally, you have to seek reprint permission from both the publication in which an image appears and from the photographer. You may be asked to pay a fee.

There are loads of websites that describe themselves as offering "free" stock photos; these can actually be pretty expensive, requiring a license or subscription fee. Watch the lingo on these sites: "Royalty free" doesn't mean that photos cost nothing.

Two sites that actually *are* free are Stock.XCHNG (**www.sxc.hu**) and morgue File (**www.morguefile.com**), but even here, you must register yourself and agree to the terms of use.

For more on copyright law and how it applies to quilters, go to the Q & A: Copyright Law for Quilters on page 515.

Surveys show that one of the major attractions of quilting to first timers is the chance to create a one-of-a-kind heirloom for a major family milestone, such as a wedding, the birth of a child, or a fiftieth wedding anniversary. With all the breakthroughs in printing photos on fabric at home, quilters are suddenly able to create quilts that feature not generic images but actual photos of their favorite people, pets, and views, thus pulling in a whole new audience to the craft—people who may have started out as scrapbook enthusiasts. These new quilters may someday gravitate toward making Log Cabin or Drunkard's Path patterns and mastering a full range of quilting skills, but for now, the main attraction for them is the chance to tell their family's story in a compelling new way.

Mary Ellen Kranz, who has quilted since childhood and long made her living teaching people how to use computers, is one of the teachers who has taken the photo quilt craze to the next level. With a coauthor, longarm quilter Cheryl Hayes, she wrote a book called *Blending Photos with Fabric* that was an instant hit in the quilt world from its introduction in late 2004.

As noted in a review of Kranz and Hayes's book on the Planet Patchwork website, many quilters start out by making photo quilts in which photos are presented in simple rows with each bordered by fabric "in the same way photos are presented on the family dresser. There is nothing wrong with this approach, but quilters are restless and endlessly inventive, so it was inevitable that they would experiment and come up with new uses for photographs in quilts." The review goes on to call *Blending Photos with Fabric* both "the technical bible of photo-quilting," and "a cutting-edge exploration of new artistic directions."

What Kranz and Hayes do, for the most part, is print out a beautiful landscape photo on the usual letter-size fabric, then create a quilt around the photo, extending the lines of the horizon and other landmarks out beyond the photo by preparing a template for cutting matching commercial fabrics that blend into the photo. By the time the quilt is all pieced together, it's hard to tell where the photograph ends and the other fabric begins.

Art quilters are playing more with photos too, including Barbara Webster, who lives near Asheville,

North Carolina, and is turning her breathtaking nature photographs into award-winning quilts. Like many others, Webster started out using photo-transfer techniques on her quilts but didn't like the results.

She discovered that she could design fabric using her own digital photos and computer graphics software and send the designs on a CD to a textile printer in New York City, who could print out the designs on fabric that was fifty-five inches wide, much broader than any home printer can tackle. Then, she could cut up these images and make quilts.

Webster's quilts are unusual. At first glance some of them look like traditional patterns in pretty colors or like the intricate design of a Persian rug, and it takes closer scrutiny to discover that the imagery comes from repeated and manipulated photos of a cherry blossom, for example. Webster is in demand as a teacher sharing these techniques but also is busy creating commissioned photo quilts.

"People see my work and realize they can commission a quilt featuring their children or their favorite place. One client flew me down to Texas and then flew me all over the state to shoot pictures of bluebonnets," says Webster. "I went home and put up lots of different designs on my website using those photos. The client was able to review my design plan and the photos and make changes. Then I printed the photos on fabric and made the quilt."

Two of Barbara Webster's intricate photo quilts: Snowfall *(top), and* Blue Spruce Star *(bottom). Both incorporate photographic images.*

Webster believes that the marriage of quilts and photography is just in its infancy, and that the growth and change in techniques to come will be dramatic, in both the realm of art quilts and the making of personal heirloom quilts.

"Anything you can photograph can be printed on fabric. That means your kids' drawings, old family snapshots, court documents, anything at all. I don't think that has really dawned on everybody. And when it does, it will be a regular revolution. The possibilities are endless." (See Webster's astounding quilts at www.starforestquilts.com.)

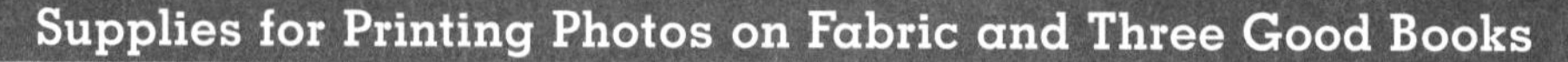

RESOURCES

Supplies for Printing Photos on Fabric and Three Good Books

Now that you've considered whether you'd like to print your photos directly onto fabric or onto photo-transfer paper first, you need to gather the appropriate supplies. Here's what you need and how to find it.

For the Paper Method

Other than an iron, photographs, and fabric, all you really need are photo-transfer sheets, which are widely available at craft shops and quilt shops, as well as from quilt e-tailers. Read the package carefully to make sure the sheets are compatible with your printer!

Soft Expressions is a well-established e-tailer for quilters and carries photo-transfer paper for both color ink-jet printers and copiers and for laser copiers.

1230 North Jefferson Street, Suite M
Anaheim, California 92807
(888) 545-8616
www.softexpressions.com

Popular teacher Ami Simms always carries her favorite brand of transfer paper on her website. The paper is designed to be taken to copy shops for printing. She also sells her two books on how to use photo-transfer paper and make photo quilts.

c/o Mallery Press
(for mail orders only)
4206 Sheraton Drive
Flint, Michigan 48532
(800) 278-4824
www.amisimms.com

For the Fabric Method

If you're planning on using pretreated fabric sheets, that's the only supply you'll need (assuming you already have a computer, scanner, and ink-jet printer). The top brands include Miracle Fabric Sheets, EQ Printables, Printed Treasures, and Color Plus. The same e-tailer recommended above for photo transfer sheets, **www.softexpressions.com,** is also a great resource for pretreated photo fabric sheets. (They even sell a sampler pack mixing all the major brands so you can compare them and see which one you like best.)

If you want to treat your own fabric sheets, here's a list of what you'll need.

- Fabric—100 percent cotton or silk is best—cut into pieces that are slightly larger than a standard sheet of typing paper, so you can trim the edges
- Freezer paper, for backing
- A plastic container in which to soak the fabric
- Rubber gloves
- The two chemical solutions Bubble Jet Set 2000 and Bubble Jet Set Rinse

Bubble Jet Set and Bubble Jet Set Rinse are widely available, but **www.softexpressions.com** carries everything you need. In addition, its website **www.softexpressions.com/help/faq/FAQbjs.htm** has an excellent tutorial on using these products.

To treat the fabric, you soak it in Bubble Jet Set for five minutes, let it dry on a towel, then iron it onto the shiny side of a piece of freezer paper. Cut the fabric-backed paper into sheets that fit your printer, and you're ready to print photos. Once the photos are printed, peel off the paper, rinse the fabric in the Bubble Jet Set Rinse, and lay the fabric on a towel again to dry. Now you can sew!

If you're looking for a fun, simple photo-quilt

design, on page 453 you'll find complete directions for making my Kiss Wedding Photo Quilt (yes, that is a picture of me and my husband kissing on our wedding day). This is a versatile pattern you can use with photos of anything you love.

Books

Quilt Savvy: Fallert's Guide to Images on Fabric,

by Caryl Bryer Fallert, American Quilter's Society; $21.95

For my money, Fallert's skinny, spiral-bound paperback is the best primer for making photo quilts. As usual, the prize-winning art quilter is ahead of the curve on technology and has produced a book that is useful, concise, and inspiring. Fallert explains how to prepare fabric sheets for ink-jet printing as well as how to use the pretreated ones, and her easy-to-follow directions are accompanied by excellent step-by-step photographs.

What I like best is that Fallert doesn't create cut-and-dried compositions that look like scrapbooks on fabric; her design ideas are fresh. Fallert even suggests such experiments as placing three-dimensional objects directly on a scanner's surface and using the images in quilts. The quilts she designed herself using scanned-in images of ordinary dandelions are stunning.

An additional resource is Fallert's amazing website, **www.bryerpatch.com**, which provides more tutorials on making photo quilts. It's also a source for all of the basic supplies used for printing photos on quilts, including Bubble Jet Set.

Blending Photos with Fabric,

by Mary Ellen Kranz and Cheryl Hayes, The Electric Quilt Company; $29.95

Two experienced quilters, one with a background in computers, Mary Ellen Kranz and Cheryl Hayes have written a primer that offers a fresh approach to using fabric photos in quilts. Their basic method is to print a photo on fabric, then create a pieced quilt that blends the photo into the patterned fabrics so it's hard to see where the photo ends and the other fabric begins.

Kranz and Hayes wisely don't assume their readers are tech savvy, so they take one step at a time, covering not just techniques for printing photos on fabric but even explaining how to take better photographs to begin with. This 128-page book offers ten quilt projects with instructions as well as a guide to shopping for computer equipment and tips for doctoring photos with special effects.

On the website for Kranz and Hayes, **www.quiltingimages.com**, you can find out when they are teaching classes and workshops, as well as buy their book and supplies, including photographs already printed on fabric sheets to be used for some of the projects in their book.

Fun Photo Quilts and Crafts,

by Ami Simms, Mallery Press; $19.95

Ami Simms is famously funny as a quilt teacher, and this book reflects her wonderful sense of humor. It doesn't matter that Simms' preferred method of making photo quilts is to use photo-transfer techniques, because the book is about much more than the how-to step of getting the picture printed. After viewing an entire show of Ami Simms' own photo quilts, I think she is a master at this craft. Her book goes way past memory quilts with rows and rows of photos. There are instructions for twenty-five projects here, including tote bags, neckties, ornaments, and vests.

At her website, **www.amisimms.com,** you can find this book and all the supplies you need for transferring photos to fabric. Ami Simms also features a gallery of her customers' photo quilts, for more design ideas.

Bison at Mission Creek, *one of Ruth B. McDowell's quilts made using only commercially available fabrics.*

CRAZY FOR COLOR: FABRIC DYEING FOR QUILTS

It has now become an accepted fact that many art quilters prefer to dye their own fabric. Art quilters, by definition, are trying to produce something unique, and controlling every aspect of quilt making, including customizing the color of each piece of fabric, is one way for them to ensure that. And so Ruth B. McDowell, one of the acknowledged masters among the ranks of quilt artists, has said she sometimes feels compelled to defend herself because she uses *only* commercial fabrics in her work.

Although at first they seem like abstract assemblages, McDowell's pieced quilts often contain images from nature. If she is depicting a leaf, she doesn't dye fabric the color of an actual leaf but finds interesting patterned and solid fabrics that together, from a distance, look leaflike. The same is true whether she is stitching fabric together to make a sky, a face, or a boat.

"My quilts are visual compositions . . . [that] must work graphically from a distance as well as reward close study of the details," she writes in the introduction to her book *Fabric Journey: An Inside Look at the Quilts of Ruth B. McDowell*. "The use of commercial fabrics contributes to this outcome, not only with their variety of colors and patterns, but also because of the historical and emotional connections these fabrics make."

McDowell's quilts are breathtaking and her artistry revered, but it's revealing that her refusal to dye her fabric has come to be seen by some of her peers as the position of a maverick. Overall, art quilters are a minority in the quilt world, which is dominated by more casual quilters who make quilts for pleasure and often prefer more traditional designs and time-saving techniques. But these days, the practice of fabric dyeing is also trickling down to the more casual and more traditional quilting population.

It isn't that the average quilter feels pressure to do this, so much as the fact that dyeing has simply been added to the growing list of techniques quilters are comfortable playing with. The more happy dyers there are in the quilt world, the more invitations there are to join the party. Guilds looking for a new program topic can easily find someone to lead a lecture/demonstration, and because gratification comes more quickly with dyeing than with many of the techniques quilters dabble in these days (including fine machine quilting), more jump on the bandwagon at each stop.

"I don't think dyeing is just for art quilters," says Carol Soderlund, an award-winning quilter and dye expert who teaches fabric-dyeing workshops at guilds and national shows. "Whether you are a traditional quilter or an art quilter or anything in between, you get this vision in your mind of a specific color you want. Even if you're making a Baltimore album quilt from a historical design, you may be driven to dye fabric in order to achieve the exact shade of deep, rich red that you want, when you can't find it at the fabric shop. Then once you get started dyeing, the process is just so much fun you keep doing it."

That certainly describes Soderlund's experience. A quilter since 1976, Soderlund got started dyeing because she was trying to make a complex quilt she designed in 1988 that looked like a three-dimensional globe. The globe shape is covered by a series of crossed arrows and Soderlund wanted to stitch the arrows of solid colors in subtle tonal gradations against the scaffoldlike globe shape that features shades of gray. But finding all the

Art quilters, by definition, are trying to produce something unique, and controlling every aspect of quilt making, including customizing the color of each piece of fabric, is one way for them to ensure that.

A Simple First Exercise in Fabric Dyeing

Low water immersion dyeing, also known as scrunch dyeing or crumple dyeing, is one of the easiest methods of fabric dyeing and a good place to start. You'll see that even in this simple technique, there are no hard-and-fast rules about dye quantities or soaking times, giving you room to play and create.

Tools and Supplies

Dyeing supplies can be found at many art supply stores and ordered from the websites listed on page 220. Buy the smallest available quantity of dyes and soda ash if you are just trying this out. Here's what you'll need:

◆ One yard of white fabric, 100 percent cotton; it must be prewashed.

◆ A small bucket or large jar for immersing the fabric: Plastic, glass, enamel, or stainless steel are all suitable. The container must be big enough to hold a yard of fabric, scrunched up, plus three or four cups of water.

◆ Procion MX dyes or other fiber-reactive dyes, in two colors; pick a wild combination of colors, such as purple and green (do not use all-purpose dyes such as Rit, which aren't specifically formulated for natural fibers and will result in a weaker, duller color).

◆ Soda ash, aka sodium carbonate—sodium bicarbonate is not a substitute.

◆ A pair of thin rubber or plastic gloves to wear when handling the dye or dye solution.

◆ Measuring cups and spoons. These cannot be used later for food: Purchase dyeing utensils from the dollar store or a garage sale. You'll use the measuring cups to mix the dye.

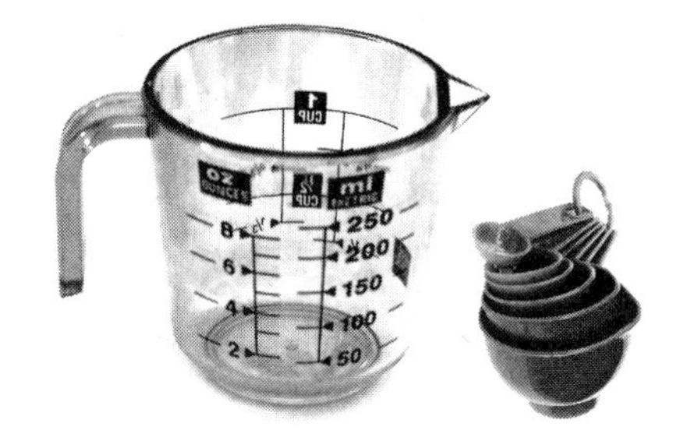

◆ A dust mask for use when handling dye powder. (This is very important.)

◆ Mild detergent or Synthrapol, a soap made especially for use with Procion dyes that is available where the dyes are sold.

Directions

Crumple the fabric and stuff it snugly into the bucket or container. It shouldn't fit too tightly or the dye won't be able to penetrate the folds of the fabric.

◆ Mix one color of Procion MX or a similar dye, measuring one teaspoon of dye into one cup of warm—not hot—water (one teaspoon is just a starting point; you can use any amount of dye from a fraction of a teaspoon up to four teaspoons to achieve different results). Some dyes will require more than five minutes of constant stirring to dissolve in water.

◆ Pour the dye mixture over the fabric in the bucket. Then, add a cup of plain water.

◆ Mix a second color of dye in water, then pour it in the bucket. *Important:* Do not stir, mix, or mush the fabric after the dye is added because you want the natural striations of the colors, not a single combined color.

◆ Be sure there is enough of the dye and water mixture to barely cover the fabric—you may have to poke at the fabric to punch down any air bubbles (add more water after the second batch of dye, if necessary). Let the dye set for fifteen minutes.

◆ Prepare the soda ash mixture: Run tap water until it is warm (but not hot), then add one-and-a-half teaspoons of soda ash to one cup of warm water and stir until the soda ash is dissolved. Pour the mixture over the fabric. Using your gloved hands, press down on the fabric to distribute the soda ash mixture. *Do not stir* the liquid. Adding the soda ash will fix the dye, making it permanent.

◆ Leave the fabric in the soda ash mixture for at least an hour. Two to four hours will create a deeper color. The color will be slightly lighter once the fabric is dry. Keep the fabric in a warm spot—in a warm room or in the sun, covered with a plastic top.

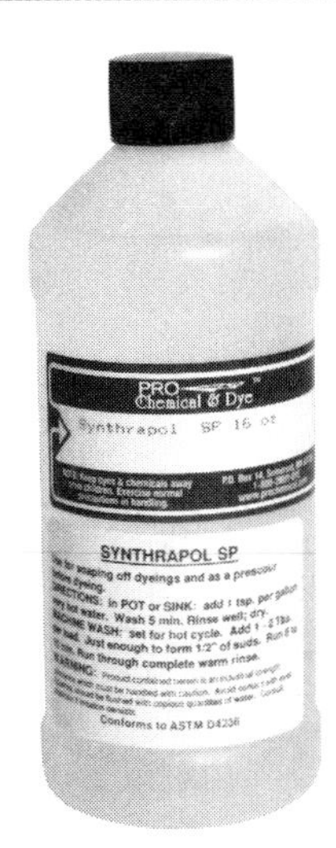

◆ Wearing rubber gloves, remove the fabric from the container, then rinse it in hot water to wash out any excess unset dye. Wash the dyed fabric in the washing machine with mild detergent or Synthrapol.

◆ Either hang the dyed fabric to dry or dry it in a clothes dryer.

This dyeing process has been adapted with permission from the website of textile artist and Ph.D. biologist Paula Burch, with the help of dyeing expert Carol Soderlund. For extensive additional information and dye recipes, go to Burch's website, **www.pburch.net**, and click on Dyeing. (If you're looking for more about low water immersion dyeing, she refers to it by the abbreviation lwi.) Hers is just one recipe for this method. Elsewhere on the Web, in dye classes, and in the books on fabric dyeing listed on pages 220–21, you'll find more recipes for low water immersion and other techniques.

different shades of color meant hours and hours of traveling from one quilt shop to the next in upstate New York—and still not finding what she wanted.

So she decided to try dyeing, following the directions in a quilting magazine. "I ordered fabric and dyes from Dharma Trading Co., it came in the mail, and within twenty-four hours, I had the most beautiful gradation of fabrics going from gray to black," marvels Soderlund. "I thought, Oh my! This is so easy, and I can have anything I want!"

In the finished quilt, called *Covenant* (you can see it on her website www.carolsoderlund.com), Soderlund ended up using 256 different colors and the quilt won Best of Show, Masters Division, at the Houston International Quilt Festival in 1989.

"Some of it was beginner's luck: I had no idea that making black was the hardest thing, like some quilters start out trying to make a king-size bed quilt," she says. "But I was sold on dyeing from the first moment."

Soderlund sought out classes and started dyeing periodically in a church basement with a friend. She read books about dyes and did tons of her own experiments, and when she began keeping a meticulous "dye notebook," she says, "my learning took off like a rocket." Then she began teaching extensively.

In 2001, Soderlund signed up a year in advance to take a ten-day course at Quilting by the Lake in Morrisville, New York, with the famously demanding quilt teacher Nancy Crow. This "improvisations" class required students to bring about one hundred yards of fabric in solid colors. Soderlund spent several months surrounded by notebooks and calculators, figuring out what she calls a three-dimensional theory of color: She wanted to create her own database of precise recipes for a very wide range of colors. She spent additional months dyeing all the fabrics and walked into Crow's class carrying 343 yards of fabric, each one a different color. "I had six or eight big Rubbermaid bins on a wheeled cart," says Soderlund. "People definitely noticed." Soon she was teaching dyeing not just locally but at Nancy Crow's Timber Frame Barn in Ohio and for one of the top commercial dye suppliers, PRO Chemical & Dye.

Soderlund is best known for her intensive five-day workshop called Color Mixing for Dyers, which

FABRIC DYEING WITH SHAVING CREAM

The list of techniques for coloring fabric just keeps growing, and these techniques can require unusual ingredients. Some dyers like to play with shaving cream, which provides a fun, easily accessible source of foam. The foam pushes the dye into wavy patterns, somewhat like marbling.

Fiber artist Jim Kankula from Winston-Salem, North Carolina, has demonstrated his shaving cream dye technique on the television show *Simply Quilts*. Basically, he mixed half a can of shaving cream with water, then spread a one-inch layer of the whipped shaving cream in the bottom of an aluminum roasting pan. Kankula mixed more shaving cream with a dye solution and poured it into an applicator bottle. He squirted this creamy dye mix in a swoopy pattern across the surface of the shaving cream in the pan and then pressed a piece of prepared fabric on the surface of the shaving cream and dye mixture.

explores the many permutations and combinations possible using just the primary colors of Procion MX dyes. The class is broken down into teams and the teams mix literally hundreds of colors: Each student leaves the workshop with a sample book of more than a thousand different dye formulas.

Although not every quilter who tries dyeing will get so immersed, so to speak, many quilters find the process appealing, even addictive. One reason is that while it's possible to get fancy by employing painstakingly complex techniques to embellish fabric, it's also possible to create beautiful effects quickly by dyeing with easily obtained materials. The Procion MX dyes favored by quilters are made specifically for natural fibers such as cotton and have been available for decades through arts and crafts suppliers. The interest in dyeing isn't so much a case of new technology but of quilters being exposed to existing tools and technology presented in a more methodical way.

"What got me started was seeing beautiful hand-dyed and hand-painted fabrics at quilt shows and thinking I wonder if I could do that?" says Lois Frankel, a quilter from Ewing, New Jersey. "It's a way to get a color or look by design that you might only find if you're lucky when shopping. It's also a way to be that much closer to the artistic process. I still use commercial fabric when it suits my project. Dyeing and painting just give me more options."

"I got into quilting because I love color and texture, so hand dyeing was a natural extension to me," says Kathy Applebaum, an art quilter from Woodland, California. "Once I started hand dyeing, the fact that I'm never one hundred percent sure of what the final product will be has kept me dyeing. Actually, hand dyeing led me to make art quilts. I started in the traditional world, but then those big hunks of hand dyed fabrics just begged to become whole-cloth quilts. Now, I make seventy-five percent art quilts and mostly make traditional quilts when my guild does them for charity."

When the dye set and the fabric was rinsed the result was swirls of color on the fabric. New Jersey quiltmaker Trina Weller, who loves to experiment with dyes, says this method is fun because "the fabric smells so good when you're done."

You'll find detailed directions for dyeing with shaving cream by going to the website of dye supplier Dharma Trading Co. (which also sells the dyes and other supplies you will need—but not the shaving cream). Go to **www.dharmatrading.com** and type Shaving Cream Dyeing in the Search box, then scroll down to the list titled Article Pages.

The PRO Chem 2007 catalog.

Like many quilters, Applebaum keeps experimenting with new techniques as she goes along, each one leading her to be more adventuresome. "In the four years I've been dyeing, I progressed from dyeing in buckets and baggies to using squirt bottles and shaving cream. I've added scrunching and tying to my repertoire, as well as multiple colors. I'm toying with the idea of adding stamping. Who knows?"

Cantilever, by Melody Johnson, made entirely with hand-dyed cotton.

Many quilters get drawn into the dyeing process because their local quilt shop is featuring mostly batiks, cute novelty prints, and some reproduction 1930s fabrics but not a wide range of the soft browns and taupes, pale blues and greens needed to complete a quilted landscape. Most now realize that by dyeing they have the option of making precisely the colors they envision. Not that dyeing is completely effortless.

"Fabric dyeing is work—just ask anyone who has had to haul buckets of water to do it because they don't have a dedicated dye room with running water and a work sink," says Larkin Jean Van Horn, who dyes fabric for both garment making and quilts and says she has dyed more than 250 yards so far. "For me, it's the magic of seeing what comes out of the dryer when the work is done. It's seeing what happened when I've tried a new formula with a pinch of this or a smidge of that."

In the end, quilters love dyeing not just because it helps them create beautiful fabrics, but because it is yet another tool that increases their control over the final product. "It goes way beyond color," says Carol Soderlund, the dye expert. "With dyeing, image transfer, and things like silk screening, the imagery you can get on cloth can be extremely personal. It can be related to your memories and things that exist only in your mind."

GETTING STARTED WITH FABRIC DYEING

Why not just jump in, and give fabric dyeing a try? Although you might expect it to be a messy process, a space the size of a card table covered in plastic is all you need to get started. The chemicals used in home dyeing are not considered toxic, but by definition they can discolor what they touch. You will need thin rubber gloves, measuring cups and spoons, a dust mask for when you're handling the dye, and a defined workspace. While some people who dye big batches of fabric use their washing machines (it sounds crazy, but if you know how to clean up, it works), you will probably want to start small, with a bucket. Don't use a sink unless it's stainless steel—porcelain will stain.

To begin with, you'll likely want to start by working with white fabric. As you would expect, the dyes in colored fabric interact with the dye you add, so submerging yellow fabric in blue dye, for example, won't give you blue fabric but some shade of green.

Whichever techniques you try, don't do anything without first reading all the instructions on the labels of the products you plan to use. That way, you'll have everything you need right in front of you *before* putting on the clumsy rubber gloves.

There are a number of fiber-reactive dyes and the most popular with quilters are the Procion MX dyes, which react to the fibers in cotton and other natural (nonsynthetic) fabrics. As fiber artist and teacher Jane Dunnewold explains in her indispensable book, *Complex Cloth: A Comprehensive Guide to Surface Design*, a chemical reaction occurs with these dyes such that the dye molecules share electrons with the fiber molecules, creating a much stronger bond than simply painting on the surface of fabric.

Small changes in the dyeing process can produce very different results. The amount of dye used will determine whether the color is light or dark, and keeping the dye bath at room temperature or above will improve results greatly. You mix the dye in water with other ingredients; depending on the process, these can include noniodized salt and soda ash. Soda ash is shorthand for sodium carbonate and acts as a fixative, so that the fabric is permanently dyed.

Small changes in the dyeing process can produce very different results. The amount of dye used will determine whether the color is light or dark.

RESOURCES

For Fabric Dyeing

Two Dye Suppliers Beloved by Quilters

PRO Chemical & Dye

Generally known as PRO Chem, this company not only supplies all the dyes and other ingredients, like soda ash, quilters need for dyeing, but also provides great instructions. Buy as little as two ounces or as much as five pounds. You can download tutorials right from the website or travel to the Fall River, Massachusetts, headquarters for intensive workshops with some of the country's top dye instructors. Among the company's regular teachers are quilter Carol Soderlund, who has developed a methodical approach that gives dyers great control over the process and a way to repeat results. "PRO Chem's online instructions are so good that I bought a binder, printed them out, put them in plastic sleeves, and I take them to the garage on 'dyeing days,'" says Maine-based quilter Sarah Ann Smith.

P.O. Box 14
Somerset,
Massachusetts 02726
(800) 228-9393
www.prochemical.com

Dharma Trading Co.

Based in San Rafael, California, Dharma Trading Co. has been selling textile craft supplies since 1969 and, like PRO Chem, is lauded for both its customer service and the instructional information available on its website. There's an excellent tutorial on the site that explains how to pick the proper dye for your project and fabric. Click on Dyes, then on Help Choosing Your Dye.

1604 Fourth Street
San Rafael,
California 94901
(800) 542-5227
www.dharmatrading.com

Four Great Books About Dyeing

Color by Accident: Low-Water Immersion Dyeing,

by Ann Johnston, Ann Johnston; $24.95

Design books for quilters by accomplished quilter and

quilt teacher Ann Johnston are considered among the best available. In addition to *Color by Accident: Low-Water Immersion Dyeing,* they include *The Quilter's Book of Design* and a second book on dyeing called *Color by Design: Paint and Print with Dye*. The website for this Portland, Oregon–based quilter is **www.annjohnston.net**.

DYES & PAINTS: A HANDS-ON GUIDE TO COLORING FABRIC,
by Elin Noble,
Elin Noble; $34.95

Elin Noble has been dyeing fabric for more than twenty years and used to be the lab manager for the dye supplier PRO Chem (see facing page). At PRO Chem, Noble tested and developed new product applications and did troubleshooting for customers. She lives in Massachusetts and teaches around the country. Noble's website is **www.elinnoble.com**.

COMPLEX CLOTH: A COMPREHENSIVE GUIDE TO SURFACE DESIGN,
by Jane Dunnewold,
Martingale & Company;
$34.95

This book by the leading expert in embellishing fabric is inspiring and practical. Jane Dunnewold goes well beyond dyeing to present instructions for fabric stamping, painting, and other techniques. Excellent photographs help make the how-to's clear. You will find Dunnewold's simple tutorial on fabric stamping on page 326. (Her profile begins on page 323.) Her website is **www.complexcloth.com**.

FABRIC DYEING FOR BEGINNERS,
by Vimala McClure,
American Quilter's Society;
$19.95

Vimala McClure is an award-winning fiber artist who may be best known as a pioneering teacher of infant massage. Many experts rate this book highly for novice dyers, who want just the basic information, clearly presented. At eighty pages, it doesn't go as deep as the others, but it does cover several techniques including tie-dye and fabric-fold methods. McClure wrote about her dyeing process in an issue of *American Quilter* magazine, and the issue was so popular, the American Quilter's Society asked her to expand the article into a book.

Bonnie Lyn McCaffery's definitive guide to painted portrait quilts.

Fiber-reactive dyes may cost a little extra but will create more vibrant, lasting hues than the dye you pick up in the laundry aisle of the supermarket. Grocery store dyes, like Rit, while fine for the occasional T-shirt, are actually a blend of many different dyes, which is why the box describes them as "all purpose." That means that they can be used with a variety of fabrics but most of the dye will go down the drain, as it isn't targeted for the particular fiber you're dyeing. What color remains will be less intense. While there are methods for using natural dyes, most beginners start with the easily available and more predictable commercial dyes, which also withstand washing and exposure to light.

Should you find the dyeing process enjoyable, you may wish to experiment more. Some quilters like to dye in groups, meeting to try different dyes and techniques and to share results. Art quilter Virginia Abrams, whose educational background was in chemistry, says she finds applying color to white fabric to be "intoxicating" and she's been dyeing fabrics as long as she has been quilting. She says her dyeing expertise grew in part from the monthly meetings she held for years in her basement with a group of quilting friends who also wanted to experiment with different dye processes. They called themselves The Dyeing Ladies.

If you're game to get started, you can certainly find lots of classes and workshops. But if you want to try first on your own, you'll find instructions for one method on pages 214–15, and you can also check out the suppliers and books listed on pages 220–21. In addition, there's an excellent website maintained by Paula Burch, a Texas-based fiber artist with a Ph.D. in biology. Go to www.pburch.net and click on Dyeing. Burch provides instructions for many methods, including tie-dyeing and dyeing in the washing machine. She also provides information about e-mail list groups for those who become serious about dyeing and want to go deeper, including a Yahoo! group that specializes in natural dyes. To subscribe to the Yahoo! natural dye group, send an e-mail to the address NaturalDyes-subscribe@yahoogroups.com.

Be warned: Many quilters find the dyeing process addictive. Some even stop quilting to concentrate on making artistic fabric.

Hollis Chatelain's Precious Water, *Best of Show winner of the 2004 International Quilt Festival.*

FABRIC PAINTING

Dyeing isn't the only technique that is growing in popularity with quilters. Fabric painting is also becoming popular as art quilters experiment with it and produce dramatic results that win awards. For example, textile artist Hollis Chatelain won the Best of Show prize at the 2004 International Quilt Festival in Houston for a quilt the surface of which was painted rather than pieced or appliquéd. Her quilt, *Precious Water,* consisted of layered images painted on fabric and then densely quilted with more than two hundred different colors of thread.

While Chatelain's quilt was widely lauded, it also created something of a controversy on the convention floor. The fact that the quilt was painted drew comments not just on Internet message boards for quilters but even in the local newspaper during the show. There were unmistakable echoes of the old "Did she cheat?" question that haunted Caryl Bryer Fallert after her machine-quilted prizewinner at Paducah in 1989.

In the end, experience and wisdom led most quilters to the conclusion that each new technique is just another tool and that the art comes from the skill and imagination with which the tool is employed and not the tool itself. Painting on fabric is no more cheating than finishing a quilt by machine is cheating. It's hard to find a discerning quilter who would disagree that both Caryl Bryer Fallert and Hollis Chatelain are accomplished artists.

There are many ways to enhance quilts by painting on fabric, and both techniques and tools vary widely. Some quiltmakers use paints to make swaths of soft color on fabric, like a watercolor painting, to fill in skies, or to make a building or object look more three-dimensional by adding shading. Sometimes paints are used to make people's features look realistic, which can be really difficult with fabric alone. Art quilter Bonnie Lyn McCaffery is famously good at painting the faces of people in quilts, a technique she teaches to others.

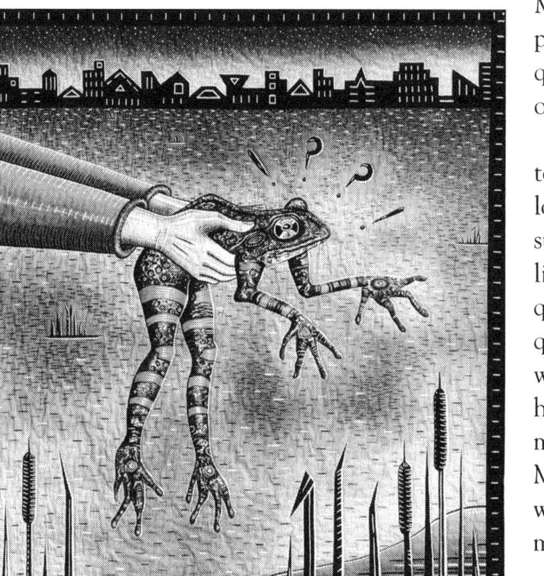

Migration of the California Red-Legged Frog, *by Linda MacDonald.*

But paint isn't always added to quilts to create a more realistic look. Susan Shie, whose quilt surfaces look raw and exuberant, like folk art, often paints on her quilts. So does award-winning quilt artist Linda MacDonald, whose whimsical nature quilts have a cartoonlike quality (you might say an editorial cartoon, as MacDonald often makes quilts with a pointed environmental message).

As fabric painting has become more popular, there has been an increase in the types of materials available for different effects. Some quilters like the intense effect of painting directly with dyes, which is Hollis Chatelain's usual method. But almost any acrylic paint can be applied to fabric. Most fabric paints, such as Setacolor, must be heat set with an iron to make them permanent, and because they lie on top of the fabric and are not chemically

Blushing Triangles I, *by Gloria Hansen; she used pastels to enhance the quilt's colors.*

bonded to it like dyes are, the paints tend to leave the fabric slightly stiffer.

Many art quilters also like to play with Shiva Paintstiks, which are oil paints mixed with wax and molded into a crayon shape. These were introduced into the general art market in the 1960s but more recently were discovered by art quilters who love new toys and relished the chance to make freehand drawings on their fabric. The marks left by a Shiva Paintstik take several days to dry, but quilt artists looking for fresh ways to transform their quilts are willing to wait.

The bottom line is that today's sophisticated quilters are very far along the learning curve. Even those who return over and over to traditional patterns and designs want to render them in a way that is both personal and current. The tools and techniques at quilters' disposal make it possible like never before for them to create the unique quilts in their minds. And their minds keep changing. As quilters keep pushing the envelope on how to make quilts, there is no way of stopping these marvelous tools from continuing to evolve. It is the awesome energy behind such innovations that keeps powering the quilt renaissance forward.

RESOURCES

For Fabric Painting

You're not likely to find fabric painting supplies in the local quilt shop. It may sell a few how-to books by quilters who like to use paint, but don't expect to find the paint there. A good art supply store or craft shop will stock acrylic paints that you could use on fabric, but a website catering to the quilt market may be your best choice if you're just starting. It will specialize in the types and brands of paints that quilters prefer and carry the books, too.

Art quilter Esterita Austin swears by Jacquard fabric paints; you can try them out by buying a special quilter's pack of nine colors that retails for $15 or less. Another paint brand that's very popular with quilters is Setacolor, made by Pébéo, which comes in dozens of colors and such finishes as opaque, transparent, and pearlescent.

Websites

Two of the best websites for fabric paint are the same two recommended on page 220 for dyes.

Dharma Trading Co., **www.dharmatrading.com** *or* telephone (800) 542-5227, has a wide variety of textile paints, plus there are tutorials to help you select the right type of paint or dye for your project.

PRO Chemical & Dye, **www.prochemical.com**, is also excellent. Phone orders may be made at (800) 228-9393.

A third site, Fabrics to Dye For, **www.fabricstodyefor.com**, sells a staggering variety of paints and dyes in quantities from a few ounces to a gallon. The site also sells fabrics that have been hand painted by the site's proprietor Jennifer Priestley or her mother. This Rhode Island–based company was founded by Priestley in 1994, after she started painting and dyeing fabric at home for her own quilts. Orders are also taken by phone at (888) 322-1319.

Books

There are few books that cover just fabric painting alone, and they are mostly not written by or for quilters. Of the four books listed here, three cover more than fabric painting. The third and fourth titles recommended are also found in resources for dyeing fabric on page 221. They cost a little more but are much more detailed.

OFF THE SHELF FABRIC PAINTING: 30 SIMPLE RECIPES FOR GOURMET RESULTS, ***by Sue Beevers, C&T Publishing; $24.95***

Quilt artist Beevers takes a playful kitchen-sink approach to fabric painting, advocating such "found" tools as leftover yogurt containers and techniques that use pantry staples like flour and cornstarch. But she also covers a lot of the standard techniques like sponging, rolling, stenciling, and finger painting and compares different types of fabric paint. Her favorites include Pébéo Setacolor textile paint and Golden fluid acrylic.

THE BASIC GUIDE TO DYEING AND PAINTING FABRIC,
by Cindy Walter and Jennifer Priestley, Krause Publications; $19.95

The section in this book on painting describes the various types of paint and such techniques as brushing, sponging, stamping, and splattering. Coauthor Jennifer Priestley is the owner of the website Fabrics to Dye For (see opposite), and the book has been recommended—"informative and inspirational"—by, among others, Dharma Trading Co. (another e-tailer that sells textile paints and dyes, as well as books on how to use them). This is a good book for basics.

DYES & PAINTS: A HANDS-ON GUIDE TO COLORING FABRIC,
by Elin Noble, Elin Noble; $34.95

The former lab manager for dye supplier PRO Chem, Elin Noble still teaches t here on occasion. Fabric painting also gets a full treatment in her book, including such techniques as stamping, stenciling, sun painting, and marbling. The best proof of the book's quality? It's recommended and sold by Dharma Trading, a PRO Chem competitor. On its website, Dharma Trading calls this book "thorough" and "a must."

COMPLEX CLOTH: A COMPREHENSIVE GUIDE TO SURFACE DESIGN,
by Jane Dunnewold, Martingale & Company; $34.95

This book covers such fabric painting techniques as brushing, stamping, silk screening, and hand painting. The directions are precise and easy to follow and are illustrated with color photographs. The book is based on the intensive workshops on surface embellishment that Dunnewold leads, and if you prefer, you can also buy a three DVD set of her Complex Cloth workshops for $65 at her website (**www.complexcloth.com**) or at Dharma Trading Co. Dunnewold's profile begins on page 323, and includes a tutorial on stamping fabric with paint.

A Gallery of Exquisite Painted Quilts

Take a moment to visit the websites of some quiltmakers lauded for their use of paint—here are six particularly noteworthy ones. Hollis Chatelain is an American who lived abroad for much of her life, including in four countries in West Africa, and many of her amazing quilts feature portraits of African people and landscapes. Her skills as a painter and a quilter are equally amazing, but what makes her quilts so powerful is also her intricate compositions. At her website, **www.hollisart.com**, you can click on Gallery and view some of her quilted paintings.

Linda MacDonald trained as a painter in the 1960s, then took up weaving and eventually turned to quiltmaking. Many of her cartoonlike quilts are whimsical but pointed, like *Tree Park*, which pictures one tall tree on display in a park surrounded by stumps. Her popular workshops are extremely detailed: She gives a three-hour workshop just on Beginning Brushes for the Textile Painter and her class on painting flowers can run from six hours to two days. See her work at **www.lindamacdonald.com**, where those who can't afford to buy her quilts can purchase posters or cards of her best known images.

Longtime quiltmaker Bonnie Lyn McCaffery has made many types of quilts and taught all over the world, but it is her portrait quilts that have made a big splash in recent years. McCaffery has won major awards and her classes on painting faces are in demand. At her website, **www.bonniemccaffery.com**, you can look at her work, view work by students who have taken her class in painting faces, and buy her book *Portrait Quilts: Painted Faces You Can Do*.

Legally blind since birth, Susan Shie works very close to the dense surfaces of her extremely tactile quilts. Often working in partnership with her husband, James Acord, Shie has lavishly embellished her works with buttons, beads, metal trinkets, and thickets of embroidery floss. These quilts are frequently covered with dense lines of black writing, like the work of some outsider artists, and Shie has said she makes "outsider art quilts." More and more in recent years, Shie says she has begun her works by "drawing first with an AirPen (like an airbrush, it's a small spray gun that uses air to apply paint) on cotton fabric, then brush painting, and writing over the colors with my AirPen again, making whole cloth quilted paintings." Go to the website of Shie and Acord, **www.turtlemoon.com**, to see some of these very unusual quilts.

One of the most popular uses of paint in quilts is to highlight shadows and textures and create an illusion of three dimensions. Esterita Austin is enthusiastically sought after as a teacher of this technique in landscape quilts; her profile can be found on page 310. At her website, **www.esteritaaustin.com** you can click on Gallery to see some of her award-winning quilts.

And, husband and wife quilt artists Inge Mardal and Steen Hougs, who live in France, have won top prizes for their painted quilts, which often feature realistic looking animals. Check out their quilts at **www.mardal-hougs.com**.

CHAPTER FOUR

Fabulous Fabric and Where to Find It

"I CAN TELL YOU IN THREE WORDS WHY QUILTERS quilt today," says one quilt store owner. "To buy fabric." There are about 2,500 quilt shops in the United States, and that number doesn't include the hundreds of shops that are exclusively web based or the fabric vendors that mostly sell their wares at quilt shows.

In any given year, an estimated 40,000 to 60,000 new fabric designs are released for the quilt market, say fabric company executives. That staggering number represents thousands of new patterns, multiplied by all the various color schemes in which each is printed. So, for example, if a fabric comes out with a pattern of fern leaves and this pattern is printed in shades of

FABRIC VS. SHEETS

For savvy consumers who buy luxury sheets with thread counts in the hundreds it might seem puzzling that quilter's cotton has a thread count so much lower—in the sixties and seventies. Isn't quilter's cotton supposed to be "the good stuff"? But a bed sheet is much stiffer and wouldn't be very easy to sew through, even using a sewing machine. A piece of cotton fabric is just one of three layers in the "quilt sandwich," and the cotton must be light enough that a quilter can easily stitch everything together. Beginning quilters have long been warned not to make the mistake of using an old sheet as the backing for a quilt: They might wear out their fingers or break sewing machine needles trying to sew through all that.

There's also the question of price. The retail price of good cotton in quilt shops is already considered high at $8 to $10 per yard. If four-hundred count Egyptian cotton sheets cost $500 for a queen-size bed, imagine what it would cost to make a quilt from that fabric.

blue, in shades of green, in shades of red, and in shades of orange, that would count as four new fabrics. There has never before been such a rich and diverse selection of fabrics for quilters, and quilters are positively intoxicated by their range of choices. It's no wonder that so many quilters are confessed "fabriholics."

Quilting has become a fashion business, with new "looks" introduced each spring and fall. Just as home cooks love to try an exotic new cuisine or experiment with this year's trendy herbs, quilters keep up with the hot trends in quilt fabrics. They will keep an eye out for the year's "challenge fabric" from Hoffman California Fabrics, check out the display of seasonal flannels, exclaim over the latest novelty prints, and seek out the latest work by gifted fabric designers like Lonni Rossi and Kaffe Fassett. The fabric manufacturers feed the sense of urgency by constantly launching new lines, allowing quilt shops to drop fabric within months if it isn't selling. Quilters have been trained to snap up a fabric that catches their eye, because it might be gone the next month.

One reason the number of new fabrics has mushroomed is that the number of companies producing fabric has grown so fast. The quilt boom in the 1980s and early 1990s attracted a lot of new players to the field. By 2005 there were about ninety fabric companies, roughly double the number a decade before. All those companies needed to differentiate their

A detail of My Mind's In a Tangle, *by Lonni Rossi.*

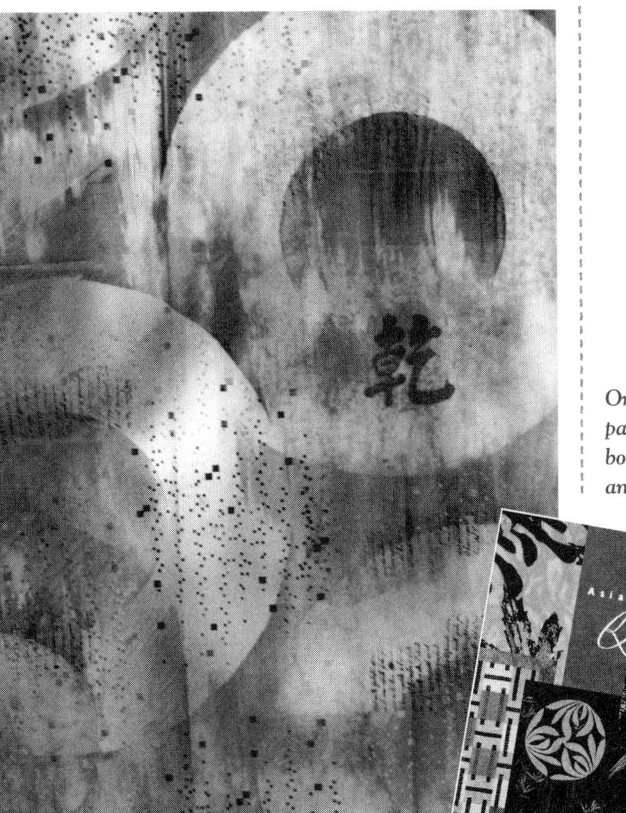

One of Loni Rossi's hand-painted silk panels, and her book on Asian-inspired quilts and fabrics.

products in order to stand out. Some became famous for bold, bright batiks; some are known for delicate pastel prints; others feature holiday-themed patterns, and so on.

Certain fabric designers allied to this company or that develop a following, as have Lynette Jensen and Jennifer Sampou. Also, fabric companies have wooed some of the best-known quilt teachers and asked them to design fabric, for which they are paid royalties. People who love the glorious flower-themed work of Jane Sassaman, for example, but could never afford to pay thousands of dollars for one of her quilts, can buy a few yards for less than $20 from the Jane's Butterfly Garden collection produced by FreeSpirit. This furthers the sense that fabric itself is a collectible.

While many fabric suppliers market their wares as the hippest new look, there are others who trade mostly in nostalgia. Some have done well offering reproductions of

Must It Be Cotton?

Cotton is king (or should that be queen?) with quilters, and for very good reasons. Good quality cotton is colorfast, wears well, feels soft, and is easy to sew, both by hand and by machine. Cotton has give to it but isn't so stretchy that you can't keep your quilt looking crisp and straight edged.

Beginning quilters should definitely start by purchasing *only* fabric that is 100 percent cotton. But things are a tad more complicated than that. Consider that the following can all be cotton fabrics (and this is only a partial list): denim, terry cloth, percale, chintz, broadcloth, damask, jacquard, chenille, flannel, corduroy, velvet, and velour. Most of these fabrics have been used in quilts at one time or another. Denim quilts have been trendy, and velvet is considered a staple in any crazy quilt, whether made in the Victorian era or today.

Irwin Bear, the longtime head of P&B Textiles, which is based near San Francisco, says there are several factors that make different cotton fabrics unique, including how tightly they are woven. Many fabric companies in the quilt market use cotton that is 60 by 60 or 68 by 68, meaning that many threads per inch going both crosswise and lengthwise. P&B often chooses cotton that measures 75 by 75, which produces a lighter, higher quality fabric, says Bear. (Flannel, in contrast, is often a 42 by 44 weave, and the cotton's surface is literally scratched to produce the nap.)

The tricky part for quilters is to combine vastly different types of cotton in the same quilt. Generally these fabrics are categorized by weight, and it can be difficult to sew together a standard quilt cotton with something heavy, like denim.

Some of the myriad cotton-based fabrics: (top to bottom) flannel, corduroy, terry cloth, and denim.

Also, some types of cotton, like terry cloth, are rather stretchy. This isn't to say any of these are forbidden to quilters. On the contrary, you can mix and match to your heart's content, but understand that, if you plan on machine quilting, some of these heavier, thicker fabrics won't move easily through your sewing machine.

Also, you will want to achieve a balance in your quilt not just of color and design but also in the weight of the fabric. You wouldn't want to make a heavy denim quilt for a newborn, nor would you want to create a crazy quilt that bunched all the heavier fabrics on one side. When opting to use a weight of cotton other than standard quilter's cotton, for example flannel, one solution is to use *only* that type of cotton in the quilt. Flannel quilts are extremely popular, and fabric stores have seen a veritable explosion in recent years of attractive flannels. While flannels used to be mostly plaids and featured dark woodsy colors, you can now find flannel fabric in wild, bright colors and a wide range of patterns.

In addition, there are some noncotton fabrics that are increasingly finding favor with quilters, including silk. A luxury fabric, silk is standard for crazy quilts, but art quilters also love its exotic texture and shimmer and use it almost as often as cotton in wall hangings.

Those pioneering art quilters love taffeta, organza, and tulle, too, and experiment with virtually every type of textile (and many nonfabric components) in their work. Why should they have all the fun? Try lots of different fabrics in your quilts, but think about how the quilt will be used. Remember that if your loved ones are actually going to sleep under the quilt, comfort and durability matter.

quilt fabrics that were popular in the thirties and forties, including novelty prints featuring toy soldiers, tiny dogs or bunnies, and the like. Reproductions of somber fabrics from the Civil War era are especially in demand.

Then there is the growing market for imported fabric from Asia, Africa, and Europe. Vendors of imports peddle rare material that looks as though it could be framed and sold as art. At a recent Paducah show, one importer displayed luscious, delicate Japanese silk hand painted by a certified "living treasure" and priced at $300 a yard.

What's making all this fabric so attractive to quilters isn't just a matter of breathtaking diversity but also the quality of what's available. The cotton used to make quilt fabrics now is undeniably finer than it was when the quilt boom began. When it comes to a quilt, things like thread and batting matter a lot, but they are nowhere near as important as the fabric. And it's the bewitching fabric that has lured many people into quilting.

Even everyday fabrics have their charms, here an assortment of soft cotton fabrics in classic patterns.

A good number of quilters who filled out the survey I circulated for this book confessed that they started quilting because they fell in love with fabric, not the other way around. Mary Shelley, who lives in Gerber, California, says she was at a boring luncheon meeting with a friend, when her friend suggested they sneak out and go to a quilt shop instead. Shelley knew how to sew and had been to fabric shops before, but "my eyes must have popped out when I saw all the fabric, sorted by colors. It looked like a candy shop!" says Shelley. "I was immediately hooked. There were samples of quilts for upcoming classes hanging there and I signed up on the spot."

To celebrate fabric and all it does for quilting, let's look at where the fabric comes from, and how to find and buy the best of it.

The fabrics available today come in a mind-boggling array of patterns, colors, and durability.

Fabric: Quality Counts

THE ATTRACTION OF WOMEN TO FABRIC RUNS deep. In her book *Women's Work: The First 20,000 Years*, scholar Elizabeth Wayland Barber argues that women have probably been making cloth since, roughly, the Stone Age. Fiber doesn't age nearly as well as dinosaur fossils, but there are preserved fibers from the caves of Lascaux, France, that date back to 15,000 B.C. Barber believes that women took up weaving, along with food preparation, because it was work that could be done at home while caring for a cave full of babies. Women have been weaving and then quilting for just about as long as anyone can remember. Although the oldest surviving quilt dates back to the fourteenth century, women were quilting garments and bedding long before that. The affinity that women have for fabric has only seemed to deepen as fabric has improved.

Even in the nineteenth century, the hands-down favorite fabric of quilters was cotton, and for good reason. Then cotton was called "wash goods" because the fabric could withstand the constant washing required for clothing worn daily, writes Harriet Hargrave in her book *From Fiber to Fabric: The Essential Guide to Quiltmaking Textiles* (now out of print). In those days, there were cotton ginghams, chintzes, dimities, and challises, but calico was the most widely used in quilts, says Hargrave, a top teacher of machine quilting who earned a degree in textiles and clothing and owns a fabric store in the Denver area.

In the twenty-first century cotton rules again, for all the reasons earlier quilters loved it. It washes well, presses flat, feels soft and supple, and lasts a long time. But in the early 1970s, at the start of the quilt revival, there was very little 100 percent woven cotton in stores. Most fabric was bought by home sewers for garment making. At that time, what quilters there were had to make do with what they could find, mostly cotton and polyester blends. These came in lots of colors, cost less than pure cotton, and were colorfast and resistant to wrinkles.

Unfortunately, there was a real downside to the blends, notes Hargrave in her book. "Polyester would not lie flat because of the permanent press finish. The fabric also tended to be more transparent than cottons, causing the seam allowances to shadow through the top layer of a quilt." But as more and more quilters began to seek out 100 percent cotton cloth, eventually more appeared, providing greater choices of color and pattern.

Although much of the cotton fabric used by quilters today is manufactured overseas, the United States is still a major producer of the raw cotton. And, as the result of improved farming methods, the cotton produced today is itself better in quality. Before it can be woven into fabric, cotton is cleaned and combed and then turned, by a machine, into strands of yarn. These yarn strands start out thick but are machine spun—pulled out until they reach the desired fineness. Those thin strands are then woven into fabric and bleached and chemically treated before being printed or dyed.

The problem today, says Hargrave, is that the quality of the fabric produced isn't uniform, and she has been on a crusade to help quilters understand the differences in quality and why it's worth paying more for the best. The fabric companies "are not out to get us," says Hargrave, but most fabric is made for multiple

FABRIC SWAPS

Susan Druding, who's the former host of the quilting forum at About.com, says fabric swaps are one of the most popular attractions for quilters at that site. "People who post regularly on the forum are often interested in fabric swaps and the variety of swaps is amazing," says Druding. "Sometimes it's a simple fabric swap involving ocean colors or conversation fabric featuring zoo animals, and in many cases, the quantity of fabric swapped is a fat quarter. Sometimes people swap finished blocks instead of fabric, and that requires a lot more organization and more work: If you sign up for a block swap and a dozen people are involved, you have to make twelve blocks."

Most of the swaps done through the About.com site are what are called centralized swaps, in that one person "hosts" the swap and receives all the fabric or blocks. Using this method for block swaps provides assurance that a diligent, creative person isn't paired with someone who does sloppy work or doesn't meet deadlines. The host uses, mostly to make clothing that isn't used as roughly as bedding. As she notes, the fabric for a simple sundress that won't be worn for more than a season doesn't have to be as durable and colorfast as the fabric in a bed quilt that will be used for years and washed often. Or, for an heirloom quilt that might be laundered infrequently but may take months to make and is meant to last generations.

"Consider that it takes the same one hundred hours to make a quilt from poor-quality fabrics as it does from high-quality fabrics," says Hargrave. "In the end, poor-quality materials will lead to a shortened life for the quilt." She adds, "You get what you pay for, and you may only save twenty dollars in materials by buying inferior-quality goods for a quilt."

One of the reasons that independent quilt shops have become such a force in the quilt world is that they emphasize top-quality fabric. Quilters may be able to buy fabric cheaper at a discounter or chain store, but the quality could well be lower. P&B Textiles sells exclusively to independent stores. Its president, Irwin Bear, explains, "In order to meet the price specifications of discounters, fabric manufacturers have to use the cheapest material to start, and then use cheaper dyes, which can be more prone to fading and also make the fabric stiffer."

The companies quilters associate with fabric are really middlemen. Called "converters," they don't generally create the material. Such well-known fabric companies as Hoffman, Robert Kaufman, Benartex, Moda, RJR Fabrics, and P&B Textiles are all converters. Converters take basic milled cotton, called greige (pronounced gray) goods—yardage that is mass-produced almost entirely in Asia now—and convert it into finished, patterned cloth. Actually, most of them don't even do the printing or dyeing themselves but send their designs to overseas plants that specialize in printing fabric. Samples of the designs are printed, then sent back to the American converters for inspection. Designers in the United States tweak the colors and other characteristics of the sample fabric, usually by computer, then send an e-mail with further instructions so the overseas printer can make

can reject poorly made blocks or low-quality fabric and will send out a neat, pretty block to someone who sent in work of that same description.

What the Internet adds to such swaps, which are plentiful in local quilting groups, is fresh ideas and the chance to connect with quilters from far away. American quilters love the chance to receive fabric from quilters abroad, and vice versa, so a good many online swaps cross international borders.

The Yahoo! group swapping2friendship welcomes participants both in and outside the country. Search for it at **www.groups.yahoo.com.**

HARRIET HARGRAVE
FROM FIBER TO FABRIC
THE ESSENTIAL GUIDE TO QUILTMAKING TEXTILES

Harriet Hargrave's authoritative guide to fabrics.

From Field to Fabric: Cotton's Journey

Step One: The Field

There are some eighty countries that produce cotton, but China and the United States are the biggest growers, each accounting for 20 percent of the world market. The American "cotton belt" produces several varieties of cotton that are highly prized because of their extralong fibers.

Step Two: The Gin

At the gin, the fibers are separated from the cottonseeds. The raw fiber, called lint, is cleaned and compressed into bales of about five hundred pounds each; a single bale holds enough cotton to make 325 pairs of jeans. The bales are shipped to textile mills in the United States and overseas.

During harvest time, a cotton gin can process up to 130 bales of cotton every twelve hours.

Step Three: The Mill

Cotton from different bales is blended and carded into a thin web, then condensed into a ropey strand called sliver (pronounced sly-ver). These strands are drawn out into thinner strands, which are twisted to make them stronger. Spinning machines pull the fibers into even thinner strands and wind them onto bobbins, and then the weaving process begins.

The woven cloth taken off the looms is called greige (pronounced gray) goods. The cloth is then treated, dyed, or printed to produce finished goods. American-based fabric companies, including those that cater to quilters, have designers in the United States who instruct textile mills, mostly in Asia, about what patterns, dyes, and designs to use.

An antique cotton gin; modern versions remain much the same.

Step Four: The Market

Fabric buyers for chain stores and independent shops choose what fabrics they want to stock after viewing the new selections each season from the major fabric companies. Some of the ordering by individual independent quilt stores is done at the two major trade shows run by Quilts, Inc., the Houston-based company that runs the International Quilt Festival. The festival is always preceded by the International Quilt Market in Houston, and Quilts, Inc. runs a second market every spring. Quilters see the fabrics at quilt shops and quilt shows, on the websites of online retailers, and in quilt catalogs, then bring the cotton fabric home to make their quilts.

adjustments. This continues until the fabric company likes the result and orders hundreds of yards of the design for sale to fabric shops, garment makers, and other clients.

Where do the designs come from? Some converters order their designs from abroad, as part of a package deal, but most fabric companies have small teams of designers and supplement their work with designs from "guest artists," some of whom are celebrity quilt artists and quilt teachers. Sometimes quilt collectors or historians share their collection of old quilts and help the fabric maker adapt much-loved historic patterns into reproduction fabrics.

"We have three designers here who design fabric," says P&B Textiles' Bear. "They study trends, go to stores to watch what sells, and do focus groups at quilt shows to ask consumers about their preferences. It's hard to turn it around fast: Once we decide on a new line, it takes between a year and eighteen months to turn that into a collection. Then, some companies only keep fabric in the line for six or seven months and don't even do reprints. We keep ours in the line for usually a year and a half to two years."

The rise of quilting has been a godsend to those fabric companies that have survived.

How Quilters Saved the Fabric Business

AMERICAN FABRIC COMPANIES OWE THEIR livelihoods to today's quilters. With the end of compulsory home economics classes and with women streaming into the workforce, starting in the sixties women in droves stopped sewing their own clothes. Fabric sales plummeted, putting some companies out of business. The rise of quilting has been a godsend to those companies that survived.

"In the early 1970s to the mid-1970s, department stores started to close their fabric departments, and that really hurt," recalls Irwin Bear. "We had a great year in 1975, but that turned out to be a peak. After that, it went into the toilet. Fabric companies were closing left and right."

Fabric patterns run the gamut from traditional to cutting-edge. Shown here is a selection from P&B Textiles.

The first Bear remembers hearing about quilting was when a shop catering to quilters opened in St. Paul, Minnesota, in 1972; it didn't last long. If only the owners had waited a few years. In the mid-1970s, Diana Leone wrote one of the first successful sampler books, which she self-published. Sampler quilts have many different block patterns, so they're great for beginners, and Leone's book received praise. She also opened a quilt shop called The Quilting Bee in Los Altos, California, around that time. Leone says that Bear advised her against going into the retail fabric business, a recommendation he doesn't recall but that sounds accurate to him.

Leone's timing was perfect; her shop's opening roughly coincided with the 1976 Bicentennial. "Quilting was part of the Bicentennial celebrations because it's part of our heritage," says Bear. "Out of nowhere came this craft that had been dormant for so long." Retail stores began asking for calico fabric, and P&B began to stock it. Bear says he searched out Leone, asking her to be his mentor in the emerging market. In 1980, Bear attended Quilts, Inc.'s annual Houston trade show for the first time; P&B sold wares to the growing number of quilt shops.

Over the years, more fabric companies saw the number of avid fabric consumers increase and jumped on the bandwagon. Many were losing clients right and left in the garment industry, as the business of making clothes moved offshore. Here was an expanding market right in the United States, and the fabric companies that switched to serve it were joined by new fabric companies springing up to cash in.

One of the new companies, Michael Miller Fabrics, was begun in 1999 by Kathy Miller and Michael Steiner in Steiner's New York apartment. Both Miller and Steiner were already working in the fabric business for one of the biggest converters but broke away to start their own company. They joined Steiner's first name and Miller's last name for their new joint venture.

By 2004, the Miller company was occupying an enormous booth at the Houston Quilt Market, cleverly designed so that the twelve salesmen's desks were covered with gorgeous bright fabrics made up to look like beds. The salesmen were kept much too busy by quilt shop owners ordering fabric to ever relax on the faux beds. "We called it our pj party and we all wore pajamas," says a company spokeswoman. "Our trademark is bright, cutting-edge prints that don't look like the usual quilt fabrics."

Kathy Miller, who had been a fabric designer for years before cofounding Michael Miller Fabrics, says quilters are the absolute best customers for a fabric company and a much easier audience to please than bargain-hunting "garmentos," as garment-industry buyers from Manhattan are known. "For quilters, it's not about the price: They want to be wowed," says Miller. "Quilters are the biggest chunk of our business. Fabric is an impulse buy for many of them. They go for bright colors and whimsical designs that make them feel good."

Without the booming quilt market, companies like Michael Miller would probably never have started, and older firms would still be shutting down. The bottom line, according to industry old-timer Irwin Bear, is that "Quilting saved the textile business."

Swatches of fabric from Michael Miller.

The Fabric Makes the Quilt

Roberta Horton, one of the pioneers of the quilt renaissance in California in the early 1970s, says there is no such thing as an ugly fabric. She proves her point dramatically during her class on making scrap quilts. Students bring fabric they think is ugly, and then Horton conducts an exercise to convince them otherwise.

After each student divides her ugly fabric into three pieces, everyone stands in a circle. Each participant puts one piece of the fabric on her shoulder, another under her arm, and a third piece in her right hand. At Horton's signal, students pass the fabric in their right hand on to the person on their right, and they add the fabric that is passed on to them from the left, to the pile on their shoulder.

More exchanging goes on (you'll have to take the class to see how the whole exercise plays out), but in the end each student has one piece of her own ugly fabric and two pieces of other people's ugly fabrics. Then Horton adds a fourth fabric she has chosen, and each student makes a block with those four colors. Later in the class all of the blocks are assembled into a single quilt. This invariably leaves the class amazed, because Horton always proves her point.

Fabric patterns are nearly infinite in variety.

Certainly, if you're making an all black and white quilt, going to the local shop and just adding a random colored fabric isn't helpful. But quilters do get overly obsessive about the fabric they pick, sometimes to the detriment of successful design. Horton provided some very refreshing and practical tips on choosing fabrics in her marvelous 1995 book, *The Fabric Makes the Quilt.*

Since that book is sadly out of print, Horton has given me permission to excerpt some of her advice on color and

Roberta Horton's fabric primer.

composition and how they relate to choosing fabrics for a quilt. Much of the book is about how to build a quilt's design around a focus fabric or fabrics that the quilter falls in love with, and Horton shares examples of her own quilts, especially a series of African-themed ones. The text that follows comes from a beginning section called The Basics.

"Every piece of fabric has three characteristics that need to be considered: color, value, and pattern. Quiltmakers need to re-order their thinking so that they buy fabric that they need rather than just fabric that they like. Sometimes a fabric that you dislike would really allow another favorite fabric to show even better."

Horton goes on to talk about color, value, and pattern, but I would like to share her six tips on color, because I think this is about the best advice a quilter can get on the topic and is succinctly put. I suggest you challenge yourself to make a quick wall hanging following the advice exactly.

One: Every color is good. Each will do something that no other color will do.

Two: Colors don't have to be used in equal amounts. One can be in the majority, the other in a minority or in an accent role.

Three: Use colors together that mismatch so that they will read as individual pieces of fabric and not all mush together.

Four: Don't worry about color schemes. Any combination goes together if you just repeat it.

Five: The warm colors come toward you and the cool colors recede. Use this knowledge to give a feeling of depth to a quilt.

Six: The greater the number of colors on a fabric, the busier it will be perceived. The same is probably true for the quilt itself.

Look for more information on Roberta Horton's quilts and her teaching schedule at her website, **www.robertahorton.com** and read more about her on page 380.

Horton's website offers a treasure trove of fabric information and history.

A COLORFUL BUSINESS: TOP FABRIC COMPANIES

Although there are roughly ninety fabric companies in the United States, only about a dozen have a high profile in the quilt world, and those are a colorful lot. Many of them work very hard to court quilters and keep them happy, both by producing luscious, gorgeously patterned fabric and through their clever marketing and promotion.

A few fabric companies are based in Texas, but most of the major companies have headquarters on the coasts, either in California or New York City. Overall, fabric companies are self divided into those that sell almost exclusively to the big, discount chain stores, like Wal-Mart or Jo-Ann Stores, which cater to crafters, and those that sell mostly to the smaller independent quilt shops.

Fabrics with metallic elements.

Wal-Mart has become a huge player in the fabric business, and when rumors surfaced in late 2006 that the retail giant planned to close the fabric departments in most of its stores, the quilt world was aghast. Petitions begging Wal-Mart to reconsider suddenly appeared on numerous websites and bloggers vented. While some quilters look down their noses at Wal-Mart and feel the quality of fabric at discounters generally is beneath contempt, there are many quilters in rural areas who say they have no other local source of fabric for quilting.

Dan Fogleman, a spokesperson for Wal-Mart Stores, Inc., told me in early 2007 that Wal-Mart plans to continue selling fabric but not in all the stores. "We have added new craft and celebration centers in our new and remodeled stores as well as in a few existing stores," said Fogleman. "These new centers will carry notions, including yarn, needles, thread, and sewing machines, but we won't be cutting fabric, selling it from bolts. The centers replace our fabric departments in these stores." But

What Price Fabric? Finding Bargains

Quilters frequently gripe about the high cost of fabric, but there really are good reasons to pay up for quality, especially if the quilt is going to be laundered and cuddled and passed down through your family.

Just how much should you expect to pay? High-quality cotton for quilters runs $8 to $10 per yard and higher in quilt shops. Fabrics that are hand dyed, imported, and/or rare will cost more, generally some multiple of those numbers. I have seen cotton hand dyed by famous teachers selling for $30 to $50 a yard and hand-painted and embellished silk for upward of $200 a yard. But there are ways to find bargains without sacrificing quality. Here are four ways to save on fabric.

◆ **Shop the sales.** Virtually every quilt shop has sales a couple of times a year, including fat quarter sales where you'll find fabric selling for half off, or better. Find out when your favorite store has sales and stock up then. This is the best time to fill in gaps in your stash and buy last year's holiday novelty fabrics for next year's holidays.

◆ **Go to flea markets and garage sales.** I know savvy quilters, especially art quilters, who rarely buy brand-new commercial fabric because they're looking not just for a bargain but for fabric that looks different. These quiltmakers swear by flea markets and garage sales, where they look for gently used clothing (especially men's shirts) and old quilts with interesting fabric that can be recycled. The bargains are amazing: You can find gently used shirts for fifty cents apiece. Another flea market find is bundles of old handkerchiefs. These can be used to make handkerchief quilts, and some quilters like to use handkerchiefs to make unusual labels for the backs of their quilts.

◆ **Swap fabric.** Like many quilt guilds, mine schedules an occasional fabric swap—ours is called Uglies Night. Anybody who brings fabric to give away is allowed to take fabric left on the table, and we draw straws to see who goes first. I've found wonderful fabric to round out my stash this way, while dumping fabric leftovers from projects (or fabric I bought that didn't look so attractive once I got home). You can go to scheduled swaps, look for swaps online, and organize casual fabric swaps with a few quilting friends.

◆ **Make a scrap quilt.** After stockpiling fabric for years, why not use your stash? If you were to make every fourth quilt entirely from fabric you already own, you could cut your annual fabric bill dramatically. There's no rule that quilt backings have to be cut from one fabric: Make a patchwork backing for your stash quilt with big swatches of similar fabrics. You'll find a pleasing collection of free patterns for scrap quilts at the website **www.scrapquilts.com,** which is run by Janet Wickell, the quilting guide at About.com.

even a partial pullback of Wal-Mart from the fabric business creates ripples in the quilt world, and some of the fabric companies that supply the retail giant soon announced cutbacks in such areas as charitable donations.

Although Wal-Mart is the Goliath of retailing and has enormous power over fabric suppliers just as it does over suppliers of most everything else, independent stores have unusual leverage when it comes to fabric. That's partly because so many of the independent quilt shops are owned by passionate quilters who demand high quality fabric and who attract like-minded quilters willing to pay top dollar for the good stuff. If a fabric company starts selling the discount chains cheaper versions of the fabric designs that company sells to the independents, the local shops will refuse to buy from that company again. The top fabric companies understand the distinction in quality perfectly well, and many trumpet it in their advertising and on their websites.

An aisle of fabric and trimmings—in most fabric stores, this is just one of many.

RJR Fabrics, for example, a family-owned company started in California in 1978, expresses its loyalties clearly on its website: "RJR refuses to sell any of its fabrics to large chain or discount stores. The company believes the independent quilt shops are by far the best avenue through which to market fabric to quilters because they have employees who are experienced in quiltmaking and are valuable sources of information."

Demetria Zahoudanis, who is a vice president of product development for RJR, explains why the company is so adamant on this score. "In the early 1980s, the president and CEO Rick Cohan walked into a little fabric shop in Southern California and asked what kinds of fabric they needed. They said they wanted 100 percent cotton, not the blends he was showing them. They complained they didn't have many choices of fabric. Cohan listened to them and began creating collections specifically for the quilt shops."

Cohan attended the first Houston Quilt Market, a wholesaler's convention (the market is annual now), to show his fabric lines to quilt shops, and soon RJR was catering exclusively to the quilt market. "Quilting is our number one industry, not a percentage of our sales," explains Zahoudanis. "Other companies sell to the home decor business and apparel companies, but not us."

The company reaches out to quilters partly through its website, www.rjrfabrics.com, with such features as free quilt patterns and a store locator. Contests and challenges run by RJR are also posted there, along with a fabric search option that lets quilters hunt for a shop that carries their favorite RJR fabric. Quilters can sign up to receive bulletins about future fabric introductions.

The company's marketing team keeps working to beef up all these online options, including the addition of a feature that lets quilters print out a design swatch on their home computer printer, complete with RJR's order number for that fabric, so they can take it to the quilt shop and ask for it by number.

A quilt made from Lynette Jensen's Arbor Town Dusk pattern uses fabric from her Thimbleberries line.

RJR's niche in the market is focused on very traditional quilting fabric, and nothing personifies that better than the fabric designed by Lynette Jensen, whose Thimbleberries line of fabric and patterns is among the most successful in the quilt world. A one-time home economics teacher who lives outside Minneapolis, Jensen started by self-publishing quilt patterns in the 1980s. Jensen's patterns were variations of standard quilt blocks in a country style, featuring a palette of browns, deep reds, and forest greens. Eventually, she decided to design fabric to match her patterns and approached RJR.

These days, Jensen is both prolific and beloved. She turns out some six collections of fabrics a year for RJR,

RESOURCES

Fabric Companies That Cater to Quilters

There are twelve to fifteen dominant fabric companies with names that will be familiar to quilt shop browsers. The twelve listed here are among the major players (although not always the largest); these are the ones that have been singled out in this chapter. None of these companies sells fabric directly to consumers, but their websites frequently include free patterns, previews of new fabric lines, and other features of interest (for more about these, see Fabric Company Goodies on page 252). If you find a new fabric you'd love to have, there is often a feature on the site that lets you locate a shop near you that carries that company's fabrics.

Alexander Henry Fabrics

Alexander Henry bills itself as offering "cutting-edge conversational print design," and few would argue. With names like Exotica and Fashionista ("for the kind of girl who likes burgers and Bergdorfs"), the fabric lines are brash and fun.

1120 Scott Road
Burbank, California 91504
(818) 562-8200
www.ahfabrics.com

Andover Fabrics

The luscious fabrics Andover carries are created by an impressive stable of designers, including the famous quilter Ruth B. McDowell (profiled on page 353) and my personal favorite, Lonni Rossi, whose vivid fabrics are almost too beautiful to cut. You'll find lots of free quilt patterns on the company's website.

462 Seventh Avenue
7th floor, New York,
New York 10018
(212) 760-0300
www.andoverfabrics.com

Benartex

Benartex has a large variety of high-quality fabric from designers that include such top quilt teachers as Paula Nadelstern, Eleanor Burns (profiled on page 319), and Caryl Bryer Fallert (profiled on page 327). A sister company to Bernina, Benartex also does a lot to appeal to quilters. To pronounce the name correctly, emphasize the first syllable, Ben: The founder was a Mr. Benardete.

1359 Broadway, Suite 1100
New York,
New York 10018
(212) 840-3250
www.benartex.com

Cranston Village

Cranston is an employee-owned company that dates back to 1824 and is rare in part because it continues to print fabric in the United States. Cranston is known for a wide selection that includes licensed kid-friendly prints, from Beatrix Potter designs to TV's Bob the Builder. The company's fabric lines include everything from reproduction Americana flag designs to cutting-edge geometrics from Robbi Joy Eklow, an art quilter and teacher. The website includes tutorials for beginners (click on Quilting under My Interests, then on Resources for a Beginning Quilter), as well as quite a few patterns.

2 Worcester Road
Webster,
Massachusetts 01570
(508) 943-0520
www.cranstonvillage.com

FreeSpirit

Not your grandma's fabric company—FreeSpirit is known for hip, fresh designs with big, bold patterns.

1350 Broadway, 21st floor
New York,
New York 10018
(212) 279-0888
www.freespiritfabric.com

Hoffman California Fabrics

In business since 1924, Hoffman was the first firm to get past dim, muted calicoes and introduce wild, bright colors to quilters back in the 1980s. Its fabrics still stand out. If you need to whip out your sunglasses at the fabric store to look at a bolt, it's probably a Hoffman fabric. Hoffman is famous for vibrant Bali batiks.

25792 Obrero Drive
Mission Viejo,
California 92691
(800) 547-0100
www.hoffmanfabrics.com

Marcus Fabrics

Family owned since its founding by six Marcus brothers in 1906, this is another company with diverse fabric designs. They run the gamut from Australian designer Jan Mullen's kicky, bright geometrics to Asian-themed collections and traditional American fabrics reproduced from the collections of museums like Old Sturbridge Village. Like some, such as Cranston Village, Marcus Fabrics sells fabrics both to chain stores and independents. Its welcoming website provides tutorials and tons of patterns.

980 Avenue of the Americas
New York,
New York 10018
(212) 354-8700
www.marcusfabrics.com

Michael Miller Fabrics

A newcomer, Michael Miller goes for both bold and nostalgic fabrics and fun prints with names like Dick and Jane and Santa Lava Lamp. The website offers an unusually large selection of quilt patterns using Michael Miller fabrics.

118 West 22nd Street
5th floor, New York,
New York 10011
(212) 704-0774
www.michaelmillerfabrics.com

Moda Fabrics

Along with beautiful retro and reproduction patterns and florals, Moda's whimsical designs include the popular Funky Monkey series. Moda's clever new products for quilters include its "jelly rolls," packs of forty different fabrics cut in two-and-a-half-inch-wide strips and wound in tight spirals. Once unwound, the forty-four-inch-long strips can be sewn into borders or cut into squares.

13800 Hutton Drive
Dallas, Texas 75234
(800) 527-9447
www.modafabrics.com

P&B Textiles

With a wide range of designers that includes such popular quilt teachers as Alex Anderson (profiled on page 307), P&B Textiles' lines like New Basics cater to quilters. The company is also very philanthropic. P&B has been especially generous to breast cancer charities.

1580 Gilbreth Road
Burlingame,
California 94010
(650) 692-0422
www.pbtex.com

RJR Fabrics

Known for a traditional look from the design powerhouse Lynette Jensen, RJR is also one of the fabric companies reaching out to younger quilters with fabric from designers like Sue Beevers, the author of a book on fabric painting, *Off-the-Shelf Fabric Painting: 30 Simple Recipes for Gourmet Results* (C&T Publishing; $24.95).

2203 Dominguez Street
Building K-3
Torrance, California 90501
(800) 422-5426
www.rjrfabrics.com

Robert Kaufman Fabrics

Robert Kaufman has a wide range of fabrics, including lots of basics and a huge selection of novelty prints. Sushi fabric? Yup, they've got it. The website makes it easy to browse through the fabric, either by designer, type (solids, novelty prints, and so on), or theme.

129 West 132nd Street
Los Angeles,
California 90061
(800) 877-2066
www.robertkaufman.com

Harvest Dance Geisha, a Lonni Rossi quilt pattern designed for and made with fabrics from Andover Fabrics.

with twenty-five to thirty fabrics in each collection. But what really drives sales of Thimbleberries pattern books and fabric are Jensen's Thimbleberries Quilt Clubs, which she initiated in the mid-1990s. These clubs, for which fabrics are designed exclusively, are held in independent quilt shops across the country once a month; there are more than one thousand of them, and each club can have up to three hundred members.

"I got the idea not just to sell more fabric but because I thought quilters were missing the social element that used to be prevalent in quilting," says Jensen. "I knew I couldn't convince them to have quilting bees in their homes and we didn't want a guild atmosphere, with officers and duties. We wanted pure, social fun."

Thimbleberries Quilt Clubs are great for shop owners too, giving them a rapt audience for all the new tools and fabrics as they come in. "The shops teach something each month, a small project or a technique," says Jensen. "They pay us a fee to start the club in their shop and we send them patterns to duplicate for club members, plus a Thimbleberries door prize they can give away each month. There is also a website just for quilt shops in the program where they can get extra ideas, projects, patterns, and a newsletter to pass along to members." The bottom line is that the Thimbleberries clubs help RJR sell more fabric. "There are fifty thousand pieces of red fabric out there, but the stores keep buying mine because they have this structure in place, and it is a structure that helps them run their stores," says Jensen.

Even with all it does, RJR faces stiff competition. Because there are so many of them, fabric companies have a tough time setting themselves apart, and many others also work hard to attract quilters. It might seem crazy that they bother to advertise in quilt magazines and promote their brands. After all, most quilters don't walk into the local quilt shop and ask, "What have you got that's new from Marcus Fabrics?" But there is method in the fabric companies' madness. Quilters respond to high quality fabric in striking designs that help them complete their quilts, so fabric companies start by printing the kinds of fabric quilters want and then alert the quilt world through extensive advertising in the many quilt magazines.

The Internet is another place where fabric companies woo quilters. Andover Fabrics boasts on its website that the New York company created a line of more than one hundred coordinated designs perfect for quilters who need closely related colors for a quilt or are building a stash. Benartex, knowing that quilters get annoyed because fabrics come and go so quickly, promises on its website that it will keep some of its most popular collections like Fossil Fern available "indefinitely." Many fabric companies offer free patterns on their websites, while some also provide tips for quilters, free newsletters, and other goodies.

One of the few fabric companies that virtually any quilter could identify by name is Hoffman California Fabrics, and it's a distinction the company has cultivated. Hoffman has deep roots in the textile business, going back to 1924. Founder Rube Hoffman started Hoffman California Fabrics to sell wool flannels to California department stores and clothing makers. Soon, he started buying greige goods (undyed fabric) to print his own designs.

Things got more interesting in the 1950s, when Rube Hoffman's two sons, Philip and Walter, both passionate surfers, joined the family business. Company lore has it that the wild colors and designs for which the company is famous come from Philip and Walter's love of looking for fabrics in exotic surfing locales. Thus, Hoffman was the first company to start printing the bold batiks from Bali that have been favorites in the quilt market for years. When the surfing brothers started at Hoffman, there was no quilting business, and much of the company's fabrics, printed with surf and underwater scenes, wound up being made into clothing, including the Hawaiian shirts that were worn in the television series *Magnum, P.I.*

Company lore has it that the wild colors and designs for which Hoffman is famous come from Philip and Walter's love of looking for fabrics in exotic surfing locales.

Fabric Company Goodies

A handful of fabric companies woo quilters directly, offering them freebies that include patterns, newsletters, quilting tips, and more. This is a list of some high-profile companies and the goodies they've been known to share. Most fabric companies provide a list of new fabrics on their websites and let you scan a list of retailers to find the nearest store carrying their fabrics. You'll find a more comprehensive list of fabric companies with extensive contact information on *pages 248–49*.

Benartex, Inc.

With a cool website that has many tantalizing features, New York–based Benartex offers a gallery of current fabrics along with a monthly e-newsletter and a project of the month. Under the community feature you can check to see if there are new quilt challenges or view the winners of previous contests.

www.benartex.com

Cranston Village

Cranston Village sells fabric to both the chains and independent quilt shops. The most unusual feature on its website is a virtual tour of the company's mill, which takes you step-by-step through the preparation and printing of the fabric (click on About Us and then click on Overview to get to the tour). Its online fabric swap forum is also unusual. In case you run out of a now "retired" fabric you can find another quilter who still has some. If you travel to Webster, Massachusetts, you can actually tour Cranston Village's plant.

www.cranstonvillage.com

FreeSpirit

A relative newcomer that started business only in 2000, FreeSpirit was a subsidiary of NTT Inc., which also owns Fabric Traditions. In 2007 FreeSpirit became a part of Westminster Fibers. To stand out, FreeSpirit stresses fresh, eye-popping designs, often from a younger generation of artists and designers. The company is trying to attract younger women to quilting by giving them tons of easy patterns that just look complicated. To that end, its website usually offers dozens of free quilt patterns to download, way beyond the token number most companies make available.

www.freespiritfabric.com

Marcus Fabrics

This East Coast company is rare in that it supplies both independent quilt shops and fabric chains. Marcus Fabrics' website is also unusual, with multiple treats for quilters. Click on Fun & Features and find things like the Guild Connection, which includes a directory of quilt guilds and news about them. There are also free tips, an e-mail newsletter, free patterns to download, and more. If you send in a tip and it gets published online, Marcus Fabrics will send you a free packet of fat quarters.

www.marcusbrothers.com

Robert Kaufman Fabrics

A family firm based in Los Angeles, Robert Kaufman Fabrics is another with a very long pedigree in the fabric business. Kaufman works with a stable of fabric designers that quilters ask for by name, such as Jennifer Sampou. Its website includes plenty of free quilt patterns to download, plus information about the Kaufman Quilt Quest challenge, which debuted in 2004. The top winners get cash prizes and their quilts tour the country, while about thirty quilts that receive honorable mentions travel in a separate exhibition.

www.robertkaufman.com

California was an early hotbed of contemporary quilting in the 1970s, and the Hoffmans soon recognized its potential. Eventually the brothers took over the business, and divided it between themselves, with Philip (known as Flippy in surf circles) running the quilt side of Hoffman and Walter running the rest. These days, the third generation of Hoffmans is in charge of the business, and Rube's grandson Marty spends half the year in Bali, supervising the company's vast production of batiks there. While the company also produces gorgeous Asian-themed fabrics in Asia, those batiks are still a huge part of the Hoffman line. The company's award-winning designer, Kathy Engle, designs roughly one thousand new batik patterns every year.

Although it had already made a name for itself among quilters with its fine fabric, Hoffman lifted its profile even higher with the announcement of its first annual quilt challenge in 1987. The rules dictated that to enter the contest quilters had to use a particular Hoffman fabric as part of their quilt, but they could use whatever other fabrics they chose to complete it. That first year, fewer than one hundred quilts were submitted. Now seven hundred or more quilts are entered in the Hoffman challenge each year, and categories have been added for dolls and garments. Hoffman advertises the challenge heavily and picks exciting vibrant patterns for the featured fabric, the annual unveiling of which is much anticipated. Every year after the winners are announced the best 150 quilts are divided into groups of 30 and sent on tour across the country. They are exhibited in quilt shows and quilt shops all over.

The jam-packed interior of the Keepsake Quilting shop in Center Harbor, New Hampshire.

In order to grab some of the glory, other fabric companies, including Benartex and Robert Kaufman

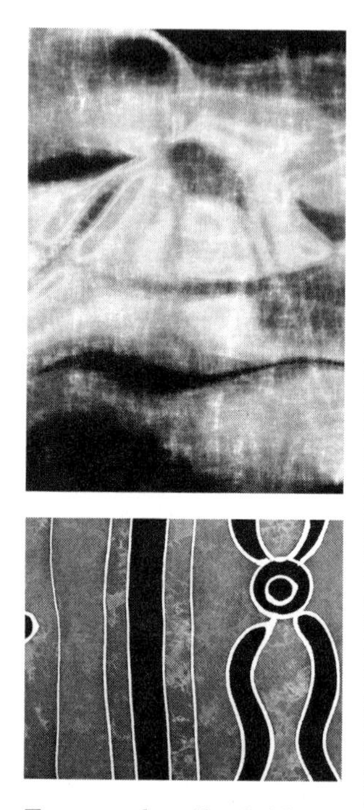

Two examples of batik fabrics using different methods.

Fabrics, have begun their own challenges and contests, but none is as well known as the Hoffman challenge. It's because of such constant marketing that Hoffman is one of the rare fabrics that quilters seek out by brand name.

Given how crowded the market for quilt fabric is already, it can be extremely difficult for a new company to get noticed. "I was asked to start a whole new fabric company in 2000, and I knew we couldn't come in looking just like Moda, RJR, or Hoffman," says Donna Wilder, who spent more than twenty years working for Fairfield, the batting manufacturer, and who also used to host a PBS television show called *Sew Creative*. At the new company, FreeSpirit, Wilder was one of four principal executives, all women, and although they had lots of expertise, they had to be creative to attract the attention of the much sought after quilters faced with many stunning fabrics.

"I felt like there was too much sameness in the fabric business," says Wilder, who is a passionate quilter herself. "I felt we were losing a sense of creativity and there was a void in larger, bolder fabrics. I also wanted to cultivate new, younger quilters."

So this became a big part of FreeSpirit's image, as Wilder sought ways to attract thirty- to forty-five-year-old women, including those who may have found knitting hip and fun but were looking for a new hobby. "This is an instant gratification generation, and these consumers are looking for quick and easy. They want fabric that helps create the quilt for them."

Wilder saw to it that many of the company's fabric designers came up with extralarge prints that could easily be cut up into big squares and assembled into quilts that had wide borders. The idea was to create quilts that were simple and quick to make but looked gorgeous and impressively complex when finished. "Large-format quilts" is Wilder's term for them, and to help novice quilters make them, the company supplies dozens of patterns that can be downloaded without charge from its website, www.freespiritfabric.com.

There are some who say that the quilt boom has attracted too many players into the fabric business and that it faces a glut. Margins are already razor thin; there could be some dropouts in the years to come. But the major players, which have been catering to quilters for years, are expected to continue for the long haul. While fabric executives complain, all the competition has been wonderful for quilters, bringing them an incredible bounty.

Famously Wonderful Fabric Stores

QUILTERS ARE ON A PERPETUAL TREASURE HUNT and they know they can strike gold in almost any fabric store, no matter what its size. But at some quilt shops, you'll feel like you've found the proverbial mother lode every time you go. It's worthwhile to take a close look at shops with national reputations—both the very large ones and those that are off the beaten path—to see what sets them apart.

Although there are thousands of local quilt shops all across the United States, a handful of megastores have become meccas for quilters. At the top of a short list are Keepsake Quilting in Center Harbor, New Hampshire, and Hancock's of Paducah, Kentucky. Both have been in business for decades; they display many more bolts of fabric than the average shop and they have furthered their

The lush fabrics at Keepsake Quilting are irresistibly displayed, making it easy for quilters to see patterns up close.

Quilt Challenges

Quilt challenges are contests with a theme. Challenge quilters don't compete simply to make the most beautiful, elaborate, or original quilt; instead, the goal is to create the best example of a quilt that meets certain established criteria.

Quilt challenges are not a new idea, but they've grown increasingly popular. Some are begun by commercial entities to advertise their products, but for many challenge originators the idea is to simply have fun and create a sense of community. In a quilt challenge, the barriers can be both creative and technical, plus there's a deadline to meet. There are often strict limits regarding materials. Quilters may have to limit themselves to certain colors or include a particular brand and style of fabric, especially when the contest is run by a fabric company.

Hoffman California Fabrics has been running a challenge since 1987 and creates a new, colorful fabric each year specifically for that purpose. All quilts entered in the challenge must contain that fabric, but that's the only design requirement. (For contest rules and photos of past winners see the website, **www.hoffmanchallenge.com**.)

Keepsake Quilting, a beloved New Hampshire–based shop, holds regular challenges that require quilters to use a group of fabrics. There is always a theme. (Learn about the most recent challenges at **www.keepsakequilting.com**.)

But challenge quilts are not only sponsored by businesses. They are sometimes initiated in order to capture a mood, commemorate momentous events, or raise awareness of an issue.

Cynthia Sullivan's winning entry in Keepsake Quilting's 2003 Eastern Inspiration challenge.

In 1998 the organization Prevent Child Abuse New York asked quiltmakers to create quilts that addressed the question of "child abuse, child abuse prevention, and violence against children." Of all the submissions received, about half of them toured in an exhibit organized to increase consciousness of the problem.

Many challenges originate online as Internet quilting groups work to create a sense of cohesion among far-flung members who rarely get to meet in person. Some of the best known are the challenges run by the online group Quiltart. A tradition has evolved wherein members throw out suggestions for possible challenges whenever inspiration strikes. Someone on the list assumes responsibility for setting the rules and keeping track of the quilts, and then the challenge goes forward. After the deadline, photos of the quilts are sent to the challenge organizer and posted on the group's website, **www.quiltart.com**.

Since the Quiltart list began in 1995, there have been more than fifty challenges, everything from making a quilt using just the colors black and white, to quilting a self-portrait. Art quilter Tomme Fent organized a Bag o' Stuff challenge, in which Quiltart members were invited to mail off a gallon-size plastic bag full of fabric, embellishments, and "found items" to Fent. The bags were randomly sent to the 130 participating quilters. At least some of the bag's contents had to be used to make the quilt.

One of the most popular Quiltart challenges was the 2005 invitation to name the eighth deadly sin and to create a quilt depicting it. The dozens of sins creatively depicted included racism, conformity, apathy, chocolate—and excessive body piercing.

Many large guilds hold challenges routinely: Some who run local quilt shows prefer to schedule challenges in the off years between their guild quilt shows. There are also challenges started by small quilt groups. Debra Eggers, an Idaho quilter, has long belonged to a group called the Monday Night Quilters, and she started its long tradition of challenges. "Challenges are sporadic," says Eggers. "Someone will say, 'Hey, Valentine's Day is coming up, let's do a challenge related to that.'"

One of the Monday Night Quilter's challenges was to make something with a heart motif, and another time members had to make a quilt using red, white, and blue fabric. Once everyone had to make a project featuring a hanky. Eggers says she used her hanky to make a butterfly, then sewed a border around that and quilted the whole thing into a wall hanging. In each case, participating quilters bring in their own completed project and swap quilts with another member of the group. For the hanky challenge, Eggers received in exchange, "a darling Sunbonnet Sue with the hanky folded in fourths to make her skirt."

Lavish awards are clearly not what lures quilters to challenges, although new sewing machines are sometimes among the prizes. Rather, quilters love the recognition. Challenge quilts are generally exhibited, sometimes quite widely. The top 150 quilts from Hoffman Fabrics' challenge travel to shows and shops all over the United States.

But the biggest rewards are personal. Many quilters seek out challenges because they find them stimulating. Instead of working with the same blocks, designs, and methods they have employed countless times in the past, challenges push them to break out of their comfort zones, try new things, and take artistic risks—sometimes radical ones.

The 2003 Eastern Inspiration second-place winner, by Monica Mercer.

Aisles of fabric at Paducah, Kentucky's famous Hancock's fabric store.

reach by producing successful mail-order catalogs and websites as well. Nonetheless, visiting both stores in person is on the must-do list of many passionate quilters.

The two fabric stores couldn't be more different. Keepsake Quilting is a trim, New England shop, located right next to pristine Lake Winnipesaukee in a town called Center Harbor. Quilts that have been entered in the two challenges Keepsake announces in its catalog each year hang from the ceiling. The store is stocked with what seems like acres of cloth, arranged in color groups; a separate room holds hundreds of pattern books and notions. Keepsake comes across as both tidy and inviting. Visitors half expect the company's mascot, a Portuguese water dog named Cisco who usually appears in the catalog, to lope down the aisle (he mostly hangs out at the warehouse and administration building, about a mile down the road).

Every summer, Keepsake Quilting stages a vast tent sale in the parking lot, and women show up as early as 3 A.M. with coffee mugs and folding chairs to get first crack at the sale fabrics, says Rob O'Brian, president of the company. Crowds of three to five hundred show up each day of the sale, which runs from two to three days, and the customer who has traveled the farthest always gets a prize (in 2006 that customer came from Michigan).

O'Brian, who spent his career in direct marketing and knew nothing about quilts until he joined Keepsake in 2005, is astonished at the passion of his customers. "The sale doesn't start until nine in the morning, but the store employees start entertaining customers at about seven, with trivia games and by spinning a roulette wheel. Prizes include fabric and gift certificates. Maybe at noon, they'll spontaneously announce that all green fabric is twenty percent off.

And every so often, a Keepsake employee will stand on the back of a truck, and auction off some of the fabric. It's a pretty big deal around here."

Hancock's of Paducah has a different flavor, but its customers are just as passionate. Hancock's has a great big blowout sale every April when the American Quilter's Society show is in town, and a good share of the 35,000 quilters who come to the AQS show make a point of stopping by.

Though a legend in the quilt world, Hancock's is housed in a nondescript sheet-metal warehouse alongside a major freeway. It's not filled with cute and cozy decorations like many quilt shops, but its attraction is simple—the biggest inventory of top-quality quilt fabric under one roof. During the show week a huge amount of it is on sale for half price. Quilters know they can snap up Hoffman batiks, RJR's Thimbleberries, and every other lavish pattern fabric they covet for a bargain price. And just seeing so much gorgeous fabric in one place makes their blood pressures rise.

The week of the show, Hancock's of Paducah (not to be confused with a national chain called Hancock Fabrics) opens early, at 8 A.M. By that time, several hundred women are usually lined up outside, and they've been known to pound on the door if the opening runs late. (During the AQS show, a sign reads, "Men who need to use a restroom can use the Porta Pottis in the parking lot." All restrooms are Ladies during the sale.)

Veteran shopper's at Hancock's know that the huge front room contains all the bolts of current fabric and that the back room has tables loaded with precut fabric, remnants from the ends of bolts, and fabric that didn't sell well. There are forty tables in that room during the April sale, says Justin Hancock, director of mail order sales, and the company sells twenty thousand yards of remnants alone during that time.

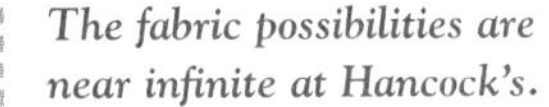

The fabric possibilities are near infinite at Hancock's.

Finding a Quilt Shop

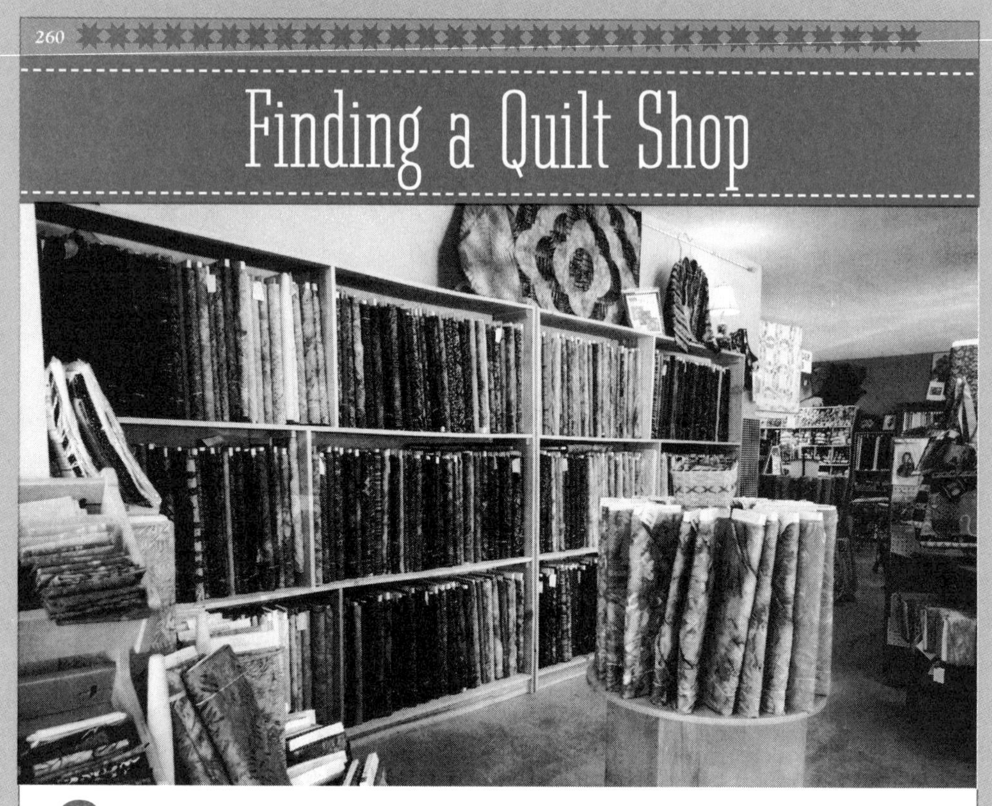

Quilt shops tend to be the epicenter of a quilter's world, the place where tools and community come together. If you're a member of a guild, you can hear lots of people opining on the best local quilt shops. Some fortunate American quilters have three or more fabulous shops within a half-hour's drive, while others have to drive for hours to find one that's only satisfactory.

But if you're new to quilting or if you're traveling, it can be a little harder to find a good shop. One of the best resources is the *Quilters' Travel Companion* (Chalet Publishing; $20), which functions like a Yellow Pages for quilt stores. Compiled by Audrey Swales Anderson and Tom Culp, the book is published in June of every even numbered year, and the most current edition boasts more than two thousand shop listings from throughout the United States and Canada.

A wall of fabric bolts at Quilts Olé in Corrales, New Mexico.

Like a phone book, there is a straightforward listing of shops by state. Stores that pay to advertise get a bigger space and a chance to list what they specialize in and brag about how many bolts of fabric they carry, but even shops that don't advertise are listed in the *Quilters' Travel Companion*. You'll find the street address, phone number, store hours, and website address, if there is one. And by going to the publisher's website at **www.quilterstravelcompanion.com**, you can find online store listings, including ones for stores that opened after the latest edition went to press.

There are a good number of other listings of quilt shops online, but many include only shops that carry a limited number of brands. For example, fabric companies will list the shops that sell their fabric lines and publishers will only point to stores that stock their books. That's not what you want if you're going on summer vacation and are just looking to find the closest good quilt store.

However, there are several excellent Web listings that tend to be pretty comprehensive. One of the best is on **www.quilt.com**; scroll down to Regional Information and click on Quilt Stores. The page gives you a list of states, and when you click on a state, you get a long list with information that goes beyond just names and addresses. For example, the listing for the Sew It Seams fabric shop in Morehead City, North Carolina (my mother's local shop for many years), describes what they carry and adds "The coffee is on and all are welcome. We even have a special husband chair."

A goodie bag from the 2007 Sisters Outdoor Quilt Show in Sisters, Oregon.

The Yellow Pages of quilt stores.

Two other good online store guides are **www.quiltwoman.com** (scroll down to the Directory of Quilting Resources and click on the word Find on the line with Quilt Shops) and **www.FabDir.com**. Quilt Woman even lists quilt shops in some foreign countries. And FabDir.com contains an unusually comprehensive guide to both fabrics and fabric shops, including those in Canada, but be warned that it contains lots of ads.

Finally, a tip from the computer guru and quilter Gloria Hansen, whose many books include *Free Stuff for Traveling Quilters on the Internet* (Watson-Guptill Publications; $16.95). Hansen says that when she's going out of town and wants to hunt for quilt shops, she goes to **www.yellowpages.com**. She types in *quilts* where it asks for a category, plugs in the address of the hotel where she'll be staying and requests a search for quilt shops within a thirty-five-mile radius. "It's easy to see from the names that come up which will do the trick," says Hansen, "Plus, you get a map and directions for each listing."

In the larger front room, women with shopping carts race around between the bolts, as scads of temporary employees help cut the fabric the shoppers select. Designated runners race the bolts back to the shelves so other customers can have a chance at them.

Staffing the sale requires many reinforcements, says Justin Hancock. "We sometimes supplement our staff of fabric cutters with twenty or so local customers, who are paid to work that week. After all, they know our inventory and where everything is. My aunt comes from Memphis with three ladies from her church, and my mom, who teaches high school locally, recruits some of her students."

The AQS sale helps feed Hancock's reputation, but what makes it possible to keep such a vast selection of fabric current in a small town is the company's much-anticipated quarterly catalog, which is mailed to thousands of quilters worldwide, and its website, which keeps improving. "According to the sales reps at lots of the top fabric companies, including Benartex, Moda, Alexander Henry, and Hoffman, we are their biggest account," says Hancock.

Hancock's of Paducah knows its power and place but tries not to compete with local shops in the kinds of extras they deliver so well. "To us, to compete with local shops on things like classes would be treading on sacred ground," says Hancock. "We have some special events but we don't do classes like shops do, and we don't offer regular things like block of the month projects."

RESOURCES

Major League Quilt Shops

The two shops that arguably occupy the top tier of the quilt shop major league are Keepsake Quilting and Hancock's of Paducah. Both have exceptional catalogs as well as "destination" shops and distinctive, user-friendly websites. Here's how to find the stores, at both their real and virtual addresses.

KEEPSAKE QUILTING

Big but cozy, Keepsake Quilting is located in Center Harbor, New Hampshire, and pulls in both loyal locals and the tourists who come to visit Lake Winnipesaukee. The Keepsake catalog, which is free, is one of those rare catalogs people save for when they can enjoy it with a cup of tea. In between fabrics and kits that range from traditional to cutting-edge are testimonials from customers who rave about Keepsake Quilting's service. (I guess this is the place where I confess that I cried the first time I visited the shop: My mother so loved the catalog and she had recently died.) Keepsake also pumps up its national audience with a quilt challenge twice a year, announced in the catalog and on the website, which it has recently improved.

The Best Local Fabric Shops

ORDINARILY, QUILTERS DO MOST OF THEIR shopping at quilt stores close to home, and the quantity and variety of wonderful local shops is astounding. Most offer an excellent, often-changing selection of fabric and tools, as well as a broad array of classes and special services.

Some quilt shops double as sewing machine dealerships, but many stock just fabric and quilt-related supplies. Owners strive to make quilt shops a comfortable place for quilters of all levels and want them to become a community hub. Browsing is definitely encouraged. The old-fashioned, personalized service that consumers moan about missing at today's megastores is automatic at most quilt stores.

Most local shops don't have a national reputation, but there are exceptions. A few have become known because they're owned and operated by famous quilt teachers. Machine quilting guru Harriet Hargrave has long owned Harriet's Treadle Arts near Denver and can be found there when not on the road teaching. Pioneering quilter Jinny Beyer opened a retail shop next to her design studio in Great Falls, Virginia, near Washington, D.C. Beyer has been a long-time designer for RJR Fabrics, and having a shop allows her to stock every single fabric she designs. This is important, as the rapid growth in the introduction of new fabric means most stores carry only a modest number of designs from each particular collection.

Oregon's famous Stitchin' Post.

Route 25B
Center Harbor,
New Hampshire 03226
(800) 865-9458
www.keepsakequilting.com

HANCOCK'S OF PADUCAH

Located in Paducah, Kentucky, this well-stocked shop always holds a humongous sale every April during the American Quilter's Society show. People come to Hancock's year-round for the staggering variety of fabric, not for classes or quaint decor, which are not part of the package. Its impressive website is well organized to help shoppers negotiate the huge array of goodies, and the catalog, which can be ordered free, will make you drool.

3841 Hinkleville Road
Paducah, Kentucky 42001
(800) 845-8723
www.hancockspaducah.com

BLOCK OF THE MONTH CLUBS

Countless quilt shops offer popular block of the month clubs, which give quilters a chance to try new techniques. Generally the way these clubs operate is that quilters sign up at the start of an annual cycle, often beginning in January or September. They pay a minimal fee, usually between $5 and $10, and are given the fabrics and pattern for a single quilt block. Most quilt shops set a certain day and time when quilters must come for the materials, like the first Saturday or third Wednesday evening of the month. While at the shop, there may be a mini class or tutorial on that first block.

There are some block of the month programs where quilters pay to participate every month, but the practice of just charging for the first block is more common. If the quilter returns at the set time with a finished first block, she will be given free materials for the second one, and so on through the twelfth. This would be a marvelous bargain except that most quilt shops use the block of the month club as a loss leader. By

One of the few other local fabric shops with a long quilting history and national reputation is the Stitchin' Post in tiny Sisters, Oregon. This shop could never boast about being biggest, but owner Jean Wells has made it a destination through her amazing annual outdoor quilt show.

Wells began her show in 1975, the year she opened her fabric shop. Quilts are displayed all over town, hanging from fences and porches and on clotheslines stretched across the sides of buildings. Always held on the second Saturday of July (it's never rained yet), the Sisters Outdoor Quilt Show attracts more than 20,000 visitors.

There were twelve quilts in the first show, recalls Wells. Now, there are more than one thousand hanging each year. Wells has insisted on keeping the show noncommercial, raising money to pay for the portable toilets and other amenities. Wells has also kept the show free. And, Wells has resisted calls to have the show last longer. "If we did it for two days, it wouldn't be special," she says.

Viewing the handiwork at the Sisters Outdoor Quilt Show.

Though the show itself doesn't make money, it has helped make Wells' shop famous. For a week before the outdoor show, the Stitchin' Post runs classes for visiting quilters, with local teachers supplemented by nationally known instructors. During the rest of the year, Wells caters to her community, knowing that tourists will come, too. Those who loved visiting the store during the outdoor show can shop year-round at the store's website, www.stitchinpost.com, where quilters can snap up Sisters Quilt Show T-shirts and posters as well as fabric and notions.

Stitchin' Post's wall of yarn.

An avid quilter, Wells has written more than twenty pattern and how-to books and travels often to teach. In one of her most popular classes she discusses how to run a quilt shop. "I find there are plenty of people opening stores who don't know the basic principles of business," she says. "I took business courses at the local community college after I had already been in business nine years, and it really opened my eyes. To be profitable, you must learn to manage inventory. You can't just buy every fabric for the shop that you fall in love with."

One of her prime lessons to would-be owners: "Keep reminding yourself that nobody has to quilt. If you think of your store as an entertainment business, that helps!"

LOCAL GEMS

For the majority of quilt shops, the clientele and their reputation are strictly local, unless the store happens to be located near a major seasonal tourist attraction. But one good way to get a glimpse of the outstanding local shops nationwide is in *Quilt Sampler*, a magazine produced twice a year by *Better Homes and Gardens*. For each of these issues, created by the staff of *American Patchwork & Quilting* magazine, ten outstanding quilt shops and their owners are profiled, with each shop providing a quilt project and pattern. *Quilt Sampler* is

requiring participating quilters to visit the shop each month, they put their customers in temptation's path. Few people can resist when they arrive at the store and see all the new fabric and other goodies.

The finished quilts are generally sampler quilts with each block having a different design, but the techniques and fabrics used vary a lot from store to store and quilter to quilter. The shop might offer one pattern per block for, let's say, an appliqué sampler but let customers choose what type of fabrics they want to use. Opting for batiks instead of reproductions of 1930s novelty prints gives the completed block of the month quilt a very different look.

Sometimes the final design of a block of the month quilt is a secret, with participating quilters seeing only the designs of the block on which they're working and those that they've completed but not how all the blocks are intended to be combined. Most of the time, however, quilt shops display a finished quilt with all twelve blocks to attract quilters to participate. Because they have a whole month to make one small block, quilters don't feel overwhelmed.

SHOP HOPS

In recent years, many independent quilt stores have organized shop hops, which encourage quilters to make the rounds of all the fabric suppliers in a particular area. The central idea is that quilters who trek to the shops during the hop will get small rewards along the way, and those who complete the entire hop circuit will be eligible for major prizes—like a sewing machine or shopping spree.

These hops, which are often held annually, vary considerably in their length, the number of shops participating, and the goodies awarded. Usually between four and twelve shops band together for the special sales, which may run for just a weekend or as long as a week or ten days. Sometimes the shops can all be visited in a single day, but more often quilters will need to stagger their trips and travel an hour or more to some stores.

Quilters who register to participate are given a document to record their visits, sometimes in the form of a "passport," which must be stamped or punched at each quilt shop in the hop. At one shop hop in Indiana, participating quilters paid

published in the spring and the fall and stays on store shelves for several months.

The articles give a sense of the stores' personalities and the regional flavor. Staff members at The Treasure Hunt, a shop in Carpinteria, California, for example, hide three colorful figurines, including a surfboard-toting lizard, among the bolts and fat quarters, and whenever a customer finds one and brings it to the counter, a prize is awarded. In Corrales, New Mexico, a shop called Quilts Olé favors extrabrightly colored fabric and the employees wear wild chile pepper necklaces.

The Quilt Box, located down a country lane in Dry Ridge, Kentucky, has developed an out-of-town following partly due to the *Quilt Sampler* and also because of a rave review on the website PlanetPatchwork.com. "It's not just a quilt shop, it's a phenomenon," wrote Lynn Holland, one of the founders of Planet Patchwork in one of her "Traveling Quilter" columns online. Holland says The Quilt Box is still perhaps her favorite fabric shop not just because the selection and service are terrific but because the setting is stunning and there is even something for her teenage kids to do while she shops.

"The shop is in a charming cottage, but the first thing you notice is the wide expanse of countryside across the lane, complete with a lake and some ducks and geese to feed, and a five-hole pitch-and-putt golf course," writes Holland in her review. While there, she paid an extra dollar to receive the quarterly newsletter "Quilt Box News," which "shows the same creativity as the store, with free patterns, pictures, and stories about customers and staff and the resident animals," which include peacocks.

Corrales, New Mexico's renowned quilting store, Quilts Olé.

Quilts Olé's airy, fabric-filled space makes shopping pure pleasure.

Lynn Holland's husband, Rob, her partner in life and in the Planet Patchwork website, actually has a different favorite, Rainbows End Quilt Shoppe in Dunedin, Florida, near Tampa. Bragging that it offers more than sixteen thousand bolts of cotton alone, Rainbows End says it is the largest quilt shop in Florida. Rob Holland loves that it's located in "a cute little town near the ocean," but he says what really won him over is "the enormous creativity. There is lots of fabric but it's arranged in a way that catches your eye and gives you ideas about how to match colors."

Most fabric shops try to create many good excuses for customers to stop by, including plenty of classes and workshops, special sales, and in-store projects—like block of the month clubs, where quilters sign up to receive materials and instructions once a month. At year's end, the quilter will, theoretically, have a dozen finished blocks that can be united in a quilt.

The quilt shop that I frequent, the Pennington Quilt Works in Pennington, New Jersey, is fairly typical. It offers twenty-five to thirty in-store classes every three months. A printed newsletter goes to every customer who signs up, listing the classes and other events. The women who run the Pennington shop along with the owner, Jan Crane, are unfailingly kind and endlessly helpful, ready to spend whatever time it takes helping a

$5 to obtain the passport and were also given a simple chain bracelet. At every subsequent quilt shop they received a charm to attach to the bracelet. Those quilters who went to every shop in the hop received a completed charm bracelet, plus a chance to win prizes.

The shop hop concept has also been adopted online, but online shop hops can require more than one hundred "visits," at which quilters just have to click a certain icon to show that they spent time browsing, if not buying. For one such online hop, go to **www.fabshophop.com** to check out the virtual shop hops run by The Fabric Shop Network, a trade group.

RESOURCES

Finding Fabric: Some Local Shops

There are many remarkable quilt shops all across the United States. The ones you'll find here have a particular claim to fame that has lifted their profile to a national level, and all of these shops are discussed in this chapter.

Harriet's Treadle Arts

Harriet's Treadle Arts is a Wheat Ridge, Colorado, quilt shop run by machine quilting expert Harriet Hargrave. (Wheat Ridge is a city near Denver.) The shop's website includes many of the fabrics and notions Hargrave likes best, including hard to find reproduction prints.

6390 West 44th Avenue
Wheat Ridge,
Colorado 80033
(303) 424-2742
www.harriethargrave.com

Jinny Beyer Studio

This full-service quilt shop located in Great Falls, Virginia, which is about fifteen miles west of Washington, D.C. The shop is run by hand-quilting guru Jinny Beyer. Beyer started selling fabric partly because no other fabric shop could possibly stock all of the fabric she has designed; it's available both in her store and on her website.

776 Walker Road
Great Falls, Virginia 22066
(866) 759-7373
www.jinnybeyer.com

Pennington Quilt Works

I'm not shy about promoting my local quilt shop in Pennington, New Jersey, which was a marvel of good taste and outstanding customer service even before it moved to a space twice as large as the original. These women have improved, even saved, so many of my quilts that I've lost count. Any day I get to go there is a good day. You can buy pretty much all the fabric stocked in the shop via its website, which also provides a great way for locals to keep up with the shop's long list of classes and events.

7 Tree Farm Road
Suite 104
Pennington,
New Jersey 08534
(609) 737-4321
www.penningtonquilts.com

The Quilt Box

You'll find The Quilt Box down a country lane in Dry Ridge, Kentucky (north of Frankfort, east of Louisville). The little shop in a cottage lacks a website and a toll-free number but still attracts tourists through great word of mouth. Most of its fabric is traditional. The Quilt Box was featured in *Quilt Sampler* magazine and got a rave review at PlanetPatchwork.com. Some groups planning to visit book in advance and preorder boxed lunches.

North Highway 467
P.O. Box 9
Dry Ridge,
Kentucky 41035
(859) 824-4007

Quilts Olé

A shop in Corrales, New Mexico, Quilts Olé was chosen by *Quilt Sampler* magazine as one of the ten featured stores in a recent issue. You can get a peek at

The rustic front porch of Stitchin' Post.

the shop and learn about classes on its website. You'll find lots of bright fabric and Southwestern patterns.

4908 Corrales Road
Corrales,
New Mexico 87048
(505) 890-9416
www.quiltsole.com

Rainbows End Quilt Shoppe

Located near Tampa and Clearwater, this creative shop claims to be the largest fabric shop in Florida. Many of Rainbows End Quilt Shoppe's fabrics and notions can be purchased via its website.

941 Broadway Street
Dunedin, Florida 34698
(800) 353-1928
www.rainbowsendquilt shoppe.com

Stitchin' Post

This lovely shop in Sisters, Oregon, is famous for sponsoring an annual outdoor quilt show that is nationally known. On the Stitchin' Post's website you can shop for gorgeous fabrics, including some designed by owner Jean Wells' daughter, Valori Wells, plus T-shirts and posters from its famous quilt show.

311 West Cascade
P.O. Box 280
Sisters, Oregon 97759
(541) 549-6061
www.stitchinpost.com

The Treasure Hunt

Occupying a beach cottage in Carpinteria, California, this little gem was chosen for a profile in *Quilt Sampler* magazine. The Treasure Hunt also sells knitting supplies. There's no catalog or e-store, but you can get a feel for the Southern California shop at its website, as well as find directions for how to get there (click on Contact Us).

919 Maple Avenue
Carpinteria,
California 93013
(805) 684-3360
www.thetreasurehunt.biz

The homey exterior of The Quilt Box, in Dry Ridge, Kentucky, and an issue of Quilt Sampler *listing the best fabric and quilting stores.*

quilter find just the right fabric to finish a project or complete the binding. The store keeps track of its customers' birthdays, and every year, customers who shop during their birthday month get a 20 percent discount on everything they purchase, plus a token gift, such as a lapel pin or note cards.

Like many quilt shops, this one has a show each year of its customers' quilts, and schedules drop-in times when the regulars can just bring along their current project and sit and sew and schmooze. Each winter, the shop has a special fat quarter sale, offering thirty fat quarters for $30. They supply the customers with pretty baskets to fill as they circle the loaded tables in the back room and make their selections. Every June, the Pennington shop has "quilting spa days" during which the staff waits on the quilters who come and sew, serving them free coffee and snacks (ordinarily, there are no snacks or coffee at the shop, and the tables in the classroom are only open to quilters taking lessons).

Such events are the twenty-first-century equivalent of an old-fashioned sewing bee. The best quilt shops feel like clubby hangouts, a sorority house for the sisterhood of quilters. What this means is that avid quilters can stop by a quilt shop virtually anywhere in the country and feel at home.

With the growth in quilt shops, so-called shop hops have blossomed nationwide, with all the shops in a community working together to create a weekend event. Typically, quilters go from one shop to the next and by getting a card punched after visiting each store, are eligible for various prizes. Individual stores go out of their way to provide compelling specials and offer food treats and other attractions to make their stores stand out during the shop hop and lure customers back.

At the quilt shops that survive in these competitive times, the day-to-day standard level of personal service is pretty amazing. Quiet satisfaction is generally the result, not something that makes headlines or will soon be turned into a reality TV show ("Let's vote this ugly fabric *outta* here!").

Buying Fabric Online

KEEPSAKE QUILTING USED TO CLAIM IT WAS THE biggest quilt shop in the country, carrying ten thousand bolts of fabric, and Hancock's of Paducah still brags it is the largest in the world. But such boasts get harder to make with the emergence of online megaretailers.

It's hard to outbrag eQuilter.com, an online quilt shop that claims to have fifty thousand bolts in its warehouse. Indeed, eQuilter.com may very well be the Amazon.com of the quilt world. Like Amazon with books, eQuilter brings shoppers a selection of fabric online that far exceeds the number of bolts local shops carry, and eQuilter has helped make buying fabric on the Internet both pleasant and simple.

Well-ordered bolts of fabric at Keepsake Quilting.

What makes eQuilter different from Amazon is that founder Luana Rubin has managed to keep the online shopping experience personal, even while sales have soared. Every order of fabric is wrapped in pretty tissue paper, like a gift. And every customer gets to choose online which of several charities will receive 2 percent of the purchase amount every time a purchase is made (eQuilter is careful to explain that this doesn't get added into the price but comes out of profits). Reflecting its philanthropic approach, the e-tailer's motto is eQuilter and You: Making a World of Difference.

Plus, the website is easy to navigate, the range of merchandise is breathtaking, and eQuilter sends out weekly e-mail newsletters featuring sale items and hot new fabrics. There are always high-quality cottons from top designers, but also popular theme fabrics featuring everything from cats to motorcycles to *Star Wars* and Christmas-related Elvis designs.

The warehouse of eQuilter.com (above), and an employee in the ordering department (right).

"My husband and I opened the business in our basement in 1999. We thought it was something I could do while our kids were little," says Rubin, who earned her degree from the Fashion Institute of Design in Los Angeles and worked in the fashion and textile business in New York. Her background in both design and retailing (she owned two shops in New York), combined with her husband Paul's expertise as a high-level web designer, were a perfect fit for the business.

"We exceeded our three-year business plan in about three months," Luana Rubin marvels. "We moved to a four-thousand-square-foot warehouse in Boulder, Colorado, and then eighteen months later, we moved to eleven thousand square feet, and then we grew some more. We have thirty-seven full-time employees, and in the first five years, donated over $300,000 to charity."

Rubin says the key to the pair's success is that they had just the right skills to meet a need that was unfulfilled. "When I started quilting, I didn't see enough of the kind of fabric I loved, which is novelty or conversational fabric," says Rubin. "There was just a little bit in each shop but nobody carried it in depth. So we have lots of that, plus ethnic and Asian fabric and the large prints that those doing contemporary quilts (traditional patterns with today's bold fabrics or nontraditional designs) want."

Rubin says she doesn't think eQuilter is competing head-on with local quilt shops so much as it is filling a niche for quilters who can't get all they want locally. And many of her customers live far away from quilt shops, especially those who send orders from Brazil, Japan, the Caribbean, and the Mideast.

THINK SMALL

There are far more small e-tailers offering specialty items for quilters than there are big ones hawking the works, and that makes economic sense. People selling only specialty threads, exotic beads, or hand-dyed fabric probably wouldn't pull in enough local traffic to justify a shop, but if their customers live all over the United States and abroad, then they can make a living with a website supplemented by vending at quilt shows.

So for example, Mickey Lawler sells her gorgeous hand-painted fabrics on her site, Skydyes.com. Lawler, who started quilting in the late 1960s when her children were young, did own a brick-and-mortar fabric shop for a while and sold her hand-painted fabrics there. In response to demand, she began selling the fabrics via mail-order also, but painting on fabric pleased her more than operating a shop. So in 1986, Lawler sold the shop but kept the Skydyes franchise, moved it into her home, and started teaching fabric painting all over the country. Later she added the website, and although she sells fabric paints and her how-to book, *Skydyes: A Visual Guide to Fabric Painting*, on the site, Lawler says 90 percent of her customers buy her already painted fabric.

Another popular specialist website is Contemporary Cloth, operated by Sondra Borrie, a quilter in Ohio whose full-time job is as a pediatric occupational therapist. Borrie clearly has a great eye for edgy modern designs—fabric that echoes the bold look of abstract paintings—and she throws in some fun retro patterns. She even sells fabric with aboriginal designs. Contemporary Cloth sends out a regular e-newsletter to customers when new items arrive, and the site, www.contemporarycloth.com, is bookmarked by thousands of adventurous quilters and fabric artists who can rarely find her product lines at their local quilt shops.

Filling niches is one way the Internet allows voracious fabric-loving quilters to find everything they want.

ONE CLICK—A THOUSAND STORES

Touching fabric before you buy it definitely adds to the pleasure. But sometimes quilters just desperately need something to finish a project and can't find the right fabric or notion close to home. Say you're making a quilt from an old issue of *McCall's Quilting*, and need the gorgeous gold Asian fabric they used for the border. Or you're down to the last block of a quilt you've been working on for months and run out of the focus fabric. Or maybe you're trying to finish a quilt for your husband's retirement party and can't find any conversation prints with sailboats that please you.

If you've already been to your local quilt shop without luck, then it's time to search the Internet. You can't exactly Google "teal with yellow polka dot fabric" and find it, but there are a couple of websites that serve as portals into vast networks of quilt shops, allowing you to search the stock of hundreds of stores all at once.

QUILTSHOPS.COM

There are well in excess of 175 quilt shops signed up

Demand for hard-to-find materials from students prompted some traveling quilt teachers to begin selling on the Internet. Liza Prior Lucy, who designs quilts and teaches quilting with Kaffe Fassett (both are profiled on page 331), says she started her website, GloriousColor.com, because "Kaffe had designed these striped fabrics that were produced in India for the Rowan company and hardly anybody carried them in retail. I was teaching all over the world and my students wanted to use this fabric and couldn't find it. So I started a very small website in 2000 so my students would have access to the fabric Kaffe designs."

The stockroom at Glorious Color.

Orders built steadily, and so did Lucy's inventory as she began to carry all of Fassett's fabric. He kept designing more, and Lucy added other distinctive designers to her roster. In 2002, her husband was laid off from his high-tech job and he started working with Lucy, running the Internet business from their home in New Hope, Pennsylvania. By 2005, with the business bursting out of their dining and family rooms and their basement and garage full of fabric, they built an addition onto their house.

"We could have rented commercial space somewhere," says Lucy, "but to me it made more sense investing in our real estate, especially with two teenage daughters at home. We want to be around for them."

Lucy doesn't have any interest in broadening her product line to include novelty patterns of snowmen or tools like rotary cutters. She prefers to be a specialist in high-end, high-quality fabric from top designers whose work excites her personally. "It is rare that we get orders from quilters in New Jersey or Pennsylvania, because there are so many good quilt shops in this area," she says. "We're meeting the needs of more isolated quilters and my customers are located all over the world. My look is offbeat and maverick, and people who live in areas where cute country brown is the norm can't find this sort of fabric."

NET WORKING

Filling niches is one way the Internet allows voracious, fabric-loving quilters to find everything they want. But there are other bonuses for savvy fabric shoppers who go online. One of the great advantages of the web is that it allows many far-flung vendors to band together in cyberspace.

The creation of websites that serve as a portal to many diverse quilting retailers has opened up a virtual nirvana for fabric hounds. One of the most established of these sites, Quiltshops.com, provides a jumping-off point for surfing through the inventory of more than 175 quilt retailers. The collective wares, instantly searchable, vastly exceed the goods to be ogled at the world's biggest quilt shows. But instead of being set up for only a long weekend, this virtual quilt show is open for business twenty-four hours a day, 365 days a year.

Jan Cabral, who is the founder and co-owner of Quiltshops.com, says she began in 1998 with thirty-five shops, and quilters immediately fell in love with the quilt search engine. The site allows a quilter who needs a particular notion or fabric to use a single query to ask all of those 175 independent member shops whether they carry that item. Quiltshops.com gets customers to register by offering them free e-mail updates and a chance to win a $500 shopping spree and other prizes on a monthly basis. From time to time, the site offers special sales that range through all the participating stores, such as its annual Super Bowl sale.

Another intriguing Internet site that serves as a retailing portal for quilters is FabShopHop.com. Modeled on regional store shop hops, where customers are rewarded for visiting a string of retailers in one area, FabShopHop.com rewards quilters who "travel" to a

on Quiltshops.com, including niche suppliers and full-service quilt shops that offer a wide range of fabrics and supplies. The Item Search function works extremely well, and there are other services at the site. You can search for guilds, shows, or workshops by state, zip code, or area code. Do sign up for the e-newsletter to learn about sales that take place simultaneously at various times of the year at all of the participating shops.

www.Quiltshops.com

FabShop Hop

Operated by the trade organization The Fabric Shop Network, the FabShop Hop website links about one thousand independent quilt shops, ones not part of a chain. The home page allows you to search the shops for either a particular product or general information on such topics as classes and newsletters. But if you have no luck with your search, there is a third option: Give as detailed a description as you possibly can of the item you can't find, and The Fabric Shop Network will send an e-mail to the entire group on your behalf.

www.FabShopHop.com

RESOURCES

Virtual Quilt Stores

There are hundreds and hundreds of virtual quilt shops now. Some are like megastores, carrying far more bolts of fabric and notions than any local shop could stock, while others are niche sellers with a staggering variety of beads, buttons, or exotic fabrics, and nothing else. It would be impossible to include them all here. The e-tailers that are listed stand out for their taste and have a good track record for quality and customer service. On pages 280–81 you'll find more specialty e-tailers that sell exotic and foreign fabrics.

Cia's Palette

Cia's Palette is a site with a distinctive look and great service. The owner lives in Minneapolis, and she only buys fabric she loves, which includes batiks, Japanese prints, folk art prints, and lots and lots of designer fabrics in bold colors. Like many e-tailers, Cia's has an e-newsletter. The telephone number is (612) 229-5227.

www.ciaspalette.com

Contemporary Cloth

A good site for those who like hip fabrics, Contemporary Cloth's stock includes a range of retro looks, bold geometrics, and edgy home decor textiles. Sign up for the e-newsletter to hear about new merchandise and sales. There's also a toll-free number, (866) 415-3372.

www.contemporarycloth.com

eQuilter.com

While eQuilter.com isn't the only Internet quilt shop trying to cover all the bases, including fabrics, notions, books, and other supplies, it's one of the first and has an extremely good reputation. Owner Luana Rubin, who also designs fabric, has a great eye and loves conversation or novelty prints. I've bought Harry Potter and Star Trek fabric from eQuilter, and when I ran out of Moda's Funky Monkey fabric (you can see how I used it in a quilt at my website, **www.megcox.com**), I found more here. Be sure to sign up for the regular e-newsletter. Rubin does a great job of organizing the fabrics by category in these missives, so you can browse methodically.

www.equilter.com

Glorious Color

The proprietor of Glorious Color, Liza Prior Lucy, designs quilts and cowrites books with Kaffe Fassett, an American artist living in England who is a prolific textile designer (read more about them on page 331). Quilters in love with Fassett's exuberant fabrics can purchase virtually all of them on this aptly named website, which also includes some select choices from others who design fabric for the Rowan company. If you prefer to call, the number is (800) 269-0309.

www.gloriouscolor.com

Reprodepot Fabrics

Reprodepot Fabrics emphasizes reproductions of vintage textiles. There are wonderful all-cotton fabrics featuring designs from the 1920s and 1930s—and the forties, fifties, sixties, and seventies—along with some very hip contemporary fabric. The site's owner resides in Easthampton, Massachusetts; the toll-free number is (877) 738-7632.

www.reprodepot.com

Skydyes

Need a hand-dyed fabric that looks like a cloudy day or a sunset or the bark of an old tree? Textile artist Mickey Lawler sells her stunning hand-painted cottons and silks at Skydyes, along with her book with instructions for painting and dyeing your own fabric.

www.skydyes.com

whole bunch of stores online. These hops are scheduled five or six times a year, and participating shoppers have to "visit" more than one hundred online shops. But they have a whole month to do it, and the top prizes include brand-new sewing machines. The gimmick is that there is a logo of a bunny hidden on a page within each participating website: When consumers click on the You Found It! bunny icon, a screen is displayed where they can type their e-mail address; this gives them credit for visiting.

The underlying purpose of the online shop hop, like the real ones, is to get quilters to visit the various participating websites. The FabShop Hop is conducted by an organization called The Fabric Shop Network, Inc., which is essentially a trade association for independent quilt shops. Most of the members of The Fabric Shop Network are brick-and-mortar shops that have a website as an adjunct. Similar to Quiltshops.com, quilters who click on FabSearch at the FabShop Hop site can use a fabric search engine to search the more than one thousand members' inventories.

Getting listed on the FabShop Hop site is just one of the benefits stores receive for becoming a member of The Fabric Shop Network, says Laurie Harsh, who started the association in 1997. Member stores also get information on marketing and promotion, a magazine that comes out every other month, access to insurance for employees, and ongoing education in good business practices.

Both FabShopHop.com and Quiltshops.com show how all the retailing categories are blurring. Quilters surfing the Internet can't tell whether a vendor exists only in cyberspace. At Quiltshops.com more than half the participating retailers have brick-and-mortar stores, but about sixty are e-tailers only. The evidence shows that quilters shopping on the web don't care which is which—as long as they can find what they're looking for.

All of these choices are a great boon for quilters, but many people predict that growth of fabric outlets has outstripped demand and that there will be some fallout among vendors in the years to come. So remember, wherever you go to buy fabric, whether you shop on the web or down the street, your money is a vote for the continued existence of that enterprise. Support the retailers you want to survive.

So remember, wherever you go to buy fabric, whether you shop on the web or down the street, your money is a vote for the continued existence of that enterprise.

A FABRIC DESIGNER'S TRIBUTE TO STASH

Quiltmaker Luana Rubin is the Boulder, Colorado–based founder and co-owner of eQuilter.com, the Amazon.com of the quilt world. Rubin loves fabric as much as any of her customers, having been a textile designer for several decades since graduating with a degree from the Fashion Institute of Design in Los Angeles.

Part of what draws customers back to eQuilter.com is the exuberant personal notes that Rubin includes every time she sends out her regular e-mail newsletter about what's new at the site. What follows is an excerpt from a mini essay Rubin wrote called "Psychology of the Stash," which appeared in one of her e-newsletters in January 2007. It struck a chord with many customers and is a good description of how quilters view their fabric collections.

I walk into my studio like a cook walks into a pantry and I start pulling out

How to Store Your Stash

THERE ARE MANY DIFFERENT WAYS TO STORE your fabric collection, but whether you choose drawers, shelves, boxes, filing cabinets, or custom-built cabinets, remember these simple rules.

- Avoid storing fabric in plastic bags, because moisture can get trapped inside and cause mildew. Cotton needs to breathe!
- Keep the fabric away from direct sunlight or it will fade. If your fabric isn't shut away in a closet or cabinets, simply cover any open shelves with a sheet or curtain. This will also cut down on dust, but it's a simple matter to give your stash a light vacuuming from time to time.
- If you keep your fabric in wooden drawers, line them first with acid-free paper or aluminum foil to protect the fabric from the acid in the wood.

Other than that, arrange your stash in a way that fits your needs best. The majority of quilters organize their fabric in color groups, just as most quilt shops do, storing the reds together, the blues together, and so forth. Some people like to keep all their tiny prints in one place, group their plaids together, and sort by style or period, keeping all their Civil War reproduction fabric in one spot, for example.

Of course the makers of fancy furniture for sewers and quilters, such as Horn or Koala Cabinets, are happy to sell you deluxe cabinets for storing your stash and other supplies, but many quilters love to improvise their storage systems.

One solution for quilters who are short on space but have a closet in the room where they quilt is to buy those closet organizers used for sweaters. These use Velcro to attach to the metal rod in the closet. They hold quite a lot of fabric, which is easy to see when you open the closet door. I use one of these sweater racks to hold fabrics that I'm gathering for projects I'm planning. I set aside one or two sections for each project: Saving the fabric there keeps it separate from the rest of my stash, which I confess is mostly piled in plastic tubs in my third-floor bathroom.

Finished quilts can be stored in a wooden cabinet.

Quilter Liza Prior Lucy (for a profile, see page 3312) says my system of stuffing lots of fabric in big closed bins would make her crazy. "I have to be able to see my stuff to be creative," she says. "I decide I want to make a certain quilt because something in my stash catches my eye. In the same way, if I were making a drawing, I'd want to look at *all* my crayons."

Lucy's perfect stash storage solution: "I buy kitchen cabinets with sturdy wire drawers that IKEA sells. I don't buy fronts for the cabinets because I want to see my fabric, but I do buy the butcher block top, which is the perfect height for cutting fabric (and veggies). The trouble with some wood and wire shelving is that it warps from the weight of the fabric, but these wire drawers are very heavy."

pieces that make me feel happy or somehow express whatever emotion I am feeling when I enter my creative space. I pile them up, spread them out, rearrange and then drip embellishments on top. If it looks like something I want to sew together, I start thinking about a design. But I always look at that pile and think "If only I had ________ it would make this composition just perfect." (Then I go shopping.)

My stash is a work in progress, with no beginning and no end.
It is the Milky Way.
It is the New York City library.
It is the Smithsonian and the Louvre.
It is looking out the window at the snowy peaks as I fly over the Rocky Mountains.
It is a collection of best-loved poems.
It is Martha [Stewart]'s spice pantry.
It holds memories.
It holds stories that are not yet written.
It is a place of infinite potential.
It is all the things in my heart that have not yet been spoken. . . .

Finding Fabric: Sources for Exotic Materials

Passionate quilters' lives are like one grand treasure hunt; they're always on the prowl for new fabric, whether it's the perfect match for a current quilt or the inspiration for a whole new project.

The suppliers here have been grouped by the type of materials for which they are best known in the quilt world. New textile suppliers continue to spring up, so compile your own lists of favorites. Try some of these if they're new to you.

Imported Fabrics

African Fabric Lady

African Fabric Lady is run by Christine Jon Covert, who buys hand-decorated cottons from artisans in West Africa. Covert sells handwoven tribal cloth, pictorial batiks, and beads, offering items for sale at quilt shows, on her website, and by appointment.

P.O. Box 236
Hancock, Maine 04640
(207) 422-9042
www.africanfabriclady.com

A selection from African Fabric Lady.

Cultured Expressions

Run by Lisa Shepard Stewart, Cultured Expressions is another supplier of African cloth. A journalist who has written books about African crafts, Stewart has a good eye for striking fabrics and also stocks kits and patterns. She carries such African fabrics as mud cloth, a hand-dyed or painted cloth made in Mali and decorated with distinctive geometric patterns. Stewart sells at quilt shows and online.

P.O. Box 356
Rahway, New Jersey 07065
(866) 683-2568
www.culturedexpressions.com

French Connections

French Connections may be located in a historic home in Pittsboro, North Carolina, but it specializes in fabrics from France and Africa, which it also sells online. You won't find thousands of bolts of fabric here, but look for stiking toiles and a good selection of fabric from Provence, as well as unusual patterned cotton from Africa.

178 Hillsboro Street
Pittsboro,
North Carolina 27312
(919) 545-9296
www.french-nc.com

Handloom Batik

Handloom Batik was a shop in Manhattan for thirty years, but now the proprietress, Usha, mostly sells her stunning Indian-style batiks at quilt shows. You can go to her website to find out where Usha will be taking her beautiful fabrics, scarves, and T-shirts next. Or, make an appointment to visit her store.

532 Warren Street
Hudson, New York 12534
(212) 925-9542
www.handloombatik.com

International Fabric Collection

A large fabric store in Fairview, Pennsylvania, International Fabric Collection is one of the best sources for foreign fabric. There is British Tana lawn fabric, African mud cloth, and fabric from Italy, Germany, Holland, Guatemala, and Japan. It also stocks seasonal prints, such as ones for Halloween and the Day of the Dead.

7870 West Ridge Road
Suite 8, P.O. Box 72
Fairview,
Pennsylvania 16415
(800) 462-3891
www.intfab.com

Mino Kame

Mino Kame sells vintage and contemporary Japanese textiles. Owner Marie Conley lives in Charlottesville, Virginia, and sells both on eBay and online, offering vintage silks and cottons. Japanese fabric sizing can vary greatly, so be sure to note the posted measurements.

www.mino-kame.com

St. Theresa Textile Trove

St. Theresa Textile Trove is the name of a funky shop and website beloved by art quilters and those with a taste for the offbeat. Owner Becky Hancock opened the store with her sister, renowned art quilter Terrie Hancock Mangat, after the death of their parents, St. Theresa being the patron saint of those who have lost loved ones. Customers come from all over the globe, and so do the fabrics.

5846 Hamilton Avenue
Cincinnati, Ohio 45224
(800) 236-2450
www.sttheresatextile.com

Hand-Dyed and Reproduction Fabrics

Artfabrik, Inc.

Artfabrik, Inc. sells well-known teacher and art quilter Laura Wasilowski's hand-dyed 100 percent cotton fabric and thread. Sales are online and at quilt shows.

(847) 931-7684
www.artfabrik.com

Jane Steinberg, Inc.

Jane Steinberg of Loxahatchee, Florida, has been dyeing silk for more than twenty-five years, and you can buy gorgeous sample packs of browns, reds, blues, and so forth at her website.

P.O. Box 1555
Loxahatchee,
Florida 33470
www.janesteinberg.com

Jeanette's Fabric to Dye For

Jeanette's Fabric to Dye For is a business run by Jeanette Viviano, who works out of her home studio in West Linn, Oregon. Viviano sells hand-dyed fabric online and at quilt shows. You can order predyed fabric or place a custom order.

www.jeanettesfabrictodyefor.com

Textile Workshop

Three artists working out of a former costume factory in Norristown, Pennsylvania, not far from Philly, run the Textile Workshop. They sell original silk-screen designs hand-printed onto velvets, silks, linens, and other sumptuous fabrics. Prices are steep, but you can also buy bargain "scrap bags"—packages of three color-coordinated fabric pieces for $18.

619 West Washington St.
Norristown,
Pennsylvania 19401
(610) 277-4500
www.thetextileworkshop.com

Reproduction Fabrics

Reproduction Fabrics has both a brick-and-mortar store and an extensive website. It sells copies of fabric made between 1775 and 1970. It claims to have the largest selection of reproduction fabrics online, and its many fans include textile expert Harriet Hargrave. You can search for fabrics by era or by type. Sign up for the free e-newsletter to hear what's new.

25 North Wilson Ave,
Suite A
Bozeman, Montana 59715
(800) 380-4611
www.reproductionfabrics.com

FOR PREWASHING

◆ You don't want to spend weeks and weeks laboring over a quilt, only to find that all your white areas turn pink from the red fabrics.

◆ You want your finished quilt to look crisp and unwrinkled and not to pucker in places when it's laundered.

◆ You've discovered that you have a sensitivity to the chemicals used to manufacture fabrics and want to wash them out before handling the material.

◆ You prefer to piece and/or quilt by hand and find that the prewashed fabric is a little softer and easier to handle.

To Wash or Not to Wash

FOR A LONG TIME, QUILTERS WERE TAUGHT THERE was a hard and fast rule: Always prewash your fabric. That way, you'd find out if the fabric was going to bleed before you spent hours cutting and piecing. Plus, you'd get any shrinkage out of the way. Like everything else in the quilt world, things have gotten more complicated over time.

Fabric experts such as quilting teacher Harriet Hargrave now argue that there are good reasons, under some circumstances, for *not* laundering fabric beforehand. Hargrave, who teaches machine quilting (for her profile, see page 342), says she prefers working with unwashed fabric partly because it flows more smoothly through the sewing machine. Sometimes, she even adds spray starch to make the fabric stiffer, so it doesn't stretch when she does elaborate stitching.

Liza Prior Lucy, another quilting teacher, is solidly in Hargrave's no-wash camp. She prefers the slightly rumpled and wrinkled look of a quilt that's been washed only after it's completed. "I want that antique look," she explains. (For more about Lucy, see page 331.)

Teachers in the opposite camp include Sharyn Craig, who says she doesn't like the slightly stiff feel that new fabrics get from the chemicals applied to them when they are sized. Once washed, fabric is more malleable, so it clings better to her flannel design wall, making it easier for her to arrange cut pieces and keep them up for weeks, if necessary. (For more about Craig, see page 379.)

As for myself, I'm definitely in the prewash camp, in part because that's what my mother taught me and because, as a hand piecer, I like the softer feel of the fabric. But sometimes I don't wash fabric until after it's been in my stash for a while, so I've come up with a system that helps me remember whether it's been washed or not. I cut one corner off the fabric right after it's washed. If I pull some fabric out of a pile and all four corners are intact, I know it hasn't been washed.

Whether you always prewash, or do it only sometimes, the experts warn that you shouldn't mix washed and unwashed fabrics in the same quilt. And, be aware that if you *don't* prewash, you do have to worry about potential bleeding. You should always do some simple tests on fabric before working with it, especially if it's red or some other dark color. Rub a white tissue against the surface of the fabric and see whether any dye rubs off. Then, cut a small square of the fabric and soak it in a glass of hot water for at least ten minutes. Place the soaked fabric on top of some white fabric or a handkerchief, and observe whether it leaves a stain.

WASHING INSTRUCTIONS

The experts always argue for extreme care when washing, but the concerns aren't the same for heirloom quilts and "utility quilts," ones made for hard use. Any quilt intended for babies or toddlers will soon be covered by drool and worse, unless you hang it on the wall and never let them touch it. But the wear and tear is part of the beauty. The first quilt I ever made was sewn entirely by hand and washed a hundred times. By the time my son was ten, it was somewhat shredded and faded but incredibly soft and still a necessary sleep companion.

Whether washing fabric or a finished quilt, do *not* use hot water or a harsh detergent. Use cool or cold water and something mild for the soap. Harriet Hargrave recommends either Orvus paste or Ivory dishwashing liquid. Orvus paste is a gentle detergent used for washing everything from livestock on farms to fine silks and rugs in museum collections. As usual, wash dark and bright colors separately. And don't let the fabric or quilt stay in the dryer until it is bone dry. There will be much less wear and tear if you remove the fabric when still slightly damp. Line dry quilts; when washing fabric, iron it dry.

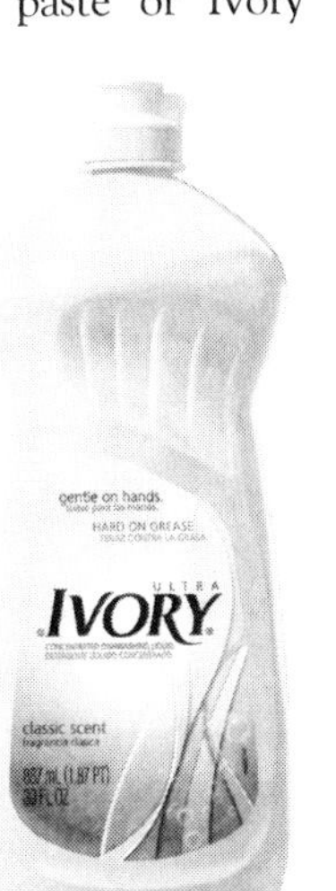

Ivory dish detergent: great for dishes and *quilts!*

AGAINST PREWASHING

- You mostly do your piecing and/or quilting by machine and find the sizing in the unwashed fabric makes it crisper and easier to work with.
- You're not going to use this fabric for a while and know that the chemicals in the fabric will inhibit mildew and fading.
- You're not sure yet what sort of quilt you'll put this fabric in, and you want to keep your options open. Once the fabric has been washed, you can't undo that process.
- You prefer that slightly crinkled, old-fashioned look that results when unwashed fabrics are sewn into a quilt and only washed when it's completed.
- You're using this fabric in a wall hanging that you don't ever intend to wash, so there is no need to worry about either bleeding or shrinkage.

THROW A BATTING PARTY

If you're curious about what different types and brands of batting are like to work with, gather together a handful of quilting friends and have a batting party.

◆ Assign each person attending the party a particular type—or several types—of batting to purchase. Have them buy the smallest quantity possible; often batting comes in folded sheets cut to the size of a quilt, so look for the crib-quilt size.

◆ Before the party, cut one twelve-inch square of every type of batting for each participant.

◆ Cut enough fabric into twelve-inch squares so that all the quilters can make a fabric sandwich with each batting sample. To figure out how many fabric squares you will need, multiply the number of quilters times the number of batting types, times two. That way there will be a top and backing for each batting sample. If you want to test the batting for bearding, use dark fabric.

◆ When the group meets, ask everyone to pin the

Batting Gets Better

THE MORE PRODUCTS THAT COME ON THE MARKET, the more craft and sewing manufacturers take notice and listen to what quilters want. One of the biggest changes has been in batting, the fluffy material that goes into the center of the fabric sandwich to make a quilt warm. When the quilting boom first began, most of the batting on the market was puffy polyester. It turned out that polyester batting was great for tied quilts—ones made using yarn or embroidery floss to tie the layers of the quilt together, scattering knots evenly across the quilt surface rather than quilting it. You didn't need a whole mess of knots to do the job; you could leave six inches or more between knots and the whole fabric sandwich would stick together smoothly and evenly.

However, polyester batting was prone to so-called bearding; its white fibers poked through the fabric's surface and gave quilts an unsightly disheveled look (batting was all white then). And polyester was slippery, making it tricky to keep the three layers of the quilt aligned during sewing.

Earlier generations had quilted with cotton batting, which didn't beard, lasted longer, stuck to the fabric, and produced thinner quilts. But cotton batting had a major drawback in the minds of modern quilters: It had to be densely quilted. According to the manufacturers' instructions, 100 percent cotton batting should be quilted leaving no spaces bigger than a quarter inch to a half inch. Since quilters in the 1970s and 1980s quilted almost entirely by hand, that dictated an immense amount of work.

The makers of batting started introducing alternatives. For those who wanted puffy polyester but wanted to disguise the bearding, dark-colored batting was introduced, so that fibers peeking out wouldn't show against dark fabrics. And then manufacturers introduced blends of cotton and polyester, which provided all the benefits of cotton but didn't have to be quilted so closely.

By the time the blended battings were on the market, many quilters had switched to pure cotton because thin quilts became the rage, partly because art quilts were becoming more popular and thin quilts looked good hanging on the wall. And, since machine quilting had become the norm, the issue of having to quilt densely stopped being a drawback for cotton: Machine quilters seem to compete to see who can quilt the most densely.

As with many of the tools of quilting, the result has been both more options and greater confusion. Quilters now have more choices of batting than ever before. In addition to cotton and cotton-poly blends, quilters can now pick silk batting or wool batting, among other choices. Wool is very warm, but there can be bearding issues. Silk is sometimes chosen for hand quilted projects but is expensive. If you're not sure what's the best choice for your next project, ask for help at your local quilt shop. These days, even some types of cotton batting can be used for tying. Before you buy, check labels carefully to see how close together your stitches must be.

In her book *Heirloom Machine Quilting*, Harriet Hargrave says that before picking a batting, quilters should ask themselves such questions as:

- Do I want my quilt to be thin or thick?
- Do I want to hand quilt or machine quilt?
- How closely do I want to quilt it?
- How warm do I need the quilt to be?
- Is the quilt going to be washed a lot, or is it just for show?
- Is the quilt going to hang on the wall or lay on a bed?

mini quilts together. Be sure to label the samples with the type of batting they contain. Then, let the quilting experiment begin!

- You can try both hand and machine quilting on the same block. (If you want to use separate blocks for hand and machine quilting, you will need twice as many fabric and batting squares.)
- Compare and record the results. Pay attention to what it's like to handle each kind of batting and whether it sticks to the fabric or is slippery. Does the thickness of the batting result in a flat or puffy quilt sandwich? Is there any bearding—white fibers from the batting sticking through the top or backing of the mini-quilt? Which batting do you like best?
- Save your quilted samples with their labels for future reference, along with any notes as to what sort of quilt the particular battings would appear to be good for.

Q & A with Fabric Designer Amy Butler

One of the hot fabric designers who has helped bring a new look to the craft, Amy Butler came into the quilt world by chance. She and her husband, Dave, were illustrators and product developers who produced lifestyle stories for *Country Living* magazine. When the craft projects—purses, eyeglass cases, and backpacks—Amy created for the magazine using vintage fabric became very popular, she started producing Amy Butler sewing patterns. Self taught as a quilter, Butler began in 1993 to make quilts that mixed her block designs with antique quilt blocks and original appliqué forms in compositions that were then painted for fine art exhibits.

She and her husband started distributing the sewing patterns from their Granville, Ohio, home and they rented a booth at the Houston International Quilt Market in 2002. Quilt shop buyers fell madly in love with what Butler describes as her "quirky vintage modern fabrics," and her whirlwind life as the "it girl" of quilt fabric was launched. After producing several fabric lines for FreeSpirit, Butler moved to Rowan, a division of Westminster Fibers. Her fabrics and patterns fly off the shelves of quilt shops. Learn more about her and download free patterns at her website, **www.amybutlerdesign.com**. Her large-patterned designs were perfect for the easy tied quilt project you'll find on page 438.

Q: What inspires your fabric designs?

A: My influences and inspiration change constantly but I do have a few core

influences. Broadly, all decorative arts and textiles have greatly influenced my work. This, of course, includes fashion. I'm hugely inspired by ethnic textiles and artifacts. My love of antique fabrics, and a collection that's been growing for twenty years now, has influenced my design eye. The natural world is also a big influence for me.

Q: Can you briefly describe the process of designing a new fabric line?

A: It usually takes me four to six weeks to complete the artwork for my collections: I design and create all of my artwork by hand. I'm always dreaming of future fabrics I'd love to sew with or use in my home. I'm always excited about a "new" color or colors. I keep an ongoing color idea stash, where I save snips of colors I love, which eventually get worked in to my palettes. When I start working on a new fabric collection, I pull my color palettes together by building color "stories" intuitively, making a collage with coloration and textures I love. I then match color chips to my color stories. I almost always make way more palettes than I need, but I love having as many options as possible. I trust my gut and go with my top three or four favorites. For my prints, my inspiration comes from antique documents that I redesign, scale, and color to fit the story of the collection I'm building.

Q: *Do you have a stable of designers? How much of your line is designed directly by you?*

A: Oh my. I do not have a stable of designers. That's flattering that you think I'm that big! Actually, I design all of my sewing patterns and fabric myself. Designing is my favorite thing to do. My husband has done an amazing job with creating my branding and giving my studio work an uplifted presence in the marketplace. I do have a group of local ladies that help me write and test my sewing instructions, but we only have one employee, Jake, our production guru who lays out and illustrates the patterns. We're just little guys doing the best we can and having a lot of fun!

Q: *What percentage of your fabric, roughly, is sold through quilt shops?*

A: I would say 90 percent.

Q: *What is your sense of what draws younger quilters into the craft today?*

A: I would say that many of them discover quilting after making clothing and home decor patterns. I think my designs appeal to a young woman who's looking to sew for herself or her family and create things for her home. The retail/design world is so sophisticated, and with the addition of the Internet, young women have a heightened sense of style. I think they're coming into quilt shops and fabric stores where they can find new products and are introduced to the special experience of great education, service, and inspiration that's been so successfully nurtured by these retailers. Once the creative fire of these women has been sparked with sewing and they build their skills and confidence, they can't help developing a desire for quilting!

Q: *Where do you think the quilt world is heading?*

A: I think it's an exciting time, with a huge influx of wonderful new designers and products hitting quilt shops. I think we'll see the quilting world explode in a new direction that envelops the art of sewing, crossing over more into home decor and fashion. Quilt shops will be multigenerational, appealing to their current customer base while also attracting new, beginner seamstresses.

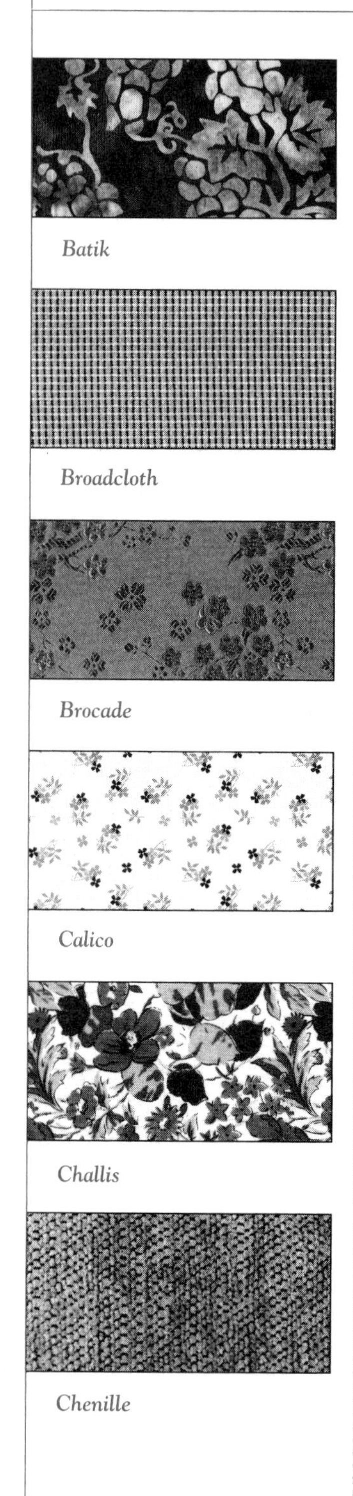
Batik
Broadcloth
Brocade
Calico
Challis
Chenille

Fabric Lingo

IS FABRIC SOUNDING LIKE A FOREIGN LANGUAGE? Here are definitions of some words and expressions related to fabric that come up frequently.

Batik: Fabric colored by a succession of dye baths, during which wax or other dye-resisting substances are applied to parts of the fabric to create a design. The colors are often intense and bright. Bali, in Indonesia, is famous for producing gorgeous batiks.

Broadcloth: A tightly woven cotton with fine, crosswise ribs that are part of the weave. Broadcloth is often used to make shirts.

Brocade: A thick, luxurious fabric, originally made of silk, into which raised patterns have been woven, often in elaborate floral patterns. Think eighteenth-century frock coats: This isn't a fabric you'd enjoy quilting.

Calico: A type of cotton, usually one that is covered with a delicate repeating pattern, often in muted shades of blue, brown, tan, or red. These fabrics give quilts the old-fashioned look that many quilters love.

Challis: A lightweight fiber woven with cotton, wool, or synthetic fibers to make it more durable. Challis is silky and has a lightly brushed surface. It is frequently printed in floral patterns and used in clothing.

Chenille: Taking its name from the French word for caterpillar, chenille is a type of cotton with a tufted pile. It's often used for fluffy bathrobes, slippers, and blankets.

Chintz: Glazed cotton fabric that is frequently used for upholstery and usually is covered with a pretty print.

Conversation print: Also called a novelty print, this refers to a print featuring not abstract shapes but images of actual objects; these can be anything from Elvis to kittens to tractors.

Damask: A glossy patterned fabric similar to brocade, damask has a much higher thread count than what is typically used in quilting fabric. It can be made from any of a number of fibers, including silk, linen, and cotton.

Dimity: A sheer but sturdy cotton cloth woven with a stripe. Dimity was mostly used for curtains and dresses and was especially popular in the late eighteenth century.

Fat quarter: One quarter of a yard of fabric, but cut to maximize its worth for quilters. Instead of cutting nine inches of fabric from the end of a bolt, which would result in a long skinny piece, quilt shops cut half yards and then cut them down the middle, resulting in a nearly square piece of fabric.

Focus fabric: A bold fabric dominating the design of a quilt that may have many other fabrics in it. Generally the other fabrics are chosen to complement or contrast with the focus fabric, which is chosen first.

Gingham: A medium-weight cotton fabric usually patterned with plaids or checks. Although it dates back to the seventeenth century and is thought of as old-fashioned, gingham still appears in everything from sundresses to bistro curtains.

Hand: The "hand" of a fabric refers to how it feels when you touch it—whether it is crisp or soft or silky, and so on. The term often comes up when quilters discuss a process like dyeing or painting fabric. The concern is generally that the process not change the hand of the fabric, making it stiff, for example.

Jacquard: This is a family of fabrics produced on a type of loom developed in the early 1800s by a man named Jacquard. The loom made it possible to weave complex embossed patterns such as those of brocades and damask used for draperies and upholstery.

Novelty print: *See* conversation print.

Organza: A sheer fabric that is stiffer than chiffon, made from silk or a synthetic material, and frequently

Chintz

Conversation print

Damask

Dimity

Gingham

Testing a fabric's hand

Jacquard

Organza

Percale

Taffeta

Toile

Tulle

used in bridal gowns. Some art quilters like to use it in their work as a partially transparent overlay.

Percale: A tightly woven, medium-weight cotton with a much higher thread count than fabric used by quilters. Percale is often used in bed linens.

Selvages: These are the tightly woven lengthwise edges of fabric, which are created during the manufacturing process to prevent fraying. They should be removed before the fabric is sewn into quilts, because their texture is different from the rest of the fabric and those edges will pucker when washed.

Taffeta: A shiny, crisp fabric sometimes made from silk or synthetic materials and often used in fancy dresses.

Thread count: The number of threads in one square inch of fabric, counting both the vertical and horizontal threads. This is a standard measure for ranking fabric on a continuum from coarse to fine, with coarser fabric having a lower count. But thread count doesn't determine everything in fabric quality—fabric is also affected by how fine the individual threads are and what sort of finish is applied to the cloth in processing.

Toile: A printed fabric, often made of cotton, that most often features a single color—say different tones of blue or magenta—contrasted with white or cream. Toile frequently depicts pastoral scenes. It became popular in France in the eighteenth century with the introduction of a new engraving process. In recent years these patterns have inspired many companies that produce traditional fabric for the quilt market.

Tulle: A gauzy, netlike material that can be made from silk, nylon, or cotton. Often used in ballet costumes and wedding veils, tulle can be used as a fun embellishment for art quilts.

Velour: A plush fabric, velour can be made of cotton, wool, or synthetics and is frequently made into coats and shirts.

CHAPTER FIVE

Great Teachers: So Many Ways to Learn

IT'S NO SECRET THAT MUCH OF LEARNING TO QUILT IS the result of trial and error. And many of today's top quilt teachers are self-taught. So you may wonder what's the advantage of taking their classes? These are people who have spent years, sometimes decades, honing their techniques and developing their styles, and the good ones can shave a lot of time off a student's learning curve. It may take one teacher months of experimenting to perfect a shortcut that can be passed on in a single workshop. Another teacher's lesson on fabric dyeing might spare you the heartache of using methods that aren't colorfast. Yet another's technique for appliqué can help you produce a more satisfying realism in landscape quilts than you might otherwise have been able to achieve.

BEGINNER-FRIENDLY TEACHERS

Here's a list of the top teachers profiled in this section who welcome beginners. This means that the less experienced won't be lost in many or most of these teachers' workshops, but you should still check the descriptions of specific classes before enrolling. While Alex Anderson, for example, is on the list, not all of her classes are good for novices. She says her classes have one of three labels describing the skill level required: all levels, basic quiltmaking skills required, or intermediate.

For more specifics on the level of students these teachers cater to, check the sidebars that accompany each of their profiles. The books by these teachers tend to be beginner friendly as well.

Alex Anderson, page 307

Esterita Austin, page 310, accepts beginners in one-day classes

Sue Benner, page 314, holds some classes for beginners

The best teachers don't just talk about their techniques and tricks, they make their lessons come alive, producing a series of transformative "aha moments" that allow students to apply what they learn immediately to their own work. In the hands of a good teacher, quilters not only learn a particular technique but also get a jolt of inspiration that pushes them to try harder and take risks. The truth is, there are thousands of quilt teachers in the United States today and many of them are excellent. The tricky part is finding the teacher who is best for you.

Daunting Choices

How does one choose among the hundreds of classes on dozens of specialized topics? Classes are held at most of the 2,500 quilt shops in the United States, plus there are classes at local YWCAs, ones included in adult education programs, and classes hosted by quilt guilds. This is not to mention the explosion of state, national, and international quilt shows and festivals, which generally offer a raft of classes and workshops. And, increasingly, there is the alternative of taking lessons on the Internet.

How is a quilter to choose? What lessons are most important? Which techniques will be most satisfying? Although many quilt teachers are excellent, they're not interchangeable. In today's sophisticated quilt world, teachers have become specialized, and it's important to know who does what—not just which particular techniques they teach but also the nuances of their teaching styles.

It's also important that students find lessons at their level: If the course is too advanced, the opportunity to work with a top teacher can be completely wasted. Finding the right teacher demands that you be honest about your current skill level. Taking basic classes that help you to master such seemingly simple skills as rotary cutting and hand quilting can be invaluable.

Indeed, teachers of advanced classes say they are shocked at the gaps in some students' educations. Because most quilters are largely self-taught, they don't

From leopard print to classic blocks, the variety of quilts is endless.

always realize what they've missed. So-called make it and take it classes that showcase one technique or one project can be very satisfying but don't give quiltmakers the foundation of skills they need to go further. Project classes generally don't focus on the fine points of craftsmanship required to make an heirloom quilt or to draft one's own original design. While the notion of absolute rules in quilting is now passé, mastering certain core skills still matters.

START CLOSE TO HOME

Many quilters start out by taking classes where they live. If you have the option available to you, it's a good way to begin. Go to a local quilt shop where you should be able to see finished quilts hanging on the wall made using the techniques and patterns being offered in upcoming classes. You'll know right away what results you can expect and whether they suit your taste.

The majority of quilt shop classes are geared to beginner and intermediate quilters and are reasonably priced, often $15 to $25 per class. They usually cover a wide range of popular techniques, including whatever new trends are popping up. Both machine and handwork classes are generally available, and you can

Eleanor Burns, page 319

Jane Dunnewold, page 323

Kaffe Fassett and **Liza Prior Lucy**, page 331, accept beginners "who know how to cut and piece"

Diane Gaudynski, page 335, accepts beginners with "some experience"

Becky Goldsmith and **Linda Jenkins**, page 339

Libby Lehman, page 350, accepts beginners with "a working knowledge of their sewing machines"

Sue Nickels, page 357

Bethany Reynolds, page 360, accepts "confident beginners"

Elly Sienkiewicz, page 363

Ami Simms, page 366

Ricky Tims, page 369

Don't Know How to Sew?

You might think: How can I quilt if I don't know how to sew, either by hand or by machine? Isn't that like asking someone to run before they can walk?

Well, not exactly. Believe it or not, you can learn to sew and to make quilts at the same time. The quilt teachers, classes, and books that embrace beginners will give you what you need. Most self-respecting sewing machine dealers are happy to show you the basics if you come try out their machines—they're hoping you'll buy one. And, if you do, you'll get extra, more detailed lessons.

In addition, starting on page 393, there is an entire chapter written especially for beginners, to take you step-by-step through all the sewing basics needed for quilting.

If this is still not convincing you, if you are one of those methodical types who want to take baby steps first, here are a few more ideas for getting started.

Fabric Store Classes

Your local quilt fabric shop, which may also sell sewing machines, will likely have classes for total beginners. These days the big fabric chains, like the Jo-Ann Stores, also offer many classes. The chains concentrate less on fabrics and tools for making clothes, emphasizing crafts, especially quilting and home decor. The classes they offer reflect this.

Books

A good book for getting started, with excellent photos and simple projects like pillows, is the spiral-bound, hardcover *Sewing 101: Beginner's Guide to Sewing*, by the editors of Creative Publishing International ($24.95), available at **www.creativepub.com.**

More books recommended for beginners:

Make a Quilt in a Day: Log Cabin Pattern, by Eleanor Burns; Quilt in a Day, Inc. ($18.95).

Quilter's Complete Guide, by Marianne Fons and Liz Porter; Leisure Arts ($22.95), which has been issued in a revised second edition.

Quilts! Quilts!! Quilts!!! The Complete Guide to Quiltmaking, by Diana McClun and Laura Nownes; McGraw-Hill ($24.95), now in a second edition.

Your First Quilt Book (or It Should Be!), by Carol Doak; That Patchwork Place, Inc. ($22.95).

Community Centers and Churches

It's best to learn from another person, and if you don't have a friend or family member who can show you how to sew, call your local Y or check at the churches in your community. There are bound to be loads of ladies who've been sewing all their lives and, for a very modest fee, would love to share their knowledge.

Sue Benner (left) helps a student in one of her classes.

-frequently choose from classes that last just a session or two or classes that meet once a week for months.

The teaching staff usually includes the shop's owner and other enthusiastic quiltmakers who work at the shop, as well as local quilters with teaching expertise. Many of today's nationally known teachers started by giving lessons at quilt shops in their own backyards, and tomorrow's star quilt teachers are out there now, looking for good students.

Furthermore, many of the top teachers have developed special relationships with shop owners and keep returning to their stores even when they become famous. Massachusetts-based Ruth B. McDowell, for example, is a legendary art quilter and teacher whose classes are notoriously hard to get into, but she returns to the same quilt shop in Montana every year. ("The owner hired me once, the class was popular, and it just turned into an annual thing," says McDowell. For more about McDowell, see page 353.) Libby Lehman travels from her home in Texas to a shop in North Carolina annually because she has developed a rapport with the owner and it's become a fun tradition to return there (you can read more about Lehman on page 350).

No matter whether the teacher is locally or nationally known, there are many advantages to these classes. You'll get to meet other quilters in your area, you don't have to travel far to learn, and for machine sewing and quilting classes, you can bring in your own machine. There's a built-in comfort level. It's a good idea to get on the mailing list of your local quilt shop: Most mail out a monthly or quarterly roster of classes. Many have websites that list such information.

Many of today's nationally known teachers started by giving lessons at quilt shops in their own backyards.

CHECK OUT THE GUILDS

Local quilt guilds also provide many wonderful learning opportunities. Quilters who belong to big guilds usually report enormous satisfaction from having the chance to take lessons from a roster of teachers with a national reputation. The quality of instruction can be very high, and again, you won't have to travel halfway across the country to receive the lessons.

When top teachers work at major quilt shows there are distractions for both the teachers and the students, but when a guild brings an instructor to its territory the focus is purely on that group, which can be very rewarding. For information about joining a quilt guild, see pages 77–80. Some guilds let nonmembers take classes, but the fees may be higher.

LEARNING ONLINE

There is a ton of practical quilting information online, at the websites of individual teachers and general sites for quilting enthusiasts (you'll find more on the latter in Quilting and Computers on pages 168–97). In addition, there are several venues for structured classes online. The oldest, called Quilt University, is run by former journalist Carol Miller and her husband, Roger, out of their Richmond, Virginia, home. At any one time, there are about thirty classes to choose from, taught by a faculty of forty teachers. Between six and eight hundred students are typically enrolled during each class period, which runs between five and ten weeks, depending on the complexity of the project or technique.

The faculty includes such popular, well-known instructors as Bethany Reynolds (see page 360) and Linda Schmidt, who was named teacher of the year in

Is This the Right Quilt Class for You?

The right quilt class can change your life, opening the doors to a fresh technique or boosting your creative achievement to a new level. But the wrong class wastes your time and money and can lead to massive frustration. I have seen students pouting or in tears because they signed up for a class but hadn't already mastered the skills needed to complete the project. And I've seen quilters bored and resentful because they weren't being challenged. To evaluate whether a quilt class is a good fit, regardless of whether the class is one offered at your local shop or a faraway quilt show, here are four important criteria to consider.

Do you need special skills or previous experience to take the class? This is the most common problem that comes up. If you're taking a class in machine quilting, say, you need to know if the class is for beginners or for people who do free-motion quilting with the ease of Tiger Woods making a putt.

Will the teacher provide individual, hands-on instruction? This isn't always made clear in class listings but may make the difference in whether you achieve breakthroughs in your quilting.

What is the purpose of the class? Will you complete a project, master a technique, or just sample some new methods or tools? Some quilters really want to take home a completed project, while others seek to improve a particular skill. You also need to know how much leeway a teacher will give you in diverting from the class agenda. There are classes that function more like master classes, where all students work at their own pace on their own projects while the teacher makes comments and suggestions. Say the assignment is to work on a self-portrait, but you want to work on a portrait of a famous person: Is that okay?

What materials and tools must you bring? Are there hidden costs? Some classes require sewing machines and some don't—make sure you know. If you need to bring fabric, be clear about the yardage and how it will be used. Also find out whether there will be quilting-supply vendors near the class in case you run out of something or brought the wrong stuff. Many classes offered in shops require you to purchase a related book. Be sure you know the cost and whether it's worth your while: Some quilters get annoyed when they have to buy a $25 book to make one small project.

Never feel shy about asking questions before signing up. Teachers would much rather teach students who are prepared and excited about what the teacher has to offer. If you have a fantastic experience in the class, you'll become a walking billboard for that teacher. When you succeed, the teacher succeeds.

2003 by *The Professional Quilter* magazine. Some of the other teachers don't have familiar names because they live in places like Kenya, Scotland, or Australia, or because they haven't written books yet or taught at national shows. But they've got quilting experience and put together a compelling course in writing.

Classes cover a wide range of topics, including such specific techniques as fabric dyeing and appliqué, as well as project classes, like making landscape quilts. There is even a class on how to run a professional machine-quilting business, taught by Carol Thelen, a well-known longarm quilter and author.

Every class is broken up into individual lessons. On a designated starting date, students can download lesson one, then they have a week to work on that lesson before the next one is posted. Lessons include written directions, supplemented by photographs and illustrations. There is a place to post questions to the teacher if you need extra help, and a response is posted within twenty-four hours. Fees are comparable to or less than those at a quilt shop, averaging about $8 per lesson. Courses generally consist of two to five lessons.

"Where am I going to find a quilt shop that offers a class at 2 A.M.?"

About 20 percent of Quilt University's students live outside the country, but others cite reasons other than distance from class for picking the online option. "Some of our students have young kids, some have demanding jobs, and some are taking care of elderly parents at home," says Carol Miller, Quilt University's "dean." "We also get e-mail from people who are deaf or who have debilitating illnesses. And there are students whose first language is something other than English: They say live classes go too fast for them."

Lois Frankel of Ewing, New Jersey, is a repeat student at Quilt University who cites a different reason for choosing the online option: She's a night owl. "I work full time and I do most of my quilting in the middle of the night," explains Frankel, whose website is www.nightstitcher.com. "Where am I going to find a quilt shop that offers a class at 2 A.M.?" Frankel has taken about ten courses online, mostly classes in design or technique, including fabric painting, surface embellishment, and curved piecing.

Carol Miller says she's tried to complement the offerings from local quilt shops rather than compete

At What Price Quilt Classes?

Fees for quilting classes range widely: A local quilt shop class might run $10 or less; a weeklong out-of-town workshop with a marquee-name teacher could cost more than $1,000, including room and board (but not travel).

Quilt shops generally offer classes at a rate of $8 to $10 per hour or $15 to $25 per class. Many classes last for several hours. For a class that requires a lot of hands-on instruction and four or five sessions, the fees might top $100. Participants will often need to buy new fabric for a class project and may be required to buy a book. Sometimes class-related materials are discounted. Quilt shops need to make a profit, but classes bring in more than fees. Luring a quilter into a fabric store is like trapping a chocoholic in a sweets shop; the temptation to buy is overwhelming.

Workshops and classes presented by guilds generally have no fee or are inexpensive because they tend to be subsidized by dues and fund-raising projects. Often, workshops led by guild members are free. Many guilds charge $20 to $50 for workshops led by prominent out-of-town teachers. These can be anything from a two-hour evening class to a full-day workshop. If nonmembers are permitted to attend, they usually pay more, and if there is a waiting list, members have the edge.

At the major quilt shows, including the American Quilter's Society show in Paducah, Kentucky, and the International Quilt Festival in Houston, many classes have waiting lists, one proof that the fees aren't considered unreasonable. For the 2007 AQS show in Paducah, half-day classes cost $40 and full-day classes ranged from $65 to $160, depending on whether there were charges for materials. The average cost was $80.

Prices for intensive seminars and retreats can be higher, but the total-immersion experience is treasured by many quilters. Five-day workshops at both the Empty Spools Seminars at Asilomar, California, and the Quilt Surface Design Symposium held in Columbus, Ohio, cost more than $1,000, including room and board. Accommodations are not deluxe, but the teachers are some of the best. For more information see Quilt Retreats and Conferences on pages 386–88.

Should you find it difficult to afford classes and workshops, check to see if there are stipends or scholarships available to help pay the fees. Some venues offer these, including Quilting by the Lake, a summer retreat in upstate New York (see page 386 for more on QBL). If there is no mention of scholarships for a given show or retreat, call or e-mail to ask.

In any case, a bargain is always in the eye of the beholder. I've had quilters tell me that they felt ripped off paying $25 for a quilt shop class because the instructor was inept and the add-on fees for fabric and a book more than doubled the cost. On the other hand, a quilter I know who spent hundreds of dollars on an intensive, multiday workshop called it "the best bargain of my quilting life," because the lessons transformed her craft.

The bottom line isn't necessarily what you pay for a quilt lesson, but what you get out of it: Shop wisely!

RESOURCES

Quilt Magazines

There are several dozen quilting magazines; new ones start all the time. I've made a partial listing here, including the most popular general quilting titles and several specialist magazines. This list doesn't include such publications as Threads *or* Cloth Paper Scissors, *which cover quilts and quilting but also feature other crafts.*

Often people start by buying single issues of quilt magazines from a newsstand to discover which match their taste and skill level. Most quilt shops carry a number of magazines, and you will also find them at bookstores, grocery shops, newsstands, and major chain stores, among other places. For more information about these and other publications, see the additional resources section on page 559.

American Patchwork & Quilting

Published six times a year by Better Homes and Gardens. To subscribe, go to **www.allpeoplequilt.com** or call (800) 677-4876.

Fons & Porter's Love of Quilting

Published every two months by Love of Quilting. To subscribe, go to **www.fonsandporter.com** or call (888) 985-1020.

McCall's Quilting

A bimonthly published by CKMedia. To subscribe, go to **www.mccallsquilting.com** or call (800) 944-0736.

The Professional Quilter: The Business Journal for Serious Quilters

A quarterly published by The Professional Quilter. To subscribe, go to **www.professionalquilter.com** or call (301) 482-2345.

Quilter's Newsletter

Ten issues a year are published by CKMedia. To subscribe, go to **www.qnm.com** or call (800) 477-6089.

Quilting Arts Magazine

Published six times a year by Quilting Arts, LLC. To subscribe, go to **www.quiltingarts.com** or call, toll-free, (866) 698-6989.

Quiltmaker

A bimonthly published by CKMedia. To subscribe, go to **www.quiltmaker.com** or call (800) 881-6634.

with them. "I've taught more than five hundred students in our beginner class called Starting from Scratch, but our most popular classes are the advanced ones. Quilt shops can't afford to offer those because they won't get enough students, but since our students come from all over, that's not a problem. The classes that do astronomically well for us are ones like Marilyn Belford's class in Realistic Fabric Portraits."

At www.quiltuniversity.com, potential students can tour the website, visiting Meet the Faculty to take a look at their bios. The teachers each list their online quilting classes, and there are photographs posted of projects made by previous students in the classes, as well as a sampling of the students' comments. The website always includes a free sample class for those who want to better understand how the Quilt University works before they make a financial commitment. And, there is also a free e-mail newsletter available, which lists upcoming classes.

LEARNING FROM BOOKS AND MAGAZINES

Not everybody has the time or money to take quilt classes, and sometimes quiltmakers have other reasons for avoiding them. Art quilter Linda McCurry of Gilbert, Arizona, who has been sewing since childhood and has a degree in fashion design, says she has consciously chosen *not* to take classes from top quiltmakers. "I don't want to make a quilt that looks like one made by Caryl Bryer Fallert or Nancy Crow," she explains. "I would prefer to study design and composition or drawing."

McCurry isn't averse to learning from books, but prefers those on specific techniques. "A few years back, I found a little book in a crafts store called *Hand-Dyed Fabric Made Easy*, by Adriene Buffington," she says. "It totally turned me into a dyeing maniac, and you can find me with colorful hands at least once a month."

Those quilters who don't start in a beginner's class at a quilt shop often start by buying a book for beginning quilters, and there are some excellent ones. The tried and true favorites include *Quilts! Quilts!! Quilts!!! The Complete Guide to Quiltmaking* by Diana McClun and Laura Nownes, which includes detailed lessons for a wonderful sampler quilt, and *Your First Quilt Book (or It Should Be!)* by Carol Doak.

MORE ONLINE CLASSES

Since the introduction of Quilt University, the use of online technology to teach quilting has grown steadily and is poised to explode. Quilters are willing to pay an enrollment fee for structured lessons. Some sites use video while others employ digital images of quilts and step-by-step how-to's in photos and text.

One newer purveyor of Internet quilt classes, QuiltCampus at **www.quiltcampus.net**, is now up and running, offering both technique and project classes.

American Patchwork & Quilting, a popular quilt magazine published by Better Homes and Gardens, announced the launch of the American Patchwork & Quilting University in the fall of 2007. The magazine's editors said APQU would start providing online classes in the spring of 2008, including on such topics as Machine Quilting 101 and How to Print Your Own Fabric. Find out more at the magazine's website, **www.allpeople.quilt.com**.

And, look for more competition in the future.

Another good bet for getting started is *Quilter's Complete Guide* by Marianne Fons and Liz Porter, who also publish a bimonthly magazine called *Fons & Porter's Love of Quilting*. And thousands swear by Eleanor Burns' Quilt in a Day book on making a Log Cabin quilt, which is one of the simplest patterns. Even experienced quilters keep resource books around to help remind them how wide to make a typical binding or the standard dimensions of a finished queen-size or crib quilt.

One of the many excellent books for the beginning quilter.

Another major source of how-to information is quilting magazines, of which there are more than a dozen published regularly. The most popular general-interest magazines include *McCall's Quilting*, *American Patchwork & Quilting*, and *Quilter's Newsletter*. They are all stuffed with patterns, projects, and general tips. *Quilter's Newsletter* provides great patterns but also contains excellent news and feature stories about the quilt world and interviews with top quilters.

Some magazines are published monthly, but many come out six times a year. *American Quilter*, which is published by the American Quilter's Society, is a quarterly magazine; receiving it is one of the chief benefits of membership in that organization.

In addition, there is another tier of magazines keyed to more specialized audiences. The lavish *Quilting Arts Magazine*, which is published every two months, is pricier than most, but art quilters call it eye candy and drool over its stunning and inspiring photographs. *The Professional Quilter* is the reverse: utilitarian rather than glitzy, but crammed with information for those trying to make a business of quilting.

Books and magazines can help teach quilting, but eventually, most quilters seek out live teachers to supplement the page-bound instructions. It's just so much easier to learn in three dimensions from a knowledgeable person who can answer questions as they arise. In past eras, those people were relatives and friends, but today's quilters—especially those just beginning—often don't know anyone else immersed in this craft. Luckily, there are lots of talented teachers.

It's Not Just the Teachers

Taking quilt classes is not just about the teachers. Not by a long shot. When quilters are asked about the benefits of quilt lessons, the experience of interacting with and learning from other students is often ranked just as high as the teacher's input.

Cindy Smith, an American living in Saudi Arabia, traveled all the way to Williamsburg, Virginia, from the Middle East to attend The Elly Sienkiewicz Appliqué Academy in 2005 and says it was the total experience that made it extraordinary.

"I went hoping merely to improve my appliqué, because I only started quilting about a year before, but the whole experience far outweighed my expectations," says Smith. "Life in Saudi Arabia is rather stark—so far from family and friends—and all of a sudden in Williamsburg I was surrounded by happy, huggy women! Each one was delighted to be away from her normal life, with no cooking, cleaning, or other obligations, just sewing and making or renewing friendships. If you wandered down to breakfast alone, there was always an invitation to join a table whether they knew you or not."

And Suzanne Louth of Springfield, Missouri, a regular at the appliqué academy, adds, "There is just so much sharing that goes on. Teachers and students alike share—techniques, meals, car rides, patterns, notions, fabric, talents, time, problems, and stories."

There are definite benefits to taking classes with friends. If you drive to the venue, you can split the driving and the expense of gas. Sharing a hotel room is a great way to reduce costs. And, every night becomes a show-and-tell session for what you learned and what you bought.

Many quilters return to the same venues and teachers year after year, often bringing friends with them or planning their classes to coincide with quilters they met the year before. Ann P. Shaw has taken more than a dozen classes from teacher Ruth B. McDowell, and the other quilters keep her coming back, almost as much as McDowell's brilliant instruction.

"I often enroll in her classes with a couple of quilting friends," says Shaw. "The three of us pretend we're a guild, which we call the Mad Madams. It all got started the first time we took Ruth's class at Asilomar on the coast of California, (part of the Empty Spools Seminars), and in a silly moment we decided to pretend we were at camp. We wore matching T-shirts and made up camp songs, and everybody in the class got involved.

"One year we all made flamingo quilts, and one of those quilts got special 'sunglasses.' Ruth made these sunglasses out of black fabric with bright stars and stuck them on my very large flamingo. The joke transformed my garish, menacing flamingo into something more like 'Joe Cool.' This led to our getting gigantic sunglasses for Ruth. I actually still have Ruth's fabric sunglasses and pin them to the flamingo quilt sometimes just for fun."

Shaw adds, "Having this sense of playfulness in the class contributes to having a good time, but I think it also helps quilters relax and open up to taking new risks with their quilts."

Why These Teachers?

THE TWENTY TEACHERS PROFILED IN THIS chapter are among the best and most sought-after quilt instructors in the country. They teach at guilds, at major shows, and sometimes at small retreats. They were chosen based on multiple criteria, including the recommendations of quilters who filled out the questionnaire I sent out to hundreds of quilters nationwide. Comments were also sought from those who run major quilt shows and know first hand whose classes sell out the fastest.

That isn't to say there aren't another twenty or fifty teachers who work at this exalted level, or near it (you'll find some of these in 27 More Quilt Teachers to Watch For on page 376). But the teachers here have earned their laurels and consistently satisfy students. There will always be a few students disappointed in a given teacher, perhaps because the student wasn't prepared for the level of work, or because the teacher wasn't feeling well that day, or the teaching style wasn't a fit with that particular student. But teachers with more than a few negative reviews didn't make the cut for this list, even those with fiercely devoted fans.

The teachers here have earned their laurels and consistently satisfy students.

You won't find some exceptional teachers on this list simply because they're slowing down their travel and teaching life. Art quilter Michael James, for one, is lauded by many advanced students, but because of his duties at the Department of Textiles, Clothing, and Design at the University of Nebraska–Lincoln and the time he sets aside for his own work, he only teaches in the United States for a few weeks each year, at most. (You can read about James on page 381 in 27 More Quilt Teachers to Watch For.)

The teachers I selected to profile here purposefully represent a wide range of techniques and styles. There are "simplifiers" who have made their reputation breaking the quilting process down into its most basic steps. There are also art quilters, whose classes can sometimes be quite advanced, appealing to students who are confident in their own creative abilities. And, many of the teachers here are specialists, known for teaching particular skills, patterns, or techniques that are especially popular now, such as machine quilting, appliqué, and fabric dyeing.

Some of these instructors are easy in their teaching style and make students laugh. Others tend to challenge and push their students. Quilters who use their vacation time for workshops and are looking for fun and relaxation may want to search consciously for a teacher with a less demanding approach. Ami Simms, Ricky Tims, and Melody Johnson are good examples of quilt teachers who have a light-hearted touch. Their students learn a lot, but have fun. Ruth B. McDowell's workshops concentrating on making nature quilts tend to be supportive of her students but intensely focused, and the same is true of Jane Dunnewold's classes in fabric dyeing.

Many quilt teachers go out of their way *not* to be negative and will look for something positive to say to each student. But if you aspire to major improvement in your craft or want to make art quilts, that isn't enough. You'll be rewarded by seeking out teachers who are known for giving helpful critiques. The very best teachers will provide assessmemts when asked and have a knack for knowing how to give advice that promotes their students' creative development.

The detailed profiles that follow are based on several sources of information. In every case, I conducted a lengthy one-on-one interview, in person when possible or by telephone. Some follow-up questions were handled in e-mail exchanges. Every teacher was asked to provide a list of previous students, so I could elicit specific descriptions of teaching styles and anecdotes about the classroom experience. And I made myself familiar with the signature quilts of each of these teachers, often by consulting one or more of her or his books.

Reading this chapter will help you distinguish among today's top teachers and also get a good idea of what sorts of classes are available now. Some of the teachers profiled in this chapter are so popular that getting into their workshops is very difficult. But, the profiles will give you an edge in knowing when and where to sign up for their classes. Almost all of the profiles include a list of that teacher's books or provide helpful tips.

WHAT WILL I NEED TO BRING?

Before signing up for a workshop, it's wise to read the list of materials required, which many quilt teachers note on their websites. In cases when the list is extensive, buying supplies can ramp up the cost of taking the class. Also, some of the products and brands the teachers recommend may need to be ordered by mail, so you'll need advance warning.

Bear in mind that there's usually a good reason for requiring those materials. Textile artist Jane Dunnewold frequently gets complaints about how many items students need to bring to her workshops on fabric dyeing and surface embellishment, but she usually covers multiple techniques, and generally, students use everything they bring.

Art quilter Nancy Crow not only requires her students to work hard and long, but she wants them to bring a lot of fabric in many different colors to her workshops so that they will have a number of choices available. Most students bring about one hundred yards of fabric for a one-week workshop.

Learning More About Teachers

How can you check out a quilt teacher before taking a class or workshop? The profiles that follow here and in 27 More Quilt Teachers to Watch For starting on page 376 are a good start. And there are several more options. First, word of mouth. Ask around at the local quilt shop and at your guild to see if anybody has taken a class with that teacher. Post the same question on quilters' message boards online.

Then, look on the Internet to see if the teacher has a website. Most quilters who make some part of their living from teaching will have one, and quite likely it will list and describe all the classes and lectures they offer on a regular basis. Look up not just the content of the classes but also check the parts of the website where the teacher displays her or his quilts. Do you find them attractive and well made? Are they done using a technique or in a particular style that you want to learn? If the teacher has won any major awards for quilts, those should be listed, often as part of the biography.

Another way to find out more about the teachers listed is from the books and patterns that many have used to record their signature techniques. There may be quilt shops that offer classes using those books as texts. There are hundreds of quilt shops where you can study specifically how to make Bethany Reynolds' Stack-n-Whack quilts, or one of Eleanor Burns' various Quilt in a Day quilts, or Ricky Tims' bold and colorful Convergence Quilts (this chapter will give a preview of some of these techniques).

Quilters can also research these and other top quilt teachers by surfing a wonderful website maintained by the nonprofit Alliance for American Quilts. The goal of this organization is to preserve the stories and traditions of great quilters and their work, and to that end, the alliance has been conducting interviews with the country's top quilters for years. Transcripts of these interviews can be read at the alliance's website, **www.centerforthequilt.org**, under the category of Quilters' S.O.S., or Quilters' Save Our Stories.

Ricky Tims discusses The Beat Goes On, *in his Q.S.O.S. interview.*

What helps keep these Q.S.O.S. interviews focused and fascinating is that each quiltmaker brings a single quilt to the interview, which is photographed and used to illustrate her or his distinctive style and quilting history. There is an alphabetical listing of all the quilters interviewed, or you can type in the name of the quilter where prompted. The interviews get extremely specific as to technique and very often give a feeling for the quiltmaker's personality.

TEACHER PROFILE

Alex Anderson

Although there are a number of quilting shows with a national television audience, Alex Anderson has a particularly large and loyal following because, starting in 1994, her show, *Simply Quilts*, was on the air for more than a decade and because of her warm and relaxed manner. In 492 episodes, Anderson showcased virtually every style and trend in quilting and interviewed almost every quilter of national repute. Thousands of women learned to quilt by watching Anderson, and many thousands more tried new techniques because she convinced them that they could.

The show's cancellation wasn't her idea, but Anderson has felt liberated by the change, which has freed her to explore new options and to expand her teaching and writing schedule. Being a resilient, upbeat person, she immediately switched media when the news came out, becoming one of the first quilt teachers making regular podcasts—free downloadable audio programs available on her website. Called the "Quilt Connection," these podcasts are generally shorter than her thirty-minute television show and feature quilting tips and interviews with quilt world personalities. For techniques that need visuals to explain them, Anderson posts photos on her site. With less to worry about, like camera angles and breaking down quilt techniques into short bits that look good on camera, Anderson is even more relaxed in these audio tapings, which allow more of her goofball, self-deprecating humor to shine through.

In 2007, Anderson launched yet another new venture, a talk show on quilting cohosted with famous teacher Ricky Tims (you'll find his profile on page 369). *The Quilt Show* broke new ground on many fronts: Not only is it taped in front of a live audience, but it airs on computer screens instead of TV screens, and viewers must pay to see it. Viewers pay a fee roughly comparable to the cost of a quilt magazine subscription, or they can wait and buy a DVD of a whole year's worth of episodes. Although there was grumbling about the cost and some early viewers said they preferred the

Alex Anderson

Cohost of the online "TV" show *The Quilt Show*, Alex Anderson specializes in updated traditional quilts.

Skill level

Classes for beginners and intermediate students.

Website

www.alexandersonquilts.com provides Anderson's teaching schedule, including information about her yearly fall retreat. In addition to an online store, which sells Anderson's books and patterns (there are also free patterns available), a quilt shop directory, and a schedule of reruns of her TV show, *Simply Quilts*, the site features Anderson's podcasts. More information about *The Quilt Show*, is available at **www.thequiltshow.com**.

Alex Anderson's Books

Alex Anderson has written more than a dozen accessible how-to and pattern books, including a series called Quilting Basics. If quilting books were counted by the keepers of bestseller lists, Anderson would have the words *bestselling author* in front of her name in print. One of her most popular titles is ***Start Quilting with Alex Anderson: Six Projects for First-Time Quilters,*** published by C&T Publishing; $12.95.

A newer title that's recommended is ***Machine Quilting with Alex Anderson: 7 Exercises, Projects & Full-Size Quilting Patterns,*** from C&T Publishing; $17.95.

heavier how-to focus of *Simply Quilts,* nineteen thousand quilters happily paid to watch Anderson and Tims in the first six months alone. The show includes interviews, technique tutorials, and even musical interludes. And the two are jointly building the new show's website into something akin to MySpace for quilters, encouraging them to post profiles and pictures of their quilts.

Whatever the medium, Anderson, who has been teaching quilting for more than twenty-five years, is the perfect host. Her manner is that of a big sister who shares a hobby and knows more than you do but is not intimidating. "My heart is in teaching and that's what I'm best at," she says. "Part of my success is that I know what needs to be asked during a demonstration so that quilters will know how to do the technique."

Anderson's fans are effusive in their praise. "I wouldn't be a quilter today if it wasn't for Alex Anderson's show," says Linda Kolber. "I was up one morning and happened to tune to HGTV. I got a glimpse of a quilt that Alex was preparing and decided 'I would love to do that.' I looked up her website, found the episode, and ordered the book the project came from. Since then, I've completed many quilts, bought a new sewing machine, and taken classes. In short, Alex Anderson changed my life forever."

Donna Allard in South San Francisco says she didn't know anybody who quilted and thought "it was just for old ladies" until she was channel surfing one morning and happened to catch an episode of *Simply Quilts*. "I guess I'm prolific, because I've made a couple hundred quilts since I first saw the show six years ago. I'm so inspired by Alex that I attended a retreat with her last year and had her autograph my sewing machine!"

The quilts Anderson makes for her own pleasure fall squarely into a style that might be called "contemporary traditional." Anderson's patterns are well-loved classic blocks, like Churn Dash, and are made from the bold patterned fabrics found in most quilt shops. The quilts tend to be machine pieced and either hand or machine quilted. Anderson got interested in quilting while working on a degree in art at San Francisco State University. She completed a quilt as part of her coursework in fiber and graphic design and also studied

Amish quilts. The passion she developed for quilts and quiltmaking hasn't abated to this day.

When Anderson began quilting in the Bay Area, the craft had just begun its renaissance and anybody who knew the basics was quickly pressed into service as a teacher. Anderson gratefully acknowledges that she soon found mentors and quilt shop owners who both exposed her to different techniques and booked her for classes. After about twenty of her individual quilt patterns had been published in magazines and books, Anderson signed a book contract with C&T Publishing, which works with many top quilters.

The book led to even more teaching engagements, and while teaching in southern California, Anderson was approached about hosting a new TV show on quilting. She describes her initial reaction as one of "extreme hesitancy," partly because it was outside the realm of her previous expertise and also because she didn't want to be away from her family. But the partnership that resulted helped lift the profile of quilting nationwide.

Yellow Rose *(top) and* Scrappy Nine Patch, *both by Alex Anderson.*

The perfect example of an accomplished multimedia quilt personality, Anderson has a reach that goes far beyond television. This includes not only her website and podcasts but the traditional print media, where she contributes articles to magazines and has written a string of books. She's also flexed her creative muscles by designing multiple lines of fabric for P&B Textiles and has become the public face of Bernina sewing machines, as a spokesperson for Bernina of America. She appears in many Bernina ads and also teaches and lectures under the auspices of the company, which sends out regular e-mail newsletters containing Anderson's tips.

For those who want to experience Anderson's teaching personally there are several venues where she holds classes regularly. Besides teaching occasionally at several Bay Area quilt shops, Anderson usually teaches

Esterita Austin

An art quilter, Esterita Austin specializes in landscape quilts and techniques for creating depth with fabric and paint.

Skill level

Classes for students of all levels; three- to five-day workshops do require previous quiltmaking experience.

Website

www.esteritaaustin.com gives descriptions of Austin's workshops and lectures, along with a calendar of engagements, a gallery of her quilts, and an online store featuring her patterns and favorite tools.

Telephone

(631) 331-3429

a five-day workshop each spring at the Empty Spools quilting seminar at Asilomar, a rustic conference center located right on the beach in Pacific Grove, California (for more information, see page 386). She also sometimes teaches on quilting cruises. And once a year, in the fall, Anderson hosts a four-day retreat at a hotel near her home (the venue varies). There are slots for about forty quilters who can choose to work independently on projects they bring or join in on the retreat's scheduled activities.

Quilters have a chance to speak with Anderson in person when she appears at national quilt shows and on her visits to Bernina dealers and quilt shops across the country. All of her upcoming appearances are listed on her invaluable website. But clearly, Anderson's greatest contribution to quilting is through the medium of television. In 2004, the American Quilter's Society of Paducah, Kentucky, asked readers of its *American Quilter* magazine to nominate and vote on which quilters had done the most to advance quiltmaking in the past twenty years. There were twenty-four nominees but only five finalists, including Alex Anderson.

TEACHER PROFILE

Esterita Austin

Called Teri by her friends and students, Esterita Austin made her reputation with an unusual specialty: creating realistic-looking rocks in her appliqué quilts. But quilters who take her classes learn about much more than rocks. They come out understanding how to use fabric and paint to create an illusion of depth and perspective in their quilts. Austin has a solid grasp of light and dark values and how shadows enhance images, and she is as gifted at teaching as she is at quilting. Since realistic landscape quilts are all the rage, her classes are popular.

Austin's reputation soared in 2001, when her quilt *The Well* won an international competition and was exhibited at the American Folk Art Museum in New York, the first of many art museums to display it. The vibrant quilt creates the powerful illusion that the viewer is looking up from the bottom of a deep well, seeing rows of stones bathed in red, yellow, and blue light and leading up to a small, circular opening far away. Many of her quilts depict stone doorways, portals, and arches and usually convey a sense of a path leading toward a mystery. In her workshops and lectures, Austin divulges the secrets of her layered looking landscapes that pull the eye forward.

Esterita Austin's award-winning quilt The Well *is in the collection of the American Folk Art Museum.*

"My career as an art quilter began as soon as I took a class from Esterita," says Lisa Chipetine of West Hempstead, New York. "I'd been quilting for a few years, using mostly commercial fabrics and patterns. I wanted to venture into art quilting, doing free-form cutting and using my own designs. I've found that many famous art quilters may be good artists but lousy teachers. Esterita is great at both. She's approachable, diligent, and allows you creative freedom, while still giving you the guidance you need. She's the only teacher I've ever had who was able to convey the ways to 'read' fabrics and deal with their values."

Another former student, Sarah Ann Smith, a Camden, Maine, resident, was hoping to take a weeklong workshop with Austin but decided on a one-day class instead because it was being held nearby. She was concerned that she might not learn much in a day but now says, "I learned more of what I needed to know [about making art quilts] from Teri in one day than I had in the previous year of reading and working independently. The key thing I learned was how to accentuate the contrast in my quilts. That nugget, combined with the exercise of doing a project for the class, helped me see things I hadn't realized before. Learning to manipulate cloth by applying paint when and where I need it has added an incredibly versatile tool to my arsenal of techniques."

Smith was also pleased at Austin's flexibility. When Smith asked if, rather than using one of Austin's photographs in the exercise, she could bring one of her own, Austin agreed. After several e-mail exchanges of images, she helped Smith select the photograph of the ruins at Machu Picchu, Peru, that would best lend itself to fabric collage.

Several things are unusual about Austin's typical classes, including the fact that they do not require sewing machines. Most are workshops with titles like Stone Portals; Painting for Illusion; and Rock, Wood, and Water, in which students create a small landscape collage by cutting and fusing fabrics, which does not require stitching (for more about fusing, see pages 163–67). Austin teaches the technique and markets her own brand of a very sheer fuse called Misty-Fuse, which can stand up to her painting enhancement techniques, while not adding bulk.

Spyrogyra, by Esterita Austin.

Once the fusing is done, Austin teaches students in many of her workshops how to paint right on the fabric to intensify the sense of shadow and light. Students have the option of taking these exercises home and turning them into actual quilts, but Austin suggests that they don't: She wants the class project to be in the nature of an experiment. "I tell them to make something *not* to save because if they try to make something perfect or great, they'll be too uptight to take risks," she explains.

Austin's teaching style has its theatrical moments. She usually begins by showing some of her own completed quilts, then she announces, in a pompous manner, "I don't expect you to do this in one day because I'm an artist, and you're not." She then plops a tiara on her head and adds, "The one thing I have that you don't is an artistic license." She whips out a laminated document with fancy lettering that reads Artistic License on the top.

While the class is still trying to figure out whether to take her seriously, Austin pulls out a sheaf of papers which are all inscribed Artistic License and proceeds to give one to each student, with her name written in. In addition, each student is given her own tiara, a small crown made of gold cardboard. The whole point, explains Austin, is to loosen up the class and keep the students from being too serious. "Artistic license is really a license for them to let go, a license to breathe."

Austin meticulously lays out the class exercise for the students, explaining her materials and methods in detail and giving them patterns to work with. "The setting up is pretty anal," she says, "but once we get to cutting and placing fabric, it's free-flowing." She talks about composition and demonstrates how to make color contrasts more dramatic. Austin circulates around the room, helping students as they put their own quilt tops up on the black design wall.

After majoring in art education at the University at Buffalo and studying for her master's in graphics and photography at Pratt Institute, Austin taught graphic arts and photography to middle school and high school students on Long Island. Like many others, after having a baby, she made her first quilt, a traditional sampler, when a friend took her to a class at a nearby quilt shop.

Austin went on to raise three children, quilting all the while. When she took art quilting classes, she began to see more and more ways in which her art background was feeding into her quilt designs. But Austin didn't hit the road teaching until her youngest finished high school.

These days, Austin teaches all over the country and abroad, at quilt shows and for guilds. She relishes the enthusiastic response of her many students. By showing them how artistic principles are applied to her own quilts, Austin gets her students to ask such questions as "From what direction is the light coming in my pictorial quilt?" and "How do I manipulate fabric and paint to show a shadow?" She shows slides of two quilts called *Into the Light* and *Out of the Dark*, depicting the inside of a cave: In both quilts, the shape and size of the design elements are the same, but all the fabric shapes that are dark in one quilt are light in the other, and vice versa. The quilts look shockingly different. She also points out that there is always one spot in her quilts where the composition "visually pops," the place where she juxtaposes her lightest fabric with the darkest.

"I've realized I'm even more of a teacher than an artist. I love watching my students have epiphanies," Austin says. "Most quilters don't have a sense of the basic artistic principles, and it's wonderful to see how quickly these lessons can transform their work."

"I've realized I'm even more of a teacher than an artist. I love watching my students have epiphanies."

Sue Benner

An art quilter, Sue Benner is known for abstract quilts in vibrant colors, often made of silk.

Skill level

Varies by class; some are open to students with all levels of quilting experience, while others specify for intermediate to advanced students.

Website

www.suebenner.com opens with Benner's artist's statement and features a listing of her gallery exhibits and shows and her lectures and workshops; there is also a portfolio of Benner's work.

TEACHER PROFILE

Sue Benner

Sue Benner's popular workshops are not just for art quilters but for any quilter who wants to fully grasp the principles of design and composition. Benner is known for her painterly abstract quilts, like *Skin Deep II*, which was chosen for inclusion in the Quilt National art quilt show in 2001. This big, brash quilt is eighty-three inches wide and thirty-four inches tall, divided into four quadrants. Each section is notable for neon bright colors, either as a background or in the painted spots that spill across the surface, resembling the mottled shed skin of some psychedelic reptile, or a microscopic close-up of dangerous bacteria.

The biological feel of the quilt is no accident. Benner majored in molecular biology and she expected to pursue a career as a medical illustrator. In a quote that accompanied the quilt when it was exhibited, Benner wrote that *Skin Deep II* represents a continuation of her "exploration of watery environments with musings about the skins of imagined fish, amphibians, and other mysterious creatures." Benner has said that she sometimes thinks of quilts as fabric "skins." If all of this sounds a bit intimidating or pretentious, it isn't. Benner's quilts are as dazzling as their maker is easygoing and down-to-earth.

Benner has her own distinct style, an unusual way of looking at quilts, and a knack for teasing out the best from her students. She is one of those gifted teachers with a flair for gently unleashing the creativity of others. Benner starts her longer workshops by asking students to write down their goals for that class, and her teaching methods include some unusual exercises to help reach those ends.

"I tell people that Sue taught me a new way of quiltmaking that fits my style and personality," says Elizabeth Byrom of Chapel Hill, North Carolina. "She pushed me to realize that my passion is France and to start a series of art quilts based on photographs I took in France. She also advised me to take art classes, which I plan on doing soon."

Seattle quiltmaker Lorraine Edmond, who took a three-day fusing class from Benner, says, "The circumstances were less than ideal, which included the classroom losing power when a fuse blew, but Sue took it all in stride. She's warm and encouraging and creates a great atmosphere for learning. She was adept at working with people at very different levels of experience. People in the workshop all seemed to turn out work that surprised them."

Edmond's comment provides a clue about how Benner's classes are different from many quilting workshops: She isn't there to hand out a pattern and get every student to rigidly copy her design. Instead, what Benner teaches is a series of composition techniques, and then she sets her students loose.

Skin Deep II *(top) and* Cellular Structure V, *both by Sue Benner.*

All of her classes include work on fusing fabric using a popular construction method (for more about fusing, see pages 163–67). Some might call this work fusible appliqué, but to Benner, it's more like fabric collage. "I work on fabric the way a painter works on canvas," she says. "My favorite workshops to teach include Quilt Fusion: Renegade Construction and Composition Trilogy." In Quilt Fusion, she teaches multiple ways to "build a quilt surface using fusibles," and then the students work on their own. Composition Trilogy

The inspiration for Benner's imagery comes from natural landscapes and sometimes from aspects of motherhood.

involves having the students focus on three different design challenges: exploring squares and rectangles, working with curved shapes, and understanding landscapes. Then, if time permits, the students practice machine quilting. Students in Benner's classes are encouraged to work quickly, so when she teaches her fusible methods in Composition Trilogy, for example, students make three quilts in three days, or four quilts in four or five days.

Benner shares her own process of quiltmaking, which involves a lot of layering of different fabrics frequently embellished by dyeing, painting, drawing, and printing. She uses mostly silks and cottons, as well as "found fabrics," such as old clothes and used linens purchased at thrift shops and garage sales. Benner's quilts often have overlays of sheer fabrics like chiffon and organza. Her palette is generally bright, with lots of primary colors, especially reds and blues. But she points out to students that these bold colors shout so loudly because they are juxtaposed with neutral tones.

The inspiration for her imagery comes from natural landscapes and sometimes from aspects of motherhood: She produced a series of quilts inspired by birds' nests, with colorful concentric circles marked by wispy, black, twiglike lines.

Benner grew up in Oshkosh, Wisconsin, and made her first quilt at the age of ten. As a teenager, she loved to design and make her own clothes and spent the summers sewing in the family's basement. Although her major at the University of Wisconsin was molecular biology, she also took classes in fabric design and art history. She moved to Dallas, Texas, for graduate school at the University of Texas Southwestern Medical School and didn't expect to stay—but her sister moved down there, and then Benner met her husband.

Benner never pursued a career in medical illustrating because her passionate sideline of dyeing and painting textiles took over her work life. "Some people in the art business saw my hobby work, and next thing you know, I was a studio artist," says Benner, whose early clients included clothing and interior designers. She adds, humbly, "Not that I was making much money at it. Just enough to pay the bills."

Sue Benner critiques a student composition.

Eventually, Benner joined her quilting background with her fiber artwork to produce startling quilts. She started lecturing as well. She was invited by Linda Fowler and Nancy Crow to teach at the annual Quilt Surface Design Symposium in Columbus, Ohio, in 1992, and her teaching career was launched.

Because her two sons are still at home and because she loves having concentrated chunks of studio time to work on her own quilts, Benner only travels for teaching gigs about six times a year. She prefers lengthy workshops lasting a minimum of four days and returns to certain venues regularly, including Art Quilt Tahoe (see page 387), the Empty Spools Seminars at the Asilomar retreat in California (see page 386), and the Quilt Surface Design Symposium in Ohio (see page 386). She also teaches dye painting classes at Nancy Crow's Timber Frame Barn in central Ohio.

Like a number of other top quilt artists, Benner prefers to work in series. She likes to fall in love with a technique and a subject matter and to keep digging deeper into a theme. "Do something twice, then do it ten more times. If it's worthwhile, do it another hundred!" Benner advises, only half joking. She also strongly urges art quilters to take drawing lessons, if they don't already have that expertise.

The exercise Benner assigns that most consistently produces an "aha moment" in her workshops is a good one for quilters to attempt at home. Benner explains, "I tell students I want them to create four panels, each six inches square. The first one is where their work is now, the second one is where they want their work to go, the third is how they are going to get there, and the fourth one is what's stopping them."

Benner tells students not to take the descriptions literally but to approach the assignment symbolically. To prevent them from getting bogged down, students are supposed to spend only about ten minutes on each panel. The instructions may vary a bit in different classes, but generally the students are limited to using half a dozen fabrics to complete the assignment. On each panel, students write a one or two word phrase relevant to their design. These panels aren't embellished or quilted; they are more in the nature of an artist's thumbnail sketch realized in the medium of fabric.

Benner once made a quilt based on imagery from a brain CAT scan.

"I get such interesting reactions!" says Benner. "People tell me later that they put the panels up in their studio at home so they can look at them all the time. Some say the panels alone made the whole class worthwhile. For many, it helps them discover what they want to do. By doing it simply and symbolically, they realize that 'It's just *me* that's stopping me,' or 'Nothing is stopping me,' or maybe it's conflicting obligations in their life."

In longer workshops Benner asks each student to quickly produce a self-portrait, which can be realistic or abstract. Sometimes she teaches a two-day workshop focused completely on the self-portrait exercise, and in that case, students are urged to bring photographs, sketches, and fabrics that have a personal meaning to them and mementos they might depict or include directly in their quilts. Benner, who once made a quilt based on imagery from a brain CAT scan, is living proof that just about any passion can translate into gorgeous quilts.

You'll find Sue Benner's quilt project Wild and Crazy Fused Ornaments on page 470.

TEACHER PROFILE

Eleanor Burns

Eleanor Burns' promotional materials say she is the "Queen of Quilting" and few would deny she has earned the title. Burns is probably the only teacher who could truly be said to have built an empire in the quilt business. "Quilt in a Day" is her promise and her trademark, and the motto graces every product she sells.

Though many quilt teachers are enterprising, the majority have a handful of employees at most. Burns runs a multimedia company with forty employees and controls all aspects of her business. Since her first how-to book on Log Cabin quilts appeared in 1978, Burns has been completely self-published. She has more than seventy books currently in print and claims to sell thousands of copies every week.

Even her television show, which airs on PBS stations all over the country, is self-produced. As part of a three-warehouse complex in San Marcos, California, Burns has her own TV studio, where her *Quilt in a Day* show has been taped since 1990. Her business compound includes editing and art departments that design all her books; a vast shipping operation for mailing her books all over the world; and a classroom full of sewing machines where local quilters meticulously test the instructions for each book.

Also on the property is a 3,200-square-foot retail store packed with Quilt in a Day merchandise, including mugs, T-shirts, and autographed plastic baggies full of fabric scraps that Burns famously flings over her shoulder on her *Quilt in a Day* TV show.

Though her greatest gifts may be for packaging and promotion, there is no denying that Burns is a gifted teacher who has turned thousands of women into quilters. There is no better teacher for the beginner.

The fervor of her fans is astounding. "Eleanor Burns is to quilting what the founding fathers were to the Revolution," declares Margaret Ann Crowder of Monmouth, Oregon. "Were it not for Eleanor's revolutionary teaching, we might all still be using paper templates."

Eleanor Burns

Head of the Quilt in a Day media empire, Eleanor Burns specializes in quick versions of traditional quilts.

Skill level

While the classes are open to students with all levels of quilting experience, Burns is exceptionally friendly to beginners.

Website

www.quiltinaday.com
Check out Burns' teaching schedule and upcoming television shows. Books, fabrics, notions, and DVDs of her classes are for sale both on the website and her San Marcos, California, and Paducah, Kentucky, quilt shops, where classes are also held.

Telephone

(800) 777-4852

BURNS' TIPS

◆ To keep your sewing machine foot pedal from migrating all over the floor while you are sewing, either wrap a large rubber band around it to make the pedal less slippery or put a computer mouse pad under the pedal.

◆ To dispose of pesky loose threads, tape a plastic baggie to the edge of your sewing table and drop them in it.

◆ Looking for an easy way to cut thread on an airplane? Use the cutter on your dental floss container.

◆ If you're stumped on picking out coordinating fabric for a quilt, look at the color bar on the selvage (finished edge) of the fabric for help: It will show the colors of dye that were used in that material.

Nevada resident Mary Henderson says her first reaction to the show was "Yeah, right. Quilt in a Day in my dreams!" But she followed the directions on the show and says, "I've become a believer. Her techniques are wonderful and she explains everything so well. I work full time outside the home and wouldn't have been able to indulge in my quilting passion without her methods."

The show has also been a lifesaver for many women who don't work outside the home, whether because they have small children, are retired, or are recuperating from an illness. "Nine years ago, I was a stay-at-home mom with three young children and going out of my mind. One day, I stumbled on Eleanor's show on PBS, somewhere between Barney in the morning and Barney in the afternoon," says Donna Peterson, who lives in Tucson, Arizona. "I fell in love with her show, her style, and her humor. Eventually, I felt inspired enough to make one of her quilts, the Log Cabin. It was as fast and easy as she promised, and I haven't stopped quilting since."

If her multimedia empire suggests she is the Martha Stewart of quilting, Burns' public persona couldn't be more different. Burns is a folksy "simplifier." A better comparison might be the easygoing style of Julia Child in her TV kitchen but without the patrician accent.

Burns will go to great lengths to entertain prospective and repeat customers. Every time she brings out a couple of new books (her rate is usually three or four a year), she creates a new live show full of corny jokes, music, slides, and outrageous sight gags. She presides over the show herself, dressed in a floppy hillbilly bonnet or a foam top hat, tooting horns, singing off-key, and generally clowning around.

Among other venues, Burns puts on these performances three times a day at the big AQS show in Paducah every spring, inside an enormous tent down the road from the convention center. As part of the 2002 show, an assistant signaled that volunteers were needed from the audience to help with a skit: "I need two people who are really energetic and just want to get close to Eleanor," said her long-time assistant, Sue Bouchard. "You'll be wearing these bird hats."

Volunteers immediately jumped up and bounded to the front of the tent, reaching for the bird hats. Burns was promoting a new pattern that year called Birds in the Air, so the women wore the bird hats while singing along with Burns to a recorded version of "Rockin' Robin" playing on a boom box.

All the frivolity has a theme and a purpose: These hour-long tent shows are free but function like infomercials. The script for the show has been carefully written to showcase the new books and the techniques involved, with Burns proudly displaying finished examples of the quilts from each book. "The idea of the show is to teach them how to use our products," says Burns. The tent is always erected right next to a building that has been absolutely packed with merchandise, including books, quilt kits (instructions plus precut fabrics), fabric by the yard, and Quilt in a Day memorabilia.

Formerly, Burns was a special education teacher and got used to simplifying the curriculum for her students. She had to learn to hold their attention from moment to moment, by keeping them constantly entertained or otherwise engaged. As she notes, she is dyslexic herself, so understands what it's like to need extra help.

"I feel I'm a teacher for beginners," she explains. "I'm completely traditional. I take an old pattern, take it apart, put it back together as simply as possible." Although her more recent quilt patterns sometimes take longer than a day to complete, it isn't by much. Burns still uses assembly-line style techniques that allow quilters to cut and sew multiple fabric patches at one time. Many of her patterns are based on simple strips of fabric, usually two and a half inches wide, which are cleverly cut and resewn to make pinwheels, nine-patch blocks, wild geese, and other simple motifs.

Burns goes to unusual lengths to make sure her instructions are clear—a panel of local students works from her guidelines printed on photocopied sheets. If anybody gets stuck, Burns adds another step or another illustration, before putting the book into final production. "People find my books easy to follow, and every year, they have to get the next one," she says.

For her television show, Burns is equally methodical. On a set that looks like it could be next door to Mr. Rogers, with her sewing machine on a table

Eleanor Burns' Books

Burns has written dozens of books, all self-published, but here are four that have been the most popular over the years. You'll find many of her books at quilt shops and almost all on her website, where some have reduced prices. There is often a sidebar showing photos of several of the patterns in specific books.

Egg Money Quilts; $27.95

Make a Quilt in a Day: Log Cabin Pattern—twentieth anniversary edition; $18.95

Quilts Through the Seasons; $27.95

Still Stripping After 25 Years; $27.95

in front of a welcoming fireplace, Burns demonstrates every step in cutting, marking, sewing, pressing, and quilting her simple patterns. And she always shows many variations in fabric selection, border styles, and ways of quilting.

Burns says that most of what propelled her in the early years was "simple survival." Born in Pennsylvania, Burns found herself in the late seventies in California, a divorced single mother with two young sons. She pleaded with the local parks and recreation department to let her teach a sewing class, and their condition was that she teach a class in patchwork because the Bicentennial was approaching. Her career as a quilting teacher was launched, and out of necessity, she self-published her first book in 1978.

Simplification is the key to Eleanor Burns' lessons.

From the start, Burns' two sisters helped with the business, and they work with her still, while her younger son, Orion, is now the general business manager. Growth was slow and deliberate at the beginning but kept building. "When I moved out of my garage to a rented warehouse, I thought, 'What have I done?!'" says Burns. "We did that in 1983, then rented a second warehouse, then a third, and in 1991, we were able to buy the whole property."

As her book sales soared and her fame grew, Burns was approached by Elna, the sewing machine company, about becoming a spokesperson. She has appeared in many print ads for Elna, and traveled often for the company. More recently, she's become the spokesperson for Baby Lock sewing machines and Garmill longarm quilting machines.

In addition to teaching at the major national quilt shows in Paducah, Kentucky, and Houston, Burns travels constantly to teach and lecture, spending about a third of her time on the road. Back home in California, she generally hosts six or eight intimate weekend quilting retreats in her private log home and usually supervises one retreat a year in a nearby church camp in Julian,

California, for about sixty students. A number of experienced teachers from Burns' Quilt in a Day staff help her with the larger retreat.

Burns says of her teaching, "People come up to me all the time and say, 'You told me I could do it, and I believed you and I did it!' It launches them into a lifetime hobby. What I'm after for these women is success."

You'll find instructions for the Scrappy Peter and Paul Quilt designed by Eleanor Burns starting on page 474.

TEACHER PROFILE

Jane Dunnewold

Dyeing one's own fabric has become standard practice for many art quilters, and even traditional quilters dabble at dyeing to spice up their projects and make them more distinctive. In recent years, there has been a big increase in the number of teachers in this field. One of the most lauded remains Jane Dunnewold, who has taught the quilt world that fabric can be a work of art all by itself.

Although she has quilted for much of her life and her quilts have been chosen repeatedly for such major art quilt shows as Quilt National, Dunnewold doesn't think of herself as a quiltmaker per se, but as a fiber artist. At her studio in San Antonio, Texas, roughly half of her advanced students are nonquilters. She produces more than one hundred lengths of one-of-a-kind fabric a year as art cloth, much of which doesn't wind up in quilts. But Dunnewold keeps at least one foot in the quilt world, teaching at quilt venues like Houston's International Quilt Festival and Nancy Crow's Timber Frame Barn in Ohio. And there is usually a waiting list for her intensive five-day classes.

Complex Cloth is both the name of Dunnewold's most popular workshop and the name of her influential book published in 1996 (for more about the book, see Four Great Books About Dyeing on page 220). The term *complex cloth* refers to white fabric with a surface that has been colored and decorated by the application of multiple patterning techniques. Dunnewold works on all sorts of fabrics, including exotic silks, rayon, and

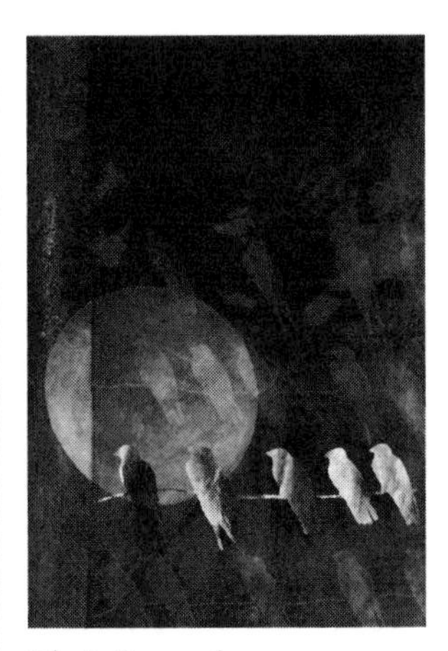

Choir Poster, *by Jane Dunnewold.*

Jane Dunnewold

A surface design authority, Jane Dunnewold concentrates on dyeing, painting, and stamping fabric.

Skill level

Classes for all levels; the specific degree of quilting experience required depends on the particular class.

Website

www.artclothstudios.com has a schedule of Dunnewold's workshops in her studio and on the road, a list of her favorite suppliers, and an online store. Some of Dunnewold's workshops are available on DVDs or CDs. On the home page you'll also find a link to her helpful glossary.

DUNNEWOLD'S TIPS

Even beginner quilters who never plan to get involved with messy dyes and other chemicals can learn some important lessons from Dunnewold's methods and philosophy. Asked to create a simple exercise in fabric embellishment for this book, Dunnewold came up with the following lesson on stamping, using inexpensive craft-store erasers.

◆ First, buy a box of a dozen white "soap" erasers (made of plastic), each measuring two inches by one inch. These are available at various craft stores, but Dunnewold suggests getting them from one of her favorite

chiffon, building up layers of color and texture through a combination of dyes, silk screen processing, paints, stencils, and stamps, among other things. She also applies metallic foils and gold leaf to fabric.

At her three-hour sampler class, held every year at the Houston quilt festival, Dunnewold quickly takes beginners through a range of techniques and lets them manipulate fabric in multiple ways. In the longer workshops that are her signature, her students explore the different methods in depth.

What makes Dunnewold unusual as a teacher isn't just the content of her classes, but also her philosophy of art and life. She says she is influenced by years of studying the *Tao Te Ching*, an ancient Chinese text, and she approaches the embellishment of fabric the way a Chinese master craftsman would. She views her work as a quest and bestows intense focus and devotion on both deepening her own knowledge and passing that knowledge on to her students. Indeed, she left the Southwest School of Art & Craft in San Antonio after chairing the surface design department for ten years to teach and create cloth full-time.

"I want my students to master the process and I never keep secrets," says Dunnewold. "I feel it's my job to tell everything I have discovered and then to encourage others to take what I know and go with it on their own."

Art quilter Barbara McKie says she has only taken a one-day class with Dunnewold in Houston but has signed up for a lengthier follow-up. "She put more in that one-day class in terms of information and suggestions to explore than anyone else." Jennie Clarke of Minneapolis was an art quilter just poking a toe into fabric dyeing when she took a two-day workshop from Dunnewold at the annual Minnesota Quilters Show in 2001. She loved the class and the teacher so much, she went on to take multiple five-day workshops from Dunnewold and then entered into an advanced program that involves an intensive correspondence course by mail. Says Clarke, "Studying with Jane has been a joy and has opened up a whole new world for me."

"She is so supportive, yet pushes you to experience outside your comfort zone without

Poster Pilgrim, *by Jane Dunnewold.*

leaving you hanging by a thread," says Lexington, Kentucky resident Heather Saunders, who took Dunnewold's five-day Complex Cloth workshop. "So what if you make a mistake? That's what the whole class was about basically, learning to deal with mistakes and make something good out of them. I learned so much."

Dunnewold grew up in a family of quilters and seamstresses in Ohio and got an undergraduate degree in psychology. She was considering divinity school when she took some time off and found herself in the first quilting class taught by quilt artist Michael James at the Massachusetts College of Art. "I was a terrible student; I didn't know how to piece well at all," says Dunnewold. "But I had been making quilts before then, and I kept quilting after."

art supply purveyors, Dick Blick Art Materials at **www.dickblick.com**, where the erasers are good quality but inexpensive.

◆ Then, cut designs into the erasers. The best tool for this is an X-Acto knife with a #11 blade. You can make curves, angles—whatever you feel like.

◆ Third, brush paint on the eraser and stamp it onto whatever fabric you choose. As a beginner, your best bet for paint is an inexpensive acrylic paint or textile paint. The most important tip is don't dip the eraser right into the wet paint, because it will be drippy and splotchy. Instead, use a small foam brush, maybe one inch wide, and dip the brush into the paint. Then paint the cut surface of the eraser. You'll get a nice clean image this way.

WHAT SHAPES TO STAMP?

Now that you've got your little box of soap erasers and your X-Acto knife, what will you carve? Here are a few simple ideas from Jane Dunnewold for some interesting shapes to try stamping on fabric. You'll find instructions for inking the stamps in Dunnewold's Tips on pages 324–25.

- Carve out squares, circles, or triangles.
- Try any geometric shape you like, but cut out the inside, so when you stamp, there will be an outline rather than a solid shape.
- Carve several small squares in a row to create a checkerboard effect.
- Experiment with a simple leaf or flower shape, solid or outlined.
- Carve some block letters: Remember they will appear reversed, so make them backward!

Dunnewold wound up moving to Texas, where her fiancé had a job, and she started taking classes at San Antonio's Southwest School of Art & Craft. After years studying there, she managed to convince the director to start a surface-design program, which she then chaired for a decade starting in 1990.

Although she teaches all around the world, Dunnewold feels particularly at home teaching at her own well-appointed studio in San Antonio. Her Art Cloth Studio occupies the third floor of a hundred-year-old Spanish-style building with stained-glass windows. Classes are limited to fifteen students, and all the students have their own six-foot-long work tables that are handy to screen-printing facilities and other tools essential for dyeing and decorating fabric, including a washer and dryer. Dunnewold's expertise is so highly valued that she offers a service critiquing the work of aspiring textile artists for $50 per hour.

Dunnewold is betting that anyone who starts manipulating the surface of fabric will want to go further, because for her, life and art are about putting one's own personal mark on things. "When people want to stamp on fabric, they start out going to Michaels [a national chain of craft stores] and buy rubber stamps with designs on them. And they like what they do, but it's not personal. So they buy a bunch of erasers and cut them and make their own stamps. First they do simple shapes, but then they go further, thinking about their own message and imagery."

Not everybody has the patience to spend so much time hovering over every inch of fabric: Many quiltmakers just want to pick out the fabric and get busy making the next quilt. Dunnewold's purpose isn't to turn quilters against the vast cornucopia of gorgeous commercial fabric now on the market. Rather, she wants to show them that they can be more deeply fulfilled if they take the fabric that's out there and give it a personal aesthetic spin.

"I think this is really just part of the long process of quilts evolving into an art form," says Dunnewold. "It's been my observation that when quilters go into the area of dyeing and printing their own fabric, they never go back. Some continue to use commercial fabrics—but they never use them just as they are."

TEACHER PROFILE

Caryl Bryer Fallert

Everything about Caryl Bryer Fallert is colorful—her flaming red hair, her vivid clothes, and especially her quilts. Fallert's award-winning quilts explode with geometric shapes and swirls in bold solid colors. Even her manner of speaking is colorful, peppered with evocative expressions. When thread gets bunched and knotted on the back of a machine-finished quilt, Fallert calls it "thread throw-up." Fussy detail work that doesn't create additional visual impact on a quilt is cited for "tediosity." The background machine quilting she does on many quilts is referred to as "swoopy, doopy stuff."

A petite, fast-talking woman, Fallert is famous for both her energy and her generosity as a teacher. Fallert has been a pioneer in several vital areas, including machine quilting, fabric dyeing, and using graphic-design software to plan her quilts. She happily shares her secrets and tricks for these techniques and more, giving some of the most thorough lectures and demonstrations in the quilt world.

If anybody deserves to act the diva, it would seem to be Fallert, whose work is in countless quilt collections and has been exhibited all over the world. Fallert is the only three-time winner of the Best of Show award at the American Quilter's Society annual show and had one of her stunning quilts chosen for the hundred best quilts of the twentieth century exhibit. But Fallert has a reputation for hard work and a pleasant demeanor that is unrivaled. Even art quilters with whom she competes adore her and come to her for advice: Among her most popular classes is one called Practical Professionalism.

Fallert's dazzling quilts are often what draws students to her classes, and they quickly find she is one of those rare creatures, a star quilter for whom teaching is also an art. "She is definitely the most professional teacher out there, and I dearly love her," says Crystal Griffith, a nurse from Baker, Florida, who has taken two classes with Fallert. "She nurtures those who need a lot of hand-holding without shortchanging the rest of

Caryl Bryer Fallert

Premier art quilter Caryl Bryer Fallert specializes in innovative computer design, photo quilts, and machine quilting.

Skill level

Classes for just about all levels; the specific degree of quilting experience required depends on the particular class.

Website

www.bryerpatch.com
In addition to posting Fallert's teaching schedule and award-winning quilts, the site is packed with tips and tricks. Fallert's hand-dyed fabrics, favorite fabric printing supplies, and CDs of her master classes are for sale online.

FALLERT'S TIPS

◆ Value is more important than color. One thing common to almost all my work is luminosity, the illusion that the light source is within the quilt itself. I create that illusion by using gradations of color. The progression of value always goes all the way from light (though I rarely use white) to dark.

◆ Improvisational piecing is a very popular technique right now. We all improvise at different stages of the process, and I do my improvising during design and quilting. I will do dozens of thumbnail sketches, then I use my overhead projector and my computer to develop a full-size design on paper. When I start to piece, I'll have a plan.

◆ When machine quilting, I never practice anything on my masterpiece quilts. Instead, I practice on another piece of cloth. For example, there is a fifteen-inch fish swimming across my big *Storm at Sea* quilt, which I practiced first on a twenty-inch square.

◆ Little stuff next to big stuff makes the big stuff look more exciting.

the class. But the real revelation was that she has developed a method of construction that is exceedingly simple yet effective and can easily be done by anybody. Of course her incredible machine quilting is something I'll never be able to do!"

"My name had been on a waiting list for two years to take a class with Caryl, and I got lucky when someone else had to cancel," says Patti Morris, a Canadian quilter. "I have never seen a teacher so devoted to her students and so patient. Her computer skills and teaching technology were way ahead of any other teacher I've ever seen, and she inspired us all individually. I took what I learned in her workshop and made a quilt for my daughter. Even though it was my first art quilt, it was chosen for the cover of the 2005 Canadian national quilt show!"

"I've taken several of her workshops, and the last one really helped me get out of a rut," says Diane Kopec, an art quilter and Web designer from Babylon, New York. "The process Caryl exposes you to in workshops is just so liberating. She shows you how to go from simple doodles to actual drawings, which then get 'appli-pieced' with her techniques. She nudges you, but you're creating your own design. And what can be more inspiring than to have actual quilts by Caryl Bryer Fallert right there for you to examine up close?"

There are waiting lists for all her classes, and Fallert loves the positive feedback she receives. "I'm old enough to acknowledge I've got gifts," she says. "What my students say is that what I taught them has made it possible for them to express themselves. I just love that!"

Fallert studied art at Wheaton College and always considered herself an artist, but for twenty-eight years she also worked as a flight attendant for United Airlines. She had tried embroidery and knitting but mostly pursued painting as a creative outlet until in the mid-1970s she and her husband bought a Missouri farm from a lifelong quilter. Fallert was inspired by this woman's work to buy a how-to book and teach herself quilting.

Some years later, during a layover between flights in Buffalo, New York, Fallert caught a lecture by pioneering art quilter Jean Ray Laury. It was the first time she encountered art quilts. Says Fallert, "It was the

Migration #2 *(left) and* Midnight Fantasy #6, *both by Caryl Bryer Fallert.*

epiphany of my life. Here was a woman who had a master's degree in design and was making these quilts as art and traveling the country talking about them. At that moment, I decided that was exactly what I wanted to do."

Fallert's work is bold and confident, and often inspired by images from nature, such as leaves, feathers, and seedpods. She frequently works in a series but seems compelled to try new things and is the art quilter most known for embracing technology head-on. It makes sense that Fallert was the first to win Best of Show at the American Quilter's Society annual show for a machine-quilted piece (in 1989), because she believed machine quilting could be used in a thrilling, creative way back when that was heretical thinking. Fallert was also early in using her computer to design quilts and has gone on to freely share her techniques in popular classes like Demystifying the New Tools.

"I believe I'm the only one teaching free-form computer design specifically for quilters," she says. While there are a handful of block-based CD-ROMs for quilters, including the popular Electric Quilt software, Fallert teaches quilters to use CorelDRAW, a program for professional graphic designers. Quilt software emphasizes a database of historical block patterns, which users can rearrange and sample in

Caryl Bryer Fallert's Book

Quilt Savvy: Fallert's Guide to Images on Fabric provides a practical and compact guide to creatively printing photos on fabric. Published by the American Quilter's Society; $21.95.

different color combinations, but Fallert uses original free-form patterns created on her computer to get an idea of what they'd look like in various fabrics.

During computer-design lectures, Fallert gives a digital presentation using a computer program called Macromedia Director, which allows her to show audiences exactly how she auditions various shapes, values, and colors along the way. "Clients who want to commission quilts from me love this feature, because I can show them numerous possible designs without the trouble and expense of making them into quilts," she tells her students. For smaller, hands-on classes, all the students come with their laptops fully loaded with software and ready to go.

Yet another technique in which Fallert has been a pioneer is in using her home computer printer to actually print her own fabric designs. With current scanner technology, quilters can download and manipulate images and create patterns they can print directly on fabric run right through their computer printer. Because quilters cut up fabric into patches for quilt tops, they have no need to print fabric the full width of commercial bolts. Fallert has published a book on creative ways to use this printing technology, and she thinks its popularity will only grow.

"To me, this is where scrapbooking and quilting merge," says Fallert. "I like that integration and the freedom of it. Plopping a bunch of your relatives in the middle of a Log Cabin block can be charming, but the technology allows us to go way past that now. You can create and manipulate wonderfully original images. If you have a great vacation, you don't have to paste all the images in a scrapbook, you can put the images right into a quilt!"

As high as Fallert's profile has become in the quilt world, it's likely to soar even higher now that she's moved her studio and living quarters to Paducah. Fallert is hoping that having a fully equipped studio there, along with a shop, classroom, and gallery, will drastically reduce her hectic touring schedule, as well as upgrade the class experience. "When I fly, I have to leave behind a lot of the teaching aids I would like to have," she says. "This way, everything I need is always here and set up, in a dedicated classroom connected to my dye studio."

For those who can't get into her sold-out classes, there are other ways to learn from Fallert. Her website, for example, is as accessible and generously informative as she is and considered one of the best in the quilt world. There are mini tutorials on a wide range of topics, including tips on machine quilting, fabric dyeing, and computer design. Fallert even answers questions about how to care for and ship quilts, what sort of lighting she uses in her studio, and how to price quilts for sale. If there's a question that isn't answered in her Frequently Asked Questions, simply click on the button that prompts you to post another.

Fallert's students are always astounded by how freely she shares tips on all the techniques she employs. She jokingly calls them "cheap tricks," because she says it isn't the techniques that are magic but "the image you create, which comes out of your mind and your heart as an artist." Fallert wants her students to know that their imagination is the greatest tool they possess, but most aspiring art quilters would argue that her so-called tricks are far too valuable to be considered "cheap."

TEACHER PROFILE

Kaffe Fassett and Liza Prior Lucy

Taking a class from Kaffe (rhymes with safe) Fassett and Liza Prior Lucy provides an opportunity to build a bridge from traditional quilts to contemporary ones. The duo love the design elements of old quilts but update them with simplified pieced construction using eye-popping colors. In their classes, both the process and the results are playful and joyful. "Kaffe and Liza are simply the best colorists I have ever worked with," says former student Claudia Chaback of Langhorne, Pennsylvania. "They have opened my eyes to a world of opportunities."

These two sometimes teach solo, but they work closely together to design quilt patterns and write books, and as a team, they are a double treat in a quilting workshop. Their usual classes revolve around one of the duo's quilt patterns, such as Gridlock, a

Kaffe Fassett and Liza Prior Lucy

Masters of color, Kaffe Fassett and Liza Prior Lucy specialize in updating traditional quilt designs using a bright, bold palette.

Skill level

All levels of quilting experience for most classes.

Websites

www.kaffefassett.com gives Fassett's teaching schedule and features photos of his designs for quilts, needlepoint, and knitwear, among other things.

www.gloriouscolor.com is the site for Lucy's online fabric shop, highlighting all of Fassett's fabrics, plus selections from other top fabric designers and the duo's books. Unless she's too busy making quilts to teach, the site also posts Lucy's teaching gigs.

Kaffe Fassett and Liza Prior Lucy's Books

Books by this duo are loaded with luscious full-color illustrations and easy-to-follow directions for twenty or more quilt projects. These are their first three, in order of publication.

Glorious Patchwork, Clarkson Potter; $34.95 hardcover

Passionate Patchwork, The Taunton Press; $34.95 hardcover, $24.95 paperback

Kaffe Fassett's Museum Quilts: Designs Inspired by the Victoria & Albert Museum, The Taunton Press; $34.95 hardcover

simple design featuring both small squares and large ones. Students are instructed to bring to class fabrics of many colors, plus tan or gray flannel with which to create a design wall. ("Never have a white design wall," advises Lucy. "It's way too distracting.")

As the class gets rolling, students spend most of their time cutting out fabrics and placing them up on the flannel to see how the colors look together. There is usually little or no sewing done during the class, but everyone leaves with a strong design that can be completed with ease once at home.

"During the class, your quilt keeps evolving," explains Rebekah Lynch, a Houston-based quilter who has taken numerous classes from the pair. "Kaffe might borrow a bit of fabric from another student, just to acquaint you with a possibility you hadn't thought of. It's a very informal class, and at the end, there's a show-and-tell segment where every student shows her quilt in progress, and Kaffe and Liza give a critique." Lynch says that taking multiple classes with the duo and making more than twenty quilts from their books "has changed both the way I quilt and the way I see color."

One of the major "aha moments" in a standard Fassett-Lucy class always happens over the issue of contrast. Quilters have the notion pounded into their heads from books, articles, and lectures that what makes a quilt beautiful and vibrant is contrast, and plenty of it. So they're always stunned when it's pointed out that Fassett's memorably brilliant color schemes ignore that inviolable rule.

"Sometimes contrast is good, but we prefer to work with close contrasts because we find that the colors bounce off one another," says Lucy. So they'll create a quilt that is mostly in the yellow/orange/red color range, but stick in some scattered shards of aqua and cobalt blue, which make the whole ensemble buzz into life. Colors used in such ways are what Fassett calls "activating agents." He says, "Any color scheme can become dead and dry looking. A yellow quilt, for example, needs a bit of lime green or lavender to activate it."

Another common lesson, tough for some quilters to swallow, is that too much sameness in pattern and type of fabric, no matter how pretty and bright, makes for a dull quilt. "Quilters love colorful batiks, but if that's *all* they ever use, their quilts look pretty boring," says Lucy. "It's so rewarding when we get a student out of a rut. I remember we taught at Houston one year, and this student had only ever worked with Civil War reproduction fabric. We told her we would help her work with that if she preferred, but she said no, she wanted to try to work with mostly yellows. She did, and by the end of class, she came up to us and said, 'The Civil War is over!'"

If Fassett and Lucy's take on quilts seems fresh, it's partly because both had their eyes "trained" in other media first. Fassett, whose parents ran a hip restaurant in Big Sur, California (where he changed his first name to that of an Egyptian boy in a book), began his career as a painter. Lucy ran an upscale needlepoint and knitting boutique, but closed it after the death of her first husband.

It was knitting that brought the two together: Fassett took up knitting in the eighties because he loved the color of yarns. He started designing groundbreaking sweaters that mixed colors in a single row and ignored all the construction "rules." By then, Lucy was working as a sales rep for a yarn company and got the assignment of taking the London-based Fassett on tour for his book *Glorious Knitting*. The pair hit it off immediately.

Lucy had become enamored of patchwork; she decided that Fassett would be a natural at quilt design and started pelting him with letters suggesting they collaborate on a pattern book. She even took the step of designing a quilt based on one of his knitwear patterns and mailed it off to convince him. The eventual result was their first book, *Glorious Patchwork*, in 1997.

The book became a model for their joint style in both quilt design and teaching and, like their other books, is a lavishly illustrated hardcover with crystal clear instructions. Fassett still lives in London and Lucy resides in rural New Hope, Pennsylvania. The two conceive of some basic designs by e-mail and telephone, then Fassett arrives in Pennsylvania for a couple of weeks at a stretch and they buy and cut fabric, arranging it on multiple design walls in Lucy's living room. Fassett can sew but rarely does. Lucy does all the patchwork, then generally sends the tops out to be machine quilted by Judy Irish, an expert quilt finisher.

LUCY'S TIPS

When buying fabric for your stash, don't stock up on too much fabric that looks cute five inches from your face because what matters is how it looks from five feet away. Tiny patterns blur at a distance and may appear as a solid color.

What's called a reducing glass is an indispensable tool. It's the opposite of a magnifying glass. Hold it up to examine quilt patches you are auditioning on a design wall and they will appear smaller. "Looking through a reducing glass makes the composition on the design wall appear tighter and more finished," Lucy explains, "so errors in color and pattern become more noticeable." You can find reducing glasses at many quilt shops.

Their inspiration for patterns comes from old quilts but also from anything they see that excites them. The Gridlock pattern, for example, is borrowed from one of Fassett's knitwear designs, which in turn was inspired by a photograph of an old carpet he saw in a book. Another quilt pattern was inspired when the two were stuck in traffic and Fassett noticed the stacks of shipping containers near the Newark, New Jersey, docks.

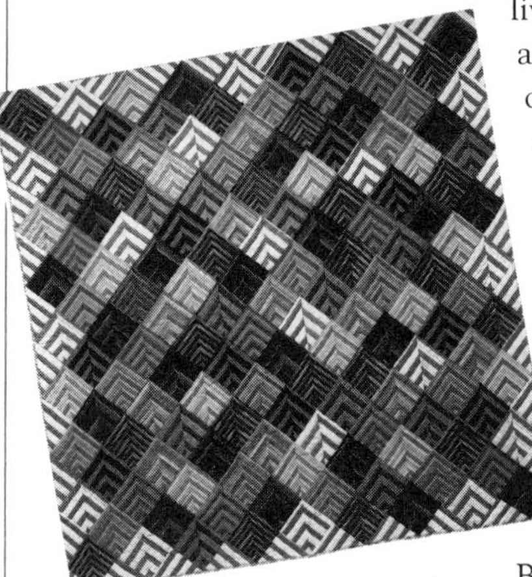

Kaffe Fassett's Fan Quilt *(top) and* Chevrons.

"I like scrap quilts based on simple geometry," says Fassett. "That's what really thrills me. Most contemporary quilts leave me cold. Old quilts give me a structure to start with, but colors are the most important part to me."

Fassett also designs fabrics and was the first living textile artist ever to have his work exhibited at London's Victoria and Albert Museum. (The size of the crowds that came to see the Fassett show was second only to the crowds that came to view Elton John's collection of jackets.)

Knowing his affinity for old quilts, the V&A museum eventually turned Fassett loose on its vast collection of antique quilts, allowing him to search the archives. He and Lucy picked out some to reinterpret for one of their gorgeous books, tweaking the complicated designs so they were easier to piece and choosing fabric with a fresh, bright palette.

Both Fassett and Lucy teach and/or lecture several times a month, but rarely in the same place, so you need to check both of their websites. Fassett teaches all over the world, while Lucy tends to teach at shops, guilds, and shows in the Northeast, partly because she still has two children at home. Generally they teach as a team annually at the Houston International Quilt Festival and separately often return to such favorite spots as the Stitchin' Post quilt shop in Sisters, Oregon, home of a yearly outdoor quilt show in July (see page 545 for more information). They jointly produce an annual patchwork pattern book published by Rowan Yarns of Britain, which includes their designs plus those of many other popular quiltmakers, such as Roberta Horton and Mary Mashuta.

Instructions for the Rosy Quilt designed by Kaffe Fassett and Liza Prior Lucy begin on page 462.

TEACHER PROFILE

Diane Gaudynski

Many quilt teachers brag on their websites about the awards they've won: Diane Gaudynski brags about the prizes won by her students. Mostly those are awards for artistic machine quilting, a skill at which Gaudynski is peerless and brilliant at passing on. Machine-quilting classes are popular everywhere quilters go to learn, but few teachers are in greater demand than Gaudynski for instruction in producing traditional patterns.

Gaudynski will take something simple like an eight-pointed star in solid colors and completely surround the points with exquisitely detailed quilted feathers. Her quilts startle partly because the normal order of things is reversed: The pieced shapes that usually dominate seem like background visuals while the quilted sections pop out impressively. Her distinctive quilts feature old-fashioned muted colors like brown, taupe, and yellow. She somehow manages to make machine quilting look sculptural and refined. As a result, she's been showered with top awards, and in 2002, her work was included in a Tokyo show called Thirty Distinguished Quilt Artists of the World. The wonder is that she teaches as well as she quilts.

"I think many times students sit down to machine quilt and are overwhelmed," Gaudynski says. "I want to help people gain confidence. I teach them to understand their tools, their threads, their body position, and so on, whether or not they want to mimic my style. I like to say that if you take my class, I want you to go up at least one level, though I have certainly had students go from being just okay to amazing."

Many of her students are astounded by the difference she has made in their abilities. "I had already won some international awards but I was looking to perfect my machine quilting," says Sandra Leichner of Albany, Oregon. "She was the only teacher I felt could help me improve and perfect my techniques as they applied to my style. She is known for her generous teaching style and enthusiasm for her students' success. I found this to be true even though I was a fellow, but

Diane Gaudynski

Virtuoso machine quilter Diane Gaudynski specializes in whole-cloth and simple pieced quilts with an emphasis on elaborate quilting as the dominant visual feature.

Skill level

Classes for students with all levels of quilting experience; however, some proficiency with a sewing machine is required.

Website

www.dianegaudynski.net is a gold mine, full of information about Gaudynski's teaching schedule, detailed tips, photos of her quilts, and more.

GAUDYNSKI'S TIPS

◆ When you're just practicing machine quilting, start right in the middle of the quilt, not at an edge. The edges are the hardest place to quilt, but it's a woman thing, I believe: We timidly start working along the edge.

◆ When you feel ready to work on an actual quilt, first stabilize the quilt sandwich by stitching along the major horizontal and vertical seams, "the construction lines." Then, quilt from the outer edges toward the center. This method is based on the theory that quilters get better the longer they work, even on the same quilt. If you save the center until last, you will do your best work in the most visible spot.

◆ Use spray starch frequently as you are quilting; it keeps the fabric from being stretched out of shape. (Some quilters also starch the fabric before cutting and piecing.)

◆ Although machine quilting can be a bit of a grind to learn, try to be playful as you work. Relax and give yourself permission to have fun.

friendly, competitor. I instantly saw improvement in my quilting the very first day in a workshop."

Leichner's quilt *American Still Life* has won multiple awards, including first place in Mixed Techniques, Professional, at the American Quilter's Society show in 2004. An earlier quilt, *Pharaoh*, has also won many awards and has been exhibited all over the world.

Another student, Cynthia Pollard Schmitz from Arlington Heights, Illinois, was impressed by how Gaudynski adapted her teaching style to meet the level of experience in her students. "I took a weekend class with her in 2000 in which there were two people who were at the very beginning of the machine-quilting process, while several of us had done rather extensive work," says Schmitz. "We all felt that we progressed from where we were to a higher level without feeling that we were either trying to slow down for someone or struggling to keep up."

Schmitz says she herself was fairly skilled at the time but had room for improvement and Gaudynski was very sensitive in her comments. "I showed her a drawing of a feather border I intended to use on a quilt. I had my doubts about the scale of the work, but it was clearly the best I was capable of at the time," says Schmitz. "Gaudynski was complimentary and made me feel it would be fine. Well, I worked very hard all weekend to improve my skills in designing feathers, and at the end of the workshop she approached me quietly and said, 'Now you might want to redraw that border.' If I hadn't progressed, I think she would have said nothing, but since I had, she pushed gently to have me do the best work I could."

Like many others, Gaudynski credits teacher Harriet Hargrave for pioneering machine quilting—and making Gaudynski's career possible. "It had started to become acceptable to quilt an art quilt on a machine but not anything else. Harriet said you can make a traditional quilt on your sewing machine. It was a huge barrier, to take a bed quilt and touch a machine to it!"

Gaudynski grew up sleeping under a quilt made by her grandmother and made her first quilt as a teenager, for her sister. Then she didn't do much quilting until the late 1970s, at which time she proceeded to hand quilt for a decade before switching to machine work.

"When I started machine quilting, it was just a faster means to an end," Gaudynski says. "But I always enjoy the process so much I don't want it to end. I can quilt quickly, but I want it to go on for months, like when you're reading a good book."

> Buy fabrics you might not ordinarily use and play with them. Sit down with purple silk and gold thread and just let yourself create something. I find my best ideas come when I give myself a period to play. At the moment, I'm working on bright red silk. I've become inspired by quilted and embroidered clothing from the 1700s.

That said, people are surprised to hear that Gaudynski had rough going machine quilting at the start, like most mere mortals. "I had a terrible time at first. I just could not do it intuitively and I simply had to persevere," she says. "I really think this is the biggest problem with my teaching. I sit down and demonstrate and make it look so easy! It is not easy."

Indeed, Gaudynski cautions that some quilters never will master this particular skill, because they just aren't wired with the "brain-eye connection" required to machine quilt well. For those still trying to puzzle out whether they've got the aptitude, here's Gaudynski's advice: "The learning curve is different for different people. But if you practice free-motion quilting [in which you move the fabric freely under the needle] for an hour a day for at least a month, you'll know. If you still can't make it work, it's either something wrong with the machine, or maybe you're just someone who won't master this."

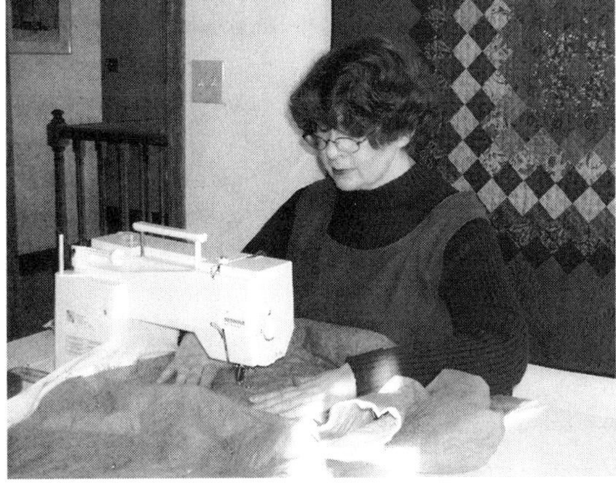

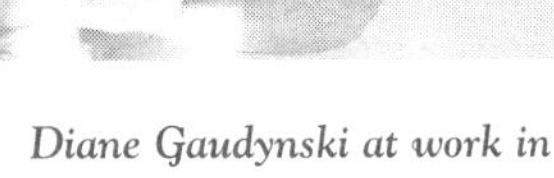

Diane Gaudynski at work in her home studio.

Still, Gaudynski loves to pass along to people wrestling heavy quilts through their truculent machines what she has spent so much time learning. "There are things that have taken me ten or fifteen years to master through my own exploration at home, and I can pass those things on so much quicker," she says.

The sad fact is that Gaudynski doesn't teach nearly as much as prospective students wish she would and it's often a "battle of postmarks" figuring out which lucky applicants will get into her workshops. For her to be able to work individually with quilters, classes must be restricted to between twenty and twenty-four students. Gaudynski limits travel from her home in Waukesha, Wisconsin, to roughly one trip per month partly because

Diane Gaudynski's Books

Gaudynski's book ***Guide to Machine Quilting*** is indispensable. Like Gaudynski's teaching, it is filled with a wealth of detail that quilters rarely find, right down to an explanation—with photos—of how to properly load a just-finished quilt into a washing machine. The book is stuffed with vital information about tools and such techniques as marking a quilt for machine work and includes patterns for three quilts, a Trip Around the World, a Basket, and a Log Cabin project. It's published by the American Quilter's Society; $24.95. Also published by the AQS as one of its small, spiral-bound Quilt Savvy titles is ***Gaudynski's Machine Quilting Guidebook*** ($21.95). It too is invaluable.

Gaudynski and her quilt Through A Glass, Darkly: An American Memory.

travel tires her and partly because of serious allergies (instructions for her workshops always include the request that students refrain from wearing perfume), but also simply because Gaudynski says she can't maintain her hard-won level of excellence if she takes weeks off at a time from quilting herself. Like a classical pianist, her proficiency is based on constant practice. "To keep up the quality of machine quilting, you really need to do it every day," says Gaudynski. "I simply can't be gone for three weeks at a time, like some teachers."

Gaudynski does usually teach at some of the major venues, like the American Quilter's Society's annual show in Paducah, Kentucky, and at various machine quilting retreats. She also travels to guilds around the country, where her visits are not to be missed.

There are other ways to tap into Gaudynski's expertise. Her website offers extensive tips. There are pages of them, everything from suggestions for the best threads and needles for machine quilting to her personal recipe for spray starch. It's worth a visit just to be inspired by her many award-winning quilts.

TEACHER PROFILE

Becky Goldsmith and Linda Jenkins

Becky Goldsmith and Linda Jenkins are known best by the name of their partnership, Piece O' Cake Designs, which is synonymous with whimsical updated appliqué patterns. Their work together is also a testimonial to the way quilting builds friendships. The two met at a meeting of the Green Country Quilter's Guild in Tulsa, Oklahoma, in 1986, and became friends before they became business partners. Both the friendship and the business have thrived, even though only Jenkins is located in Tulsa now. Goldsmith lives in Texas, where her husband is a biology professor.

Appliqué, sewing fabric shapes onto the surface of a quilt top, is a very popular style of quilting. What's different about the Piece O' Cake women's style of appliqué is both their technique for doing it and the aesthetic of their original patterns. And, while some quilt teachers teach machine appliqué, Goldsmith and Jenkins do it by hand.

The Piece O' Cake method is a technique called needleturn appliqué. While it is faster than many other methods, it requires skill and patience. The fabric shape to be appliquéd is cut and pinned onto the quilt top, then sewn on, using a needle or finger to turn the raw fabric edges under as you sew.

Jenkins and Goldsmith are pros at teaching this style and presenting it in their very detailed books. *The Appliqué Sampler*, for example, takes sixty-four pages to give the directions for one quilt. Each step is presented thoroughly, with lots of drawings picturing exactly how to do the different stitches and appliqué a variety of shapes. They even have illustrations for those who are left-handed.

"People think appliqué is hard, but if you know the technique, it's easy," says Goldsmith. "You need to learn the basic invisible appliqué stitch, plus how to do inner and outer curves and points." The name of the pair's business came from the fact that, early in their

Becky Goldsmith and Linda Jenkins

Masters of hand appliqué, Becky Goldsmith (right) and Linda Jenkins (left), concentrate on needleturn appliqué technique used in fresh, contemporary patterns.

Skill level

Classes for students with all levels of quilting experience.

Website

www.pieceocake.com lists Goldsmith's and Jenkins' teaching schedules (the two often teach solo). The online store sells their books, DVD, patterns, notions, and the like.

GOLDSMITH AND JENKINS' TIPS

If you frequently need to trace a pattern onto fabric, you'll find that if you are working on any kind of smooth surface the fabric slips and slides and you can't achieve a neat, reliable line. What you need is something called a sandboard. Larger than a sheet of legal paper—approximately twelve by sixteen inches—a sandboard has sandpaper on one side to grip the fabric.

When you are doing needleturn appliqué, to trace the fabric that is being appliquéd, place it on top of the sandboard's rough side with the right side facing up. Then place the template on top of the fabric and trace around it. Marking the top of the fabric will show the line where the fabric is to be folded under. You cut around but not on the line—leave a narrow margin of fabric that can be turned under with the help of a needle. Then you tack the cut shape to the quilt top using an appliqué stitch.

Sandboards are available at quilt shops and are also sold on the Piece O' Cake website.

friendship, Jenkins would ask Goldsmith how to do something and the answer was almost always preceded by "It's a piece o' cake!"

Goldsmith and Jenkins have a wonderful color sense and use some unexpected fabrics in their creations. Many appliqué quilts feature mostly solid fabrics, but the two delight in using lots of plaids and pretty prints in their designs. "It's been surprising to me, but not to Becky, that starting with our second book people began recognizing our work as a Piece O' Cake design without seeing the name," says Jenkins. "There are a lot of people out there doing appliqué, but ours doesn't look the same as everybody else's."

Once they started their business, the books and patterns came out fast: In the first twelve years, they produced nineteen books and patterns for approximately 150 different blocks. They also started designing fabrics, and their teaching schedules are packed, both solo and as a team. Their classes are popular partly because Goldsmith and Jenkins have been ahead of the curve on classroom technology. The two were among the first quilt teachers to employ a digital camera and projector for their classes.

"It's a live video feed of me or Linda sewing, projected on a wall and magnified about ten times," explains Goldsmith. "Not only can all the students see us, but it's like they're looking through our eyes. It's hard to see a needle in someone's hands from eight or twelve feet away, but with this technology they can all see perfectly."

"First we demo a technique, say for how to stitch an outer point," says Jenkins. "The students watch the live demo, then try the technique themselves, and we go around the room and work with them. Then we go on to the next technique, followed by practice time and one-on-one assistance. Students say they don't usually get that much of a teacher's individual attention."

Both of the teachers routinely get rave reviews from their students. "Becky's style is upbeat, friendly and fun, fast-paced, and thorough," says Stephanie Brokaw of Carmel, Indiana. "She came and taught at my guild and I was so impressed by the level of detail and how clearly she demonstrates. My technique improved immediately!"

Recent fan mail received by Linda Jenkins included a note from Canadian quilter Lori Slack saying, "I just took your How Do You Do That?! course, and I can honestly say it was the best quilting course I have ever taken!" Another satisfied quilter wrote to her: "I want to thank you for your patience. The feedback from your class has been overwhelming. I finished my tulips, and I'm proud to say they *look* like tulips." It's the small details that really work that are the kind of gems students pick up in classes with Goldsmith or Jenkins.

Goldsmith's quilting history is typical of many quilters today. Nobody in her family made quilts and she never thought about making one until her two sons were one and three and a half. "We bought bunk beds and I made two quilts from a pattern in a newspaper article," she says. "I progressed from the newspaper quilt to a quilt book, and then to a quilt class."

Jenkins says that her husband's grandmother quilted, but her real inspiration was a regular client at the beauty salon Jenkins owned who used to hand piece quilts while sitting under the hair dryer. "I just knew I wanted to do that, so I took every class at the local quilt shop, then started traveling to take more," she says. When the two met, Jenkins had just sold the salon and was poised to seriously ramp up her quilting activity.

The good thing about a partnership like this is that it doubles the opportunities for students. Goldsmith and Jenkins teach jointly on some occasions but are more likely to teach alone. Both travel extensively, an average of one to two weeks per month. The two often teach at major quilt shows, such as the annual quilt festival in Houston. They also frequently visit guilds. The best way to keep up with the classes taught by both ladies in Piece O' Cake is on their website.

Linda Jenkins and Becky Goldsmith's Books

Books by the Piece O' Cake duo are easy to follow and well illustrated. Some feature complete projects, others provide a choice of blocks you can combine to make a wall hanging or quilt. Their books may have fewer projects than some others, but that's because teaching appliqué technique takes so many steps and because their books always include full-size patterns. The pair are prolific, sometimes publishing more than one book a year. Here are five of their most popular titles; all are from C&T Publishing.

Covered with Love: Kids' Quilts & More from Piece O' Cake Designs; $26.95

Amish-Inspired Quilts: Tradition with a Piece O' Cake Twist; $26.95

The New Appliqué Sampler: Learn to Appliqué the Piece O' Cake Way; $26.95

Appliqué Delights: 100 Irresistible Blocks from Piece O' Cake Designs; $24.95

Quilts with a Spin: 7 New Projects from Piece O' Cake Designs; $24.95

Harriet Hargrave

A master machine quilter, Harriet Hargrave specializes in teaching machine quilting on a home sewing machine.

Skill level

Classes for just about all levels; the specific degree of quilting experience required depends on the particular class.

Website

www.harriethargrave.com lists Hargrave's teaching itinerary. The fabrics—including Hargrave's favorite hard to find reproduction fabrics—notions, scissors, batting, and books found at her Denver quilt shop are also available through the website.

Telephone

(303) 424-2742

TEACHER PROFILE:

Harriet Hargrave

Harriet Hargrave can be found at the top in the pantheon of those who teach machine quilting. Hargrave gets credit for pioneering the machine-quilting movement, which most agree was formally launched with the 1985 publication of her book *Heirloom Machine Quilting*. This is still considered one of the best books on the subject and has been updated multiple times.

"There are few people that machine quilt who have not taken a class from me, or from a teacher that took my class or was influenced by my book," says Hargrave. From someone else that might sound like boasting, but from her, it's the simple truth.

Among the prize winning quilters who say Hargrave liberated and inspired them are Caryl Bryer Fallert and Diane Gaudynski, both famous for their virtuoso machine quilting. In the introduction to her 2002 book *Guide to Machine Quilting*, Gaudynski writes that Hargrave's first book "sent me into a world of discovery, of joy, of completion."

Completion is the name of the game. With the introduction of the time-saving methods of rotary cutting and machine piecing, quilters found themselves with a growing pile of unfinished quilt tops. Because it wasn't considered kosher or even possible to quilt by machine, the quilting part of the process became a logjam for many. To finish a beautiful quilt top within days or weeks, then have to spend months quilting it by hand was a major source of frustration.

Then Hargrave came along. She not only gave everyone permission to finish quilts by machine, but she showed them how, proving that with the right materials and techniques, machine quilting on a home sewing machine could be as beautiful and personal as hand quilting. Within a decade, machine quilting became the norm instead of the rare exception.

"I've been making quilts for more than twenty years, and until I took Harriet's machine-quilting workshop, I was sending all my quilt tops out to have someone else finish them [by machine]," says Karen

Azevedo of Fort Collins, Colorado. "My daughter and I took her four-day class and went to bed dreaming of quilting. It was an intense program, and since then, I've quilted all my tops, except for one that was queen size. My daughter has only been making quilts for a year, and she's machine quilting her tops, too."

"Harriet's workshop changed my life, my quilting life anyway, and probably my other life too," says Havrilla Stephens, who lives in Durham, New Hampshire. "She showed me how to achieve a beautiful, traditional look with a domestic sewing machine to make the kind of quilts I wanted to make. And convinced me I could do it."

The following customer review on Amazon.com, where Hargrave's *Heirloom Machine Quilting* gets an average rating of five stars (out of five), gives the standard reaction succinctly: "The first book you need on machine quilting. There is no better. The rest just supplement this one."

Listing these laurels might imply that Hargrave is lying around somewhere resting on them, but it couldn't be further from the truth. Hargrave is one of the busiest quilt teachers in the country. She spends roughly twenty-seven weeks a year teaching on the road, and the other half of the time she can be found at the Denver-area quilt shop she has owned for twenty-five years, Harriet's Treadle Arts. She gives classes at the shop, too.

Hargrave calls herself a "maverick traditionalist" and that is because, although she uses the latest techniques and technology to make quilts, the quilts she makes and teaches are themselves completely traditional. Antique quilts are her passion.

The shortest class she gives in machine quilting is two days, since she feels there is so much ground to cover. "It can't be done in one day, even though I cram ten hours of teaching into six hours," she says. "We don't take breaks, and we don't sit around and chat. There are no cell phones allowed in class, and I tell my students if they don't do their homework, don't come back. I'm a taskmaster, but I find the students really respond to that."

She doesn't tolerate whining. "Quilters can do it themselves, but they have to learn it isn't instant

HARGRAVE'S TIPS

The hardest thing for students to get over is that machine quilting is an ongoing skill—you need to keep practicing. After you learn my machine quilting techniques you must spend at least ten to twenty minutes a day practicing them for a full six months.

If you are trying to teach yourself, don't practice on a large project, or on anything pieced, but on simple squares of fabric layered around batting. Build up a little at a time. Start with fourteen-inch squares to learn the basic movements, then go to twenty-four inches, then thirty-six inches, and so on. Just keep quilting bigger pieces and eventually, 90 by 108 inches will no big deal.

Harriet Hargrave's Books

In addition to her must-have book ***Heirloom Machine Quilting*** (C&T Publishing; $29.95), Harriet Hargrave cowrote ***The Art of Classic Quiltmaking*** (C&T Publishing; $34.95) with Sharyn Craig and

wrote ***Mastering Machine Appliqué*** (C&T Publishing; $29.95). She is also the author of ***From Fiber to Fabric: The Essential Guide to Quiltmaking Textiles***, an excellent reference book on how fabric is made that is, sadly, out of print.

gratification," says Hargrave. "At the beginning of workshops I hear the same thing: 'I can't do it. I tried a queen-size quilt in my machine and I can't do anything bigger than a placemat.' I tell them it's damn hard work when you start but it's worth it. Over and over, I tell them to shut up and buck up, and just do it! I'm in their face about it, and by the end, whenever I start saying 'Buck up!' they're saying it with me."

One of the things prospective students should know is that Hargrave does not give project classes. You won't come out of her workshops with a finished quilt to throw on your bed or hang on your wall. She doesn't create or sell patterns either. What she does do is teach everything you need to know about a sewing machine and every aspect of machine quilting, including picking the proper batting. She provides a wealth of information about threads, fabric, bobbins, marking techniques, even the proper way to sit while sewing.

She starts by trying to change the way students even *think* about quilting by machine. As she says in the first line of her book, "You are not machine quilting. You are hand quilting with an electric needle." Hargrave tells her students that guiding that electric needle is a lot like driving a car. "You have to look ahead, look back, and look at where you are all the time," she says. Not to mix metaphors, but dancing is another favorite of hers. "I try to teach my students to build a rhythm," says Hargrave. "We dance with our sewing machines. The motor is our orchestra, and we dance with our hands."

Quilting is something Hargrave grew up with, but she didn't like the handwork from the start. "My family were homesteaders in Kansas, and I come from generations of quilters," says Hargrave. "My mother taught me, and she was a hand quilter. I thought that was ridiculous." At one point, when her mother was making an exquisite wedding quilt, Hargrave decided to prove she could copy it but make it by machine. She succeeded. Then, she fell in love with her mother's worn old traditional quilts and decided to copy all those quilts using her machine.

After having designed ski clothing when she was in college and made custom wedding gowns, as a young mother Hargrave earned money by selling crafts on the weekends. By applying her own sewing skills and taking adult education classes in machine embroidery, she became a master machine embroiderer. Her most popular items at craft shows were baby quilts with machine-embroidered motifs on them; she turned the quilts out at the rate of one a day. Eager customers started asking, "Can you teach me to do this?" and in 1978 Hargrave's teaching career was launched. Within two years, she had opened her quilt shop.

One of Harriet Hargrave's machine-quilted masterpieces.

Hargrave teaches all over the country, but increasingly she has been concentrating on longer retreats held closer to her home. Working with her daughter Carrie, Hargrave offers a number of four-day retreats each year, sometimes at a Colorado dude ranch called Peaceful Valley. These in-depth workshops start with the basics, but by the end of the last day, "students are doing machine trapunto with silk thread," says Hargrave (trapunto is a technique in which extra padding, sometimes in the form of yarn, is added under the top layer of fabric). In addition to machine quilting retreats, there are retreats at the ranch that focus on machine appliqué and on machine piecing.

Concerned that too much emphasis has been placed on longarm machines and that owners of regular home sewing machines have been neglected, Hargrave organized an annual four-day conference for home machine quilters. This popular event occurs at a Colorado conference center and welcomes quilters of all levels, including beginners. Hargrave teaches along with five or six others, including prize winning quiltmakers like Diane Gaudynski and Sue Nickels.

Melody Johnson

An art quilter, Melody Johnson specializes in appliqué by fusing, with an emphasis on bold colors.

Skill level

Classes for students with all levels of quilting experience.

Website

www.wowmelody.com
View Johnson's teaching schedule and read her thoughtful musings on making art. Johnson's quilts are also for sale online. Her blog is **http://fibermania.blogspot.com.**

TEACHER PROFILE

Melody Johnson

Melody Johnson is a curious hybrid in the quilt world. Most of the quilting "simplifiers" are teachers who make traditional quilts less difficult; Johnson "simplifies" art quilts. Viewed from a distance one of Melody Johnson's distinctive quilts might be mistaken for a painting. Her quilts are full of dazzling colors that seem splashed across the surface, and they often have saucy names like *Technique Rebellion*. There is a free-form, casual feeling to the shapes, which sometimes echo traditional geometric forms, like those found in abstract paintings, and sometimes take the natural shapes of leaves or flowers. Many have remarked that her quilts "look happy."

Johnson's favorite technique is fusing, a simpler alternative to appliqué. Fusing allows quilters to essentially glue pieces of fabric together (for more about fusing, see pages 163–67). Many quiltmakers who fuse finish the process by stitching around the edges of the fused-on shape to prevent the fabric from fraying. But not Johnson. She has developed materials and a technique that allow her to skip the stitching and still eliminate the problem of unraveling fabric. This fits beautifully with her philosophy of liberating quilters from drudgery and freeing them to play with color.

"My students get to realize their ideas immediately and don't have to go through all that slow construction," says Johnson. "If they choose to, students can use what they make in my class simply as a design sketch for a quilt. Or, the classwork could be their final result. My purpose is to get students to play because I think that's where discoveries are made."

That was certainly the experience of Cheryl Ryan Harshman, an academic librarian from West Virginia, who took a three-day workshop with Johnson in Indiana. Harshman had been sewing since girlhood but had only recently begun quilting. The two traditional quilts she had tried seemed "too fastidious" and dull, so she searched the Internet for quilt teachers whose work inspired her. "Fusing with Melody's hand-dyed fabrics was like swimming in pools of color. As a teacher, she was organized, encouraging, and unflappable—even when we blew out the circuit box and half of us had no electricity, she forged right ahead."

Once you've seen Johnson's quilts, it isn't surprising to learn that she started out as a painter. "As a child, I thought being an artist meant being a painter, so I did everything necessary to live out that role," says Johnson. But after earning a degree in painting "I felt that it wasn't as fulfilling as I expected." Johnson, who had been sewing since the age of nine, became captivated by quilts while she was in college. For roughly the first decade of her quilting career, Johnson specialized in teaching machine quilting and embroidery but found after a while that other concepts excited her more. She switched to teaching fusing, design, and the use of color and emphasized wall quilts rather than bed quilts.

Johnson's plunge into experimental fusing resulted partly from sheer desperation.

Johnson's plunge into experimental fusing techniques happened in the early nineties and resulted partly from sheer desperation. She had seven quilts entered into a show in Indiana, and after they had been boxed up and prepared for shipment back to her, four of the quilts were stolen. "Most of those quilts were supposed to go into my master's show: I was using them to earn my master's thesis," Johnson explains. "I had to work fast to remake the lost quilts, so I started fusing like crazy."

The techniques Johnson invented became her preferred work method, and subsequent quilts won top prizes, even at fairly conservative national shows. "In 1995, I entered the AQS show at Paducah with an all-fused raw-edge quilt and it won best wall quilt." After that, Johnson says there was no question as to whether fusing was a legitimate style.

Students have flocked to Melody Johnson's classes because they are full of epiphanies fueled by her techniques and laid-back style of teaching. Like many quilt teachers, she tends to start with a slide show of her own work and that of previous students. "The slides elicit questions and clarifications and that gives me an idea of the level of the students' experience," she says.

Her next move is highly unusual: Johnson will break into a song and sometimes a dance, about a mythical quilting school called the Chicago School of Fusing. This pretend school was born of long car rides with a

JOHNSON'S TIPS

Here's a speed secret to fusing: Fuse the web to the fabric *before* cutting out the shapes you want. Johnson prefers the fusible web Wonder-Under, which comes in thirty-five-yard bolts that are seventeen inches wide. To prepare the fabric, first cut off a forty-four by eighteen inch piece of fusible web. Then cut a forty-four by eighteen inch piece of the fabric you want to fuse.

Lay the fabric out flat on an ironing board, back (dull) side up. Place the fusing web, glue side down, on top of the fabric (the protective paper backing will be faceup).

Using a hot, dry iron, begin ironing in the center of the paper backing, working out toward the edges. Now you have a piece of fabric that is completely covered with fusible web, ready to cut into whatever shape you want. If you keep a stash of different colored fabrics that have already been fused, you'll always be ready to go.

Peel off the paper backing before you cut out your pieces, but don't do this until the fused fabric

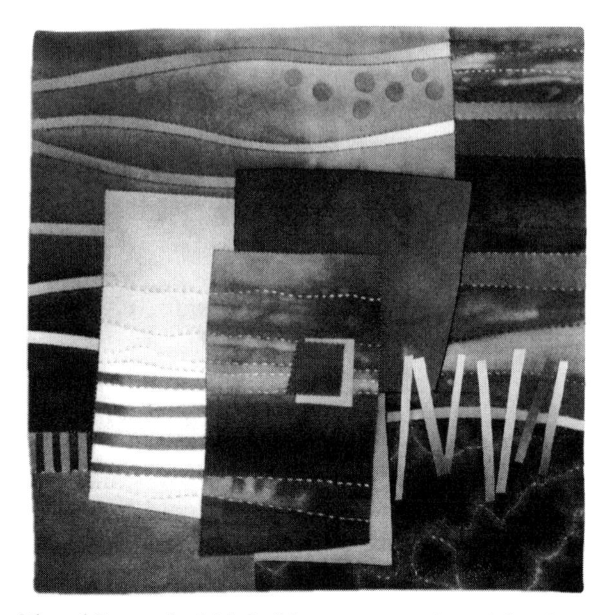

Silt and Pepper, *by Melody Johnson, was made with hand-dyed cottons.*

former business partner, and extolling its faux history and folklore has become an expected ritual in all of Johnson's classes. The school's theme song begins "I'm proud to be a fuser from Chicago," and the ditties that follow include a fight song. If Johnson doesn't think it will offend any of her students, she will also sing an antipiecing song that starts, "If I were a piecer . . ."

Johnson's repeat students demand more anecdotes and more songs about the Chicago School of Fusing. Her introduction has grown longer, but that's okay with her. "I feel it relaxes everyone and gets them ready for having fun," she explains. "I think that part of my job is show business, especially when it's a four or five day class. My students use vacation time for this class, and I want to give them their money's worth."

Although Johnson does offer five-day classes, many of her lessons are one-day workshops. They often emphasize a themed project, such as making the small whimsical floral quilts she calls Bodacious Bloomers. Another popular class, which she gives in versions that last between one and five days, is called Releasing the Creative Block: An Introduction to Working in a Series.

With her long career and art background, one might assume that Johnson would prefer intermediate

Johnson's Technique Rebellion III Redux.

and advanced students, but she welcomes all levels and has a special fondness for those just starting. "I love beginners because they don't have bad habits yet," she says. "They may feel freer to let loose and experiment, whereas an experienced quilter who is a perfectionist may balk at not getting finite rules to follow. Many of my students have never worked so directly before, without a pattern to follow and relying on intuition and quick decisions."

Johnson is one of those teachers, like Libby Lehman (see page 350), who puts all of her art into making quilts and teaching and she isn't particularly interested in writing books. She values immediacy and is a born teacher. This spirit extends to Johnson's unusual website. She also is an enthusiastic blogger and goes into great detail explaining the evolution of the quilts she is making. Unfortunately, Johnson has been making comments about slowing down her teaching schedule, even retiring completely. Jump at any chance to take a class with her! If you don't get that opportunity, do sign up for a class with one of the other faculty members of the Chicago School of Fusing, Laura Wasilowski (you can find out about her classes at the Artfabric website, www.artfabrik.com) or Frieda Anderson (www.friestyle.com).

is cool. Removing the paper pulls at the threads on the edges of the fabric, so peeling off the backing first will help prevent the edges of the cut out pieces from fraying.

One of those skinny, lightweight "irons on a stick" is great for fusing the pieces onto the quilt surface because it makes it easier to iron edges and skinny pieces such as flower stems. The irons are sold as quilter's or craft irons.

Hand-dyed fabrics, which don't have a commercial finish, are ideal for fusing because they don't need to be stitched down.

Commercial fabrics have a tendency to peel away at the edges once fused. To prevent this you have a couple of options: Stitch along the edges as part of the quilting process or reinforce the edges with a zigzag or satin stitch.

Libby Lehman

An art quilter, Libby Lehman is known for dazzling embroidery and other machine-quilted effects and embellishments.

Skill level

Classes for all levels; the specific degree of quilting experience required depends on the particular class.

Website

www.libbylehman.us
Download Lehman's teaching schedule and take a look at a gallery of her quilts, many of which are for sale. (Lehman can also be reached by e-mail at threadplay@aol.com.)

Telephone

(713) 688-7681

TEACHER PROFILE

Libby Lehman

Many people have heard of the "horse whisperer" and a woman who calls herself the "baby whisperer." Quilt teacher Libby Lehman has been called a "machine whisperer," because of her awesome ability to control that notoriously wild beast known as the sewing machine.

Lehman, a lifelong Texan who has been quilting since 1971, is known for lavish, bold machine stitches that make her quilt designs pop right off the wall. One of the pioneers who created a whole new aesthetic for machine quilting, Lehman uses her sewing machine not just to outline or echo shapes she has pieced but to create the illusion of painting with thread. Ribbonlike swirls dance through her quilts, their curves contrasting with the sharp angles of the pieced shapes. Lehman uses dazzling metallic and other glossy threads with a density and bravado that wasn't seen in the quilt world before her.

Her quilt *Joy Ride*, made in 1996, was included in the exhibit The Twentieth Century's Best American Quilts. The quilt's name is evocative of both Lehman's ebullient style and her personality. *Joy* is a word that comes up a lot with Lehman, and also the word *play*, something she encourages her students to do. Indeed, for many years her most popular class has been what she calls Threadplay, which she teaches either as a basic one-day class or in a more advanced form lasting from three to five days.

Like many others whose love of quilting dates to the early days of the current boom, Lehman didn't start out quilting by machine. In 1971, Lehman was pregnant with her first child, and her mother suggested they take a basic quilting class. "It was so much fun learning something together and going into something as equals," says Lehman. Both were immediately hooked on quilting, and within a few years, Lehman's mother was the co-owner of a Houston quilt shop called The Quilt Patch. Lehman got to meet all the nationally known teachers who were booked there and says she was allowed to take their classes free "as long as I brought lunch for Mom and the teacher." Before long, she was teaching at the shop herself. Lehman switched from making very traditional quilts to art quilts after she and her mother took classes from the pioneering art quilters Nancy Crow and Michael James.

Having grown up in a big family that camped often, Lehman says she can sleep anywhere and finds travel exhilarating. With her son grown, Lehman spends the majority of her time on the road, teaching two to three weeks a month except for December and August. That's good for people eager to take her classes, because many of the teachers at her level of expertise, with twenty-five years' experience under their belts, have cut back substantially on their travel for teaching.

Machine quilting takes lots of time to master, but Lehman says one thing that helped her was finding the right sewing machine. "There are other wonderful machines out there, but the Bernina tolerates what I call weird sewing," says Lehman. "It makes it easy to use things like the unusual decorative threads I favor." Still, Lehman has made it her business to work on all the major models of sewing machines, so she can help her students no matter what machine they use.

Teaching is clearly Lehman's favorite way to pass on knowledge. Other top teachers have written piles of books and created elaborate websites and videos and other teaching aids, but Lehman can't stand to stop teaching and quilting long enough to transfer her know-how to the page. One of the few books she has written, *Threadplay with Libby Lehman: Mastering Machine Embroidery Techniques*, remains extremely popular.

Her teaching style is gentle and patient, and Lehman is the sort of teacher whose students gush, "She changed my life." Betty Cavallucci, who first took a five-day Threadplay class from Lehman at Art Quilt Tahoe, says, "I have sewn and quilted for so many years, but she made me understand everything in a new way. She gave me this incredible confidence. She taught us so much about thread and what happens to your stitches. She spent half a day just on sewing machine needles. Now, I can solve problems. If I don't like how the stitches look, I know how to fix them."

With her relaxed manner and emphasis on playfulness, Lehman gets her students to loosen up and

LEHMAN'S TIPS

The metallic threads Lehman loves to sew into her quilts are extremely slippery—"the problem children of the sewing world." Many of the headaches they cause can be eliminated by doing these four things.

1. Use a Topstitch needle that's size 90/14 on your sewing machine. These needles are widely available and work on most any machine. They have an extradeep groove and other features that help keep decorative threads from fraying and breaking.

2. When you've got metallic thread loaded into the top of your machine, use 60-weight polyester thread in the bobbin (50 weight is considered medium and the higher the number of the weight, the finer the thread, so 60 weight will be less bulky).

3. Decrease the top tension.

4. If the thread seems tight, don't pass it through the final thread guide, the one closest to the needle.

Deluge, by Libby Lehman.

One of Lehman's mantras is "Make visual decisions visually."

try new techniques. One of her mantras, borrowed from the book *Design Essentials: The Quilter's Guide*, by Lorraine Torrence, is "Make visual decisions visually." By this she means that quilters shouldn't just imagine how something will look in their quilts but actually arrange a sample on a table or design wall using the colors and shapes they want. She advises cutting out shapes from freezer paper first and placing them on a design wall. "Say it's a leaf shape, and the first one I cut just seems too small or not the right design," she explains. "It's very easy to cut new ones out of paper until I have the shape I want." Only then will she cut the fabric, thereby avoiding waste.

Those who want to study with Libby Lehman will find her most years at the major quilt shows, including Houston and Paducah. She also gives classes to guilds around the country.

Instructions for Libby Lehman's Falling Leaves quilt project begin on page 498.

TEACHER PROFILE

Ruth B. McDowell

Among the top quilting teachers in America, none inspires more awe for sheer bravura than Ruth B. McDowell, the Michelangelo of pictorial piecing. Although she has made vividly detailed quilts featuring people, trees, fish, chickens, boats, and even hobbits, McDowell is particularly famous for her stunning flower quilts. It's not that her quilted daylilies, for example, look as realistic as a photo of daylilies but that they seem to express the colors and shapes of these flowers with a greater intensity. McDowell doesn't attempt to "disguise" the fabric or thread and even uses unexpected plaids and vivid patterns clearly not found in nature. But her design and workmanship create a rich textural composition, making her quilts appear three-dimensional and full of life. McDowell isn't trying to rival a photo for its realism, but as art.

"The seeds for my quilts spring from things that absolutely amaze me in themselves: a tree or a place, a group of people or a plant, a ship or a stone," she writes at the beginning of her 2005 book *Fabric Journey: An Inside Look at the Quilts of Ruth B. McDowell.* "My quilts are an attempt to record and celebrate the unique characteristics of these subjects and my response to them."

Although appliqué is a very popular way of creating quilted landscapes, McDowell's complex quilts are almost completely pieced. She might appliqué a tiny eye onto a bird, but that's about it. If she's quilting a tree, every curve of every branch is joined at a seam with other fabrics: There may be hundreds of tiny triangles and fabric shards joined together to make the sky behind the tree. "There is an integrity to a top that is assembled this way," says McDowell. "The seam lines in my quilts are related to the leaf or the flower like the skeleton of the thing, and they're intimately related to the way the pieces go together."

McDowell's gift is abundant and abundantly shared. Quilters say, in hushed tones, that she can piece anything, piece it so it's smooth, without bulges, and then teach the whole process to a roomful of students.

Ruth B. McDowell

Art quilter Ruth B. McDowell's quilts feature intricate landscapes pieced from commercially printed fabric.

Skill level

McDowell's classes are not open to beginners.

Website

www.ruthbmcdowell.com (the middle initial is essential) has McDowell's teaching schedule, but you'll need to book well in advance. You can also read her artist's statement in the About Ruth B. McDowell section; see her quilts, some of which are for sale; or purchase patterns, books, and note cards from the online shop.

Ruth B. McDowell's Books

If Ruth B. McDowell's classes are all full or you feel too intimidated to study directly with the

master, there are classes at quilt shops all over the country that teach McDowell's methods. She purposely wrote several of her books to be used as texts, including ***Pieced Flowers*** (out of print, but worth buying used) and ***Pieced Vegetables*** (C&T Publishing; $27.95). These books include detailed instructions and patterns, and the classes based on them are sometimes taught by quilters who have studied with McDowell. McDowell's ***Piecing: Expanding the Basics*** (C&T Publishing; $27.95) also provides thorough how-to instruction for pieced quilts.

McDowell's method starts with a meticulous drawing, and it isn't a thumbnail sketch but the same size as the finished quilt will be. She begins with the outline of the shapes she is depicting, say a set of maple leaves, drawing on whatever paper she has at hand. Then, she puts tracing paper over the drawing and adapts it, adding lines that will become the seams of the pieced quilt. There is a mosaic or puzzle quality to her quilts: She won't cut one big leaf shape out of an orange fabric, but breaks that shape down into shardlike segments and mixes different tones of orange fabric together, some with hints of other colors. Her extremely detailed sketches end up resembling architectural blueprints. The drawings are then pinned to the wall, and different bits of fabric are cut and pinned in place to "audition" them in context. Although her quilts are pieced by machine and usually quilted by machine as well, McDowell's process is painstaking and patience is a must. Unlike the many quilt teachers who streamline techniques and use their machines for speed, there are no quickie shortcuts with McDowell. Her workshops, all titled Designing From Nature, run for four and five days.

"What sets Ruth's classes apart is that everyone does their own original design," says Carmen Holland of Dallas, Texas. "It sounds intimidating for the first-timer, but she gives you all the tools you need to get it done. It's a huge learning experience to watch all the students work on their very different projects."

"Some of my students will have taken my workshops repeatedly and bring a difficult design or photo with them, while others will work on translating a simple leaf into a quilt," says McDowell. "After more than twenty years of teaching, I know how to approach the information in a way that is accessible to everyone. People learn at their own pace, and students must have a safe place to try new things. So I explain different ways to work through the material. I work with each student, but after the first day or two, I let them do as much on their own as they want."

Oakton, Virginia, resident Ann P. Shaw has taken McDowell's classes at least eight times. Says Shaw, "You don't just learn one technique in Ruth's classes, but many simultaneously. Also, her classes are just a hoot. There's a camplike atmosphere, a feeling of playfulness and fun, and Ruth jumps right in. So one is likely to create enduring new friendships as well as to create great quilts in her class."

While many quilters embrace her techniques and leave transformed, there are some who gain enormous respect for McDowell's process but decide it isn't for them. "I learned more math from Ruth McDowell than I ever did in school," says North Carolina–based quilter Meg Manderson, "but I also learned that at heart I am not a piecer!" Manderson, who teaches quilting herself, prefers to appliqué her landscape quilts.

That's fine with McDowell. "The point of taking classes is partly to learn what you like and don't like," she says. "Even if you don't like it, it gets you further down the road in figuring out your own style. The style of quilting I do appeals to people who are interested in structure: It's like building a house."

McDowell, who lives in Massachusetts, graduated from the Massachusetts Institute of Technology in 1967 with a B.S. in art and design. She worked as an illustrator for several years and began quilting in 1972. Those were early days in the quilt renaissance, and McDowell learned to quilt from one of the few how-to books that was then available, *101 Patchwork Patterns*, by Ruby McKim.

McDowell began making traditional quilts and discovered immediately that piecing was her passion. Her technique evolved, and she was soon making art quilts of her own design. She has made more than four hundred unique quilts so far and is widely considered one of the country's top art quilters. McDowell's fairy tale quilt *The Twelve Dancing Princesses*, made in 1982, was selected for the book and exhibit The Twentieth Century's Best American Quilts, and in 2004, the American Quilter's Society named her one of the five most influential people involved in promoting contemporary quilting.

One thing that becomes clear in McDowell's classes and books is that she simply loves fabric, and she has a lot of great advice for quilters about shopping for and using commercial fabrics. She has written that there are times it would be easier for her to dye a patch of fabric to get exactly the effect she wants, but she believes that the challenge of having to find existing fabric that works has

McDOWELL'S TIPS

McDowell has this advice in her book *Fabric Journey: An Inside Look at the Quilts of Ruth B. McDowell* (C&T Publishing; $25.95):

Keep a large fabric stash and don't be afraid to buy on impulse. Most often you won't need to buy more than a yard. Select fabric using the following criteria—

Look for unusual colors, patterns, and reproduction fabrics.

Seek out fabrics with tiny splashes of bright white, because they add visual sparkle to the quilt. "A lot of quilt teachers teach students to never use white—that's an error."

Seed Catalog Series: Pansies, *by Ruth B. McDowell.*

brought an extra richness to her quilts.

McDowell makes a unique use of border designs in many of her quilts. Traditionally, trained quilters tend to make borders, often between two and four inches wide, that are rigidly symmetrical on all four sides. McDowell's borders are variable. They might be sewn only on two sides of the quilt or they might weave in and out of the picture on some of the edges. Her quilted plants and animals can reach all the way to the very edge, creating the illusion that they are standing closer to the viewer than the other creatures and objects in the quilt.

McDowell prefers not to sell her quilts through middlemen. She always takes recently completed ones on her teaching trips, and many times, she doesn't have to pack the quilts for the return because students purchase them on sight. "About ninety percent of my quilts are bought by other quilters," she says.

McDowell spends about a third of her time teaching, much of it overseas. In the United States, she teaches her long workshops mostly at regional retreats like the Empty Spools Seminars at Asilomar in northern California (see page 386). In addition, she teaches for several weeks each year at the Quilt Gallery, a quilt shop in Kalispell, Montana, near Glacier National Park. If you are thinking of taking her class, bear in mind that you should be comfortable with a sewing machine and know how to piece traditional blocks, but you don't have to know how to draw. McDowell's workshops generally fill up more than a year in advance, so be advised to sign up early.

TEACHER PROFILE

Sue Nickels

Sue Nickels is one of a number of top quilt teachers whose popularity was boosted by winning a major prize. She is notable not just for her considerable skills in machine quilting and machine appliqué but for updating the visual vocabulary of quilts, stretching the notion of what could be pictured.

Her two best-known quilts, made with her sister, Pat Holly, are hip and current, featuring not recycled appliqué patterns from the nineteenth century but inventive designs related to pop culture and modern history. One pays tribute to the Beatles and the other to the history of NASA and space exploration. Both are offbeat and full of unusual colors. The two quilts' fame has helped inspire other quilters to produce work drawn from their own time and personal passions.

Nickels and Holly's Beatles quilt won the Best of Show award in 1998 at the American Quilter's Society show in Paducah, Kentucky. Like any album quilt, every block is different, but the notion of an album becomes a visual pun, since each block illustrates one of the band's record albums. There is a folk art aesthetic to the appliqué images of a yellow submarine, the octopus's garden, and so forth. The quilt's palette of lime green with pinks and blues was borrowed straight from the costumes on the Sergeant Pepper album cover.

This remarkable quilt helps explain everything that makes Nickels tick as a quilter and as a quilt teacher. "I am inspired by antique quilts, looking at them for ideas in design and symbolism," says Nickels. "High-quality workmanship is important to me. I also like when quilts tell stories about their makers and their times." And her Beatles quilt is a case in point. Nickels and Holly, who had collaborated on a few previous quilts, decided to make the Beatles project while watching a 1996 television documentary about the rock group. They reminisced about how big a role certain Beatles songs played in their middle school and high school years, growing up in Ann Arbor, Michigan. Then they planned the design and divided up the work.

Sue Nickels

Appliqué art quilter Sue Nickels concentrates on machine appliqué featuring contemporary themes and color schemes.

Skill level

Classes for all levels; the specific degree of quilting experience required depends on the particular class.

Website

www.sue.nickels.com (don't omit the period between her first and last names)—look up Nickels' teaching schedule, read her biography, view her prizewinning quilts, and buy her books and thread.

NICKELS' TIP

The advice dispensed by Nickels covers a wide gamut and includes solutions to nitty-gritty, everyday problems. One unusual tip of hers has to do with trying to get traction when pushing the three layers of a quilt through a sewing machine after they're basted together. There are special gloves and other items available to aid with this, and some quiltmakers apply a sticky substance to their fingertips. Nickels' trick is to control the quilt sandwich during free-motion quilting by wearing rubber gloves from which the first and second fingers have been cut off.

"Not surgical gloves, but the ones you use to wash dishes," Nickels explains. "I buy small ones so they fit snugly, and I cut the fingers down to the hand part. I find these gloves are the grippiest of anything available and let you have a very light touch on the quilt. The harder you push down on the quilt, the jerkier and more uneven your stitches," so you want to be able to push lightly but stay connected.

Sue Nickels' The Space Quilt, *with NASA-inspired imagery.*

A few years later, when deciding on a new joint project, they agreed that one of their most vivid childhood memories was seeing a man walk on the moon. Their father was a test pilot who was passionate about the space program and watched every launch with with his daughters. So both these quilts capture peak moments in the lives of Nickels and Holly, at points where they intersected with the larger culture.

Although Nickels and her sister enjoy making quilts jointly, they frequently work on separate projects, Nickels in Ann Arbor and Holly in Muskegon, Michigan. Their collaborations rarely extend to joint teaching assignments, as Holly has young children at home. Nickels' two daughters are grown, however, and she loves to teach—which her hectic travel schedule makes clear. The craftsmanship is impressive in all of Nickels' work and craftsmanship is the principal theme of all the classes she teaches. "Some of my quilts have taken one hundred hours or more just to do the machine quilting part, and a single appliqué block can take eight to ten hours doing the machine appliqué," says Nickels. When you consider that Nickels and her sister took the time to write the lyrics to all 181 original Beatle songs in fabric marker on the back of their quilt, where few people will see them, it's clear that they take joy in the process and not just the accolades.

"I try to teach quality workmanship above all else," says Nickels. "I think having patience is what has made me a successful machine quilter, and this is so important in teaching. Most quilters think by choosing machine techniques you will finish quilts quickly. Well, you will work faster on the machine than by hand, but it takes time. Good workmanship should never be compromised for speed."

Like many quilters, Nickels grew up sewing but didn't decide to try quilting until she had a child. When she took her first class in a quilt shop in 1978, handwork was the rule, so she learned to make a quilt by hand. But she always preferred machine sewing, and when the first few books came out about machine techniques, she happily switched in the early nineties and hasn't looked back.

Nickels' most popular workshop is called Machine Quilting Essentials, and in it she passes on some of the basic techniques she uses in her masterpiece quilts. Many of her quilts are made using raw edge fusible appliqué (for more about fusing, see pages 163–67). Nickels teaches fusing and other styles of appliqué, including invisible appliqué in which the stitches attaching the cut shape to the background don't show.

The projects in her classes and books tend not to be as complex as her award-winning quilts. Nickels teaches how to make the fairly traditional flowers, leaves, and wreathes found in album quilts, employing very meticulous methods, all executed using a sewing machine. She jokes that she doesn't offer advanced classes because the underlying skills are pretty basic. Thus, almost all her workshops are one-day lessons.

Nickels always brings her own quilts along as models to show her students. Since the top winners in Paducah are required to give their winning quilts to the American Quilter's Society for its museum collection (they can keep the quilt if they elect not to take the prize money), she and her sister made a second, smaller Beatles quilt so they could share with students some of the techniques they used.

Students praise Nickels for her soft-spoken manner, warmth, and humor, but especially for her generosity.

Sue Nickels' Books

The books here offer a lot of the same lessons and techniques as Nickels teaches in her most popular classes. The first two she wrote solo, and the last one, on raw edge appliqué, was cowritten with her sister, Pat Holly. All three are published by the American Quilter's Society.

Machine Appliqué: A Sampler of Techniques; $22.95

Machine Quilting: A Primer of Techniques; $24.95

Stitched Raw Edge Appliqué; $22.95

"She shares her approach to designing unique quilts, brings resource material for students to browse for ideas and talks freely about her own inspiration," says quiltmaker Annie Smith of San Jose, California. Smith ought to know about other teachers, as she has taken classes from many top teachers and has taught quilting herself for more than twenty years. Smith finds Nickels so inspiring and helpful that she's taken half a dozen different classes with her and says Nickels' influence on her has been enormous. "I've designed several quilts using Sue's method but my own style," says Smith. "I also started my own pattern company, thanks to Sue's encouragement and am planning to write a book."

Says another quilter, Bev Burris from Greenville, Illinois, "I first sought out Sue as a teacher because of her award-winning Beatles quilt. After one class I was hooked, and I've taken many since. I have become pretty good at machine quilting and machine appliqué, and it is all because of Sue. I would recommend her to any quilter, no matter how novice or how advanced. You *will* learn!"

Lucky for those who want to study with her, Nickels travels a lot, teaching often at major quilt shows and also at regional and local guilds. She also teaches regularly near her home, at The Icehouse Quilt Shop in Grayling, Michigan, and usually runs a January retreat there.

Instructions for the "All That I Am" quilt project designed by Sue Nickels begin on page 490.

Bethany Reynolds

A designer of quick, colorful quilts, Bethany Reynolds is the originator of the Stack-n-Whack method of making quilts using a rotary cutter

Skill level

Classes for students with all levels of quilting experience.

Website

www.bethanyreynolds.com lists Reynolds' teaching schedule and features a gallery of her quilts and those of her students. Click on Cool Stuff and you'll find free patterns and quickie tutorials.

TEACHER PROFILE

Bethany Reynolds

There is no better example of a career built around an original technique than that of Bethany Reynolds, the innovator behind the Stack-n-Whack quilt designs. Reynolds' method involves using a rotary cutter (a circular rolling blade attached to a handle) to cut multiple layers of fabric at a single time, then she joins the pieces to create unusual visual effects. Lots of quilters began using rotary cutters in the early 1980s, but Reynolds added ingenious nuances to the cutting technique and procured a trademark on the name Stack-n-Whack. She spent lots of time playing with patterned fabric and design software to create patterns for quilts that look like they would be difficult to make—but aren't. Reynolds' know-how comes from years of experimentation and from a decade of owning a quilt shop in Maine.

"Students are frequently surprised at how easy my techniques are because the results look complicated," says Reynolds. "People often come to class with some anxiety about whether the fabric they brought will work and worry that they'll cut something wrong. I let them know early in the class that there's no mistake they can make that we can't fix."

Total novices might be a little lost in her classes, but quilters with at least some experience flourish. Mostly she teaches full-day or half-day workshops. Reynolds is famously methodical in her teaching style and generous in sharing tips. When quilting, for example, Reynolds advises: "One general rule is that what you see is what you *don't* quilt. When you want something to stand out, quilt around it."

Her classes are project oriented and use the colorful commercial cottons with repeating motifs that today's quilters love. Many of her designs are based on popular traditional block patterns like fans, stars, and kaleidoscopes, but Reynolds simplifies the construction and adds a visual twist that makes the quilts look fresh. Because her technique keeps evolving and she continues publishing new books and patterns, many of her students are happy repeaters.

"I've taken five classes from her and look forward to taking more," says Jo Reid of Scottsboro, Alabama. "Her teaching style is relaxed, and she shares her keen eye for color and design choices with her students. She never stops moving around the room, making sure that everybody understands."

Bethany Reynolds' Paisley Vignettes.

Bethany Reynolds' Books

Reynolds' books give concise directions with lots of tables, black-and-white illustrations, and color photos. The books are listed in the order in which they came out, starting with the most recent. All are published by the American Quilter's Society.

Magic Quilts by the Slice; $25.95

Stack-n-Whackier Quilts; $21.95

Magic Stack-n-Whack Quilts; $19.95

REYNOLDS' TIPS

Reynolds gives lots of advice to her students about the proper, safe way to use rotary cutters.

◆ Always cut away from the body, holding the cutter at about a 45 degree angle from the mat.

◆ Many people have trouble with the ruler slipping on the fabric when they're cutting against it. Your arm puts pressure on the ruler as you cut, so it may slip; make sure that at least one finger is off the ruler—the left pinky if you are right-handed—so you can brace that finger against the ruler to keep it from slipping. But make sure your thumb isn't down on the cutting side! (Although Reynolds constantly issues warnings to her students to be careful with the sharp cutters, there are occasional accidents. "I always have Band-Aids with me," says Reynolds.)

◆ Some quilters use spray starch to stiffen and stabilize their fabric so the grain stays straight, but Reynolds prefers to use spray sizing. "Starch can flake off," she explains, and may attract insects.

Debbie Best from Missouri City, Texas, is another of Reynolds' repeating students; she loves the methods so much, she began teaching them. "I first signed up for her class at a guild," says Best. "I love to take all her different classes, then bring the techniques to my students. I've taught LeMoyne Star, Hexagon Star, Morning Star, Pinwheel, Lazy Daisies, Butterflies, and Flip-Flop Fans, among others. Bethany is great. She keeps updating her techniques. She has so many shortcuts to make the process easy. And she's organized about things like dividing the class into two sections and making sure we're not all in line to iron at the same time."

Reynolds comes from a long line of quilters, though her mother mostly sewed clothing. Her family has lived in Maine for generations, and as a young woman, she left the state to work for a wholesale fabric company in Manhattan. When the city proved too expensive, her father told her there was a fabric store for sale in her hometown. She and her husband bought the store, then called Union River Fabrics, in 1982. They were both twenty-three years old. "It had been an outlet for a woolen mill, but the previous owner had added some quilt fabric," says Reynolds. "We picked up on that and started adding classes."

After Reynolds' son, Sam, was born in 1992, they closed the shop, and Reynolds gradually turned her hand to designing quilts and teaching quilters how to make her designs. Reynolds' first book, *Magic Stack-n-Whack Quilts*, was an almost instant hit when it was published in 1998, thanks to a demonstration of the technique on the popular television show *Simply Quilts*. "Within a week after that show aired, the first edition sold out," marvels Reynolds. By that time, she had already been teaching her method for about four years.

"I was playing with a rotary cutter and cutting eight squares and stacking them up and cutting them into triangles for a kaleidoscope quilt," says Reynolds. "I realized I could stack big rectangles and cut whatever shape I wanted." She started honing and teaching the technique and didn't consider going to the bother of getting a trademark until "I'd get these phone calls from someone saying they were having trouble with a pattern of mine they picked up in a class, and it was a class that had nothing to do with me."

In the years that followed, Reynolds wrote more books, made patterns for quilts and drawstring backpacks, and produced tools such as rulers to complement her books. She began designing her own fabric lines for several fabric companies.

Reynolds teaches often, especially at guilds. She frequently teaches at the Houston quilt festival and the American Quilter's Society show in Paducah, Kentucky, as well as at such regional shows and retreats as the Vermont Quilt Festival and A Quilter's Gathering in New Hampshire. Reynolds also teaches online, through Quilt University, which is great for people who can't travel to quilt classes and for students who live outside the United States. Students download the lessons sequentially, and if they have questions or problems, they can ask for help on a central message board, which Reynolds checks daily. At the end, students can submit digital pictures of their finished quilts, which will be posted with those of their "classmates." (For more information, see Learning Online on page 296 or visit the "university's" website, www.quiltuniversity.com.)

TEACHER PROFILE

Elly Sienkiewicz

Elly Sienkiewicz is the foremost expert on the Baltimore album quilt, a challenging appliqué style, and its astonishing revival is due largely to her hard work. These ornate quilts, which had their heyday in Baltimore in the 1840s and 1850s, are typically dominated by red and green designs against a white background. They are called album quilts because each block is different, just as a photograph album would feature many different photos. Certain images are very common in these quilts, including baskets and bouquets of flowers, wreaths of leaves, eagles, flags, hearts, doves, monuments, and institutional buildings.

Sienkiewicz (pronounced sin-KEV-itz), has been teaching modern quilters how to make Baltimore album quilts for more than twenty-five years and has published at least nineteen books on quilts. Some of

Elly Sienkiewicz

A hand appliqué master, Elly Sienkiewicz specializes in both traditional and contemporary Baltimore album quilts.

Skill level

Classes for students with all levels of quilting experience.

Website

www.ellysienkiewicz.com
Read Sienkiewicz's biography and take a look at her teaching schedule, along with in-depth information about her annual appliqué academy held every February in Williamsburg, Virginia. There are lists of instructors and downloadable application forms for the upcoming session, plus a portfolio of finished projects from the last one.

Elly Sienkiewicz's Books

Sienkiewicz is a prolific author but not all of her titles are still in print. The ones listed here are among her most popular books. All are published by C&T Publishing.

Baltimore Beauties and Beyond: Studies in Classic Album Quilt Appliqué, Volume One; $24.95

Baltimore Elegance: A New Approach to Classic Album Quilts; $29.95, features smaller, more simple quilt blocks than those in many of Sienkiewicz's previous books.

her books include historical accounts, but most are how-to books with patterns and instructions. Sienkiewicz is active on the teaching and lecture circuit but best known for the annual weeklong Elly Sienkiewicz Appliqué Academy, which is held every February in historic Williamsburg, Virginia (for more about the academy, see page 388). Sienkiewicz usually teaches only one-day classes in other venues, so the academy provides the rare chance to get her expertise in depth.

"Every year, I travel from northeast Pennsylvania to Williamsburg, Virginia, to study with Elly," says Deborah Gale Tirico. "I've read all her books, made many of her blocks, and have heard her speak on numerous occasions. She opened my eyes to innovative techniques in appliqué and has given me a love of the craft. It's not just her teaching skill; she has the ability to transport her students to another time in history through the stories of tradition, folklore, and the family quilters who came before her."

"My daughter and I have been attending the academy for eight years, and we call it our 'running away time,'" says Kathy Tennyson of Chestertown, New York. "We've taken several classes with Elly, and she is such an inspiration. She gets the class going with their stitching, and then she keeps us entertained the entire time. She will read us poetry, tell us stories of her childhood, and then move to the white board to sketch a stitch or technique she wants us to see."

Similar comments come from those who have taken her classes at other locales. Her scholarly knowledge is as impressive as her craftsmanship, but the words used most often to describe Sienkiewicz's teaching style are *gentle*, *patient*, and *enthusiastic*. "Elly is one of the most giving teachers I have ever had," says Susan Slesinger, a resident of Seal Beach, California. "She's willing to repeat demonstrations until every single student 'gets it,' and then she'll go around the room to help anybody who needs her."

In a casual quilt world where many students favor denim and sweatpants, Sienkiewicz stands out, an old-school dame draped in colorful shawls and wearing elegant brooches. She speaks softly and has exquisite penmanship. She graduated from Wellesley College,

Classic Revival: Alex's Album, *a group quilt made under Elly Sienkiewicz's direction.*

earned a master's degree from the University of Pennsylvania, and taught history for seven years.

Sienkiewicz started quilting with the birth of her second child. She had been an accomplished needleworker all her life, which is one of the reasons Baltimore album quilts bowled her over. Many are lavishly embellished with embroidery used to add detail to the pictorial aspects of the quilts, such as putting faces on the people. Sienkiewicz says her passion was unlocked by viewing a show of these quilts at the Baltimore Museum of Art. "As I stood there, I felt tears welling up," she recalls. "I felt as though I was looking into the soul of the women who made these quilts."

Sienkiewicz's first book told the story of the album quilts and decoded their common motifs. It was called *Spoken Without a Word: A Lexicon of Selected Symbols with 24 Patterns from Classic Baltimore Album Quilts*. After immersing herself in the quilts' history, Sienkiewicz wrote the book quickly, sending her husband and three kids off for a beach vacation so that she could write without interruption. Sienkiewicz slept in four-hour segments "because I read that Benjamin Franklin did that." She self-published her first book in 1983 and began selling it by mail. Running the mail-order business was wearing her

The Best of Baltimore Beauties: 95 Patterns for Album Blocks and Borders; $24.95

The Best of Baltimore Beauties Part II: More Patterns for Album Blocks; $24.95

Sweet Dreams, Moon Baby: A Quilt to Make, A Story to Read; $14.95
A free-style contemporary pattern book that includes five projects. The main one is a charming baby quilt.

Ami Simms

Light-hearted quilter Ami Simms specializes in hand quilting, with an emphasis on photo quilts.

Skill level

Classes for students with all levels of quilting experience.

Website

www.amisimms.com
Simms' amusing website has not only her teaching schedule and an online store where you can buy her books, patterns, and fabric, it also includes information about the quilt exhibits and sales Simms has organized to raise money for Alzheimer's research.

Telephone

(800) 278-4824

out, she says, when she realized "I had found paradise in teaching." So Sienkiewicz sold her mail-order business through an ad in *The Wall Street Journal*.

As Sienkiewicz's expertise grew, so did the number of her fans and the number of her books in print. Baltimore album quilts became much better known, leading directly to numerous major exhibitions. Her impact is all the more impressive considering that the original quilts were something of a fad, in fashion for fewer than twenty years, and that the number of first-rate Baltimore album quilts that survived from the nineteenth century is relatively small. Many awards have been bestowed upon Sienkiewicz by the quilt world, including the prestigious Silver Star Award, which Quilts, Inc., the company that runs the International Quilt Festival in Houston, gives each year to someone whose career has furthered the art of quilting.

In addition to her appliqué academy, Sienkiewicz teaches regularly at venues that include the Empty Spools retreat at Asilomar on the coast of California; Appliqué by the Bay, an annual conference in Delaware; and the International Quilt Festival in Houston.

By combining her love of lore and history with her skills in needlework and teaching, what Sienkiewicz has done is to usher in a revival that spurs modern women to make their own versions of the Baltimore album quilts. They have the choice of copying the patterns and colors of the originals or learning the style and then updating it with their own personal imagery. Sienkiewicz encourages both approaches.

TEACHER PROFILE

Ami Simms

If the quilt world has a class clown, it's Ami Simms. Even explaining how to pronounce her name is an opportunity for a joke. "Ami rhymes with salami," she explains, "but I answer to any lunch meat."

Simms falls in the category of the "simplifiers," those whose lectures, workshops, patterns, and books cover a lot of the basics. What sets Simms apart is a self-deprecating sense of humor that keeps quilters in stitches (pun intended). Almost all of Simms' endeavors, including her free monthly e-mail newsletter and her website, poke fun at her own foibles and reassure quilters that they're doing just fine.

To promote her book *How Not to Make a Prize-Winning Quilt*, in which she confesses every mistake she ever made personally, Simms created the Worst Quilt in the World Contest. People entered hundreds of quilts, and her sponsors paid thousands of dollars in prize money. Entrants were sent lapel pins that read Thank Goodness I Didn't Win the Worst Quilt in the World Contest! and some got Abominable Mention awards.

Ami Simms arrives at a quilt show.

Although the contest only ran from 1995 through 1997, Simms continues to post photos of the awful quilts on her website and offers a popular lecture about the contest. She shows photographs of quilts that are miserably off-kilter, lumpy where they ought to be flat, and full of the overly large stitches quilters deride as "toe-hookers." The contest even gave an award in the category of Most Disgusting (But Fitting) Name for a Quilt. One year it went to an entry titled *Kitty in the Blender*.

With the contest and her other work, Simms' message is twofold: She tells quilters that no matter how klutzy their work may be, it could be worse, and even if it is this bad, hey, at least they can laugh. At the same time, she promises to patiently help them improve.

"My teaching style is to take one skill, break it down to its simplest components, and build it back up again," says Simms. "My goal is to present a skill so students can conquer it and make it their own. I try to do that through clear explanations, demonstrations, and humor."

Her students are very appreciative. "I was new to quilting and had never tried appliqué, but I was looking for a class to take at the Houston quilt festival and saw that Ami is left-handed, too. So I thought I might learn something," says Sally Becker of Wausau, Wisconsin. "Did I ever! She taught us her infamous ladder stitch, which I consider invaluable. I use that stitch on any quilt where I have to hand sew the binding down. At the end of class that day, I said to Ami, 'I could just kiss

Ami Simms' Books

Simms has self-published the books here, through her Mallery Press. They come in paperback only and are available from her website; many are also found at quilt shops and through Amazon.com.

Creating Scrapbook Quilts; $14.95

How Not to Make a Prize-Winning Quilt; $8.95

Invisible Applique; $9.95

Picture Play Quilts; $22.95

you!' I was that excited about the whole experience." Adds Battle Creek, Michigan, resident Kay Carr, "Ami's sense of humor is delicious, and her attention to each individual in the class endears her to the students."

Simms clearly loves to teach, and she also has a maverick can-do spirit that leads her to try things nobody else would consider. For example, once in the mid-nineties, Simms announced on a quilter's message board on the Internet that she was flying home from Texas and would have a four-hour layover in Pittsburgh. She said she was planning to offer an appliqué class right there in the airport terminal, if anybody would care to sign up.

Laura Rohwedder, who took the airport class that day with her mother, says it was an experience she'll never forget. "There were about ten students, and after going through security with our fabric and scissors and all, we met Ami at her gate and walked to another gate that wasn't being used," Rohwedder recalls. "We sat in a big circle on the floor, and our class began! Some people stared but nobody asked what we were doing there. Ami's spirit of fun and excellent teaching made it a great class!" So it wasn't a big surprise that *The Professional Quilter* magazine gave Ami Simms its coveted Teacher of the Year award in 2005.

"I tell students to be gentle with themselves," says Simms. "Goals are good, but only if you can achieve them nine times out of ten. Anything more difficult than that and you should take up brain surgery."

One of Simms' signature classes focuses on making photo-transfer quilts, one of the technological trends fueling the quilting renaissance (for more about photo transfer, see pages 199–211). Simms gives popular workshops and has written several books on the topic. Beginning quilters frequently tell her that they want to start with a photo quilt, but are afraid that they're "supposed" to start with a sampler quilt. Her response is typical Simms: "There is no sense in making a sampler if you don't want to own a sampler. Your first quilt should be a quilt you're committed to."

Given her reputation as a humorist whose favorite target is herself, it might seem that Simms doesn't take her own quilting seriously, but much of her work is wonderfully creative and executed with superb craftsmanship. Many of her elaborate photo quilts, which have been exhibited widely, appear in her book *Creating Scrapbook Quilts*, including one made for her mother's seventieth birthday that features 180 photographs on the front and another 50 on the back. Simms often sews little trinkets and mementos onto her photo quilts, including a fork dripping with spaghetti (actually it was a glow-in-the-dark shoelace) on a quilt made as a tribute to the city of Rome.

Simms learned to quilt when she visited the Old Order Amish in Indiana while working on an undergraduate thesis in anthropology. After college, Simms became a second-grade teacher and an adult education teacher. She began teaching quilting in 1982. For years, she has stuck close to her home in Flint, Michigan, first because she had a young daughter and later because her mother, who has Alzheimer's disease, lived with the family. As a result, Simms usually only schedules one teaching trip a month. Her calendar is booked at least three years ahead, with classes at various regional and national shows and, often, at guild events. So when the chance arises to take an Ami Simms class, don't hesitate. In addition to photo transfer, Simms' popular classes include hand quilting, invisible appliqué, and string quilting, a technique of sewing together narrow "strings" of fabric to make pretty patterned blocks, using up lots of scraps in the process.

Who but Ami Simms would invite quilters to show her their stashes and then post photographs of people's shelves and closets bulging with fabric? She says her personal favorite is the woman who sent a photo of fabric in her refrigerator.

Instructions for Ami Simms' Fruit Tart Pincushion quilt project begin on page 482.

TEACHER PROFILE

Ricky Tims

Ricky Tims takes the notion of quilt teacher as entertainer to a whole new level. A soft-spoken Texan in a black cowboy hat, Tims has wed his first career in music with his second career in quilting and taken the quilt world by storm. His weekend seminars attract huge crowds that cheer both his colorful

Ricky Tims

Musical art quilter Ricky Tims is known for his distinctive designs and techniques for making contemporary quilts.

Skill level

Classes for students with all levels of quilting experience.

Website

www.rickytims.com
Not only can you check out Tims' teaching schedule, you can view a gallery of his quilts and shop for his book, patterns, thread, hand-dyed fabric—even coffee mugs. There are instructional quilting DVDs, too, and CDs of his original piano music.

Telephone

(303) 252-0579, for bookings

quilts and his heartfelt piano playing. And now he's blazing new media trails by teaming up with Alex Anderson (see her profile on page 307) to cohost an innovative new program on the Internet, *The Quilt Show,* that viewers must pay to watch.

An award-winning quilter, Tims creates his own designs, which include bold geometric grids pieced from dazzling hand-dyed fabrics. While he sometimes transforms traditional designs into contemporary expressions and often creates laborious art quilts, Tims is known for his relatively simple techniques that allow quilters to make a big visual impact with a few fabrics.

Tims' Convergence Quilts, for example, involve taking two fabrics with gradually changing horizontal design elements, cutting them into strips of various widths, then merging the two sets of strips together. The checkerboard-like quilts look like colorful, clever puzzles. Tims' instructions are so clear that Convergence Quilts are virtually no fail. Even timid beginners produce beautiful quilts and feel creatively unleashed. "I make easy quilts that look difficult," is how Tims describes his work.

South Cheyenne Canyon, *by Ricky Tims.*

Atlanta resident Patricia Kilmark says of the class she took on Convergence Quilts, "I was so amazed. Right there, before my eyes, 'converging' strips of fabric in his style, I was able to make the most wonderful creation I'd ever seen!" Kilmark's quilt from that class was selected as one of the student examples for Tims' how-to book on Convergence Quilts, and she has been teaching the technique herself ever since.

One fast-growing part of Tims' burgeoning empire is the two-day seminars he created to keep up with the demand for his teaching services. Normally, hands-on classes in which students work at sewing machines and get some one-on-one interaction with the teacher can't exceed twenty-five or thirty students. Tims' seminars, which don't involve sewing, are limited only by the size of the halls, and audiences generally run into the hundreds.

The big crowds justified the expense of purchasing a truck and large trailer to haul Tims' collection of more than fifty quilts to venues—along with quilt stands, a sound system, and a good selection of his merchandise. Thus, the two elements quilters love most are added to the classroom experience: shopping and looking at beautiful quilts.

But just as Tims anticipated, there was initial resistance to the idea of the large seminars. People he first approached thought quilters would get bored sitting for that long and wouldn't learn as much from the lecture format. Tims persisted, explaining that for every ninety minutes of instruction, there would be a thirty-minute break. He spent time, money, and effort to create sophisticated audiovisual demonstrations of each of his techniques, so that every person in the room could see how he performed each step in the process. And each student would receive an exclusive bound syllabus, with thirteen chapters of concise instructions.

After several trial runs, positive word of mouth made booking easy. There were 60 students at his first quilting seminar and 250 at his fourth. The swelling crowds prompted Tims to package "Super Quilt Seminars" beginning in 2007, in which he shares the stage with such other quilt stars as Libby Lehman (see page 350) and Alex Anderson.

"I'm used to hands-on classes so I was really questioning the whole ordeal," says Glenda Farrell, a quiltmaker who took Ricky Tims' seminar at the Houston quilt festival in 2004. "I couldn't imagine what a person could talk about for two whole days but I had heard wonderful things about Ricky. Anyway, I came away from the seminar so inspired and fired up. The way he explains and demonstrates his techniques is easy to understand. Even without any hands-on experience, I came away being able to do all the things he taught us. He is such a breath of fresh air!"

"Right there, before my eyes, 'converging' strips of fabric in his style, I was able to make the most wonderful creation I'd ever seen!"

Tims says with a laugh that when people hear he plays piano they expect either Liberace—or Garth Brooks, because of the cowboy hat. But, the most fitting description of his performance style comes from his partner Justin Shults, who describes Tims as

TIMS' TIP

Many quilters baste the three layers of a quilt together by hand with thread before quilting, but Tims says when he began doing more dense machine quilting it was difficult to remove all the basting threads. While safety pins are a popular alternative to basting, Tims feared he'd snag the fabric with a pin and rip his quilt.

"Instead, I use thin, lightweight water soluble thread for basting," he says. "I spread my quilt out on the floor and do a moderate amount of basting by hand, then I bring the quilt to my machine. I put the water soluble thread in both the top (I may loosen the tension so it doesn't break) and the bobbin and continue basting by machine in straight lines. I do regular-size stitches and free-motion quilting. It's great because I keep flipping the quilt upside down to look for puckers. If I find any, all I have to do is spritz with water, dissolve the basting stitches, let it dry, and rebaste. And when I'm done quilting with regular thread and wash the quilt, all the basting stitches dissolve!"

"George Winston [New Age pianist] meets Jeff Foxworthy [comedian known for redneck jokes] meets Dr. Phil [the therapist Oprah made famous]."

Nan Maples, a marketing analyst who has taken three of Tims' regular hands-on classes, says he has an uncanny ability to "meet each student at exactly where they are at that particular moment." She says she won't forget either his skillful, personalized teaching or his colorful speaking style. "As I presented a woefully mangled attempt at a wiggly seam that wouldn't press flat, Ricky said, while drenching the seam with water from a spray bottle, 'Don't worry. We'll just iron [pronounced arn] the snot out of it.' And we did!"

Tims' rise in the quilt world has been nothing short of meteoric. It's not just that he stands out because he's a man—there were prominent male quilt teachers before him. Tims represents a kind of star phenomenon more common to the world of pop music than the world of crafts: Middle-aged women who flock to Tims' workshops and seminars jokingly refer to themselves as "groupies." Tims' career path doesn't look remotely like that of anybody else in the quilt world.

While many of the top teachers profiled in this book started quilting and teaching in the seventies and eighties, Ricky Tims didn't start quilting until 1991, when he inherited a sewing machine from his grandmother. At the time, Tims was living in St. Louis, working as a freelance music producer, and had time on his hands. He decided to sew a shirt but concluded that was too difficult for a novice, so he bought a book on sampler quilts. He made one, and then more. He hadn't been quilting long when he ran into a woman at the local five-and-dime store who invited him to a guild meeting, which changed his life.

"I really believe it was divine providence!" he says. "There were two hundred and fifty ladies there for a lecture on the design elements of art. I thought, 'Wow, these are exactly the elements I use to create music. Line in visual art is like melody in music. Moods of color are like harmony.' Pretty soon, I went to the guild and said 'I have an idea for a program about how music and art relate.' "

Thus was born Tims' first lecture, a slide show with music that he presented all over St. Louis. "First I would play a few pieces on a keyboard or piano," he says. "Then I would explain what a motif was in a symphony by Beethoven or a song by Andrew Lloyd Webber and show them a slide of a quilt with a repeating motif."

By 1995, one of Tim's quilts had been accepted into the big national quilt show in Paducah, Kentucky, and he was flying all over the country doing what he called his "dog and pony show." At the time, he was also working full-time as the music coordinator for a large Presbyterian church, composing his own music, and running a small-scale recording studio out of his home.

Bohemian Rhapsody,
by Ricky Tims.

Deciding that he could make a living in the quilt world if he gave it his all, Tims quit his job in 1998. He put out the word he was available to teach and lecture, and his bookings escalated immediately. Now living in the tiny mountain town of La Veta, Colorado, he and his partner own a gallery devoted to art quilts, which is the home to Tims' popular weeklong La Veta Quilt Retreat (held several times annually). His gallery is also the base of operations for the Tims Art Quilt Studio, with space for hand dyeing fabric, plus video and recording production facilities.

This sleepy mountain town is where Tims and his cohost Alex Anderson are taping episodes of their new Internet-based "television" program, *The Quilt Show.* When the first episode began airing in the spring of 2007, many quilters grumbled at having to pay for quilt programming they were used to watching for free. Others were miffed because they didn't have the high-speed connection needed to watch the show. But within six months, nineteen thousand quilters had paid for the first thirteen episodes. Whatever venture he presents to the quilt world next will be worth watching.

You'll find instructions for Ricky Tims' Quilted Keepsake Greeting Cards on page 467.

"Ricky said, while drenching the seam with water from a spray bottle, 'Don't worry. We'll just iron [pronounced arn] the snot out of it.' And we did!"

Quilt Class Etiquette

Paying attention to the details in a quilt class.

A quilt class can be virtually ruined by a single student who is late, loud, and disorganized. Many of the rules of etiquette are those that apply in most group-learning situations, but they are still worth going over. Whether it's a hands-on workshop offered to twenty or thirty students or a lecture being delivered to a packed auditorium, it's important to be respectful. Here are six simple rules that will enhance quilt classes for both the teacher and your fellow students, no matter what the venue.

1. Days or weeks before the class, take the time to read the list of necessary materials and assemble them. You might need to buy special supplies. For a machine-quilting class, you may be asked to prepare a "sandwich" of batting between two layers of fabric, basted together with pins. That way, you can begin sewing immediately in class. Scrambling to buy supplies from the teacher or borrow them from your fellow students will delay the class.

2. Be on time. A lot of ground gets covered at the beginning, even while students are getting settled in their seats. Teachers tend to give an overview of the lesson to come, and some use this time to show examples of their own work. A late arrival means you'll miss this valuable introduction, and you'll also make it harder for everyone else to concentrate. There are quilt classes where early arrival and set-up are either allowed or encouraged: Check beforehand.

3. Don't interrupt the teacher except in an emergency. If it's a workshop, most teachers spend plenty of time walking around the room and making sure all the students get what they need. If it's a lecture, there will almost always be time for questions at the end.

Naiad, *by Charlotte Warr Anderson.*

4. Don't hog the teacher's time or distract your fellow students. In many classes there are periods, sometimes hours at a time, during which students work away at the project or technique of the day and a low conversational buzz is perfectly acceptable. Use your common sense. If you have a problem, don't be shy about raising your hand and asking for help, but respect the needs of your fellow students in this regard as well. It can be particularly distracting if you spend your time and that of the teacher on a project or technique that isn't part of the lesson as advertised. Don't go there!

5. There are copyright issues related to the works and ideas of the teacher that must be taken into account. It's common courtesy to ask a teacher's permission before photographing any samples or finished works. The strictures are even greater against reproducing any of the teacher's handouts or other class materials and using them to teach the techniques to your local guild or any other group. There are some well-known teachers who permit their books and classes to be taught by other people, sometimes after special training, but permission is always required and there may be fees. (For more about copyright questions, see page 515.)

6. If after a class begins you find yourself either bored or unable to keep up, stick with it at least until there is a declared break. Chances are there will be at least some lessons you'll learn, even if they aren't exactly what you expected or they merely serve to prove that this particular technique isn't your cup of tea. Some teachers take a while to hit their stride, and sometimes, tips that were mere tangents to the main lesson turn out to be the unexpected bonus you never forget. It's likely that you'll have a chance to evaluate teachers and classes later on, and these surveys are taken seriously both by the teachers and the venues that book them.

27 More Quilt Teachers to Watch For

The next Eleanor Burns or Ricky Tims is already perfecting techniques and developing a unique teaching style.

YOU'LL FIND INFORMATION HERE ABOUT SOME additional famous teachers and other first-rate ones who aren't household names. Some of the up-and-comers may not have written a book, and some don't have a website yet: They're on this list because their classes fill up and their students rave.

I've selected these teachers after considerable research, asking many quilters across the country to tell me which teachers made the biggest difference to them. These teachers are experts in a wide variety of quilting techniques, and the information here will help you pinpoint not just who is teaching but what sorts of classes you're likely to find. It's an abbreviated listing so it won't give you full biographies and such, but I've identified the specialties of all of the teachers and highlighted some of their signature classes and books, listing websites when possible.

The list is meant to supplement the top teachers profiled at length starting on page 307, but I don't want to suggest that this list is comprehensive either. There are hundreds of terrific quilt teachers out there, with new ones turning up constantly. The next Eleanor Burns or Ricky Tims is already perfecting techniques and developing a unique teaching style: Maybe someone that spectacular will offer a workshop at your guild next month.

I suggest that you go right ahead and appoint yourself a "talent scout." Go to lectures at your local guild and take classes at shows, big and small. Watch the quilt television shows and read the quilt magazines to see what new work excites you and what new patterns and techniques are appearing. Ask your friends to recommend new teachers they've tried. And, for more advice on how to pick the right class for you, go to page 297.

CHARLOTTE WARR ANDERSEN
PICTORIAL APPLIQUÉ

Based in Salt Lake City, Utah, Charlotte Warr Andersen is famous for her lush, detailed pictorial quilts, especially landscapes. Her quilts have won many awards and she has published two books on her techniques. Andersen teaches both hand and machine appliqué. Her website, www.charlottewarrandersen.com, includes an e-store where you can buy her favorite tools.

CHARLOTTE ANGOTTI
QUICK MACHINE PIECING

Fans of mystery quilts flock to Charlotte Angotti's classes. Students in her workshops often don't know until the end of the lesson how the simple blocks they make will fit together into a quilt. Angotti is a famously funny teacher and also streamlines the quilting process. For those in a hurry, Angotti sells precut kits for her quilt patterns. Get her schedule at www.charlotteangotti.com.

JINNY BEYER
MASTER OF HAND QUILTING

One of the pioneers of the quilt boom, Jinny Beyer is still going strong after thirty-some years. Beyer doesn't teach as much as she used to, but she still runs a popular weeklong seminar at Hilton Head, South Carolina, every winter. The author of at least ten books about quilting, Beyer is also one of the most prolific fabric designers. All her colorful fabrics (and a lot more) can be purchased on her web shop or at her brick-and-mortar store in Great Falls, Virginia. Beyer is passionate about handwork, and her book *Quiltmaking by Hand: Simple Stitches, Exquisite Quilts* is indispensable. Her website is www.JinnyBeyer.com.

Windows, *by Jinny Beyer.*

JEAN BIDDICK
MOSAIC QUILTS AND BLENDED BACKGROUNDS

Looking High and Low, *by Jean Biddick.*

JEAN BIDDICK BELONGS TO THE GROUP OF QUILT teachers whose hard-won knowledge draws from years of co-owning a quilt shop and solving quilters' problems daily. Though Biddick has won top awards at the major quilt shows, she sees herself as a teacher and quiltmaker, not an artist, and she breaks intricate patterns into doable steps for students at all levels. She is a technique teacher more than a design instructor, emphasizing machine piecing. Her favorite classes include Piecing Mosaic Tile Designs and Blended Backgrounds. Go to www.jeanbiddick.com.

JUDI WARREN BLAYDON
MAKING SENSE OF DESIGN

A FORMER ART TEACHER WITH AN M.F.A. AND MANY prizewinning quilts to her credit, Judi Warren Blaydon is widely cited as one of the best quilt teachers on the circuit. Her specialty is teaching both hand and machine quilters the principles of art and design, helping them to reach new levels in their work. She teaches regularly at the major venues, including the American Quilter's Society show in Paducah, Kentucky, and Quilting by the Lake, a summer retreat in upstate New York.

JOAN COLVIN
NATURE QUILTS

ANOTHER QUILTMAKER WHOSE STUNNING QUILTS HANG on museum walls, Joan Colvin was a very popular and creative teacher. Colvin favored "fast machine appliqué" in her own work but was an expert in using both hand and machine techniques for different effects. She often taught at venues that cater to art quilters, such as Art Quilt Tahoe. Unfortunately, you can no longer take her classes—she passed away just before this book went to press—but keep an eye out for her terrific book *Nature's Studio: A Quilter's Guide to Playing with Fabrics & Techniques*. One customer review on Amazon.com reads "This is a must-have for folks who make or want to make landscape/art quilts."

SHARYN CRAIG
TRADITIONAL BLOCKS MADE EASY

SHARYN CRAIG HAS A DEGREE IN HOME ECONOMICS and has been teaching quilting since 1980. Like a number of teachers in this chapter, she was voted Teacher of the Year by *The Professional Quilter* magazine (she won in 1985). The author of several books, Craig mostly teaches one-day workshops focusing on piecing such beloved traditional patterns as Log Cabin by machine. Her website is www.sharyncraig.com.

It Takes a Village, *by Sharyn Craig*

CAROL DOAK
PAPER PIECING

CAROL DOAK IS BEST KNOWN FOR HER MANY BOOKS AND workshops on a popular technique called paper piecing, which allows quilters to make complicated blocks from tiny pieces of fabric by attaching the fabric to a paper pattern and sewing through that. Doak, who lives in New Hampshire, teaches all over the country and also designs fabric. The word *easy* appears in many of her book titles, and her goal is to simplify a technique that seems daunting at first. Her most popular books include *Easy Machine Paper Piecing* and *300 Paper-Pieced Quilt Blocks*. Doak's excellent website, www.caroldoak.com, includes free patterns, an online store, her workshop schedule, and a show-and-tell section where you can see previous students' work.

CYNTHIA ENGLAND
EVOKING REALISM IN FABRIC

TRAINED AS A GRAPHIC ARTIST, THIS DICKINSON, Texas–based quilter has won many of the top prizes at major shows, including the American Quilter's Society People's Choice award. Cynthia England has developed a special technique she calls Picture Piecing that allows her to use her sewing machine to create stunningly realistic looking pictorial quilts. Many of her quilts depict natural landscapes, but she's equally adept at creating indoor scenes. England

has produced more than fifty patterns and several books. You can find her workshop schedule (click on Contact Info), free patterns, and a gallery of student work at her website www.englanddesign.com.

JOHN FLYNN
TEACHER AND QUILT FRAME MAKER

ONE OF THE MOST VISIBLE MALE TEACHERS ON THE circuit, John Flynn is a trained engineer who used to build bridges for a living. He designed a quilt frame to help his wife, Brooke, then took up the craft himself. He still makes and sells his Flynn Multi-Frame System, which allows quilters to finish their quilts without basting the three layers together. Some of his classes focus on using his trademark frame, while others concentrate on how to cut and machine piece such traditional patterns as the difficult but popular Double Wedding Ring pattern. One of his best-selling books is a workbook about that design. His website is www.flynnquilt.com.

KLAUDEEN HANSEN
SIMPLIFYING THE CLASSICS

HER NAME MAY NOT BE FAMILIAR, BUT KLAUDEEN Hansen's classes are some of the first to fill up every year at the American Quilter's Society show in Paducah, Kentucky. Hansen is an experienced quilt judge and chooses quilts for the AQS annual calendars. Her workshops are often devoted to cutting and machine piecing classic patterns like Delectable Mountains, but Hansen keeps the projects small and doable, so students usually leave her workshops with a finished project.

ROBERTA HORTON
GLOBAL INFLUENCES

ANOTHER ONE OF THE MUCH LAUDED PIONEERS, Roberta Horton has taught quilting for more than three decades. She has taught in almost every state and thirteen foreign countries, and Horton gathers fabric and design inspiration from every corner of the globe. She has inspired many quilters to add Japanese and

African fabrics to their quilts. Almost all of her classes require a sewing machine. One of her most popular ones focuses on scrap quilts. Horton's website is www.robertahorton.com.

Dutch Treat, *by Roberta Horton.*

MICHAEL JAMES GROUND-BREAKING ART QUILTS

A GIANT IN THE PANTHEON OF PIONEERING ART quilters, Michael James is noted for his graphic abstract quilts. He helped to reinvent the genre and to get quilts taken seriously as art. James is a full professor at the University of Nebraska at Lincoln, and his quilting classes are few and far between. Generally he gives week-long design seminars for advanced students. In recent years, James has been a pioneer in transferring photographs to large-scale art quilts. Even if you are not an art quilter, don't turn down the chance to hear him speak or see his distinctive quilts. The website at www.unl.edu/mjames_quilts provides a look at his work.

NATASHA KEMPERS-CULLEN COLLAGES

AFTER SIXTEEN YEARS OF TEACHING ART IN PUBLIC schools, Natasha Kempers-Cullen knows how to help quilters create playfully. She calls her own art quilts collage constructions and the techniques she teaches include painting on fabric, design and composition, and "over-the-top" quilted embellishment. Although Kempers-Cullen uses both hand and machine techniques in her own work, she says most of her workshops "are like note taking and sketching and are not about creating finished works." Students in her classes start looking at their quilts as abstract art works and loosen up creatively. Kempers-Cullen's quilts can be found in such museum collections as the Smithsonian's Renwick Gallery. They can also be seen on her website, www.natashakempers-cullen.com.

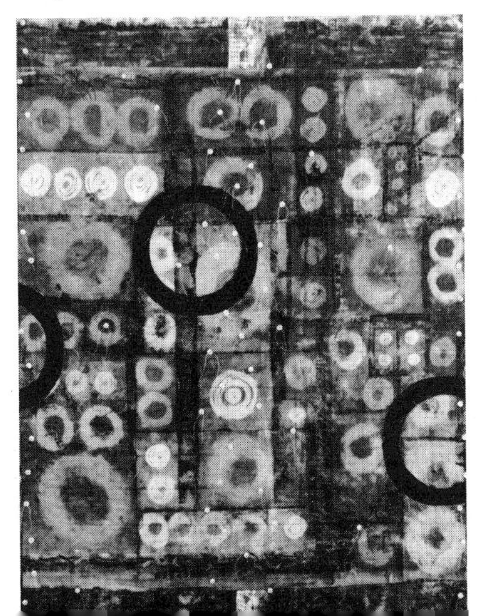

Blowing Bubbles, *by Natasha Kempers-Cullen.*

RESOURCES

Quilt Tours and Cruises

Tour director Jim West and Beth Hayes, editor in chief of McCall's Quilting, *at Rome's Trevi Fountain.*

Quilt travel is getting to be a big business. There are more quilting cruises than ever before, plus quilt-related tours to exotic locales everywhere from Iceland to South Africa. And there are companies that specialize in domestic quilt trips, usually by bus, taking quilters to the big shows and to quilt havens like the Amish country in Pennsylvania.

The resources listed here represent a small fraction of those available but come highly recommended. Quilt travel can be one of the few aspects of this craft that rivals sewing machines in price, so do your homework before you make a booking. Get feedback at your local quilt shop and guild, and post your queries online.

Quilt Tour and Cruise Agencies

COUNTRY HERITAGE TOURS

With two decades of service, the Amherst, New Hampshire–based Country Heritage Tours has an excellent track record as a specialist in the quilt tour business. The organization brings multiple busloads of quilters to Paducah, Kentucky, every year for the American Quilter's Society show in April but it also offers, among other excursions, fall foliage tours to New England with quilt stops, and excursions to the big quilt shows in Houston and Chicago. Although most of its trips are domestic, Country Heritage Tours does have some overseas packages as well.

For more information, call (800) 346-9820 or go to **www.countryheritagetours.com**.

Sew Many Places

Veteran cruise director Jim West runs Sew Many Places out of offices in Spring Valley, Illinois (his other subsidiaries offer travel packages catering to everyone from honeymooners to Catholics). Sew Many Places has organized quilt cruises for such major players in the quilt world as the American Quilter's Society and *McCall's Quilting* magazine, traveling to enticing locations like China, Bali, the Greek islands, and the Caribbean. Well-known quilt teachers like Eleanor Burns (find her profile on page 319) offer lessons on the cruises, which stop at regular tourist destinations as well as those of particular interest to quilters. In China, Sew Many Places stops at not just the Great Wall but also travels to such spots as a silk factory. This isn't for bargain travelers but there are options in several price ranges.

For more information, call Sew Many Places toll free at (877) 887-1188 or go to **www.sewmanyplaces.com**.

Quilt Ventures

Another outfit with a good record, Quilt Ventures offers quilt packages within the continental United States and cruises to places like Hawaii and England. For more than a decade Quilt Ventures has produced a week-long quilt show with classes at different locations in Hawaii. Sponsors of this annual event include the American Quilter's Society, and you'll find such experienced teachers as Charlotte Angotti (see page 377 in More Quilt Teachers to Watch For) and Dierdra McElroy, one of the thimble experts profiled on page 93. Sightseeing is mixed with lessons on topics like Hawaiian quilting, and there is a substantial show of quilts to view.

For more information, call one of the principal partners in Quilt Ventures, Faye Labanaris at (603) 742-0211 or go to **www.quiltventures.com**.

Ricky Tims in Talkeetna, Alaska (top), and quilt tourists at a castle in Ireland.

Tours Led by Quilters

A growing number of popular quilting teachers are sharing their wanderlust, putting together quilt tours all over the globe. Some of these feature quilting classes in a gorgeous tourist spot, such as Tuscany, and add on side trips. Other trips don't include actual lessons but focus more on the indigenous textile culture; this can include trips to factories and mills, museums, and even local quilters' homes. Keep an eye on the websites of your favorite teachers to see if they are traveling. In addition, here are three well-known teachers who often lead tours.

The quilts of renowned art quilter **Nancy Crow** have frequently been inspired by her travels. She has led tours to such far-flung destinations as Mexico, Guatemala, South Africa, and France. Go to **www.nancycrow.com** for information about upcoming tours.

Beading expert **Mary Stori** is a frequent teacher on quilt cruises and has been known to lead tours. Catch up with her at **www.marystori.com**.

And, art quilter **Esterita Austin** conducts classes as part of her tours of Tuscany. See her website, **www.esteritaaustin.com**, for details.

BILL KERR AND WEEKS RINGLE HIP MODERN QUILTS

BILL KERR AND WEEKS RINGLE TAKE A FRESH ANGLE ON quilting. Both have master's degrees in design, and Kerr is a graphic design professor. The married couple makes striking commissioned quilts (priced from $1,000 to $5,000) at their design studio, FunQuilts, outside Chicago, and they design fabric for RJR. Their book *The Modern Quilt Workshop: Patterns, Techniques and Designs from the FunQuilts Studio* teaches how to make bold geometric quilts. About eight times a year, they hold workshops with titles like Design for the Adventurous Quilter that range from one to five days. The intensive tutorials on color and composition help quilters express their ideas more powerfully. "We think everybody has a unique design voice, and we want to help them develop that," says Ringle. "We're proud of how radically different the quilts are in each of our workshops." See the duo's gorgeous quilts and check their teaching schedule at www.funquilts.com.

BONNIE LYN McCAFFERY PORTRAIT QUILTS

PORTRAIT QUILTS ARE A HOT SPECIALTY, AND BONNIE LYN McCaffery is one of the top experts; her classes always fill up at the International Quilt Festival in Houston. Her workshop on painting faces, in which she teaches how to paint features right on the fabric, is especially popular. Those who can't take the class will want her book, *Portrait Quilts: Painted Faces You Can Do.* McCaffery also gives workshops on machine techniques for kaleidoscope quilts, creative layering of fabrics on quilts, and free-form appliqué, among other topics. Her website is www.bonniemccaffery.com. There you can download her free "VidCasts," video demonstrations.

KATIE PASQUINI MASOPUST COLOR AND COMPOSITION

KATIE PASQUINI MASOPUST CALLS HERSELF A FIBER artist and one of her artworks, *Rio Hondo,* was chosen as one of the top one hundred quilts of the twentieth century. That quilt was part of a series of what Masopust calls "fractured landscapes," complex abstractions of scenery that display her confidence with colors.

In many of her popular workshops, Masopust shares her vast artistic knowledge, as she does in the book, *Color and Composition for the Creative Quilter: Improve Any Quilt with Easy-to-Follow Lessons*. The book is cowritten with studio artist Brett Barker. Masopust's website is www.katiepm.com.

Rainbow Lilies, *by Kate Pasquini Masopust.*

MARGARET MILLER
SIMPLE QUILTS THAT LOOK HARD

A VERY POPULAR TEACHER, MARGARET MILLER OFFERS workshops that often cover new arrangements of familiar patterns. Her AnglePlay classes feature rectangles. Miller stresses easy strip piecing and other simple machine construction methods that produce fresh, graphic looks. Her website is www.MillerQuilts.com.

JUDY MURRAH
QUILTED CLOTHING

PATCHWORK GARMENTS ARE A MAJOR PART OF THE ongoing quilt boom, and Judy Murrah is one of the pioneers. She specializes in machine-made jackets and vests, often in bold colors. Murrah also works as the head of education for Quilts, Inc., the outfit that puts on the big quilt show in Houston every year. Her own classes are very popular, as are her books *Judy Murrah's Jacket Jackpot* and *Jacket Jazz: Five Great Looks . . . Over 30 Patchwork Techniques*.

VELDA NEWMAN
COLOR, SHAPE, AND TEXTURE

VELDA NEWMAN'S QUILTS GENERALLY DRAW ON LARGE-scale shapes from nature, such as flowers or shells. With

titles like Creating Realism or Texture and Form, her workshops sound like formal art classes, but they focus on creating quilts with a wide range of collage techniques. Students use such tools as paints, dyes, crayons, ink, and machine stitching to add depth and dimension to art quilts. Newman teaches at many of the main venues, such as the Houston International Quilt Festival, as well as for guilds. Her website is www.veldanewman.com.

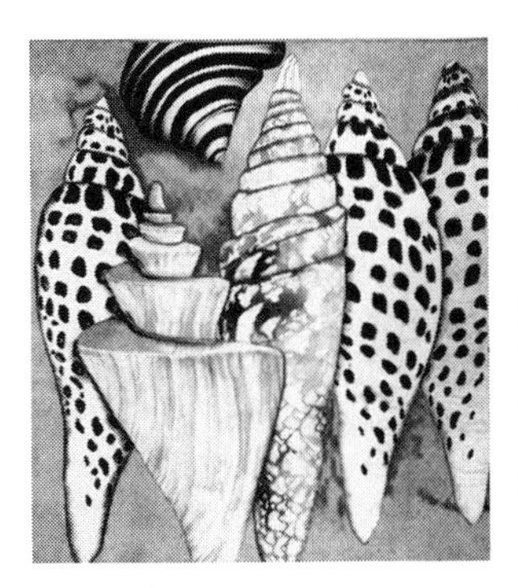

Shell, *by Velda Newman.*

RESOURCES

Quilt Retreats and Conferences

A comprehensive list of national and regional quilt retreats and conferences would be nearly impossible to compile, partly because new ones are constantly springing up. Here, listed by season, are some of the best-known quilting learn-a-thons, those that have been in existence for a number of years and have received good reviews from participants.

This list does not include quilt retreats abroad or those conducted on cruise ships—for information about these, see Quilt Tours and Cruises on page 382. And quilt shows are described separately, starting on pages 543–49. Most shows tend to offer classes, sometimes quite a few, but the major concentration is on looking at quilts and buying quilt-related merchandise. Some of the retreats and conferences here also display quilts and a few have vendors present, but learning is the principal focus. The essence of a retreat is that quilters leave home and go someplace special to immerse themselves in their passion without real-world interruptions. Generally class sizes are small enough for personal attention.

The websites provided here have information about which classes and lectures are offered in a given year, by whom, and detail the fees. Some retreats supply sewing machines free, some require that participants pay to rent them, and some conferences specify that attendees bring their own machines. There are conferences that are run for profit and some that are not.

Summer

QUILT SURFACE DESIGN SYMPOSIUM
Columbus, Ohio

Arguably the most serious annual conference for art quilters, don't go to the Quilt Surface Design Symposium for scenic views but for immersion in quilting with legendary teachers. The sessions at the conference center include about thirty-five different classes, some lasting two, five, or seven days. The conference was established in 1989. Students come from all over the world to take intense classes in nontraditional quiltmaking from the likes of Sue Benner (see page 314) and Esterita Austin (see page 310).

For information, call (614) 297-1585 or go to **www.qsds.com**.

QUILTING BY THE LAKE, Morrisville, New York

This two-week conference has classes that last two days, three days, or five days. In addition to the instruction, Quilting by the Lake always includes a quilt show and a merchant's mall where quilt supplies are sold. Founded in 1981, it was once on a lake but now takes place on the campus of a state university, so housing is in dorm rooms (but at least there's a pool). Classes lean toward sophisticated techniques in design, construction, and embellishment, but more traditional quilters will also find classes to their liking.

For information, call (315) 255-1553 or go to **www.quiltingbythelake.com**.

EMPTY SPOOLS SEMINARS
Pacific Grove, California

Housed at Asilomar Conference Grounds, part of a state park south of San Francisco, the Empty Spools Seminars are a series of five-day quiltmaking workshops. There's a gorgeous beach but accommodations are a bit rustic—no phones, no TV. The seminars boast a roster of ten to twelve top-flight national teachers with a range of styles from appliqué to art quilts.

For information, call (925) 930-7893 or go to **www.emptyspoolsseminars.com**.

Quilters at the Cowgirl Quilt Retreat in Gallatin Gateway, Montana.

Fall

COWGIRL QUILT RETREAT
Gallatin Gateway, Montana

An intimate annual one-week program, Cowgirl Quilt Retreat features relaxed classes with two nationally known teachers, Charlotte Warr Andersen (see page 377) and Georgia Bonesteel, a pioneer in the quilt renaissance famous for inventing the portable lap-quilting method. At a Montana dude ranch, the duo teaches four mornings, usually leading students in making a machine-pieced and appliquéd wall hanging with an animal motif (examples include moose, rabbits, bears, and trout). Afternoons are for trout fishing, horseback riding, hiking, or shopping.

For information, call the ranch, (406) 995-4276, or go to its website **www.ninequartercircle.com**; click on Activities at the bottom of the page.

BEAVER ISLAND QUILT RETREAT
Elk Rapids, Michigan

Located at the hundred-year-old White Birch Lodge, this retreat consists of four sessions, each lasting four days. Beaver Island Quilt Retreat has been led for several decades by quilt teacher Gwen Marston, a prolific "simplifier" known especially for folk art quilts and appliqué. She has produced more than twenty books on her "liberated" techniques for Log Cabin and other traditional patterns. Each retreat focuses on one pattern, for example, basket quilts: In that class, the dominant design element in the machine-pieced quilts will be baskets.

For information, visit Gwen Martson's website, **www.gwenmarston.com**; click on Quilt Retreat at the bottom of the page. Or, contact the lodge at (231) 264-8271.

QUILTING IN THE TETONS
Jackson Hole, Wyoming

The weeklong annual Quilting in the Tetons workshop features half a dozen well-known teachers. Classes focus on traditional blocks, like the Log Cabin, but also on such topics as fabric painting. The workshop is held in nonglamorous venues, including the local 4-H building, and students find their own housing in local motels. A nonprofit conference, it does include a quilt contest with cash prizes for top winners.

For information, call (307) 733-3087 or go to **www.quiltthetetons.org**.

ART QUILT TAHOE
Squaw Valley, California

The teachers are the cream of the crop at this annual quilt conference, known for attracting such renowned art quilters as Libby Lehman (see page 350) and Jane Sassaman (see page 389) to teach. The faculty of top prizewinners and innovators bring their quilts to show. Art Quilt Tahoe lasts five days and is fancier than many retreats, with resort accommodations and a gorgeous locale. The prices reflect this.

For information call (530) 887-0600 or go to **www.artquilttahoe.com**.

Winter

JINNY BEYER QUILTING SEMINAR
Hilton Head, South Carolina

Pioneering quilt teacher Jinny Beyer has hosted this retreat for more than twenty-five years. The five-day event, which gives you the option of adding a second two-day workshop, features classes with top teachers supplemented by lectures and quilt-related entertainment. Each year Beyer picks a theme and about 250 quilters come, including many repeaters. This is a quilt retreat at a resort for those who don't like roughing it. (For more about Beyer, see page 377.)

For information, call (866) 759-7373 or go to Beyer's website **www.jinnybeyer.com**; click on Quilting Seminar Info.

THE ELLY SIENKIEWICZ APPLIQUÉ ACADEMY
Williamsburg, Virginia

A four-day conference held every February in historic Williamsburg, the academy is a must experience for those who do traditional appliqué. The lessons emphasize meticulous handwork, although there is one big-name teacher who specializes in machine appliqué. About a dozen teachers preside, led by Elly Sienkiewicz, the top proponent of Baltimore album quilts (for more about Sienkiewicz, see page 363).

There's some sightseeing, but quilting takes center stage; you can add on one or two more days of classes. One ritual that has evolved at the academy is the Saturday night dessert—in a bow to earlier traditions all the participants wear hats and gloves that could have belonged to their mothers.

You'll find more information about the academy at Elly Sienkiewicz's website, **www.ellysienkiewicz.com**.

Spring

QUILTERS' ESCAPE
Eureka, California

Begun in 2003, this relaxed four-day retreat with half a dozen top teachers is run out of a conference center on the Eel River. Quilters' Escape classrooms open at 6 A.M. for the early birds and stay open until midnight for the night owls. You can choose from a wide variety of techniques to study. Many quilters extend their stay in the area so they can explore the redwood forests and spend time on the beach.

For information, call (707) 442-0081 or go to **www.quiltersescape.com**.

LA VETA QUILT RETREAT
La Veta, Colorado

Popular teacher Ricky Tims (see page 369) offers several five-day retreats each year in the picturesque Colorado mountain town where he lives. These aren't classes per se but a period of independent study that includes pep talks, performances, and meals with Tims. The retreat is held at a gallery owned by Tims in La Veta, with students staying at an inn next door. Only ten quilters attend each session, so the waiting list is long and attendees are picked through a lottery system. The time for these retreats varies each year, but most occur in spring and1 summer.

For information, go to the website **www.rickytims.com** and click on Retreats. Or call (719) 742-3755.

JACKIE ROBINSON
FAST MACHINE PIECING

Jackie Robinson has a degree from New York's Fashion Institute of Technology and used to own a fabric shop in a St. Louis suburb. Now based in Montana, she has written many books on quilting and is a busy teacher offering a wide range of classes. Whether the pattern to be shared is one from her popular book *Tesselations*, her Ultimate Log Cabin, or one of her designs based on art glass by Frank Lloyd Wright, Robinson knows that her students are pressed for time and stresses quick methods with clean results. Her website is www.animas.com.

JANE SASSAMAN
GLORIOUS FLOWER QUILTS

Jane Sassaman's award-winning quilts feature abstracted images taken from the natural world, especially flowers, often done in machine appliqué. Sassaman's workshop on floral quilts is her most popular, but those who love her work can also learn from her terrific book, *The Quilted Garden: Design and Make Nature-Inspired Quilts*. There probably isn't a more beautiful quilt website than www.janesassaman.com, where fans can order from her fabric line as well as buy kits featuring simplified versions of some of her most famous quilts. The kits include one for Sassaman's quilt *Willow*, voted one of the hundred best quilts of the twentieth century.

Magic Forest Quilt, *by Jane Sassaman.*

SHARON SCHAMBER
"PIEC-LIQUÉ"

This former owner of a wedding gown factory started sewing sophisticated clothing as a preteen. Sharon Schamber retired from her wedding dress business in 1994 and turned to quilting. Along the way, Schamber developed a technique she calls "Piec-liqué," combining piecing

and appliqué, which Schamber claims "allows people to sew curved seams with incredible accuracy." She also teaches classes in using longarm sewing machines and made history in 2005, when her quilt *Scarlet Serenade* was the first one quilted on a longarm to win the top prize at the Houston International Quilt Festival. Schamber's website is www.sharonschamber.com.

KAREN STONE
FOUNDATION PIECING FOR PRECISION

KAREN STONE'S QUILTS HAVE BEEN SEEN ON MANY magazine covers and calendars, chosen for their bright colors and complex piecing. She favors such difficult traditional patterns as New York Beauty, but she often updates these classics. This Texas-based quilter produced an unusual book, *Karen K. Stone Quilts*, that traces her development and methods as a quilter, while also providing patterns for some of her most popular quilts. The book was published by Electric Quilt, a maker of quilt software, which sells a companion CD-ROM that allows quilters to make templates for the quilts or adapt them. Stone says her favorite classes to teach are "technique classes with lots of color work, based on ideas present in quilts I've made."

MARY STORI
BEADING FOR QUILTERS

A FORMER COOKING INSTRUCTOR, MARY STORI IS arguably the best-known teacher of beading and embellishment techniques for quilts and garments. She teaches quilters how to attach "beads, charms, buttons, trinkets, and unusual objects" onto their projects. She provides tips and tricks about good design as well as practical considerations for this fine handwork, such as how to keep heavy beads from sagging off the cloth. Her book *Beading Basics: 30 Embellishing Techniques for Quilters* is quite popular. For information on classes, go to www.marystori.com.

RESOURCES

Quilt TV

If somebody finds a way to make quilting as competitive and compelling as NASCAR races or poker, there'll be lots more on television. Isn't someone inventing a quilt version of the hit reality show *Project Runway*, featuring quiltmakers not dress designers?

Most quilt programs are rather methodical, step-by-step demonstrations of techniques. Still, quilting shows have been on television for decades, mostly on cable and PBS, and they aren't likely to disappear, given the niche-happy world of broadcasting.

Here are four of the most successful shows, now that HGTV has stopped broadcasting new episodes of *Simply Quilts*. Each of these are produced by the teachers who host them: Three are exclusively about quilts and quilters. All are broadcast by public television stations.

Quilt in a Day

Hosted by the media mogul of quilting, Eleanor Burns (profiled on page 319), this homespun show features Burns demonstrating her quick techniques for making traditional quilts. The show is taped at Burns' production studio in her California headquarters.

For more information, go to **www.quiltinaday.com**.

Love of Quilting

Marianne Fons and Liz Porter jointly host a show taped near where they live in Winterset, Iowa. Called *Sew Many Quilts with Fons and Porter* when it began in 1995, the show features the pair interviewing many of America's top quilters and quilt teachers. Fons and Porter are the authors of several popular books, including *Quilter's Complete Guide* (Oxmoor House; $22.95), and publish a popular quilt magazine, *Fons and Porter's Love of Quilting*.

For more information, go to **www.fonsandporter.com**.

Kaye's Quilting Friends

Kaye Wood is another quilt teacher with a long track record, having written twenty books and taught many classes. Her show covers a wide range of techniques, including how to make quilted clothing and purses.

For more information, go to **www.kayewood.com** and click on Kaye's TV Show.

Sewing with Nancy

Nancy Zieman, who sells notions from her website, Nancy's Notions, and lives in Beaver Dam, Wisconsin, hosts this half-hour sewing show, which frequently has episodes on quilting topics and techniques. *Sewing with Nancy* has aired on PBS since 1982.

For more information, go **to www.nancysnotions.com** and click on sewing with nancy.

QNNtv

One other important resource for viewers is QNNtv, which describes itself as "quilting television on the Internet." QNNtv, which began in 2005 as Quilters News Network, is a sort of hybrid: The web-based channel runs a number of quilting shows that also air on PBS, including episodes of *Quilt in a Day*, *Love of Quilting*, and *Sewing with Nancy*. To keep running 24-7, QNNtv also produces its own programming, segments that vary in length from three to thirty minutes. There are some free videos, but in the fall of 2007 QNNtv switched to a paid membership model. Access to the full content requires an annual member fee.

For more information go to **www.qnntv.com**.

GABRIELLE SWAIN
HAND APPLIQUÉ FROM A MASTER

A self-described former theater rat, Gabrielle Swain creates graphically sharp leaf quilts that could also be called dramatic. The Texan has won many top prizes in national quilt shows and is a popular teacher at such major venues as Quilting by the Lake. Hand appliqué is her preferred style and one of her most popular courses, but Swain also lectures on Designing from Nature and The Creative Spirit. At her website, www.handapplique.com, you'll find DVDs of several of her master classes.

JOEN WOLFROM
COLOR AND CURVES

Many quilters say the lessons they learned from Joen Wolfrom on color radically improved their quilts. Her fifth book, *Color Play: Easy Steps to Imaginative Color in Quilts*, is a classic: In her workshop of the same name, students "play" with colors both in paint and fabrics. One of a number of celebrity teachers who lives on Puget Sound in the Northwest, Wolfrom offers many other classes, including several on piecing curves, landscape quilts, and how to draw and adapt traditional patterns to any desired size. Wolfrom's own work and her classes focus on machine techniques. Her website is www.mplx.com/joenwolfrom/.

Northern Lights, *by Joen Wolfrom.*

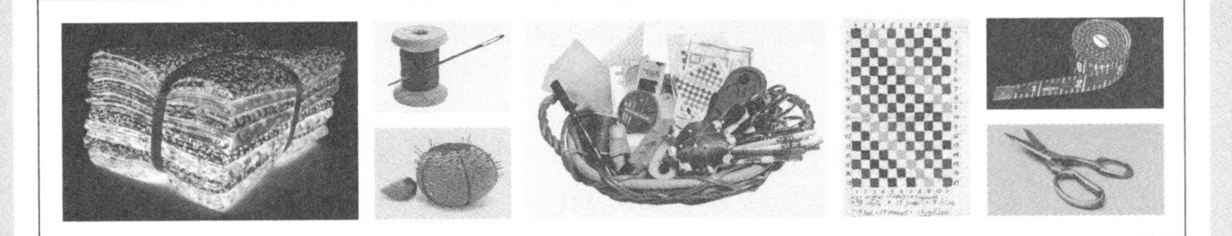

CHAPTER SIX

For the Beginner

QUILTING IS A FORGIVING CRAFT. GRATIFICATION IS nearly instant and the basics are easy to learn. The quilt boom is no nostalgia fad. The quilt renaissance isn't about emulating our foremothers in tedious manual labor. You won't see me signing up for a PBS reality show where you sit around the old quilting frame when not churning butter and plowing fields. The point is to use high-tech tools and tricks that allow us to make cooler quilts far more quickly than earlier generations could even imagine.

You can make a simple quilt in a day or a weekend. But the process is so satisfying, you may prefer to stretch it out and take your sweet time. Don't worry about whether you already know how to sew or whether you own a sewing machine. Anybody can sew; everybody can quilt. Honestly. If you have ever tacked up a falling hem or replaced a single button, you can make a quilt.

Making a small quilt by hand is a great way to begin. That's what I did—it's the quilting equivalent of the first scarf knit by a novice knitter, and not much harder. One option for the beginner is to purchase a quilt kit in which the fabric for the project has been precut. But then you'd miss what's possibly the most fun step in quilting: choosing the fabric.

If you've got a sewing machine and know how to use it, that's great. But rest assured, you don't need a $1,000 machine to make quilts. In fact, you don't need a sewing machine of any kind to make the majority of the projects in this book. For most of them, you'll find instructions for both handwork and machine work versions. Even though I've had a lot of experience using a sewing machine and own a fairly high-end model designed for quilters, I prefer to piece and quilt mostly by hand, so I've insisted on giving you the choice.

Of the dozen projects in this book, seven were created by some of the top quilt teachers in the United States, but most of these are not terribly hard. They're labeled according to the level of difficulty, so if you're a novice, you can make an appropriate choice. One of the major causes of beginner burnout among quilters is choosing a pattern that's the hiking equivalent of scaling Mount Everest, like a Double Wedding Ring quilt. If you follow the guidelines in the how-to and project sections, sewing your first quilt will be a lot more like the proverbial stroll in the park.

Hand quilting on a Double Wedding Ring quilt.

You could choose one of the five projects for beginners that I designed. The three quilts, tote bag, and purse are quite simple but lovely, allowing you to play with pretty fabric, hone some core quilting skills, and complete a truly memorable gift in a short time (if you can bear to give it away). You'll find all of the quilt projects beginning on page 438.

Getting Help

Beginners often need some hand-holding as they make their first few quilts. You'll always be welcomed back at the quilt shop for follow-up tutorials and tips, but there are other good resources for novices as well.

It's never too early to join a quilt guild. You may be thinking, "But why would they want me? I don't know anything yet." That's precisely the point. Joining a guild before you finish your first quilt isn't just considered acceptable, it's considered smart.

Guilds welcome people with a very wide range of expertise, including plenty of beginners and some amazingly advanced veterans. Indeed, some guild members don't quilt at all personally but love to be around quilts and quilters. At meetings, which are usually monthly, your fellow guild members can provide tips and tricks, alert you to big sales at local fabric shops, and tell you about upcoming shows in the area. If you strike up friendships, you'll have people to phone or e-mail between meetings when you need a little help.

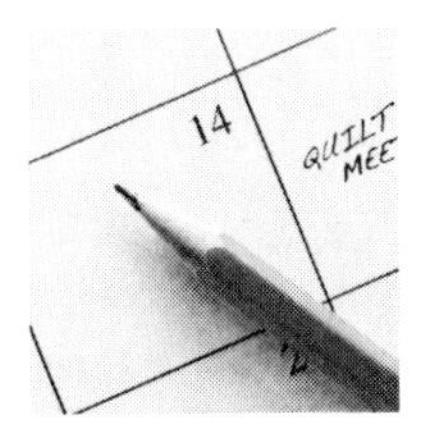

Joining a guild right away is guaranteed to smooth out and speed up your learning curve. If I hadn't had my mother to call up every time I got stumped, I probably would have joined a guild years sooner and would have gotten better quicker—my mother lived hundreds of miles away and I only saw her a few times a year.

The two easiest ways to scout for guilds are to ask the local quilt shop for information or check on the Internet. One good site is **www.quiltguilds.com**. You just click on your state and then search for the listings for the city nearest you. You'll find the name of the group, where and when they meet, and how to contact them. (For more on guilds, see pages 77–80.)

Surf the Web. The sisterhood of quilters occupies a vast amount of real estate on the Internet. You can download free patterns, shop for exotic fabrics, even take online classes. Most important, you can easily find free ad vice on whatever has you stumped, night or day. (One day, just for the heck of it, I Googled the phrase "How to make a quilt binding" and there were 582,000 listings!) There are any number of message boards and e-mail groups where more experienced quilters are happy to answer questions and share hard-won wisdom.

You'll find lots of detailed information on specific Web services throughout this book, but for starting out, here are two websites that are especially rich in resources for beginners: **www.quilt.com**, which is also known as the World Wide Quilting Page, and **www.planetpatchwork.com/beginners.htm** (aka Planet Patchwork). On both sites, if you scroll down the home page to click on the references to beginners or basic how-to's, you'll see lots of links, resources, and step-by-step directions.

The vibrant interior of Deer Country Quilts in Seeley Lake, Montana.

Get Thee to a Fabric Shop!

FOR ABSOLUTE BEGINNERS, MY ADVICE IS SIMPLE. As soon as possible, go to the quilt shop nearest you. If you don't know where it is, check the Yellow Pages. Once you walk in the door, prepare to fall in love. Walk all the way around the shop, looking closely at any bolt of fabric that catches your eye. This may take some time, as the average fabric shop has hundreds of bolts. Be sure to touch the fabric!

Note the selection of patterns and books and the tools and accessories as well. Have a good look at any completed quilts that are hanging on the walls to advertise upcoming classes or kits for sale (as if you haven't been sneaking peeks at them already). Do any of the quilts cause your breathing to quicken? Start picturing in your mind which of the gorgeous fabrics might look good in that pattern.

Walk up to one of the quilt shop staffers and introduce yourself as a novice. Chances are excellent that she (or, occasionally, he) will do everything in her power to help you. She will tell you when the shop has its next class for beginners. It may have separate introductory classes for handmade and machine-made quilts.

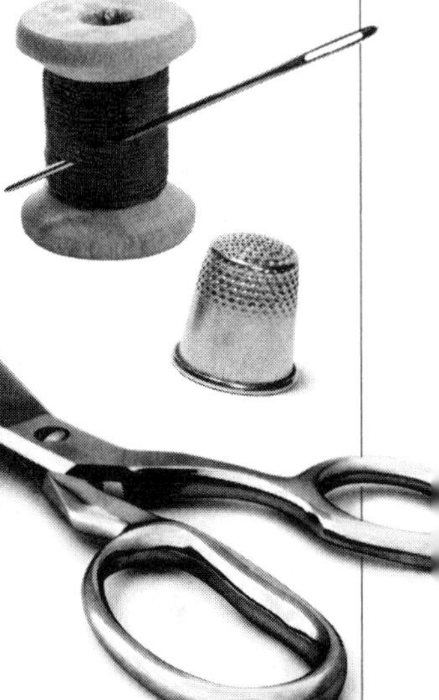

If your schedule is just too hectic for a regular class, ask which books for beginners the quilt shop sells and recommends. (You can also check the resources section on page 563 for some excellent beginner books.) And you can start quilting with the book you're holding now, which includes basic how-to directions (see page 416), along with many beginner-friendly projects. More experienced quilters will turn directly to the directions for the individual projects, but if you are a beginner, start by reading this step-by-step guide.

Once you've figured out the design for your first quilt, ask the clerk in the shop to help you choose all the fabric and tools you need to get started, including thread, scissors, and needles. There is lots of basic advice for beginners on these tools in the pages ahead.

So now, you've got no more excuses! After buying your fabric and tools, go straight home and start your quilt.

Buying Fabric

LET ME START BY SAYING THAT THERE ARE NO hard rules about buying fabric and no single method of building a fabric stash. I personally didn't start collecting fabric for years because my first few quilts were made completely from my mother's scraps and I had a tiny apartment with a single closet at the time. Boy, was I missing out.

Now, I tend to indulge my fabric lust on a regular basis. I'm not one of those women whose weakness is shoes, or handbags, or clothes. Fabric is my addiction, and just touching and buying it is a high. That may sound weird, but I know that as a fabriholic, I have lots of company. (If you doubt me, go to the website www.quiltaholics.com, and click on Confessions.)

So this book and this chapter should probably come with a caveat something like this: WARNING! The purchase of quilt fabric is potentially highly addictive. Do not begin quilting without being aware that possible side effects include a depletion of your bank account and diminished interest in all activities other than quilting and buying quilting supplies. Now you know.

Like many quilters, I feel it is always a good time to buy fabric. I like to buy it for now—and for later. I love to come up with projects that use up fabrics in my stash, like an all black and white quilt. But no matter how vast my stash, when I start cutting and sewing, I discover there are gaps, and I usually end up buying a few filler or border fabrics to complete the design. There are some projects for which I've been collecting fabrics for years: I've almost got enough flannels to make a Log Cabin quilt for relatives who live in New Hampshire.

It's also very satisfying to buy all the fabrics for a new quilt in one visit to the quilt shop. I walk out of the store feeling that I've already accomplished something, when I haven't even taken the first stitch.

Nothing beats cruising the shows and shops for fabric that sings to me. Sometimes it's a delicate period pattern with horizontal designs that would make great borders, so I'll buy two or three yards. More often, if I find a fun novelty print with lizards (for my reptile-loving son) or some other appealing motif, I'll buy just one yard.

I had no idea how I would use the Mary Engelbreit fabric with children reading books and the word *read* in big block letters, but it was perfect later for a quilt I made for my son's fifth-grade class. The colors and print of that single yard of fabric dictated the whole design of the school quilt (see the quilt on page 9).

Here is some very general advice to get you started buying and collecting fabrics. If you're not at all sure you'll continue quilting, buy fabric for just the first quilt you plan to make. But if you can already tell this is for you and want to start building a stash, I would make several general recommendations. When you begin, it's sort of like stocking a kitchen with such basic supplies as flour and salt and canned soup. You wouldn't buy just beans for your pantry, so don't buy only one color or type of fabric. Spread out your choices across all styles of fabric and throughout the color wheel. Pick up some sunny batiks, some cute reproduction prints with patterns from the thirties and forties, and some big, bold contemporary prints—whatever it strikes your fancy.

FABRIC MATH

Okay, so you decided to make a simple Log Cabin quilt and you've fallen in love with some contrasting colors, but you aren't sure how much of each fabric to buy.

If you're using a quilt pattern from a kit or a book, the recommended yardage will be listed, like the ingredients in a cooking recipe, near the beginning of the instructions.

If you've designed the quilt yourself, maybe using a block pattern that you saw in a book or on the Internet, ask the quilt shop clerks to help you. That's always my fallback option.

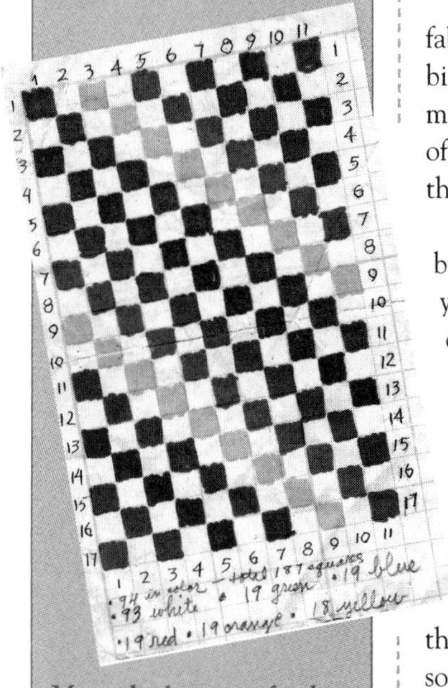

My mother's pattern for the first quilt I made.

Buy 100 percent cotton. Experienced quilters often choose to work in silk, wool, rayon, and other fabrics, but the best choice for beginners is pure cotton. Most shops that cater directly to quilters won't carry blends—fabrics that mix cotton with other fibers, such as polyester—but it's always a good idea to read the information on the end of the bolt and make sure it says 100 percent cotton. While flannel and chintz are cotton fabrics, they're more difficult to work with than plain cotton, so it's not a good idea to start out quilting with those.

Quarter yards and half yards build your stash. New quilters always want to know how much to buy when they are building up a collection of fabrics. Quarter-yard and half-yard cuts are very good for filling in the holes in your collection: Try to cover the color wheel basics. Also, these are good amounts for scrap quilts. However, if you find a fabric with a large pattern you think could dominate a quilt, or a wide-banded pattern that would be perfect for a border, you may want to buy two or even three yards.

A great way to build up your collection is by buying fat quarters, pieces of fabric that are approximately eighteen inches by twenty-two inches (picture a piece of fabric one half yard long that's been cut in half parallel to the selvages, resulting in two quarter-yard pieces—the fat quarters). Frequently, fat quarters are packaged by color in bundles of six or more pieces, which are even better for building a stash. Veteran quilters love to shop fat quarter sales to fill in colors that they generally neglect: I'm always looking to add some brown, orange, and tan, colors that add balance to a quilt but don't bring me joy in themselves.

Fat quarters.

You shouldn't worry about your gaps yet, but get a variety of fabrics you like. (For lots more about how fabric is made and great places to buy it, see Fabulous Fabric and Where to Find It, pages 229–90.)

I often design very simple gift quilts that involve square blocks framed by strips of fabric to set them off. I make little drawings on quilting graph paper (which is broken up into quarter-inch squares), and I multiply the amount of fabric I need by the number of blocks to compute how much fabric to buy. Whether I use an existing pattern or my own, I always ask the savvy clerks at my local quilt shop how much they think I should buy of each fabric for a project. Often, I tack on a quarter yard to what they suggest. This gives me room to make mistakes, tinker with my design, or add to my stash for scrap quilts.

When you get more advanced, the quilt-design computer software on the market includes features to compute yardage. And there are hand-held electronic devices similar to calculators that do the fabric math while you're standing in the quilt store.

Just remember, this is called *patchwork* for a reason. Running out of a fabric you planned to use is a design opportunity, *not* a disaster. Making do is part of the creativity of quiltmaking.

How Big Is Your Quilt?

Just like everything else in quilting, deciding on the size of your project isn't always as simple as you expect. Of course, if you are making a wall hanging, the size is up to you. It can be influenced by everything from the wall space to the dictates of your design.

Bed quilts are trickier. It's true that mattresses come in fairly standard lengths and widths, but some are about ten inches thick and others are nearly twice that. Some quilts are designed to cover only the top of the bed, while others drop over the edges like comforters. You might want your quilt to come down just to where the box springs start, because you want to show off a pretty dust ruffle underneath, or you may want it longer. All of these are essentially decorating decisions, and they directly affect the dimensions of your quilt.

A special word about baby quilts: There is much more variety in crib mattress sizes than in those for adult beds, and it is inadvisable to completely cover a baby sleeping in a crib for fear that the infant will get trapped in the bedding. Baby quilts are often used outside of cribs anyway, so consider how you expect that quilt to be put to use. If it's meant primarily to be a floor throw—a safe, clean spot to set the baby down on—then you might want to make it bigger than a crib quilt, and you may choose to make it square.

Before you start cutting or sewing—even before you buy the fabric—calculate the dimensions of your finished quilt. For an adult's bed quilt, measure how many inches you want the quilt's border to reach down the sides of the bed, multiply that number times two (for both sides of the bed), and add that to the width of the mattress top. The length will be affected by how much you want to tuck in at the bottom of the bed and how high you want the quilt to reach at the top. Some people want the quilt to reach to the headboard and arrange their pillows on top of it. If you want to tuck the pillows under the quilt, it needs to be longer. Still can't figure it out? Simply measure a comforter or blanket that you use regularly that's got the dimensions you'd like to duplicate.

There are some good tables on the Internet to help you determine the size of a quilt. One put together by quilting expert Susan Druding can be found at **www.equilters.com/library/quilt_issues/quilt_sizes-bed_sizes.html**—it's worth typing all that in for the information she provides.

Many quilting books also provide measurement tables for quilts and can help you figure out things like border dimensions and how many triangles or squares you'll need to produce a certain size quilt. One of the most thorough books on quilt layouts and sizes is *The Art of Classic Quiltmaking* (C&T Publishing; $34.95), cowritten by Harriet Hargrave and Sharyn Craig, two top quilt teachers.

Standard American Bed Sizes

Crib	23 to 26 inches by 46 to 48 inches
Twin bed	39 inches by 75 inches
Double bed	54 inches by 75 inches
Queen-size bed	60 inches by 80 inches
King-size bed	78 inches by 80 inches

Mix solids and prints. Many beginners fall in love with print fabrics and ignore the solids. Both are important. Remember that from a distance, tiny prints will appear to be solid.

Stand back to audition fabric. Fabric might look great when it's five inches from your nose, but most people will see it in a quilt from across the room. So, stand back to see how the fabric appears from ten feet away. You're also getting an atypical view of fabric when you study the whole surface of a bolt laid flat. You will probably only see the fabric in small pieces in your finished quilt. To get a similar effect, stand the bolt of fabric up on one end so you look at just the edge, like the way you'd see the lengthwise spine of a book.

Tool Basket for Beginners

BEGINNER COOKS DON'T NEED MANY TOOLS AND neither do first-time quilters. When my mother taught me how to quilt, she put together a simple collection of tools in a pretty basket, and I wish I could give one to every beginning quilter. In the basket were:

- Two pairs of scissors—one large pair for cutting fabric and a small pair for cutting thread. Mine are made by Gingher, an excellent brand.
- Several spools of white and off-white cotton thread, also some light gray and some black.
- A pincushion full of pins. Make sure they are quilter's pins, which are slightly longer and thinner than regular ones.
- Several paper packets of needles for hand sewing and quilting.
- A white fabric-marking pencil; its marks show up well on dark fabric but come out in the wash. And a regular No. 2 pencil, which shows up on most lighter-colored fabrics.
- A thimble. I don't usually use one when piecing, but it's very helpful for quilting. Most people use a thimble on the index or the middle finger of their dominant hand (right for me), to push the needle down through all

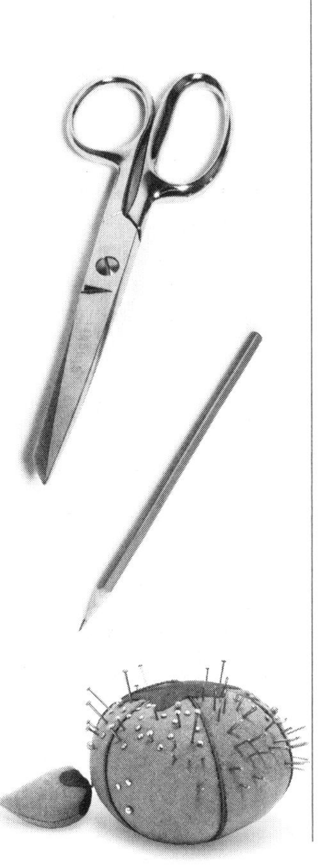

PIN PRIMER

Silk pins are the finest, the least apt to leave holes. Flower pins are flat and let you place a rotary cutter ruler on top of them. Beaded-head pins are easy to handle and pull out. Pick the pins that are best for your needs.

three layers. Start with a simple metal thimble from the quilt shop that fits securely. If you become an avid quilter, there will be plenty of time to buy customized, fancy ones (for more about these, see page 93).

Note: Although my mother didn't stick a seam ripper in my tool basket, many quilters find one indispensable. Whether you work by hand or machine and whether you're a beginner or a prizewinning master quilter, you will often need to cut out stitches that aren't where they should be. A basic acrylic quilter's ruler is also a good beginning purchase, especially one that measures six by twenty-four inches.

The only other thing in my basket was the fabric for the crib quilt I was making, which my mother had already cut out for me and arranged in little piles, one pile per row. And, for the first seven or eight years that I made quilts, those were pretty much all the tools I required, since I always worked by hand and never used a frame for quilting. Occasionally, I would buy thread of another color, although I use off-white most of the time. I would buy batting once the top was pieced together. But my needs were simple, my work was portable, and I still use that same basket.

If you already own a sewing machine, then feel free to use that for piecing. I wouldn't head out to buy a sewing machine unless you're sure you'll stick with quilting or plan to use it for other purposes, such as making clothes or home-decor items like curtains. And if you're going to try quilting by machine, please practice at the beginning on something other than your first quilt top! Just put batting between two layers of scrap fabric and practice sewing lines.

When it comes to stocking your beginner's tool basket, you'll find all these items at virtually any fabric store. If you go to the local quilt shop and feel overwhelmed by all the choices of thread, needles, scissors, and pins, simply ask someone on the staff to recommend good choices for a quilter starting out. And if it turns out that the quilting process brings you great joy, there will be plenty of time later to invest in fancy gizmos, and by then, you'll know which are the ones you'll use.

THREAD BASICS

Crazy as it sounds, thread is one of those basics that have gotten complicated since the quilt boom exploded. When I learned to sew, most thread was polyester and the only real choice you had to make was color. Not anymore. Now there is thread made of silk or rayon or nylon or cotton, not to mention polyester-wrapped cotton. Do you want domestic or imported thread? Plain or metallic? Two-ply or three-ply? Solid colors or variegated ones? How about some water-soluble thread?

Spools of metallic thread—tricky to use, but they produce striking results.

When you're a beginner, thread is something you take for granted. It's about as exciting as glue, just something to hold together the three layers of your quilt—which is fine, really. But once you get to a certain comfort level with the basics of quiltmaking, you will begin to view thread as another exciting design element. You can play with wild colors and different sheens and textures, and you'll come to appreciate why some expert quilters think of thread more as paint than glue. If you are a machine quilter, you can experiment with things like using one color for the bobbin thread and another for the needle thread, so your quilt will have different colors on the top and the bottom.

Should you become a quiltaholic, you can dabble in all the thread varieties. But if you're just starting out as a quilter, stick with the basics. One of the cardinal rules is to match the content of the thread to that of the fabric, using cotton thread for cotton fabric, silk thread with silk fabric, and so on. If you use a thread that is stronger than that in your fabric, over time the threads may weaken or wear through your fabric. Many man-made threads like polyester are stronger than natural fibers like cotton, so you wouldn't want to use polyester thread on a cotton quilt. Since most beginner quilters wisely stick with cotton fabric, choose cotton thread.

It's worth spending the few extra cents for good-quality thread. Quilt shops generally don't sell the lowest-quality thread, but if you are in a discount store, don't buy the cheapest.

NEEDLE THREADING TIPS

Whatever size needle you choose, the local quilt shop probably carries a version with a bigger than normal eye to make it easier to thread. If you are having trouble

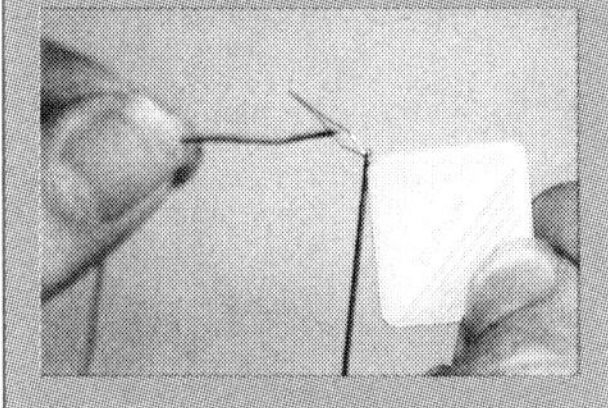

threading a needle, flip it and try entering the eye from the other side. Due to the manufacturing process, the eye of a needle is generally smoother on one side than the other. Or you can buy a needle threader, a small, inexpensive device that helps pull the thread through the eye.

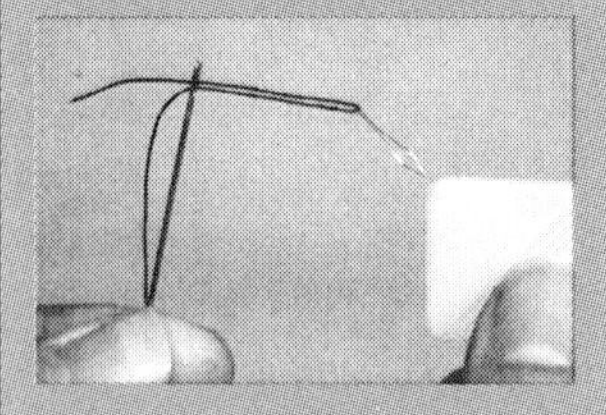

To thread a needle with a simple needle threader, insert the wire loop through the eye, then pass the thread through the loop. When you pull the loop out of the eye, the needle will be threaded.

Threads are numbered for thickness and weight, and it seems as if the numbering system runs backward: the lower the number, the thicker the thread. So a thread numbered 80 or 60 will be finer, less thick, than a thread numbered 50, 40, 30, and so forth. There is a second number on the label that refers to the number of strands of fiber twisted together to make that thread: 50/2 thread would be two-ply; 50/3 has three strands twisted together and is slightly stronger. A good medium-weight thread that can be used on cotton fabrics for both hand and machine quilting is the type marked 50/3. Finer threads, with a number higher than 50, are harder for a beginner to manage.

When you first shop for quilting thread, stock up on white and off-white. As you go along, you can buy colors to match the fabrics in a particular quilt. Remember that quilting in thread that matches the color of the fabric will make the stitches nearly invisible, while using contrasting colors in the quilting thread will make the stitches stand out.

NEEDLE BASICS

One of the smallest tools in quiltmaking is one of the most vital. Whether you piece and quilt by hand or by machine, needles matter. Quilt teacher Ami Simms has confessed that the first time she made a quilt she used a tapestry needle and struggled mightily to make the tiny stitches she wanted. No one had explained to her that the smaller the needle, generally, the smaller the stitches you can make. Tapestry needles are enormous, needle-wise, so you can see why she was fighting a losing battle.

Learn from her mistake: If you choose the right size and type of needle, the job will be easier. Machine and hand needles are classified by both type and size. Both hand and machine needles must be discarded when they get dull. The following guidelines will help you make smart choices.

Hand-Sewing Needles—Handwork needles come in packages that specify the size and use of the needles. The diameter of the needle is used to specify its size, which can range from 1 to 28. The bigger the number, the larger the diameter of the needle. Tapestry needles, some of the fattest, range from 13 to 28.

Thread 101

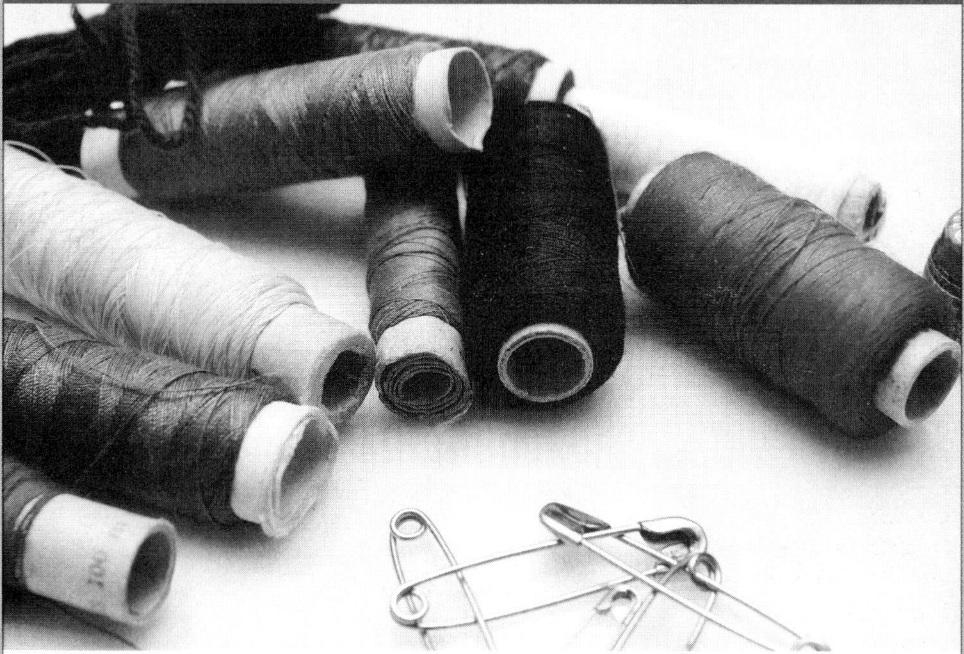

When beginning to quilt, it's best to buy all-cotton thread that's marked 50/3. Buy spools of white, off-white, charcoal, and gray. For piecing quilts, it's fine to use the same thread to piece together the entire quilt top. Don't switch colors for different patches. Choose a neutral color thread that is similar in darkness or lightness to most of the fabric.

Type of Thread	Description	Uses
Cotton	sturdy, not too stretchy	great for piecing and quilting
Metallic	comes in gold, silver, and shiny colors	creates shimmery effects in machine quilting, but you must adjust the tension and use the proper needle
Nylon	comes in clear or smoke colors; also called monofilament	popular with machine quilters because it is nearly invisible and so mistakes don't show
Rayon	colorful, shiny, and strong	good for machine embroidery
Variegated	has a color or tone that changes	creates fun visual effects for hand or machine quilting
Water soluble	dissolves in water	good for basting

REPLACING YOUR SEWING MACHINE NEEDLE

Some experts say a good rule of thumb is to replace your needle after every ten hours of use, but others such as machine-quilting maven Harriet Hargrave say simply put in a new needle every time you begin a new project.

For hand piecing and hand quilting, you want to use the shorter, skinnier needles called sharps and betweens, which range in size from roughly 4 to 12. Both are made of fine wire, so they are strong and flexible. Sharps are all-purpose sewing needles for piecing quilt tops and for appliqué work.

When hand quilting you want to use betweens, which are stubbier than sharps and are often labeled quilting needles. For novices, they will seem awkwardly small, like doll-size needles, but you do get used to using them. Experts prefer a size 10 or 11 between, but a good size for a beginner is 8 or 9, a slightly longer needle.

As you learn new skills to embellish your quilts, such as fancy embroidery stitches and beading, you'll need other types of needles. They'll be labeled as to their use, so they will be easy to identify.

Because even the best sewing needles on the market don't cost much, it makes sense to buy top quality. Some big-name quilters recommend needles made by the British manufacturer John James. You can purchase a package of thirty John James needles in an assortment that includes betweens, sharps, and big tapestry needles for less than $3.

Sewing Machine Needles—The needle is one of the least expensive parts of your sewing machine and arguably the most important. The wrong needle may result in problems like thread breakage and skipped stitches.

Sewing machine needles are made of steel wire, which comes to a sort of rounded ball point, so as to make as small a hole in the fabric as possible. Sizes are determined by measuring the width of the needle blade. There are usually two numbers on machine needles: the first is the European size and the second is the American size. When piecing and quilting cotton fabric, a common choice is 75/11.

For basic piecing and quilting, you can probably just use the standard needle that comes on your machine, but make sure it is sharp. If you get more deeply involved in quilting, you will find there are nuances in needles, just like everything else. You can buy special needles for use on flannel and denim and for doing embroidery stitches.

In their excellent primer *The Art of Classic Quiltmaking*, respected teachers Harriet Hargrave and Sharyn Craig recommend using a Schmetz brand needle, known for its consistently high quality. Most makes of sewing machines will take a Schmetz needle, except for Singers.

Keep a good supply of machine needles handy. Prizewinning machine quilter Diane Gaudynski says she has used up to two full packages of needles to complete a project with elaborate stitching.

Four Secrets to Success

HUNDREDS OF EXPERIENCED QUILTERS FILLED out a questionnaire I circulated when I started writing this book. They described their personal quilt histories—I wanted to know how they began quilting and why they loved it so much. But I also asked them to list the best quilting advice they ever got. I found that a few answers cropped up over and over and were the same principles that helped lift the quality of my own quilting. So here is the very best advice for beginners: Heed these four directives and your work will improve radically.

Just remember the fifth great piece of advice; it also came up often, attributed to a variety of wise teachers: "If a person galloping by your quilt on horseback can't spot the mistakes, they're not significant."

One more tip: If you've started a project and have come to hate the design, yes, you can toss it out and start over. There are always bumps on a learning curve, but never forget, quilting is supposed to be fun!

Measure twice, cut once. This is true whether you're using templates and drawing around them, or manipulating a ruler and rotary cutter to cut fabric. Once you cut into a piece of fabric, you can't undo that action and, if you messed up, you might not have enough fabric to carry out your planned design. Although it seems that measuring twice will slow you down, I guarantee that if you follow this simple rule, you'll save yourself time, money, fabric, and frustration.

Using Templates

Templates are actual-size patterns for the individual fabric pieces in a quilt. Typically templates are made of thin, flexible clear plastic, called quilter's template plastic. Sometimes this is crisscrossed with quarter-inch lines. When you cut out the fabric for a quilt, you place the template on the wrong side of the fabric (where the design and color are fainter) and draw carefully around the plastic with a pencil. After you draw an entire row of squares, triangles, or whatever the shape may be, you cut the fabric.

Typically in quilt books and magazines you'll find diagrams of the templates needed to make a quilt top. Sometimes the diagrams will be scaled-down versions of the actual size, but often they will be true to scale. In that case, you can place a piece of see-through template plastic right on top of the diagram. Using a ruler, carefully trace the shape, and cut it out to create the template.

You'll need to pay attention to whether the diagrams for the pattern pieces are drawn with a single or double line. If there are two lines, the inner one will be the seam or sewing line, typically one quarter of an inch inside the cutting line. Understand that if you want to make a quilt that will have three-inch squares when it's completed, you need to cut fabric pieces that are three and a half inches square. When you factor in a quarter inch for the seam allowance at both the top and bottom of each square, that adds a half inch in length. And, when you do the same for the sides, it adds a half inch in width.

This is true no matter what the size of the square: If you are making a quilt with ten-inch squares, you still need to add a half inch to the length and width, so the template must measure ten and a half inches by ten and a half inches. Whatever the pattern shape: triangles, hexagons, rectangles—or what have you—you have to figure in the seam allowance when you cut fabric pieces so they turn out the correct size when pieced. The instructions for the projects in this book give you dimensions for pattern pieces that include the seam allowance.

When creating templates and cutting fabric consider whether you will piece the quilt top by hand or by machine. If you

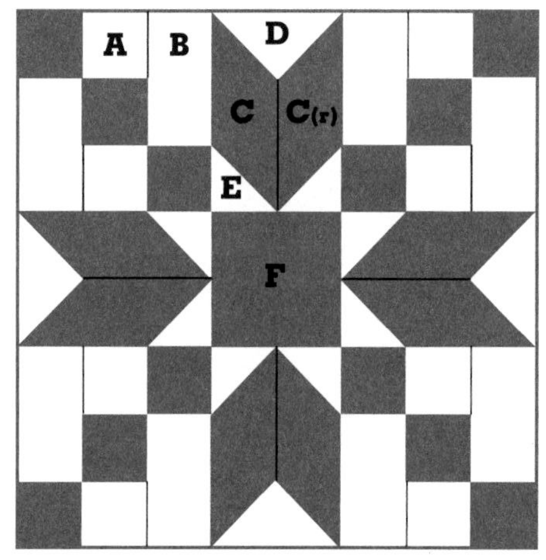

Good Cheer block

Cut out a plastic template for each of the different shaped pieces of fabric in the block you want to sew—precision counts! The illustration on the bottom of the opposite page shows one way you might arrange the templates along the straight grain of the fabric.

are machine piecing, you don't need to mark the sewing line: You line up the fabric under the needle to sew one quarter inch from the raw edge, using the marks on the sewing machine to guide you. When you sew by hand you are still sewing one quarter inch from the edge, but in order to stitch a straight line, you need to have a pencil line to follow.

Hand piecers have a second template option, a trick my mother taught me that makes it unnecessary to draw both the cutting and sewing lines. You make a template that is the size of the fabric piece in the finished quilt. For a quilt with three-inch squares, your template will be three inches square. Draw carefully around the template on the wrong side of the fabric, and that mark becomes the sewing line, *not* the cutting line.

Then, you must remember *not* to cut on the pencil line! Make a visual estimate and cut about a quarter inch outside the pencil line, all the way around the shape. It doesn't have to be exact because the sewing line *is* exact, but you don't want it to be too wildly off. Too skinny a seam allowance and your quilt might unravel in the wash; too fat and it won't press smooth.

This method works well, but you have to be careful and consistent. How can you remember whether your template shows the sewing line or the cutting line? My advice is to write the dimensions right on the plastic. I switch back and forth between hand and machine work, and I can't tell you how many times I've made the mistake of cutting the wrong dimensions. Then, I try to put my quilt top together and find it doesn't fit! If it seems too confusing, always make templates that include the seam allowance. You can pencil in the sewing line if you piece by hand.

Sometimes precut templates are available: You can buy a whole set of different-size stars, triangles, or squares. But, the plastic templates you make yourself are equally sturdy. Mine last for years and I've used them for multiple quilt projects. I keep all the templates for one project together in a large plastic baggy with a label.

As for rotary cutters, while there are some extrathick template materials on the market for use with these, in general, quilters who use rotary cutters rely on their rulers when cutting the shapes they need instead of using templates.

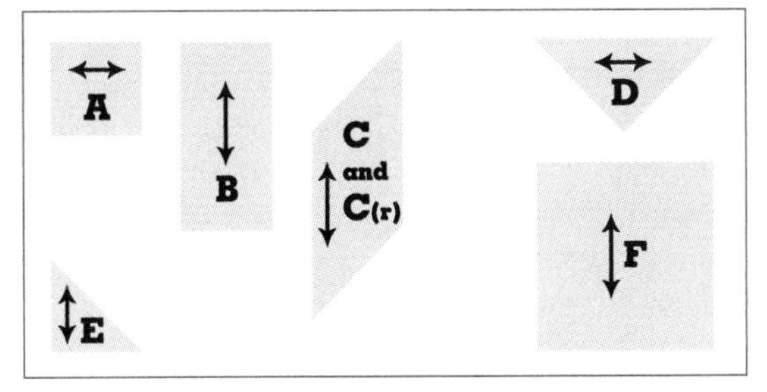

Templates for a Good Cheer block.

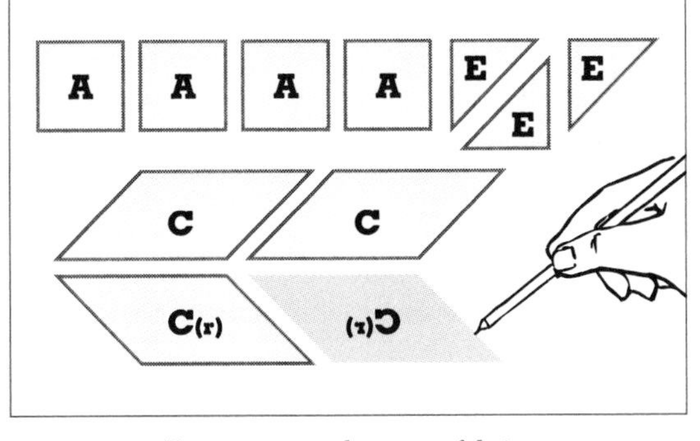

Tracing a template onto fabric.

MARKING FABRIC

The simplest way to mark your quilt fabric is with a plain old No. 2 pencil. If the fabric is dark and regular pencil marks won't show, use a white or silver marking pencil. These are sold at craft shops and quilt stores. There are other marking tools on the market, including soapstone and tailor's chalk. Some stores carry "disappearing ink" markers for quilting that supposedly wash out, but the experts caution that these don't always work as advertised.

It's one thing to trace around a template on the wrong side of your fabric, where no one will see it. Greater caution must be exercised when marking a quilt top for the actual quilting process. Sometimes you don't need to mark your quilt top, because you're quilting right next to the seam lines or echo quilting—quilting around features in the pattern, such as a flower shape. Machine-quilters may opt to do what's called stippling or meander quilting, where you just sew random wavy lines, like doodling with a pencil on paper. (You'll find examples of this on page 430.)

Mind the grain when cutting. The grains of a piece of fabric are determined by the direction of the strands of yarn (yes, yarn, but much thinner than that used to knit) that are woven to make it. The lengthwise grain runs parallel to the selvages, the extrathick edges along the length of the fabric (these edges are woven tight at the factory so they won't fray before the fabric is sold). The crosswise grain runs perpendicular to the selvage.

The reason you need to pay attention to the grain is that fabric is stretchier depending on its orientation, and you don't want to cut pieces of fabric at an angle that will make them stretchy and unruly. The next time you have a piece of fabric cut off a bolt, give it a tug; you'll notice that it gives more if you pull on it crosswise than if you pull on it lengthwise, and that it's as elastic as Silly Putty if you tug it on the diagonal (called the bias).

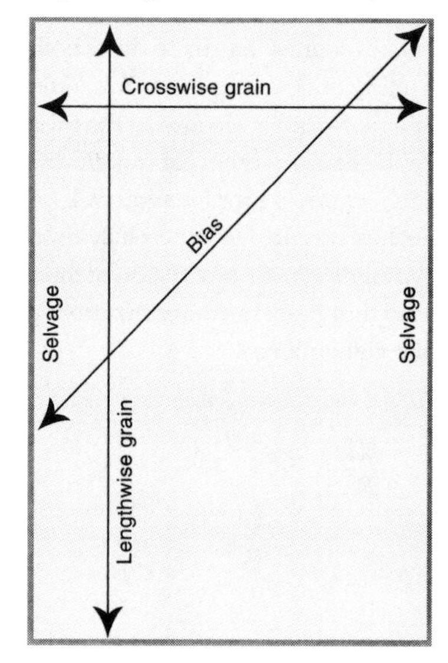

This diagram clearly shows the grain lines of a piece of fabric. Cutting parallel to the grain, rather than at an angle, will make your fabric pieces fit together more cleanly.

Whether you use templates to cut your fabric pieces or use a rotary cutter and ruler, the straighter you make your cuts, the less distortion you'll have. Most patterns and commercial templates come with a line that shows where to cut to take advantage of the grain to avoid distortion. But, don't include any of the selvages in the pieces for your quilt; if you do, it can cause the quilt to pull and pucker.

Naturally, when you cut a triangle or diamond, it isn't possible to have all the edges in line with the grain. Occasionally, you're also going to do something called "fussy cutting" where you cut around a design or shape in the fabric and you may be cutting against the grain in places.

Be precise with your quarter-inch seams. Let's face it: Quilting is a great activity for those who are good at coloring inside the lines. Precision in every aspect vastly increases your chance of success, and that is nowhere more true than in producing a straight seam exactly one-quarter inch in from the edge of the fabric. If you cut your pieces exactly and then sew precise seams, your quilt will fit together as neatly as a Lego project.

The seam allowance is especially important when you piece by machine, because the sewing line or seam line is not marked on the fabric. Instead, you position the fabric under the needle exactly one quarter inch from the edge, using the marks on the machine to guide you. Many quilters use a special quarter-inch foot on their machine, which makes it easy to stay on the quarter-inch line as you sew, but you must be diligent about checking it.

Generally, when you do your piecing by hand, you'll want to mark the quarter-inch sewing line right on the fabric. Expert hand quilters like Jinny Beyer say this measurement is so burned into their brains, they can get away with just "eyeballing" the fabric and start stitching, but this is *not* recommended for beginners.

Press every seam. I hate to iron clothes, but when I'm piecing a quilt top, I iron a lot. Pressing as you go gives your quilt a neater, flatter look and makes the pieces fit together better. This doesn't mean you have to jump up and iron every time you join two blocks. I like to take quilt projects on long car trips and may not get back to my ironing board for hours, even days. So after joining seams, I "finger press" them using my index finger. Then when I go to join a whole row, the seams are more or less where I want them.

There's a difference of opinion among quiltmakers as to whether the seam allowance should be pressed open down the middle, or pressed to one side or the other. Jinny Beyer says she never presses seams open but always to one side, and many top teachers are in her camp.

So, how do you know which side to press the seam allowance toward? The rule of thumb is that you press it toward the darker fabric, otherwise a dark line may be visible through the lighter fabric.

It's especially important to give your quilt top a good pressing before layering it with the batting and backing and starting to quilt.

Whether you are sewing by hand or machine, it's trickier if you want to quilt such elaborate patterns as fans and feathers, but your local quilt shop will have many tools to help you do this. You can buy see-through plastic stencils for quilt squares and borders; just trace along the precut slots.

Also, there are what are called tear-away materials that are preprinted with a design. You place the pattern right on top of your quilt, sew along the design lines, then gently rip away the papery sheet, leaving only the line of thread. These tear-away sheets also come unmarked so you can create your own design.

Or, you can be resourceful and just draw around items you've got at home: I've done lots of scallops by using the bottom of a spice jar as my template, and you can also draw around cookie cutters for any number of shapes.

Remember: It's fine to use pencil on your quilt top if you're planning to wash the quilt. If you're using materials that aren't washable, choose an option like tear-away sheets that won't leave a mark.

No Mistakes, Only Opportunities

Sooner or later, every quilter has that sinking feeling: Oh no, my quilt is *ruined!* It might be because of a rip in the pieced top, or a pet who used the quilt as a bed or, worse yet, a chew toy. But not to worry, there are few mistakes or accidents that can't be rectified, sometimes in ways that result in a more original and striking finished quilt. Quilters who have been there can provide hints and tips about possible ways to salvage a quilt. Here are some of the tried-and-true methods.

Use patches and embellishments. If a quilt is made from a big, busy pattern, sometimes it's possible to take leftover fabric and cut around the dominant shapes, like flowers for example, then appliqué them right on top of any small rips, stains, or other blemishes. You may want to do this in several places on the quilt, so it looks like an intentional design.

Pets figure in many quilt-disaster stories, including that of Cindy Sisler Simms. She had left a nearly finished quilt in an eighteen-inch circular hoop, with the back of the quilt facing up. While she slept, her cat decided to snuggle with the quilt and wound up shredding the backing fabric inside the hoop with his claws. "I wasn't going to lose all that work on my Mariner's Compass quilt," says Simms, "So, I went to the fabric store and searched for ready-made flower appliqués. I sewed one over each tear in the backing fabric." Simms says she always tells her students, "No matter how awful a mistake seems at the moment they make it, if they stop, put the quilt away,

and then come back to the problem, there is always a solution."

Robbin Neff was making a quilt that featured a blue heron against a background of sky and marsh grasses. Her project was nearly done when her scissors slipped while she was adding beads and other embellishments, leaving a small hole on the top of the quilt. To remedy the problem, Neff says she grabbed a skein of fluffy white yarn and decided to use that to make clouds in the sky, thus covering the hole. "The clouds add another dimension and technique to the quilt, which is better than my original plan," she says.

Some quilters add clever embellishments at the end not because a quilt is ruined, but because they want to distract attention from work that simply isn't their best. Kaffe Fassett once made a quilt for a book and decided that the chartreuse fabric he had chosen wasn't working in the color scheme. He considered tossing the quilt out of the book but instead densely embroidered petal shapes over the chartreuse, so what people notice is little sunflowers rather than the color. The quilt stayed in the book. (For more about Fassett, see page 331.)

Eithne Taaffe recalls the time she decided to make a little quilt for her nieces to take on family car trips. "I foolishly started too late in the evening, when I was tired after work. Of course, I proceeded to make a pig's breakfast of it," says Taaffe. "I made a mess of a simple pattern and the colors were flat and boring. I was going to chuck the quilt, when I decided to sew on a little quilted mitten I'd made to put on my Christmas tree. It looked fabulous, so I made a few more and sewed them to the most offending areas of the quilt and the whole thing sprang to life. It won't win any awards, but it has delighted my nieces: They love the mitten quilt."

Fabric paints cover a multitude of sins. There are wonderful fabric paints on the market now, and sometimes quilters are able to paint over disaster areas. That was the case for Linda Hall, who had forgotten to prewash some of the fabrics in a quilt. She finished a scrap quilt with fan shapes. The top row was in shades of red that bled onto a white background when she washed the quilt. Hall says she painted over the stains using white acrylic craft paint and adds, "The Quilt Police haven't caught me yet." (Hall also says that she might not have used paint for a bed quilt destined to be washed many times, but for a wall quilt she didn't expect to wash again, the paint was the perfect solution.)

Try cutting and reshaping. If you've already decided that all is lost, that the damage or design is beyond repair and you may as well throw the quilt in the garbage, then you've got nothing to lose and you may as well do something truly drastic.

Peg Keeney says there was a quilt she had been working on "forever" but it wasn't coming out the way she wanted. "So one afternoon, I simply cut the quilt apart and sewed it back together in a new configuration. I did a lot of thread-painting on the surface and voilà, a wondrous piece."

Another version of this is the road taken by Francie Gass of Bellingham, Washington, who turned one bad quilt into three good ones. She says she had embarked on a mystery quilt project, not knowing what the finished quilt would look like. "Along the way I realized my fabric choices weren't good for the design of this particular quilt. Rather than finish a 'bad' mystery quilt, about three quarters of the way along, I broke it up and made three smaller quilts that I really liked."

When all else fails: Have a sense of humor. Liza Prior Lucy, an accomplished Pennsylvania quilter who is one of the teachers profiled in this book (see page 331), wasn't too thrilled when a family member let his dog sleep on the lovely quilt she gave him. But it got worse when the dog took a bite out of the binding on the quilt's edge. Rather than trying to patch the jagged spot and attempt to make it disappear, Lucy decided to make it a focal point: She made the edge even more jagged but finished it so it wouldn't unravel. Next to the bitten area, she appliquéd a "nasty looking dog" cut from some printed fabric she found.

How to Care for Your Quilts

I WAS ALMOST TOO SCARED TO USE THE FIRST QUILT my mother gave me, because it came with a list of rules as long as my arm. (You can get a taste of them in the sidebar at left. While my mother's last rule may sound like a stealth abstinence program, I was thirty-five and divorced at the time.)

My mother *was* technically correct: Anything that pulls or crushes a quilt may break the threads that hold it together or damage the fabric. Happily, I ignored pretty much every one of her rules. Twenty years later, I still have the quilt and it's in fine shape, although it's not without wear.

Nonetheless, my mother's rules are good when it comes to heirloom and masterpiece quilts. If you are working on a quilt that you expect will win major prizes or hang in the Smithsonian, then you should pay close attention to those nine commandments.

Pay particular heed to the advice to limit washing. If you must wash your quilt, use cold water and very mild soap; set the washing machine on the gentle cycle. Line dry the quilt if possible.

And avoid plastic bags, whether or not your quilt is a work of art. Storing a quilt in plastic, where the fabric and thread can't breathe, will hasten its deterioration. Many people store their quilts on shelves in closets and refold them several times a year so they don't develop permanent creases. Other quiltmakers pile their masterpiece quilts up on a bed in a spare room, making sure a sheet or comforter tops off the pile to protect the quilts from sunlight and dust.

However, except for those masterpiece quilts, feel free to ignore the rest of my mother's advice. In my book, any quilt not destined for a museum is a utility quilt, and you and your loved ones should just love the stuffing out of it.

MEG'S MOTHER'S RULES FOR THE QUILT

Never sit on the quilt.

Never eat on the quilt.

Never put heavy objects on the quilt.

No children allowed near the quilt.

No dogs or cats on the quilt.

Keep the quilt out of bright sunshine.

Never put the quilt in a plastic bag.

Wash the quilt seldom, if ever.

Never, ever have sex on the quilt.

CHAPTER SEVEN

Putting It Together

Basic Quilt How-To's and Directions for Twelve Projects

IF YOU'RE NEW TO QUILTING, YOU'LL WANT TO READ THE how-to instructions here before beginning any of the twelve quilt projects that follow. The how-to instructions describe the basic techniques for cutting, sewing, and quilting. You'll read about ◆ How to prepare and cut fabric ◆ How to sew quilt blocks together ◆ How to prepare the quilt "sandwich" ◆ How to quilt a quilt ◆ How to bind and finish a quilt.

Once you've reviewed the how-to information, you'll be ready to start quilting. We went out of our way to make the directions for the projects in this chapter easy to follow. First you'll find instructions for five projects that are designed for total novices. Many of the seven projects contributed by prominent quilt teachers that appear afterward are also simple to make. They are ranked by level of difficulty on a scale of one to five.

Each quilt project is ranked as to its level of difficulty. Don't be intimidated if the instructions look complicated on first reading: Like cooking directions, they will make much more sense to you when you're actually following them. Do start out by reading all the way through the instructions for a given project, as you would before trying a recipe, then go back to the beginning and follow each step to make the quilt.

BASIC HOW-TO'S

This book isn't called The Quilter's Bible *because I don't believe there's only one way to do* any *of this. Here is some good general advice that has worked for me. There are many other methods—choose what works for you.*

First the Fabric

Fabrics—in all their infinite variety—are the foundation of a quilt.

YOU'LL AVOID MANY HASSLES IF YOU STICK TO THE lightweight 100 percent cotton fabric made for quilts, sometimes called quilter's cotton. This fabric is easy to sew and to handle, washes and irons well, and is usually colorfast. It's readily available in quilt stores. If the fabric in a shop isn't labeled as to content, ask a salesperson.

Quilt shops carry most of their fabric wrapped on bolts, and the material usually measures forty-four or forty-five inches wide. Customers carry the bolts they like to cutting counters, where employees will cut partial yards or multiple yards as instructed. Precut fabric is also displayed on shelves and in baskets, generally in the form of fat quarters. A conventional quarter yard measures approximately nine by forty-four inches, while a fat quarter is about eighteen by twenty-two inches, closer to a square in shape.

Quilters often buy what they need for a given project, and at the same time pick up yards or fat quarters of whatever else grabs their attention. Quilters like to build a "stash" of fabrics in lots of colors and patterns, so they'll have material on hand for scrap quilts or fabrics to inspire a future design. There's more about building a stash—and about fabric in general—in the chapter on fabric, which starts on page 229.

The quantities of fabric listed as needed for each of the projects in this book are meant to be plenty to complete the design as given. In many cases, you'll have a bit left over; save this for future scrap quilts. Anytime you use an existing quilt pattern in a book or from a website, the fabric requirements will be listed. Once you begin to create your own quilt designs, you'll learn to compute how much fabric you need, although I still usually ask the quilt shop ladies to check my math.

If you plan on washing your quilt project someday, you'll probably want to prewash the fabric so any shrinkage will occur before the quilt is made. (For more information on the pros and cons of prewashing fabric, see page 282.) Gently wash similarly colored fabrics together in the washing machine with mild soap or detergent. Avoid hot water. Tumble fabrics in the dryer, but take them out when they're still slightly damp. Press the fabric dry with an iron set on permanent press.

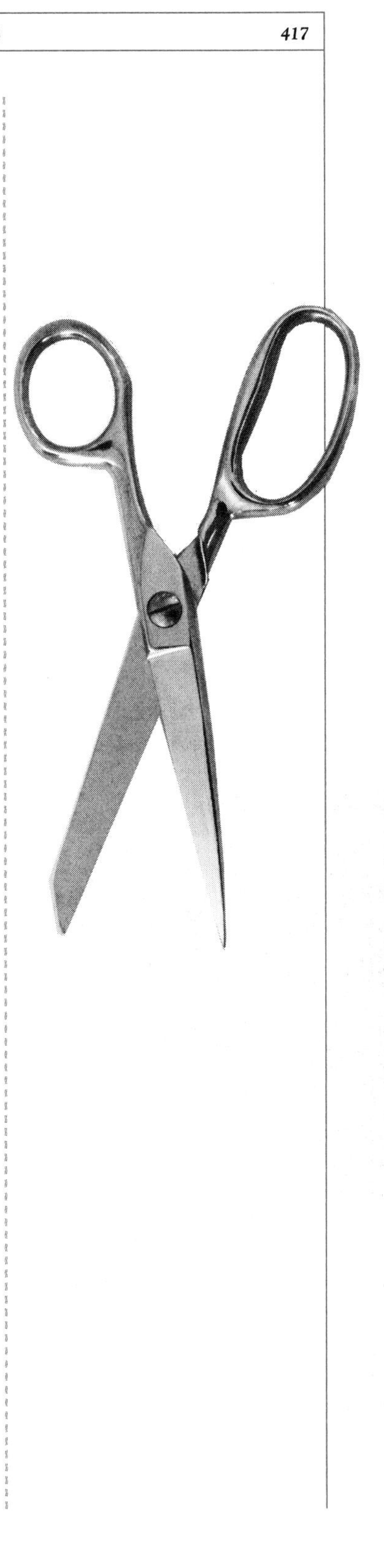

Fabric Cutting

CHOOSE YOUR WORKING METHODS. IN THE TOOL Basket for Beginners on page 401 you'll find a list of the basic tools essential for making quilts. But, you need to decide whether you want to cut the fabric with scissors or a rotary cutter. And, do you want to piece and quilt by hand or by machine? If you're planning on using a sewing machine, make sure it is in good working order. Consult the manual for cleaning instructions and get a tune-up from your local sewing machine shop if it's been more than a year since the last one. Install a sharp new sewing machine needle: 70 or 80 are good sizes for most of the projects in this book.

Remove the selvages when you are cutting out fabric pieces. Selvages are the thicker, more tightly woven edges that run lengthwise down both sides of the fabric. If you don't cut them off, they'll distort the quilt and they're difficult to sew through.

Basic How-To's for Rotary Cutting

Rotary cutting is an intrinsic part of quiltmaking today for many quilters. It speeds things up so that cutting hundreds of patches is no longer daunting. Plus, rotary cutting using rulers marked at one eighth–inch intervals adds precision to your work.

Rotary cutter blades are sharp—or should be. If you find you're not getting a good clean cut, replace the blade. And since the most important aspect of rotary cutting is safety, follow these tips.

- Be sure the lighting is good and stand over your cutting table, if possible.
- Keep the hand that holds the cutter away from the blade.
- Press your other hand, with the fingers splayed, firmly on the acrylic ruler; be sure it's away from the cutting edge.
- Keep the blade of the rotary cutter against the edge of the acrylic ruler.
- Cut away from your body.
- Cover the blade with the built-in blade guard after every cut.

When you are cutting multiple blocks, keep the fabrics folded lengthwise in half (so that the edges with the selvages are together). For accuracy, cut no more than two layers at a time. For speed, however, you may prefer to cut strips across the doubled width of fabric, then layer two doubled strips and cut square patches or other block shapes from four layers of fabric until you have enough. For an illustration of how to cut triangles using a rotary cutter, see page 159.

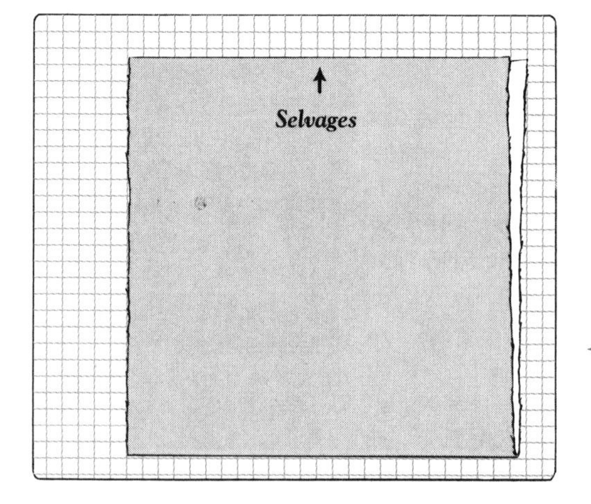

STEP 1

The first thing you want to do is square off the sides of the fabric. Fold the fabric in half with the selvage edges together. Arrange it on the cutting mat so that the fold is flush against a grid line near the bottom of the mat.

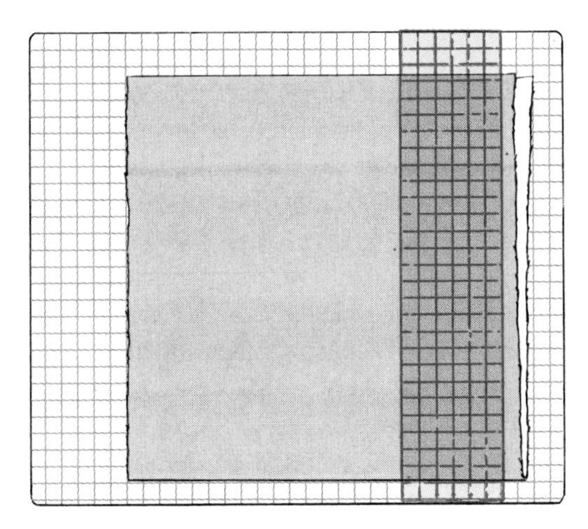

STEP 2

Place a 6 by 24–inch acrylic ruler along the right edge of the fabric, aligning it at a 90 degree angle to the fold.

STEP 3

Starting from the fold at the bottom, cut off the ragged edge. Press firmly on the rotary cutter. It's good to position your little finger off the ruler and on the fabric to keep a good grip. Note that all fingers are safely away from the cutting edge.

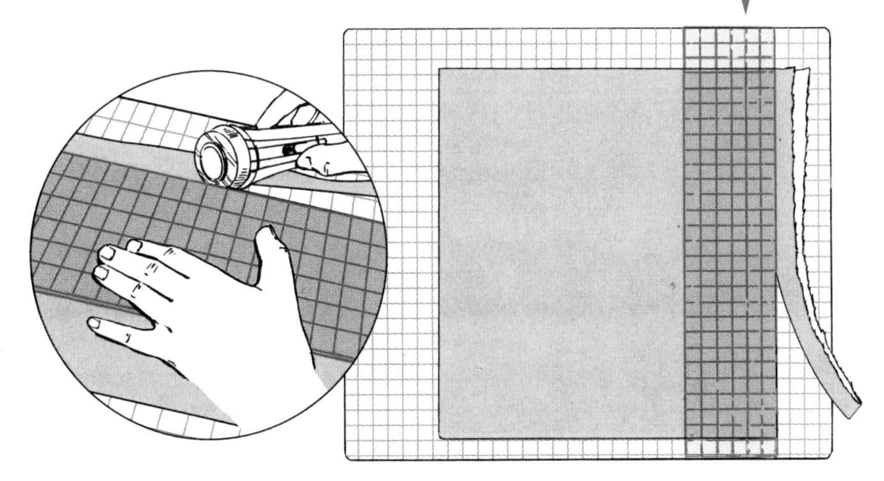

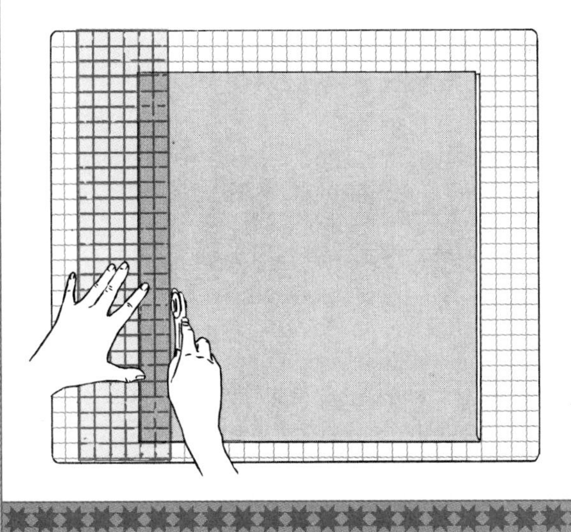

STEP 4

Once you have trimmed the ragged left edge the same way, use the grid lines on the mat and ruler as a guide to cut a strip of fabric to the width you need for the quilt pieces. Keeping the fabric lined up, you can make additional parallel cuts of the desired width.

If you are cutting the fabric with scissors, you will either need to measure with a ruler or you'll need to make templates from template plastic for the quilt pieces. Flip the fabric over so the back side is up and trace around a template using a No. 2 pencil or, if the fabric is dark, a white fabric-marking pencil. Before you begin tracing, look closely at the placement of the template on the fabric to make sure that the threads of the fabric run straight, not at an angle to the sides of your cut shape. You want to align the template with the crosswise or lengthwise grain of the fabric. One way to test this is to lift up the fabric under both sides of the template and pull on it: There will be much less give if you are pulling on the crosswise or lengthwise grain than on the bias. (For more about templates, see page 408.)

You need to decide whether you want to cut the fabric with scissors or a rotary cutter.

If you are planning to quilt by hand, you will need to take a ruler and mark a sewing line around the shape one quarter inch in from the edge of the fabric. (If you piece by machine, you'll use the machine's guidelines for seam width.)

If you are using a rotary cutter, you'll want one that has a sharp new blade. Unless otherwise indicated, the projects here can be made using a standard 45-millimeter blade. You'll also need an acrylic ruler six by twenty-four inches and a cutting mat—the larger the better: Twenty-four by thirty-six inches is best! You'll find step-by-step rotary cutting instructions on page 418.

Sewing the Quilt Top

WHETHER YOU SEW BY HAND OR MACHINE, THE basics of piecing a quilt top are the same. First, arrange the pieces of fabric you want to sew together so that they are right sides together, making sure the edges are even. Insert pins at the corners first, then pin at intervals in between, if needed to keep the fabric edges together. Now you are ready to sew the pieces together. Strive to consistently sew exactly one quarter inch from the edge.

If you are working by hand, the sewing line you've drawn on the wrong side of each of the quilt pieces will be your guide. Following that line, use a running stitch to sew the two pieces together: Gather up three or four small, even stitches on the needle each time before pulling the thread through the fabric.

If you are sewing on a machine, use a quarter-inch presser foot or a stitching guide adhered to the throat plate of the machine. Some people stick a piece of masking tape on the one quarter–inch line. It's best to practice sewing seams, measuring the seam allowance to be sure it is consistently exactly one quarter inch. Include the stitching line in the quarter inch—you can move the needle position one stop to the left or right to compensate if the seam allowances are a hair too narrow or too wide. Remove pins as the machine needle comes to them; machine needles sometimes break if they rub over a pin.

PRESSING

Pressing is important because it helps keep seams flat and makes everything fit together more neatly. But overly aggressive ironing can actually distort fabric and seams, making things wonky. Some people avoid using steam when pressing quilt seams, but the most important thing is to press with a light hand. Just touch the iron down lightly on the back of the seam, don't drag and whack like you're beating the fabric into submission. Be sure to press every stitched seam before sewing another one across it.

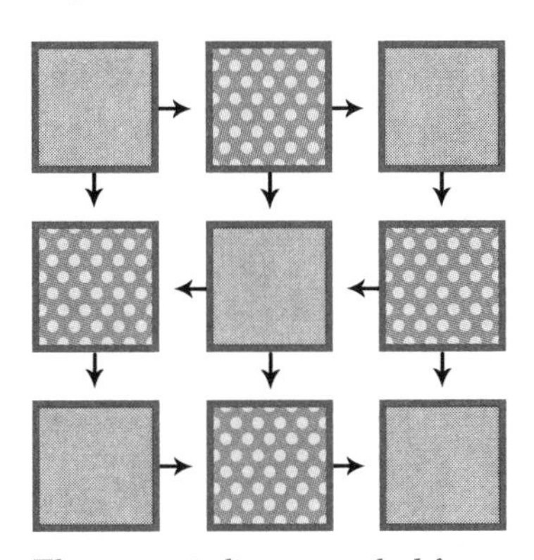

The arrows indicate a method for pressing seam allowances when the color of the fabric is not a factor.

In general, you want to press seam allowances toward the darker patches of fabric so the darker fabric does not show through the lighter. When the color of the fabric is not an issue, you want to press all of the seams in a single horizontal row of quilt pieces in the same direction, then press all of the seams in the row below in the opposite direction. That way you avoid having four thicknesses of fabric sewn together when the horizontal rows are joined.

PRESSING "TOOLS"

Here are the tools that you'll need to press your quilt tops flat while keeping your iron clean.

- A steam iron, preferably one that does not turn off automatically; while you will need to remember to turn the iron off when you're completely done, this lets you press seam allowances as you go without waiting for the iron to reheat.
- An ironing board or other surface that is protected by a cover.
- A pressing cloth—this is especially useful when fusing fabric and for protecting metallic threads. Teflon pressing sheets are good for this (for more about pressing cloths, see page 165).
- A dampened pressing cloth for ironing out stubborn creases.
- A tube of iron cleaner for those times when you do get some fusible web on the iron.
- Spray bottles or plant misters filled with water to spray on the fabric when you are steaming out wrinkles.

Design Wall 101

No matter how good your eye, it's hard to really know how the elements of a quilt will look together until you make it. But there is a very helpful shortcut that many quilters swear by that allows them to visually preview and edit a quilt design in progress. A design wall is a big open space on which you can stick your pieces of fabric together and experiment with different fabrics and shapes: How would the design work if you put the squares on

Liza Prior Lucy and Kaffe Fassett work out block placement on a design wall.

a point, like diamonds? How would this quilt look with a pink border instead of a yellow one?

Sometimes people affix flannel or other "nappy" fabric directly to an existing wall and then position quilt pieces on the flannel. But most quilters prefer to use a nonstructural wall, some flat surface they can move from the sewing room to the den or stick in the attic when it isn't needed.

You can buy commercially made design walls; many cost more than $100. A popular model, created by a quilter in Oregon, consists of a six by six–foot piece of white flannel stretched over slender fiberglass tent poles. Called Cheryl Ann's Design Wall, it's portable, weighing less than six pounds. Quilters can pack it up and take it to quilt classes. For details, go to **www.cherylannsdesignwall.com**.

But here is a simple, durable homemade design favored by the popular quilt teachers Liza Prior Lucy and Kaffe Fassett (profiled on page 331). Lucy says she has made several for her house and that they've lasted for more than a decade. She adds, "I have never seen one that works better." Simply go to the local do-it-yourself supply store or lumberyard and buy two sheets of insulation board (one brand is Homasote) that each measure four by eight feet. These boards are lightweight; they're usually covered with foil on one side and colored paper—pink or blue—on the other. Two sheets of this insulation board will make a design wall big enough to enable you to work on a queen-size quilt.

Glue good-quality cotton flannel, preferably a neutral color like taupe or light gray, to one side of each of the boards, then trim the edges. (Some people lap the flannel over the edges and use a staple gun to secure the fabric on the back of the boards.) Use duct tape to make hinges to hold the two boards together: Attach three hinges on the wrong side of the boards, making sure the hinges are loose enough to allow the boards to fold with the flannel sides together. Lucy says that if there is just a tiny bend at the hinges, the wall will be freestanding. When's she's having company and needs to whisk the wall out of sight, she places paper over her work, folds the boards together, and slides the design wall under a bed.

Preparing the Rest of the "Sandwich"

ONCE THE QUILT TOP IS PIECED, IT'S TIME TO assemble the other layers so that you can baste together the quilt sandwich in preparation for quilting. Both the backing and batting should be about three inches larger on all sides than the finished quilt top. This assures that you won't have gaps later in the filling or back that must be patched. When you're sending quilt tops out to be quilted by longarm finishers, they may need the back and batting to extend four inches or so beyond the quilt top, to enable them to be attached to the machine's rollers.

TIP

A bed-size quilt will require between three and nine yards of fabric for its backing, depending upon the width of the fabric, the dimensions of the quilt, and whether you are piecing the backing. You need to plan the back of the quilt as well as the front.

Four of the possible ways to piece fabric for a quilt backing.

BACKINGS

If you are making a large quilt, you will need to piece the backing: The fabric on bolts is usually forty-four or forty-five inches wide, but most quilts are wider. You can sometimes find superwide cotton (104 to 115 inches) for backing, but there is little choice of color and pattern. Before you piece the backing, make sure you remove the selvages. Beginners may want to stick with making a backing out of only one fabric, but more experienced quilters often get adventurous with their backings. This is a purely aesthetic decision, but some quilters avoid backs that pair a wide chunk of fabric with a thin add-on strip: They try to even out the size of the attached pieces (see the illustration above for some suggestions). One possibility: a patchwork backing that combines big squares of fabric that is left over from your quilt top.

Machine Appliqué

The French word *appliqué* means applied, and it involves cutting out shapes in fabric and then sewing them on top of a background material. Many quilts combine appliqué and piecing techniques, with individual blocks being pieced together after each is embellished with appliqué shapes. Hand appliqué is still widely practiced, but machine appliqué is especially popular: You'll find instructions for it here because it's used in the quilt projects of Sue Nickels (on page 490) and Libby Lehman (on page 498).

All of the appliqué projects in this book can be done by raw edge, machine appliqué. Fusible web, a nonwoven fiber with a paper backing, is a webbing of adhesive that melts with the heat of an iron and enables fabrics, or fabrics and batting, to bond together. There are a variety of fusible products, but you'll want a lightweight fusible web, such as Wonder-Under, which is made by Pellon (you'll find more about fusibles on pages 163–67). You'll need to protect your ironing surface, your iron, and other areas of the fabric from adhesive where you don't want it. Using a Teflon pressing cloth is a good idea if you fuse and so is a product for cleaning the iron plate.

When using fusible web, follow the manufacturer's instructions that come with it and apply the fusible web to the wrong side of the fabric. Let fusible web–backed fabrics cool for a few seconds before handling them. Once you remove the paper backing, you can position the piece to be appliquéd on its background or layer it on another appliqué piece. Pin until you are content with the arrangement and then touch the tip of the iron to the appliqué to lightly secure it in place. Finally, place a pressing cloth over the piece, and iron each part of the surface of the appliqué in overlapping sections for a few seconds, or as indicated in the instructions. To ensure a good bond, also press the wrong side of the fabric.

Over time, fused appliqués will pull off, at least around the edges. It's important to secure appliqués by sewing them on. This can be done using machine stitching or machine quilting. One way is to sew an outline around the raw edges, using a blind stitch with invisible thread, a satin stitch with bold thread in a contrasting color, or a decorative machine stitch, such as buttonhole, sewn in black or a matching color. Alternatively, you can work a quilting pattern over the appliqués, making sure that at least two lines of stitches cross over each fused piece to secure it.

Machine appliqué seen up close.

BATTINGS

There are now more choices of batting material than ever before. In addition to cotton, polyester, wool, silk, and blends of all of these, there is even a batting from Mountain Mist made from processed corn plants, called EcoCraft batting. Batting comes in white, off-white, and black (slate gray, actually) and varies from very thin—about an eighth of an inch—to several inches thick (called high-loft batting). As a general rule, the thicker the loft, the warmer the quilt will be.

How to decide what to use? Mostly it's a matter of preference and style, but one important factor is how the quilting will be done. The default choice for many quilters today is a thin cotton batting, which is easy to machine quilt and produces a fairly flat quilt. But many brands of cotton batting must be closely quilted to keep the layers from slipping. A blend that is mostly cotton with some polyester is also a good choice.

For tied quilts, like the one on page 438, polyester batting or a blend may be best because you can place your ties as much as ten inches apart without the fabric sliding (always read the packaging to find out how closely you need to space the ties). Polyester battings give a puffier look to quilts.

Generally, batting is produced in flat sheets that are folded into bags, although some big stores carry batting on rolls. The bags are labeled by the size of a project, such as crib or queen-size, as well as the length and width in inches of the batting sheet. If you can't find something with the exact dimensions you want, buy the next largest size. No matter what size the quilt, you'll probably need to smooth out the wrinkles when you remove the batting from the bag.

LAYERING AND BASTING

Before you assemble your quilt sandwich, press the quilt top smooth. Then, place the quilt backing, wrong side up, on a flat surface large enough to accommodate it. I usually use my living room floor, after rolling up the rug in front of the couch. Tape the edges of the backing at frequent intervals, so it is smooth but not pulled taut. Smooth the batting out over the backing. Finally, center the quilt top on the batting and baste all three layers together. Use an extralong needle and make big

STANDARD BATTING SIZES

Batting comes in precut pieces and sometimes on big rolls, where it's sold by the inch. According to Leggett & Platt, one of the top batting manufacturers, these are the standard sizes of packaged batting.

Craft .... 36 by 45 inches

Crib ..... 45 by 60 inches

Throw ... 60 by 60 inches

Twin ..... 72 by 90 inches

Full ...... 81 by 96 inches

Queen ... 90 by 108 inches

King ..... 120 by 120 inches

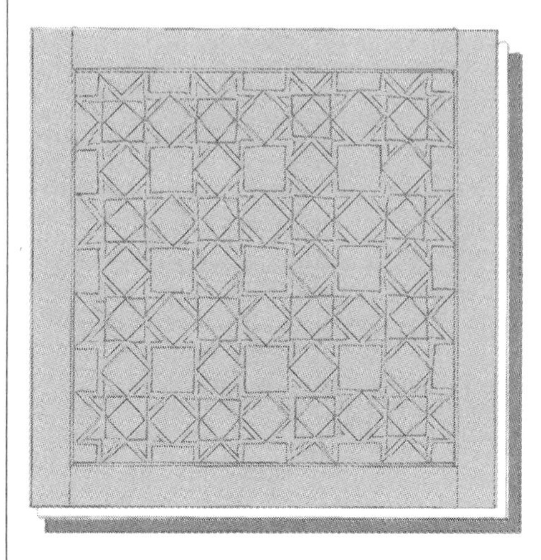

STEP 1. Layer the batting and quilt top over the backing for the quilt.

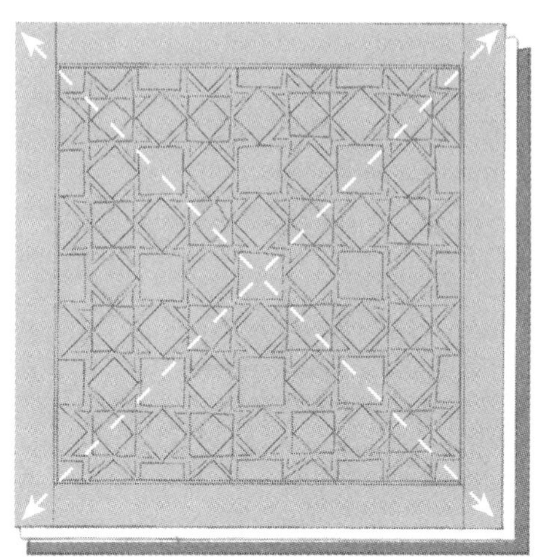

STEP 2. Baste the quilt "sandwich" on the diagonal.

stitches, about three inches long, in an X pattern starting at the center. Then, stitch a series of horizontal and vertical lines spaced about four inches apart—in each case, begin basting from the center of the quilt, working out to the edges to keep the layers smooth and stable. Only after you have finished quilting your project should you trim the batting and backing even with the quilt top. That's also the time to cut the basting threads and pull them out.

Note: If you need to mark the quilting design on the quilt top, do so *before* you layer the quilt sandwich unless you are using a chalk wheel to mark (the chalk may rub off as you baste). None of the projects in this book requires marking a quilting design, but if you want to do this, use a marking pencil you've tested to ensure the marks will come out later. You can use a stencil, trace around a pattern, or transfer a pattern to mark the quilting design.

There are several alternatives to basting with thread. Many machine quilters prefer to pin baste, inserting safety pins every three to four inches—you still want to work from the center out. If you use pins, the basting thread doesn't get mixed up in the quilting thread, but you do have to take out each pin before it gets too close to the sewing machine needle.

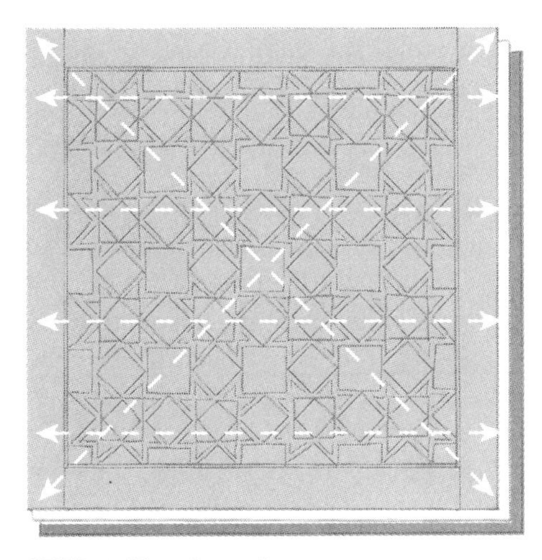

STEP 3. *Next, baste the "sandwich" crosswise.*

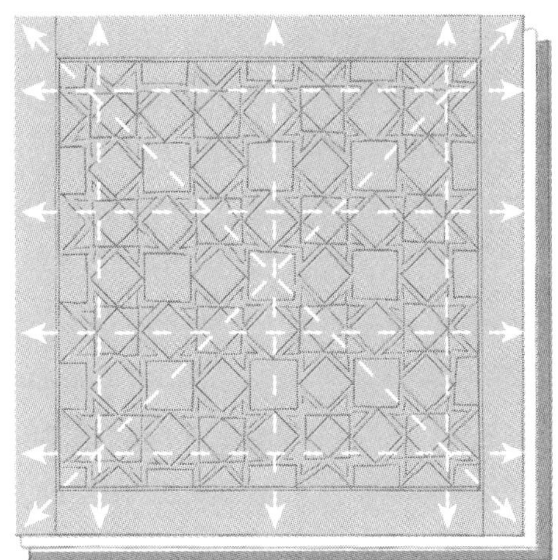

STEP 4. *Finally, baste the "sandwich" lengthwise.*

Quilting

MY MOTHER ALWAYS USED TO SAY "IT ISN'T really a quilt until you sew the three layers together." Before that, no matter how intricate your piecing, appliqué, or embellishment, it's just a quilt top. To a beginner, quilting can seem daunting and less fulfilling than the other stuff. But as your skills grow, it becomes both easier and a bigger part of your design vision. It's important to understand the various quilting alternatives and match the best one to your specific project.

HAND QUILTING

Although the projects in this book were mostly machine quilted and the majority of quilters today quilt by machine, hand quilting survives because it is relaxing, portable, and cheap. It isn't that hard to learn, either. If this is going to be your first quilt, you don't own a sewing machine, and can't tell yet if you'll love quilting, I suggest you either try hand quilting or hire someone else to finish the quilt.

Hand quilting up close.

The little crib quilt on page 443 is a great starter project for hand quilting. Being small, it won't require even a little frame to quilt: You can simply work in your

TIP

So you don't have to keep stopping and starting as you are hand quilting, thread a number of needles ahead of time. Knot the ends of the threads, then stick the threaded needles in your pincushion.

lap. Also, the hand quilting won't take forever on such a small project. Another argument in favor of starting with hand quilting—it's a lot easier to rip out than machine stitching when you start sewing crooked or mess up in some other way.

To hand quilt, thread a short needle with a piece of cotton thread that is about eighteen inches long, and tie a knot in one end (they sell extrastrong thread for hand quilting). For the first stitch you make with every new length of thread, you don't want to poke the needle through all three layers of the quilt because you want to "bury the knot." Push the needle through just the top layer about an inch away from where you want your first stitch to show. Poke the needle up at the spot you want your quilting to begin and pull on the needle. When you get to the knot at the end, the thread will catch, and you want to tug gently until the knot makes a little popping sound and gets embedded in the batting (I find this very satisfying).

You then use a simple running stitch, gathering up three or four small, even stitches on the needle each time before pulling the thread through. It is more important that your stitches are even than that they are tiny. Experienced hand quilters develop a rhythmic rocking motion, moving the fabric toward the needle from the left (if they are right-handed) while moving the needle up and down. Remember to check the back of the quilt from time to time to see that your stitches are quilting through all of the layers. Stop when you still have several inches of thread left, make another knot on the end, and then "bury" that one too before pulling the needle free.

For more on hand quilting, ask your local quilt shop if they give lessons. One of the best books for learning the technique is Jinny Beyer's *Quiltmaking by Hand: Simple Stitches, Exquisite Quilts* (Breckling Press; $29.95).

TYING QUILTS

Also called tufting, this method of securing the layers of a quilt together is quick and easy; it's the method used in the quilt project on page 438. The little knots and fringes—or tufts—of thread add an attractive design element to a quilt.A tied quilt may not hold up to frequent machine washing so it isn't practical if you are making a quilt for a baby or toddler. But if you are making a wall hanging, a decorative table covering, or a sofa throw, tying may be a wise choice. You will be able to finish the project faster by tying than if you either hand or machine quilt.

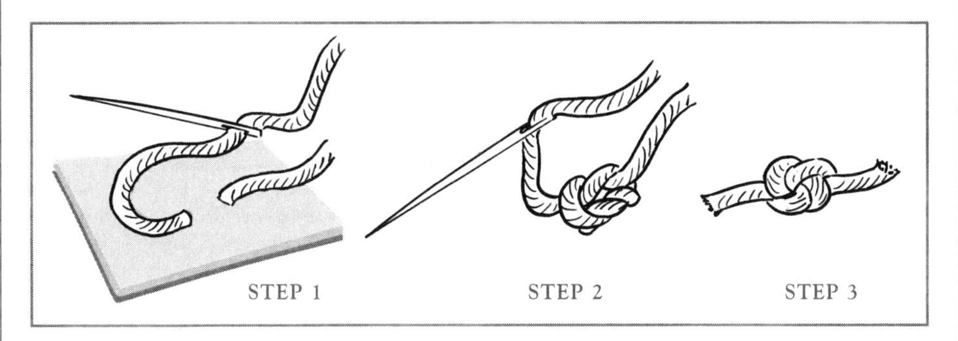

To tie a quilt, stitch the thread through all three layers of the quilt "sandwich" (Step 1); tie a double knot (Step 2); and trim the ends (Step 3).

To tie a quilt, thread a large-eyed embroidery needle with pearl cotton, crochet cotton, or six-strand embroidery floss. Starting from the front at the place where you want a tie, insert the needle, then bring it back to the top, an eighth of an inch away, and tie a square knot—basically a double knot. Cut the thread ends, leaving a quarter or half inch as a "fringe."

MACHINE QUILTING

I'm the first to admit that machine quilting isn't easy. I've taken the beginning machine quilting class at my local quilt shop twice. But practice helps enormously: Just ten minutes a day will vastly increase your control.

The first thing you need to do is to thread your machine: If you are new to machine quilting, use thread that matches the fabrics, and stitch "in the ditch," or right along the seam lines, so mistakes will be camouflaged. If you are ready for adventure, consider quilting in threads with contrasting colors. Try shiny rayons and metallics, or exciting variegated threads for your work.

Then, you need to fit the quilt under your sewing machine needle. The basic idea is to make sure that your quilt sandwich doesn't flop over the edges of your sewing table: Its weight can pull on the needle and distort your stitches. Many quilters fold parts of the quilt they aren't stitching—or roll them up like a log—to keep them out of the way, sometimes securing the

TIP

Some of the new, very pricey machines on the market have a stitch regulator, which reduces the challenges of free-motion quilting (see Chapter Two for more about sewing machine features and brands).

TIP

Award-winning machine quilter Diane Gaudynski gives great advice on ditch quilting in her book *Guide to Machine Quilting*. She says to quilt all the vertical lines first and then go back and do the horizontal ones. Start in the center and quilt a series of lines on the right, top to bottom. Then, turn the quilt to do the left side.

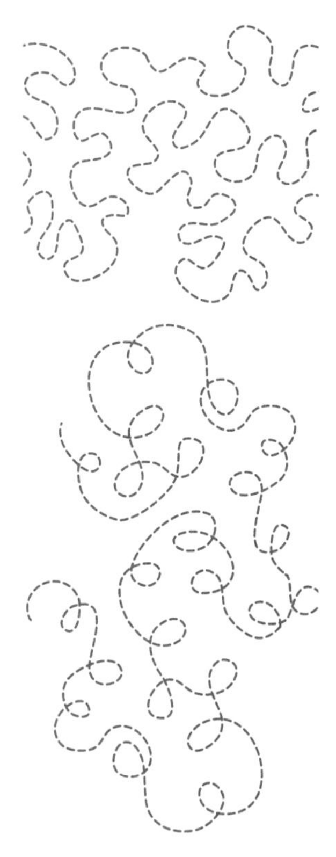

Free-motion machine quilting patterns: stippling (top) and loop-the-loop (bottom).

bulk with clips or pins. But this method can restrict the movement of the quilt under the needle, especially in free-motion quilting. In that case, machine-quilting guru Diane Gaudynski says she likes to "gently mush" her quilt on both sides of the needle, with part of the quilt puddling up in her lap and across the tabletop surrounding her machine. (You may need to place a table behind your sewing machine if your work surface is narrow and there isn't room for the quilt there.) As a beginner, you can avoid these difficulties by sticking to smaller quilts and wall hangings for machine quilting—for example, the crib quilt on page 443, photo quilt on page 453, or other small projects.

To start sewing, turn the flywheel and take a single stitch. Pull the thread end to bring up a loop of the bobbin thread, then pull on the loop to bring up the end of the thread. Lower or cover the feed dogs (see your sewing machine manual) and decrease the stitch length all the way down to 0. Take three or four stitches without advancing the needle. Once you've sewn a short line of stitches, you can cut the two thread ends even with the quilt surface. But, try to avoid lots of stops and starts; use continuous line quilting patterns and-or start and end at the edge of a quilt.

You have three machine quilting options.

Machine-guided quilting is what sewing machines traditionally were built to do: The presser foot and the feed dogs pull layers of fabric under the needle where they are stitched together. You set the stitch length and the pace, but basically, you're just feeding fabric under the needle. As long as you're going to quilt straight lines, you can use your machine set up the same way as for regular sewing. Harriet Hargrave, a pioneer of machine quilting, refers to this as "straight-line quilting," and it works best for standard practices like quilting "in the ditch," along the edge of straight seams.

To do this, you may want to replace your regular sewing foot with a walking foot, also known as an even-feed foot. While bulky, this foot keeps the layers from shifting, so the back of your quilt will look as nice as the front—or nearly as nice. Set the stitch length to about ten stitches per inch. You can also experiment with decorative machine stitches that penetrate all layers of the quilt. For very small projects, there's no need to use a walking foot but for something bigger, the walking foot will increase your control.

There are several ways to finish machine-guided quilting. Some machine quilters switch to making very tiny stitches about one inch from the end of a row. You can also make the end of the quilting line secure by going into reverse for six or eight stitches. Then clip the threads on the front and back.

Free-motion quilting: Some machine quilters prefer to lower, or at least cover, the feed dogs because it gives them more freedom of movement. The key to this popular technique is using a darning foot, which has a coil in its mechanism that releases the quilt when the needle is in the up position. At this point, you are free to move the quilt sandwich in any direction. The trick is getting stitches that are even in length. The rate at which you move the piece and run the machine must be smooth and consistent. This takes a lot of practice, and you'll want to do your practicing on a test piece that is similar in thickness to your project. Work on a test sandwich until you are comfortable with the technique and satisfied with the quilting. Three common free-motion patterns that fill space are the meander stitch, stippling, and loop-the-loop curlicues. A meander stitch is made up of random wavy lines that are used to fill in a space, and the lines can cross over one another at places. Stippling is similar, but the lines are very close—no more than an eighth of an inch apart—and never cross. And, loop-the-loop quilting is just like it sounds.

To end a line of free-motion stitching, take three or four stitches in place. Make a longer stitch to bring up a loop of the bobbin thread, and cut both thread ends even with the quilt top surface.

Professional quilt finishers provide a third alternative—paying someone else to do the quilting. To find a reputable quilt finisher in your area, consult your local quilt shop or guild, or see page 520 for other resources. Even if you go this route, I must plead that somewhere along the line, you learn how to do every stage in the quiltmaking process yourself. It's like cooking from scratch: Sometimes you need the shortcuts, but the greatest feeling of accomplishment comes from doing it all on your own.

TIP

Quilting teacher Karen Musgrave was the first person to suggest that I practice free-motion quilting by writing my name over and over in thread on a test square. It's easier to get into a rhythm with your machine and get even stitches because you're not nervous about whether you can stipple properly or make a perfect star shape. You sign your name without thinking, so this will relax you. This is what got me to start enjoying machine quilting. Now I like to write words in the borders of most of my quilts. It's so much easier than embroidering words by hand.

How to Bind Your Finished Quilt

Most beginners are intimidated by making a quilt binding, especially when it is a stretchy bias binding. But if you cut the fabric carefully and follow directions, it's not that hard. The directions given here are for a double-fold binding: These are the most common and durable.

For a finished binding along the quilt edges that is a quarter of an inch wide, begin by cutting fabric strips that are two and a quarter inches wide. If you are making a bed-size quilt, you may want a wider binding: Consult your quilt shop about how much fabric you'll need.

Before you attach the binding, remove any basting threads or pins from the quilt. Then trim the batting and quilt back so that they are precisely even with the quilt top. You want the edges to be sharp and clean.

You can make bindings cut straight across the width or length of the fabric, but bindings cut on the bias last longer and fit better. A bias binding is made by cutting strips along the diagonal of the fabric. To get the 45 degree angle you want, start by cutting your binding fabric into a square. The easiest way to do this is to fold the piece of fabric for the binding wrong side out, positioning the left side edge on top of the top edge. Following the right side edge, cut off the rectangle of fabric extending to its side **(see Step 1)**.

Leave the fabric folded. Using a large quilter's ruler as a guide, draw a line parallel to and two and a quarter inches away from the fold. Draw another parallel line two and a quarter inches away from the first. Continue drawing parallel lines that are two and a quarter inches apart until you get to the corner **(see Step 2)**. Unfold the fabric and cut out the binding strips along the

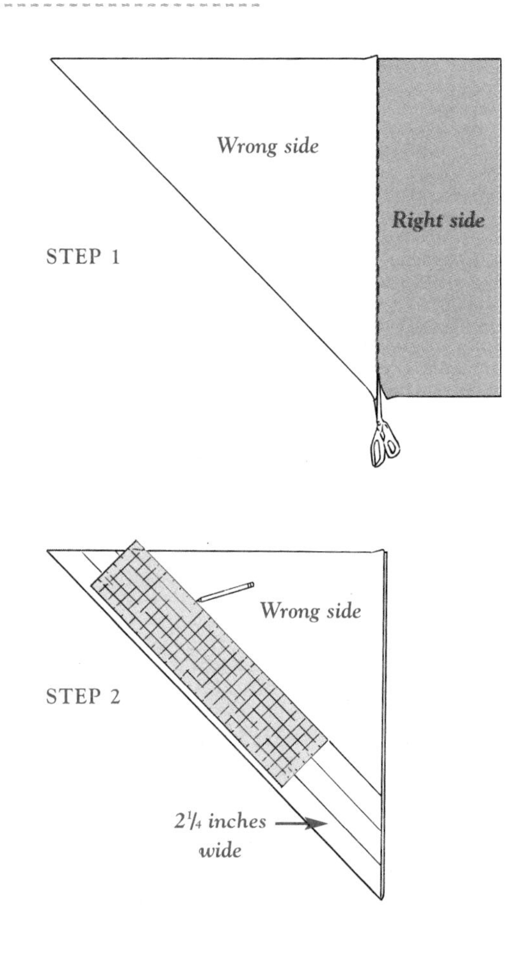

lines. Using the ruler, draw a line parallel to and two and a quarter inches away from the diagonal cut line on the remaining piece of fabric **(see Step 3)**.

Piece the strips of binding together using diagonal seams sewn with a quarter inch seam allowance. To do this, arrange one binding strip on top of another so they are right sides together and at a right angle **(see Step 4)**. Draw a diagonal line across the middle of the overlapping box; this will be your sewing line. Sew the two strips together along that diagonal, then trim off the triangle one quarter inch outside of the seam.

The simplest way to determine the length of binding that you will need for your quilt is to measure the four sides of the quilt top and add fifteen inches to that total. Keep measuring, cutting, and piecing strips of binding together until they are at least that long. Press the seams open; the result will look like the binding strip in **Step 5**. Fold the joined strips together lengthwise in half, with the right side facing out **(Step 6)**. Press the folded strip of binding.

Whether you attach the binding by hand or machine, the method is similar. Start at the bottom of the quilt top a few inches from a corner. Leaving a roughly five-inch tail, pin the pressed binding to the front of the quilt top: You want the raw edge of the binding strip to be positioned on top of and even with the raw edges of your quilt sandwich. Working

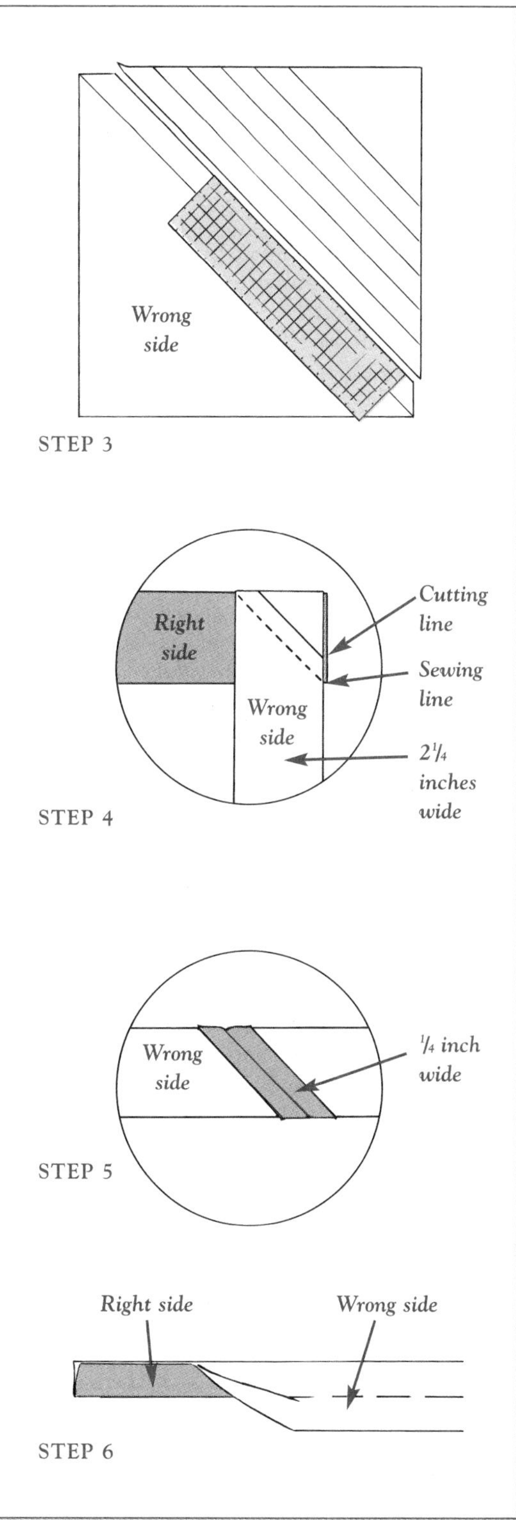

either by hand or by machine, sew the binding to the quilt one quarter inch from the raw edges, removing the pins as you come to them **(Step 7).**

When you come to a corner miter it as follows: **If you are machine sewing,** stop stitching a quarter inch from a corner and take a backstitch. Remove the quilt from under the presser foot, and fold the binding up so it is flush with the next edge you will attach it to, creating a 45 degree angle fold line **(Step 8).** Finger press the fold, then fold the binding down again **(Step 9),** aligning its raw edge with the unbound edge of the quilt. Insert the needle a quarter inch from both edges of the corner, take a couple of stitches and a backstitch, then proceed on down that side of the quilt until you come to the next corner **(Step 10).**

If you are hand sewing, the process is similar but somewhat simpler. You don't lift the presser foot when you start down the second side, you just rotate the quilt in your lap and, starting a quarter inch from both edges of the corner, continue sewing the binding to the quilt.

Sewing corners seems tricky until you get the hang of it. If you follow this method, you'll see that when you fold the binding over to the back of the quilt, mitered corners will result automatically.

When you are about ten inches from the point at which you first started attaching the binding,

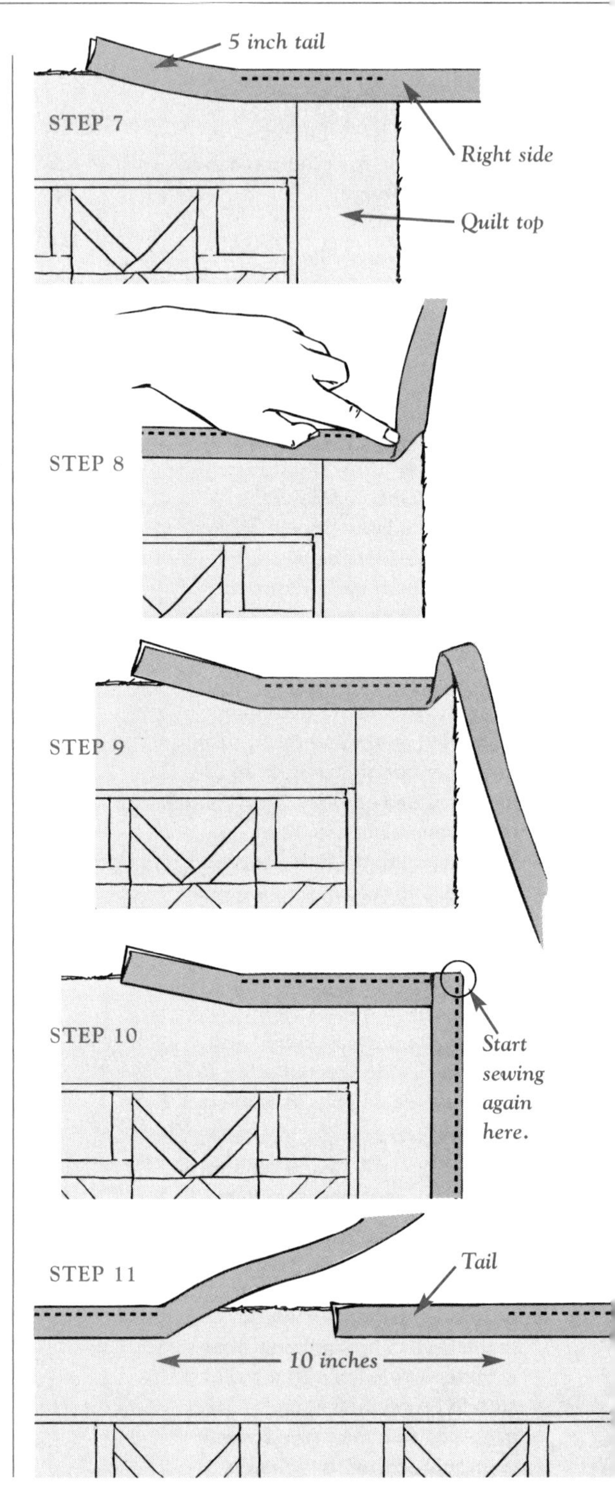

position the tail at the beginning of the binding so that its raw edge is aligned with the edge of the quilt **(Step 11).** Position the other end of the binding on top of it. Finger press the end of the top binding where it meets the cut end of the binding tail underneath **(Step 12).** Starting at that crease, measure a distance that is equal to the total width of the unfolded binding strip (following the instructions above, that will be two and a quarter inches). Cut the top binding at that point **(Step 13).**

Unfold the two binding tails and align them at a right angle, right sides together. As you did when piecing the strips for the binding, draw a diagonal line across the middle of the overlapping box; this will be your sewing line **(Step 14).** After checking to see that the two strips of binding are not twisted, sew them together along that diagonal, then trim off the triangle one quarter inch outside of the seam and press the seam open. Fold the binding strip in half lengthwise as before; it should lie flat **(Step 15).** Finish stitching the unattached binding to the quilt.

Finally, fold the binding over the edge of the quilt sandwich from the front to the back, and pin it to the backing. Whether you have attached the binding to the quilt top by hand or machine, the last step is done by hand. Using thread in a color that matches the binding, slip stitch the binding neatly to the backing of the quilt **(Steps 16 and 17),** folding under the mitered corners as you go.

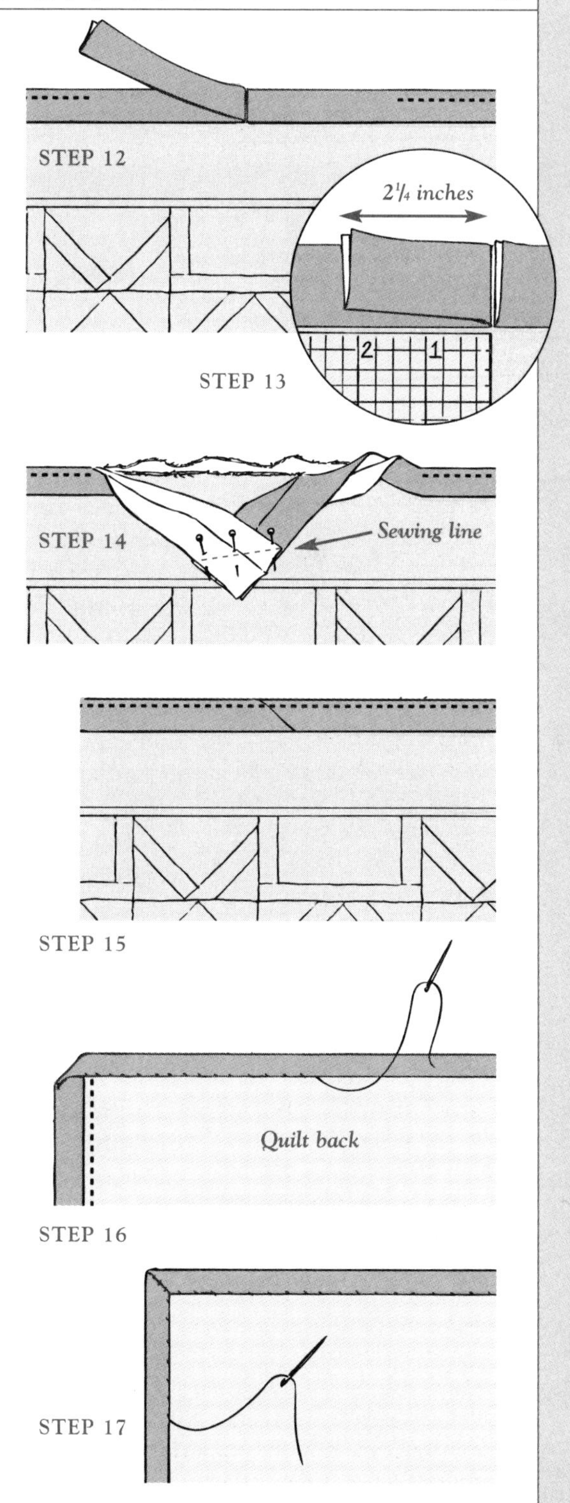

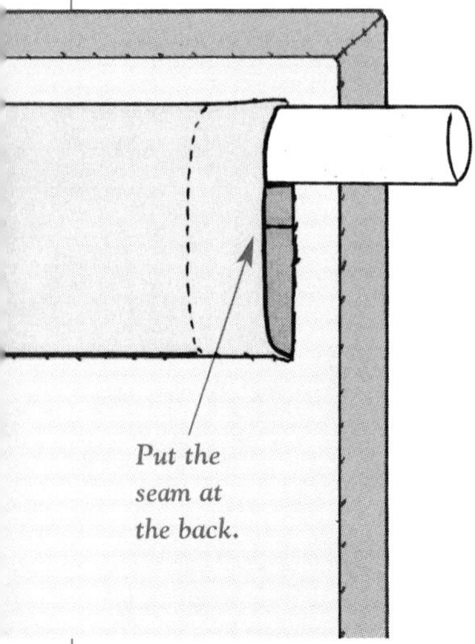

Put the seam at the back.

Hanging sleeves should not show from the front or top: Make the sleeve less wide than your quilt.

Attaching a Hanging Sleeve

EVEN FOR SMALLER WALL QUILTS, IT'S GOOD TO GET in the habit of making a hanging sleeve for the back. A hanging sleeve makes it possible to safely and easily display the quilt. The directions that follow here are for the size hanging sleeve required for most quilt contests, but this is also a good basic size for hanging quilts displayed at home.

You can use leftover fabric from the quilt itself or scrap fabric. I often use plain unbleached muslin. The minimum size for most quilt contests, where typically quilts are hung on thick poles, is a sleeve that is four inches wide. To wind up with a sleeve of that width, cut a strip of fabric that is eight and one half inches wide. To compute the length, make a pencil mark on the back of the quilt that is two inches in from each side (you want the finished sleeve to be skinnier than your quilt). Then, cut a strip of fabric that is that many inches long, plus one half inch more for turning the edges under.

Hem the short ends of the strip of fabric, fold it lengthwise, and press it, right sides together. Then stitch the long edges together. Turn the sleeve inside out, so that the seam line doesn't show after the sleeve is attached, press it so that the seam line runs down the middle. Center the sleeve at the top of the quilt back, seam side down. Sewing by hand and being careful not to sew through all three layers of the quilt (you don't want the stitches to show on the front of the quilt) slip stitch the sleeve to the back of the quilt, along the top and bottom edges of the hanging sleeve. Don't pull the sleeve taut against the quilt back; you need to leave some slack so there is space for the pole to slide through.

For those who hate making hanging sleeves or who decide at the last minute to enter a quilt in a contest and don't have the time to put a sleeve together, there's a new product that can help. Quilter's Hangup, introduced in 2006, is a presewn quilt sleeve that is 4 by 108 inches (three yards). You can attach it as is or cut it to fit. So far it only comes in unbleached muslin. To learn more, go to www.quiltershangup.com

Finishing a Quilt

ONCE YOUR QUILT IS COMPLETED, YOU MAY WISH to rinse out any spray starch, dots of glue stick, or any markings you made in cutting, tracing, or quilting. Finally, make a label for the back of the quilt. You will be signing your work of art, adding a personal message for the receiver, and documenting it for generations to come. And, whether you are keeping the quilt or giving it away, take a photo.

HOW I LABEL A QUILT

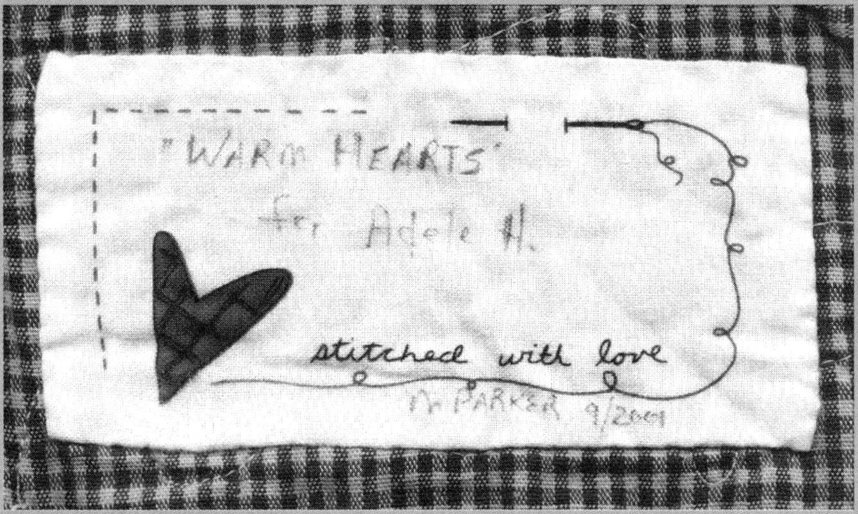

Label on a lap quilt made by Marilyn Parker of Lawrence, Kansas.

My usual style is to make a simple label cut from unbleached muslin and decorate it with washable fabric markers. I always write when the quilt was finished, where, and my name. I specify if the quilt was made for a special occasion. If you like, you can also add the name of the quilt. Decorate the label before sewing it on. Then fold under the edges to prevent the fabric from unraveling and attach the label to the back of the quilt using a slip stitch.

I sometimes include washing instructions on the label if the quilt is a gift to a friend or for a charity.

You'll find more ideas about how to label quilts on page 524, but the best advice is to be as creative and personal with the label as you are with everything else about your quilt.

TWELVE PROJECTS

First, you'll find five supereasy quilt projects of my own design here. Then, I've assembled projects from seven of the twenty top teachers profiled in Chapter Five. You'll find a mix of quilts and wall hangings, cute bags—even quilted greeting cards and Christmas ornaments. The projects grow progressively more ambitious.

Need a Gift Next Week Tied Quilt

BY MEG COX
Level of difficulty: ■ □ □ □ □
Can be pieced by hand or machine

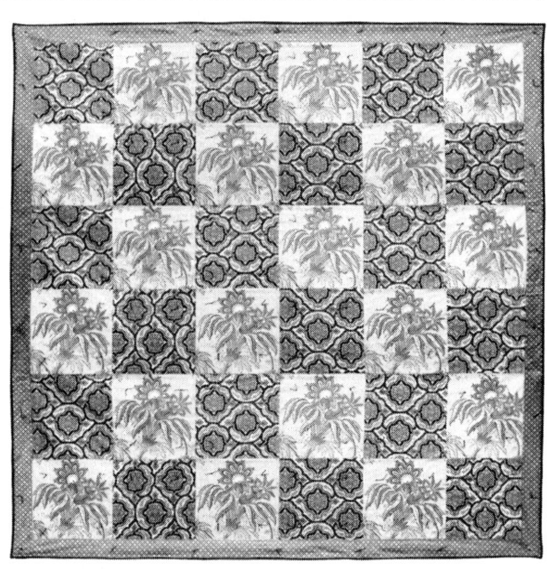

When my sister asked me to teach her how to quilt, this is the project I picked for her first effort. A very basic project, the quilt isn't really any harder to make than the crib quilt on page 443, which was my first quilt project. It goes particularly fast because the squares are large and also because the three layers are tied together rather than quilted. Tied quilts may not hold up well under frequent washing, so you won't want to use this technique for bed quilts. But tying is perfect for wall hangings or something decorative to drape on a sofa.

The design for the quilt consists of alternating ten-inch squares cut from two different fabrics. What makes this quilt dramatic is the choice of stunning fabric from one of today's hot designers, Amy Butler. Like many who design fabric for the quilt market now, she creates a lot of very bold prints that are perfect for this style of quilt: There is so much going on visually in her fabric that you don't need to add embellishments such as fancy patchwork or appliqué. This fabric begs to be left big, not cut up into tiny pieces.

As you can see in the photo of Project 1 in the color insert, I selected a

12 PROJECTS
from Renowned Quilters

TAKE A PICTURE THIS MORNING, turn it into a cute purse this afternoon. I've used digital photos of my book's cover; my son Max; and Tulip, the cover dog for *Mark Lipinski's Quilter's Home* magazine. Your bag could feature any image that strikes you—a perfect flower, a glorious sunset. Print the photo on fabric with a home ink-jet printer: no special software is required. Both sides of the bag can be either tied or quilted (by hand or machine).

1. Meg's Bag

by Meg Cox

FINISHED SIZE:
about 6 by 8 inches

LEVEL OF DIFFICULTY: ■□□□□
< beginner....advanced >

Project instructions begin on page 457.

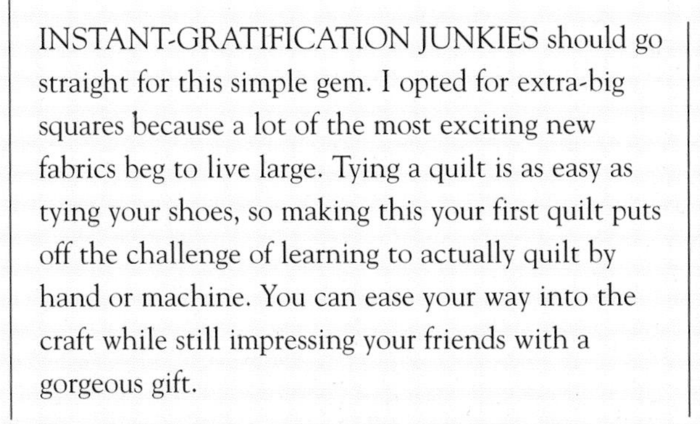

INSTANT-GRATIFICATION JUNKIES should go straight for this simple gem. I opted for extra-big squares because a lot of the most exciting new fabrics beg to live large. Tying a quilt is as easy as tying your shoes, so making this your first quilt puts off the challenge of learning to actually quilt by hand or machine. You can ease your way into the craft while still impressing your friends with a gorgeous gift.

2. Need a Gift Next Week Tied Quilt

by Meg Cox

FINISHED SIZE:
about 65½ by 65½ inches

LEVEL OF DIFFICULTY: ■□□□□
< beginner....advanced >

Project instructions begin on page 438.

3. Jo Cox's Crib Quilt

by Meg Cox

FINISHED SIZE:
about 33½ by 51½ inches

LEVEL OF DIFFICULTY: ■□□□□
< beginner....advanced >

Project instructions begin on page 443.

SIMPLE SQUARES make a sweet quilt that beginners can embrace. I love the purity of white in a baby quilt, but you can choose any colors or patterns you like. It's my mother's design and was the first quilt I ever made; I did both the piecing and quilting by hand. Although I pieced the version shown here by hand, the quilting was done by a hired professional so I could meet my deadline!

THIS FUN AND MANAGEABLE tote bag is a great way to practice quilting, since you don't have a vast expanse to cover. It also makes it a good project for a first timer. Because it's the first tote bag I made myself, I didn't go for lots of flaps, pockets, and embellishments. I stuck with a basic, sturdy tote that would let the fabric and the stitching make a statement. This bag would look great made from batiks or funky novelty prints.

4. Showcase Your Stash Tote Bag

by Meg Cox

FINISHED SIZE: an approximately 15 by 19–inch tote bag

LEVEL OF DIFFICULTY: ■□□□□
< beginner....advanced >

Project instructions begin on page 448.

5. Rosy Quilt

by Kaffe Fassett and Liza Prior Lucy

FINISHED SIZE:
about 60 by 78 inches

LEVEL OF DIFFICULTY: ■■□□□
< beginner....advanced >

Project instructions begin on page 462.

FOR ME, KAFFE AND LIZA'S PATTERNS are as addictive as popcorn, and this is one of their classics. The simple pattern is perfect for a beginner or for an experienced quilter who wants to make a quick throw for the family room sofa. Kaffe and Liza delight in taking old quilt patterns and breathing fresh life into them with today's thrilling fabrics.

6. Quilted Keepsake Greeting Cards

by Ricky Tims

FINISHED SIZE:
makes three 5 by 7–inch greeting cards

LEVEL OF DIFFICULTY: ■■□□□
< beginner....advanced >

Project instructions begin on page 467.

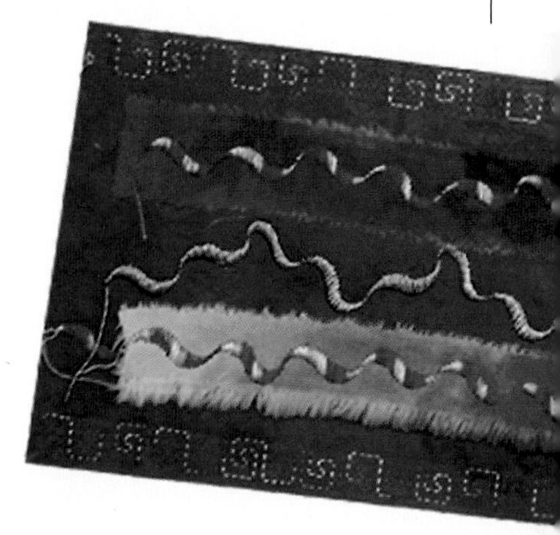

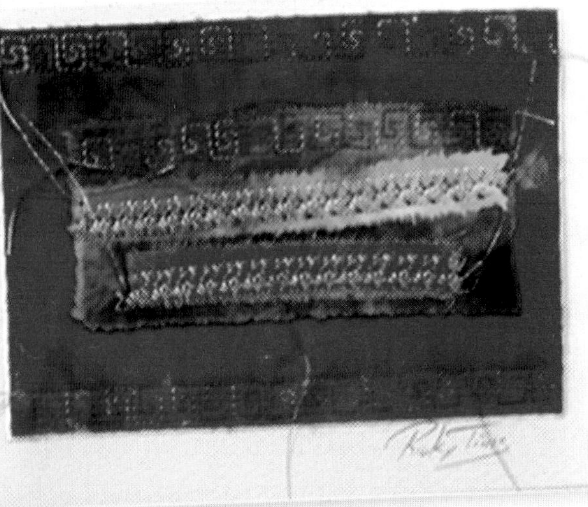

THESE SIMPLE CARDS showcase Ricky Tims' taste for flamboyant colors and virtuoso machine quilting. The project employs raw-edge appliqué, but the edges are purposefully left raw. Bright, dangling threads add to the sense of bursting energy that the fabric and paper collages emit. It's a terrific excuse to play with decorative stitches on your sewing machine and turn out an easy gift for friends.

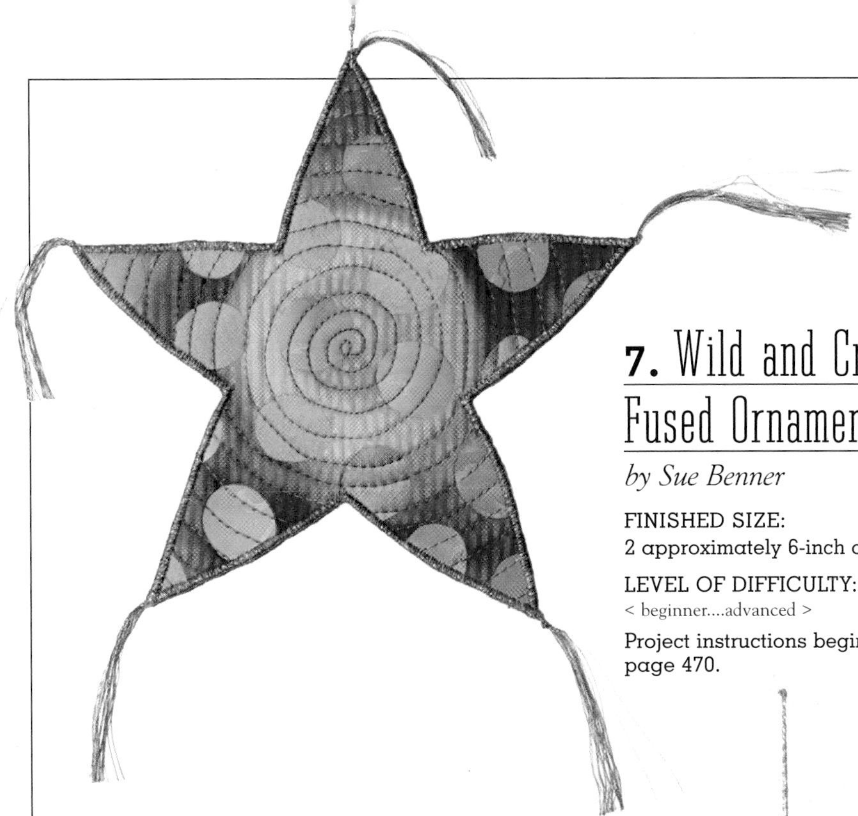

7. Wild and Crazy Fused Ornaments

by Sue Benner

FINISHED SIZE:
2 approximately 6-inch ornaments

LEVEL OF DIFFICULTY: ■■□□□
< beginner....advanced >

Project instructions begin on page 470.

THESE STUNNING ORNAMENTS are shockingly simple to make. On one side, you use a quarter as a template to cut out circles. For the other, you just cut pretty silks into simple shapes to create a fabric collage. There is very little stitching because the fabric is fused to the background. Here is a great opportunity to experiment with quilting stitches to make an irresistible present for your lucky family and friends.

Geraldine Brooks

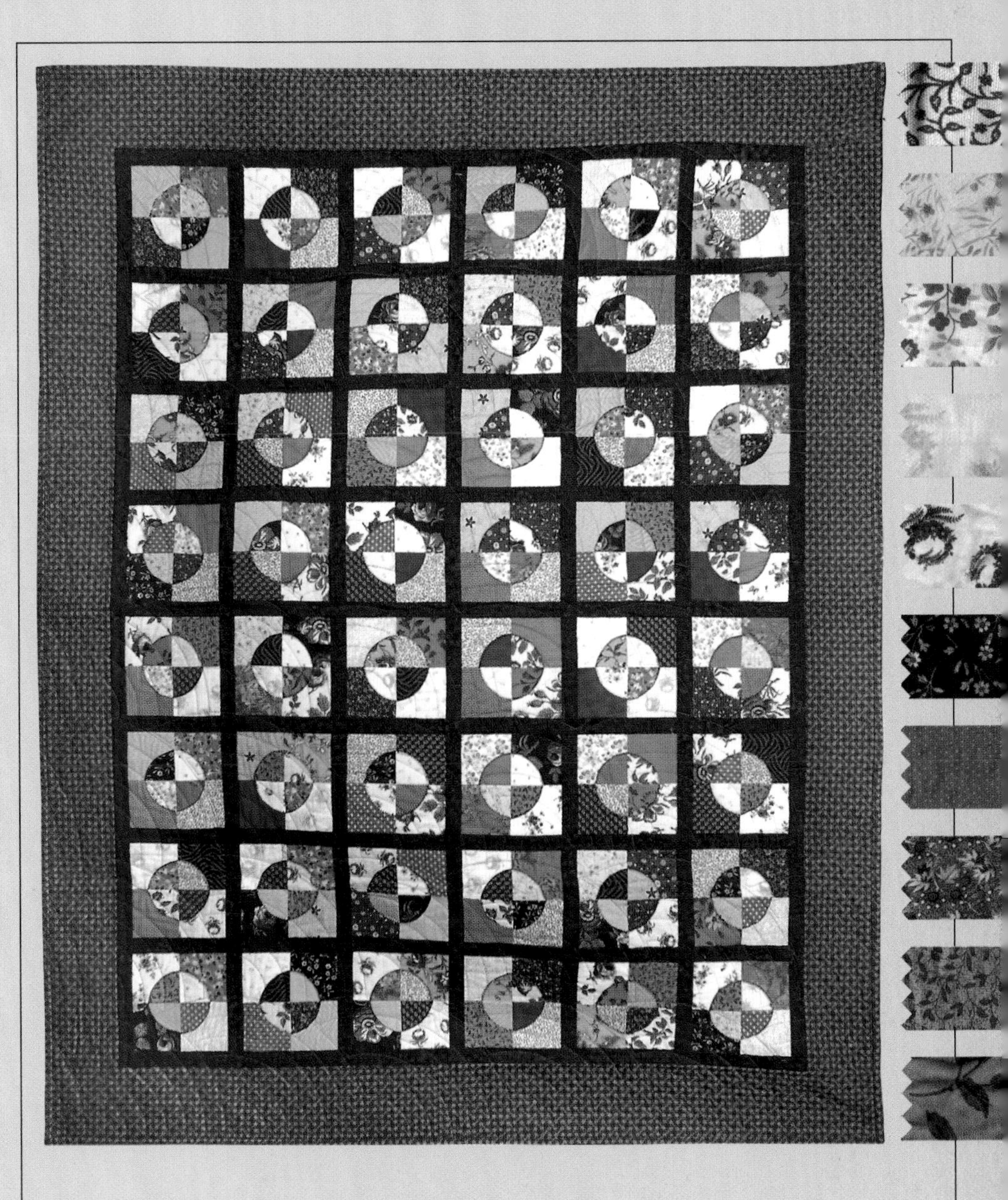

FAMOUS "SIMPLIFIER" ELEANOR BURNS does her thing with the old standard quilt pattern Robbing Peter to Pay Paul. For those who find curved seams a form of torture, Eleanor devised a plan that has you fusing circles to squares, cutting them into quarters and then doing a massive mix and match to create this striking quilt. It's a good introduction to her quick methods of cutting and piecing. For a different look, use bright, sassy fabrics.

8. Scrappy Peter and Paul Quilt

by Eleanor Burns

FINISHED SIZE:
about 52 by 66 inches

LEVEL OF DIFFICULTY: ■■■□□
< beginner....advanced >

Project instructions begin on page 474.

9. Fruit Tart Pincushion

by Ami Simms

FINISHED SIZE:
makes one 5½-inch tart

LEVEL OF DIFFICULTY: ■■■□□
< beginner....advanced >

Project instructions begin on page 482.

THE FAMOUSLY FUNNY AMI SIMMS knows that quilters love a visual joke. A fairly simple project, this pincushion looks good enough to eat and makes a great gift. Essentially, you're sewing an elasticized fabric top for an actual tart tin, which is filled with stuffing. The decorative stitching can be done by hand or machine and enhances the illusion.

RAW-EDGE APPLIQUE is all the rage in quilting because it liberates quilters from a lot of tedious edge turning. This lovely project combines that technique with a charming traditional looking pattern created by prize-winning quilter Sue Nickels. There are lots of options here: You can machine quilt, like Sue, or finish the edges of the appliquéd shapes using hand embroidery. Make a pillow or turn this into a small wall hanging.

10. "All That I Am" Pillow

by Sue Nickels

FINISHED SIZE:
about 16 by 16 inches

LEVEL OF DIFFICULTY: ■■■■□
< beginner....advanced >

Project instructions begin on page 490.

A. B. C.

11. Falling Leaves Wall Hanging

by Libby Lehman

FINISHED SIZE:
about 12 by 14 inches

LEVEL OF DIFFICULTY: ■■■■■
< beginner....advanced >

Project instructions begin on page 498.

KICK YOUR MACHINE-EMBELLISHMENT skills up a notch by making a small wall quilt that Libby sometimes teaches in her popular machine-quilting classes. You'll be working with appliqué and reverse appliqué techniques, sheer fabrics like organza, and shiny metallic sewing machine threads that require special handling. Unlike most of the projects in this book, this one isn't recommended for beginners, but the results are stunning.

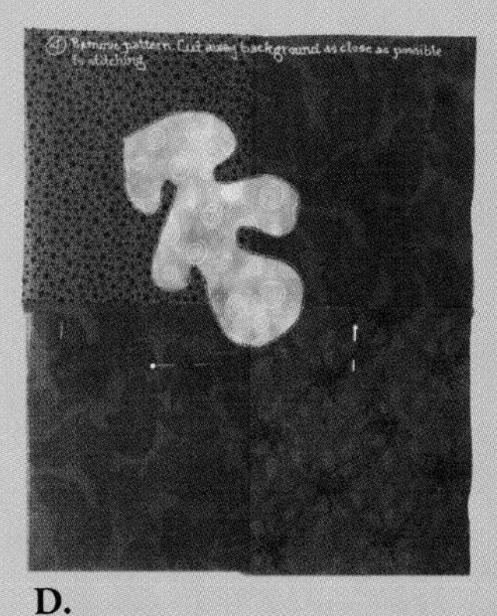

D.

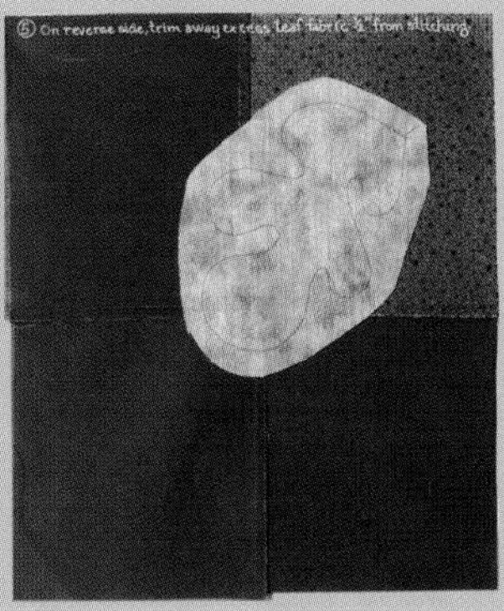

E.

F.

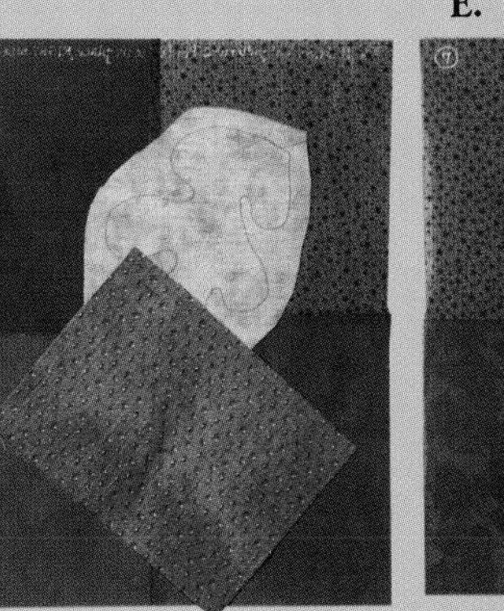

G.

H.

I.

J.

K.

L.

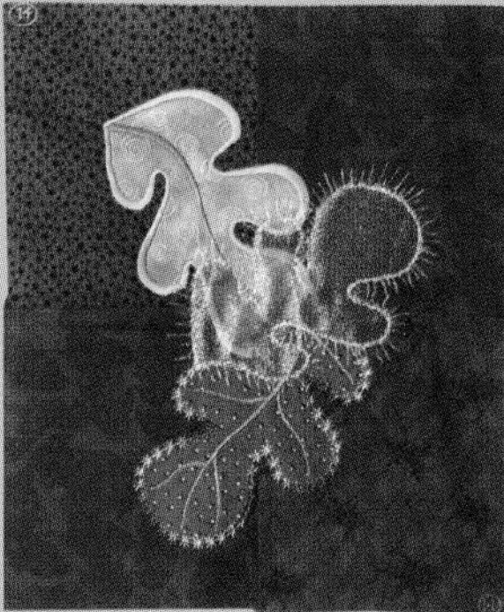

M.

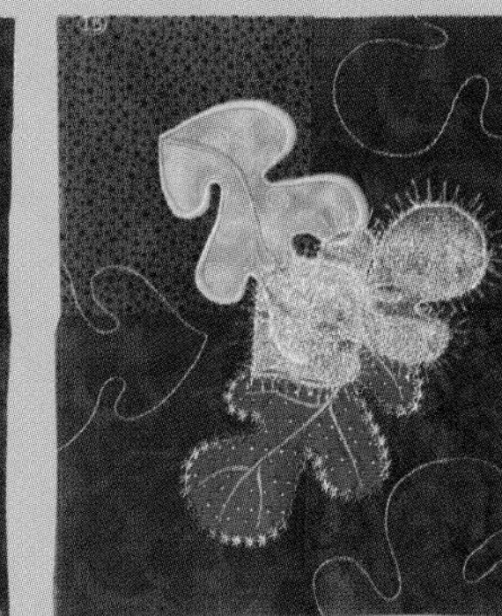

N.

These pictures show the actual class samples Lehman uses when teaching each step of this project. They demonstrate both the complexity of her technique and her generosity in sharing explicit details of her process. Prizewinning quilts today often feature lavish machine embroidery and gorgeously layered fabrics, so this tutorial is especially valuable for quilters who aspire to do cutting-edge work.

12. Kiss Quilt

by Meg Cox

FINISHED SIZE:
about 29 by 31 inches

LEVEL OF DIFFICULTY: ■□□□□
< beginner....advanced >

Project instructions begin on page 453.

THIS IS A PERFECT FIRST PROJECT, teaching you how to make a simple quilt and how to print photographs on fabric using the printer of your home computer. Although I used the same picture from my wedding four times, Andy Warhol–style, you can use four different photos. Make a fun quilt about your kids or cats or best friends, or make a breathtaking souvenir for a milestone event like your parents' golden wedding anniversary.

striking green, brown, and pink all-over pattern (this is Fabric A) and a pink and brown cotton with a repeating floral motif (Fabric B). Since these two prints were so striking and busy, I paired them with a small print for the border, echoing the pink and brown, and used a solid brown for the binding. What made picking these fabrics a breeze was that the three prints were all part of the same collection of fabrics designed by Amy Butler. Many fabric companies introduce new fabrics in collections that are color coordinated, but you don't have to stay within one "family" of fabrics like that. Instead, you can find one bold print you like, then run around the fabric shop with a bolt under your arm, until you find a second big print that sets it off. Ideally, you want two prints that complement one another, sharing some of the same colors or shapes. When you select the thread for tying, look for a color that contrasts with the fabric for the large squares—I used dark brown.

In the case of this particular floral print fabric, there was one element of Butler's design that I especially loved, so I cut around those big flowers and excluded other parts of the design. This is called "fussy cutting." Be aware that if you decide to fussy cut your fabric, you'll have to buy extra. I don't consider this wasteful; I like to have plenty of bits for scrap quilts. But, fussy cutting is certainly optional; if you decide not to, you'll get to the sewing part even faster.

Makes an approximately 65½-inch-square quilt; see Project 1 in the color insert.

For this project

- All fabric should be 100 percent cotton and 44 to 45 inches wide.
- Remember to remove the selvages from the fabric.
- All of the seam allowances in the quilt are ¼ inch.
- Press the quilt top smooth on the right side before sandwiching the layers together.

MAKING THIS A BED QUILT

Look in the popular home-furnishing catalogs and you'll frequently see beautiful quilts made of big squares in arresting fabrics. In many cases, these are no more complicated to make than the quilt here. Why not make your own? You'll save money and you can pick colors and patterns that perfectly complement your bedroom's decor.

To make this quilt for a bed, simply convert it to the dimensions of your favorite comforter or bedspread (or see the bed size chart on page 400) and quilt the three layers together instead of tying them. You'll find basic quilting instructions on page 427.

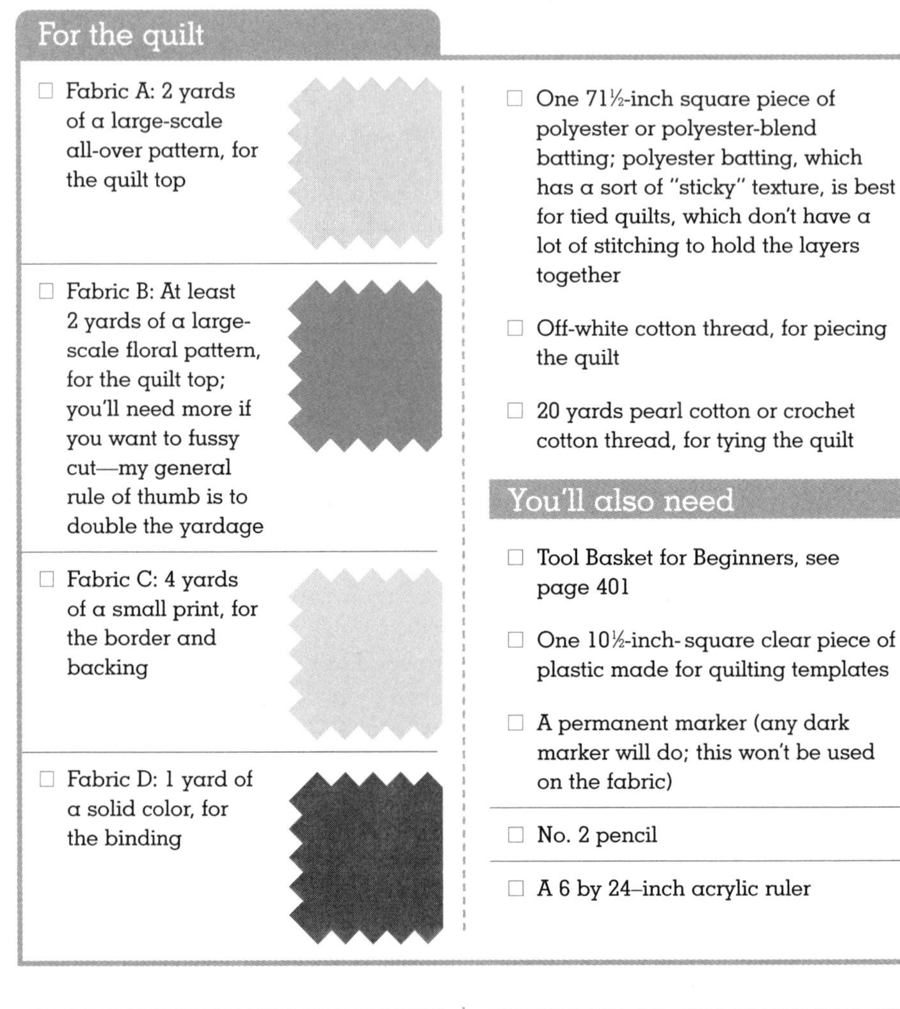

For the quilt

- ☐ Fabric A: 2 yards of a large-scale all-over pattern, for the quilt top
- ☐ Fabric B: At least 2 yards of a large-scale floral pattern, for the quilt top; you'll need more if you want to fussy cut—my general rule of thumb is to double the yardage
- ☐ Fabric C: 4 yards of a small print, for the border and backing
- ☐ Fabric D: 1 yard of a solid color, for the binding
- ☐ One 71½-inch square piece of polyester or polyester-blend batting; polyester batting, which has a sort of "sticky" texture, is best for tied quilts, which don't have a lot of stitching to hold the layers together
- ☐ Off-white cotton thread, for piecing the quilt
- ☐ 20 yards pearl cotton or crochet cotton thread, for tying the quilt

You'll also need

- ☐ Tool Basket for Beginners, see page 401
- ☐ One 10½-inch-square clear piece of plastic made for quilting templates
- ☐ A permanent marker (any dark marker will do; this won't be used on the fabric)
- ☐ No. 2 pencil
- ☐ A 6 by 24–inch acrylic ruler

Cut out the quilt blocks

1. Using scissors or a rotary cutter, cut 18 blocks from fabric A, each 10½ inches square. Cut on the crosswise grain—this means that you will cut squares in a straight row across the width of the fabric.

2. Cut 18 blocks from fabric B, each 10½ inches square. To help you position one of fabric B's large floral motifs identically in each block, make a template: Place the clear square of plastic flat on the fabric so that a floral motif is centered or positioned as you would like it to appear on the block, then use the permanent marker to trace some of the motif's outline on the clear plastic. Arrange the template on the fabric, aligning the *MARKED* outline with the pattern on the fabric (see Diagram 1), then using a pencil, trace around the edges of the template—these will be your cutting marks. Repeat, aligning the outline on the template with the fabric pattern, until you have 18 blocks.

3. If you are going to be piecing the blocks by hand, draw a sewing line on the wrong side of each ¼ inch inside the edge.

DIAGRAM 1

Make the quilt top

4. Arrange the blocks of fabrics A and B in six rows of six, alternating the fabrics as shown in Diagram 2.

5. Pin and then stitch the blocks together in each row. Press the seam allowances in the directions shown in the arrows on the blocks in Diagram 2.

A →	B →	A →	B →	A →	B →
B ←	A ←	B ←	A ←	B ←	A ←
A →	B →	A →	B →	A →	B →
B ←	A ←	B ←	A ←	B ←	A ←
A →	B →	A →	B →	A →	B →
B ←	A ←	B ←	A ←	B ←	A ←

DIAGRAM 2

6. Pin and then stitch the rows of blocks together. Press these seam allowances toward the bottom of the quilt.

Make and attach the border

7. Cut fabric C crosswise in half.

8. Cutting along the lengthwise grain of one piece of fabric C, cut four 3-inch strips for the border. Set aside the rest of this piece of fabric for the backing.

9. Pin and then stitch one 3-inch border strip to the top edge of the quilt top and one to the bottom, then press the seam allowances toward the outside edge. Trim off the ends of the attached strips so that they are even with the quilt top.

10. Pin and then stitch the remaining two 3-inch border strips to the sides of the quilt, press the seam allowances toward the outside edge, and trim off the ends so they are even.

Make the backing

11. Pin and then stitch one of the 2-yard-long sides of each of the two remaining pieces of fabric C together to make the backing; you will have a roughly square piece of a little more than 70 inches. Measure the completed quilt top and trim the pieced backing and the batting so that they are 3 inches larger than the quilt top on all sides.

Assemble and tie the quilt

12. When tying the quilt, you want to place the knots so that they accentuate the patterns of the fabric. They don't need to be any closer than 10 inches apart. You can tie the quilt freehand, but if you want to duplicate the knots in my quilt, follow Diagram 3 and mark the placement of the knots on the quilt top using a No. 2 pencil. First mark the ties for the quilt blocks: Working from the corners of each block, measure and mark 2 inches on the diagonal toward the center of the block.

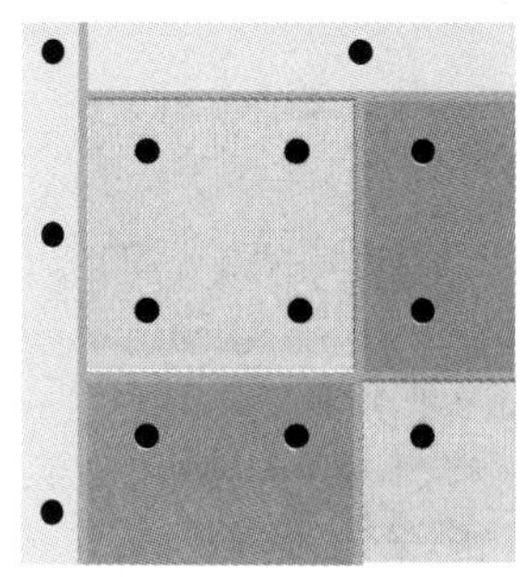

DIAGRAM 3

13. Then, to mark the placement of the knots in the borders, for the top and bottom borders, align the ruler with the seam of each pair of blocks, locate the center of the border, and place the mark there. Mark the placement of the knots on the side borders by centering them at the midpoint (5 inches) of each block. Then, mark a knot in each corner of the quilt border, centering it on the diagonal.

14. Press the quilt top smooth.

15. Following the Basic How-To's on pages 423 and 425–26, sandwich the quilt top, batting, and backing together and baste or pin them.

16. To tie a knot of pearl cotton or crochet cotton at each mark, cut a 4-inch length and thread a large embroidery needle with it. Working from the top of the quilt, punch the needle through all three layers of the quilt and make a single short stitch that is about 1/8 of an inch long. Tug on the ends of the thread until they are even, then tie a double knot. After you have made all of the knots, using scissors, trim the ends of the threads to a length that suits you; the threads on this quilt are roughly 1 inch long. You'll find an illustration of tying on page 429.

Bind the quilt

17. Trim the edges of the batting and backing so that they are even with those of the quilt top.

18. To make a bias binding that is approximately 1/4 inch wide, cut fabric D on the diagonal into strips that are 2 1/4 inches wide, piece them together, and attach them to the quilt following the instructions on pages 432–33. When finished, if you like, make a label for the quilt.

Jo Cox's Crib Quilt

BY MEG COX
Level of difficulty: ■□□□□
Can be pieced and quilted by hand or machine

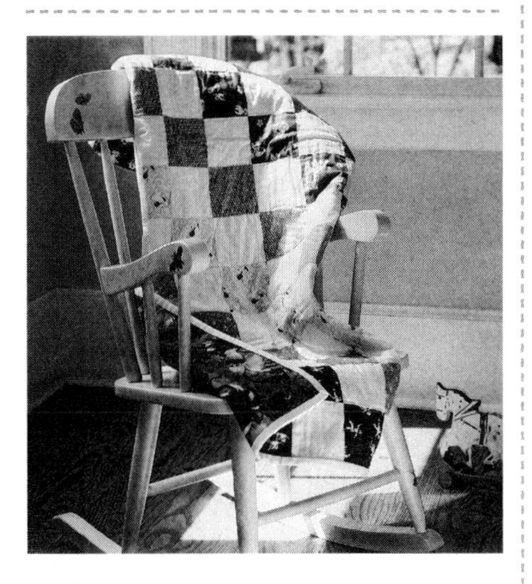

A BASIC PATCHWORK CRIB QUILT IS a great starter project, the quilting equivalent of a scarf for knitters. This pretty example is a copy of the first quilt I ever made. It was designed by my mother. Alternating white and colored three-inch squares create a diagonal pattern across the surface. My mother chose solid colored fabric—red, yellow, green, orange, and blue—but I thought it would be fun to use some of the charming vintage reproduction prints available now.

My first quilt was both pieced and quilted by hand. I didn't own a machine at the time, and I still often prefer handwork. Don't worry that this will make a delicate quilt that can't stand up to active infants and toddlers. My son slept with his handmade quilt for years, and it was washed a hundred times. Eventually, the fabric softened and frayed, but that's inevitable, even with a machine-sewn quilt, and proves that the quilt is loved!

For all my quilts in this book, I pieced the patchwork squares by hand. But due to the pressure of deadlines, the quilting was done by machine. I hired a friend from my local guild, Sandy Merritt, to do

To make this beginner project even simpler, don't worry about arranging the fabrics to make diagonal lines; simply alternate white squares with colored ones, perhaps prints that are from one color family. You could sew an all blue and white or all pink and white crib quilt.

For this project

- All fabric should be 100 percent cotton and 44 to 45 inches wide.
- Remember to remove the selvages from the fabric.
- All of the seam allowances in the quilt are ¼ inch.
- Press the quilt top smooth on the right side before sandwiching the layers together.

the quilting with her longarm machine. Most guilds have members who work as professional quilt finishers, or a local quilt shop can recommend someone. If you choose to quilt by machine, or hire a finisher, and want to copy the pattern used on my version of this project, it is illustrated on page 447. There are also directions for hand quilting.

You don't have to have a particular baby in mind to make a crib quilt. I made my first one three years before I married my husband and five years before our son was born. I saved it because I was proud of my first effort. My second was a crib quilt also, for a friend's first baby. By then, quilting seemed like second nature.

Makes an approximately 33½ by 51½–inch quilt; see Project 2 in the color insert.

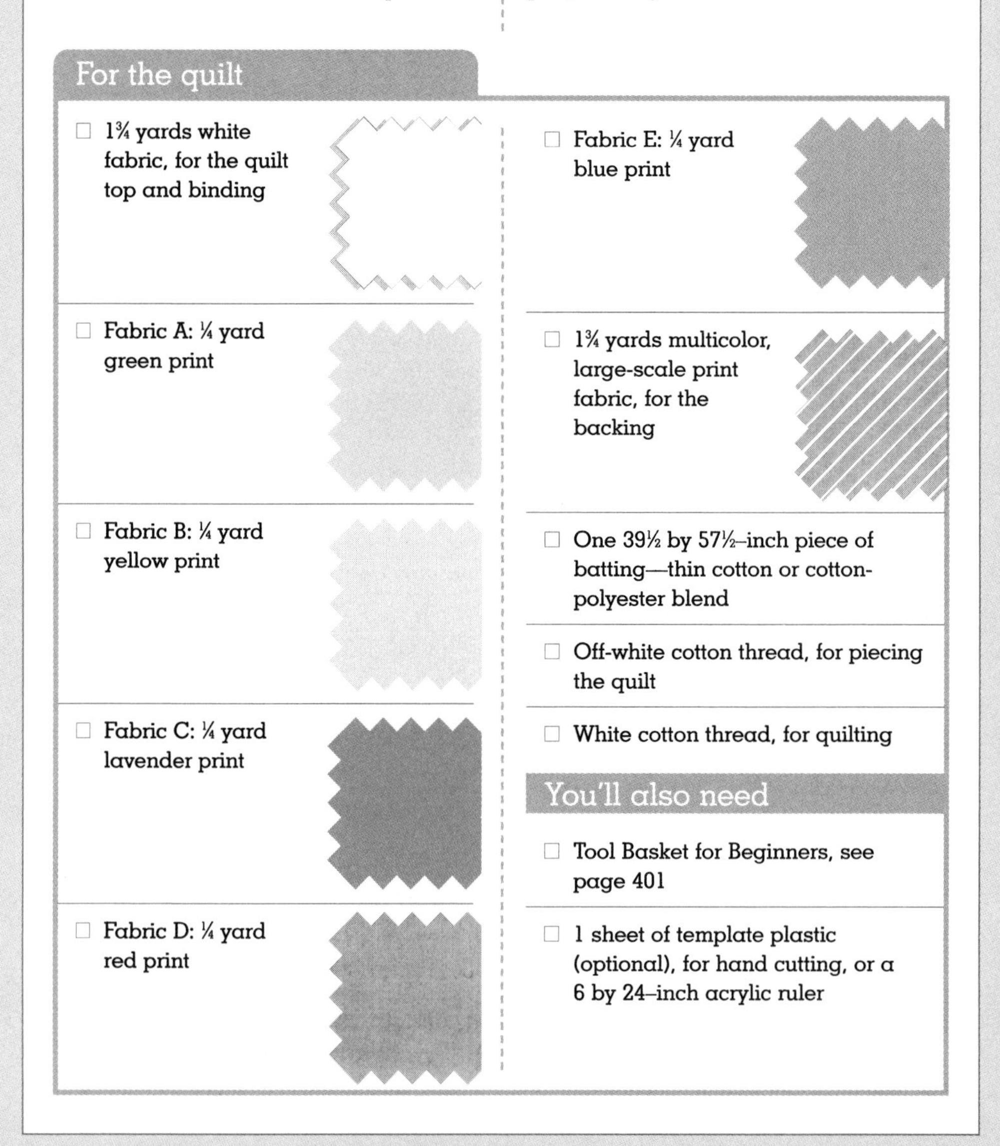

For the quilt

- ☐ 1¾ yards white fabric, for the quilt top and binding
- ☐ Fabric A: ¼ yard green print
- ☐ Fabric B: ¼ yard yellow print
- ☐ Fabric C: ¼ yard lavender print
- ☐ Fabric D: ¼ yard red print
- ☐ Fabric E: ¼ yard blue print
- ☐ 1¾ yards multicolor, large-scale print fabric, for the backing
- ☐ One 39½ by 57½–inch piece of batting—thin cotton or cotton-polyester blend
- ☐ Off-white cotton thread, for piecing the quilt
- ☐ White cotton thread, for quilting

You'll also need

- ☐ Tool Basket for Beginners, see page 401
- ☐ 1 sheet of template plastic (optional), for hand cutting, or a 6 by 24–inch acrylic ruler

QUILTING STRAIGHT LINES

Because of the deadline, I sent the crib quilt pictured on page 443 to a longarmer in my local quilt guild to do the quilting by machine. But when I made a quilt like this as my first project, I did all the quilting by hand. What helped me a lot to sew in a straight line was quarter-inch masking tape, which you can find in most quilt shops.

Machine quilters use the markings on their machine to help them quilt in straight lines. For a beginner, hand quilting is easiest if you stitch right along the edge of the seam lines, but that usually isn't enough stitching to secure a quilt. I used quarter-inch masking tape to help me sew straight diagonal lines through each block. You carefully position the tape where you want to sew, quilt right along the edge of the tape, then pull it off when that line of stitching is done. Generally you can reuse the same strip of masking tape several times before it loses its stickiness.

Cut out the quilt blocks

1. Cut ¾ yard crosswise off the white fabric and set it aside for the binding.

2. Cut the fabric for the quilt top into 3½-inch squares, cutting on the crosswise grain—this means that you will cut squares in a straight row across the width of the fabric.

To cut out the quilt blocks with scissors, use a ruler to mark rows of squares, or make a template out of template plastic that is 3½ inches square. Draw around the template on the wrong side of the fabric. If you plan to piece by hand, use the ruler to mark a ¼-inch seam line.

If you are using a rotary cutter, follow the Basic How-To's on page 418 and keep the fabric folded lengthwise in half (so that the edges with the selvages are together). Cut across the doubled width of fabric in 3½-inch strips, then layer two doubled strips together and cut 3½-inch squares from the four layers of fabric until you have as many squares as you need (there will be extra squares).

Cut the remaining yard of white fabric into 93 squares (from eight strips, if rotary cutting).

Cut the green print fabric (A) into 19 squares.

Cut the yellow print fabric (B) into 18 squares.

Cut the lavender print fabric (C) into 19 squares.

Cut the red print fabric (D) into 19 squares.

Cut the blue print fabric (E) into 19 squares.

Make the quilt top

3. Following Diagram 1 on page 446, arrange the blocks in seventeen rows of eleven blocks, alternating white blocks with colored blocks and creating diagonal rows of a single color.

C ←	→	B ←	→	A ←	→	E ←	→	D ←	→	C
→	C ←	→	B ←	→	A ←	→	E ←	→	D ←	
D ←	→	C ←	→	B ←	→	A ←	→	E ←	→	D
→	D ←	→	C ←	→	B ←	→	A ←	→	E ←	
E ←	→	D ←	→	C ←	→	B ←	→	A ←	→	E
→	E ←	→	D ←	→	C ←	→	B ←	→	A ←	
A ←	→	E ←	→	D ←	→	C ←	→	B ←	→	A
→	A ←	→	E ←	→	D ←	→	C ←	→	B ←	
B ←	→	A ←	→	E ←	→	D ←	→	C ←	→	B
→	B ←	→	A ←	→	E ←	→	D ←	→	C ←	
C ←	→	B ←	→	A ←	→	E ←	→	D ←	→	C
→	C ←	→	B ←	→	A ←	→	E ←	→	D ←	
D ←	→	C ←	→	B ←	→	A ←	→	E ←	→	D
→	D ←	→	C ←	→	B ←	→	A ←	→	E ←	
E ←	→	D ←	→	C ←	→	B ←	→	A ←	→	E
→	E ←	→	D ←	→	C ←	→	B ←	→	A ←	
A ←	→	E ←	→	D ←	→	C ←	→	B ←	→	A

4. Pin and then stitch the blocks together in each horizontal row, then press the seam allowances toward the colored fabrics, following the direction of the arrows in Diagram 1.

5. Pin and then stitch the rows together. Press these seam allowances toward the bottom of the quilt.

Assemble and quilt the crib quilt

6. Press the quilt top smooth.

7. Measure the completed quilt top and trim the backing fabric and the batting so that they are 3 inches larger than the quilt top on all sides.

8. Following the Basic How-To's on pages 423 and 425–26, sandwich the quilt top, batting, and backing together and baste or pin them.

9. The simplest way to quilt this, whether you are working by hand or machine, is to "stitch in the ditch." For every seam between two blocks of fabric

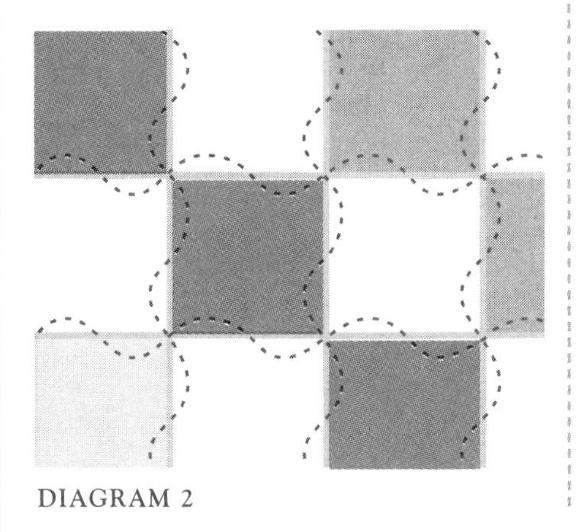

DIAGRAM 2

DIAGRAM 3

you'll see that one side is higher than the other. You stitch in the ditch by sewing in a straight line right along the lower edge of each seam. Quilt the vertical lines first, followed by the horizontals.

To duplicate the quilting design used in quilt Project 2 in the color insert, follow the pattern of intersecting wavy lines shown in Diagram 2. Or you can quilt it on diagonals the way I did when I made the quilt the first time, as shown in Diagram 3.

Bind the quilt

10. Trim the edges of the batting and backing so that they are even with those of the quilt top.

11. Using the remaining white fabric, make a bias binding that is approximately ¼ inch wide by cutting the white fabric on the diagonal into strips that are 2¼ inches wide, piece them together, and attach them to the quilt following the instructions on pages 432–33. When finished, if you like, make a label for the quilt.

Showcase Your Stash Tote Bag

BY MEG COX

Level of difficulty: ■ □ □ □ □

Can be pieced and quilted by hand or machine

THIS TOTE BAG IS EASY AND FAST. The project is essentially two original and contemporary patchwork blocks, with a filler to make them sturdy, a lining with an inside pocket, and handles secured with whimsical buttons. The construction is so quick, why not whip one up for yourself and another as a gift?

This is a good project for using up scraps or an excuse for buying precut fat quarters at the quilt shop. You can choose from a family of fabrics all designed by the same person or mix and match colors and patterns. I picked three lighter-colored and three darker-colored fabrics.

All six fabrics that I used were from my stash: I had long been looking for a project to showcase the fabric with rows of leaves, which was designed by Nancy Crow, one of my favorite art quilters. You can choose to make the tote bag using gorgeous, bright batiks or some of the fun novelty prints that are on the market. There are patterns featuring cats, dogs, cowboys, movies, sports themes, fruits, vegetables—you name it.

As with most of the projects I designed for the book, I did all the piecing by hand but sent it out to my guild friend, Sandy Merritt, for the quilting. Whether you choose to quilt by hand or machine, the sewing is done on just two layers, not three; you quilt together the patchwork sides of the tote and the interfacing/batting.

Unlike most quilts, which stay at home, this quilted bag will travel wherever you go. If you make it quirky and personal, you'll be sure to turn heads and start conversations.

Makes an approximately 19 by 15–inch tote bag; see Project 3 in the color insert.

For this project

- ◆ All fabric should be 100 percent cotton and 44 to 45 inches wide.
- ◆ Remember to remove selvages from the fabric.
- ◆ All of the seam allowances in the tote bag are ¼ inch.

For the tote bag

- ☐ ¼ yard or 1 fat quarter of each of 3 coordinating light-colored fabrics
- ☐ ¼ yard or 1 fat quarter of each of 3 coordinating dark-colored fabrics
- ☐ 1 yard heavyweight fusible interfacing, see pages 163–67
- ☐ 1 yard fabric for the lining and handles; I used black
- ☐ Off-white thread, for piecing the outside of the tote bag
- ☐ Thread of a contrasting color, for quilting
- ☐ 4 large sew-through buttons
- ☐ Black thread, or a color that matches the lining

You'll also need

- ☐ Tool Basket for Beginners, see page 401
- ☐ No. 2 pencil
- ☐ A 6 by 24–inch acrylic ruler
- ☐ 2 pieces of freezer paper, each at least 20 by 15 inches, for making templates
- ☐ Pressing cloth, see page 165

Prepare the templates

1. Using the pencil and ruler, draw two copies of the pattern block on the freezer paper, using the dimensions indicated in Diagram 1 on page 450.

2. Following the diagram, label each template with a letter from A to F; you will have two templates for each letter.

3. Cut all of the templates apart along the lines.

Make the quilt blocks

4. Arrange the two templates labeled A facedown on the wrong side of one of the ¼ yard pieces of light-colored fabric, so that the two long edges are along the crosswise grain. Pin the templates to the fabric, then cut out the quilt pieces. Label the wrong side of each of these quilt pieces A. Repeat with the remaining templates and ¼ yards of fabric.

5. Arrange one of the pieces labeled A on top of one labeled B, right sides facing, so that both corners on the short side are aligned (see Diagram 2 on page 450). Pin the pieces of fabric together. Stitch the pieces together, sewing along the edge of the fabric that is the same length on both sides. Press the seam allowance toward the darker fabric.

6. Pin and stitch one of the pieces labeled C to the AB patch the same way, then press the seam allowance toward the darker fabric. Sew pieces D, E, and F together in the same manner.

DIAGRAM 1

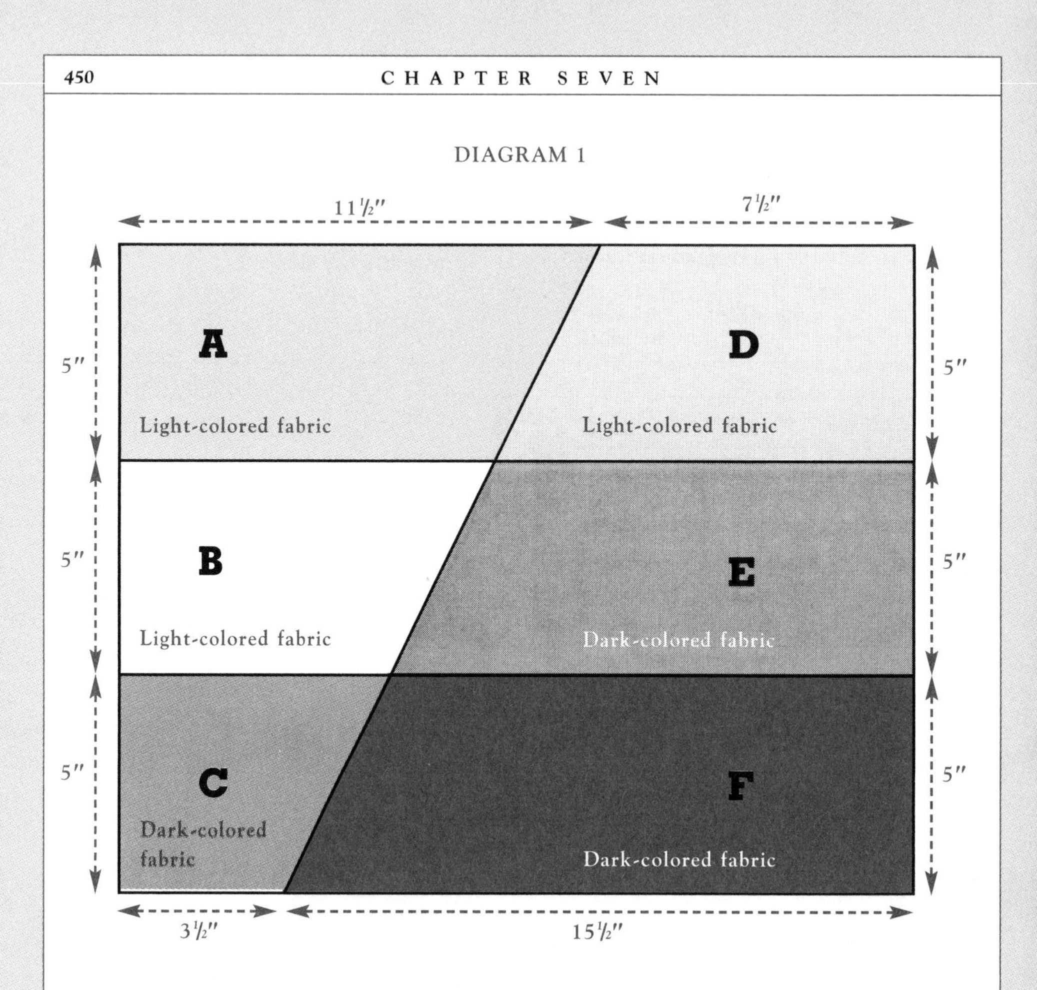

7. Arrange the ABC and DEF patches together, right sides facing, so that the diagonal edges align and the horizontal seams match (see Diagram 3). Pin the patches, then gently stitch them together along the diagonal, ¼ inch from the edge; take care not to stretch the fabric along the bias. Press the seam allowance to the darker side.

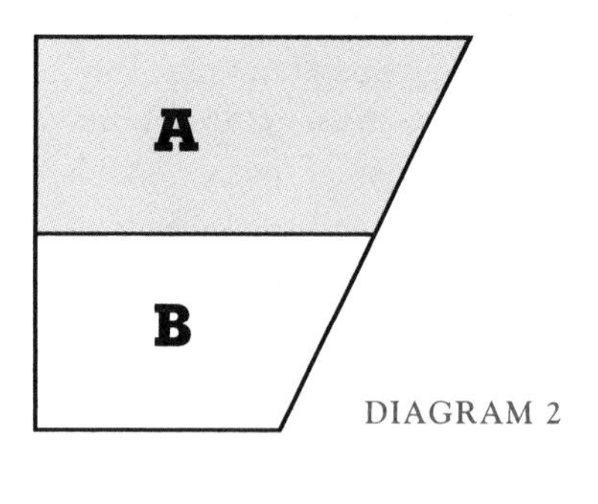

DIAGRAM 2

8. Using the remaining fabric patches A through F, sew together a second quilt block for the other side of the tote bag.

Quilt the blocks

9. Pin the two quilt blocks together with the right sides facing and stitch them together at the bottom (patches C and F). Press the seam allowance to one side.

DIAGRAM 3

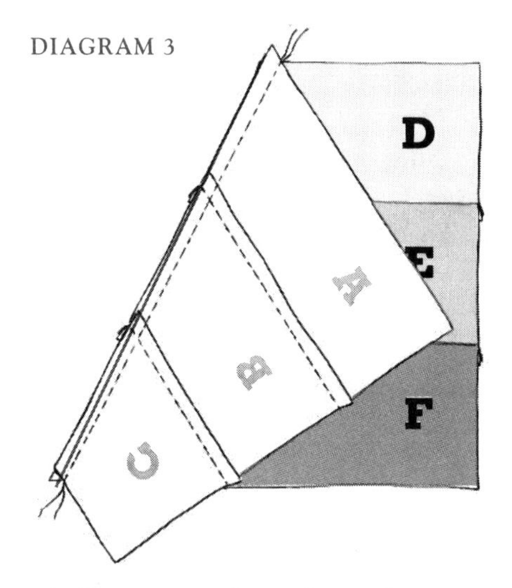

10. Cut a piece of interfacing that is ¼ inch smaller on all sides than the joined quilt blocks. Center the interfacing on the wrong side of the joined blocks and fuse it in place following the manufacturer's instructions and using a pressing cloth to protect your iron and ironing board from the sticky stuff in the interfacing.

11. Quilt the outside of the tote either by machine or by hand; the tote pictured on page 448 was quilted by longarmer Sandy Merritt in what she calls a tight feather meander pattern, but this is a good small size for quilting on your machine at home. Try a spontaneous pattern of loops and swirls, or do echo quilting around the patterns in the fabric. You can hand quilt similar designs or try quilting a series of angled lines parallel to the diagonal seam line on both sides.

Make the lining and handles

12. Using the lining fabric, cut two 3½ by 36–inch strips for handles, cutting along the lengthwise grain (parallel to where the selvages were). Then cut a rectangle for the lining that is the same size as the quilted, joined blocks. Cut two 5½-inch squares from the remaining lining fabric, for an inside pocket.

13. Cut 2 pieces of interfacing for the handles, each 1½ by 35½ inches. Position one strip of interfacing on the wrong side of one of the handle strips so that it is approximately ¼ inch from the edge and, using a pressing cloth, fuse it in place. Repeat with the second handle strip and interfacing.

Attach the pocket

14. To make the inside pocket, pin the two squares together, right sides facing, aligning the edges. Stitch around the pocket square, leaving a 2-inch opening on one side. Turn the pocket right side out and press it, folding the unsewn edges inside.

15. Position the pocket on the right side of the piece of fabric for the lining so that it is 2¼ inches below one of the short edges and centered between the two long edges. Make sure the unsewn edge is at the bottom of the pocket. Pin the pocket to the lining, then using matching thread, whipstitch along the sides and bottom of the pocket sewing it to the interfacing and lining.

Assemble the tote bag

16. Press the outside of the tote bag smooth on the right side.

17. Place the lining on top of the outside of the tote bag, right sides together. Pin, then stitch the lining and quilt blocks together on all sides ¼ inch from the edge, leaving a 4-inch opening along the short edge near the pocket. Clip across the seam allowances at the corners, close to the stitching, so that they will turn neatly.

18. Turn the tote bag right side out and pick out the corners with a pin or other tool (see page 496). Press the tote bag, turning the unsewn edges at the top of the tote bag inside; then, using matching thread, whipstitch these edges together. Using a double strand of thread, whipstitch the sides of the tote bag together.

Attach the handles

19. Place the handles wrong side up. Starting at a short end, press ¼ inch of the handle toward the interfacing; repeat with the remaining short ends. Then, fold in and press ¼ inch along each of the long edges. Fold the long sides in half together and press. Sew topstitching all around the handles ⅛ inch from the edges.

20. Using a double strand of thread, securely stitch a button to each end of the handles about 1 inch from the end.

21. After the buttons are attached, pin one end of a handle to the tote bag 4½ inches from a side seam and 2½ inches from the top edge. Pin the other end of this handle 4½ inches from the opposite side seam and 2½ inches from the top edge (see Diagram 4). Repeat with the remaining handle on the reverse side of the tote bag. Sew the handles securely onto the tote by using a double strand of thread to whipstitch around the edges of the handles where they come in contact with the patchwork sides.

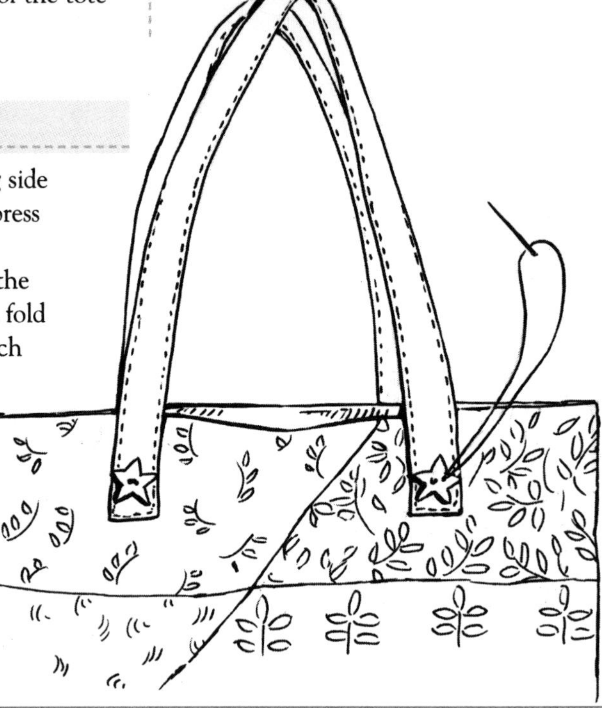

DIAGRAM 4

Kiss Quilt

BY MEG COX

Level of difficulty: ■ □ □ □ □

Can be pieced and quilted by hand or machine

THE TECHNOLOGY FOR TRANSFERRING photographs to fabric is push-button easy and provides yet another compelling argument for starting to quilt. Like the other projects before it, this quilted wall hanging is simple enough to be the first quilt project you make. I used a single photograph of my husband and me kissing at our wedding and printed it multiple times, but you could just as easily use four different photographs. Your photo quilt can feature whatever you love in life: your kids, your pets, your closest friends, the beach house you rent every summer. . . . Photo quilts are fantastic gifts for milestone events—weddings, anniversaries, major birthdays,

For this project

- ◆ All fabric should be 100 percent cotton and 44 to 45 inches wide.
- ◆ Remember to remove the selvages from the fabric.
- ◆ All of the seam allowances in the quilt are ¼ inch.
- ◆ Press the quilt top smooth on the right side before sandwiching the layers together.

PRINTING PHOTOS ON FABRIC

If you have a scanner or another way of manipulating images, the photographs you use for the photo quilt can be just about any size. The photo I used was roughly four inches square, but I printed it as a five-by-seven image on fabric.

If you want to get deeper into photo-transfer techniques, you'll find that there are cheaper but more time-consuming ways to do this that can give you greater creative leeway and let you work on larger pieces of fabric. There are many books and classes available for these other techniques: You'll find more information starting on page 199.

reunions, graduations, and retirements, among others.

I chose to use the same print fabric in four different colors to frame my photos, but you could pick four distinct but related fabrics, such as ones that contain the same shade of green—or even four wildly different but compatible fabrics. My only advice would be to stay away from big, busy prints: With a solid color or small print, the photos will stay the central focus.

When I made my Kiss Quilt it was the very first time I used photo transfer technology and I'm a total technophobe. If I can do this, anyone can! First I scanned the photograph I wanted to use into my computer. Then, I printed the photo on paper to see how it would look and to judge whether I wanted to crop the shot or adjust colors. Then, I put a sheet of paper-backed fabric into my printer and printed the photo on the treated cotton, using one of the most commonly available brands of paper-backed fabric, Printed Treasures. (Most quilt shops sell this and other brands in packs of between five and fifty sheets; for more information on photo-transfer options and where to purchase photo-printable fabric, see page 205.) Don't stack the fabric sheets in your printer as you would ordinary paper—it will work best if you print each sheet one at a time.

After peeling off the backing paper from the fabric, I was ready to make my quilt.

Makes an approximately 29 by 31–inch quilt; see Project 4 in the color insert.

For the quilt

- ☐ 1, or as many as 4, horizontal photographs, each 5 by 7 inches; scan the photo(s) into a computer or download digital photos(s)
- ☐ 4 pretreated fabric sheets such as Printed Treasures' Sew-On or EQ Printables, for printing photos using an ink-jet printer
- ☐ 1 fat quarter each of 4 print fabrics, for framing the photos
- ☐ ½ yard white fabric, for the inner border
- ☐ ½ yard dark-colored print fabric for the outer border
- ☐ 1½ yards bright batik fabric that complements the outer border, for the backing and binding
- ☐ One 35 by 37–inch piece of batting—thin cotton or cotton-polyester blend
- ☐ Off-white cotton thread, for piecing the quilt
- ☐ White thread, for quilting

You'll also need

- ☐ Tool Basket for Beginners, see page 401
- ☐ Color ink-jet printer
- ☐ A 6 by 24–inch acrylic ruler

TIP

If the paper backing on the photo transfer is hard to remove from the fabric, gently scoring the paper with dull scissors or heating it with a hair dryer will make pulling it off easier.

Transfer the photos to fabric

1. Before you print the photos on the fabric, make a test print on sheets of plain paper, adjusting your printer's settings as needed for the best quality. That way you can tweak the colors, crop the pictures or make other changes, and be sure you've got the images you want for your quilt without wasting any of the fairly expensive fabric sheets. You can also use the printer settings to reverse the image, as was done for two of the photo transfers in the quilt on page 453. You can use your scanner to enlarge and crop photos before you print as well.

2. Print one photo on each of the four fabric sheets, following the manufacturer's instructions for the pretreated fabric sheets you are using.

3. Peel the backing paper off each of the photo prints.

"Frame" the photo transfers

4. Trim the fabric sheets with the photo prints so that they are 1/4 inch larger than the images.

5. Cut two 3 1/2 by 5 1/2–inch rectangles and two 3 1/2 by 13 1/2–inch rectangles from each of the four fat quarters of fabric to use as framing strips.

6. Using two pieces of the same color, arrange one smaller framing strip on each of the shorter edges of a photo transfer, with the right side of the fabric facing the photo; make sure the edges are even. Pin the edges together, taking care to pin through the seam allowances only, not the printed fabric photo—pin marks in fabric photos are hard to "erase." Working on the wrong side of the photo transfer, stitch the frame to the photo, using a 1/4 inch seam allowance. Make sure there are no white spaces along the edges of the photo: Increase the seam allowance width if necessary.

7. Press the seam allowances toward the framing strips. Carefully pin the longer framing strips to the top and bottom edges of the photo transfer and side strips and stitch as before. Again, press the seam allowances toward the framing strips.

8. Make the remaining three photo blocks in the same way.

Make the quilt top

9. Arrange the photo blocks in two rows of two as shown in the diagram of the Kiss Quilt top on page 456. Stitch the blocks of each row together, then press the seam allowances toward the darker-colored fabric.

10. Pin, then stitch the two rows together. Press the seam allowances toward the bottom of the quilt.

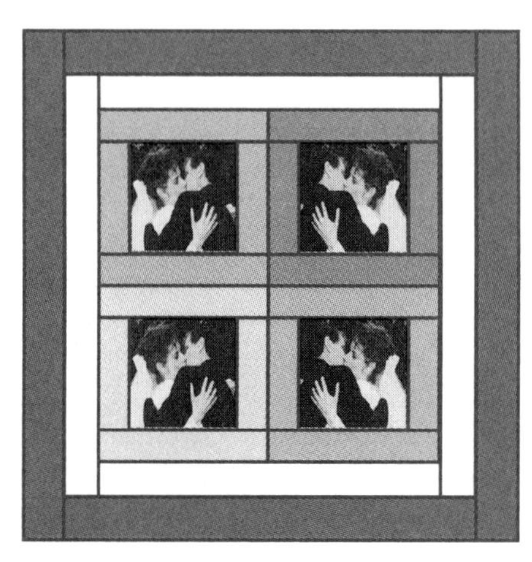

Kiss Quilt

11. Cut the white fabric for the inner border of the quilt top: You will need two 2½ by 23½–inch pieces for the top and bottom and two 2½ by 26–inch pieces for the sides. Pin and then stitch the shorter white borders to the top and bottom of the quilt, then pin and stitch the remaining white pieces to the sides.

12. Cut the dark-colored print fabric for the outer border of the quilt top: You will need two 2 by 29½–inch pieces and two 2 by 31½–inch pieces. Pin and then stitch the shorter borders to the top and bottom of the quilt, then pin and stitch the remaining pieces to the sides.

Assemble and quilt the photo quilt

13. Measure the completed quilt top and cut the batting and the backing fabric so that they are 2 inches larger than the quilt top on all sides. Since you are using the same batik fabric for the backing and binding, cut out the backing first. With a quilt that is this small, you will be able to cut one piece of backing without having to stitch together pieces of fabric. Then take the remaining piece of batik backing fabric, which will be about ½ yard, and cut it crosswise into four 2 inch–wide straight strips. (Although I prefer making a bias binding, I don't want you to run out of fabric. If you want to make a bias binding, I'd suggest starting with a bigger, 1¾ yard piece of backing fabric.)

14. Following the Basic How-To's on pages 423 and 425–26, sandwich the quilt top, batting, and backing together and baste or pin them.

15. Quilt the photo quilt by machine or by hand, taking care not to quilt over the photo transfers. The Kiss Quilt was quilted in the ditch—right over the seams—to outline each of the photos, and the longarmer who did the quilting chose a pattern of delicate ivy leaves for the framing strips and borders, picking up the leaf pattern in the outer border. This is also an excellent project for hand quilting because of its small size. You could quilt heart shapes or do echo quilting following the lines of the fabric's design. Another idea would be to quilt a series of parallel straight lines around each photo, accentuating the frames around your treasured photos.

Bind the quilt

16. Trim the edges of the batting and backing even with those of the quilt top.

17. Piece the binding strips together and attach them to the quilt following the instructions on page 433. When finished, if you like, make a label for the quilt.

Meg's Bag

BY MEG COX

Level of difficulty: ■ □ □ □ □

Can be pieced and quilted by hand or machine—or tied

I FIRST MADE THIS LITTLE PURSE TO advertise my quilt book before it was in the stores. I simply printed a digital image of the book's cover art onto fabric and used it to create a simple bag about the size of the book you're holding. I liked to wear it to quilt shows, where it started many conversations.

After that, I realized that any photo could be used to make a cute but dramatic small bag and that it was the perfect project for quilters who need a little instant gratification. It doesn't take very much in the way of supplies or experience, yet making this quick project will let you play with some of the hottest techniques in quilting today. You print a photo on fabric using your own computer printer. Then, you make two mini quilts and sew them together to make the purse. If you like you can try hand or machine quilting on a very small scale. For the "Tulip" bag here, I did the simplest possible form of quilting—stitching around the shapes in the photo of Tulip, the dog, on the front of the purse, and around the pattern of the fabric on the back. When I made my "book bag," I used the quickest quilt finishing technique—tying.

If you've been quilting for years, I urge you to bring your own aesthetic to this exercise. Instead of making the back of the purse out of a single piece of fabric,

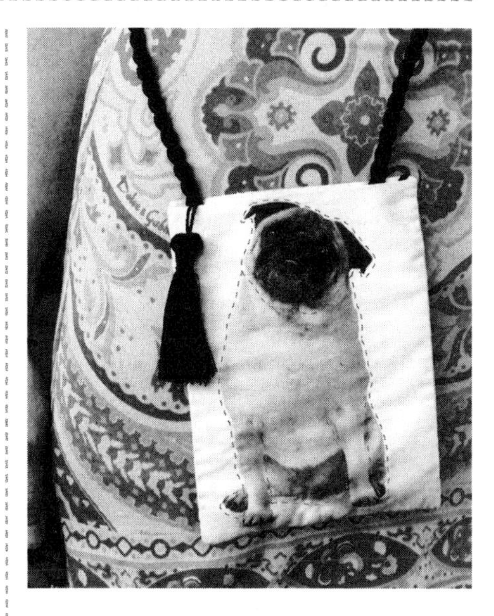

create a patchwork design. Try a crazy quilt style or make the purse out of silk rather than cotton. You can embellish the front and back of the purse as much as you like by adding beads, trinkets, ribbons, and more. There's been a trend of making very small art quilts lately, some the size of postcards; here's a chance to make art quilt bags that aren't much bigger or more time-consuming.

Finally, there's no rule that only one side of the purse has to be a photograph. Your quilted bag can include photos on both sides: two views of something you love, two different people you care about. Or, you can use the same photo on the front and the back. (For more about photo transfer see pages 199–211.)

Makes an approximately 6 by 8–inch purse; see Project 5 in the color insert for a photograph of one version of the purse.

For the purse

- ☐ 1 photo, any size (either a digital photo you can download to your computer or a photo you've scanned into your computer)
- ☐ 1 pretreated 8½ by 11–inch fabric sheet, such as Printed Treasures' Sew-On or EQ Printables, for printing a photo using an ink-jet printer.
- ☐ ⅛ yard fabric with a print outline that will be fun to quilt, or a scrap from your stash that is at least 6½ by 8½ inches, for the back of the purse
- ☐ ⅛ yard fabric for the lining; choose something that picks up one of the colors in the photograph or backing fabric, or use plain black, which won't show stains
- ☐ ⅛ yard lightweight interfacing or fusible web, such as Pellon Wonder-Under, see page 167
- ☐ Thread for quilting the purse, either a neutral color or if you are a confident quilter, a bright color that will really show up; or 1½ yards of quarter-inch ribbon, for tying the purse
- ☐ Off-white cotton thread, for piecing the purse
- ☐ 1 to 1½ yards twisted silk cord, black or any color you wish, for the strap
- ☐ 2 silk tassels in a color that matches the silk cord (optional)
- ☐ Black thread (optional), for sewing on the straps
- ☐ Clear nylon thread such as the kind that's using in stringing beads, for sewing the sides of the purse

You'll also need

- ☐ Tool Basket for Beginners, see page 401
- ☐ Color ink-jet printer
- ☐ A 6 by 24–inch acrylic ruler
- ☐ Pressing cloth, see page 165
- ☐ Point turner or chopstick, see page 496
- ☐ Transparent tape

For this project

- ◆ All of the fabric should be 100 percent cotton.
- ◆ Remember to remove the selvages from all fabric.
- ◆ All of the seam allowances in the purse are ¼ inch.

Transfer the photo to fabric

1. Before you print the photo on the fabric, make a test print on sheets of plain paper, adjusting your printer's settings as needed for the best quality. That way you can tweak the colors, crop the picture or make other changes, and be sure you've got the image you want for your bag without wasting any of the fairly expensive fabric sheets. I don't have any

TIP

Big craft shops like Jo-Ann's carry twisted silk cord in several thicknesses and some quilt shops may carry it as well. I used one yard of cord for the strap for the "book bag." For the purses I made with photos of my son and of Tulip the dog, I wanted to be able to drape the strap across my shoulder, so I made a longer strap of one-and-a-half yards.

In order to keep the cord from unraveling, tape the cut ends with transparent tape (it may even come that way). Frequently when you buy a length of cord from a craft store they wrap a piece of tape around the place where it will be cut. Then they cut through the center of the tape, leaving both cut ends protectively wrapped.

fancy editing software for photos so I'm not able to print out a photo that is exactly the size I want (I find the standard photo size of 5 by 7 inches a tad small for a purse). Instead, I set the size of the photo to fill a letter-size page and print the photo at that size.

2. Once you have a photo image that suits you, follow the manufacturer's instructions for the pretreated fabric sheets you are using to print the photo on the fabric, then trim the fabric photo to make a 6½ by 8½–inch rectangle.

Prepare the rest of the fabric

3. Cut out a 6½ by 8½–inch rectangle from the print fabric for the back of the purse.

4. Cut out two 6½ by 8½–inch rectangles from the fabric for the purse lining.

5. Cut two 6 by 8–inch pieces of fusible interfacing.

6. Place one piece of the lining fabric on an ironing board wrong side up. Arrange one piece of interfacing sticky side down (the tiny raised dots are on the sticky side) on top of the piece of lining fabric, adjusting it carefully so that it is centered with an even edge of lining fabric on all four sides of the interfacing. Following the manufacturer's instructions, fuse the interfacing to the piece of lining by pressing them carefully on both sides, using a pressing cloth to protect your iron and ironing board.

7. Repeat with the second piece of lining fabric and fusible interfacing.

Sew the lining to the purse

8. Place the piece of photo fabric faceup on your work surface. Position one of the lining pieces on top, right side down, so that the edges are exactly flush. Pin the edges together, taking care to pin through the seam allowances only, not the printed fabric photo—pin marks in fabric photos are hard to "erase." Stitch the photo fabric and lining together on all sides ¼ inch from the edge, leaving a 2-inch opening so that you can turn the pieces inside out.

9. Clip across the seam allowances at the corners, close to the stitching so that they will turn neatly. Turn the front of the purse inside out, then use a chopstick or point turner to poke out the fabric in the corners, so that they

TIP

Most pretreated fabric transfer sheets work only on ink-jet printers, so make sure that yours isn't a laser printer. Color ink-jet printers can be purchased for less than $80 and are well worth the investment for quilters who want to use photos in their work.

have a crisp edge. Press the front of the purse so that it is flat and even. Using a slip stitch (see Diagram 1), carefully stitch up the opening in the edge.

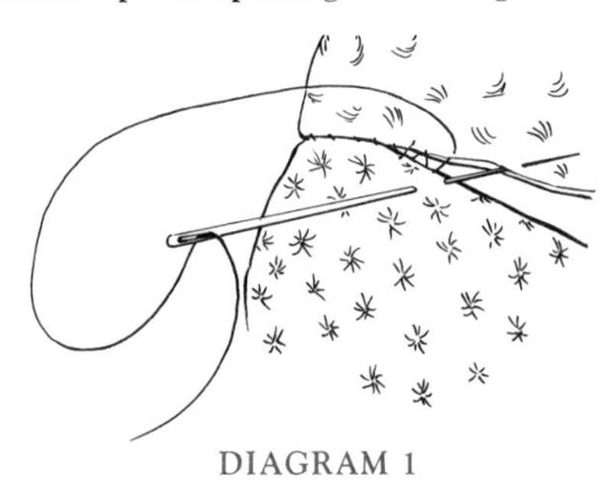

DIAGRAM 1

10. Repeat with the fabric for the back of the purse and the second piece of lining fabric.

Quilt the purse

11. You've now got two mini quilts that are each approximately 6 by 8 inches and ready for the actual quilting. If you want to tie both sides of the purse instead of quilting them, decide on where you want the ties to be placed and how many there should be (in Diagram 2 you'll see how I tied the back of the "book bag"). Cut a piece of ribbon that is about 3 inches long and thread it on an embroidery needle with a large eye. Poke the needle down into the quilt and pull it back up about ⅛ inch away. Tie a double knot (for more about tying see page 428). Repeat, tying as many knots as desired. Trim the ties or leave them as they are.

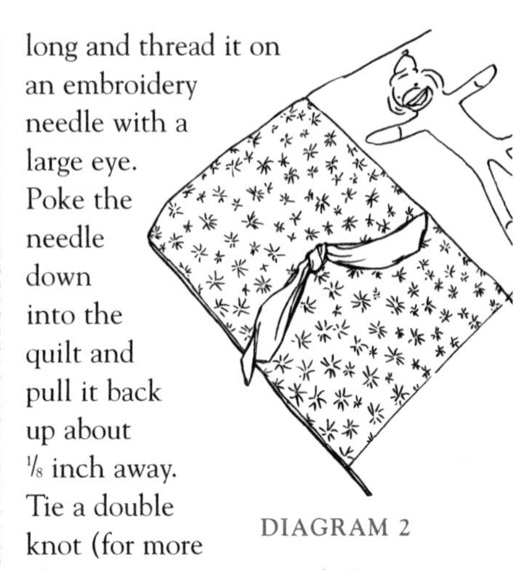

DIAGRAM 2

If you want to quilt the purse, whether you are working by hand or machine, the simplest approach is to quilt around the dominant lines of the photo on the front and of the fabric on the back (see Diagram 3). You'll find instructions on hand quilting on page 427; for machine quilting, see page 429.

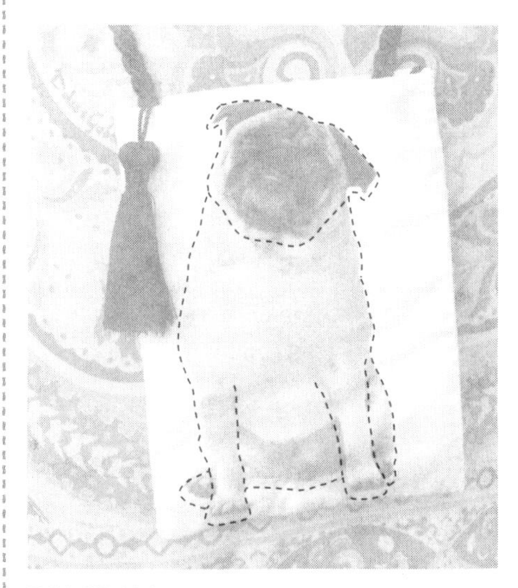

DIAGRAM 3

Attach the strap

12. Cut the silk cord to the length you wish, 36 inches for a strap for a shoulder bag or 54 inches if you want to be able to drape the strap around your neck and have the purse fall below the waist. If they are not taped already, tape the ends of the cord.

13. Attach the strap to the back of the purse by positioning the end on the inside at a side edge so that the cord extends down about 1½ inches from the top. Using either black thread or clear nylon thread, sew the end of the strap firmly in place, being careful not to poke the needle through the outside of the back. If you are adding tassels, slip the loop at the top of one of the tassels over the end of the cord before you position it on the back of the purse, sliding it up a few inches so that it is out of the way when you stitch the cord to the purse (see Diagram 4). Then, slide the tassel back down the cord and take a few stitches to secure the loop the tassel hangs from to the purse (Diagram 5).

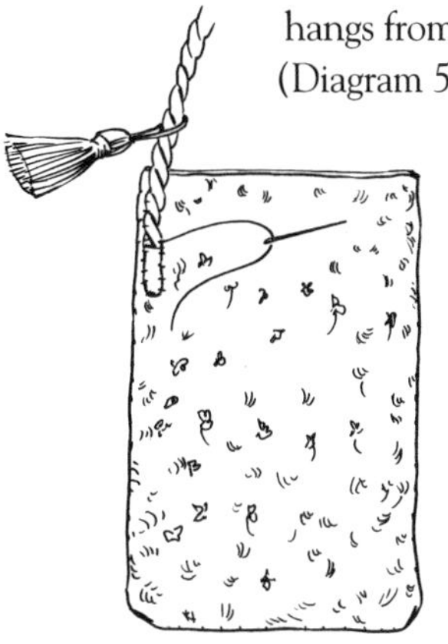

DIAGRAM 4

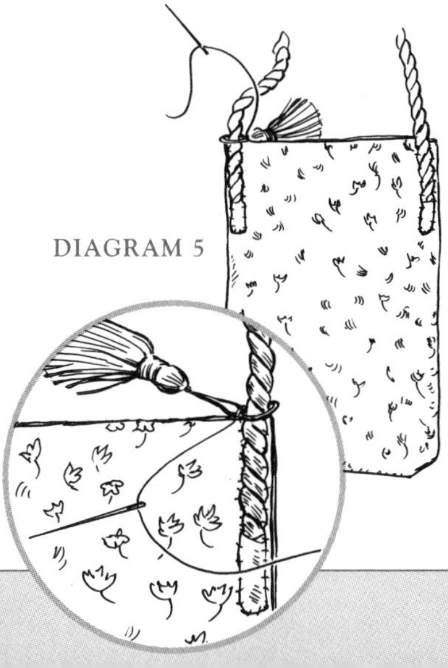

DIAGRAM 5

TIP

Normally the three layers of a quilt are quilted together and the raw edges are covered with a binding. Here, and in the tote bag on page 448, interfacing or fusible web takes the place of batting. And, you are sewing the pieces for the front and back to the lining pieces the way you would sew a pillow. The seams will create a finished edge when the pieces are turned inside out. You will need to leave an opening in one of the seams so that you can do this. Make sure to sew extra stitches on both sides of the opening so it won't pull apart when the pieces are turned inside out.

14. Attach the loose end of the cord and the remaining tassel, if there is one, to the other side of the purse the same way.

Assemble the purse

15. Place the purse lining side up, on a work surface. Arrange the photo front of the purse, lining side down, on top of it. Using pins, secure the front and back together, then slipstitch the edges together with clear thread. Start by stitching the bottom seam, then sew both sides. Now, it's time to carry your purse in public and show off!

Rosy Quilt

BY KAFFE FASSETT AND LIZA PRIOR LUCY

Level of difficulty: ■■□□□

Can be pieced and quilted by hand or machine—or tied

IT MIGHT NOT BE OBVIOUS LOOKING AT this striking quilt, but the design is among the simplest in this book. The basic pattern consists of alternating plain fabric squares with easy Nine Patch blocks. And the border is simply made of smaller plain squares. Rank beginners should feel perfectly comfortable trying this project. One of my first quilts was also a Kaffe and Liza creation, and I know from experience their quilts look harder to make than they actually are.

You can recognize a quilt designed by Kaffe and Liza from a mile off: The dazzling colors hit you right between the eyes. Their secret is that they violate what many quilt teachers think is an absolute rule, the old saw about using contrasting colors. Rather than mixing dark, medium, and light colors, Kaffe and Liza use similar tones and often just a few colors. One of their quilts might be composed mostly of shades of blue with a little white, but there will be dozens of different fabrics of varied shades and patterns. The quilt will look vibrant, not merely busy, as the blueness pulls the whole quilt together. Also, the two observe in their books that tiny patterns appear like solids from a distance, but give off more energy and intensity than solid colors.

Kaffe and Liza return again and again to simple patterns they love, such as this

one. The first time they used this pattern, they tried to make it using only fabrics that featured roses or flowers. They've done versions in all shades of leafy greens, deep jewel tones, and drab repro-

For this project

- ◆ All fabric should be 100 percent cotton and 44 to 45 inches wide.
- ◆ Remember to remove the selvages from the fabric.
- ◆ All of the seam allowances in the quilt are ¼ inch.
- ◆ Press the quilt top smooth on the right side before sandwiching the layers together.

For the quilt

- ☐ ½ yard each of at least 10 different large-scale prints
- ☐ ¼ yard each of at least 10 different small-scale prints
- ☐ ¾ yard each of 2 different striped fabrics
- ☐ 4 yards fabric for the backing; Liza suggests using your favorite fabric from the quilt top
- ☐ ¾ yard small-scale print fabric, for the binding
- ☐ One 63 by 81–inch piece of batting—Liza prefers thin cotton batting or, if you tie the quilt, wool batting
- ☐ Neutral-colored thread, for piecing and quilting
- ☐ Pearl cotton or crochet cotton thread for tying the quilt (optional)

You'll also need

- ☐ Tool Basket for Beginners, see page 401

duction fabrics from bygone eras, but it is still known as the Rosy Quilt. Kaffe almost exclusively uses fabric he designs in his quilts. If you want to use his fabric but it's not at your local quilt shop, you can order it from Liza's Web-only quilt shop, www.gloriouscolor.com.

For more about master quilt teachers Kaffe Fassett and Liza Prior Lucy see page 331.

Makes an approximately 60 by 78–inch quilt; see Project 6 in the color insert.

Cut out the quilt blocks

1. Using scissors or a rotary cutter, cut eighteen 9½-inch squares from the large-scale fabrics for the plain blocks.

2. Cut 3½-inch squares for the Nine Patch blocks from the small-scale fabrics: You will need 17 sets of 5 squares, each set cut from a single fabric pattern, and 17 sets of 4 squares.

3. Cut twenty-six 5-inch squares from each of the striped fabrics for the inner border, for a total of 52 squares.

4. Cut 3½-inch squares for the outer border from any of the leftover large- and small-scale fabrics; you will need 88.

TIP

Liza Prior Lucy says this is meant to be a "scrappy" quilt, so the fabric yardage is really simply a guideline. You can include more—or fewer—different fabric patterns to suit yourself. Feel free to use some of the large-scale pattern fabric when you cut out the smaller blocks. Cutting extra 3½-inch large- and small-scale fabric patches will give you more options when you arrange the blocks for the outer border. And when quilting, pick a thread color that's subdued and don't quilt too densely; you want the fabric to take center stage.

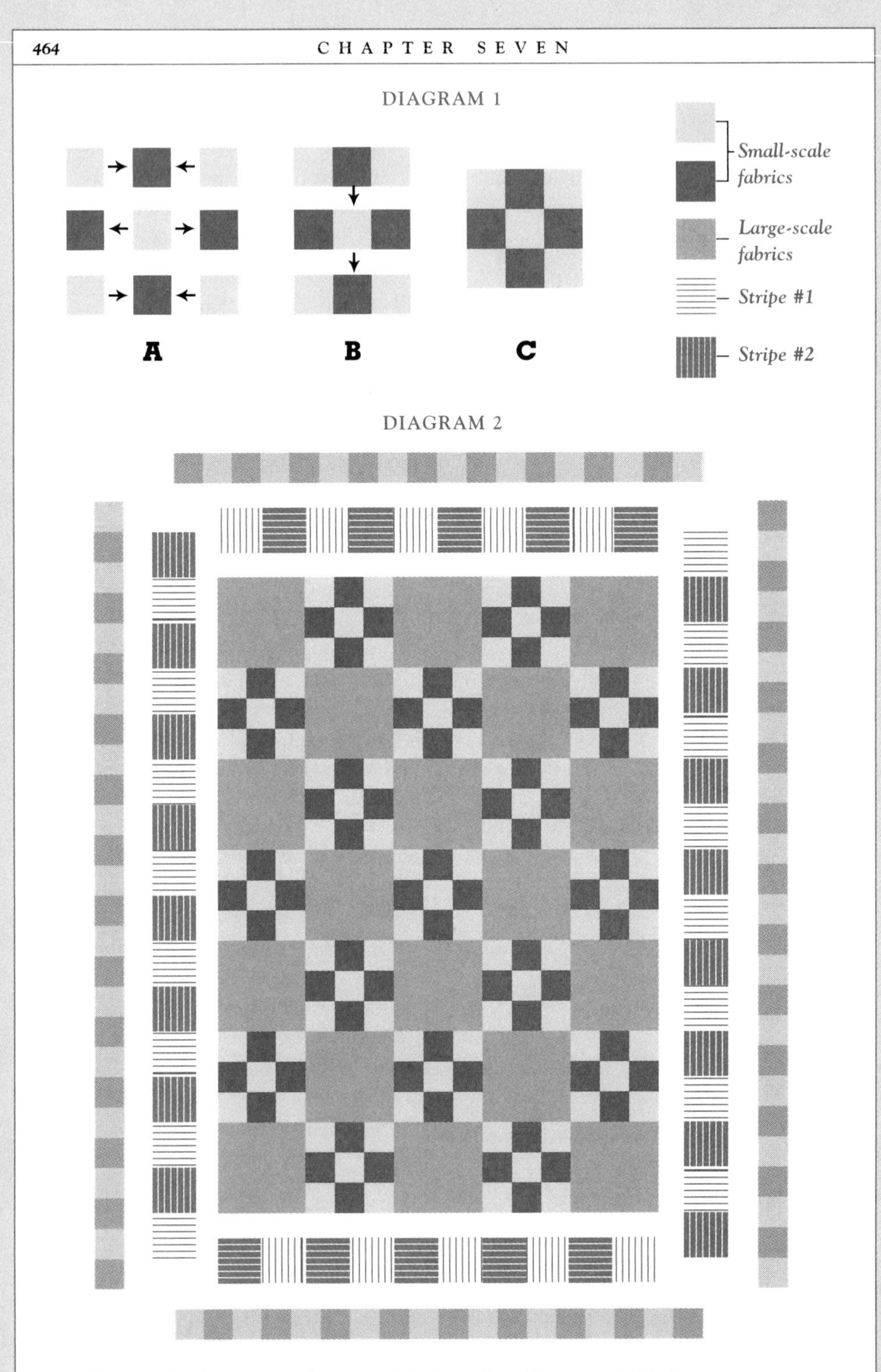

The outer border consists of squares of both small- and large-scale fabrics.

Make the Nine Patch blocks

5. Make 17 Nine Patch blocks: For each block, choose five 3½-inch squares from one small-scale fabric and four 3½-inch squares from a different small-scale fabric. Arrange the squares to form a Nine Patch block as shown in Diagram 1-A.

6. Pin and then stitch the horizontal rows of squares together. Press the seam allowances in the direction shown in the arrows in Diagram 1-A.

7. Pin and then stitch the rows of squares together. Press these seam allowances in the direction shown in the arrows in Diagram 1-B. The result will be Nine Patch blocks as shown in Diagram 1-C.

Assemble the quilt center

8. Alternate the 17 Nine Patch blocks with the 18 plain blocks to make a checkerboard pattern following the design in the center section of the quilt top assembly shown in Diagram 2. Play with the positions of the blocks until you are satisfied with the balance of colors and fabric patterns, substituting extra blocks, if you have them. The photos of Project 6 in the color insert will give you an idea of the overall effect.

9. Pin, then stitch the blocks of each horizontal row together. Press the seam allowances toward the plain blocks.

10. Pin, then stitch the horizontal rows together. Press these seam allowances downward.

Make and attach the inner border

11. Arrange the striped fabrics in two rows of 10 squares and two rows of 16 squares as shown in Diagram 2, alternating the two fabrics and positioning them so that the stripes of one fabric square are horizontal and the stripes of the fabric squares next to it are vertical. Pin, then stitch the squares of each row together.

12. Pin, then stitch the two rows of 10 squares to the top and bottom of the quilt center. Press the seam allowances toward the borders.

13. Pin, then stitch the remaining two rows of 16 squares to the two longer sides of the quilt center and press the seam allowances toward the borders.

Make and attach the outer border

14. Arrange fifty-two 3½-inch squares in two rows of 26. Arrange thirty-six 3½-inch squares in two rows of 18. Pin, then stitch the squares of each row together.

15. Pin, then stitch the two rows of 18 squares to the top and bottom of the quilt top. Press the seam allowances toward the outside edges.

16. Pin, then stitch the two rows of 26 squares to the long sides of the quilt top. Press the seam allowances toward the outside edges.

Assemble and quilt the Rosy Quilt

17. Press the quilt top smooth.

18. Piece together the fabric for the backing: First cut it in half crosswise, then pin and stitch two of the longer edges together. Trim the backing fabric so that it is at least 63 by 81 inches large.

19. Following the Basic How-To's on pages 423 and 425–26, sandwich the quilt top, batting, and backing together and baste or pin them.

20. Quilt or tie as desired; Kaffe and Liza's quilt was quilted with an overall meander stitch done in free-motion quilting (see page 431). If you are hand quilting, Liza suggests a repeating leaf or flower pattern. Because she and Kaffe Fassett love to make quilts using vivid, busy fabrics, you won't need to rely on the quilting for visual interest. You might choose to just quilt around existing design elements in the fabric of each square: This is easy for even a beginner and it will make the shapes in the fabric "pop" out more boldly.

Bind the quilt

21. Trim the edges of the batting and backing so that they are even with those of the quilt top.

22. To make a bias binding that is approximately 1/4 inch wide, cut the binding fabric on the diagonal into strips that are 2 1/4 inches wide, piece them together, and attach them to the quilt following the instructions on pages 432–33. When finished, if you like, make a label for the quilt.

Quilted Keepsake Greeting Cards

BY RICKY TIMS
Level of difficulty: ■ ■ □ □ □
Can be pieced and quilted by hand or machine

Ricky Tims combines fabric and paper to make fun greeting cards that their recipients will treasure. It's fitting that the poplular teacher came up with outside-the-box "quilts" that look harder than they actually are.

Like the lovely ornaments offered by Sue Benner, this project is something that grew out of Ricky's own life and his impulses to both design and give quilted items to people he loves on special occasions. "Over the years I began using leftover fabrics to make personalized greeting cards," he says. "There are three designs shown here which are simple and quick to make. Use these as stepping-stones for your own ideas. Once you see how easy it is, you might become addicted to creating your own unique cards using a few scrappy bits of fabric and those wonderful decorative machine stitches."

Ricky uses his own hand-dyed fabrics to make his cards, using shiny and variegated threads in decorative sewing machine stitches. You can order Ricky's hand-dyed fabric from his website, at www.rickytims.com, or use any colorful fabric you wish.

For more about master quilt teacher Ricky Tims see page 369.

For the greeting cards

- ☐ Three 5 by 6–inch pieces of background fabric in different colors
- ☐ Assorted scraps of hand-dyed or other brightly colored fabric in a variety of colors
- ☐ 3 pieces of thin cotton batting, each approximately 5 by 7 inches
- ☐ 3 blank 5 by 7–inch greeting cards with matching envelopes
- ☐ Cotton or polyester thread in vibrant, variegated colors
- ☐ Yellow-orange polyester or rayon thread

You'll also need

- ☐ Tool Basket for Beginners, see page 401
- ☐ Glue stick
- ☐ A sewing machine that can sew decorative stitches (optional)

Makes three 5 by 7–inch greeting cards; see Project 7 in the color insert.

Assemble the appliqués

1. Position each rectangle of background fabric on top of a piece of batting.

2. Tear six to nine smaller rectangles and strips, ranging from ½ to 4 inches in width, from fabrics of contrasting colors. Refer to the cards in the color insert for inspiration.

3. Arrange these smaller rectangles of fabric on the fabric backgrounds. When you are satisfied with the results, use dabs of the glue stick to hold the appliqués lightly in place.

4. To machine appliqué, using variegated or contrasting thread in the needle and either the same or a neutral thread in the bobbin, machine stitch the appliqués to the fabric background and batting. Use a wide, decorative stitch, if available.

To appliqué by hand, use variegated or brightly colored thread to attach the fabric pieces to the background by embroidering a satin stitch or other decorative stitch.

In some of Ricky's cards he sewed embroidery stitches using only bright orange thread; in others he used the orange thread for decorative touches and used a variegated thread as well—the complexity of the design and whether you use more than one type of thread is up to you. Don't trim the ends off of the threads; leave all of them loose for an artistic effect.

Quilt the greeting cards

5. To machine quilt the cards, thread your sewing machine with variegated thread in the needle as well as in the bobbin and set the machine for an open decorative stitch sewn with straight stitches, rather than a dense pattern that includes satin stitching. Trim each piece of appliquéd background fabric with its attached batting to 4 by 6 inches. Center each on the front of one of the blank cards and secure it in place with the glue stick.

Unfold a blank card (you don't want to sew the two halves of the card together) and stitch along the long edges of the background, ⅛ inch from the edge of the fabric, sewing through the paper. Repeat with the remaining two cards.

To hand quilt the cards, trim each piece of appliquéd fabric with its attached batting to 4 by 6 inches, then using decorative embroidery stitches, quilt through the two layers. Center each mini quilt on the front of one of the blank cards and secure it well in place using the glue stick.

Finish the greeting cards

6. Sign your quilted artwork and send the greeting cards off to your friends.

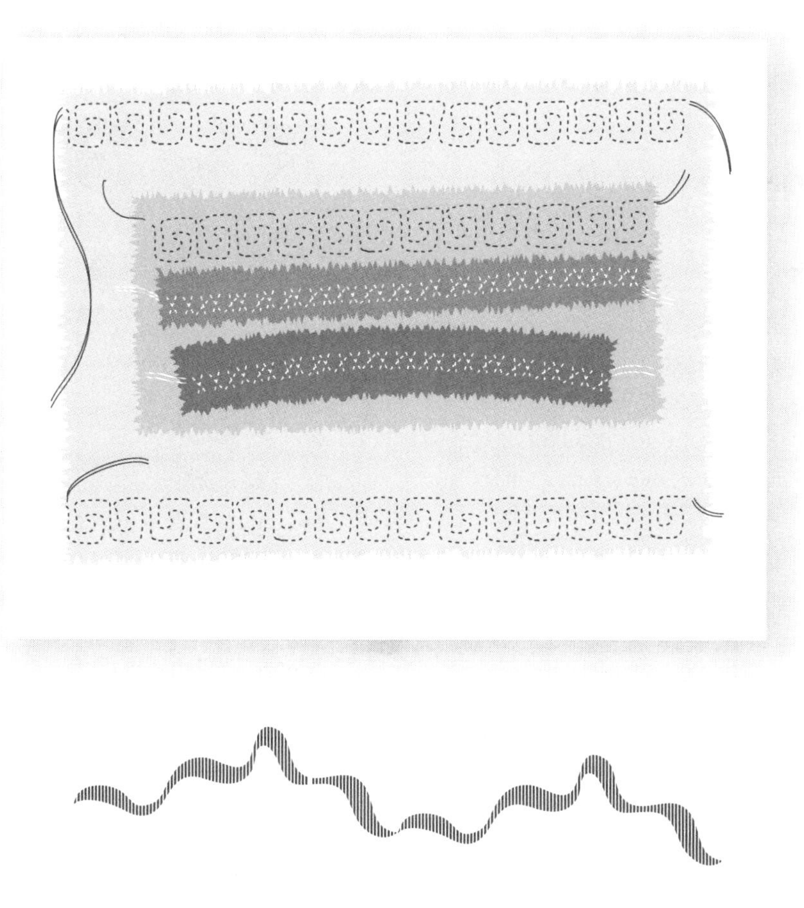

Wild and Crazy Fused Ornaments

BY SUE BENNER
Level of difficulty: ■■□□□
Can be quilted and finished by hand or machine

EVERY YEAR ART QUILTER SUE BENNER makes a new Christmas ornament for each of her two sons. Whether or not you decide to adopt this lovely tradition, following her patterns and directions is a great way to sample some of the design and construction techniques that make her work stand out.

These star and heart ornaments are made by fusing fabric scraps to simple background shapes. One side is covered like a crazy quilt, but because it's fused, you don't have to do any stitching. Sue embellishes the ornaments using free-motion quilting, a satin stitch edging, and other techniques, but you could also embellish them by hand, using simple embroidery stitches. Many novice quilters stick exclusively to cotton: One of the fun aspects of this project is that it gives you permission to play with some

For the ornaments

- ☐ 2 pieces of colorful silk fabric, each approximately 6 inches square
- ☐ 4 to 10 scraps of different fabrics—silk, cotton, or polyester—in a variety of colors and patterns
- ☐ ⅜ yard lightweight fusible web, see page 167, such as Pellon Wonder-Under
- ☐ 2 pieces of 100 percent cotton needle-punched batting, each approximately 6-inches square
- ☐ Colorful cotton and gold metallic thread or embroidery floss

You'll also need

- ☐ Tool Basket for Beginners, see page 401
- ☐ Iron
- ☐ Pressing cloth, see page 165
- ☐ A quarter coin, for a template (optional)
- ☐ Two 6-inch square pieces of tracing paper

TIP

Slippery metallic thread is not easy to use and requires special sewing machine needles. Beginners may want to stick with brightly colored cotton threads. You'll find tips on using metallic thread in your sewing machine, in Libby Lehman's profile on page 350.

beautiful silk. Sue says she acquired much of her silk stash by buying old blouses at flea markets; you can try that approach or buy a small quantity of pretty silk at your quilt shop or from an Internet shop.

For more about master quilt teacher Sue Benner, see page 314.

Makes 2 ornaments approximately 6-inches in size; see Project 8 in the color insert.

Make the foundations for the ornaments

1. Cut two pieces each approximately 6-inches square from the fusible web.

2. Fuse one square of web to each 6-inch square of silk, following the manufacturer's instructions and using a pressing cloth to protect your iron and ironing board.

3. Peel the paper backing off the fused web on one piece of silk and fuse one square of batting to it.

4. Repeat with the remaining web-backed square of silk and square of batting.

Decorate the polka-dot sides

5. Fuse web to the wrong side of several small scraps of fabric in colors that will contrast brightly with the background colors fused to the batting.

6. Remove the paper backing from the fabric and then working freehand or using a quarter as a template, cut a number of approximately 1-inch polka-dot circles.

7. Scatter polka dots, web side down, over the fabric-covered side of one of the 6-inch squares, arranging them about ¼ inch apart. Using a pressing cloth, press the polka dots to fuse them in place.

8. Repeat with the second 6-inch square of fabric.

Cover the crazy quilt sides

9. Fuse web to the wrong side of more fabric scraps in assorted colors.

10. Remove the paper backing from the fabric and cut out a variety of shapes—squares, quadrangles, and strips—that are approximately ½ to 4½ inches long.

11. Place one of the 6-inch squares batting side up. Arrange the pieces of silk, web side down, over the batting so that they cover it completely, making a random, crazy-quilt design. When you are pleased with the result, using a pressing cloth, press to fuse everything in place.

12. Repeat with the second 6-inch square of fabric.

Quilt the fabric-covered squares

13. Machine quilt each 6-inch square, using free-motion meander quilting or the pattern of your choice (see page 429) or hand quilt or embellish the squares as you like.

Cut out the ornaments

14. Fold a square of tracing paper in half. Place the folded edge on the line of dashes in the half star outlined in Diagram 1. Trace the half star onto the folded tracing paper. Leaving the tracing paper folded, cut out a half star following the traced marks. When you unfold the tracing paper, you will have a full-size star pattern. Pin the star on one of the fused and quilted squares and cut out the ornament along the outline.

15. Fold the second square of tracing paper in half. Place the folded edge on the line of dashes in the half heart outlined in Diagram 2. Trace the half heart onto the folded tracing paper. Leaving the tracing paper folded, cut out a half heart following the traced marks. When you unfold it, you will have a full-size heart pattern. Pin the heart on the second fused and quilted square and cut out the ornament along the outline.

Finish the ornaments

16. Using cotton thread or embroidery floss that matches or contrasts with the

DIAGRAM 1

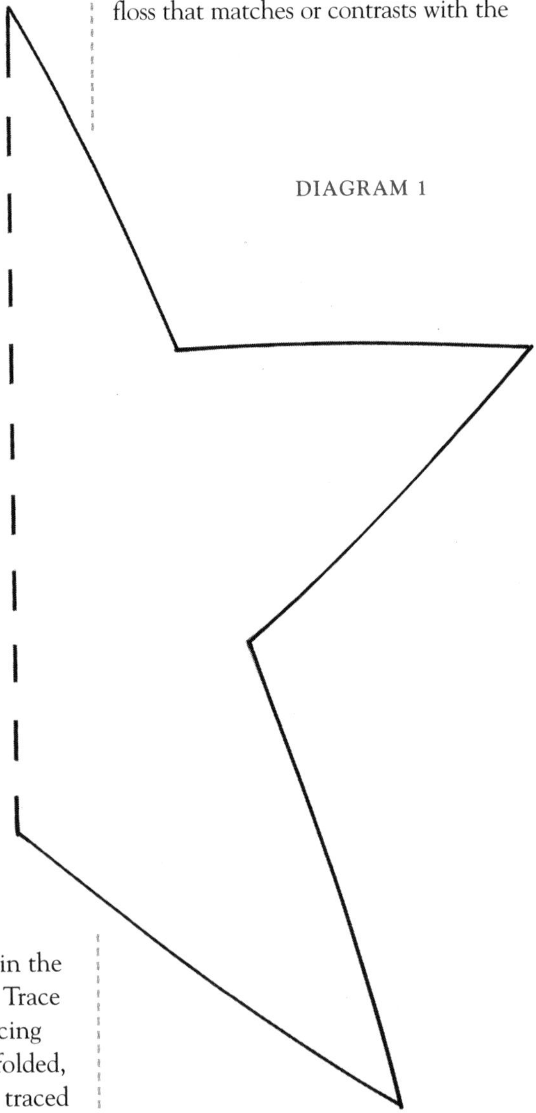

background fabric and leaving about 4 inches of thread at each place you start and stop, stitch around the edge of each of the ornaments. For the star, start at the tip of each point and stop at the tip of an adjacent point. For the heart, start at the top center and stop at the bottom point.

If you are using a sewing machine, set it for a wide satin stitch. If you are sewing by hand, first run a black permanent marker around the outside edge of the ornaments to hide the batting. Then, use a blanket stitch to finish the edge.

17. Using a different color thread or floss, sew a second line of stitching around the ornaments; do not trim the ends of the thread.

18. Using metallic thread, stitch along the edges of both ornaments once more; the colored threads should show under the metallic ones.

19. Tie the loose threads together in knots close to the ornaments. To make a hanging loop, tie the loose threads at the top of each ornament together at the end farthest from the ornament. Trim all the other threads to create little tassels, about 1½ inches long for the points of the star and 2½ inches long at the bottom of the heart.

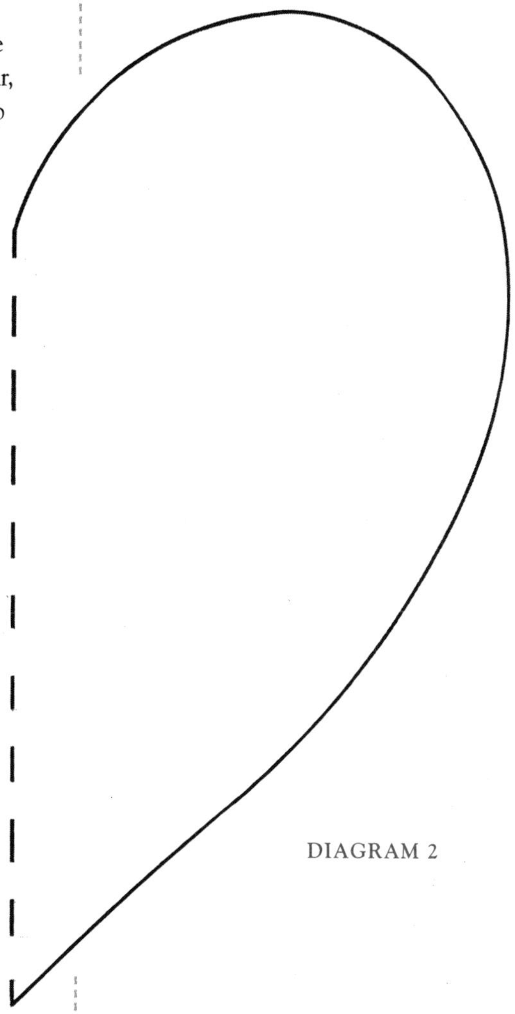

DIAGRAM 2

TIP

When working with fusible web, you need to match your iron temperature to the fabric. Cotton and silk can be fused with a hot iron. Polyester needs a cooler one.

Scrappy Peter and Paul Quilt

BY ELEANOR BURNS

Level of difficulty: ■■■□□

Can be pieced and quilted by hand or machine

ELEANOR BURNS IS BELOVED BECAUSE she has taken so many popular, classic quilt patterns and simplified them, taking advantage of today's tools and techniques. In this project, Eleanor simplifies the traditional Rob Peter to Pay Paul quilt pattern, employing the sort of shortcuts for which she is famous. Rather than having to piece the pattern's curved lines together, you simply fuse circles onto large fabric squares, cut them into quarters, and then mix and match the quarter pieces. Be warned that this project isn't as basic as some of Eleanor's earlier patterns for her Quilt in a Day product line, for example her Log Cabin pattern. However, if you follow these step-by-step directions precisely, you'll find that they

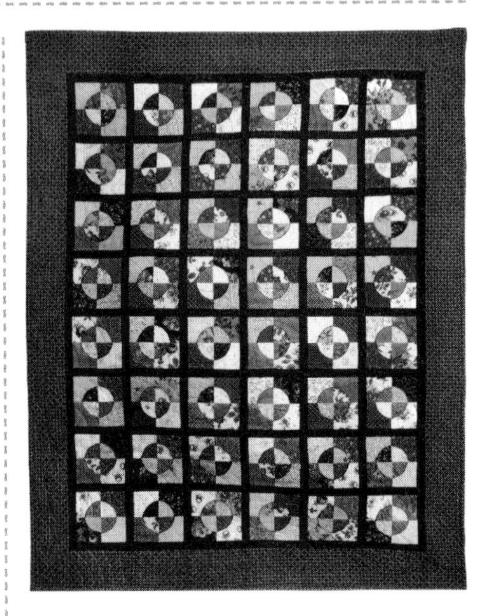

CHOOSING FABRIC

Eleanor Burns suggests selecting a theme for your quilt. You could make a Civil War quilt out of 1860s reproduction fabrics, a Depression-era quilt in 1930s fabrics, or a bright contemporary quilt from batiks. Once you've decided on a theme, look for fabrics with different scales—small, medium, and larger prints—and with varying color values. You'll need twelve different light-colored fabrics and twelve different dark-colored fabrics for the quilt blocks. (Project 9 in the color insert has photos of color swatches of some of the fabrics Eleanor used in her Scrappy Peter and Paul Quilt.)

For the border and binding, look for a fabric that appears solid from a distance and ties all the scrappy fabrics in the blocks together. As for the back, Eleanor used a glowing gold floral print that echoes the colors of some of the light-colored fabric in the quilt top. It's easiest to choose the fabric if you select from a fabric line put together by a single designer.

For this project

- All fabric should be 100 percent cotton and 44 to 45 inches wide.
- Remember to remove the selvages from the fabric.
- Press the quilt top smooth on the right side before sandwiching the layers together.

work like a dream, and it's really fun to mix and match all the colors and patterns in the quilt.

Part of what makes this quilt so much of a pleasure to plan and assemble is that the blocks use twenty-four different fabrics. Quilt shops normally have baskets and baskets stuffed with fat quarters, so you have a perfect excuse for checking them all out and buying a bagful. Or, if you have been quilting awhile and love to find gorgeous scrap quilts to use up some of the fabrics tucked away in your stash, this is the perfect project.

For more about master quilt teacher Eleanor Burns, see page 319.

Makes an approximately 52 by 66–inch quilt; see Project 9 in the color insert.

For the quilt

- ☐ 1 fat quarter or ¼ yard each of 12 light-colored fabrics
- ☐ 1 fat quarter or ¼ yard each of 12 dark-colored fabrics
- ☐ 1 yard fabric for the lattice; Eleanor Burns used a subtle black print
- ☐ 1⅝ yards fabric for the border and binding
- ☐ 3¾ yards fabric for the backing
- ☐ 2 yards lightweight nonwoven fusible interfacing (not fusible web), see pages 163–67
- ☐ One 58 by 72–inch piece of batting—thin cotton or cotton-polyester blend
- ☐ Neutral-colored cotton thread, for piecing and quilting
- ☐ 25-weight black thread, for machine blanket stitching, or black pearl cotton, for hand embroidery

You'll also need

- ☐ Tool Basket for Beginners, see page 401
- ☐ A 4½-inch square of template plastic
- ☐ Felt-tip marking pen with permanent ink
- ☐ A roughly 6-inch square piece of sandpaper
- ☐ Point turner or chopstick, see page 496
- ☐ Iron
- ☐ Open toe presser foot, if you are machine quilting
- ☐ A 9½-inch square acrylic ruler

Cut out the quilt blocks

1. Cut two 7-inch squares and two 5¼-inch squares from each fat quarter or ¼ yard of both the light- and dark-colored fabric. You will have 24 light-colored squares of each size and 24 dark-colored squares of each size.

2. Cut forty-eight 5¼-inch squares from the fusible interfacing.

3. Following Diagram 1, use the marking pen to trace a 4½-inch circle on the template plastic, then trace the marks at each quarter of the circle. Cut out the circle template.

4. Place a square of interfacing, smooth side up, on top of the sandpaper, to keep it from slipping. Place the template on top of the interfacing and trace the circle and the quarter marks. Lift off the template and extend the quarter marks slightly down into the center of the circle. Repeat with the remaining squares of interfacing.

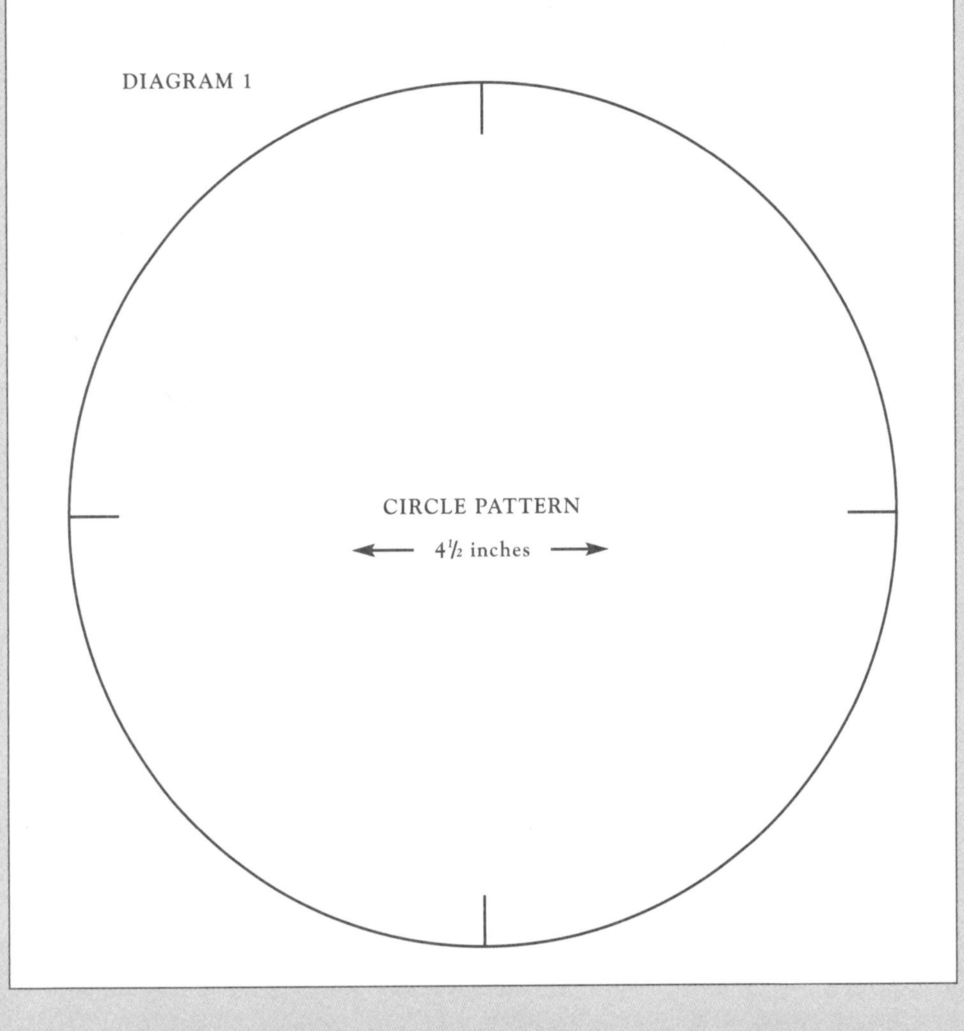

Make the circles

5. Place a square of interfacing, with the marked side up and the textured side down, on the right side of a 5¼-inch fabric square. Align the edges of the two squares and pin them together to secure (see Diagram 2). Repeat with the remaining squares of interfacing and 5¼-inch squares of light- and dark-colored fabric.

DIAGRAM 2

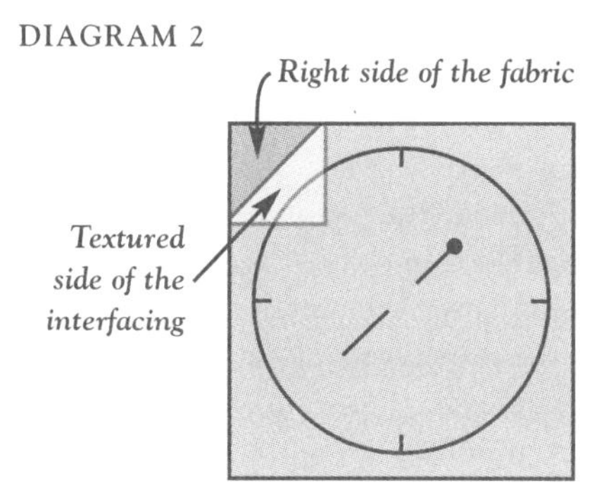

6. Using small stitches (about 20 stitches per inch if you are working on a sewing machine), sew over the circle marked on each 5¼-inch square; overlap the beginning and ending stitches.

7. Trim off the fabric and interfacing around one of the stitched circles, leaving a seam allowance of ⅛ inch. Using a seam ripper or small pair of scissors, cut a small slit in the middle of the interfacing (Diagram 3-A). Turn the circle right side out by pulling it through the slit. Run a point turner or chopstick along the inside edge of the circle to push the seam out evenly all around (see Diagram 3-B). Repeat with the remaining stitched circles; you should have a total of 48 circles.

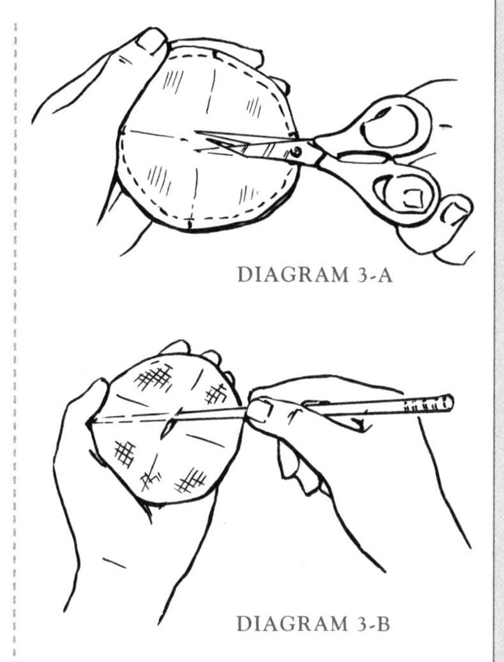

DIAGRAM 3-A

DIAGRAM 3-B

Make the patches

8. Fold all of the 7-inch squares in half lengthwise and press them. Then, fold the squares in half again crosswise, to make quarters, and press again. Unfold a dark-colored square and center a light-colored circle on it with the right side of both pieces of fabric facing up. Carefully align the quarter marks on the interfacing of the circle with the creases on the square so that the circle is perfectly centered—see Diagram 4 on page 478; this will ensure that circles on the finished blocks will align. (You will be able to see the quarter marks through the interfacing.) Pin the circle to secure it to the square.

9. Following the manufacturer's instructions, fuse the circle to the square by steam pressing it; press both

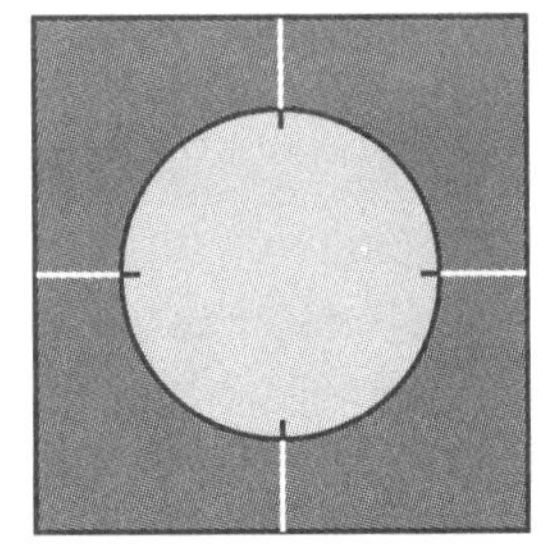
DIAGRAM 4

the right and wrong sides. Repeat with the remaining circles and squares, positioning light-colored fabric circles on top of dark squares and dark-colored circles on top of light squares.

10. Cut each square lengthwise and crosswise in half to form four 3½ inch–square patches with quarter circles (see Diagram 5). You should have 192 patches.

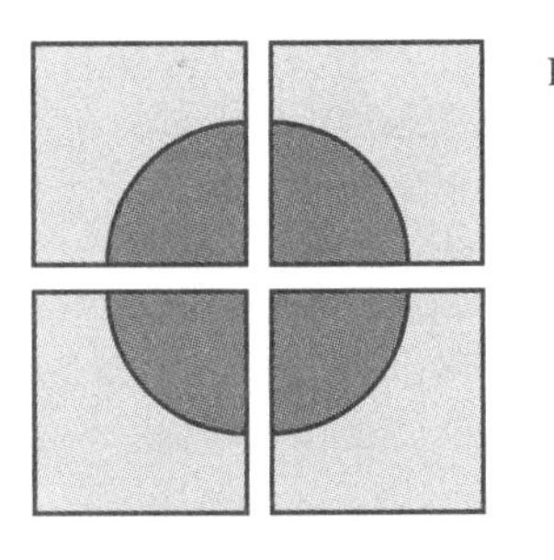
DIAGRAM 5

Assemble the quilt blocks

11. For each block, combine four different patches to form a circle within a square, as shown in Diagram 6: Arrange two different light-colored quarter circles diagonally opposite each other and two different dark-colored circles diagonally opposite each other. Try to match patches so that edges of the circles meet neatly, but don't worry too much about this—the blanket stitching on top will cover up imperfect alignments.

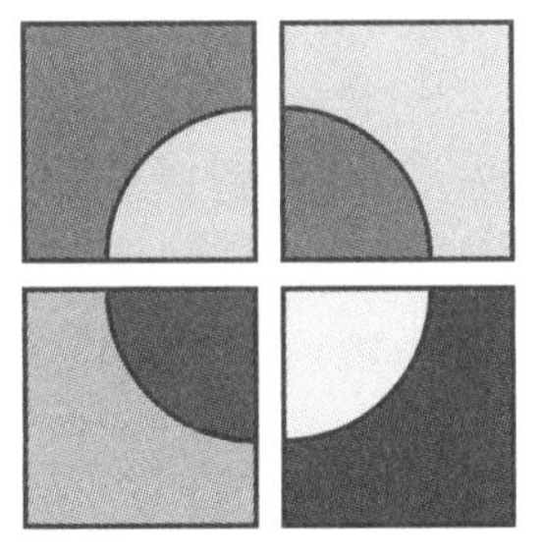
DIAGRAM 6

12. Stitch the quilt block by placing the two patches on the top row right side together, taking care to match the curves of the circle. Pin, then stitch the center seam. Repeat with the two patches on the bottom row.

13. Arrange the top and bottom rows of the block right side together, taking care to match the curves of the circle. Pin the rows together and stitch them, finger pressing the seam allowances in different directions so that they do not overlap (see Diagram 7).

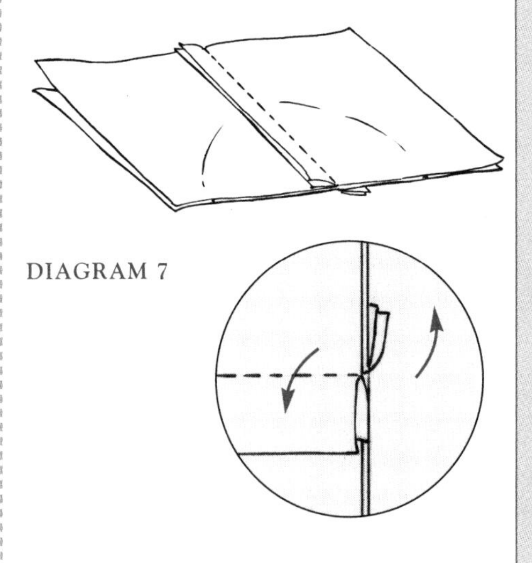
DIAGRAM 7

14. Cut through the thread of the stitch that is at the very center of the quilt block (see Diagram 8).

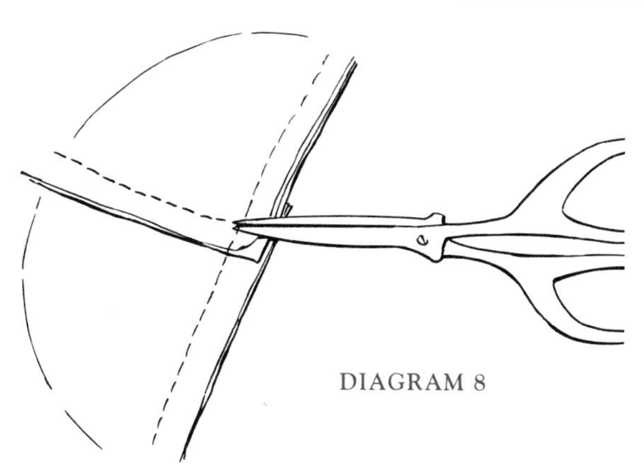
DIAGRAM 8

15. Place the quilt block wrong side up and finger press the seam allowances in the directions as shown in Diagram 9. Spread out the seams at the center; they will form a tiny Four Patch, reducing the bulk at the center of the quilt block. Using an iron, press the seams counter-clockwise around the block.

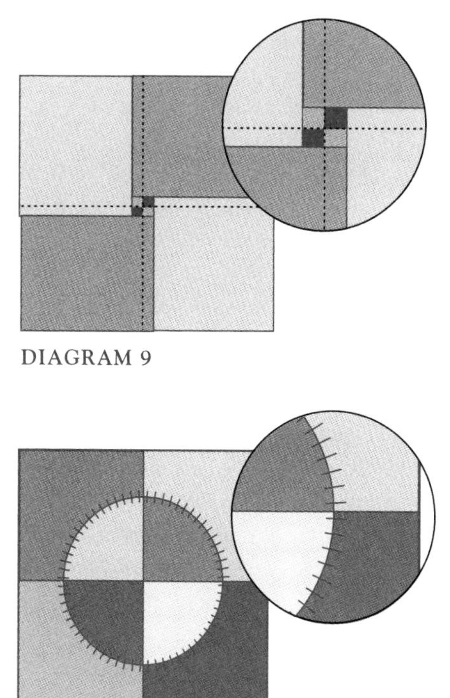
DIAGRAM 9

DIAGRAM 10

16. Repeat assembling quilt blocks until you have used all of the quarter circles.

17. Working with black thread or pearl cotton and using a sewing machine or sewing by hand, embroider a buttonhole or blanket stitch around the edge of the circle in each quilt block (see Diagram 10).

Assemble the quilt center

18. Cut the lattice fabric crosswise into eighteen strips each 1½ inches wide (you will have some fabric left over). From these strips cut 40 strips that are 6½ inches long.

19. Arrange the quilt blocks in eight rows of six, positioning the lighter quarter circles so that they are in the upper left and lower right corners. Starting with the top row of six, place one of the 6½ inch–long lattice strips between each pair of quilt blocks (Diagram 11 on page 480 shows the quilt top). Pin, then stitch the blocks and lattice strips together. Press the seam allowances toward the lattice strips. Repeat with the remaining horizontal rows.

20. Measure several horizontal rows of quilt blocks (they will be approximately 41½ inches long). Cut nine of the remaining 1½ inch–wide strips of lattice fabric to this length. Place one of these lattice strips above the top horizontal row, then starting at the bottom of that row, place a lattice strip between each horizontal row. Place the remaining

DIAGRAM 11

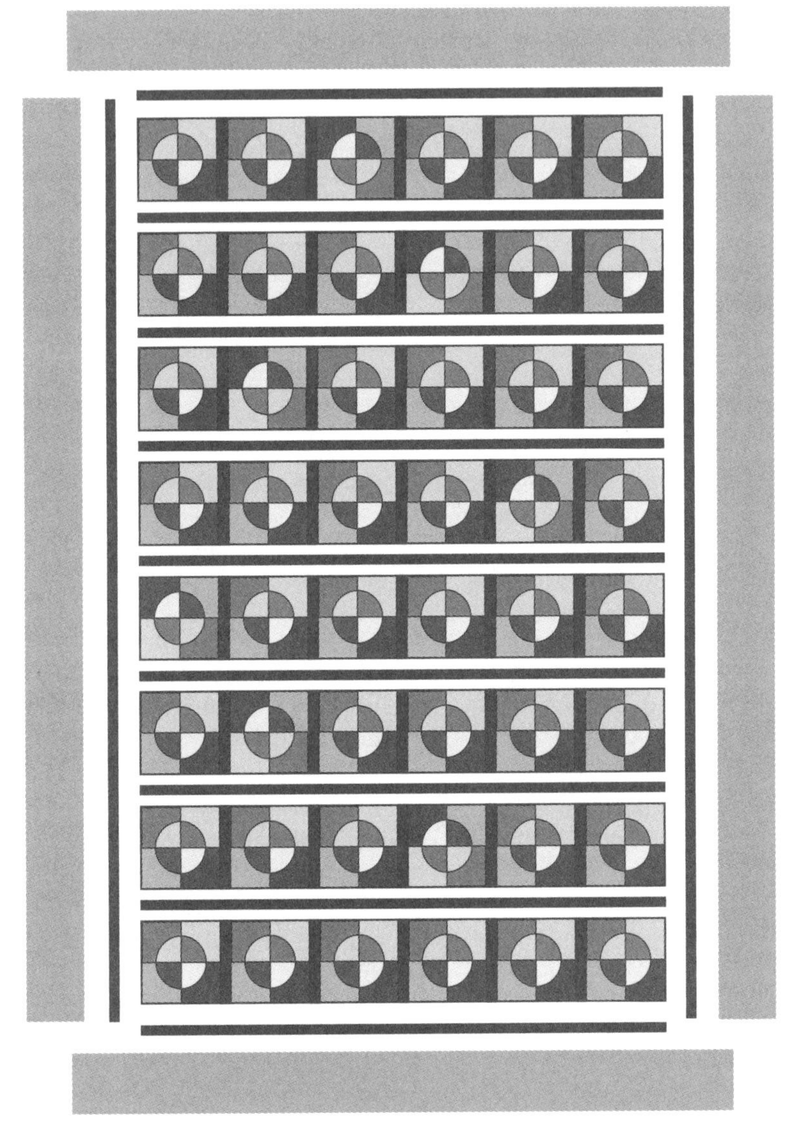

lattice strip at the bottom. Pin, then stitch these lattice strips and rows together. Press the seam allowances toward the lattice strips.

21. Measure the long sides of the quilt top (they will be approximately 57½ inches long). Sew enough of the remaining 1½ inch–wide strips of lattice fabric together to make two strips of this length (remember to add a seam allowance of ¼ inch when piecing these strips). Pin, then stitch one of these lattice strips to each long side of the quilt top. Press the seam allowances toward the lattice strips.

Make and attach the border

22. Cutting across the width of the fabric, cut six 5 inch–wide strips from the border and binding fabric. Piece enough of these strips together to make a border for the two long sides of the quilt top. Sew the long side border strips to the quilt top and press the seam allowances toward the borders. Trim the ends of these border strips even with the center of the quilt top. Piece enough of the remaining border strips together to make borders for the two short sides of the quilt top. Sew these borders to the top and bottom of the quilt, press the seam allowances toward the borders and trim the borders so that they are even with the center of the quilt top.

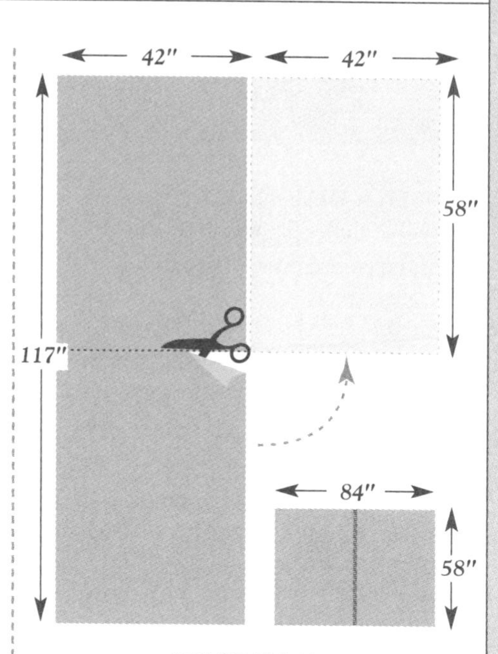

DIAGRAM 12

Assemble and quilt the Scrappy Peter and Paul Quilt

23. Press the quilt top smooth.

24. Piece together the backing fabric so that it is about 58 by 72 inches large: Cut the backing fabric in half across its width. Pin the two pieces right side together and sew a seam down one long side (see Diagram 12).

25. Following the Basic How-To's on pages 423 and 425–26, sandwich the quilt top, batting, and backing together and baste or pin them.

26. Quilt as desired; Eleanor's quilt was machine quilted in a pattern of concentric quarter circles. You can also hand quilt this project. Since there are so many colors and patterns of fabric and the blanket stitching around the circles is so prominent, you don't want a busy quilting pattern. Keep it simple, perhaps just quilting in the ditch, along the seam lines.

Bind the quilt

27. Trim the edges of the batting and backing so that they are even with those of the quilt top.

28. Make an approximately ½-inch-wide bias binding with the remaining border fabric by cutting the fabric on the diagonal into strips that are 3¼ inches wide. Piece these strips together and attach them to the quilt following the instructions on page 432. When finished, if you like, make a label for the quilt.

Fruit Tart Pincushion

AFTER A DESIGN OF AMI SIMMS
Level of difficulty: ■■■□□
Can be pieced and quilted by hand or machine

A PERFECT INTRODUCTION TO THE wacky world of Ami Simms, this quilted pincushion looks so much like a real tart, your mouth will water. The bottom of the pincushion is a small metal tart pan, which is filled with stuffing. It's topped with a circular piece of fabric quilted to look like a pie crust. The fruit filling, a fabric layer, is sewn to a "crust" that has an elastic that makes it stretchy like a shower cap so it can cover the tart pan. If your local fabric shop doesn't have any fabric with blueberries, strawberries, or other fruit filling, try doing a search in the online stores, such as www.equilter.com or www.quiltshops.com.

Although the project may look difficult at first, if you follow the directions and diagrams carefully it will come together perfectly. Serve up a pincushion tart as a gift for your favorite quilter.

For more about master quilt teacher Ami Simms, see page 366.

For the tart

- ☐ ¼ yard pale tan fabric for the crust and lattice
- ☐ ¼ yard fabric with a fruit design that looks like pie filling
- ☐ "Invisible" thread
- ☐ Tan thread to match the pastry fabric
- ☐ One 6-inch square of thin cotton batting
- ☐ ¼ yard fusible web, such as Steam-A-Seam 2, see pages 163–67
- ☐ 12 inches round cord elastic
- ☐ One 5-inch metal tart pan

You'll also need

- ☐ Tool Basket for Beginners, see page 401
- ☐ 3 pieces of tracing paper
- ☐ No. 2 pencil
- ☐ Pressing cloth, see page 165
- ☐ Sewing machine with buttonhole or similar stitch (optional)
- ☐ Tweezers (optional)
- ☐ Point turner or chopstick, see page 496
- ☐ A safety pin
- ☐ A handful of fiberfill or plastic pellets, to put inside the tart

Two 8-inch squares of tan fabric for the bottom crust.

Three 6-inch squares of tan fabric for the top crust and lattice.

One 6-inch square of "pie filling" fabric.

Makes one tart, 5½ inches in diameter and 1½ inches tall; see Project 10 in the color insert.

Cut out the fabric squares

1. Cut two 8-inch squares from the tan fabric; these will be used for the bottom of the tart crust.

2. Cut three 6-inch squares from the tan fabric; these will used for the top crust and lattice.

3. Cut one 6-inch square from the "pie filling" fabric.

For this project

- ◆ All of the fabric should be 100 percent cotton.
- ◆ Remember to remove the selvages from the fabric.

Make the templates

4. Fold a piece of tracing paper in half lengthwise, then fold it in half again crosswise. Crease the folds and unfold the tracing paper. Place one quarter of the tracing paper on Template A (see page 484), aligning the creases with the dash lines. Trace the solid quarter circle line of Template A, then refold the tracing paper. Following the line, cut out the template and label it A; this is the template for the bottom of the tart crust.

5. Fold a second piece of tracing paper in half lengthwise, then fold it in half again crosswise, creasing the folds. You will use

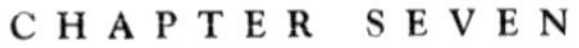

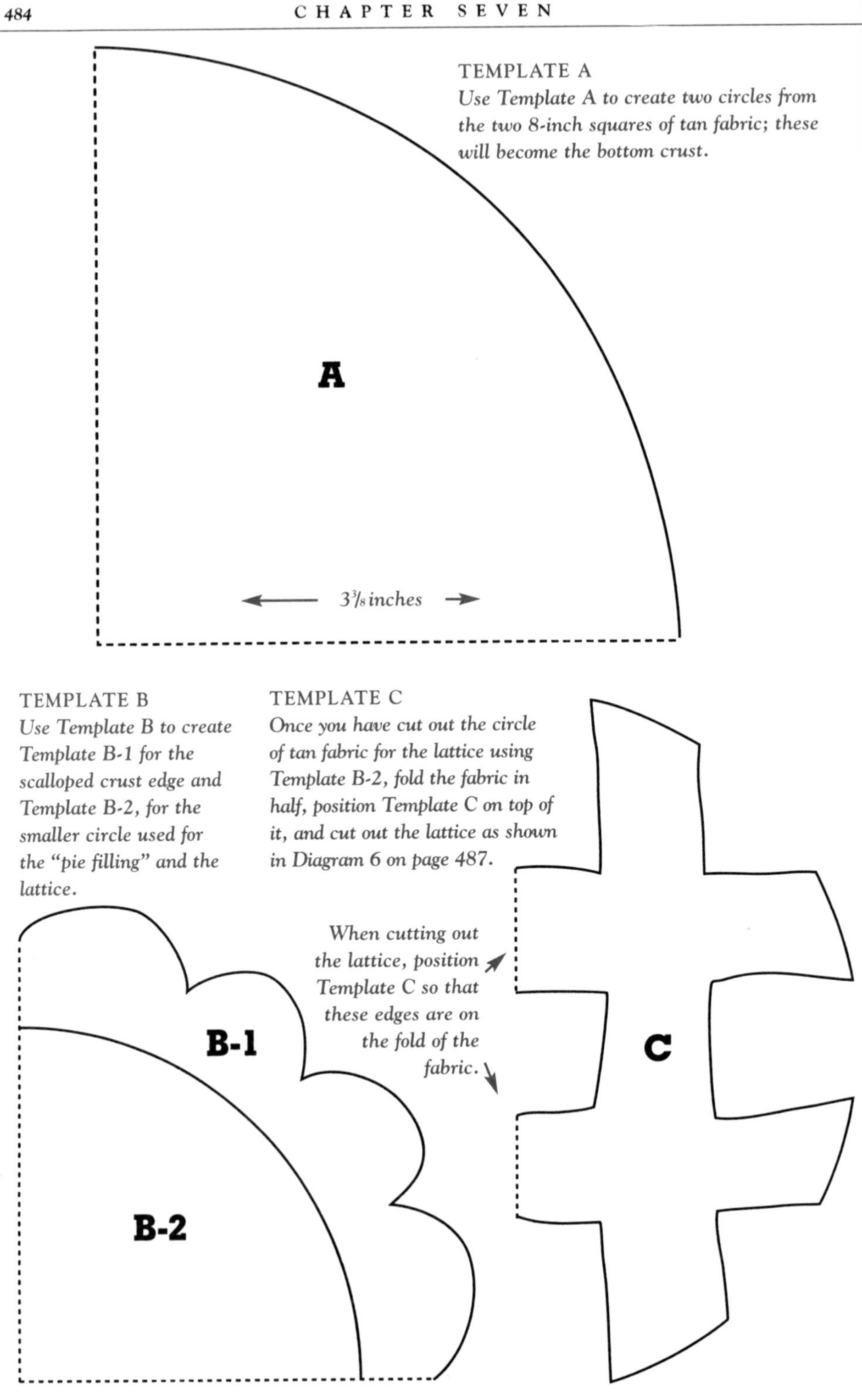
TEMPLATE A
Use Template A to create two circles from the two 8-inch squares of tan fabric; these will become the bottom crust.
A
3 3/8 inches
TEMPLATE B
Use Template B to create Template B-1 for the scalloped crust edge and Template B-2, for the smaller circle used for the "pie filling" and the lattice.
TEMPLATE C
Once you have cut out the circle of tan fabric for the lattice using Template B-2, fold the fabric in half, position Template C on top of it, and cut out the lattice as shown in Diagram 6 on page 487.
When cutting out the lattice, position Template C so that these edges are on the fold of the fabric.
B-1
B-2
C

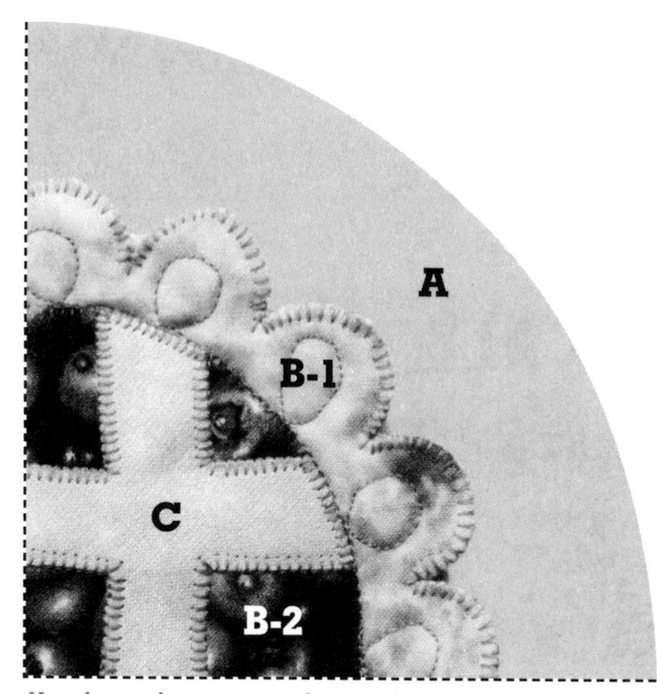

How the templates come together to make the tart.

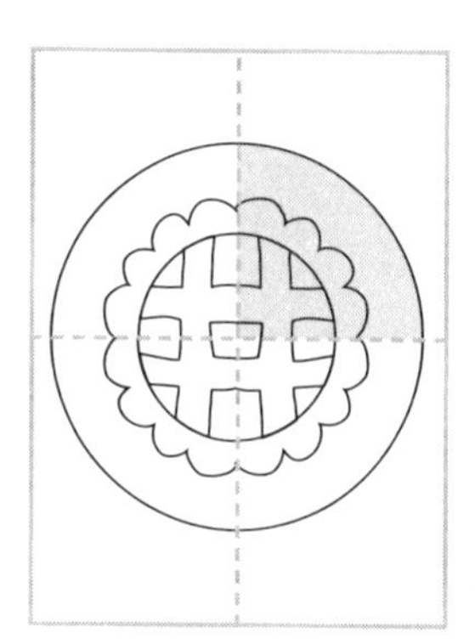

Templates A and B outline one quarter of the fruit tart. After drawing these templates on tracing paper, fold the paper back in quarters. Once you cut out and unfold the paper, you will have templates for the full-size tart.

this piece of tracing paper to make Templates B-1 and B-2. Unfold the piece of tracing paper, align it with the dash lines of Template B, and trace the scalloped edge and the smaller circle inside it. Refold the tracing paper and then cut out the scallops as shown in Diagram 1-A. Next cut out the small inside circle as shown in Diagram 1-B. Unfold the scalloped piece (Diagram 1-C) and label it B-1; this will be the template for the crust edge. Label the small circle B-2; this will be the template for the "pie filling" and the circle of fabric from which the lattice will be cut.

6. Place the remaining piece of tracing paper on top of Template C and trace

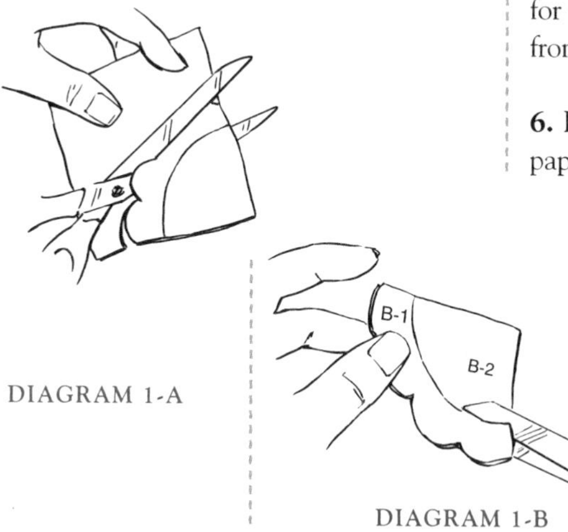

DIAGRAM 1-A

DIAGRAM 1-B

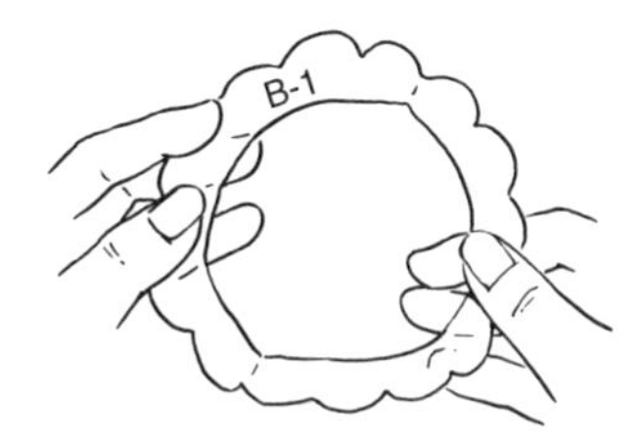

DIAGRAM 1-C

the lattice outline, then cut it out. Label this C; it will be the template for cutting out the lattice.

Prepare the crust and filling

7. Trace around Template B-2 twice on the fusible web (Diagram 2) and cut out both circles. Center one circle of web on the wrong side of one of the 6-inch squares of tan fabric. Following the

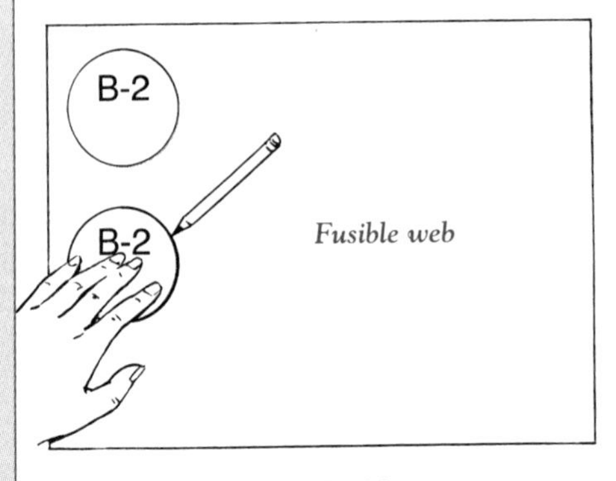

DIAGRAM 2

manufacturer's instructions and using a pressing cloth to protect your iron and ironing board, fuse the web circle to the fabric. Trim the fabric to the outside edge of the small circle and set it aside for the lattice (Diagram 3).

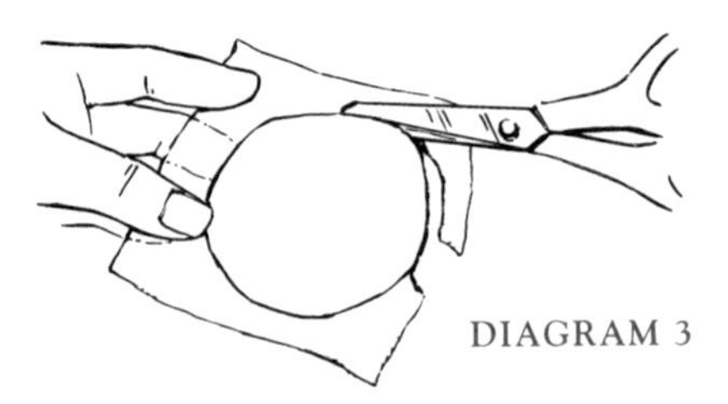

DIAGRAM 3

8. Peel back the edge of the release paper from one side of the second circle of web and trim off ¼ inch of paper, exposing the web (Diagram 4). Center the web on the wrong side of the "pie filling" fabric with

TIP

The fusible web Ami Simms uses to make the Fruit Tart Pincushion needs to be double sided—that is, both sides can be fused. A layer of release paper covers both the top and bottom of the fusible web. Ami recommends using Steam-A-Seam 2.

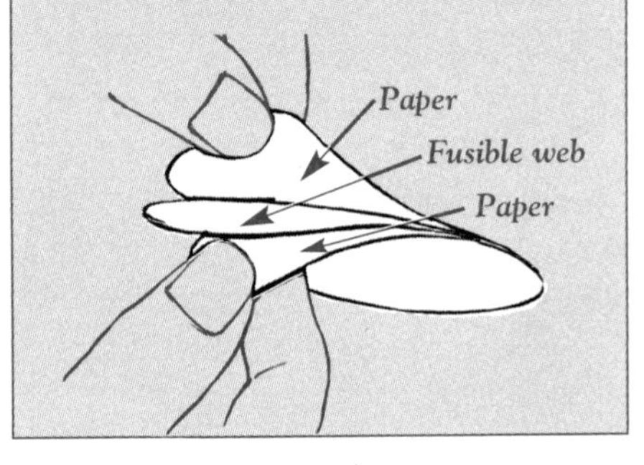

the exposed edge of fusible web against the fabric (Diagram 5). Fuse the web to the fabric, trapping the smaller piece of release

DIAGRAM 4

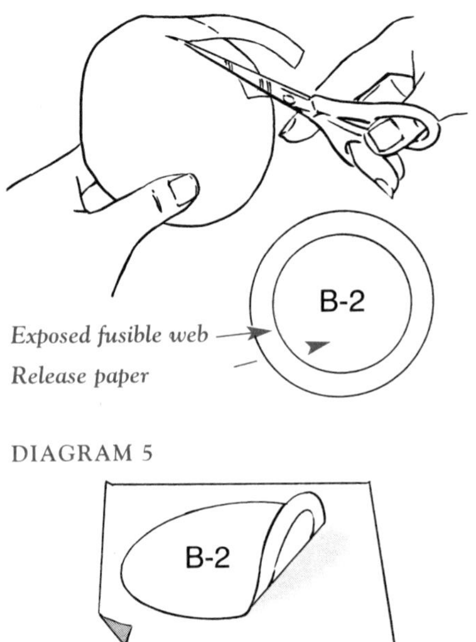

DIAGRAM 5

paper between the web and the fabric—this will help to reduce the bulk of the fabric later. Trim the "pie filling" fabric to match the outside edge of the web.

Add the lattice crust

9. First make the lattice. Remove the paper backing from the fusible web on the small tan circle and fold the circle in half. Position template C on top of the circle and pin it in place. Following the template, cut away pieces of fabric (Diagram 6). Don't worry about duplicating the lines exactly; you want the tart to look homemade.

DIAGRAM 6

10. Position the lattice web side down on top of the pie filling fabric and fuse it to the filling. Trim the edges of the "pie filling" and lattice so that they are even (Diagram 7).

DIAGRAM 7

Fillling *Lattice* *Combined*

Assemble the top of the tart

11. Remove the release paper from the back of the pie filling fabric. Center the "pie filling" fabric on the right side of one of the 6-inch squares of tan fabric (Diagram 8), then fuse them together. Using "invisible" thread, appliqué the filling to the tan square without stitching through the release paper.

DIAGRAM 8

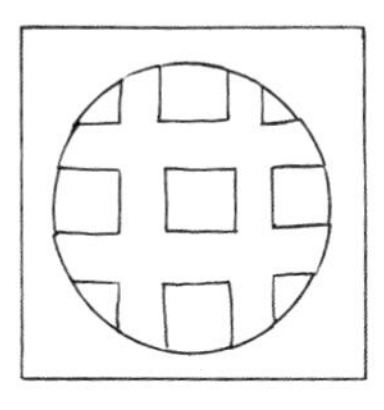

12. To cut out the excess fabric and remove the trapped release paper, pinch the "pie filling" at its center and pull it away from the crust fabric (Diagram 9).

DIAGRAM 9

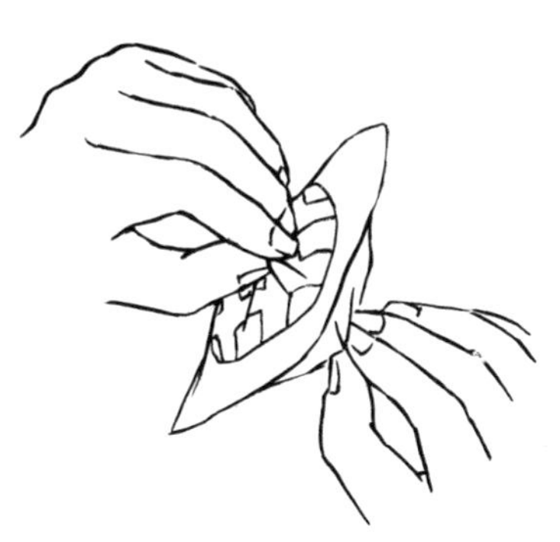

Insert the tip of a pair of scissors and make a slit in the back of the crust, then trim away the center by cutting as close to the appliqué stitching as possible (Diagram 10-A, page 488). Using your fingers or tweezers, pull the exposed release paper off of the "pie filling" (Diagram 10-B, page 488).

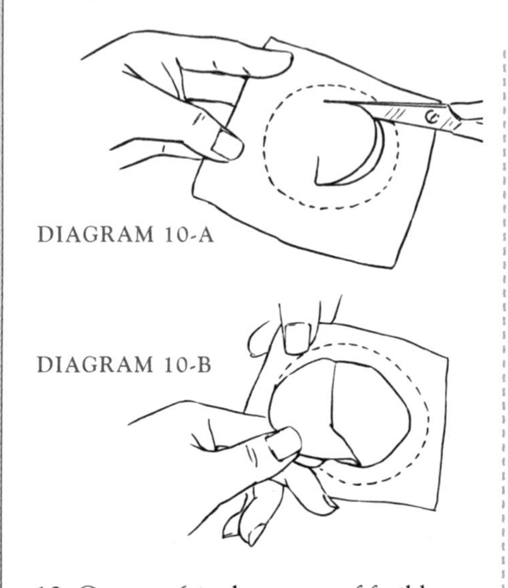
DIAGRAM 10-A

DIAGRAM 10-B

13. Cut two 6-inch squares of fusible web. Arrange one piece of web on one side of the square of batting and fuse them together. Fuse the second square of web to the other side of the batting.

14. Center the square with the "pie filling" on the batting and fuse them together. Center the remaining 6-inch square of tan fabric on the other side of the batting and fuse them together.

15. Arrange template piece B-1 over the top of the tart so that the "pie filling" is centered under the circular hole in the middle of the scallops. Pin the template to the fabric (Diagram 11) and then cut through the layers of fabric and batting following along the scalloped edge.

DIAGRAM 11

Quilt the tart

16. Using a sewing machine or working by hand, quilt the tart top using tan thread. Start by sewing a buttonhole stitch on the edge of the scallops. Then, quilt along the edges of the lattice strips using a buttonhole stitch. Quilt a loop on each scallop of the crust to simulate thumbprints (see Diagram 12).

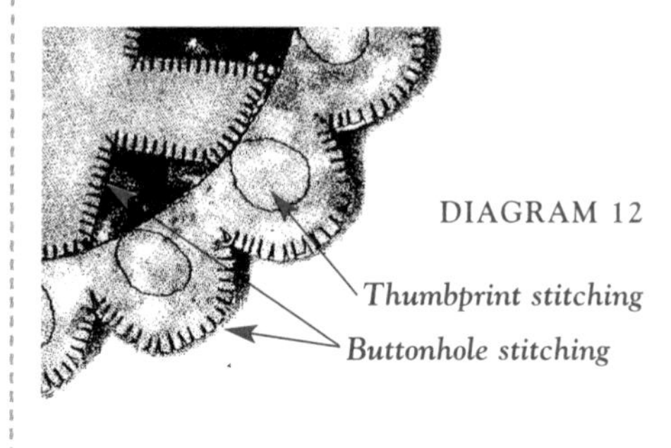

DIAGRAM 12

Make the bottom of the tart

17. Trace pattern piece A on the wrong side of each of the two 8-inch squares of tan fabric, then cut out the circles; these will be the bottom of the tart.

18. Pin the two large circles right sides together. Using a scant ¼-inch seam allowance, sew them together, leaving a 2-inch opening (Diagram 13). Turn the circles right side out. Run a point turner or chopstick along the inside edge to push the seam out evenly all around; the tart bottom should be round. Fold under the raw edges of the seam opening. Press the tart bottom.

DIAGRAM 13

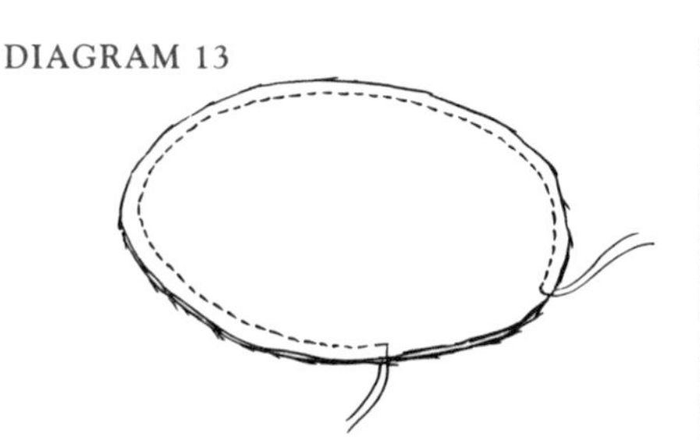

19. Using tan thread, sew all the way around the tart bottom ⅜ inch from the turned edge to create a channel for the elastic (see Diagram 14). If you are sewing by machine, backstitch to secure the threads when you have completed the circle.

DIAGRAM 14

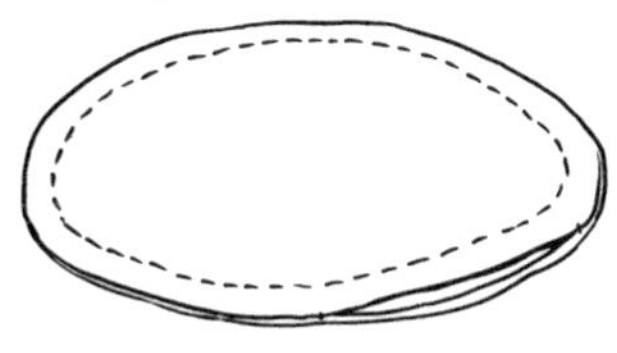

Attach the tart top to the bottom

20. Center the quilted tart top on the tart bottom as shown in Diagram 15, filling side up (the tart bottom doesn't have a right or wrong side). Pin through the scalloped edges to secure the top and bottom of the tart together.

DIAGRAM 15

21. Using tan thread, attach the tart top to the bottom by stitching through all of the layers along the outside edge of the "pie filling." If you are sewing by machine, use an even-feed foot.

22. Tie the elastic onto a safety pin. Starting at the opening in the edge of the tart bottom, thread the elastic through the channel. Tighten the elastic so that the tart bottom folds in on itself and lays almost flat against the underside of the tart top without causing the top to curl (see Diagram 16); do not overtighten the elastic.

DIAGRAM 16

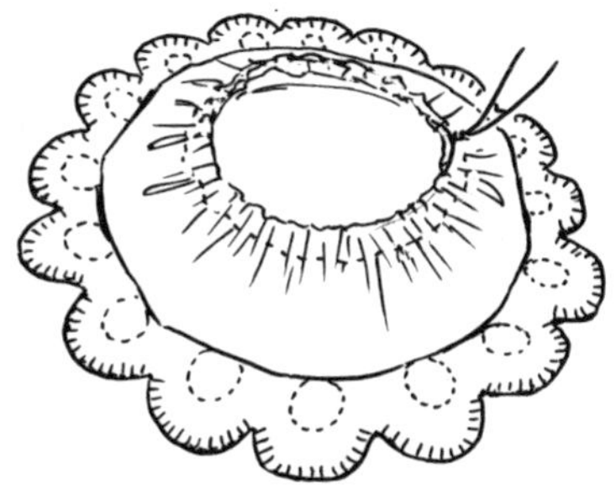

23. Cut off the excess elastic and tuck the ends into the channel. Using tan thread, slip stitch the opening in the pie bottom closed.

Put the tart together

24. If desired, fill the tart pan with fiberfill. Or, place plastic pellets in a plastic sandwich bag, place this in the tart pan, and tape it to the bottom of the pan.

25. Pull the tart bottom over the rim of the tart pan and you're done.

"All That I Am" Pillow

BY SUE NICKELS

Level of difficulty: ■■■■□

Can be pieced and quilted by hand or machine

FEATURING A PERIOD STYLE AND colors plus a wonderful quote from Abraham Lincoln, this might look like a very traditional project, but the techniques employed are fresh and new. Sue Nickels is a master at machine appliqué and has often used such decidedly contemporary themes in her quilts as the Beatles and NASA.

This sweet, small project provides a great chance to explore an appliqué technique that involves cleaning up raw edges with machine embroidery. The vine shape is a standard in appliqué work; here's an opportunity to practice this and quilting feathers on a small scale. Flowers and hearts are also common appliqué shapes. Turn Sue's design into a pillow or a wall hanging—either way, it makes a great gift.

For more about master quilt teacher Sue Nickels, see page 357.

For this project

- All of the fabric should be 100 percent cotton.
- Remember to remove the selvages from the fabric.
- Press the quilt top smooth on the right side before sandwiching the layers together.

Makes an approximately 16-inch square quilt or pillow; see Project 11 in the color insert.

Cut out the fusible web

1. You'll find a template with all the pattern pieces for this project on pages 492–93. Arrange the fusible web paper side up on top of the pieces of the pattern for the woman, the heart, and the flower and trace each piece, leaving some space between the individual pieces. The dotted lines indicate edges of the pieces that are covered by another

TIP

Lightly spraying the wrong side of the quilt background fabric with spray starch will stabilize it. Spraying the appliqué fabrics with spray starch is also helpful. Use a regular, not a heavy-duty, spray starch.

For the quilt

- ☐ One 20-inch square of solid-colored fabric, for the front of the quilt
- ☐ One 20-inch square of a complimentary print fabric, for the quilt back
- ☐ Scraps of 8 to 10 different fabrics for the appliqués, including a green for the stems and leaves and a flesh color
- ☐ ⅛ yard fabric for the narrow border (in Sue's quilt this is the same light gold print used in the appliqués)
- ☐ ¼ yard fabric for the binding (in Sue's quilt this is the same red print used in the appliqués)
- ☐ ½ yard lightweight paper-backed fusible web, see pages 163–67
- ☐ Cotton thread in colors that correspond to the appliqué fabrics, for stitching the appliqués
- ☐ Cotton thread in a color that matches the front of the quilt, for quilting
- ☐ One 20-inch square of batting, preferably a blend of cotton and polyester

You'll also need

- ☐ Tool Basket for Beginners, see page 401
- ☐ Tracing paper
- ☐ No. 2 pencil
- ☐ Spray starch
- ☐ Iron
- ☐ Pressing cloth, see page 165
- ☐ Fine-tip black fabric pen, such as a Pigma Micron 01
- ☐ An open toe or appliqué presser foot, if you are machine quilting

appliqué piece; include these in the outlines. Trace the outline of the bodice and skirt of the dress as a single piece.

(see Diagram 1). You do not need to cut the center out of the smaller pieces, like the hands, legs, and shoes.

2. Cut out the pieces of fusible web, cutting about ¼ inch outside the traced pattern lines. Then, to reduce the amount of fusible web, cut out the center of the larger pieces, cutting about ¼ inch inside the traced pattern line

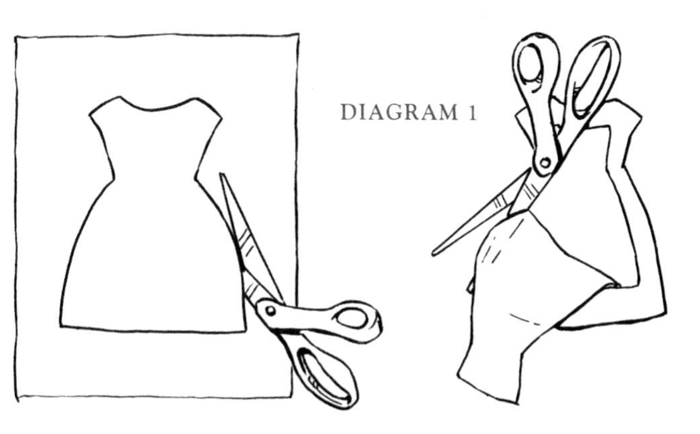

DIAGRAM 1

TEMPLATE

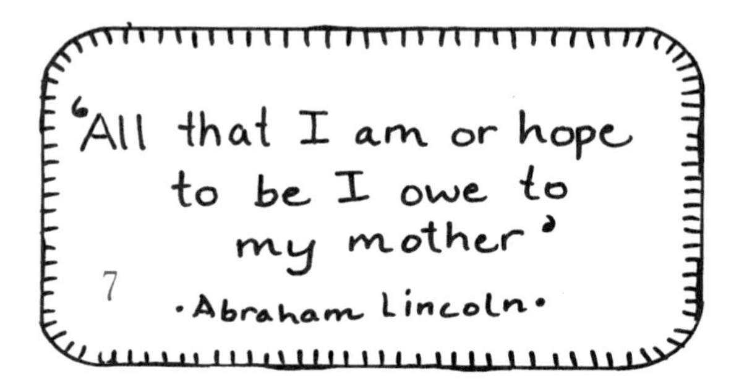

"ALL THAT I AM" QUILT FABRICS

Here's a key to the colors of the fabrics used in Sue Nickels' pillow (see Project 11 in the color insert). Feel free to substitute whatever colors and prints you like—just assign to each the number of the color being replaced so you can keep track of where to position it.

1. BLACK
2. GREEN PRINT
3. SOLID RED
4. RED PRINT
5. LIGHT GOLD PRINT
6. DARKER GOLD PRINT
7. TAN
8. BROWN

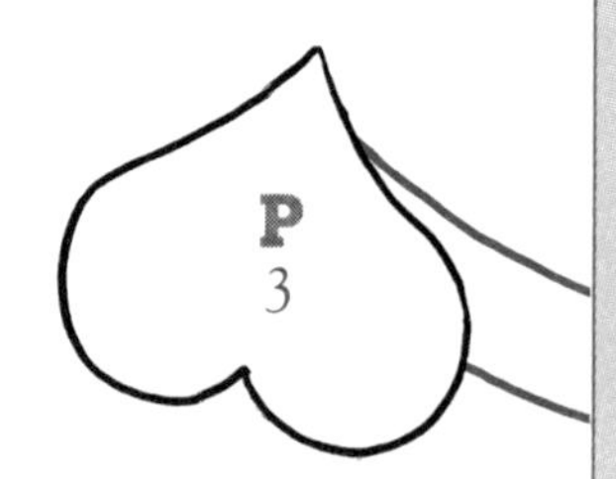

A
6
B
5
C
4
D
2
E
1
2
F
2
G
2
H
2
I
2
J
3
K
2
L
3
M
2
N
3
O
3
P
3
Q
3
R
1
DIAGRAM 2

3. Trace the right half of the floral design on tracing paper. Fold the tracing paper in half and, following the lines you have drawn, trace the design on the other half of the tracing paper. Unfold the tracing paper and you will have a full-size pattern. Use this to trace the individual pieces on the fusible web as you did with the pattern pieces in Step 1. To help keep track of the pattern pieces in the floral design, label each piece with the letter that appears on the pattern, writing close to the traced outline.

4. Cut out the pattern pieces, cutting about ¼ inch outside the traced lines. Cut out the center of the fusible web in the larger pieces.

Cut out the appliqué pieces

5. Arrange the pieces of fusible web paper side up on the wrong side of the corresponding pieces of fabric following the color key on page 492. Following the manufacturer's instructions and using a pressing cloth to protect your iron and ironing board, press the fusible web to fuse it to the fabric.

6. After the fusible web has cooled, cut out the appliqué pieces following the traced outlines. Remove the paper backing, then arrange the pieces on a work surface so that they correspond to the pattern.

7. Using the black fabric pen, draw the face on the woman and write the motto on the label for the front of the quilt.

Make the quilt top

8. Find the center of the fabric for the front of the quilt by folding it in half lengthwise and then in half crosswise. Mark the center point with a pin. Place the fabric on an ironing board.

9. Arrange the appliqué pieces on the fabric for the front of the quilt following the design in Diagram 2. Place the center of the woman's dress in the center of the fabric, removing the pin. Arrange the head and neck, sleeves, hands, pantaloons, and ankles underneath. Place the hair, apron, belt, and shoes on top.

DIAGRAM 2

10. Center the label with the motto 1¼ inch above the woman's head. Position the stems on either side of the woman, then place the print heart upside down over the bottom ends of the stems. Center the two-layered flower below the print heart.

11. Arrange the three-layered flowers over the top ends of the stems. Position the solid-colored hearts, leaves, and small circles so that they correspond to the pattern.

12. Following the manufacturer's instructions and using a pressing cloth, fuse all of the pieces to the quilt top.

13. Using thread that matches each fabric and working in a small buttonhole or blanket stitch, stitch around the edges of the appliqué pieces. Use thread of a contrasting color to stitch around the label with the motto. If you are sewing using a machine that does not sew a buttonhole stitch, substitute a zigzag or blind stitch.

DIAGRAM 3

Assemble and quilt the quilt

14. Press the quilt top smooth.

15. Following the Basic How-To's on pages 423 and 425–26, sandwich the quilt top, batting, and backing together and baste or pin them.

16. Quilt as desired; Sue's quilt was machine quilted in a pattern of free-motion feathers and stippling (see Diagram 3; you'll find more about machine quilting on page 429). You can also hand quilt this project.

17. Trim all the edges of the quilt so that the appliqué design is centered in a 16-inch square.

Make and attach the border and binding

18. Cut four crosswise strips of the narrow border fabric that are 1 inch wide and 16 inches long. Fold the strips in half the long way, right side out, and press them. Pin one of the strips along each edge of the quilt so that the raw edges are together and the ends of the strips overlap (see Diagram 4, page 496). Topstitch along the fold of the border.

MAKING CORNERS SHARP

Whenever you sew a corner seam and then turn it inside out, the fabric in the inside of the corner bunches up, preventing you from making a crisp corner. There are a number of tricks and tools for fixing this problem. Clipping across the seam allowance at the corner helps reduce the bulk. Then, some people push the corner out from the inside using the eraser end of a pencil or a chopstick.

Others pick at the outside of the corner seam using the point of a sewing pin to tease out more of the bunched up fabric and create a clean angle. In addition, there is an inexpensive tool called either a point turner or a pointer and creaser. These are usually made of plastic or wood—sometimes bamboo—and sell for $2 to $3 each. One end comes to a point and the other generally has a curve. You stick the point inside your seam and gently push out the fabric in the corner.

19. To make a bias binding that is approximately ¼ inch wide, cut the binding fabric on the diagonal into strips that are 2¼ inches wide. Piece these together and attach them to the quilt following the instructions on page 432. When finished, if you like, make a label for the quilt.

DIAGRAM 4

To Turn the Quilt into a Pillow

For the pillow

- ☐ ½ yard of a complementary print, for the pillow back
- ☐ 2 yards ruffled eyelet trim with a bound edge
- ☐ One 16-inch pillow form

1. Cut two 16½ by 20½–inch rectangles from the fabric for the back of the pillow. Fold each piece in half, right sides together, to form two 10¼ by 16½–inch rectangles.

2. Using a ¼-inch seam allowance and leaving a 3-inch opening on the side opposite the fold, stitch around the raw edges of each half of the pillow back. Clip across the seam allowances at the corners, close to the seam, so that they will turn neatly. Turn the two halves of the pillow back right side out, then use a chopstick or point turner to poke out the fabric in the corners so that they make a crisp edge. Fold ¼ inch of the open edges inside the backs and press them.

3. Arrange the two halves of the pillow back alongside each other, with the open edges at the far left and far right sides. Pull one folded edge up over the other so that it overlaps 4 inches and the overall dimensions of the pillow back are 16 inches on each side, matching the quilt top (see Diagram 5). Pin and baste along the overlap to secure it.

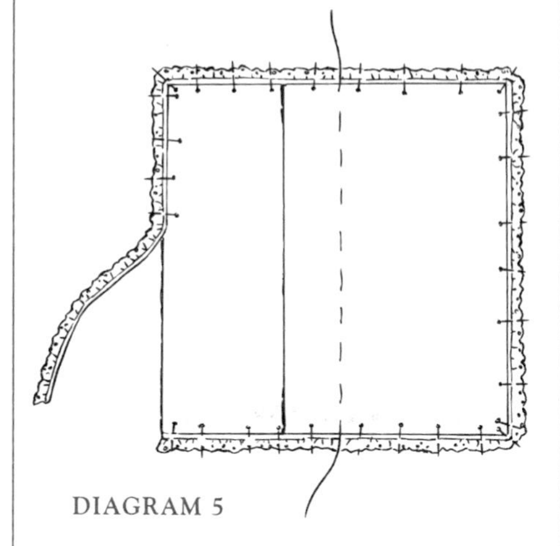

DIAGRAM 5

4. Starting at one of the bottom corners, pin the bound edge of the ruffled eyelet trim along the outer edge of the two overlapping panels. Using thread that matches the color of the eyelet in the needle and thread that matches the pillow back fabric in the bobbin, zigzag stitch along the bound edge of the eyelet (as you stitch, you will be topstitching the openings in the sides of the pillow back closed). Curl the two ends of the eyelet trim together and slip stitch them.

5. Place the pillow back on a work surface with the bound edges of the eyelet facing down. Place the quilt on top, matching the edges, and pin the top and back together. Using thread that matches the quilt in the needle and thread that matches the pillow back in the bobbin, straight stitch all around the quilt close to the edge. Remove the basting threads and insert the pillow form through the opening.

Falling Leaves Wall Hanging

BY LIBBY LEHMAN
Level of difficulty: ■■■■■
Can be pieced and quilted by machine*

LIBBY LEHMAN IS A REVOLUTIONARY, one of those pioneers who changed machine quilting from a guilty shortcut to an envied accomplishment. Her small wall hanging is the perfect size for exploring some of the masterful techniques she calls threadplay and is based on a pattern she uses frequently in her workshops.

Libby starts with the simplest of pieced backgrounds, but the focus is on reverse appliqué and machine appliqué. In reverse appliqué, instead of stitching a shape to a backing, you cut the top fabric away to reveal the shape of another layer of fabric below it. Here Libby uses the decorative stitches and exotic threads for which she's famous. You can see the quilt evolve in the sequence of photographs in the color insert for Project 12. This project is ranked as difficult because the quilting techniques take some time and experience to master. Although this is not a large quilt, making it could be challenging for someone who has not had a lot of

experience using a sewing machine or has never machine quilted. But learn from a master and you'll dazzle your friends.

For more about master teacher Libby Lehman, see page 350.

Makes an approximately 10 by 12–inch quilt; see Project 12 in the color insert.

For this project

◆ **Remember to remove the selvages from the fabric.**

◆ **All of the seam allowances in the wall hanging are ¼ inch.**

Make the background

1. Arrange the four 6½ by 7½–inch pieces of green fabric for the background as shown in Diagram 1. Pin and then stitch the top and bottom rows together, using dark green thread. Press the seam allowances in the directions shown in the arrows on the blocks in Diagram 1.

2. Pin and then stitch the top and bottom rows together. Press the seam allowances toward the bottom of the quilt.

*Although you could choose to execute Libby Lehman's project by hand, using beautiful embroidery stitches to edge the appliquéd shapes, machine quilting is Lehman's specialty and the directions read accordingly.

For the wall hanging

- ☐ Four 6½ by 7½–inch pieces of dark green print fabric, for the background
- ☐ One 8-inch square piece of lime green print fabric, for leaf #1
- ☐ One 8-inch square piece of rusty red print fabric, for leaf #2
- ☐ One 6-inch square piece of sheer copper-colored fabric, such as organza, organdy, or chiffon, for leaf #3
- ☐ One ¼ yard or fat quarter of dark green print fabric, for the backing
- ☐ One ¼ yard or fat quarter of dark green print fabric, for the binding
- ☐ One 12 by 13½–inch piece of medium-weight tear-away stabilizer
- ☐ Dark green sewing thread to match the background fabric or polyester monofilament
- ☐ Copper-colored sewing thread to match the sheer fabric
- ☐ Light green thread for quilting
- ☐ Colorful thread for decorative top stitching and bobbin drawing
- ☐ One 14-inch square of cotton batting

You'll also need

- ☐ Tool Basket for Beginners, see page 401
- ☐ Freezer paper
- ☐ Fabric marking pencil
- ☐ Temporary fabric-spray adhesive

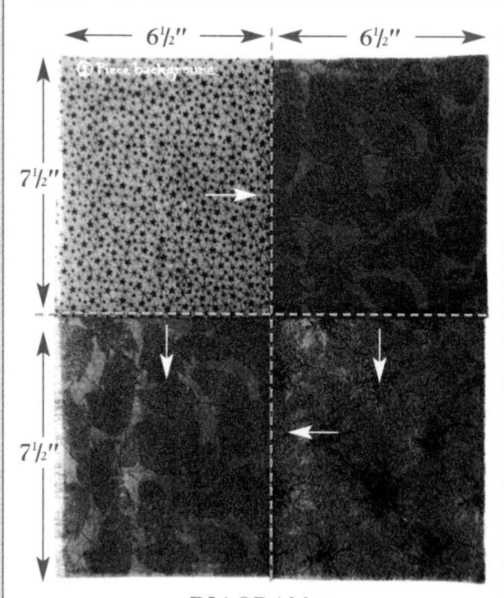

DIAGRAM 1

TIP

For the decorative top stitching, Libby Lehman used a medium and a light green thread, plus a variegated thread in shades of red and white. She used a heavier bright green metallic thread for bobbin drawing.

Reverse appliqué the leaves onto the background

3. Enlarge the four leaf templates on pages 500–501 by 133 percent; you can use a copy machine to do this. Then, trace the leaf templates on the nonslick side of the freezer paper, numbering each. Trace and number two more templates for leaf #4.

TEMPLATES

These templates are printed at 75 percent of the actual size. Enlarge them by 133 percent to get the correct size for the wall hanging. You can use a copy machine to do this.

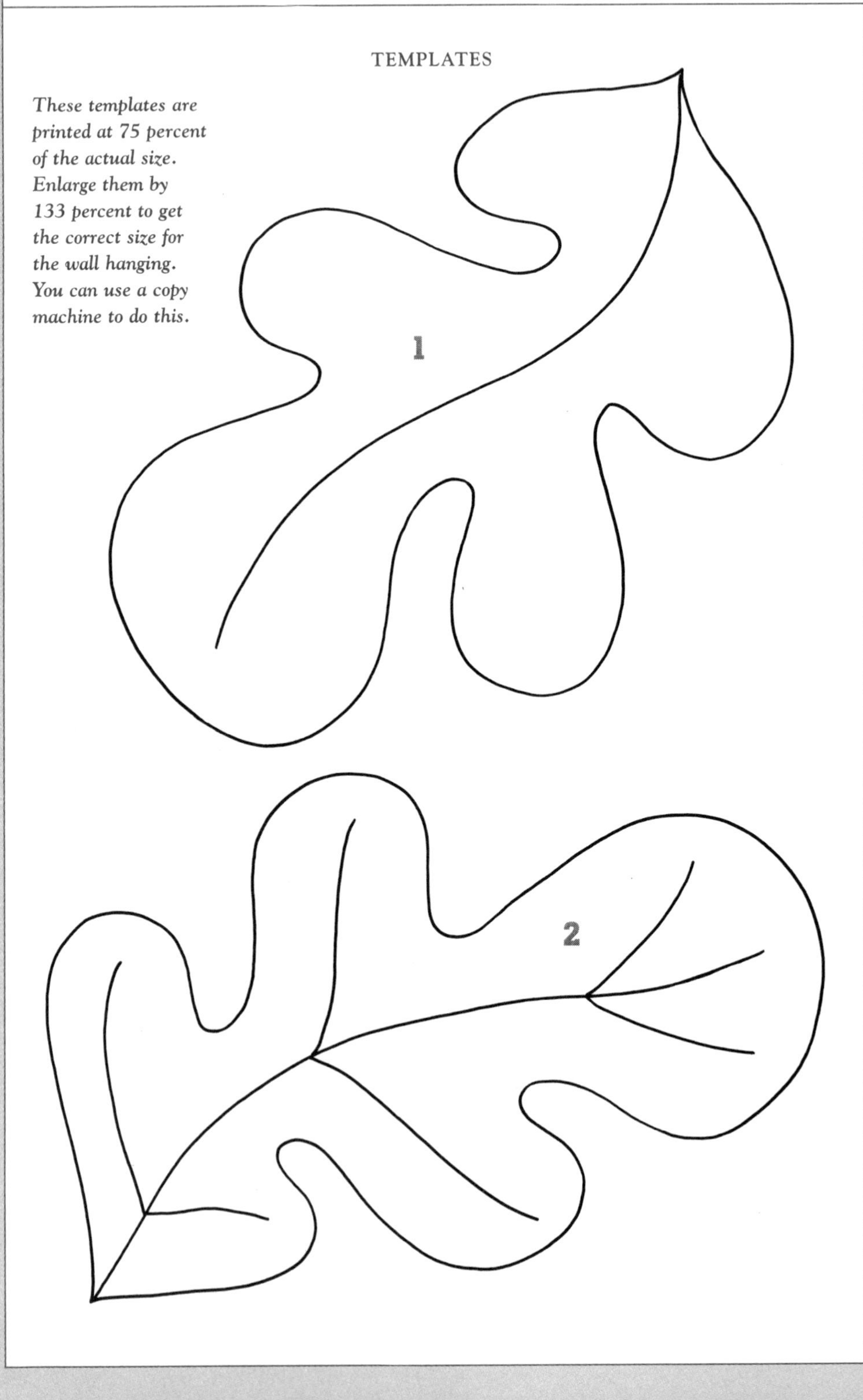

3
4

4. Iron the template for leaf #1 diagonally on the upper left corner of the right side of the quilt background as shown in Diagram 2 (you may also want to secure the template with a pin).

5. Turn the quilt background over and pin the lime green fabric for leaf #1 right side down over the upper right corner so that it corresponds to the placement of leaf #1 (see Diagram 3).

6. Turn the quilt background right side up. Using dark green thread and sewing with a very short stitch length, machine stitch around the template for leaf #1. Remove the template and cut away the background fabric in the center of the stitching to reveal the lime green fabric underneath; you want to cut as close as possible to the stitching (see Diagram 4). Then, turn the quilt over and trim the excess fabric from around the outline of the leaf, leaving about ½ inch of fabric outside the stitch line (see Diagram 5).

DIAGRAM 2

7. Iron the template for leaf #2 diagonally on the lower right corner of the right side of the quilt background as shown in Diagram 6 (you may also want to pin it).

8. Using the rusty red fabric and the dark green thread, reverse appliqué leaf #2 to the quilt background, as you did leaf #1. See Diagram 7 for the placement of the fabric on the back of the quilt background.

DIAGRAM 3

Embroider the leaves

9. Using a fabric marking pencil, draw the center veins on leaves #1 and #2, then add the smaller veins to leaf #2 as shown in the template on page 500.

10. Use the temporary spray adhesive to attach the tear-away stabilizer to the back of the quilt top. Using a green thread, embroider the veins in a satin stitch. Start with the center vein of

DIAGRAM 4

DIAGRAM 6

DIAGRAM 5

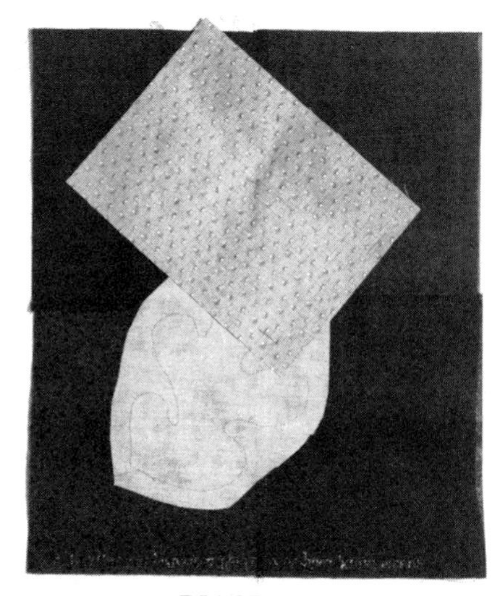

DIAGRAM 7

leaf #1, beginning at the pointed end with wider stitches and tapering to narrow stitches at the other end—tapering is simply reducing the stitch width as you sew. (Diagram 8 shows the decorative stitching for leaves #1 and #2.)

11. Stitch the smaller veins on leaf #2 first, making them wider at the center and tapering them toward the edge. Then stitch the center vein, tapering it the same way as on leaf #1.

12. Sew a satin stitch around the edge of leaf #1, tapering the stitches on the inside curves.

13. Choose a different decorative thread and another embroidery stitch for the edge of leaf #2; Libby used a red and

DIAGRAM 8

white variegated thread. Make sure the embroidery stitch covers the raw edge of the fabric where the background has been cut away from the leaf underneath.

Appliqué leaf #3 onto the background

14. Iron the template for leaf #3 onto the right side of the sheer fabric. Use temporary spray adhesive to glue the fabric and template onto the quilt top, positioning it as shown in Diagram 9.

TIP

The tear-away stabilizer will stabilize the quilt background as you sew the decorative embroidery stitches. Once you've set up your sewing machine for decorative stitching, it's a good idea to practice sewing on a scrap of fabric and stabilizer before you work on the quilt.

Using the copper-colored thread and sewing with a very short stitch length, machine stitch around the template for leaf #3. Remove the template and trim away the excess sheer fabric, cutting as close to the stitching as possible (this is what is shown in Diagram 9).

15. Using a new decorative thread and a darning foot, stitch around the edge of leaf #3 with a free-motion zigzag stitch as shown in Diagram 10.

Add the outlines of leaf #4

16. Turn the quilt top over. Arrange the three templates for leaf #4 at the edges of the tear-away stabilizer as shown in Diagram 11. Iron the templates onto the stabilizer (you may want to do this one leaf at a time).

17. Set up your sewing machine for free-motion bobbin stitching, using a topstitching needle, a darning foot, and

DIAGRAM 9

dark green thread in the needle of the machine. Use the heavier bright green metallic thread in the bobbin; it may be necessary to hand wind this onto the bobbin.

18. Working with the wrong side facing up, stitch along the outlines of the three templates for leaf #4. Use a slightly longer stitch to accommodate the thicker thread.

DIAGRAM 10

Assemble and quilt the wall hanging

19. Tear off the tear-away stabilizer.

20. Set the iron on the wool setting to keep from melting the sheer fabric, then press the quilt top smooth.

21. Following the Basic How-To's on pages 423 and 425–26, sandwich the quilt top, batting, and backing together and baste or pin them.

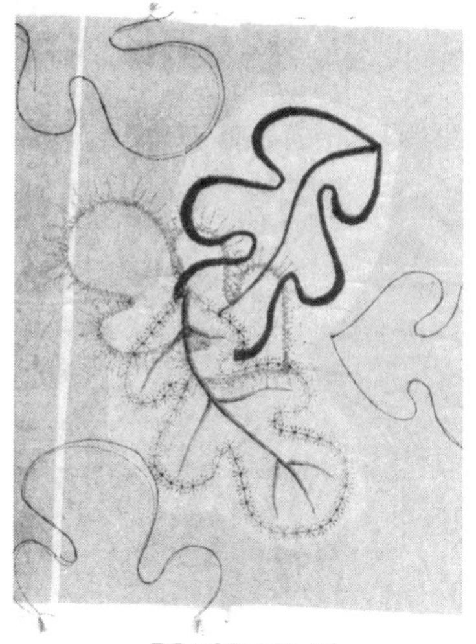

DIAGRAM 11

22. Machine quilt the quilt with light green thread using free-motion quilting (see page 431). Libby's quilt was quilted

TIP

Bobbin drawing is the perfect technique when you want to use a thread that is too thick for the needle of your machine. Threads thicker than size 12 and up to size 3 can be used for bobbin drawing (for more about thread see pages 403 and 405).

Depending on your machine, you will need to lessen the bobbin tension or bypass it altogether. To bypass the bobbin tension, place the bobbin in the case and draw the thread directly through the throat plate. To lessen the bobbin tension, adjust the screw by turning it to the left until the bobbin tension feels the same as a normal tension. Libby does this adjusting over a magnetic pincushion. That way, if the screw falls out, it will fall onto the pincushion, not onto the floor.

with echo quilting around the outlines of leaves #4 and an overall loop-the-loop pattern (see Diagram 12).

Bind the wall hanging

23. Trim the backing and batting so that they are the same size as the quilt top.

24. To make a bias binding that is approximately ¼ inch wide, cut the binding fabric on the diagonal into strips that are 2¼ inches wide, piece them together, and attach them to the quilt following the instructions on pages 432–33. Bobbin stitch a decorative edge of green metallic thread along the edge of the binding.

25. When finished, if you like, make a label for the quilt.

DIAGRAM 12

CHAPTER EIGHT

Shoot It, Show It, Ship It, and More!

MAKING QUILTS IS JUST THE BEGINNING. TO BE SURE, your satisfaction will deepen as you produce more quilts and learn new techniques. But your quilts won't have the maximum impact in today's world unless you verse yourself in some other aspects of quiltmaking. This chapter gives you the latest scoop on everything needed to expand your horizons. You'll learn how to enter contests and find tips on photographing your quilts so you can submit them. You'll find out how copyright law applies to quilters. And, there's a listing of all the major annual quilt shows, with insider tips on tracking down elusive hotel rooms in Paducah and Houston. Let's start with a primer on finding a great block pattern for your next quilt: Here's a wealth of quilting advice from top experts.

RESOURCES

Free Quilt Patterns on the Internet

The Internet is one of the best sources of free patterns and quilting directions, but many of the Web resources are inconsistent in quality or provide only a few designs. The major fabric companies will usually have some good free patterns, as will the websites for quilt magazines, so be sure to go there. These six websites have been around for a good while and provide a rich range of diverse patterns and how-to's.

Quilter's Cache

Marcia Hohn says she has posted more than a thousand block patterns on Quilter's Cache; it's probably the best-known site for free patterns. There are several ways to search, including by the title and size of block. You'll find all the most recognizable historical blocks and many minor ones, too. More than three hundred of the blocks are new designs, and Hohn has a dozen volunteers across the country who test each new pattern before she posts it. The site doesn't just show a schematic for a given block but also gives both cutting and sewing directions.

www.QuiltersCache.com

How to Find Quilt Block Patterns

The names of quilt blocks are as beguiling and evocative as a faded daguerreotype. Churn Dash, Storm at Sea, Delectable Mountains, and Drunkard's Path are among the best known. Many quilters become fascinated by the quaint names of and the histories behind the classic block patterns. What are the origins of the Log Cabin and Sunbonnet Sue? Why do some blocks have multiple names? How many different quilt blocks are there?

Renowned quilt historian Barbara Brackman became so obsessed with such questions that she spent more than a decade trying to document every quilt block in existence. She gave up in 1970 after identifying more than four thousand different ones.

One of the things Brackman discovered is that the naming of quilt blocks is far from an exact science. In the preface to her *Encyclopedia of Pieced Quilt Patterns*, which includes drawings of all the blocks she found, Brackman says she was forced to conclude that "the right name for a pattern is the name you call it." She says she learned that some of the common terms we use for very old patterns like the Lone Star and Mariner's Compass were "apparently unknown to nineteenth-century quilters" who made quilts in those patterns.

Brackman tracked down newspaper quilt columns from the 1930s and 1940s, which helped circulate the patterns and their names. She interviewed a retired woman's page editor from *The Kansas City Star*. "She told me that if she couldn't find a name for a block, she would just make it up. And I hear that over and over,"

says Brackman. "I used to think that quilt block names were true folklore. But the older and wiser I get, I realize that it's more of an informal and sometimes commercial thing."

Brackman has spent a lot of time reading diaries from the nineteenth century and trying to figure out the nomenclature of earlier eras, but the quilters of the day didn't make it any too easy. "People rarely mention the name of the blocks. They'll write 'I finished the blue quilt' or 'I finished the red quilt.'"

It simply isn't possible to discover the true histories of many block names. In her 1929 book *Old Patchwork Quilts and the Women Who Made Them*, historian Ruth Finley includes a short chapter on the origin of quilt names, but many of her observations are general. She notes that early Americans tended to be quite religious and that many quilt blocks were given biblical names, such as Jacob's Ladder and Crown of Thorns. Other names were descriptive of the natural world, such as Bear's Paw and Flying Geese. And some were named for political movements or historical events, like Whig Rose or Fifty-Four Forty or Fight, referring to an 1844 land dispute between the United States and Canada.

Attempting to learn more specific histories of these blocks usually results in frustration, says historian Brackman. She cites as an example the still-popular pattern Drunkard's Path. According to Brackman, some historians have suggested in recent years that the block was invented specifically to send an anti-alcohol message during the temperance movement, but she says, "Nobody really knows for sure."

Just one of the infinite number of quilt blocks.

Block Central

Another awesome compilation, Block Central is also a labor of love, kept running by high school band director Kim Noblin. She says her alphabetical listing includes three thousand different blocks, and her site offers a lot more resources, including forums and block exchanges.

www.BlockCentral.com

The following websites are also good sources for free patterns.

About.com's quilting page:
www.quilting.about.com

FreeQuilt.com:
www.freequilt.com

Scrapquilts.com:
www.scrapquilts.com

World Wide Quilting Page:
www.quilt.com

Five Popular Block Patterns Close-Up

There is something so appealing about many of the shapes in favorite quilt blocks that you have to wonder if the basic designs don't satisfy some primal pattern recognition part of the brain. The collection of rectangles, triangles, and curves featured in popular quilt patterns have turned up again and again in manmade designs all over the world and through the ages. For example, you can find patterns that echo what quilters call Wild Goose Chase everywhere from cathedral floors designed in the Middle Ages to centuries-old Asian wall tiles.

Block patterns are, of course, the building blocks of traditional quilt designs—quilts made either from one block pattern repeated in row after row or in combinations with other block patterns. In what are called medallion quilts there will be a very busy, big design feature in the center, but then frequently blocks of stars or triangles or other patterns may appear in the borders that surround the central design. Or, you can make a sampler quilt that combines a lot of different block patterns; these are often appealing to beginning quilters.

While there are hundreds of traditional block patterns, here let's take a look at a handful of some of the most enduring ones.

Log Cabin

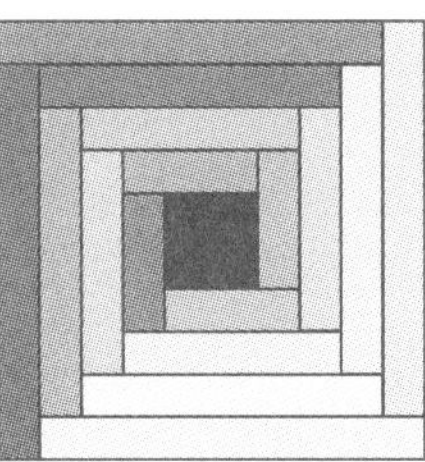

One of the most popular quilt block designs, the Log Cabin is also one of the simplest. It consists of a center shape, generally a square, framed by narrow strips of fabric that grow progressively longer the farther away they are from the center. Sometimes the quilt block's design is enhanced by using varying shades of dark and light fabrics, which add nuance to the block pattern, creating a sense of alternating light and dark triangles.

Many early Log Cabin quilts feature red centers, and some people believe that these are meant to symbolize the hearth inside a cozy home. In his book *The American Quilt: A History of Cloth and Comfort 1750–1950* (Clarkson Potter; $27.50), Roderick Kiracofe says that the center square in a Log Cabin block is referred to as the chimney.

Log Cabin quilts reached the height of their popularity in the second half of the nineteenth century, but today this design is still considered a beautiful and versatile pattern. In early days, Log Cabin quilts were often made of scraps and almost always tied together rather than quilted. Historians say that's because these blocks were often pieced from different types of fabric, making it difficult to quilt them.

Contemporary quilters have found ways to create more complex Log Cabin–inspired patterns, often using coordinated fabrics purchased for the project and finishing it with hand or machine quilting. When Log Cabin quilts are made of tiny strips, quilters often use foundation-piecing techniques, in which some sort of backing is used to stiffen the fabric. When larger strips are used, this shouldn't be necessary, but piecing Log Cabin blocks can be an excellent introduction to foundation piecing.

For a free pattern: Susan Druding, who for many years ran the quilting forum at About.com, has compiled excellent research and patterns for many standard quilt blocks. When she left About.com, Druding took her content with her, much of which can be found at her new website **www.equilters.com**. The exact address for her wonderfully detailed directions for making a simple Log Cabin block is **www.equilters.com/library/logcabin/easy_log_cabin_part1.html**. (Don't forget the "s" in the first part of the address or you will wind up at the home page for online quilt retailer eQuilter.)

Wild Goose Chase

Also called Flying Geese, this design consists of a row of triangles pointing in one direction, giving it the appearance of geese flying in formation. Another ubiquitous and endlessly adaptable pattern, Wild Goose Chase dates back to the 1800s. Like the Log Cabin block, it is easy enough for beginners, but is frequently used by accomplished quilters as well. One simple version has repeated rows of triangles that run the full length of the quilt. Some patterns feature lines of triangles crisscrossing on the diagonal, and wild geese blocks also make a great border pattern for a quilt.

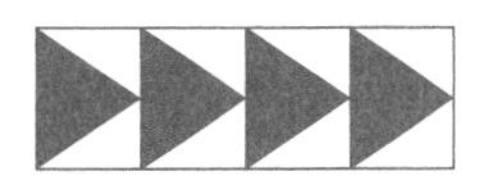

As far as how-to books go, a beginner wanting to make a Wild Goose Chase quilt couldn't do better than to look at Eleanor Burns' book on that topic in her Quilt in a Day series. She presents one basic design but shows the results of many different fabric choices. As usual, she includes specific instructions for rotary cutting, as well as for piecing and quilting by machine.

For a free pattern: There are two websites that provide very different versions of Wild Goose Chase. *Quiltmaker* magazine presents its design at **www.quiltmaker.com/patterns/patt13b/**. Another excellent online source for free patterns is Quilter's Cache, where you will find a beautiful version of this popular block at **www.quilterscache .com/W/WildGooseChase2Block.html**.

Bear's Paw

The combination of a square and some triangles looks something like the footprint of a bear in this pattern. It's slightly more complicated than the Log Cabin and Wild Goose Chase blocks, but not much. In her book *Old Patchwork Quilts and the Women Who Made Them,* first published in 1929, Ruth Finley says that this pattern was very popular in the early to mid-1800s, but that this isn't the only colorful name given to it. Some call it Duck's Foot in the Mud, she reports, and others call it Hand of Friendship. Bear's Paw is one of the block patterns Diana McClun and Laura Nownes teach in their excellent book *Quilts! Quilts!! Quilts!!! The Complete Guide to Quiltmaking*. The two include this block in the sampler quilt presented in the book.

For a free pattern: There are several good sources for free Bear's Paw patterns on the Internet. You'll find one in the fantastic resource known as the World Wide Quilting Page (a misnomer, since it is made up of thousands of Web pages), which provides detailed directions for making a fourteen-inch Bear's Paw block. Go to **www.quilt.com/Blocks/BearPaw/ BearPaw.html**. (The address is case sensitive, so don't forget the capital letters!) On the site for *McCall's Quilting* magazine there is a pattern based on a vintage Bear's Paw quilt. You'll find it at **www.mccallsquilting .com/legacy/v08_pattern/**.

Drunkard's Path

One of those wonderfully evocative block names, Drunkard's Path refers to a pattern with curved lines that seem to stagger across the surface of the quilt. Historians speculate that there is a connection between Drunkard's Path and the Temperance Movement: There are quilts made in the late 1800s that use this design in the movement's signature colors of white and blue. One version of this ingenious design is sometimes called Robbing Peter to Pay Paul (for a variation on that pattern, see the quilt project on page 474 created by Eleanor Burns).

Not surprising, given the repeating curves, the Drunkard's Path pattern can be somewhat challenging for beginners,

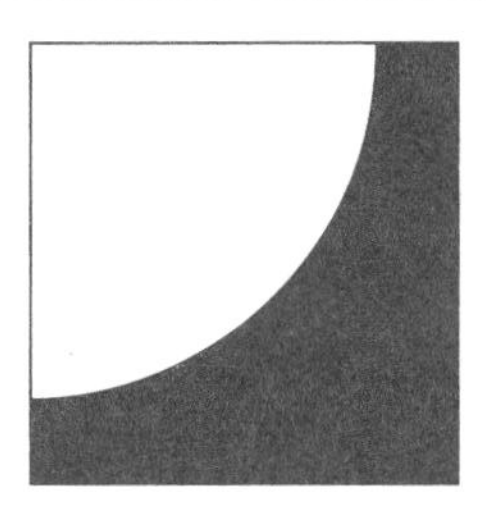

but it really takes just a little patience and a few strategic cuts on the inner curves. All in all, this block offers an excellent way to practice piecing curves. Try a single block, even if the thought of making a bed-size quilt in this design seems daunting.

For a free pattern: Quilter's Cache has good free directions for Drunkard's Path. Go to **www.quilterscache.com/D/DrunkardsPathBlock.html.**

Sunbonnet Sue

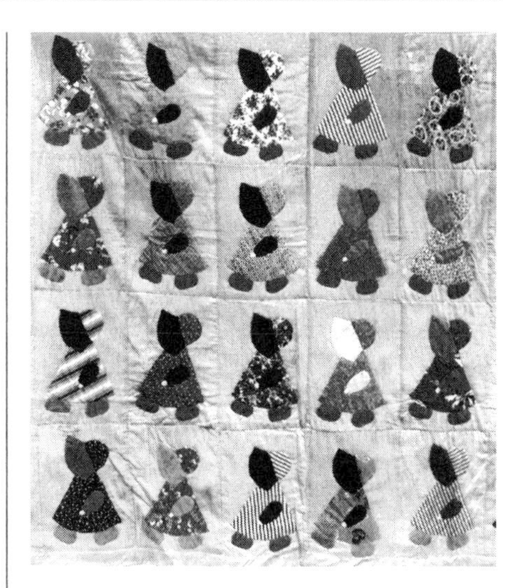

In the early 1900s, appliqué block patterns soared in popularity and one of the most beloved was Sunbonnet Sue, who had first turned up in drawings of the period and then in embroidery patterns. A little girl, viewed in profile with a big sunbonnet obscuring her face, this sentimental favorite has appeared in countless children's quilts.

Today, quilters either love or hate Sue. Those who find her cloying and annoying started a whole genre of "Bad Sue" quilts in which Sunbonnet Sue either engages in bad behavior (sometimes with Sunbonnet Sam) or is killed in any of multiple, creative ways. Nonetheless, making a Sunbonnet Sue block is one way to practice appliqué. This is a technique in which fabrics are not pieced together to form a block; instead, the Sue figure is cut out of fabric and then laid on top of a background fabric and stitched or fused in place.

For a free pattern: There is an entire website devoted to Sunbonnet Sue—a good place to download free patterns. Go to **www.sunbonnetsue.com**, where you can view a wide range of Sue quilts, including a series inspired by Beatles songs. The site is run by Sue devotee Kim Bunchuck of Greenport, New York, who sells books and fabrics devoted to Sunbonnet Sue and sends out a newsletter. Bunchuck also runs a sister site featuring Sue's darker alter ego: Go to **www.badsuequilts.com.**

RESOURCES

Books on Quilt Block Patterns

The design of new quilt blocks has never ended. Quilters today frequently invent their own, and many prominent teachers have copyrights on their designs. But there are thousands of blocks in the public domain from which to choose and a wealth of books on the subject. Here are some of the better ones.

ENCYCLOPEDIA OF PIECED QUILT PATTERNS,
by Barbara Brackman American Quilter's Society; $34.95

Brackman's encyclopedia is still the bible of quilt blocks, the definitive list. Indeed, the numbers she assigned to each of the blocks are widely used by scholars and appraisers and are known as the Brackman numbers. Brackman devotes an entire page to airplane blocks, assigning each a number; when possible, Brackman lists where and when that design originated. Block no. 906 is Lindbergh's Night Flight and was created by Ruby Magness in 1977 (one of the few blocks Brackman documents from after 1970). Quilters can use this fat volume as a source of ideas, but there are no patterns, templates, or sewing directions. For those who prefer software, there is a CD-ROM version of the encyclopedia called BlockBase, available from The Electric Quilt Company. (Electric Quilt automatically includes a database of hundreds of block patterns in its popular quilt-design software.)

501 QUILT BLOCKS: A TREASURY OF PATTERNS FOR PATCHWORK & APPLIQUÉ,
by Joan Lewis and Lynette Chiles Better Homes and Gardens; $19.95

505 QUILT BLOCKS: PLUS 40 BEAUTIFUL PROJECTS TO MAKE,
Better Homes and Gardens; $34.95

These two books from Better Homes and Gardens cover many of the best-known blocks in Brackman's volume, providing how-to instructions with color photos and lots of patterns.

5,500 QUILT BLOCK DESIGNS,
by Maggie Malone, Sterling Publishing Co.; $24.95

Here's another great resource for quilters who want to view a wide range of patterns, although Malone's book doesn't include projects or directions. While the Brackman book is black-and-white, Malone presents the quilt blocks in bright colors and gives tips on how to transfer them to graph paper.

DEAR JANE: THE TWO HUNDRED TWENTY-FIVE PATTERNS FROM THE 1863 JANE A. STICKLE QUILT,
by Brenda Papadakis, Ez Quilting by Wrights; $25.95

This 1996 book about a quilt made during the Civil War from 225 distinctly different blocks has fueled a fad. Teacher and quilter Brenda Papadakis saw Jane Stickle's quilt in a book and took it upon herself to draft templates for every single block, an enormous undertaking. Others became obsessed with Jane Stickle, and there are more than one thousand people on a Dear Jane e-mail list: They call her quilt "the Mother of All Quilts," and all the quilts they make borrowing Stickle's designs are her "babies." This book covers the history of the original quilt and includes the patterns in it. Quilters can also buy quilt software from The Electric Quilt Company that provides the patterns, lessons, and a gallery of Stickle-inspired quilts.

Q & A: Copyright Law for Quilters

Copyright law isn't something quilters used to spend much time stewing about, but that has changed in recent years. There has been a flurry of high-profile controversies about who owns the rights to various quilt designs and how those people should be compensated. Copyright law has become one of the hot topics at guilds and on online message boards.

As a quilter, you'll see photos and patterns daily in books and magazines, at quilting classes, and on the Web, and you may think: I'd love to use this in a quilt. But there are strict laws on copyright, and consequences if you break them. In 2004, a woman made a quilt patterned after one in a popular book, then listed the quilt top on eBay for $1,200. The author of the book containing the original quilt contacted that quiltmaker and reportedly said the author was entitled to 12 percent of whatever was the quilt's selling price. Eventually the two women reached a private settlement, but all over the country, quilters panicked at the news. Some vowed to stop making projects from books. In another instance, a woman won a prize for her quilt at the county fair. The creator of the pattern she used demanded a share of the prize money.

How will you know if you've broken the law by violating a copyright for a quilt pattern or photo?

As a quilter who has created distinctive quilt patterns, how can you prevent others from stealing your ideas?

To help sort out these thorny issues, attorney David Koehser, a Minneapolis-based specialist in intellectual property law whose clients include quiltmakers, answers some burning questions. For more information, his website is www.dklex.com.

Q: I just recently learned that any original work, including a quilt design, gets copyright protection automatically when it's made. I know quilters who

Copyright law has become one of the hot topics at guilds and on online message boards.

always write the word *copyright* along with the date and their name on the label of every quilt they design. Why is it worthwhile to take the extra trouble of formally registering a copyright?

A: Copyright refers to a bundle of exclusive rights, consisting of the right to make copies of the work; the right to distribute copies of the work to the public; the right to display the work to the public; and the right to prepare works based on or derived from the work. Like any other design, a quilt design is automatically protected by copyright as soon as the creator of that design puts the design on paper, on a computer file, or in some other tangible form from which it can be perceived by others.

So, registration of the copyright with the U.S. Copyright Office isn't required. However, there are two benefits to registration. First, registration is a prerequisite to bringing a lawsuit against anyone who violates any of the exclusive rights in the copyright. While it is possible to register after an infringement has been discovered and then file a lawsuit when the registration becomes effective, it is usually more efficient to have a registration in place prior to any infringement. Second, if the copyright has been registered beforehand, the copyright owner may seek statutory damages ranging from $750 to $30,000, as determined by the court, as well as attorney fees. But if copyright is registered after infringement, the copyright owner will be limited to actual damages suffered.

Q: Copyrights cost $45 and the procedure can be done by downloading the VA (for visual arts) forms from the government's website, www.copyright.gov. Other than the form and the fee, all that is required is to mail in a photo of the quilt or quilt design. Is this the best and easiest way to register and how long does it take?

A: This is the only way to register a copyright in the United States. The Copyright Act states that a registration will become effective on the day that the application for registration, the registration fee, and a photo are received by the Copyright Office.

RESOURCES

Copyright Resources

To obtain a copyright on your original quilt designs, go to the website for the U.S. Copyright Office, **www.copyright.gov.** On the home page, click on Visual Arts. You can download the VA (Visual Arts) form there. Send a photograph of your quilt design to the Washington, D.C. address provided, along with the form and a check for the amount specified. There is also information on the site about current copyright laws.

You'll find an overview of how copyright law applies to commercial quilt patterns on the website of fabric and pattern designer Amy Butler, **www.amybutlerdesign.com.** Click on FAQs (frequently asked questions) for a description of what is and isn't legal. For example: It is perfectly legitimate to use Amy Butler's fabric to make a quilt of your own design and then sell it. But it is *not* legal to sell a quilt, purse, or other item you made using an Amy Butler pattern—with or without her fabric.

Q: Some quilters have told me that instead of filing separately for each of their original quilts, they file a bunch of quilts at once and list them as a "collection." Is this permitted? Is there a limit on the number of items that can be covered in a single registration?

A: Copyright regulations permit the registration of a collection of unpublished designs on a single registration application paid by a single fee, if the designs are assembled in an orderly form, the collection bears a single title, and the same person is the copyright claimant for all designs. There is no limit on the number of designs included in a collection.

Q: Do you recommend that quilters register every new design?

A: The decision is entirely up to the copyright owner. One of the factors to consider is the likelihood of the design being infringed. If the quilt isn't going to be shown to many people or doesn't appear to be particularly unique, the owner may decide to forego the registration. On the other hand, if the design is one that will get a lot of exposure (such as being entered in national shows), the owner may want to register the copyright.

Q: Why do you think quilters have become so concerned about copyright? Have people been brought to court, charged with fines?

A: I have heard of at least one case in which a quilter has alleged that one of her designs was copied without permission, for use on carpets. Infringements can also occur in other settings. In one high-profile case, story quilter Faith Ringgold brought a copyright infringement suit against a television producer who included a poster depicting her *Church Picnic* story quilt in a TV sitcom episode.

"A quilt design is automatically protected by copyright as soon as the creator of that design puts the design on paper."

Q: I think quilters are surprised that if they make a quilt from a kit, a pattern, or a workshop project, they don't have the right to sell it. Period. When you make a quilt from a pattern, what rights do you have?

A: The design depicted in a pattern is protected by copyright. Any reproduction of that design, including reproduction in the form of a quilt, and any distribution of quilts containing that design will constitute copyright infringement unless permission has been granted by the copyright owner. In most cases, the pattern or pattern book will contain a statement granting the user permission to use the designs for certain limited purposes, such as producing one or more quilts for personal use. Absent a broader grant of permission, any other use will constitute copyright infringement.

From the collection of Shelly Zegart, a floral appliqué quilt in a Garden Maze pattern, signed Elizabeth Cary, 1859, Indiana.

Q: Many traditional quilt patterns date back to the eighteenth and nineteenth centuries, and designs that originated before 1923 are available to anyone as part of the public domain. Does that mean quilters can use old-style block patterns like Log Cabin and Bear's Paw without any qualms?

A: A work in the public domain can be freely used by anyone. However, if someone creates a different version of a familiar pattern, the changes they made to the design are protected by copyright, even though the underlying pattern, say a Log Cabin block, remains in the public domain.

Q: Of course, quilt designs are not the only creative objects protected. Photographs have become a major component in today's quilts and I, for one, see images every day I'd love to use. Please clarify the rules for transferring images onto a quilt. For example, I've been saving a touching news photo that ran on the front page of *The New York Times* several years ago. I assume it would be a copyright violation to print it on fabric and sew it into a quilt even if I don't sell or publicly exhibit that quilt?

A: Yes, it would. A copyright includes the exclusive right to make copies of the copyrighted work. You could get permission to use the photo from the owner of the copyright—in this case, *The New York Times*. If an individual is depicted in the photo, there may be additional issues relating to that person's rights of privacy.

Q: Are quilters better off using only photos and other images they create personally (drawings, photographs, and so on)? Isn't it also acceptable to acquire so-called stock images and clip art from the public domain, via websites, software, and other resources?

A: Quilters should only use images they have created *or* images for which they have received permission from the copyright owner. Stock images can be a problem because the stock house purporting to grant a license for use may not hold the copyright. If this turns out to be the case, the copyright owner can sue the quilter. Clip art should be used only if it comes from a reliable source and it comes with a statement expressly granting rights to its use.

Q: Should quilters know about other issues in copyright law?

A: Yes: When you create something, don't give away more rights than you have to! A copyright can be transferred in its entirety by an assignment, or limited rights can be licensed for a limited term. As a general rule, copyright owners should only grant licenses for the specific uses intended. If your pattern is being published by a company that only produces books on paper, in English, in the United States, then those are the only rights they should be assigned. The quilter is then free to sell the patterns in other forms, such as electronic books and DVDs, and in other countries.

"When you create something, don't give away more rights than you have to!"

Finding Someone to Finish Your Quilts

For many quilters, designing and making the quilt top is pure joy but the actual quilting is pure drudgery. With all the time-saving tools and techniques, making a quilt top can be done faster and more easily than ever, but quilting still takes time. If done by hand, it can take months. If done by machine, it won't look good without regular practice. So it's no surprise that more and more quilters are sending their tops out to be finished, often by a professional custom finisher who owns a big, professional longarm sewing machine. But how do you find someone you trust, someone who won't ruin your heirloom quilt and will charge you a reasonable price?

Lydia Wengerd stitches a quilt sent to her by Emma Witmer.

HAND QUILTED IS STILL AN OPTION

While the bulk of custom finishing work is done by longarmers, there are still hand quilters who will finish your quilts for you. One excellent resource is Homemade Stitches, a group of eighty-nine Amish and Mennonite women scattered across five Midwestern states. Most don't have phones or computers, but the business end is handled by a "worldly" Mennonite lady, Ruby Nelsen, who lives outside Minneapolis. Turnaround time is three to four months, and the cost is one dollar per yard of thread used, which comes to more than $250 for a quilt that fits a queen-size bed. Go to www.homemadestitches.com or call Nelsen at (952) 997-2019.

ASK AROUND

Many professional machine quilters say most of their business comes through word-of-mouth referrals. Chances are someone in your guild either provides this service or other guild members can recommend someone. If you don't belong to a guild, go to the local quilt shop and ask the owner: It's very likely he or she will know quilters who do this type of work, and there may even be a shop employee who does custom finishing. If you still come up short, there are places to go on the Internet to search, including the website for the International Machine Quilters Association, at www.imqa.org. On the home page, if you click on Member Business Listing, you can pull up lists of machine quilting businesses in all fifty states and various foreign countries. All of these businesses are members of the IMQA, although the association can't guarantee the quality of the results. Another excellent resource is the Professional Longarm Yellowbook, a state by state (and Canadian) listing created by the Sewing Dealers Trade Association. Paper copies of this guidebook are printed annually; you'll find the easy-to-use online version at www.quiltingprofessional.com.

Most professional quilters have a library of designs to choose from.

BE SPECIFIC

"The most important thing is good communication between piecers and longarmers," says longarm guru Marcia Stevens, who teaches classes on running a successful quilting business. "It's not helpful to just tell the longarmer 'Do what you think is best,' because you may wind up with something you don't like." If nothing else, provide photos or descriptions of other quilts you love. Was the quilting very dense? Was it an overall repeated pattern or did it vary across the surface? Was it plain stippling (random wiggly lines spaced only about an eighth of an inch apart), or was the quilting done in flower shapes or some other shape? Were there multiple colors of thread? Do you want a very flat surface or should some design elements literally "pop" out of the quilt? What sort of quilting would further your design intentions for this particular quilt?

Most professional quilters will have a library of designs to choose from—commercial quilting patterns that they've acquired and have permission to duplicate or patterns of their own invention. Steve and Jan Rondeau, a couple who run a longarm finishing business in Johnstown, Colorado, boast on their website, www.quiltedexpressions.net, that they have 2,500 patterns for customers to pick from. Such popular shapes as feathers, stars, hearts, and flowers come in countless variations, or the finisher can do an "echo" pattern—that is quilt around dominant shapes in the quilt top.

If the quilting is too elaborate, it might compete with a quilt top that is vibrant and complex. Provide a sketch if you can and look at samples of the quilter's other jobs for additional ideas. If the person doing quilting is supplying the batting, she will also need to know whether you want a thick, warm quilt for the bed, or a thin one to hang on a wall. And, you'll need to pick a thread color, or colors, for the project.

DETERMINE A FAIR PRICE

Prices for professional quilting vary widely, affected by where you are located, the amount and difficulty of the work to be done, and the expertise of the quilt finisher. Some quilters charge by the inch and some by the hour, and rates can range from $10 an hour to more than $50. It's a good idea to try to get a rough estimate of the final price before having the job completed. Usually, the customer delivers or mails the quilt top to the quilter along with any other materials that will be needed, although some quilters do supply batting. A simple repeat pattern or stippling will cost the least and generally can be completed fairly quickly—within days, unless the quilter has a backlog of work. For custom designs, quilting will take much longer and the time spent designing may be added to the bill. If the quilter is going to add the binding to the finished quilt, that will also affect the fee. Some people prefer to do this final step themselves, especially if the quilt is a special gift.

ALLOW ENOUGH TIME AND PUT DETAILS IN WRITING

Just because yours is a simple job that could technically be finished in an afternoon doesn't mean you can send out a quilt top two days before your cousin's wedding and expect to have it back in time. The best professional finishers have waiting lists ranging from several weeks to several months. Plus, it takes time to unload one quilt and load another one on a longarm machine. If there's a must-have date for the quilt, such as a wedding or baby's due date or a deadline for entering

QUILT JOURNALS AND SCRAPBOOKS

Most people who quilt want to keep a record of their creative output. One way to do this is in a quilt journal or scrapbook. You can purchase commercial versions that provide a space for a photograph of each quilt and some text.

What to write? The quilt's name, when and where you made it, and for whom. Also include the name of the pattern and its source, or whether it's your own design. Some other information to add: the sources of your inspiration; any special materials or techniques used; the name of the quilter who finished the quilt for you; and awards the quilt received.

Quilt historians comb through the papers of long-ago quiltmakers; some quilters kept meticulous scrapbooks filled with samples of the fabric they used in their quilting and other needlework. Keep a fabric journal and incorporate your design doodles along with photos of art, architecture, and decorative details to translate into quilts.

a quilt contest, tell the quilt finisher and ask to have the quilt returned to you in advance of that date.

All of these details should be put in writing, in a simple document that both parties sign, with each receiving a copy of the agreement. Professional quilters will have forms on hand or you can draft one. If it's not a superquick job, it's also a good idea to schedule a progress report along the way.

SHARE THE CREDIT

Not only do quilt finishers deserve to be paid fairly, they should also be properly credited for their work. Anytime you display a quilt that was finished by another quilter, her or his name should be listed along with yours. This is especially true if the quilt is entered in a contest, photographed for publication, or hangs in a show somewhere. Indeed, some machine quilters who have gotten burned in this regard stipulate that such credit be promised before they sew the first stitch: Some add language to that effect in the signed agreement they require from prospective clients.

Naming Quilts

Unless they are just practice samples or projects made from a kit using somebody else's design, many quilters routinely name the quilts they make. When asked why, their reasons vary. Some quilters say that having a name makes it easier to keep track of their various works in progress. Others say they've gotten into the habit of naming quilts because they enter many quilts in shows and the entry form always has a space to list the name, not just the dimensions.

"I don't name quickie projects," says Della Alice Cruz of Omaha, Nebraska. "My first quilt names in the late seventies were just descriptions, like *Wren's Baby Quilt* or *Lion King* quilt. But after taking my first quilt class in the mid-nineties, I was taught that every quilt should have a label. Well, you need a name to put on that label."

Airmail for Harry, *by Valli Schiller.*

Cruz says that her naming process has evolved since. "I actually have two names now, the working name and the 'real name.' The working name might describe the intended recipient of the quilt, my reasons for making it, or the technique or pattern I'll be using. The real name develops while I'm making the quilt." A project called "baby quilt" on Cruz's work-in-progress list was eventually named *Hidden Rainbow*. One listed as "self-portrait quilt" became *Alice's Brain*.

Some quilters say the name comes first and helps inspire the design, but for many, the name has to bubble up during the creative process. There are quilters who love puns and wordplay in their quilt names, and others, like quilter Kevin Key, who take the names from favorite songs. "Unless the quilt was inspired by a particular phrase I heard or an idea, I'll pick a song title," says Key. "My blue and yellow quilt is called *Flies on the Butter* because I couldn't help thinking about the song by the Judds. Other songs that have become quilts include 'Golden Slumbers' after the Beatles' song, and 'Psychedelic Shack' from The Temptations."

Stumped for a name? You can always just use words that describe a quilt's colors and/or patterns, like *Batik Log Cabin*. But give yourself a chance to become more imaginative in naming your quilts, and it may well loosen you up to be more creative in your piecing and quilting as well.

LEARNING ABOUT LABELS

The best source of information about quilt labels is a terrific nonprofit website at **www.lostquilt.com**. You can click to find advice about labeling quilts and also about how to photograph and store them. The site advises quilters not to sew the label on as a final step but to attach it *before* the quilting is done. That way, the label will be much harder for a thief to quickly remove, and there is a way to find the owner if the piece is lost or stolen before the quilting is completed. Also at this valuable site are photographs of lost quilts and information about reporting losses. Best of all: You can read some happy stories about recovered quilts. (For more about Lost Quilt Come Home, see page 531.)

A Label for Every Quilt

QUILTERS ARE BUSY AND WAY TOO MODEST, SO they often neglect to stitch labels onto their quilts. They rationalize this by saying: "Hey, it's not some masterpiece" or "Well, everyone knows I made it for Aunt Betty's fiftieth wedding anniversary." But these are precisely the reasons quilters *should* be labeling their quilts as they go. Future historians trying to document today's quilt renaissance will probably have tons of information about the quilt masterpieces that survive but will be desperate to uncover all the nuances of everyday quilts. Which materials and techniques did quilters use? Who were these quiltmakers?

A quilt label with a wealth of personal detail: the recipient, the occasion, the date, the maker, and the maker's home.

What inspired them?

And, it may turn out that Aunt Betty's children's children actually won't have a clue who the person was who made the quilt or why they made it. I'm still kicking myself that I never asked who stitched the Grandmother's Flower Garden quilt I slept under as a child. Now, the quilt is long gone and there is no one alive who remembers its story. There was no label on the back. Labeling leaves a trail of information for two very different audiences—the descendents of the quilter and the rest of the future world, led by historians who will interpret the meaning of the quilts.

There is another vital reason for making a label; it makes it much, much easier to find a quilt that has been lost or stolen. The Lost Quilt Come Home website is pretty emphatic about trying to foil would-be thieves and make up for the vagaries of life that separate quilts from their makers. The website has stories about quilts that had been accidentally left on car roofs winding up on freeways and of moving men wrapping furniture in quilts they considered just another packing tool. There are also stories of people who found quilts and diligently tracked down their owners, guided by the names and towns that were listed on the labels. (For more about Lost Quilt Come Home, see page 531.)

So what information do historians and appraisers today wish they had on every quilt they see? Quilt appraiser Bunnie Jordan says the absolute minimum information to include on a quilt label is:

The name of the quilt's maker.

The date when the quilt was made, either the start and finish dates or just when it was completed.

The location(s) where quilt was made.

The title of the quilt or its pattern name—whatever the quilter calls the quilt.

Additionally, Jordan says quilters might want to add "the reason the quilt was made, such as a special occasion." And, if the quilt wins an award, that information can be added, too.

Labels can convey a quilt's essential information.

Some thorough quilters include a great deal more. Lisa Portwood, an Ohio quilter who gives lectures and classes on labeling quilts, likes to include "where I got the inspiration for the quilt, or the pattern name or book if it's not my design. If it's the result of a class I took, I like to include that, too. If others were involved, whether it's a group quilt or someone else did the quilting, I like to give them credit. Finally, if I remember to track it, I'll write down the number of hours spent making the quilt: People ask me that all the time, so why not put it down?"

It might seem that all that information would take up a great deal of space, but an amazing amount can be included on a label that is four by six inches, or six by eight inches, says Caron Carlson, a quilter who has also done presentations on how to label and document quilts. Carlson says there is a member of her large guild who also adds extensive instructions on her labels about how to take care of the quilts. "She even goes so far as to write down which batting she used, so she can see how the different battings perform over time," says Carlson. "She also writes on the label what was going on in her life at the time, such as 'during construction I celebrated my thirty-first wedding anniversary.'"

Some quilters make very elaborate labels, but labels can also be extremely simple. Just cut a square or rectangle of plain, off-white muslin and write the information on it using a fabric marker with permanent ink. Attach the label by folding under the raw edges and sewing it on using a simple whipstitch.

How to Hang a Quilt

TODAY'S QUILTERS USUALLY HAVE FAR MORE QUILTS to display than they have beds to cover. And with their new status as art, why not hang quilts proudly on the wall, for all to admire? Before considering how to hang your quilt, think about where is the best place to display it. Just like paintings, quilts will fade if they are hung in a sunny room. Keep them out of direct sunlight.

A quilt can make a beautiful wall hanging.

When it comes to hanging a quilt, choose a method that won't stretch it out of shape. You need something strong enough to hold the weight of the quilt but that won't mark the fabric or weaken the stitching. While quilts are occasionally put into a frame and then hung as one would a painting, this is rare. Most quilts don't have a solid frame to attach to the wall so you can't use the hardware you would use to mount a photograph, painting, or poster.

Many quilters sew a hanging sleeve across the back of their quilts, an inch or two from the top (you'll find directions for doing this on page 436). They do this

MAKING HANGING SLEEVES

A hanging sleeve is a simple fabric rectangle folded lengthwise in half and sewed together, leaving the ends open. The length of the sleeve is determined by the width of your quilt. But how wide should the sleeve be? Most quilt contests require hanging sleeves that are at least four inches wide, because show quilts are often hung on very thick poles. If your hanging sleeve is too skinny for the pole, the people hanging the quilts are not going to sew on another one.

Plan on making sleeves that are four to six inches wide, even if you're not sure whether you will ever enter your quilt in a show or contest. The formula for how much fabric to cut is this: desired sleeve width times two plus a half inch. So if you want a four-inch hanging sleeve, cut an eight-and-a half-inch-wide piece of fabric.

even if they plan to use the quilt as a throw or a bed quilt because they want the option to display the quilt on a wall or hope it will be in a quilt show sometime.

Some quilters use unbleached muslin for the sleeve, which won't show when the quilt is hanging. Nancy Breland, a prizewinning quilter from Pennington, New Jersey, has an alternative idea. She always uses some fabric left over from the quilt top for the hanging sleeve. That way if the top is damaged in some way and needs to be patched, Breland knows right where she can find more of the principal fabric.

Some quilt hangers add architectural interest.

A hanging sleeve doesn't extend all the way to the side edges of the quilt because most people don't want the rod holding the quilt to stick out on the sides, yet the rod has to extend far enough beyond the sleeve so that you can hang it on nails in the wall. Unless your quilt is a small wall hanging, you will want to have two or more hanging sleeves spaced a few inches apart. This leaves a space in the middle for an extra nail or two, which will provide added support for a bigger, heavier quilt.

There are various types of rods you can use to hold a quilt. One popular choice is inexpensive wooden dowels from the hardware store. For most wall hangings, a quarter-inch diameter rod will be fine, but if your quilt is big or especially heavy, choose a thicker rod.

Another simple option that can be decorative as well is to use thin metal curtain rods threaded through the hanging sleeve. You'll need to screw in the wall-mounted brackets at the ends. Choose an adjustable rod that extends at least the full width of your quilt. Using this option, you probably won't hide the decorative bulbs on the ends of the rod, so the rod will have to be slightly wider than your quilt.

It's also possible to sew decorative fabric loops, several inches wide, to the top of your quilt, and thread a wooden or metal rod through those.

There are many wooden quilt-hanging systems on the market that are widely available in quilt catalogs and online. These include wooden clips that attach to nails on the wall. You use as many clips as you need to secure the top of the quilt. A screw in the clip allows you to loosen the grip and feed the quilt edge between two blocks of wood, then you tighten the screw and the quilt stays held in place. There are also long wooden strips that come in various sizes and can grip the entire top edge of the quilt.

How to Photograph a Quilt

I KNOW I'M NOT THE ONLY QUILTER WITH A BOX full of photos in which my disembodied head seems to float just above the quilt I'm holding. Sometimes you can't see my head—instead my feet stick out underneath the handheld quilt. Not a pretty picture.

Photographing a quilt is not simple unless the quilt is small. It's hard to get the whole thing in the shot, but if you throw the quilt over a porch railing or the sofa, you've cut off half of the quilt's design. Sometimes a quilter just wants a simple snapshot of a quilt and then it isn't necessary to get fussy. But there are many good reasons for taking a professional-looking photograph of a quilt. You'll want a high-quality quilt photo if:

- You're giving the quilt away and want to keep a record of it in your quilt scrapbook or journal.
- You're shipping the quilt to a show or a contest and want a good record in case it's lost.
- You're entering one of the many shows or contests where the first round of judging is done solely from photographs. A poor photo can prevent your masterpiece from getting the attention it deserves.
- You'd like to get a magazine or newsletter to feature your quilt; they're not going to publish the photo unless the quilt looks great.

Here's a quilt I made from a pattern by Jan Mullen, an Australian quilt designer whose patterns and fabrics I love. Do check out Mullen's website, www.stargazey.com, but when you photograph your quilts don't commit all the faux pas seen here! The tips at right will help you take better quilt photos.

There *is* a better way to take quilt pictures: Art quilter Holly Knott and photographer Andy Baird have some basic tips for taking quilt photos.

- Shoot the quilt indoors, where you have more control over background and light.
- Shoot against a neutral background that will set off the quilt rather than distract from it. Some experts like a medium-gray fabric as a background, but Knott and Baird prefer a background that is white or black and often use black knit polyester "because it doesn't attract lint and pet hair like felt, flannel, or cotton does."
- Hang the quilt carefully. Many quilters tack quilts in some way to the design wall they use to audition fabrics and patterns. If you don't have a design wall, see page 422 for a simple one you can make.
- Alternatively, if you've got the proper hardware, such as wooden clip quilt hangers, you can photograph a quilt hanging on a wall in any room in your house, as long as there is sufficient room in front for lights and your camera.
- For a clear image, use a tripod to hold the camera still.
- Position the camera so that you are shooting into the center of the quilt.

On Knott's website, www.hollyknott.com, Knott and Baird provide a detailed free tutorial on taking good digital pictures of quilts. You can find the complete directions by clicking on Shoot That Quilt!, which includes advice on buying a digital camera, cheap and easy ways to rig up good-quality lights, and how to convert your photos to slides.

How to Safely Ship a Quilt

IT'S A SCARY THING TO TRUST YOUR ONE-OF-A-KIND quilt to the postal service or a private shipper, but quilters do it every day for a variety of reasons: To send a quilt to a friend or relative as a gift. Because it's been accepted into a quilt show somewhere out of town. Or, perhaps a magazine is featuring that pattern and needs the quilt to take photographs.

Lost and Found

One benefit from pairing the "hard" high-tech and "soft" quilt mediums is obvious at the Lost Quilt Come Home Page, which is "dedicated to displaying lost and stolen quilts and to providing information on protecting quilts." This unusual website, **www.lostquilt.com**, is operated by art quilter Maria Elkins, who works full time in Dayton, Ohio, as an assistant to an engineer.

"At work, I do computer drafting, secretarial work, accounting, purchasing, graphic design, and mailing—everything except take out the trash," says Elkins. Somehow, in her spare time, she also maintains a website that is a benchmark of the online quilt world's generosity.

Elkins says she went on the Internet in 1999, "when one of my quilts was lost by a shipping company." She was frantic to find the quilt because it had been accepted into an international quilt show. "The shipping company was helpful and concerned but they still couldn't find my quilt," she recalls. "That's when I got the idea to start a website for lost and stolen quilts. I began www.lostquilt.com and spent hours contacting other sites, quilt stores, and guilds to tell them about it. I was fortunate that my quilt was eventually found after being missing for nearly two months."

After the shipping company recovered her quilt, Elkins didn't close down the website. Instead, she thought it would be a great way to share the lessons she learned, while helping other quilters find quilts that had gone missing. "I learned a lot from my own experience, and it changed how I package my quilts," says Elkins. She discovered that she did some things right. "Fortunately, I did have pictures of my quilt that I could post on the site. It's amazing how many people don't photograph or document their quilts, and without that, it becomes nearly impossible to recover a lost quilt." (For information about photographing quilts, see pages 529–30.)

"It's always amazing to hear about the different ways quilts become missing," Elkins says. "It can be anything from simply forgetting it in a public place to a home burglary where the thief used the quilt to carry things away. I'm always sad to hear about quilts stolen from quilt stores or shows, because it seems like those should be the most secure places. It's heartbreaking to hear about beautiful, one-of-a-kind quilts which have been placed in plastic trash bags and got accidentally thrown away."

Though Elkins has posted extensive information on how to ship, store, photograph, and generally protect quilts, the Lost Quilt website mostly functions as a catalog of missing quilts, with photos and details of last sightings (about one thousand quilts are currently posted). Thanks to Elkins there are also some stories with happy endings. "I posted one story about two quilts that were lost in tornadoes and one of them was later recovered," she says. "There's also a heartwarming story of a Christmas gift quilt, which was wrapped and packed with other items on the top of a car. It apparently slid off the car and a highway worker found the quilt and tracked down the quiltmaker by looking up her name on the Internet."

SHIPPING INSURANCE

Typically, a quilt is covered under your homeowner's policy while at home, and under the quilt show's insurance policy while it's hanging in a quilt show. But neither of those policies will cover a quilt in transit. You can always pay extra to insure your quilt when you take it to a delivery service, but how do you know what price to write? All the experts agree that if you're sending an heirloom-quality quilt, you had better get a formal appraisal or you haven't much hope of a decent payout should your quilt have the misfortune to be lost.

Lost Quilt Come Home (**www.lostquilt.com**) has lots of information about finding an appraiser; one reliable resource listed there is the Professional Association of Appraisers (**www.quiltappraisers.org**).

Even if you are not shipping your masterpiece quilts, you will still want to get them appraised. Most homeowner policies regard quilts as "blankets" and pay only about $50 for them, unless you've got a written appraisal proving a higher replacement value.

Most of the quilts arrive at their destination without being damaged on the way. But there are plenty of horror stories—UPS trucks have caught on fire. People have ripped open cartons with scissors or box cutters and sliced through precious quilts. But there are precautions you can take. Here are a number of helpful tips for safely shipping quilts, adapted with permission from the Lost Quilt Come Home Page at www.lostquilt.com. (Should you, sadly, ever lose a quilt, you can post its picture on this nonprofit website, just as you might tack a photo of your lost cat on a community bulletin board: Quilts *have* been recovered.)

Don't just label your box, label the quilt, too. Be sure it has a label sewn to the back that details your name and hometown, at a minimum. Many quilters also attach a business card to the quilt with a safety pin.

Always put your quilt in a clear plastic bag before placing it in a carton. Never use a garbage bag that is opaque! Someone could easily throw your quilt away without looking inside. One lady put her precious crazy quilt in a garbage bag during a move, and a well-meaning friend took out her trash. Another woman brought three quilts to a quilt show in brown plastic bags, and they were never seen again. (However, don't use plastic bags for long-term storage: Quilts need air.)

Use a permanent, waterproof marker to label the clear plastic bag. Mark the bag with *both* the address the quilt is being shipped to and your return address.

Include a preaddressed return label if your quilt is to be returned to you. Quilts are usually returned from contests and shows; supply a preaddressed label so there's no question about where to send it. Make sure you use a shipping label that has a tracking number, and don't forget to write this number down before you send off the quilt.

Use a strong, new box. Boxes are put through a lot of stress during shipment. Purchase a box that will not be crushed or break open.

Before you close the box, put a piece of cardboard on top of your quilt to protect the quilt if a knife is used to open the box.

If you use a cardboard tube instead of a box, which some quilters prefer because folding a quilt can leave wrinkles, be sure to stuff crinkled newsprint or tissue into the ends of the tube. That keeps the quilt from shifting and also protects against knife cuts.

Insure your quilt. If you don't insure your quilt, the courier service you are using has no obligation to pay you any more than the minimum reimbursement, usually about $100. There were two prizewinning quilts lost in a UPS truck fire, but since they weren't insured, the quilter received only $100 in compensation. The cost of insuring your quilt is relatively small compared to the trauma of a lost quilt.

If you are flying, carry your quilt on board, if possible. Luggage is frequently lost. Put your quilt in a carry-on bag and keep it with you.

Entering Contests

DON'T THINK THAT JUST BECAUSE YOU'RE A beginner, you can't enter a quilt contest. In fact, you might even win! According to one estimate, there are more than two thousand quilt shows a year in the United States, and many are welcoming to beginners. Not only that, individual quilt shops have contests, as do quilt catalogs and quilt websites. Some of the best-known contests are those run by manufacturers of quilt products, especially fabric companies.

Almost every quilt guild in the country stages a contest annually or biennially, and many of them award blue ribbons to the

Karen Kay Buckley's Sunny Side Up, *first place winner in the category Innovative Appliqué–Large at the 2004 International Quilt Association judged show in Houston, Texas.*

THREE TIPS FOR ENTERING CONTESTS

ONE: Plan Way Ahead Think today about what contests you'd like to enter a year from now. Most major contests require the quilts or slides of quilts to be sent in months before the show. It takes time to create a masterpiece, and if you produce a fabulous quilt top and then surround it with a sloppy, last-minute binding, your quilt will be passed over.

Take a look at the section starting on page 544 that lists the major national shows and go to their websites to find out when quilts are due. For quilters at the top of their game, *The Professional Quilter* magazine includes a listing of upcoming competitions in each quarterly issue under the heading Professional Opportunities (**www.professionalquilter.com**).

Best First Quilt. My mother's first quilt won a blue ribbon from her local North Carolina guild, and she entered my first quilt into competition about five years later. I didn't win a ribbon, but it sure was a kick seeing my quilt hanging in a show. Entering local shows first is a good idea. Remember that while you usually can't reenter the quilt in the same show, most shows don't rule out quilts that have been exhibited or won prizes elsewhere.

Some contests, including those for guilds, shops, and county fairs, don't limit entrants to a certain style of quilt. Whatever you made, you can bring and have it hung. You can enter these contests when you're especially proud of a quilt you made and want to show off, but the contest doesn't dictate what you make. Also, in these sorts of casual contests, the quilt doesn't have to be an original design. It can come from a kit, a class, or a book.

Other contests have strict requirements: If you enter a miniature quilt show, your quilt must fit the specified dimensions. Many contests have a theme that is required to be reflected in your design, such as a garden or a patriotic motif.

If a company is running a contest, you generally have to use its products to have your quilt accepted. Hoffman California Fabrics, famous for its gorgeous batiks, has its annual Hoffman challenge, which requires the use of a particular fabric designed by Hoffman (for contest rules go to www.hoffmanchallenge.com).

Keepsake Quilting, a national retailer, stages two quilt challenges every year. The winners are published in its catalog and displayed at the New Hampshire shop. Entrants must purchase a medley of six fat quarters and use at least four of those fabrics in the quilt. (Go to www.keepsakequilting.com and click on News and Events for details.)

What are the rewards? Except for major quilt shows, you normally won't get a fat check. While the Hoffman challenge hands out cash as well as ribbons for the top quilts in half a dozen categories, Keepsake Quilting gives gift certificates to the top winners. But even when money isn't part of the haul, winners get plenty, including having their quilts tour to shops, shows, and museums. The biggest reward is the validation—recognition that your quilting skills and designs are viewed as exceptional.

Beginners do win national contests. "We have lots of beginners who enter, and we've had quilts win from people who have only quilted for a year or two," says Bonnie Knott, a spokesperson for Keepsake Quilting. "We love to see that." When attempting to make a winning quilt, remember that judges have only a very short time to evaluate each entry. While workmanship is important, creating instant visual impact with color and design choices matters just as much, if not more. (For more information on what judges look for in a winning quilt, see the Interview with a Quilt Judge on page 536.)

Diane McClure and her quilt that won second place in the 2006 Childhood Days Keepsake challenge.

Although entries for local shows will be judged by looking at the quilt itself, judges for national contests and those bound for distant venues often rely on photographs, so it's important both to make a handsome quilt and then to take good quality photos of it (see pages 529–30 for tips on taking great quilt photographs).

Sewing quilts for contests is a completely personal choice. Mostly, you should concentrate on making quilts that seem like winners to you. If you've got that Girl Scout gene and want to rack up some ribbons and prizes, I say go for it. You'll find more contests than you could possibly have time to enter.

TWO: Research the Contests and Be Realistic Be honest with yourself about your skill and experience levels and concentrate on contests where you have some chance of success. The winners at major shows like the International Quilt Festival in Houston are among the best in the world, so the competition is beyond fierce. If you're an intermediate but promising quiltmaker, try entering regional shows or competitions run by national companies like the Hoffman challenge. Wouldn't you have more fun piling up ribbons than rejections?

THREE: Follow Directions Carefully
Even fabulous quilts will be losers if the paperwork comes up short or you botch a required step. Shows are carefully planned: If the dimensions of your quilt don't match the contest requirements, it has no chance. The quilt is also out of the running if you don't read the fine print about hanging requirements and don't attach the proper size hanging sleeve. Attention to details is a must.

Karen Kay Buckley and a little bit of her fabric stash.

Q & A: Interview with a Quilt Judge

There are many quilt shows, including those mounted by local shops and guilds, where all of the quilts submitted are accepted and displayed. But quilters also love to enter competitive shows and contests, where only some projects are chosen. In the major shows, top winners receive cash awards as well as recognition. Winning a major prize has catapulted many a quilter into the ranks of the top teachers: These quilters' classes fill quickly and sales of their books often soar.

There is a difference between juried and judged shows. A juried show uses a selective process to determine which quilts will be displayed; some entries get rejected, possibly due to poor quality or because they don't fit the stated theme or size requirements. A judged show means that the accepted quilts compete against one another and prizes are awarded.

Even among judged quilt shows procedures differ. Judges may just evaluate a quilt by making check marks on a list or they may make specific comments and suggestions for improvements. Shows frequently use volunteer helpers, who run around after the judges and write down what they say about each quilt.

Karen Kay Buckley is an accomplished quilter living in Pennsylvania who has made more than 250 quilts and garnered many honors, including multiple Best of Show awards. Her quilts have appeared on many magazine covers, and in 1997 Buckley was named teacher of the year by *The Professional Quilter* magazine. So, it's not surprising that Buckley is often chosen to judge quilt shows.

Here Buckley answers some frequently asked questions about what judges look for in a winning quilt.

Q: How did you become a judge?

A: After having entered so many shows and being lucky enough to often win a ribbon, groups started asking me to judge. While there is a certification program offered by The National Quilting Association, I am not certified.

Q: In your opinion, what are the top five qualities judges look for in a prizewinning quilt?

A: Visual impact is number one; the overall impression you get needs to be powerful. That is followed by execution of chosen construction techniques, execution of quilting techniques, use of color, and balance of design.

Q: Describe the judging process.

A: Sometimes there is a single judge, and sometimes two or three. Three is good for breaking a tie. The judges may work together and give one critique for each quilt. Other times, every judge is given a critique form to complete for each quilt entered in the show. Most forms include a comment section. Some shows use scribes, and the scribes must remain silent during the judging process. The final decision is often based on the comments as discussed among the judges during the process. In some cases a number system is used, and whichever quilt gets the highest number in each category will take first place in that category. After a first, second, and third place and an honorable mention quilt are selected for each category, all the first-place quilts are looked at again. One of these will be named the Best of Show.

Judging at the 2006 Enterprise Quilting contest in Fort Collins, Colorado.

Q: Typically, how many quilts will you judge in a single show?

A: In a guild show the number is generally between one hundred and two hundred quilts. For a national show, it is often around 350 or 400 quilts. Due to the large numbers, the judges may spend only a minute or two looking at each quilt. The most I've ever judged for a single show was 340, which we did over the course of three days.

Q: What is the best advice you can give quilters who want to win awards?

A: I often advise anyone interested in entering a quilt show to start with the annual National Quilting Association show (for information go to its website www.nqaquilts.org). There are no monetary prizes, just ribbons. Of all the shows I have entered, its evaluations have been the most complete. They often included fifteen written comments. Considering that hundreds of quilts are being judged in a couple days, the number of comments is amazing (the judges do use scribes). When I first started entering shows, I was looking for feedback to know how and what to improve, and the judges' critiques were often no help, like the one who wrote "Excellent workmanship . . . lacked spontaneity." But the NQA judges will do a very thorough evaluation, which will both let you confirm your skills and help you improve your quilts.

Q & A: How to Sell Your Quilts

MANY QUILTERS ARE PERFECTLY CONTENT TO GIVE away most of their quilts to family, friends, and the occasional charity, but sooner or later, someone will inevitably say: "Your work is so gorgeous! Why don't you try selling your quilts? I bet you could make a fortune!"

If only.

As anyone who has ever tried to peddle his or her work can attest, consumers used to cheap, imported goods are rarely up for paying the actual worth of unique, handmade crafts. Even though quilts have attained the status of museum-quality art, the

THE TWENTIETH CENTURY'S BEST QUILTS

It was a big job choosing the best hundred quilts of the last century, and it took a panel of twenty-nine historians, appraisers, collectors, and quiltmakers to do it. The experts each picked quilts they thought were both beautiful and exemplary, winnowing their selection down to one hundred. The final selection ranged from very traditional quilts from the early 1900s to abstract and photo-realistic quilts from the 1990s.

The quilts were shown in a 1999 exhibit at the International Quilt Festival in Houston, and a companion book, *The Twentieth Century's Best American Quilts: Celebrating 100 Years of the Art of Quiltmaking*, was published that included a photo of each quilt.

The selection process and the quilts were showcased in a 2001 PBS documentary "A Century of Quilts: America in Cloth." It is available on both DVD ($24.99) and VHS ($19.98). Look for it on websites like **www.amazon.com** or **www.pbs.org**.

population of serious collectors is small. And just because Caryl Bryer Fallert has a quilt priced at $30,000 on her website doesn't mean that your masterpiece art quilt can fetch $10,000: With quilting, as in everything, celebrity matters.

Most quilters realize the sad fact that if they added the actual cost of their materials to the value of their time, they'd come up with a figure far greater than what anyone would pay them. Although a quilt may be priceless to the maker, potential buyers might balk at paying $500 when they can get a quilt in a catalog or chain store for a fraction of that. This doesn't mean you shouldn't try to sell your quilts—or that you won't succeed. You just need to adjust your expectations to the sobering realities of the marketplace and do your homework so you fetch the best price.

Here is some advice from Morna McEver Golletz, editor and publisher of *The Professional Quilter* magazine; she not only publishes articles on the subject but has also sold her own quilts. If you hope to be compensated for any aspect of quiltmaking, her quarterly magazine is a good place to start looking for advice. Check out the website, www.professionalquilter.com, where you can also buy books on such topics as how to get quilt patterns published and the nuts and bolts of selling crafts online.

Quilter Morna McEver Golletz is editor and publisher of The Professional Quilter.

Q: What is the first step someone should take when planning to sell quilts?

A: Start by evaluating what you want to accomplish. Do you really want a business or just to make a little extra money to offset your fabric expenses? If you want to have a full-fledged business, spend time figuring out what you want that business to be. To set up a business, you need to: outline your goals and create a mission statement; evaluate your financial resources and arrange financing if needed; prepare a business plan; set up a business checking account; choose a business name; comply with any state or local business filing requirements; obtain a sales and use tax license, if applicable; get business cards and stationery; line up suppliers; apply for a Web domain name; and create a marketing plan. And that's before you make all the quilts!

Q: What mistakes do novices make when they try to sell their quilts?

A: I think the biggest mistake is underpricing the work, setting a price by what they think someone will pay. It's important to consider not just the cost of fabric and your time but also overhead costs—things like hosting costs for your website and maintenance on your sewing machine. You need to give yourself a fair hourly rate, which will depend partly on your experience and credentials. And don't forget to add in a profit!

Q: I notice there are some websites such as QuiltBroker.com that provide an online marketplace for selling quilts, but the commissions seem pretty hefty—40 percent in that case. What are the pros and cons of selling this way?

A: I don't know how well quilts sell from this specific website, but I do know quilters who have made sales via the Internet. Options range from www.guild.com for high-end art quilts to eBay for just about everything else. Also, many quilters sell their quilts on their own websites. I think it's all about getting your name and/or quilts known in the marketplace. Before selling online, quilters need to ask for references—that is, the names of quilters who have sold work through particular sites. And a 40 percent commission is pretty standard for gallery work (some charge even more). You have to decide if you want to pay someone to handle the marketing or whether you have the time and expertise to do this yourself.

Examining a quilt at a quilt festival.

Q: What are the various options for quilters who want to sell locally?

A: This depends on a quilter's marketing plan and price point. When I first sold my work, I had booths at juried shows, was a member of a fine-crafts cooperative, and took commissions, which came largely through word of mouth. Other local options include consignment or home holiday shows, both venues I used. Once you determine your price for a particular quilt, it should remain consistent regardless of the venue. If you sell the quilt outside the gallery venue you bring in some extra money, but it isn't professional to offer the same quilt at different prices in different retail venues.

Q: **Lots of prominent teachers seem to sell their quilts on their own websites. What are the pros and cons of doing this?**

A: This is such a positive way to market one's work, and students love to have their teachers' quilts. Of course you have to be wary of credit card mail-order fraud, where a stolen card is used to make purchases and the merchandise is shipped to a fake or forwarding address. Accepting checks doesn't always solve the problem either, as we've seen the rise in fake official, certified, and bank checks. In the case of both methods of payment, the quilts may be shipped before the fraud is detected and the quilter is cheated out of the quilt *and* the money. I would suggest a practice of taking payment but advising buyers that shipping won't take place until funds have cleared.

Q: **I went to the annual show of the Asheville Quilt Guild in North Carolina and saw that some of the quilts displayed were for sale, with their prices listed. The guild says on its website that it takes a 10 percent commission on the sale. Do lots of guilds sell quilts at their shows?**

A: I think actual sales at shows are an exception, not the norm, but it's a good idea. Of course, the guild has to be set up to process credit cards and handle sales tax. But a 10 percent commission is a real bargain for quilters when galleries charge 40 percent or more. At quilt shows in my area, quilters can indicate that their work is for sale, and if someone shows interest, the guild puts the quilter in touch with that person. Even if you don't get an immediate sale from a show, shows are a great way to get your work better known.

"Even if you don't get an immediate sale from a show, shows are a great way to get your work better known."

Q: Prominent quiltmakers are frequently approached by corporations and individuals to make customized quilts. What's the best way for quilters to attract commissions?

A: If you'd like to get commission work, you need to get involved in the art scene where you live. Join the arts council. Look for exhibition opportunities. Today, more and more galleries accept fiber work, especially quilts. Try to join an art quilt group in your area, and if you can't find one, start your own. Also, Studio Art Quilt Associates (www.saqa.com) is a wonderful organization to check out. Talk about quilts publicly: You never know where this will lead. Let your dentist know that you quilt; perhaps he needs a quilt for the waiting room. And always hand out your business cards!

Q: Do you have any other tips for quilters who want to sell their wares?

A: Something we see more of lately is the selling of smaller pieces, such as journal-size quilts (letter-size or even smaller). These more affordable pieces are sometimes easier to sell. I think we're also going to see more use of the Internet as a marketing vehicle, whether that's via virtual tours of galleries or showcasing quilts via blogs or e-zines.

I should also mention that selling quilts is very competitive and not many quilters make a living just from selling their quilts. Even most top art quilters also make money by teaching and selling books and patterns.

My final tip would be: Just go for it. The quilt and art worlds are big, with room for all of us. You'll find your niche, be challenged, and grow. Good luck!

"My final tip would be: Just go for it. The quilt and art worlds are big, with room for all of us."

Quilt Shows

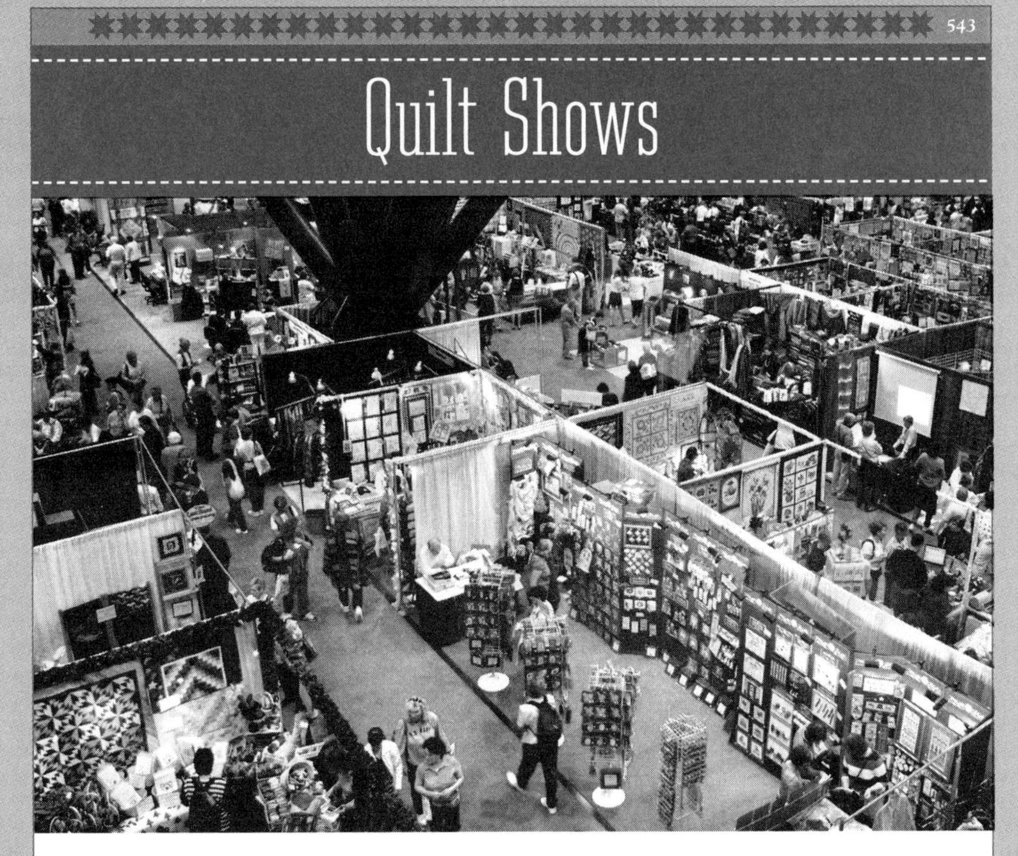

In the past decade, there has been an explosion in the number of regional quilt shows, while the national shows just get bigger and bigger. Quilt shows are a jackpot for passionate quilters. In one place they can see quilts, buy quilt things, and make quilts. The quilts on display are often dazzling, giving attendees a chance to view the best local quilts, along with the quilts in national and international touring shows. Many quilt shows have contests, so there is a chance to win awards and possibly pocket some prize money.

The biggest shows have hundreds of vendors, and quilters get a chance to spot new tools and techniques and collect exotic specialty fabrics they might not find at home. There may be a vendor selling, for example, *only* imported Japanese silks or African batiks, fabrics rarely found in local quilt shops in any quantity. There's an opportunity to try out the latest models of sewing machines and other new gadgets, and some of these may be offered at special "quilt show prices."

The International Quilt Festival in Houston, Texas.

In the 2003 Primedia study of quilters, 98 percent of those who had been to a show in the past year said they attend shows to see quilts. About three quarters said they attend to buy quilt supplies, and 36 percent said they go for the classes and lectures. At many quilt shows, only about 10 percent of attendees actually take classes, but one explanation for this is that the classes fill up quickly: The average hands-on quilt class can take a maximum of twenty-four students.

For those who enroll early, quilt shows can be terrific venues for learning. The major shows offer a wide variety of classes, often with top teachers. Being surrounded by prize-winning quilts, the newest fabrics, and others who share their passion can really inspire quilters to do their best—and they don't have far to go if they run out of supplies to finish the class project. Workshop registration starts six months before most shows, sometimes even earlier, so plan way ahead if you want to take a class with a popular teacher.

Even if classes fill, most shows also offer lectures by famous teachers, who bring slides and/or some of their best work to show and often lecture to hundreds at a time in an auditorium or banquet hall. There may also be fashion shows of quilted garments and other types of entertainment, such as charity auctions.

You'll find both national and regional shows on the list here, but it is not comprehensive by far. New shows spring up frequently and may not last more than a year or two. It would take too much space to list the annual shows of all the guilds around the country. The shows here are well-established events that receive good word-of-mouth reviews from quilters.

Quilt National, Athens, Ohio
The oldest, biggest, and best show of art quilts in the country, this biennial event began in 1979 and takes place in odd-numbered years. Quilt National is unusual because the show lasts all summer and boasts its own venue. It has become *the* showcase for art quilters, and it offers a chance to discern emerging trends and hot new artists. Despite the name, quilts are sent from all over the world to compete for the honor of being included in this prestigious juried show; between eighty and eighty-five quilts are selected. After Labor Day, the quilts are broken into three collections to tour. The hardcover book that catalogs the quilts chosen for each show is a must-have for art quilters.

For information, call (740) 592-4981 or go to **www.quiltnational.com.**

NQA Quilt Show, Columbus, Ohio
The National Quilting Association boasts the oldest national quilt show in the country; it's been in existence for more than thirty-five years. This nonprofit's show is smaller and less commercial than the show in Paducah, Kentucky, run by the American Quilter's Society, but has a lot to offer. About four hundred quilts and garments are displayed, and there is an extensive vendor mall and more than fifty lectures and classes. NQA is also unusual in being a nonjuried show, so it's not hard to get quilts accepted. The NQA simply accepts the first four hundred submissions that meet its minimal requirements—quilts must be clean, smoke free, have a hanging sleeve, and so on. After the NQA has received four hundred quilts, all additional entries are mailed back, regardless of their artistry. "We're an educational organization and we think it's encouraging for attendees to see different levels of work displayed," says NQA's former president Lynn Kough. The show is

judged, but winners receive ribbons rather than monetary prizes, as at the AQS show and others. The NQA is based in Columbus, Ohio, and most years that is where the June show can be found.

For information about the NQA and its quilt show, call (614) 488-8520 or go to its website, **www.nqaquilts.org**.

Sacred Threads, Reynoldsburg, Ohio
This unique, nondenominational quilt show has a mission to explore themes of spirituality, inspiration, joy, healing, and grief. About two hundred quilts are displayed in a local high school, and each quilt is accompanied by an artist's statement explaining its story. Quilts are selected from slides but are not judged or awarded prizes. Viewers are given a blank piece of paper as they enter the show, so they can write down their reactions to the quilts. These notes are filed and given to the quiltmakers when the quilts are returned. The show runs for two weeks, coinciding with several other local events for quilters including the Quilt Surface Design Symposium in Columbus, Ohio. Sacred Threads is biennial, always taking place in odd-numbered years. "I think we're the only quilt show that provides Kleenex for our viewers," says art quilter Vikki Pignatelli, who founded the show.

For information go to **http://home.att.net/~sacredthreads/**. (Please note, that's a squiggly tilde, not a hyphen, before sacredthreads in the Web address.)

Vermont Quilt Festival,
Essex Junction, Vermont
Billed as New England's oldest annual quilt show, the four-day Vermont Quilt Festival includes a display of more than four hundred quilts and hosts dozens of quilt vendors and quilt classes. There are many big names teaching, mostly full-day and half-day classes, as well as lectures. And people are invited to bring old quilts to have them appraised.

For information, call (603) 444-7500 or go to **www.vqf.org**.

Sisters Outdoor Quilt Show,
Sisters, Oregon
Organized by Jean Wells, owner of the Stitchin' Post quilt shop, this legendary event began in 1975. Hundreds of quilts are displayed outdoors all over town on the second Saturday in July. Although the town of Sisters has a population of one thousand, the one-day show typically attracts twenty thousand people. For the week leading up to the show, quilters can choose from more than twenty classes, part of a program called a Quilter's Affair, also run by the quilt shop. Teachers include a mix of locals and national names. There are lots of outdoor quilt shows now, but this is the original.

The Sisters Outdoor Quilt Show in Sisters, Oregon.

For information call the Stitchin' Post at (541) 549-6061 or go to its website, **www.stitchinpost.com**.

Quilt Odyssey, Hershey, Pennsylvania
A four-day show, Quilt Odyssey has been running annually since 2000. The judged and juried quilt show offers more than $10,000 in cash prizes. Attendees can expect classes taught by nationally known teachers and a merchant mall with ninety vendors.

For information, call (717) 423-5148 or go to **www.quiltodyssey.com**.

American Quilter's Society Quilt Exposition, Nashville, Tennessee
Run by the American Quilter's Society, Quilt Exposition is a baby sister to its Paducah show. Begun fifteen years later, it echoes many of the same elements, only on a smaller scale: Cash prizes total about a third of what they are at the big Paducah spring show. About 25,000 quilters attend annually. There are a wide variety of classes taught by well-known teachers, lots of quilts on display, and dozens of vendors. The exposition takes place at the Gaylord Opryland Resort & Convention Center, which by itself has more hotel rooms than the entire town of Paducah, so it's loads easier to book a room.

For information about the AQS and its quilt shows, call (270) 898-7903 or go to its website, **www.AmericanQuilter.com**, and click on Shows & Contests.

International Quilt Festival,
Long Beach, California
As of this writing, a significant new quilt show is planned to begin in July 2008. Its producer, Quilts, Inc. is known for its must-see quilt shows, starting with its annual Houston Quilt Festival (see below), which sets a high standard.

For more information, call Quilts, Inc. at (713) 781-6864 or go to its website, **www.quilts.com**, and click on Shows.

International Quilt Festival,
Houston, Texas
The ultimate annual quilt-world event, the International Quilt Festival is a vast and overwhelming convention hall show that bills itself as the World's Fair of Quilts. It's a truly Texas-size gathering with about 2,000 quilts on display, 1,000 vendor booths, and more than 450 classes and lectures. More than fifty thousand quilters attend annually from all over the world. This is the place to catch the buzz on new trends, products, and techniques. If your goal is to take a class with a star teacher, pay attention to when the class roster will be released, and sign up immediately.

The crowd at the Houston quilt festival.

For information about the International Quilt Festival, call Quilts, Inc., which produces it, (713) 781-6864, or go to its website, **www.quilts.com**.

Pfaff shows off its wares in Houston.

A Quilter's Gathering,

Nashua, New Hampshire

A four-day conference started by two friends in 1989, A Quilter's Gathering features a juried quilt show, about sixty classes and lectures, and a merchants' mall. It's very popular in New England and has a loyal following. There are no big corporate sponsors, so A Quilter's Gathering is smaller and more personal than many of the larger regional shows.

For information, go to **www.aquiltersgathering.com**.

American Quilter's Society Quilt Exposition,

Des Moines, Iowa

Having had such success with its add-on show in Nashville, the American Quilter's Society is starting a third show in Des Moines, Iowa. The AQS announced October dates for an exposition there in 2008 and the following two years. Look for a classy, well-run show that should prove popular: Quilting is big in the Midwest.

For information, about the AQS and its quilt shows, call (270) 898-7903 or go to its website, **www.AmericanQuilter.com**, and click on Shows & Contests.

Road to California,

Ontario, California

Promoted as the largest quilt show in California, this popular event provides quilters with an excellent excuse for a sunny vacation in January. Road to California started in 1987 purely as a quilt conference featuring classes. A quilt show and vendors were added in 1995. An impressive faculty presides over about seventy-five classes. There are approximately five hundred quilts on view, generous cash prizes, and loads of vendors. The four-day show draws roughly twenty thousand attendees.

For information, call (909) 946-0020 or go to **www.road2ca.com**.

Mid-Atlantic Quilt Festival,

Hampton, Virginia

Held annually since 1989, this four-day show displays more than six hundred quilts and hosts dozens of vendors and up to eighty workshops led by top-ranked national teachers. The Mid-Atlantic Quilt Festival is a commercial show, not affiliated with any quilting organizations. Run by the Mancuso brothers, David and Peter, who are also known for their antiques shows, this event held near Williamsburg was their first foray into the quilt world. The Mancusos followed it with others, establishing a reputation for the overall quality of their quilt shows. Their two fall shows, the Pacific International Quilt Festival, in California, and the Pennsylvania National Quilt Extravaganza, are also very popular.

For information, call, the Mancuso Show Management at (215) 862-5828 or go to its website, **www.quiltfest.com**.

Indiana Heritage Quilt Show,
Bloomington, Indiana

This Midwestern state has long been a quilting hotbed, and the nonprofit Indiana Heritage Quilt Show goes back more than fifteen years. It's an annual three-day show at a convention center featuring more than three hundred quilts, plus many vendors and classes. The money awards exceed $15,000.

For information, go to **www.ihqs.org**.

The Nebraska State Quilt Guild displays its work at the 2003 Nebraska State Fair.

A Mountain Quiltfest,
Pigeon Forge, Tennessee

The city of Pigeon Forge, which produces the Mountain Quiltfest, sees bringing quilts to this picturesque town as a magnet for tourists. Admission is free to the show at the Smoky Mountain Convention Center, plus there are more than seventy classes taught by both regional and national quilt teachers. Annual attendance is about twenty thousand.

For information, call (800) 251-9100 or go to **www.mountainquiltfest.com**.

American Quilter's Society Show & Contest, Paducah, Kentucky

A bookend event to the fall International Quilt Festival in Houston, the Paducah show is the other hot ticket for quilters in the know. The AQS show isn't as big as the Houston event, but its impact is enormous while the feel is totally different, since the convention takes over the entire town and fills up hotels fifty miles away (some locals let quilters stay at their homes for a fee). Every firehouse and church caters to quilters with chicken and biscuit dinners.

There are more than four hundred quilts on display, competing for prizes in about fifteen categories. Winners collect a total of more than $100,000 in prize money. The prizes are a record in the quilt world, but it's a purchase prize and the top quilts become the property of AQS. Previous winners can be seen at the lovely AQS museum, which is in walking distance from the convention center. There are more than 300 vendors and about 150 quilt classes. Paducah calls itself Quilt City, U.S.A., and while the AQS show is on, there are quilts and quilters everywhere.

For information about the AQS and its quilt shows, call (270) 898-7903 or go to its website, **www.AmericanQuilter.com** and click on Shows & Contests.

Sharon Schamber accepts the Best of Show award at the 2006 Paducah quilt show.

Quilters' Heritage Celebration,

Lancaster, Pennsylvania

A well-established commercial show, Quilters' Heritage Celebration runs for four days in Amish country, so there are wonderful places for sightseeing and quilt shopping nearby. The show, which started in 1988, is judged and juried and features roughly 300 quilts on display, plus another 250 to 300 quilts in special exhibits. The main quilt exhibit is organized each year around a theme, such as Quilts for a Cause. About twenty thousand people attend the show, and you can expect approximately eighty vendors.

For information, call (217) 854-9323 or go to **www.qhconline.com**.

Fat quarters abound at quilt festivals.

International Quilt Festival,

Chicago, Illinois

An offshoot of the megaquilt show that takes place in Houston every fall, the Chicago International Quilt Festival is growing fast. Held at a convention center near O'Hare International Airport, it features more than 900 quilts on display, about 400 vendor booths, and well in excess of 125 classes and lectures.

For information about the International Quilt Festival, call Quilts, Inc., which produces it, at (713) 781-6864 or go to its website, **www.quilts.com**.

Machine Quilters Showcase and Machine Quilters Exposition,

Overland Park, Kansas, and Manchester, New Hampshire

Machine quilters now have two major shows, both taking place in the spring, and more shows are in the works. Started in 1995 by the nonprofit International

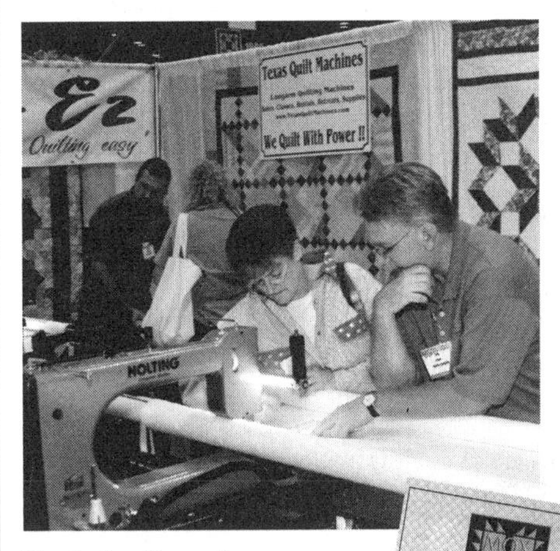

Festivals offer a chance to try out the newest machines.

Machine Quilters Association, the Machine Quilters Showcase was the first of its kind. This show, which takes place in Overland Park, Kansas, boasts about seventy-five classes and four hundred quilts, plus a large number of vendors. For information about the showcase, call (713) 781-6864, or go to **www.imqa.org**.

Catching up fast is the newer Machine Quilters Exposition, or MQX, which was started in 2003 by two professional longarm quilters. On page 149 you can read more about the MQX, which is held in Manchester, New Hampshire. The MQX website is **www.MQX.com**.

Doing the Big Shows

The megaquilt shows in Houston and Paducah, Kentucky, can be overwhelming, especially for first timers. To help you get the most out of the time and money you spend there, here are some tips for attending both Houston's International Quilt Festival and Paducah's American Quilter's Society Show & Contest. The tips come either from quilters who have attended many times or from the shows' managements.

Booking a Room

One of the hardest parts about attending either show is finding an affordable room, especially one nearby. Houston has far more hotel rooms than Paducah, but the ones near the show get snapped up fast, particularly those discounted for quilt show attendees. In Houston, be aware that more discounted rooms are often added later or open up due to cancellations, so you need to keep checking. Also, to get the show discount, you have to give the hotel the code for the discount, and you must make reservations using a local phone number rather than a hotel's national, toll-free number. For both shows, booking superearly is your best bet. Almost all hotels have cancellation policies, so you won't lose money if you cancel before the deadline. Many hotels near the shows are booked a year ahead.

To save money, many quilters come with friends and share rooms. One group who had booked three adjoining rooms at a Houston hotel showed up to find that the rooms were filled, so the hotel gave the ten of them the presidential suite for the same price. They never stopped partying!

For the Paducah show, go to the website **www.Paducah-tourism.org**, click on AQS Quilt Show, and then click on the AQS-approved accommodations list. If you can't find a room anywhere nearby, the Paducah visitors bureau coordinates a home bed-and-breakfast service for the AQS and can help you find lodging with a family in town. Literally hundreds of people use this service, but to do so you must be a member of the American Quilter's Society. Forms for requesting a room at a local home are available from the visitors bureau, (800) 723-8224, starting on February 1. A month later, the bureau matches up quilters and home owners and sends their names to each other (the AQS show is always in April).

Seeing Quilts

The quilts are the primary attraction. They include hundreds entered into the annual shows, along with many other special quilt shows and traveling exhibits. The total number of quilts on display exceeds what you would see in a major museum, and many are of museum quality.

Membership always has its privileges. For both shows, you get free or discounted tickets and other extras if you are a member of a quilt association affiliated with that show. The Paducah show is run by the American Quilter's Society, so there are benefits for AQS members. The Houston show is run by an organization called Quilts, Inc., which shares

Masterpieces on display at the Houston quilt festival.

management and office space with the International Quilt Association (IQA).

At the Houston show, IQA members can go to a special members-only preview at 5:00 P.M. on Wednesday night (otherwise, the doors open at 7:00 P.M.) and members can also get into the show at 8:30 A.M. Friday, even before the vendors open; this is billed as a photo op. Members say it's really worthwhile to come at these times because it's less crowded.

In Paducah, among other benefits, AQS members get a reduced admission fee and pay much less to enter the show contest. The special sneak preview at the Paducah show is not just reserved for AQS members. It takes place on the Tuesday night of the show week and is held as a benefit for the Museum of the American Quilter's Society. Attendance is limited so it's never crowded.

Another way to get special privileges is to volunteer to be a "white glove lady," which means you hang out by a particular quilt or quilts on display and, when viewers want to see the back, you use your gloved hands to turn over a corner. The Houston show especially rewards the white glovers, whom it calls Quilt Angels. If you provide this service for six hours during a given show, you will be mailed the next year's class catalog a full week ahead of everybody else (and you'll get a special pin). White-gloved hostesses in Paducah get the collectible show pin as a thank-you and free admission on the day they volunteer.

In terms of avoiding the crowd, regulars report that the worst crush in Houston is on Saturdays, making that an excellent day to sign up for classes. In Paducah, Saturday has the lightest traffic of the week; Thursday and Friday are the most crowded.

Taking Classes

The classes of the most popular teachers fill up immediately after the roster gets mailed. In order to get in, regulars start checking the show websites daily at about the time the schedules are usually released (July for Houston, November for Paducah) to find out if the announcement of teachers is imminent.

If you want to get the class list for Houston a little earlier, the best advice is to work as a show volunteer. For Paducah, if you order the registration guide before November, you will be among the first to get the schedule by first-class mail.

For both shows, whether you get the class information by mail or on the website, many regulars believe the best bet for speed is to sign up by fax. There are some classes that fill up just from the first day or two of faxed and e-mailed registrations. By the time registrations that have been sent by mail arrive, some of these hot classes will be closed. Advance registration is recommended—the sooner, the better. Nonetheless, if you are tardy there may still be hope: Both the AQS and Quilts, Inc. have bulletin boards at the convention center where people can buy, sell, or trade classes.

Show veterans warn against signing up for too many classes the first time you attend. They are time and energy consuming. Make sure you leave plenty of time for looking and shopping.

Lectures and Demonstrations

Both venues offer numerous lectures. This is a great way to get off your tired feet and, for not much money, listen to a renowned quilter and see his or her work. Lectures are generally held in big rooms, so they rarely sell out and, except for lunch lectures, you can decide at the last minute to attend.

As for demos, Houston has a special area set up on the show floor where the technique and project demonstrations are pretty much continuous. The teacher is on a raised platform, and there are chairs to sit on and video monitors to help you see. This is a great place to "teacher shop" for future shows—see whose work and personality are just what you need. In the Teach America 2 Quilt area Paducah has free demonstrations, where vendors and authors share their latest techniques.

Shopping

Bring a notepad and pen with you, and write down the vendor booths and the particular items you think you want to buy, say experienced show goers. After a while, your brain may shut down from the overload of visual stimulation, but t his way, you can take a look at all the stuff that's for sale, then go back and locate those must-have items. Another suggestion is to make check marks on the floor plans handed out to attendees. Put a check by the booths where the merchandise caught your eye.

Some people bring an empty suitcase to fill with purchases, which is fine if you come by car or bus, but airline luggage restrictions can be tight. Both venues offer packing services, so for a reasonable fee, you can mail your purchases (or your clothes) back home.

Don't Miss These Extras

In Houston: The Tiara Parade—following a colorful tradition, members of the online Quiltart group troop through the convention center on Saturday just before lunch, wearing elaborate handmade tiaras. You don't have to be a member of the art quilter group to watch the parade or cheer on the participants. The tiara ladies parade for Karey Bresenhan, founder and head honcho of the Houston show, and she picks the winners. The parade doesn't always take place in the same spot, so ask around.

Art quilters rave about the High Fashion Fabric Center, a vast showroom full of designer fabrics and trims. Located at 3101 Louisiana Street, it's a short cab ride from the convention center. For more information about the High Fashion Fabric Center, call (713) 528-7299 or go to **www.highfashionfabrics.com**.

The Houston Center for Contemporary Craft, at 4848 Main Street, makes a great side trip; call (713) 529-4848 or go to **www.crafthouston.org** for information.

In Paducah: Fabric lovers always fit in a trip to Hancock's of Paducah, a huge fabric store that regularly has a super sale during the AQS show. While the show is on, Hancock's opens early, and if you don't want to drive to the shop, there are free buses available from the convention center. Hancock's is located at 3841 Hinkleville Road; call (800) 845-8723 or go to **http://hancocks-paducah.com** for information.

The Museum of the American Quilter's Society is a short walk from the convention center and definitely worth a visit. Its address is 215 Jefferson Street; for details, call (270) 442-8856 or go to **www.quiltmuseum.org**.

Folksy "simplifier" Eleanor Burns (you'll find her profile on page 319) usually has her tent program in nearby Carson Park, where she puts on daily seminars and classes. These are free and extremely entertaining.

The most unusual thing about the AQS show is the way that it takes over the entire town. Take time to check out the quilts displayed in downtown windows and other venues. There are free buses that go to the civic center, which always has an antique quilt exhibit during this time, and to the hotels.

What to Wear

"Fashion ends at the knees" is the standard saying for both shows. Comfortable shoes are a must, and loose, comfortable clothing is a good idea also. You will see quilters wearing gorgeous quilted garments or vests decorated with the commemorative pins from every show they've ever attended, but you won't see high heels or people wearing their Sunday best. Jeans and sweats are fine. Many repeat attendees suggest bringing two pairs of comfy shoes, so you can alternate between them.

Paducah paramedics say the biggest problem is blisters and the second biggest is dehydration, so break in those shoes ahead of time and drink plenty of water.

Eating

Convention center food can be expensive and unhealthy. Many show goers pack healthy snacks and bring a water bottle in a tote or backpack. Those who drive bring coolers. In Houston try the restaurants near the convention center and the eateries in the Houston Center mall across the street. In Paducah, there are chicken and biscuit dinners or pancake breakfasts at local churches and firehouses.

Q & A: Tips from a Top Quilt Collector

"You could put together a terrific collection of small works by contemporary art quilters . . . that would be easier to pay for, care for, and display than . . . large masterpiece quilts by the same quiltmakers."

SINCE SHELLY ZEGART FELL IN LOVE WITH OLD QUILTS in the 1970s, she has been sharing her passion. A collector and appraiser living in Louisville, Kentucky, Zegart ran the first-ever state quilt documentation project, starting in 1981.

Zegart's collection of classic quilts made between 1820 and 1982 was acquired by The Art Institute of Chicago in 2002. I talked to her about how to start a quilt collection.

Q: Jonathan Holstein, who organized the Whitney museum's famous quilt show in 1971, has said that he and his wife bought their first Amish quilt for $11 and that by the mid-1980s, the best old Amish quilts were fetching upward of $20,000. Can quilt collectors bank on good returns for their investment?

A: Nobody should do this expecting to get rich. The quilt market peaked in about 1989, and prices for top items have probably fallen 50 percent from what they once were. Also, it's much harder to find undiscovered heirloom quilts in good condition: The really good old stuff has been pretty picked over by now.

Q: A gold standard in antique quilts, the ornately appliquéd Baltimore album quilts from the nineteenth century fetch $45,000, even in a cooled-down quilt market. Works by famous contemporary art quilters like Nancy Crow and Michael James can go for even more. The same is true of some of the quilts made by the women of Gee's Bend, Alabama. Even with the current dip in value, it still seems that quilt collecting is only for the rich.

A: Definitely not. Old quilts, sometimes just tops or blocks, can still be picked up at flea markets and

antiques shops for as little as $10 or $20. They might not be museum quality, but someone interested in quilt history can begin to collect examples of patterns or periods or styles they love. People can set parameters for a collection that make it simpler and less costly, such as only collecting kit quilts from the 1930s, or only collecting small quilts. You could put together a terrific collection of small works by contemporary art quilters, for example, that would be easier to pay for, care for, and display than a collection of large masterpiece quilts by the same quiltmakers.

Q: What's your advice on getting started? And, how did you begin?

A: First of all, I have a tremendous amount of intellectual curiosity. I just looked and looked and went and went and talked and talked. I tell people to pay their dues, do their homework. Go to exhibits, read books, talk to dealers and appraisers and quilters. Some people think they can just do it by going on the Internet, but that isn't a substitute for seeing and touching quilts. Some people set out to buy an encyclopedic collection, or just buy blue and white quilts, or Amish. But I really believe you should buy what you love. I learned over time that the things I had to reach deeper to pay for because they made my heart go pity pat were the ones that over time increased the most in value.

Q: Could you describe a quilt that captured your fancy and turned out to be a wonderful, valuable find?

A: One is a quilt made in 1877, which is now in the collection of the Art Institute. It's called the *Old Maid Quilt*, and I saw it in a show in 1981. I knew the people who owned it were dealers and that because it wasn't an especially pretty quilt there would be less buyer interest: I let them know I'd be interested if they ever wanted to sell it. I wanted to know more about the story behind the quilt and, after I bought it, did research at a historical society in upstate New York near where the quilt was made. It had been a tradition that when a young woman got engaged, all her friends got together and made an album quilt, with each one contributing squares.

RESOURCES

QUILTED JACKETS

Judy Murrah provides great instructions and cool patterns for jackets—see her

popular book *Jacket Jackpot* (Martingale & Company; $22.95). For single jacket patterns, you'll find some striking designs from an outfit called Moonlight Design Quilts and Wearables Inc. These all start with a sweatshirt, which works like a batting layer to give the garment its shape and structure. Go to **www.moonlightdesignquilts.com** (the company also sells purse patterns).

Another fun option is the Rag Fur Jacket pattern sold by quilt teacher Ami Simms (who is profiled on page 366). This garment isn't quilted; it's made by sewing half-inch fabric strips cut on the bias. Simms sells the pattern on her website, **www.amisimms.com**, where you can see photos of the wildly colorful jackets made by some of her customers.

Quilted Clothing

Quilted clothing has a long and illustrious history. In ancient times, quilted garments were the precursors of polar fleece and Gore-Tex. (Even now with high-tech fibers, look at how many ski parkas and coats are still made in a quilted style.) Medieval knights wore quilted clothing under their armor, as did their horses.

Warmth wasn't the only factor: Quilted garments that have survived through the ages include examples of high style and exquisite workmanship. In her book *Quilted Planet: A Sourcebook of Quilts from Around the World* (Clarkson Potter; $40), Celia Eddy shows a stunning photo of a lady's quilted traveling costume made around 1745; every inch of the jacket and skirt is covered with elaborate stitching. Eddy describes a patchwork jacket from Indonesia that is said to have had magical powers of protection and writes that some tribes in Ghana wore appliquéd robes as proof of their status.

A quilted kimono designed by Yvonne Porcella.

Today, style rules. Quilted garments have been a small but vitally creative segment of the quilt renaissance since the boom began in the late sixties and early seventies. Yvonne Porcella was one of the pioneers in this field, making patchwork garments that were displayed in galleries starting in the early 1970s. She was especially known for her gorgeous kimonos, which were made exclusively to be displayed on walls, never to be worn.

This was the time of hippies and tie dye, when everyone played with crafts and adorned their bodies with the fruits of their creative labors. So why shouldn't quilted garments have been part of the mix? Another pioneering art quilter, Jean Ray Laury, wrote magazines and books on quilted clothing, and Porcella remembers Laury saying in those days, "If you made a quilt for your bed, no one saw it. So why not make quilts for your body?"

Vests, jackets, and skirts were the principal garments being made, often of patchwork, sometimes in the crazy quilting style, with elaborate embroidery stitches, trinkets, and beads. Eventually, some of these gorgeous garments appeared in books and art galleries, and then formal challenges and contests came along devoted to this branch of quilting. The Hoffman challenge, begun by the California fabric company of that name in the late 1980s, initially focused just on quilts, but soon a clothing category was added (as were dolls).

Later, a special fashion show was started at the Houston International Quilt Festival, sponsored by the Fairfield company, a maker of batting. When in 2001 sponsorship shifted to Bernina, the sewing machine company, the requirement

Project Runway *has sparked renewed interest in sewing.*

to use batting in the entries was dropped. There was an immediate decrease in the number of quilted garments. These days, the Bernina show (all participants enter by invitation only) features jaw-dropping designer garments. Though not all of the garments are quilted, the recent trends closely follow those in the quilting field.

"Now that Bernina is the sponsor and the batting requirement is lifted, the garments have gotten lighter and have more drape and float factors," says accomplished quiltmaker and teacher Larkin Jean Van Horn. "The days of jackets made of Log Cabin blocks quilted in the ditch over thick polyester batting are long gone. The use of color and materials is now more sophisticated, and there are these incredible thin battings available so garments don't look so much like a quilt you threw over your shoulders!"

Van Horn notes that Bernina show entrants are big on using their digitized embroidery attachments these days, as are quilters, and also follow the quilt world trend of using lots of hand-dyed and hand-painted fabrics.

There are a number of other fashion shows that are annual events at major quilt shows, like the one sponsored at the American Quilter's Society show in Paducah, Kentucky, every year by the Hobbs batting company. Generally these shows, including the Bernina one, travel to other venues around the country as well. But overall, insiders say the category of quilted garments has dwindled in popularity. Texas-based Judy Murrah, who has been teaching classes in how to make quilted garments since the 1970s and whose 1993 book *Jacket Jazz* was one of the bestsellers in the field, estimates that only 5 or 10 percent of quilters make quilted garments.

Porcella believes there are several reasons the trend peaked some time ago. "In recent years, women got bigger, and who wants to draw attention to that?" says Porcella. Not only that, she says, many of those who embraced the trend early on got bored and tried something else: "A lot of us moved on to make quilts because how many wearables can you make? How many closets can you fill?"

Add to that the younger quilters coming on the scene now who didn't have obligatory high school home economics sewing classes (though the hit TV show *Project Runway* is getting more young sewers interested). No matter—the new hot thing in quilted fashion pieces is the quilted tote bag, which works for women of all ages and figures. There has been an explosion of patterns and styles—backpacks, duffle bags, diaper bags, purses, iPod cases, and totes of every size and shape. They can be personalized using all the latest photo-transfer technology and embellished with embroidery. These quickie projects are perfect for an age that craves instant gratification and are a great way to show off your quilting accomplishments in public. On page 457 you'll find instructions for an easy-to-make purse.

This was a quilt made for a young woman who had vowed at an early age she would never marry. For her thirtieth birthday, she asked her friends to make her an album quilt anyway, and this is it. Although I never set parameters to start with, I began to realize later that my chief criterion in choosing a particular quilt was that I wished I could have met the maker, and that was certainly true with this quilt.

Q: What are some of the ways that collectors can educate themselves?

A: The best is to see and study lots of quilts. There are two especially good websites, including that of The Alliance for American Quilts, (www.centerforthe quilt.org) and the site for University of Nebraska's International Quilt Study Center (www.quiltstudy .org). A good book on identifying period quilts is *Clues in the Calico: A Guide to Identifying and Dating Antique Quilts*, by Barbara Brackman. It's harder to find resources on prices; most of the services that list auction prices for arts and crafts provide the information only to paid subscribers. But you can ask the auction houses and top dealers for price histories.

"I never object to paying a high price, but I want to be sure it's really a great quilt and properly dated."

Q: How should budding quilt collectors protect themselves? Is it safe to buy quilts online?

A: Sadly, it is very much a buyer beware situation. Reproductions of period fabrics are widely available and there are people who will stoop to artificially fading new quilts to make them look old. It requires a trained eye to discern the differences. One option is for collectors to hire savvy, experienced dealers or appraisers before buying expensive examples. You wouldn't put a huge amount of money into a new investment vehicle without an expert to advise you, and it's the same with art and collectibles. If you buy an older quilt, you will want a guarantee in writing that what you are buying is authentic and that if any repair or conservation has been done, it must be listed. When buying quilts on eBay, I would check for sellers who have loads of good feedback from previous buyers and who guarantee authenticity.

ADDITIONAL RESOURCES

Associations and Membership Organizations for Quilters

AMERICAN QUILTER'S SOCIETY
P.O. Box 3290
Paducah, Kentucky 42002-3290
(270) 898-7903;
www.americanquilter.com

Membership benefits include a subscription to the quarterly *American Quilter* magazine, discounts on books sold by the American Quilter's Society, and reduced admission to the annual AQS shows in Paducah, Kentucky; Nashville, Tennessee; and Des Moines, Iowa.

INTERNATIONAL MACHINE QUILTERS ASSOCIATION
P.O. Box 419
Higginsville, Missouri 640371
(660) 584-3841; www.imqa.org

A trade organization for those who use sewing machines to quilt professionally, especially those who use longarm sewing machines to finish quilts for others. The IMQA stages an annual show, publishes a quarterly magazine, and provides other services to educate members.

NATIONAL QUILTING ASSOCIATION
P.O. Box 12190
Columbus, Ohio 43212-0190
(614) 488-8520; www.nqaquilts.org

Membership benefits include a subscription to *The Quilting Quarterly* magazine. The National Quilting Association holds an annual quilt show in Columbus, Ohio. There are local chapters as well as the national organization, which is a nonprofit.

STUDIO ART QUILT ASSOCIATES
P.O. Box 572
Storrs, Connecticut 06268-0572
(860) 487-4199; www.saqa.com

Membership includes publications and invitations to regional and national shows, workshops, and other events. The Studio Art Quilt Associates provides lots of resources for professional art quilters and wannabes.

Quilt History Resources

THE ALLIANCE FOR AMERICAN QUILTS
125 S. Lexington Street, Suite 101
Asheville, North Carolina 28801
(828) 251-7073;
www.centerforthequilt.org

An ambitious nonprofit, The Alliance for American Quilts runs one of the best quilt-related websites, period. I'm not just a fan because I'm on the board, but that does help me appreciate how hard they work. By partnering with various universities that study and preserve quilts, the alliance helps support a huge database of historic quilts at the Quilt Index. Also, it runs several oral history projects, and on the alliance's website you can look at great quilts by living quiltmakers and read the quilters' personal histories. The alliance does creative things to raise money, including selling gorgeous calendars. Sign up on the website for a free newsletter to keep up with the alliance's projects.

AMERICAN QUILT STUDY GROUP
1610 L Street
Lincoln, Nebraska 68508-2509
(402) 477-1181;
www.americanquiltstudygroup.org

A terrific nonprofit group for those who love quilt history. The American Quilt Study Group's membership of about two thousand includes both amateur and professional historians as well as appraisers, collectors, and others. Membership benefits include a quarterly newsletter, *Blanket Statements*, and an annual journal, *Uncoverings*. Since 1980, the AQSG has held an annual seminar featuring a keynote speaker, presentation of scholarly papers, and tours of local quilt sites. If you want to go deeper into quilt history, learn to date fabrics, and so forth, this is the organization for you.

Two Terrific History Websites

www.antiquequiltdating.com

The New Pathways into Quilt History website is maintained by quilt historian and collector Kimberly Wulfert. Wulfert is fascinated by dyes and mill history and all the little clues that help tell when fabric and quilts were made. There is lots of information on the site about dating quilts, details of Wulfert's classes and lectures, and lists of books she recommends.

www.historyofquilts.com

An awesome labor of love, the Patches from the Past website is maintained by retired teacher Judy Anne Johnson Breneman, who provides dozens of links to facts and stories. She adds new articles about once a month, and her site is especially rich in resources for teachers who want to use quilts to teach history. Breneman is scrupulous about the validity of the information she posts.

Quilt Museums

Some of the major museums that have significant quilt collections include New York's American Folk Art Museum and The Metropolitan Museum of Art; The Art Institute of Chicago; The Newark Museum located in Newark, New Jersey; and the Shelburne Museum in Vermont.

In addition, there are a number of museums that feature quilts and textiles exclusively.

INTERNATIONAL QUILT STUDY CENTER
University of Nebraska–Lincoln
Department of Textiles, Clothing & Design
234 Home Economics Building
Lincoln, Nebraska 68583
(402) 472-6549; www.quiltstudy.org

Closely affiliated with the University of Nebraska–Lincoln, the International Quilt Study Center boasts a first-rate quilt collection, which can be studied online, and hosts many exhibits, educational programs, and symposia. Renowned art quilter Michael James chairs the university's department of textiles, clothing, and design and has been an advisor to the center (for more about Michael James see page 381). As this book went to press, the International Quilt Study Center was finishing up a new 37,000-square-foot headquarters in Lincoln that will include three exhibition galleries and greatly enlarged quarters for all its programs. Look for exciting new educational programs and more chances than ever to view the center's outstanding collection of more than two thousand quilts.

LA CONNER QUILT & TEXTILE MUSEUM
703 South Second Street
P.O. Box 1270
La Conner, Washington 98257
(360) 466-4288;
www.laconnerquilts.com

A Victorian mansion first built in 1891 is home to the La Conner Quilt & Textile Museum, which offers national and international quilt exhibits year-round. Open since 1997, the La Conner museum showcases both contemporary and vintage quilts. One way it raises money is by asking quilters whose work is exhibited to donate one of their quilts: Go to the website to see what's for sale; some cost as little as $100.

LANCASTER QUILT & TEXTILE MUSEUM
37 Market Street
Lancaster, Pennsylvania 17603
(717) 299-6440;
www.quiltandtextilemuseum.com

Tucked in the scenic heart of Pennsylvania's Amish country, the Lancaster Quilt & Textile Museum is a great place to view Amish quilts. In 2002 the Lancaster heritage center acquired the well-known Esprit Collection of Amish quilts, which now forms the core of the museum's permanent collection.

MUSEUM OF THE AMERICAN QUILTER'S SOCIETY
215 Jefferson Street
Paducah, Kentucky 42001
(270) 442-8856; www.quiltmuseum.org

The couple that started the American Quilter's Society, Bill and Meredith Schroeder, founded this museum in 1991, and it is a must-see for those who attend the annual AQS show in Paducah. The permanent collection includes most of the top winners from previous AQS shows (if winners accept the generous cash prize, they must agree to donate their quilts to the museum), and there are several other galleries where exhibits rotate. You'll find lots of educational programs here and a nice gift shop.

NEW ENGLAND QUILT MUSEUM
18 Shattuck Street
Lowell, Massachusetts 01852
(978) 452-4207;
www.nequiltmuseum.org

Located in historic Lowell, Massachusetts, the home of America's earliest textile mills, this commendable museum exhibits both old and new quilts. The New England Quilt Museum boasts a good library and gift shop and is very active in the community, hosting all kinds of monthly events, including a book group that reads quilt-themed books.

THE QUILTERS HALL OF FAME
926 South Washington Street
Marion, Indiana 46952
(765) 664-9333;
www.quiltershalloffame.org

Like the Rock and Roll Hall of Fame, The Quilters Hall of Fame inducted honorees for some years before settling into a permanent home. Now it resides in a colonial revival house once occupied by Marie Webster, who in 1915 published the first serious history of American quilting. Webster ran a successful quilt pattern company out of this house, which now features exhibits on quilt history and her life.

ROCKY MOUNTAIN QUILT MUSEUM
1111 Washington Avenue
Golden, Colorado 80401
(303) 277-0377; www.rmqm.org

A lively, small museum that opened in 1990, the Rocky Mountain Quilt Museum presents ten exhibits a year featuring everything from historical quilts to contemporary art quilts. One unusual tradition here is the museum's promise to hold a biennial exhibit of quilts made by men.

SAN JOSE MUSEUM OF QUILTS & TEXTILES
520 South First Street
San Jose, California 95113
(408) 971-0323;
www.sjquiltmuseum.org

Founded in 1977, the San Jose Museum of Quilts & Textiles claims to be the country's oldest quilt museum and is a great place to view work by the pioneering art quilters of California. The wide-ranging textile exhibits have made it one of the top attractions in this vibrant city. It has lots of educational programs, including a monthly Kids Create activity on Sunday afternoons. This area has been a hotbed of innovative quilting since the 1970s, and there are great quilt shops and retreats in the vicinity.

Quilting Magazines

AMERICAN PATCHWORK & QUILTING
published by Better Homes and Gardens
1716 Locust Street
Des Moines, Iowa 50309-3023
www.allpeoplequilt.com

American Patchwork & Quilting is an extremely popular magazine published six times a year since 1993. It includes both traditional and contemporary projects. Its website is crammed with free patterns, how-to videos, and more. The magazine also publishes several special issues each year titled *Quilt Sampler,* which feature top quilt shops around the country, including a project from each shop.

FONS & PORTER'S LOVE OF QUILTING
P.O. Box 171
Winterset, Iowa 50273
(888) 985-1020; www.fonsandporter.com

Published every two months, *Fons & Porter's Love of Quilting* includes fun patterns for quilters of every skill level. Marianne Fons and Liz Porter have been hosting a quilt TV show together for years and write good quilt guidebooks. Their magazine also includes information, such as how to shop for a sewing machine and how batiks are printed. (The website is for both the magazine and TV show, and you can use it to order from the brick-and-mortar quilt shop on the ground level of Fons and Porter's Winterset, Iowa, offices.)

MARK LIPINSKI'S QUILTER'S HOME
published by CKMedia Inc.
13 Pickle Road
Califon, New Jersey 07830
(908) 876-1208;
www.quiltershomemag.com

An offbeat bimonthly, *Mark Lipinski's Quilter's Home* is the first lifestyle magazine for quilters. Editor in chief Mark Lipinski, a former television producer, mixes product reviews and decorating tips with funky features on such topics as quilt tattoos. There are only three or four projects per issue, but the editor's "posse" always reviews quilting supplies like rotary cutters or batting. The magazine reflects Lipinski's larger-than-life antic personality, which I find refreshing: Check *Quilter's Home* out on the newsstand to see if it's for you. The last page is always a Q & A with a quilt celebrity. Only in *Quilter's Home* would you learn that A-list quilt designer Denyse Schmidt once posed nude for Andy Warhol.

McCALL'S QUILTING
published by CKMedia Inc.
741 Corporate Circle, Suite A
Golden, Colorado 80401
(800) 944-0736; www.mccallsquilting.com

One of the top quilt magazines in terms of readership numbers, *McCall's Quilting* is a bimonthly with tons of projects, often using the latest fabrics. The editors get personal with their readers, coming along on quilt-themed cruises and trips to exotic locales like Tuscany. The top editors teach classes themselves onboard. *McCall's Quilting* website includes free patterns and other features.

THE PROFESSIONAL QUILTER
22412 Rolling Hill Lane
Laytonsville, Maryland 20882
www.professionalquilter.com

A quarterly publication, *The Professional Quilter* is not a glossy consumer magazine and it contains no patterns. Instead, it's full of tips and advice for those who want to earn a living from quilts, whether as a teacher, shop owner, designer, pattern maker, or quilt finisher. There is also a free monthly e-mail newsletter you can order on the website. Both the magazine and e-newsletter contain good listings of upcoming quilt shows to enter.

QUILTMAKER
published by CKMedia Inc.
741 Corporate Circle, Suite A
Golden, Colorado 80401
(800) 881-6634; www.quiltmaker.com

Published six times a year, *Quiltmaker* emphasizes quilt tips and techniques and has plenty of easy projects. *Quiltmaker* boasts that the majority of the projects in its pages come from readers and that its projects range across all tastes and levels of skill.

QUILTER'S NEWSLETTER
published by CKMedia Inc.
741 Corporate Circle, Suite A
Golden, Colorado 80401
(800) 477-6089; www.qnm.com

Like the other pattern magazines listed here, *Quilter's Newsletter* is glossy and full of fun projects. It comes out ten times a year. But, one of the first quilt magazines, it stands out because it includes not just patterns and techniques but also news about trends and people in the quilt world. Its website offers many resources including tips, patterns, a chat room, and links.

QUILTING ARTS MAGAZINE
P.O. Box 685
Stow, Massachusetts 01775
(866) 698-6989;
www.quiltingarts.com

After years of being published quarterly, *Quilting Arts Magazine* now comes out six times a year. This stunning magazine has been called "eye candy" by its fans. Patterns are few, but this is a gorgeous publication that is full of inspiration, artist interviews, and technique demos. It's also a good source for information on upcoming quilt contests, shows, and challenges. Quilting Arts runs a brick-and-mortar store in Stow, Massachusetts, as well as an online shop that carries the beads, ribbons, and other special embellishments art quilters love. Subscribers to the magazine shop at a discount.

Quilt Books

Just because Amazon.com lists thousands of quilt books and your local chain bookstore has a huge craft section, doesn't mean they've got all the worthwhile quilting books or that they'll offer the best price. One good reason for joining the American Quilter's Society is its discounts on books; the more books you buy at one time, the bigger the discount. The AQS regularly mails a lengthy list of all the books it carries, not just the ones the society publishes. The quilt shop Keepsake Quilting has clubs you can join (for a fee); members receive a 20 percent discount on books, plus hundreds of fabric swatches. Some of the mail-order book clubs for crafters also offer bargains. And, there are several excellent websites devoted to quilt books, including Quilt Books USA at ***www.quiltbooksusa.com****.*

What follows are my suggestions for books worth seeking out to build a comprehensive quilt library. They are arranged by subject matter.

Books for Beginners

THE ART OF CLASSIC QUILTMAKING,
by Harriet Hargrave and Sharyn Craig
C&T Publishing; $34.95

Two first-rate quilting teachers have joined together to produce a reference book that is unusually thorough. It also includes a large number of color photographs of finished quilts to inspire you. (You'll find more about Harriet Hargrave on page 342 and about Sharyn Craig on page 379.) They give excellent advice on how to plan and design quilts based on a variety of popular block patterns. The machine piecing instructions are especially thorough. For quilting how-to's, whether by hand or machine, look elsewhere, including Hargrave's groundbreaking book *Heirloom Machine Quilting: A Comprehensive Guide to Hand-Quilted Effects Using Your Sewing Machine*.

QUILTER'S COMPLETE GUIDE,
by Marianne Fons and Liz Porter
Oxmoor House; $22.95

Multimedia pros Fons and Porter really understand what beginners need. Their book contains lots of photographs and sketches showing how to do all the major techniques, plus there are plenty of appealing projects. The revised edition (2004) includes a few timely additions, such as information on photo quilts, but the original edition is also excellent.

QUILTS! QUILTS!! QUILTS!!! THE COMPLETE GUIDE TO QUILTMAKING,
by Diana McClun and Laura Nownes
McGraw-Hill; $24.95

This book was my quilt bible in the early years and I still refer to it. It's got lots of attractive quilt patterns, many of them simple, but it's also organized so that you can combine a number of block patterns into an attractive sampler quilt. Many beginner guides have been published since, but lots of quilt shop owners still recommend this one. I used the first edition (1988), but get the second, from 1998; it's fifty pages longer, with more patterns and how-to help.

Virtually any book by Eleanor Burns is great for beginners. Burns breaks things down, tests all her instructions with real people, and tries to live up to her company's name—Quilt in a Day. Her first book, *Make a Quilt in a Day: Log Cabin Pattern*, is still her best seller. (You'll find a profile of Eleanor Burns on page 319.)

Quilting Techniques

QUILTMAKING BY HAND: SIMPLE STITCHES, EXQUISITE QUILTS,
by Jinny Beyer
Breckling Press; $29.95

If you want to learn to piece and quilt beautifully by hand, there's no better resource. Jinny Beyer has produced a book as beautiful and detailed as her prize winning quilts. It includes great step-by-step photographs, lots of suggestions for borders, and a wealth of information on the nitty-gritty of hand quilting, plus appealing patterns on which to practice. (Find more about Jinny Beyer on page 377.)

BALTIMORE BEAUTIES AND BEYOND: STUDIES IN CLASSIC ALBUM QUILT APPLIQUÉ (Volume One),
by Elly Sienkiewicz
C&T Publishing; $24.95

There isn't a better-known proponent of classic Baltimore album quilts than Elly Sienkiewicz, and this book is a great way to learn about them. It includes a dozen lessons, more than two dozen patterns, and careful explanations of the various stitches and appliqué techniques necessary for making these quilts. (Read more about Elly Sienkiewicz on page 363.)

MACHINE APPLIQUÉ: A SAMPLER OF TECHNIQUES,
by Sue Nickels
American Quilter's Society; $22.95

For those who want to do appliqué on their sewing machines, this is a wonderful book by a master of the art, award-winning quilter Sue Nickels (profiled on page 357). She keeps it simple and gives thorough directions.

Any of Becky Goldsmith and **Linda Jenkins'** books of patterns. Known as Piece O' Cake Designs, the two (profiled on page 339) specialize in hand appliqué and create fresh updated patterns with very easy-to-follow directions.

Color and Design for Quilters

COLOR AND COMPOSITION FOR THE CREATIVE QUILTER: IMPROVE ANY QUILT WITH EASY-TO-FOLLOW LESSONS,
by Katie Pasquini Masopust and Brett Barker
C&T Publishing; $24.95

Masopust is one of those teachers who really energizes students and gets them to see differently. Here she is paired with a studio artist, and the two of them provide such useful exercises as creating a color wheel from fabric scraps.

COLOR PLAY: EASY STEPS TO IMAGINATIVE COLOR IN QUILTS,
by Joen Wolfrom
C&T Publishing; $27.95

This isn't a project book or a how-to book, but it takes quilters all the way through the color wheel, hue by hue, and gives them a better understanding of how colors play off one another. There are tips on how to use color in quilts to create the illusions of depth, luminosity, transparency, and other effects.

THE QUILTER'S BOOK OF DESIGN, *by Ann Johnston* Quilt Digest Books; $27.95

Johnston's book is a revelation, full of simple exercises that apply such basic design elements as line, color, value, and texture to quilts. An award-winning quilter, Johnston explains each element and illustrates it with photos of quilts. Toward the end of the book, she tests what readers have learned by having them analyze some quilts and then design their own, emphasizing certain features. Johnston's two books on fabric dyeing, *Color by Design: Paint and Print with Dye* and *Color by Accident: Low-Water Immersion Dyeing*, are also very popular.

QUILT STUDIO: INNOVATIVE TECHNIQUES FOR CONFIDENT AND CREATIVE QUILTMAKING AND DESIGN, *by Pauline Burbidge* Quilt Digest Press; $29.95

Burbidge is arguably the most lauded art quilter in Britain, but this is an accessible book, broken down into "workshops" on the techniques for which she is well known. These include how to dye and paint on cotton and how to design big, bold patterns. Even if I never try these things, I love to look at Burbidge's clean, graphic designs and drool over her well-equipped studio.

Quilt History

THE AMERICAN QUILT: A HISTORY OF CLOTH AND COMFORT, 1750–1950, *by Roderick Kiracofe and Mary Elizabeth Johnson* Clarkson Potter; $27.95

The paperback edition of this fine book is extremely affordable, making it a must-have. The text explains how quilts fit into the history of the United States, and the photographs are striking. When the paperback was issued, a reviewer in *Publishers Weekly* wrote: "This is something that an overcrowded market actually needs." In a perfect world every quilter would own this book.

AMERICAN QUILTMAKING: 1970–2000, *by Eleanor Levie,* American Quilter's Society; $25.95

Levie filled a glaring gap in quilt history with her well-researched and thorough investigation of the modern quilt renaissance. Who were the early trailblazers and what moved them? Levie lays all that out and illustrates it beautifully. I found this book to be an invaluable resource long before I tapped the writer to help edit the directions for the quilt projects in this book.

AMERICA'S PRINTED FABRICS 1770–1890, *by Barbara Brackman* C&T Publishing; $29.95

Brackman is the dean of American quilt historians and is known for creating a numbering system for block patterns. But she is also an expert on fabric history, critically important for doing the detective work to figure out when a vintage quilt was made. This book isn't a dry, scholarly tome, but an inviting tool for quilters, appraisers, and others who use the information professionally. Good history on fabric is cleverly combined with attractive, doable quilt patterns.

For Inspiration

ART QUILTS: A CELEBRATION: 400 STUNNING CONTEMPORARY DESIGNS, *introduction by Robert Shaw* Lark Books; $24.95

If you care at all about art quilts, this book is essential. It's a compilation of four hundred quilts chosen for the biennial Quilt National show in Athens, Ohio, between 1995 and 2003. Each quilt is beautifully reproduced in color and paired with the artist's statement, but because the book has been published in paperback, it is very affordable.

The Art Quilt,
by Robert Shaw
Beaux Arts Editions; $85.00

Yes, this coffee-table book is expensive and may give you a hernia, but it's the ultimate publication of its kind. Folk art historian and curator Shaw has packed the outsize volume with a fascinating history of the art quilt movement, loads of lavish photos, and fascinating sidebars on such pioneering figures as Nancy Crow, Michael James, and Therese May. This 1997 book is no longer in print, but it's not hard to find used copies, often for half price or less.

The Quilts of Gee's Bend,
by William Arnett, Alvia Wardlaw, Jane Livingston, and John Beardsley
Tinwood Books; $45.00

The women of the backwater Alabama community of Gee's Bend have become famous for their stunningly vivid quilts, which are documented in this oversize book. I was blown away by the simple beauty and purity of the quilts when I saw them at the Whitney museum in New York. This is the book published in conjunction with the 2002 exhibition: It's now out of print, so snap it up if you find a reasonable copy.

Nancy Crow,
by Nancy Crow
Breckling Press; $65.00

This book showcases a number of different series of art quilts designed by the renowned art quilter Nancy Crow since 1988. Crow's work often resembles abstract art, and she is one of the most rigorous risk takers in the field. She's a pioneer who never stopped developing, and it's exciting to see all of these beautiful quilts in one book. True, it's expensive, but to me, worth every penny.

Some of My Other Favorite Quilting Books

Any of Jennifer Chiaverini's *Elm Creek quilts novels—these are a series of novels about a group of quilters, including the main character who runs a quilt retreat in her beautiful mansion. While there are other quilt novels, I find these are especially deft, and I like the characters. It's fun to read about people who love to quilt and have quilts threaded through their lives and family histories. I've read almost all of Chiaverini's books, but especially liked* The Cross-Country Quilters. *The author has also designed fabric and patterns—check out her website,* ***www.elmcreek.net****.*

The Quiltmaker's Gift,
by Jeff Brumbeau, with illustrations by Gail de Marcken
Scholastic Press; $17.95

I bought this book for my son's first-grade class and fell in love with it. It's an illustrated children's book that tells the story of a greedy king. The one thing he can't have are the beautiful quilts made by a mysterious old woman who only gives them to the poor. The king goes on a quest of generosity and earns his quilt.

Scholastic published a how-to companion book called *Quilts from the Quiltmaker's Gift*, which is perhaps even more magical. Written by Joanne Larsen Line and Nancy Loving, this special book shows kids helping to make the quilts and provides wonderfully clear directions. The patterns vary in complexity, but many are pretty basic; I made one for my son and found the book easy to use. Meanwhile, the original storybook has taken on a life of its own: There are sequels to both the picture book and the how-to book, and *The Quiltmaker's Gift* has been turned into a musical for children.

A GLOSSARY OF COMMON TERMS

Album quilts

Just as photo albums are a collection of different pictures, album quilts join together a variety of quilt BLOCKS. Although the blocks vary, they are usually all made in a similar style, such as folk art APPLIQUÉ. Baltimore album quilts of the 1840s and 1850s were intricate appliquéd quilts, lavishly embellished with embroidery. During the nineteenth century, album quilts were frequently made for friends and family for special occasions, such as weddings. The blocks were sometimes crafted by lots of people and at other times all sewn by the same quiltmaker.

Appliqué

In piecing a quilt, two pieces of fabric are sewn together at an edge and pressed flat with the seam between them. Appliqué involves cutting out fabric shapes and then sewing them on top of a background fabric. This technique is extremely popular partly because there are so many ways to do it, both by hand and using a sewing machine. The edges can be meticulously folded under and stitched down, or quilters can choose raw-edge appliqué, which is best used for a wall hanging or quilt that won't be washed repeatedly (the edges of the fabric tend to fray).

Attaching fabric shapes to a background has become easier thanks to new products and techniques like fusing—essentially gluing the fabric on. Appliqué allows quilters unlimited choices in the shapes they can use on their quilt tops. With reverse appliqué, a layer of fabric is added *under* the fabric for the quilt top. A shape is cut out of the top fabric and the raw edges are turned under and stitched down, revealing the fabric underneath.

Note: On page 288 you'll find a glossary devoted entirely to fabrics.

Backing

The fabric that is sewn to the back of a quilt—the bottom layer in the quilt "sandwich." Quilt shops now sell extrawide fabric that enables quilters to use a single piece of fabric to cover the entire back of a quilt. But most fabric comes on bolts that are 44 or 45 inches wide, and quilters usually have to piece together their backings. For a very long time it was the general practice to choose just one fabric for the backing, in a pattern or color that complemented the quilt top. As contemporary quilters have gotten more creative and willing to experiment, some use lots of colors and fabrics in their backings to make their quilts distinctive. And there are the occasional reversible quilts.

Basting

Once a quilt top is completed, the three layers of the quilt need to be held firmly together so the quilting can be done without the fabric and BATTING shifting. Basting is the process of temporarily securing the three layers, and it can be done in several ways. Basting with a needle and thread involves sewing long, loose running stitches, which can easily be cut out later. As more quilters have turned to quilting by machine, some eschew the use of thread because those threads get tangled in the machine. They prefer to use safety pins, which they unhook and remove as they sew. And, some swear by basting sprays, adhesives that hold the quilt layers together but will wash out later, or prefer water-soluble thread, which also comes out in the wash.

Batting

The middle, or filling, layer of the quilt "sandwich," batting makes it warmer and adds texture. There are a number of choices for batting: polyester, cotton, silk, wool, and blends—and more. Some battings are thin, excellent for a wall quilt decorated with a complex APPLIQUÉ pattern, and others are thick, perfect for a puffy quilt to keep on the sofa in winter. The thickness of a batting is referred to as its loft. It's often best to buy batting for one quilt at a time, so you choose the best one for that project.

Betweens

Short, fine needles used most often for hand piecing and quilting. There are two general rules to remember with needles. First, the smaller the needle, the shorter the stitches you can make with it, which is considered desirable in quilting. Second, although it sounds backward, the higher the number of the needle, the shorter it is: A size 12 between is shorter than a size 9 and would probably be very frustrating for a quilter who's just beginning.

Binding

The narrow strip of fabric that goes around the edges of a finished quilt. Commonly these fabric strips are only about a quarter or a half-inch wide. Attaching a binding is extremely gratifying because it's the last step in making a quilt. A binding evens everything out and covers up any fraying edges on the quilt top and BACKING. Many bindings are made of one color or pattern of fabric, but they can also be pieced together from scraps and become another creative, colorful design element in a quilt.

Block

The basic unit of design in a quilt top is called a block, or sometimes a square. A block can be pieced or APPLIQUÉ and can be an original pattern or a well-known one like Sunbonnet Sue. The same block design may be repeated over and over, or there may be many different kinds of blocks in one quilt. One-block quilts are made with a single block pattern, such as Log Cabin, that is repeated to form the quilt top. Although a popular block size is twelve inches square, many quilts feature six-inch or eight-inch blocks, and miniature quilts are often made from blocks that measure a square inch.

Borders

If the BINDING is like the frame around a photograph, the border is like the mat—strips of fabric that surround the central design of the quilt. Like mats, quilt borders come in many different widths. Borders can be made from a single fabric, or they can be pieced together in designs that complement the quilt's main design. Some quilts are made with multiple borders of varying widths.

Challenge

A quilt contest in which all entrants must work within certain parameters. Sometimes the requirements are that certain fabrics must be used, as in the annual challenge run by Hoffman California Fabrics, which creates a special new fabric every year for its Hoffman challenge. At other times a challenge involves making quilts of a certain style or related to a particular theme, such as gardens or friendship. Guilds and other groups often sponsor challenges. One quilting group in Portland, Oregon, called the Book Club Quilters sets itself the task of making four quilts a year that celebrate books they've read.

Charm quilt

In a charm quilt, every single piece is cut from a different fabric. Some charm quilts are made from hundreds of fabric bits and others from thousands. This is a sort of gimmick quilt with a cyclical popularity. Near the end of the nineteenth century there was a craze for charm quilts featuring one thousand fabrics, while at the dawn of the latest millennium, lots of quilters made charm quilts with either 2,000 or 2,001 different fabrics. The explosion in fabric companies makes it easier to amass a vast collection now, as does the Internet: Quilters love to swap fabric with quilters across the country and around the world. Many charm quilts are simple in design, with a geometric shape like a square or triangle repeated over and over. Variety is the hook here, not complexity.

Crazy quilt

A fad in Victorian times, crazy quilts feature patchwork tops made of odd-shaped fabric patches of rich fabrics like silks and velvets. Crazy quilts are generally heavily embellished with fancy embroidery, beads, lace, and ribbons. These were not exercises in frugality but statements of conspicuous consumption, showing off the finest in imported fabrics and the needle skills of the maker. With more choices than ever of exotic fabrics and embellishments, quilters still love to make crazy quilts. After laboriously following nitpicky BLOCK patterns, it's liberating to make a quilt with wild angles and lots of bling.

Cutting mat

An essential tool for anyone using a ROTARY CUTTER, these plastic mats protect tabletops from the cutter's sharp blades while keeping fabric from shifting as it's being cut. Cutting mats come in sizes ranging from small to huge, and the best are labeled self-healing because cuts don't penetrate the mat top, leaving the surface smooth.

Design wall

A vertical wall with a surface that fabric can stick to, so quilters can "audition" different colors and shapes for a quilt before sewing the fabric together. Some lucky quilters have design walls permanently erected in their studios, but many make do with ad hoc arrangements they can put up and take down. In a pinch, it's possible to simply tape a bed-size piece of flannel or felt to your wall and stick the fabric onto that. For smaller projects like wall hangings, some people improvise, using folded cardboard panels from office supply stores or the simple wooden screens that are sold as room dividers at home improvement stores. Sometimes just changing one fabric in a quilt can jolt the whole design into life. A design wall is a like a science lab for testing colors and is the source of many "eureka" moments.

Fat quarter

A fat quarter is one quarter of a yard of fabric that has been cut to maximize efficiency for quilters. If quilt shops took one-quarter yard cuts straight off the end of a bolt, you'd wind up with a skinny hunk of fabric 9 inches wide and 44 or 45 inches long. Instead, they cut "fat" quarters by cutting half yards, then splitting them down the middle, producing a nearly square piece of fabric about 18 by 22 inches. This gives quilters a lot more flexibility to cut different shapes and sizes for their BLOCKS. When quilters love a fabric they may buy at least a yard, but fat quarters are perfect for SCRAP QUILTS, with lots of little pieces, or when you're buying colors that will only provide accent notes in a quilt. Many quilt shops package their leftover fabric in fat quarters, which are rolled, tied, and arranged by color families in pretty baskets. Fat quarter swaps are very popular with guilds—they're an easy way to trade fabric with friends.

Feed dogs

For anyone who ever felt that her machine looked like it devoured fabric, this is the perfect term to describe the piece underneath your sewing machine needle that looks like a row of metal teeth. These teeth pull fabric through the machine from the bottom, which is great for machine piecing. But when quilting on a sewing machine most people like to be able to move the fabric freely with their hands rather than have the machine move the fabric, so it is necessary to lower the feed dogs or disengage them to keep them from pulling on the quilt's bottom layer. (See the machine's manual for instructions.)

Finger pressing

Anytime you're piecing a quilt but aren't near a hot iron (such as when you bring quilt piecework on car trips or other outings), it's a simple matter to take your index finger and press the seams flat. To be effective, you need a hard surface, such as a table or hardcover book to press against. Finger pressing works fine as a short-term measure, but when you start assembling your quilt BLOCKS into a finished top, you'll want the extra precision of an iron to flatten the seams.

Foundation piecing

See PAPER PIECING.

Free-motion quilting

This is the most popular method of quilting using a sewing machine: In addition to lowering the FEED DOGS, quilters use a special quilting foot that allows them to freely move the fabric around. Using this method, quilting becomes more like drawing than sewing, and the results can be exquisite. However, quilters have learned at their peril that this isn't a quick, easy option. Successful free-motion quilting requires patience and practice.

Fusible web

A big factor fueling the boom for APPLIQUÉ, fusible web comes in lightweight fuzzy-looking sheets that adhere to fabric when ironed. What's great about fusible web is that it allows quilters to cut virtually any shape they can imagine out of fabric, then essentially glue that shape to a background fabric. They can then add decorative stitches around the edges to keep the fabric from fraying, confident that the adhesive web will hold the shape in place—thus, no pins and no BASTING. (Remember: After placing fusible web against the wrong side of the fabric, you want to iron on the right side, not the fusible web side, or you will be left with a horrible sticky mess on your iron.) There are types of interfacing that are also fusible but are thicker than fusible web; these are used to stiffen fabric, not just make it sticky.

Grain

Fabric is woven from threads that run crosswise and lengthwise, and the direction in which the threads run is called the grain. Working with the grain helps you create a quilt that is stronger and fits together more neatly. The lengthwise grain is the strongest and least stretchy—the width of a piece of fabric has a bit more give. When cutting fabric, position your TEMPLATE or ruler so that the straight lines of your cut fabric will be parallel to either the lengthwise or crosswise grain. What you want to avoid most of the time (except when making a bias binding) is cutting on an angle, where the fabric is extremely stretchy.

Hanging sleeve

This is a long, narrow tube of fabric stitched to the back of a quilt that allows the quilt to be hung on a wall. A hanging rod of wood or metal can be threaded through the sleeve, so even a heavy quilt can be suspended safely. Such sleeves are required by most quilt shows. Like everything else, some people get very creative with their hanging sleeves, but mostly they're a utilitarian add-on made of unbleached muslin or fabric left over from the quilt.

Medallion quilt

A quilt dominated by a large central design, such as a Mariner's Compass or Lone Star, which is surrounded by several BORDERS and sometimes BLOCKS. This English tradition was picked up enthusiastically by colonists in America. These are magnificent quilts that stand out at shows and contests but generally aren't a good choice for a beginning quilter.

Mystery quilt

A mystery quilt is one in which participating quilters are given instructions for just one BLOCK or section of a quilt at a time. The overall design of the project remains a surprise until the quilt is sewn together at the end. Instructions for mystery quilts are doled out in many ways, including through guilds, in quilt shop groups that meet weekly or monthly, and increasingly, online. Part of the fun is comparing finished projects with others who followed the same "clues." Quilters really love this stuff: When I Googled the words *mystery quilt,* there were nearly half a million results, many linked to free patterns available on the Internet.

Paper piecing

In paper piecing, also sometimes called foundation piecing, paper TEMPLATES are made for each piece of fabric in a quilt, and the fabric is actually basted onto the paper. It's easier to cut precise shapes in paper than fabric, and pressing the edges of fabric against the paper edges keeps fabric from stretching and makes the lines more crisp. Later, when the quilt top construction is complete, the BASTING threads are cut and the paper templates are removed (they can be reused), but the fabric retains its shape. Paper piecing is often used for meticulous, demanding designs like Grandmother's Flower Garden, which is made of rings of small hexagons. Although the technique is ancient, originating in England, it's had a resurgence in popularity because it allows for great accuracy in highly complex patterns, and quilters have adapted the technique to machine piecing as well as handwork.

Rotary cutter

These simple devices that look like pizza cutters are used to quickly and accurately cut multiple layers of fabric at once. Since their introduction in the early 1980s rotary cutters have revolutionized quilting, inspiring many time-saving techniques for cutting and assembling quilt tops. The supersharp cutters are great but require two other implements: a CUTTING MAT, to protect the tabletop, and a special quilter's ruler to create a cutting guide. Quilters must be careful to keep the blade closed when the rotary cutter is not in use and always cut away from their body! (See page 418 for step-by-step instructions for using a rotary cutter.)

Sampler quilt

In a sampler quilt each BLOCK is different, making it a great project for a beginner. Sewing the same pattern block after block, especially something tricky and curvy like Drunkard's Path, can be tedious, but with a sampler quilt, you never get bored and are sure to find patterns you love and enjoy making. Then, you can always go on to make a quilt that is all Log Cabin blocks, or all Bear's Paw, or anything else you like. Sampler quilts can be made entirely of pieced blocks, or entirely of APPLIQUÉ blocks, or the two techniques can be mixed in the same quilt. To give a sampler quilt a unified look, quilters often use the same fabrics over and over, sometimes sticking to just a few colors. Sampler quilts also invite you to try different quilting patterns for the various blocks.

Scrap quilt

These are quilts made from lots and lots of different fabrics, sometimes cut in very small pieces. Despite the use of the word *scrap*, it would be wrong to suppose that these quilts are always made from old clothes and leftover snippets of material. Scrap quilts are more about style than they are about saving money, and indeed, many quilters make them entirely from new fabric. Those who love to make scrap quilts may collect fabrics for years, stocking up on FAT QUARTERS and buying half yards at quilt shops and shows. Like SAMPLER QUILTS, scrap quilts are fun and never boring because they contain so much variety.

Seam allowance

The distance between your sewing line and the rough edges of the fabric is the seam allowance. When you are quilting, the standard seam allowance is one quarter of an inch. The current generation of quilters loves to say there are no rules anymore, but this is an exception to the no rule rule: If you don't keep your seams uniform, your quilt won't fit together cleanly, no matter whether it's a BLOCK pattern that dates back a century or a design you invented last week.

Selvage

In order to keep the lengthwise edges of fabric from fraying during production, fabric manufacturers make the weave extratight for about half an inch along each side. Fabric makers print their names on the selvages, along with the name of the fabric line, and there will be a row of dots showing the colors used to dye the fabric. The selvages on both sides of a piece of fabric will pucker when washed and shouldn't be included in a quilt. Most quilters keep the selvages on until they're ready to cut out pieces from the fabric: The selvages identify the lengthwise GRAIN and will help you make sure that you cut pieces of fabric along a straight grain.

Template

Templates are used to trace shapes onto fabric so the cutting will be more precise. Most templates are made from plastic, but the basic requirement is that the template be stiff and sturdy. Paper templates will do in a pinch, but quilt shops sell wonderful template plastic that has grid lines right on the plastic sheets. This can be used over and over. Savvy users of ROTARY CUTTERS use fewer templates because they know how to cut to get the shapes they want by making angled cuts in an assembly-line fashion. Templates are also used to draw patterns on a quilt top before it is quilted.

Tied quilt

The simplest and quickest method for attaching the three layers of a quilt together is to tie them with yarn or embroidery thread—or sometimes with narrow ribbon. Using a needle, a length of yarn or thread is pulled through the three layers leaving two even end pieces on the quilt's surface. Once tied into a secure knot, the ends are cut to a uniform length, usually one to three inches. Care must be taken that the ties aren't too far apart or the layers of the quilt will slide.

This technique is great for beginners and quilters with a tight deadline who want to make something fast, like a "utility quilt" to throw on the family room sofa. Tied quilts, also called tufted quilts, have a puffy, unfussy homemade look to them. Do bear in mind that tied quilts may not hold up well to repeated machine washing. Ties of a color that matches the fabrics in the quilt will blend in and disappear, but quilters often pick contrasting colors so the ties stand out and function as a decorative focal point.

Whole-cloth quilt

Remember that a quilt is a fabric sandwich: What makes it a quilt is that it is quilted, not that the top is made of patched together pieces of fabric. As the name suggests, whole-cloth quilts are those where the entire top is made from a single fabric. Sometimes there are several pieces sewn together, but they are all from the same fabric, often in a solid color. Most of the oldest known quilts are whole cloth, and this is the style of quilt the earliest colonists would have brought from England. Because the fabric doesn't vary, it doesn't compete with the quilting stitches, and whole-cloth quilts are a great showcase for those with exquisite needle skills. Many whole-cloth quilts are made by hand, but as sewing machines get more sophisticated and machine quilters hone their skills, more are being sewn by machine. Machine-quilting guru Diane Gaudynski in particular has made whole-cloth quilts her trademark, creating stunning thread designs on brilliant silks.

BIBLIOGRAPHY

Anderson, Alex
Hand Quilting with Alex Anderson: Six Projects for Hand Quilters. Lafayette, Calif.: C&T Publishing, 1998.

Start Quilting with Alex Anderson: Six Projects for First-Time Quilters. 2nd ed. Lafayette, Calif.: C&T Publishing, 2001.

Anderson, Audrey Swales, and Tom Culp, editors
Quilters' Travel Companion.
Old Forge, N.Y.: Chalet Publishing, 2004.

Arnett, William, Alvia Wardlaw, Jane Livingston, and John Beardsley
The Quilts of Gee's Bend. Atlanta, Ga.: Tinwood Books, 2002.

Barber, Elizabeth Wayland
Women's Work: The First 20,000 Years: Women, Cloth, and Society in Early Times. New York: W. W. Norton & Company, 1995.

Barnes, Christine, and Steve W. Marley
Quilting, Patchwork & Appliqué.
Tampa, Fla.: Sunset Publishing Corporation, 1981.

Beyer, Jinny
Quiltmaking by Hand: Simple Stitches, Exquisite Quilts. Elmhurst, Ill.: Breckling Press, 2004.

Bissell, Don
The First Conglomerate: 145 Years of the Singer Sewing Machine Company. Brunswick, Maine: Audenreed Press, 1999.

Bonesteel, Georgia
Lap Quilting Lives! Bothell, Wash.: Martingale & Company, 1999.

Brackman, Barbara
America's Printed Fabrics 1770–1890. Lafayette, Calif.: C&T Publishing, 2004.

Encyclopedia of Pieced Quilt Patterns. Paducah, Ky.: American Quilter's Society, 1993.

Facts & Fabrications: Unraveling the History of Quilts & Slavery. Lafayette, Calif.: C&T Publishing, 2006.

Brandon, Ruth
A Capitalist Romance: Singer and the Sewing Machine. New York: Kodansha America, 1996.

Brumbeau, Jeff
The Quiltmaker's Gift. New York: Scholastic Press, 2001.

Burbidge, Pauline
Quilt Studio: Innovative Techniques for Confident and Creative Quiltmaking and Design. Lincolnwood, Ill.: Quilt Digest Press, 2000.

Burns, Eleanor
Make a Quilt in a Day: Log Cabin Pattern. San Marcos, Calif.: Quilt in a Day, 1998.

CKMedia
Quilting in America. N.p.: 2006.

The Twentieth Century's Best American Quilts: Celebrating 100 Years of the Art of Quiltmaking. Golden, Colo.: Primedia Special Interest Publications, 1999.

Colvin, Joan
Nature's Studio: A Quilter's Guide to Playing with Fabrics & Techniques. Lafayette, Calif.: C&T Publishing, 2005.

The editors of Creative Publishing International
Sewing 101: A Beginner's Guide to Sewing. Chanhassen, Minn.: Creative Publishing International, 2002.

Crow, Nancy
Nancy Crow. Elmhurst, Ill.: Breckling Press, 2006.

Darling, Sharon
The Quilter's Review Guide to Picking a Sewing Machine You'll Love. Seattle: Trillium Publishing, Inc., 2003.

Dobard, Raymond G., and Jacqueline Tobin
Hidden in Plain View: A Secret Story of Quilts and the Underground Railroad. New York.: Anchor Books, 2000.

Dunnewold, Jane
Complex Cloth: A Comprehensive Guide to Surface Design. Woodinville, Wash.: Martingale and Company, 1996.

Eddy, Celia
Quilted Planet: A Sourcebook of Quilts from Around the World. New York: Clarkson Potter, 2005.

Fallert, Caryl Bryer
Quilt Savvy: Guide to Images on Fabric. Paducah, Ky.: American Quilter's Society, 2004.

Fassett, Kaffe
Glorious Patchwork. New York: Clarkson Potter, 1997.

Passionate Patchwork. Newtown, Conn.: The Taunton Press, 2001.

Fassett, Kaffe, and Liza Prior Lucy.
Kaffe Fassett's Museum Quilts: Designs Inspired by the Victoria & Albert Museum. Newtown, Conn.: The Taunton Press, 2005.

Ferrero, Pat, Elaine Hedges, and Julie Silber
Hearts and Hands: Women, Quilts, and American Society. Nashville, Tenn.: Rutledge Hill Press, 2000.

Finley, Ruth E.
Old Patchwork Quilts and the Women Who Made Them. Charlottesville, Va.: Howell Press, Inc., 1929.

Fons, Marianne, and Liz Porter
Quilter's Complete Guide. 2nd rev. ed. N.p.: Leisure Arts, 2000.

Freeman, Roland L.
A Communion of the Spirits: African-American Quilters, Preservers, and Their Stories. Nashville, Tenn.: Rutledge Hill Press, 1996.

Fry, Gladys-Marie
Stitched From the Soul: Slave Quilts from the Antebellum South. Chapel Hill, N.C.: The University of North Carolina Press, 2002.

Gaudynski, Diane
Gaudynski's Machine Quilting Guidebook. Paducah, Ky.: American Quilter's Society, 2006.

Guide to Machine Quilting. Paducah, Ky.: American Quilter's Society, 2002.

Goldsmith, Becky, and Linda Jenkins
Amish-Inspired Quilts: Tradition with a Piece O' Cake Twist. Lafayette, Calif.: C&T Publishing, 2006.

Appliqué Delights: 100 Irresistible Blocks from Piece O' Cake Designs. Lafayette, Calif.: C&T Publishing, 2004.

The New Appliqué Sampler: Learn to Appliqué the Piece O' Cake Way. Lafayette, Calif.: C&T Publishing, 2005.

Gordon, Maggi McCormick
The Quilter's Resource Book. London: Chrysalis Books Group, 2004.

The Ultimate Quilting Book: Over 1,000 Inspirational Ideas and Practical Tips. London: Collins & Brown Ltd., 1999.

Gutcheon, Beth
The Perfect Patchwork Primer. New York: D. McKay Co., 1973.

Hall, Carrie A., and Rose G. Kretsinger
The Romance of the Patchwork Quilt in America. New York: Bonanza Books, 1935.

Hargrave, Harriet
From Fiber to Fabric: The Essential Guide to Quiltmaking Textiles. New York: Watson-Guptill Publications, 1997.

Heirloom Machine Quilting: A Comprehensive Guide to Hand-Quilting Effects Using Your Sewing Machine. 4th ed. Lafayette, Calif.: C&T Publishing, 2004.

Hargrave, Harriet, and Sharyn Craig
The Art of Classic Quiltmaking. Lafayette, Calif.: C&T Publishing, 2000.

Hayes, Cheryl, and Mary Ellen Kranz
Blending Photos with Fabric. Bowling Green, Ohio: The Electric Quilt Company, 2004.

Hedrick, Virginia "Rusty"
Quilt Savvy: Hand Quilting. Paducah, Ky.: American Quilter's Society, 2003.

Heim, Judy, and Gloria Hansen
Free Stuff for Quilters on the Internet. 2nd ed. New York: Watson-Guptill Publications, 1999.

Hewitt, Barbara
Blueprints on Fabric: Innovative Uses for Cyanotype. New York: Publishers Overstock Unlimited, Inc., 1995.

Hicks, Kyra
Black Threads: An African-American Quilting Sourcebook. Jefferson, N.C.: McFarland & Co., 2003.

Hopkins, Mary Ellen
The It's Okay if You Sit on My Quilt Book. Lafayette, Calif.: C&T Publishing, 2006.

Horton, Laurel, editor
Quiltmaking in America: Beyond the Myths. Selected Writings from the American Quilt Study Group. Nashville, Tenn.: Rutledge Hill Press, 1994.

Horton, Roberta
The Fabric Makes the Quilt. Lafayette, Calif.: C&T Publishing, 1995.

Hughes, Robert
Amish: The Art of the Quilt. New York: Alfred A. Knopf, 1990.

Johnston, Ann
Color by Accident: Low-Water Immersion Dyeing. Ashland, Ohio: Ann Johnston, 1997.

The Quilter's Book of Design. Lincolnwood, Ill.: Quilt Digest Books, 2000.

Kerr, Bill, and Weeks Ringle
The Modern Quilt Workshop: Patterns, Techniques, and Designs from the FunQuilts Studio. Gloucester, Mass.: Quarry Books, 2005.

Kiracofe, Roderick, and Mary Elizabeth Johnson
The American Quilt: A History of Cloth and Comfort 1750–1950. New York: Clarkson Potter, 1993.

Laury, Jean Ray
The Photo Transfer Handbook: Snap It, Print It, Stitch It! Lafayette, Calif.: C&T Publishing, 1999.

Levie, Eleanor
American Quiltmaking 1970–2000. Paducah, Ky.: American Quilter's Society, 2004.

Lewis, Joan, and Lynette Chiles
501 Quilt Blocks: A Treasury of Patterns for Patchwork & Appliqué. Des Moines, Iowa: Better Homes and Gardens, 1994.

Line, Joanne Larsen, and Nancy Loving Tubesing
Quilts from the Quiltmaker's Gift. New York: Scholastic Press, 2001.

Malone, Maggie
5,500 Quilt Block Designs. New York: Sterling Publishing Co., 2003.

Martin, Judy
Judy Martin's Ultimate Rotary Cutting Reference. Paducah, Ky.: Collector Books, 1997.

Mazloomi, Carolyn
Spirits of the Cloth: Contemporary African American Quilts. New York: Clarkson Potter, 1998.

McClun, Diana, and Laura Nownes
Quilts! Quilts!! Quilts!!! The Complete Guide to Quiltmaking. New York: McGraw-Hill, 1998.

Quilts Galore! Quiltmaking and Techniques. San Francisco: Quilt Digest Press, 1990.

McDowell, Ruth B.
Fabric Journey: An Inside Look at the Quilts of Ruth B. McDowell. Lafayette, Calif.: C&T Publishing Inc., 2005.

Pieced Flowers. Lafayette, Calif.: C&T Publishing, 2000.

Pieced Vegetables. Lafayette, Calif.: C&T Publishing, 2002.

Piecing: Expanding the Basics. Lafayette, Calif.: C&T Publishing, 1998.

McMorris, Penny, and Michael Kile
The Art Quilt. Lincolnwood, Ill.: Quilt Digest Press, 1996.

Mech, Susan Delany, M.D.
Rx for Quilters: Stitcher-Friendly Advice for Every Body. Lafayette, Calif.: C&T Publishing Inc., 2000.

Nickels, Sue
Machine Appliqué: A Sampler of Techniques. Paducah, Ky.: American Quilter's Society, 2001.

Machine Quilting: A Primer of Techniques. Paducah, Ky.: American Quilter's Society, 2003.

Nickels, Sue, and Pat Holly
Stitched Raw Edge Appliqué. Paducah, Ky.: American Quilter's Society, 2006.

Orlofsky, Myron, and Patsy Orlofsky
Quilts in America. N.Y.: Abbeville Press, 2005.

Pahl, Ellen
Quilter's Ultimate Visual Guide. Emmaus, Pa.: Rodale Press, 1994.

Papadakis, Brenda
Dear Jane: The Two Hundred Twenty-Five Patterns from the 1863 Jane A. Stickle Quilt. Paducah, Ky.: EZ Quilting by Wrights, 2003.

Pritchard, Gayle
Uncommon Threads: Ohio's Art Quilt Revolution. Athens, Ohio: Ohio University Press, 2006.

Sassaman, Jane
The Quilted Garden: Design and Make Nature-Inspired Quilts. Lafayette, Calif.: C&T Publishing, 2000.

Schmidt, Denyse
Denyse Schmidt Quilts: 30 Colorful Quilt and Patchwork Projects. San Francisco, Calif.: Chronicle Books, 2005.

Shaw, Robert
The Art Quilt. New York: Beaux Arts Editions, 1997.

(Introduction). *Art Quilts: A Celebration: 400 Stunning Contemporary Designs*. New York: Lark Books, 2005.

Sienkiewicz, Elly
Baltimore Beauties and Beyond: Studies in Classic Album Quilt Appliqué. Vol. 1. Lafayette, Calif.: C&T Publishing, 1995.

Baltimore Elegance: A New Approach to Classic Album Quilts. Lafayette, Calif.: C&T Publishing, 2006.

Design a Baltimore Album Quilt! A Teach-Yourself Course in Sets & Borders. Lafayette, Calif.: C&T Publishing, 1992.

Sweet Dreams, Moon Baby: A Quilt to Make, a Story to Read. Lafayette, Calif.: C&T Publishing, 2003.

Simms, Ami
Creating Scrapbook Quilts. Flint, Mich.: Mallery Press, 1993.

Fun Photo Quilts and Crafts. Flint, Mich.: Mallery Press, 1999.

Stanley, Isabel, and Jenny Watson
The Ultimate Quilting and Patchwork Companion. London: Hermes House, 2003.

Stemer, Linda
Blueprints on Fabric: The Magic of Cyanotype. N.p.

Taylor, Linda
The Ultimate Guide to Longarm Machine Quilting. Lafayette, Calif.: C&T Publishing, 2002.

Waldvogel, Merikay
Soft Covers for Hard Times: Quiltmaking & The Great Depression. Nashville, Tenn.: Rutledge Hill Press, 1990.

Wasilowski, Laura
Fusing Fun! Fast, Fearless Art Quilts. Lafayette, Calif.: C&T Publishing, 2005.

Webster, Marie
Quilts: Their Story and How to Make Them. Detroit, Mich.: Omnigraphics, 1992.

Winston, Kimberly
Fabric of Faith: A Guide to the Prayer Quilt Ministry. Harrisburg, Pa.: Morehouse Pub., 2006.

Wolfrom, Joen
Color Play: Easy Steps to Imaginative Color in Quilts. Lafayette, Calif.: C&T Publishing, 2000.

Zegart, Shelly
American Quilt Collections: American Quilt Masterpieces. Tokyo: Nihon Vogue, 1996.

METRIC EQUIVALENCIES

Inches are rounded to the nearest tenth of a centimeter; yards are rounded to the nearest hundredth of a meter.

Inches to Centimeters

Inches		Centimeters
1/8	=	0.3
1/4	=	0.6
3/8	=	1.0
1/2	=	1.3
5/8	=	1.6
3/4	=	1.9
7/8	=	2.2
1	=	2.5
1 1/4	=	3.2
1 1/2	=	3.8
1 3/4	=	4.4
2	=	5.1
2 1/2	=	6.4
3	=	7.6
3 1/2	=	8.9
4	=	10.2
4 1/2	=	11.4
5	=	12.7
6	=	15.2
7	=	17.8
8	=	20.3
9	=	22.9
10	=	25.4
11	=	27.9
12	=	30.5
13	=	33.0
14	=	35.6
15	=	38.1
16	=	40.6
20	=	50.8
30	=	76.2
40	=	101.6
44	=	111.8
45	=	114.3

Yards to Meters

Yards		Meters
1/8	=	0.11
1/4	=	0.23
3/8	=	0.34
1/2	=	0.46
5/8	=	0.57
3/4	=	0.69
7/8	=	0.80
1	=	0.91
1 1/8	=	1.03
1 1/4	=	1.14
1 3/8	=	1.26
1 1/2	=	1.37
1 5/8	=	1.49
1 3/4	=	1.60
1 7/8	=	1.71
2	=	1.83
2 1/8	=	1.94
2 1/4	=	2.06
2 3/8	=	2.17
2 1/2	=	2.29
2 5/8	=	2.40
2 3/4	=	2.51
2 7/8	=	2.63
3	=	2.74
4	=	3.66
5	=	4.57
6	=	5.49
7	=	6.40
8	=	7.32
9	=	8.23
10	=	9.14

INDEX

D

G

I

PHOTO CREDITS

COVER CREDITS:

All images Courtesy of the International Quilt Study Center, University of Nebraska-Lincoln (*except RF). All images are details from original quilts.

LEFT TO RIGHT
ROW ONE: 1997.007.0125 © Michael James, 1999-007.0001 © David Hornung, 1997-007.0516 Maker Unknown,
ROW TWO: 2000-004.0001 Maker Unknown (and spine), 1997-007.1094 © Elizabeth Cave,
ROW THREE: 1997-007.0450 Maker Unknown, 1997-007.0181 Maker Unknown, 1997-007.0125 Maker Unknown
ROW FOUR: 2000-007.0072 Maker Unknown, *Royalty Free © Shutterstock

INTERIOR CREDITS:

Color Inset Photography by Tria Giovan

AGE Fotostock: 112 (left), 279, 293, 374; AP/WideWorld: xi, 18, 20, 21, 22, 28, 36, 38, 44, 45, 52, 53, 58, 72, 84, 86, 90, 92, 100, 113, 238, 256, 396, 520, 537, 548, 557; Art Resource: 11, 12 (top), 13, 23, 39; ClipArt: 190; Corbis: 112, 527; Getty Images: 79, 91, 117, 194; Library of Congress: 12, 14, 15, 25, 26, 40, 46, 69, 104, 106, 185, 195, 513; Meredith Corporation, Creative Collection: 270 (bottom), 300 (top); The Granger Collection: 10, 49, 101

Thank you to the following for providing photography:

Alex Anderson; American Professional Quilting; American Quilter's Society; Ami Simms; Amy Butler Design; Ann Johnston; Anna Williams; Arrow Sewing Cabinets; ArtFabrik; B&J Fabrics/Karlé J. Meyers; Barbara Webster; Bermina of America, Inc.; Beth Gutcheon; Bethany Reynolds; Blueprints on Fabric; Bonnie Lyn McCaffery; Brother International Corporation; C & T Publishing; Carol Bruce; Caryl Bryer Fallert; Chalet Publishing; Charlotte Angotti; Charlotte Warr Andersen; Collection of Kathleen and Robert Kirkpatrick; Cultured Expressions, Inc.; Cynthia England; Dawn Cavanaugh; Diane Gaudynski; Dierdra McElroy/Roxanne International; Elin Noble; Elly Sienkiewicz; Elna Inc.; eQuilter.com; Esterita Austin; Faith Ringgold; Festival of Quilts; Gabrielle Swain; Gammill Quilting Machine Company; Georgia Bonesteel Films; Gingher; Gloria Hansen; Handi Quilter; Harriet Hargrave; Hinterberg Design; Hobbico Inc.; Hollis Chatelain; International Quilt Study Center; Jackie Robinson/Animas Quilts; Jane Dunnewold; Jane Sassaman; Janome America, Inc.; Jeri Riggs; Jinny Beyer; Joan Colvin; Joe Cunningham; Joen Wolfrom; John Flyyn/Flynn Quilt Frame Company; Judy Martin; Kaffe Fassett Studio; Keepsake Quilting Inc.; Kyra Hicks; Linda's Electric Quilters; Liz Berg; Lonni Rossi; Machine Quilters Exposition; Marilyn Belford; Marilyn Parker; Martingale & Co.; Mary Stori; McCall's Quilting; Meg Cox; Melody Johnson; Michael Miller Fabrics; More Than Warmth; Mulhern & Company Advertising, Inc.; Nancy Crow; Natasha Kempers-Cullen; Nolting Manufacturing; OLFA; On-Word Bound Books, LLC.; P&B Textiles; Pennington Quilt Works; Penny Mateer; Pfaff Sewing Machines; Piece O' Cake; Plumb Memorial Library; PRO Chemical & Dye; Quilt Box; Quilt in a Day with Eleanor Burns; Quilt University; Quiltaholics.com; Ricky Tims; Roberta Horton; Ruth B. McDowell; Sandy Merritt; Scott Murkin; Sharon Schamber; Sharyn Craig; Shelly Zegart; Singer Sewing Company; Stitchin' Post; Sue Benner; Sue Nickels; Sunset Publishing; Susan Shie; Suzanne Mouton Riggio; Taunton Press; The Alliance for American Quilts; The Electric Quilt Company; The Professional Quilter Magazine; The Quayside Publishing Group; The Quilt Index; The Warm Company; Thimble Lady; Thimbleberries; Vallie Schiller; Velda Newman.

Additional Photography by:
Dietrich Gehring and Jenna Bascom